THEN CAME EACH ACTOR

Other Books by Bernard Grebanier

The Heart of Hamlet
The Truth About Shylock
The Great Shakespeare Forgery
The Uninhibited Byron: An Account of His Sexual Confusion
Thornton Wilder
Edwin Arlington Robinson
The Enjoyment of Literature
Playwriting
Racine's Phaedra, *an English Acting Version in Verse*
Molière's The Misanthrope, *an English Acting Version*
Armenian Miniatures

POETRY

The Angel in the Rock
The Other Love
Mirrors of the Fire
Fauns, Satyrs and a Few Sages
(ed.) *Pegasus in the Seventies*

Charlotte and Susan Chapman as Romeo and Juliet. Engraving, 1879.
(Courtesy of The Museum of the City of New York, Theatre and Music Collection)

THEN CAME EACH ACTOR

Shakespearean Actors, Great and Otherwise,
Including Players and Princes, Rogues, Vagabonds
and Actors Motley, from Will Kempe to
Olivier and Gielgud and After

BERNARD GREBANIER

POLONIUS: *The actors are come hither, my lord.*
HAMLET: *Buzz, buzz!*
POLONIUS: *Upon my honour—*
HAMLET: *Then came each actor on his ass—*
                                    Hamlet, II, ii.

David McKay Company, Inc.

NEW YORK

Library of Congress Cataloging in Publication Data

Grebanier, Bernard D   N   1903–
   Then came each actor.

   Bibliography: p.
    1. Shakespeare, William, 1564–1616—Stage history.
2. Actors—Biography. I. Title.
PR3112.G73   791'.092'2   74–82983
ISBN 0–679–50507–5

Preface

While my Byron book was being seen through the press, my agent phoned to tell me that an editor at David McKay wished me to do a book on Shakespearean actors. He had noted my many references to actors in my books on Hamlet, Shylock, and the young forger, William Henry Ireland, and thought me suited to the undertaking. I had two weeks for my enthusiasm to develop the possibilities in such a work before meeting the editor.

When we met I began to expound my plans: the book must not be a mere chronicle, but entertaining, too; it should be full of anecdote and interesting biography; it ought to afford a view of changing modes and tastes in acting, production, audiences, and the theaters themselves during the nearly four centuries since Shakespeare began to write. He stopped me in the middle of my excited exposition to say: "Oh no! That's not the book I had in mind. I was thinking of the actors who were Shakespeare's contemporaries." At once I was deflated. When I recovered I said, "That is a book I shall never write. We know all that we are likely to know on that subject, and what we know would be only faintly interesting to the general reader. But the book I *thought* you wished interests me very much, and if you do not want it, I shall take the idea to another publisher." He asked for some examples of what I was going to write about. I sketched some of it and told him some of the anecdotes, including the one herein narrated about Salvini. He seemed intrigued, and asked me to give him a few days to consult his staff. Two days later my agent had a letter from him saying that everyone at McKay thought my idea much more fascinating than his. As it turned out, it was just as well that he was convinced, for several months later a book on his original idea was published in England: *Shakespeare and the Actors,* by my friend Ivor Brown, prolific writer and critic of exquisite taste and prodigious learning, and one of the finest stylists of our century. Had I accepted the editor's idea, I obviously could not have finished *that* book once Brown's was issued. The gods had clearly not forsaken me.

While I am gratified with the possession of all I have learned in my studies for this book, I am not sure that I should have so eagerly undertaken it had I had a firmer knowledge of the monumental amount of research it would require—for centuries almost every actor appeared in Shakespeare!—or that, even after I had decided to omit hundreds of lesser or uninteresting players, it would end by being nearly twice the size of any book I have heretofore published. For instance, before I could determine whom to omit, it was necessary to study their careers just the same. Finally, after a process of elimination, though I deal with legions of British, American, and foreign Shakespearean actors and actresses, I flatter myself that there is not one here who has not his or her peculiar interest. Some were great, some were absurd; some led tragic, melodramatic, or comic lives. I have not overlooked the attempts to transfer the plays to film, both silent and talking. I have dealt with players who were magnificent in their craft, players who could fail, players who had good lives, frustrated lives, self-destructive lives, players who were loved and players who were hated, and players who were unknowingly the victims of their times.

I am happy to bring before the public again men and women whose very names are already undeservedly unknown or forgotten, players who had the courage to bring back, after traditional depredations, the vitality and incomparable poetry of the world's greatest poet-dramatist and subtlest psychologist. Nor have I spared those anxious for their own sensational ends to distort and vulgarize his works—an enterprise that is particularly thriving these recent decades.

I wish to thank Carl Willers and Louis Rachow of The Players' Library for their assistance in plumbing the resources of their fabulous collection, which was invaluable as a supplement to my own and to what I found at the Theatre Wing of the New York Public Library and in the British Museum.

BERNARD GREBANIER
Castalia, 1974

Contents

THEN CAME EACH ACTOR

Actors, Acting, and the Performing of Shakespeare

When I was twelve I had my first conscious experience of beauty in human beings. This overwhelming occasion took place at a nickelodeon, as movie houses were then called because of the price of admission, which was showing a film featuring Jane Cowl. At a certain moment I was made aware of her hands, and in the next of how beautiful they were. That hands could be beautiful was an astonishing idea, and for the rest of the movie my attention was fixed on them. When I returned home, sputtering with excitement over my discovery, my mother, who missed the point entirely, merely assured me that Jane Cowl was a very famous actress.

Decades later, after having seen Miss Cowl in every Broadway play in which she had appeared (my first play was *The Crowded Hour* during World War I, while I was in high school), I had the good fortune to meet her in Blanche Yurka's dressing room. Later, when I knew her better, I felt I could speak frankly without sounding fatuous; I told her of my boyish transport over her beautiful hands. She threw back her lovely head, laughed, and then cried, "Ridiculous! I've always had hideous hands. Just look at them." She extended them, and I was shocked to see that they actually were ugly. "I realized early," she continued, "that *because* they are hideous I had to learn to use them beautifully." It flashed through my mind that in every play in which I had seen her she had kept her hands extraordinarily busy. She went on, insisting I agree with her on their ugliness. Avoiding a direct reply, I said in all sincerity, "You are the most beautiful woman I've ever watched on the American stage." She laughed again and murmured, "That's nonsense, too." She placed one hand on the hollow of her throat and said, "Down to here, yes, not bad—perhaps even very good. But from the shoulders down, ugh!" She shuddered. "My mirror taught me while I was still young to wear the sort of clothes I do to conceal the bitter truth." It was true that, as at that moment, she usually wore clothes with flowing lines. She added: "My only capital has been my face, my voice, and, of course, whatever talent I've developed."

Certainly, personal beauty is no essential to the success of an actor in the theater. What matters is his ability to project, when necessary, the illusion of beauty. Some actors of both sexes who are distinctly plain-looking have been able to create that impression. Dame Judith Anderson is one of them. Like Jane Cowl, she is gifted with a glorious voice and enormous talent but —and I intend no incivility—unlike Miss Cowl she does not possess a single attractive feature. It does not matter. I have seen her again and again create perfectly the illusion of great beauty and voluptuousness.

The history of acting on the stage proves that there are no aesthetic endowments indispensable to the performer, not even a good voice. Henry Irving, the idol of the late Victorian age, reflected at the summit of his career: "How strange it is that I should have made the reputation I have as an actor, with nothing to help me—with no equipment. My legs, my voice, everything has been against me. For an actor who can't walk, can't talk, and has no face to speak of, I've done pretty well." Thomas Betterton, who dominated the Restoration stage, is described by his admiring contemporary, Anthony Aston, as laboring "under ill figure, being clumsily made, having a great head, a short thick neck, stooped in the shoulders, and had fat short arms, which he rarely lifted higher than his stomach . . . He had little eyes, and a broad face, a little pock-fretten, a corpulent body, and thick legs with large feet. . . . His voice was low and grumbling." The celebrated Mrs. Abington had a voice described as "not naturally pleasing to the ear"; and Louis XIV's favorite, Sophie Arnould, owned "the finest asthma ever heard." Among other greats, Garrick was conspicuously below average height, as was Kean, who had the added disadvantage of a voice neither melodious nor strong. Sarah Siddons, the greatest tragic actress of the English-speaking stage, had a nose too long for beauty—Gainsborough, for whom she sat, complained that there was "no end to it"—and her voice when calm was downright dissonant.

Personal beauty is of so little importance to the actor that it may easily escape the notice of the audience and may, moreover, incline him to get by on his looks without mastering his art, if that beauty is unaccompanied by a gift few possess. I was made aware of a quality quite apart from beauty or voice years ago, when I was teaching a course in playwriting and theater workshop. As I asked young men and women to mount the stage and read their fellows' scripts, I was astonished at a recurring phenomenon. Often, those who were attractive and possessed good voices became common the instant they were on stage. While others, who appeared rather ordinary in person or had unpleasant voices became luminous, as if magically transformed. This incandescence does not seem to be related to any other quality —not even intelligence—yet it is an invaluable gift. A performer who has it is blessed; one who does not may become accomplished but will never be great. The records show that Garrick, Mrs. Siddons, Kean, Henry Irving, Ellen Terry, and Eleanora Duse possessed it in abundance. Judith Anderson, John Gielgud, and Ralph Richardson have it today, while Garbo is one of the few screen actors so gifted.

Similarly, the sort of intelligence indispensable, for example, to the critic may be of little use to an actor. The wife of a well-known actor has repeatedly said to me that her husband might have gone even farther if he had not been too intelligent for the theater. She may be right. Of more importance than brains is the actor's spontaneous reaction to language. A friend of mine, a superb actress, generously offered to make a recording of some of my lyrics, which were written on the whole in the simplest of words. The result was wonderful: I thought that she made the verses sound better than they actually were, and that I should never again hear them so well read. As we listened to the recording, she gracefully inclined her head and said, "You know, I am just *beginning* to understand them!"

Considering how unrewarding the acting profession was in the past, one wonders why anyone wished to enter it. For a long period in the history of their art, players were looked upon as little more than the dregs of society. In England, before the first theater was built, strolling players were considered so much of a threat to decency that it was thought necessary to keep track of every one of them in the kingdom; each had to hire himself out as a servant to some powerful lord, who became his company's patron. In Henry VIII's time when a strolling player was found not to be a member of such a company, the penalty was to have an ear or a nose cut off. The justification for this harshness was that the same actor who played a noble role on Monday might very well slit a man's throat for his purse on Tuesday. In France, as late as 1673, Molière, the greatest dramatist and actor of his age and a favorite of Louis XIV, was refused Christian burial because of his profession.

The profession was unrewarding indeed. While dramatists of quality like Shakespeare, Webster, Congreve, Goldsmith, Sheridan, and Wilde could hope to live on in their plays and continue to have life every time their works were performed or read, the actors who first gave their comedies and tragedies a hearing before a public, and those who bestowed on them new life by reviving them on the boards, had to be content with the ephemeral approval—when they could get it—of a limited number of their contemporaries. The very names of those who were praised are, with few exceptions, now forgotten, and those few are little more than names to the most literate. They would be lost in oblivion were it not for writings, like the present one, which undertake to resuscitate their memories. Even actors who glorified the stage in this century are already dim figures. Mention the names of Julia Marlowe, E. H. Sothern, Richard Mansfield, Maude Adams, Elsie Ferguson, Margaret Anglin, Robert Mantell, or Walter Hampden to anyone in his or her twenties, and you will be greeted with a blank stare.

Although well aware of the shortcoming of players, Hazlitt wrote sympathetically of them in 1816,

Actors have been accused, as a profession of being extravagant and dissipated. . . . It is not to be wondered at. They live from hand to mouth; they plunge from want into luxury; they have no means of

making money *breed,* and all professions that do not live by turning
money into money, . . . spend it. Uncertain of the future, they make
sure of the present moment. This is not unwise. Chilled with poverty,
steeped in contempt, they sometimes pass into the sunshine of fortune, and are lifted to the very pinnacle of public favour; yet even there
they cannot calculate on the continuance of success, but are, "like the
giddy sailor on the mast, ready with every blast to topple down into
the fatal bowels of the deep!" . . . Again, with respect to the habit of
convivial indulgence, an actor, to be a good one, must have a great
spirit of enjoyment in himself—strong impulses, strong passions, and
a strong sense of pleasure: for it is his business to imitate the passions,
and communicate pleasure to others. . . . The neglected actor may be
excused if he drinks oblivion of his disappointments; the successful
one if he quaffs the applause of the world, and enjoys the friendship
of those who are the friends of the favourites of fortune, in draughts
of nectar. There is no path so steep as that of fame. . . . If there is any
tendency to dissipation beyond this in the profession of a player, it is
owing to the prejudices entertained against them—to that spirit of
bigotry which . . . slurs over their characters, while living, with a half-
witted jest. Players are only not so respectable as a profession as they
might be, because their profession is not respected as it ought to be.

Well, their profession has become in our own time more than respectable.
Actors, especially the movie contingent, have become the new aristocracy;
very few of them, unfortunately, have the necessary qualifications. Publicity
having become the sine qua non of their success, they are often forced to
live their private lives in public—though it is clear enough that too many of
them enjoy that obligation—to the extent that they find it impossible to live
private lives at all. The most talked-about among them—not necessarily the
most gifted—are entitled to a cordon of police wherever they appear, like
visiting potentates. They are encouraged to write articles and books—or to
have books written for them, the "nonbooks" of this epoch—in which their
drinking habits are extolled and their amorous experiences anatomized.
Worst of all, in these lucubrations they are encouraged to mouth vulgarities,
platitudes, and idiocies which would disgrace a high school sophomore. It
makes one wonder whether or not the old days of injustice were not better
after all.

For actors are generally ill equipped to strut before the world in their own
persons. How can they be, when so few of them have any idea of who they
actually are? That is, most touchingly, their occupational hazard, and it is
what most entitles them to our compassion. An actor, if he is a good one,
becomes so accustomed to identifying himself, as he must, with an ever-
changing series of characters in different plays that before long he begins
to lose touch with his own identity. Most men and women have, it is true,
the unfortunate habit of bringing their businesses and professions home or
into company with them; the lawyer boasts of how he has helped the party
of the first part cheat the party of the second part of twenty-five dollars; the

mother entertains with stories of the archness of little Johnny; the surgeon, as he carves the turkey, is reminded of an interesting appendectomy he recently executed. But the temptation is even greater for an actor who must have enormous strength to avoid acting off as well as on stage.

Jean-Paul Sartre's play *Kean*, an adaptation of a drama by the elder Dumas, has as its absorbing subject the struggles of a great actor to escape in private life the tentacles of attitudes and postures he has held in his various roles in the theater. In a moment of self-revelation, the hero declares:

> You act to lie, to deceive, to deceive yourself; to be what you cannot be, and because you have had enough of being what you are.

And later, in a fit of desperation, he addresses the audience in the playhouse:

> I was wrong just now to mention Kean. Kean the actor died very young.
> (Laughter) Be quiet, murderers, it was you who killed him!

In this play, Kean, the great Shakespearean actor of his time, inevitably finds himself adopting the attitudes and postures of Shakespearean heroes at crucial moments in his own life.

Of course, this dilemma must be unknown to the crop of actors who during the last few decades have debased the stage, the film, and television, those actors who, students of The Method, do not identify themselves with the roles they are called upon to play, but who distort them until they are no more than an expression of the actor's own personality. For a long time now we have been treated to a parade of thoroughly uninteresting self-portraits on stage and screen—not infrequently self-portraits which are repellent, though none the less praised by the critics because they are "natural." We have watched scratchings of ears, noses, and scalps, because *those* are "natural," mumblings and inaudible mouthings and slouching all over the stage, on the same grounds, and because that is the way the actor comports himself, it is presumed, at home. Perhaps in so-called naturalistic plays—though that is a contradiction in terms; the very conditions under which drama is presented in a theater of any kind could not be more removed from "real life" than they are—it does not matter so much if we are compelled to look at all that unloveliness, since the theory seems to be that the grossness itself will be good for us. But in the great classics of the theater (and there exist those who would banish the great classics from the theater forever) it ruins dramatic effectiveness. Let us leave Shakespeare out of the argument for a moment. Conceive, if you can, a company of Method actors performing *The Importance of Being Earnest!*

The theory behind Method acting in the United States goes to extremes. "Without the actor and without assuring the final supremacy of the actor," declares William Redfield in *Letters from an Actor*, "there is no truly great theatre. . . . The playwright . . . is not the *sine qua non* of the theatre . . . The center of the theatre is the actor." Even the director, he thinks, should be reduced to minor significance, because the "director can only coordinate." The actor must be "true to himself." To expect the actor to present "the *ideal* Hamlet . . . is to deny the human condition . . . Directors sometimes pretend that the character is everything and that the actor must adjust no matter how uncomfortable it makes him, but the actor's job is to preserve himself."

The bright star among Method actors is, for Mr. Redfield (as well as for many others, including some critics), Marlon Brando. Since 1949, he tells us, no one has appeared in the New York theater who can "be seriously thought of as Hamlet . . . Brando was the American challenge" to the British, and with him the United States was saying to England, "He does it without your damned elocution lessons, your fruity voices. . . . He throws away your books and he burns your academies. He does it from within. And he is better than all of you!" Redfield goes on to praise Brando for what was undeniably his best performance, as Kowalski in *Streetcar Named Desire.* Are we to understand that playing Kowalski was a preparation for enacting Hamlet? Astonishingly, Redfield also acclaims Brando for one of his worst pieces of acting, Antony in the film *Julius Caesar,* and praises him for the "clarity" with which he spoke. Brando was unquestionably a Roman beautiful to behold, but his speech—! It was Kowalski all over again, and sounded rather as though the actor's mouth were filled with mashed potatoes. In certain roles, when Brando has been able to repeat his Kowalski without any conflict with the character he is portraying, his performances have been admirable enough. But when he undertook the role of Napoleon, the results were ridiculous— even though this time he made no attempt to turn him into Kowalski. Similarly, Rod Steiger reenacted his pawnbroker role when he made the film in which *he* was supposed to be Napoleon. The Lord forfend that we should ever be treated to a quasi-Kowalski Hamlet. The Prince of Denmark has had enough mayhem committed upon him in our time.

In the United States The Method had its first important exponents in the Group Theatre, some forty years ago. Like many contemporary Method teachers, Morris Carnovksy is a veteran of the Group Theatre. Though he is a far more significant practitioner of The Method than Mr. Redfield, and more moderate and less egocentric, the two men have basically the same views on acting. Failing to distinguish between the true creator (the playwright or the composer) and the interpreter (the actor or the musician), Carnovsky believes that all "artists" wish above all in their work "to find out how to say himself. I as an actor want to find out how to say myself, through O'Neill, through Shakespeare, through Chekhov, through whoever." I think Mr. Carnovsky is less an exemplar of The Method than he imagines himself to be. He does not hesitate, thank Heaven, to use his beautifully resonant voice to rhetorical advantage, he does not scratch head or nose, he has an impressive bearing and dignity consonant with the noble roles he enacts. A few years ago his brilliant Shylock rescued *The Merchant of Venice* at Stratford, Connecticut, from the outrages of the director's interpretations. I number myself among his sincere admirers. Nevertheless, it must be conceded that Mr. Carnovsky so much seeks "to say himself" that he makes his Priam and his Lear faintly Yiddish. To be faintly Yiddish as Shylock is perfect, but it is a little disturbing to expect Priam or Lear momentarily to break into some anecdote à la Sholom Aleichem.

I once had an unnerving experience with a Method actor. I had given him the role of Edmund in a *Lear* I was directing because he had seemed very promising. But in rehearsal he grew worse and worse until there was some danger that he would ruin the entire production. Finally, as opening night neared, I lost my patience and demanded to know what had happened to him. He explained: "You see, as Edmund I'm supposed to hate Edgar but I find I can't." "Why not?" "Because the actor doing Edgar happens to be my best friend. How can I hate my best friend?" As I began to explode, he tried to calm me by saying, "But don't worry. I've found a way to lick this. I hate my uncle, so I'm going to pretend to myself that my best friend is my uncle." It was useless to ask him why he could not pretend simply that he was Edmund and his friend Edgar.

The Group Theatre and Method acting look to the old Moscow Art Theatre as the fountainhead of their theory. It is therefore refreshing to hear all the Method nonsense utterly swept aside by one of the most highly gifted actresses of our century, Alla Nazimova, who herself had acted with the Moscow Art Theatre. "Like the aeolian harps that used to be in the trees to be played upon only by the breeze, the actor should be an instrument *played upon* by the character he depicts. All the impulse which sets him free . . . should stem from the creature of the dramatist's imagining. The actor himself should be a creature of clay, of putty, capable of being molded into another form . . . I am nothing. I am nobody. I have to reconstruct my whole self into this woman I am to portray—speak with her voice, laugh with her laughter—move with her motion."

In complete accord with this conception of the actor was John Barrymore: "A man isn't an actor until he commands a technique which enables him to get an impression across into the heart of an audience without reference or relation to his own individuality."

Strictly speaking, of course, one would have to agree that the theory behind the histrionic art does not matter so long as the actor knows how to act. But the views of Nazimova and Barrymore are fairly descriptive of what has for centuries been the tradition in England, ever since Hamlet gave Shakespeare's advice to the players, certainly emphasizing the need for actors to acquire a discipline in the objective techniques of their art. The incomparable Garrick, who ruled the stage during his lifetime as no actor has done since, was said by his old teacher and friend, Samuel Johnson, to have "left nothing to chance. Every gesture, every expression of countenance and variation of voice was settled in the closet before he set his foot upon the stage." This mastery of technique was so perfect that Garrick's own wife did not recognize him when he appeared upon the boards as a country bumpkin. But even The Method will do if in the end the actor succeeds in identifying himself with the role he is playing. He is, however, beyond hope if he despises the technical requirements of his profession and insists on transforming the character into his own far less interesting self, instead of transforming himself into the character he is to portray.

From the mid-eighteenth century through the early decades of the twentieth century to be a leading actor in the English-speaking world meant to be a Shakespearean actor, even though the player might appear occasionally in contemporary plays. In England this is still somewhat the case. Whatever the play being performed in a London theater today, the biographical notes in the program will tell you that the men and women in both major and minor roles have had years of experience—I prefer to think of it as training —in the plays of Shakespeare at Stratford-on-Avon, in London with the Royal Shakespeare Company or at the Old Vic, in touring or stock companies at Manchester, Bristol, Birmingham, and other cities of "the provinces," in Great Britain, Ireland, and Australia. That is why a cast of British-trained actors in a modern play can be relied upon to deliver a fine performance, no matter how inferior the play itself. Indeed, they often make a play seem much better than it is. (I shall never forget the disappointment I felt on reading T. S. Eliot's *The Cocktail Party* because the splendid performance I had witnessed had caused an inept play to seem brilliant.) American actors, not having the opportunity for a comparable grounding in the classic repertory, are by and large inferior, and at their worst in these classics. Many of them are capable of playing only themselves on stage, and have no conception of style, which they have been taught to think of as artificial. They are usually insufferable when they attempt Shakespeare; they do not know how to speak verse; their English is likely to bear the stamp of their native locale or else of that Brooklyn inflection which most of the Actors Studio students for some reason acquire; they have not learned how to walk or move with grace—or, more importantly, when *not* to move. There seems to be a fear, even a dread of Shakespeare among actors, doubtless initiated by the endeavors of schoolteachers to render the world's greatest and most adult dramatist and poet distasteful and boring to the young. At the Lambs' Club, one of the most celebrated of our low-comedians, in absolute panic, rejected a request to participate in an evening of fun in the Pyramus and Thisbe episode—because it was Shakespeare! Though no subtlety or high imagination is called upon for the enacting of Bottom, he would not undertake the role even for its twenty minutes of duration; he had never done Shakespeare, he said, and frankly admitted his terror of doing *any* Shakespearean part, even so easy a one as Bottom.

Alas! Though training in the plays of Shakespeare has been (except in the United States in our own time) the rule for English-speaking actors, it has been only by exception—as in the instance of such devoted men as Samuel Phelps—that those plays have been performed according to Shakespeare's intentions. At one time I seriously thought of calling this book: "What the Actors Have Done to [not *for*!] Shakespeare."

What would a sincere lover of music think of a rendition of Beethoven's Seventh Symphony in which a passage from *Billy the Kid* were introduced into the midst of the Dionysian revelry—or, say, a passage of rock music. (As I write, a highly successful—I mean financially successful—rock version of *Othello* is holding its own in London.) Yet this sort of thing has been done to the plays of Shakespeare ever since the 1660s. The reason for such ravages visited upon masterpieces was not so long ago summed up and justified by Jack Landau, director at the time of the Stratford (Connecticut) Playhouse, a theater presumably built to present Shakespeare's plays under the best possible auspices, and where the record of violence done to those plays is staggering. Mr. Landau asks what is the point of producing the plays "the way they were done for an Elizabethan audience? Doesn't it make more sense to find out what the plays mean for us in our time?" According to Mr. Landau, what the plays mean for us in our time has required his converting *Measure for Measure* from exquisite poetry and mordant satire into slapstick farce, and *Troilus and Cressida* into a magnolia-scented reproduction of the American Civil War, pierced with loud rebel yells. (Of that performance, Howard Taubman of *The New York Times* said that it "verges on puerility. It achieves a noisy silliness worthy of Westerns but not of Shakespeare.") More recently the same theater, under other direction, gave a production of *The Merchant of Venice* in which Antonio and all his friends were obvious homo-sexuals—Antonio was grief-stricken at Bassanio's marriage!—and Portia was described by her portrayer, Barbara Baxley, as a "brazen bitch." In New York we have been treated by a British company to a *Love's Labour's Lost* become quaint in a Victorian setting and a *Troilus and Cressida* equally so in an Edwardian setting. In the 1971 season the Royal Shakespeare Company presented Peter Brook's lavishly praised (Brendan Gill and John Simon, whose heads are clearer, dissented strongly from the encomia) *A Midsummer Night's Dream,* which was more like a three-ring circus than a play. It had the added attraction of gratuitous lecheries totally disastrous to the delicately balanced tone of the comedy, such as Lysander's caressing Puck's crotch, Bottom as an ass waving a colossal phallus, and the lovers at the end indulging in mutual groping. As for the infectious Pyramus and Thisbe episode, all the fun had been drained out of it—I've seen kids do a far superior job with it a dozen times. The audience, laughing constantly at the director's shenanigans, never found anything to laugh at in the lines of the play itself.

With vast sanity Joseph Papp once wrote that to enable audiences today to identify with the characters, the plays must be directed "without sacrific-ing the form and poetry of Shakespeare, and without vulgarizing the pe-riod." Sad to relate, after this sound counsel, Mr. Papp some years later gave us a *Hamlet* in which the prince was wheeled out in a coffin-on-wheels, and in which the "Too too solid flesh" speech was rendered novel by having Hamlet rip off the coverlet from the bed on which, on stage, his mother and uncle were cozily ensconced.

This spurious method of adapting Shakespeare to the times has been going on ever since D'Avenant. In the 1660s he transported Beatrice and Benedick from the sparkling milieu of *Much Ado about Nothing* and squeezed them into his version of the acrid *Measure for Measure*. His *Macbeth* witches flew about on "machines," dancing and singing. His tasteless rewriting of lines in these plays and *Hamlet* need not detain us, but his gifts as a poet may be gauged from this excerpt of one of the songs allotted to the witches:

> Black spirits, and white,
> Red spirits and gray;
> Mingle, mingle, mingle,
> You that mingle may.
> Tiffin, Tiffin, keep it stiff in,
> Fire-drake Puckey, make it lucky;
> Liar Robin, you must bob in.

Nahum Tate's perversion of *King Lear* (c. 1680) had Edgar in love with Cordelia; her interest in him became the cause for her defying her father. A scene was introduced in which Edmund and Regan were "amorously seated" in a grotto. Edgar and Albany came to the rescue of Lear and Cordelia at the end, in the style, later made familiar by silent movies, of American government troops arriving in time to defeat the Indians. The play concluded with Lear, his kingdom restored, bestowing it upon Cordelia before her marriage to Edgar. Her lover spoke the last line of the play: "Truth and Virtue shall at last succeed." Samuel Johnson approved of this travesty of one of Shakespeare's sublimest achievements and Tate's outrage passed as Shakespeare's *King Lear* for one hundred fifty years and more!

Garrick, for all his sincere devotion to Shakespeare, worked similar depredations upon a number of the plays. His conclusion to *Hamlet* will indicate how far his bad judgment could go: The prince bursts in upon Claudius and Laertes. Laertes reproaches him with the deaths of Polonius and Ophelia. The king interposes saying that he will no longer put up with Hamlet's disobedience (as manifested by his refusal to go to England) and threatens the prince with his wrath. "First feel you mine," cries Hamlet, and at once stabs him. The queen rushes off stage, shrieking that she must be saved from her son. Laertes finds the moment opportune for stabbing Hamlet, who is grateful for that "precious balm," the stroke of death, and declares it was Heaven which directed Laertes's hand. Word is brought that Gertrude has fallen into a trance. Hamlet hopes that she may repent before madness seizes her, and joins the hands of Laertes and Horatio, entreating them to unite and "calm the troubled land." This atrocity was, of course, concocted to satisfy the Good Taste stipulated by the eighteenth century!

What would a sincere lover of music think of a performance of Beethoven's Third, Fifth, Sixth, Seventh, Eighth, or Ninth symphony which truncated, without a by-your-leave, whole segments of the composition? Yet this is the sort of thing which has been happening to Shakespeare's plays for a very long time now. It was for many decades customary to bring down the final curtain on the death of Hamlet (dispensing with the entry of Fortinbras, as did Garrick) and on the deaths of Romeo and Juliet—as in Gounod's saccharine opera (thus dispensing with the reconciliation of the hostile families). This amputation of the Shakespearean catharsis is precisely comparable to a performance of Strauss's *Death and Transfiguration* which would lop off its marvelous final pages.

Indeed, it is only on the rarest occasions that any of the plays have been given uncut. Maurice Evans produced one such memorable *Hamlet*. The experience of witnessing the play as Shakespeare had written it was so astounding that the critics thought they had been treated to a new interpretation, only because that *Hamlet* at last made some sense. Lawrence Olivier's movie of the play cut out about one-third of the tragedy in order to make room for far-from-subtle Freudian suggestions, and completely left out Rosencrantz and Guildenstern, who are necessary to the resolution of the plot. But that was merely an extreme instance of the general practice of clipping Shakespeare's lines in all of his plays. It is hardly surprising that the plays have given rise to so much discussion as to their meaning when it is remembered that this generous slashing of passages creates an overall imbalance of plot and characterization, so that the "meaning" of the play is inevitably distorted. That the plays survive and continue to amaze new generations with their magnificence is therefore the more remarkable. That they do so is probably due to the fact that they are read. Though Shakespeare's plays cry out for acting, a man or woman with imagination is bound to get more out of them in the library so long as this mad cult of novelty remains the rule.

I know of only one instance when a Shakespearean play was cut and did not suffer from the omissions, and that revision was made either by Shakespeare himself while he was still living or his fellow actors shortly after his death. *Hamlet* is an extraordinarily long play even for the age in which it was written. (One might say of it, as Schumann said of Schubert's Symphony in C, that it is "of heavenly length.") Sometime between its composition in 1602 and the first folio publication of 1623, 218 lines (a mere handful, considering the length of the tragedy) were excised. This slightly abridged version was obviously the acting text of Shakespeare's company by 1623. A careful comparison of that text with the text of the *Hamlet* quarto edition of 1604 will reveal that the 218 lines omitted in 1623 are, by and large, passages which could be cut from any performance of *Hamlet* without jeopardy to the health of the tragedy.* Oddly enough, although the play is always being unmercifully cut, these passages are usually retained.

There is no reason why the theater should not avail itself of all the increased resources of the modern stage. Of greatest value are the magical and endless possibilities of lighting and the peculiarly appropriate use of the

*See the present author's *The Heart of Hamlet* (New York: Apollo Editions, 1967), pp. 317–8, 333–4, 335, 425–6, 431–3.

black-out in Elizabethan drama which renders the cumbersome lowering and raising of the curtain superfluous. As for scenery, I have serious reservations. There exist two schools of scenic design: one, an extension of the Victorian, goes in for elaborate scenic effects, and in Shakespeare I deplore it; the other, which for Shakespeare's plays is ideal, prefers simplicity, even bareness.

Just as surely as a painter's work varies with the size and shape of the canvas or panel he has chosen, so the work of a dramatist is conditioned by the kind of stage for which he is writing. Greek drama was conditioned by the theater in which it was presented, and is still most effective when the physical limitations of the Athenian stage are approximated. Shakespeare and his fellows were inevitably limited by the theater for which they wrote: a theater open to the sky, without lights, almost without any kind of scenery, and with no curtain to separate the stage from the audience. It was Shakespeare's unwillingness, despite the lack of a curtain to shut off the stage, to have the corpses of the queen, the king, Laertes, and Hamlet walk off at the end of the play, which forced him to invent an expedient for having the bodies carried off with dignity. It was for this that he needed Fortinbras and, needing him, he wove him into the background of the play. A consummate artist, Shakespeare then used the final Fortinbras scene to magnificently increase the catharsis of the play's conclusion. To end the tragedy in the modern theater by dropping a curtain on Hamlet's death and omitting the Fortinbras scene is to cheat the tragedy of its splendid final tone.

In the last act of *The Merchant of Venice*, the serious business of the Shylock story having been rounded off, the dramatist exercises all the sorcery of his art—and a powerful witchery it is—to lead back into the ways of comedy and romance a play that almost crossed the borderline into tragedy. This feat of legerdemain is achieved through his exquisite poetry. The scene opens with Lorenzo and Jessica walking Portia's garden at Belmont in moonlight and shadow. If that passage were to be presented using all the resources of the modern theater to supplement with modern decor Sir Herbert Beerbohm Tree's turn-of-the-century style, one might have on stage the trees, the flowers, the grass, the moon, and off stage a wind machine gently wafting the branches and leaves about; as Lorenzo and Jessica come in, the moonlight could tenderly bathe Jessica's hair, and beams from her locks rebound to glint in Lorenzo's eyes—to melt the hearts of the spectators. If desired, there could be a stagehand in the wings pumping perfume into the atmosphere with a spray gun.

On Shakespeare's stage that scene was presented on a wooden platform and exposed to the same light (or fog or rain) of a London midafternoon as was its audience. How was a dramatist to convince that audience that what they were seeing was a moonlit garden in Belmont? Such a bare, unlit stage devoid of scenery would, on the face of it, seem enough to cripple any writer's talent. Actually, it proved a blessing, for it posed a challenge of the kind which only stimulated the great creator. It explains in part why Marlowe, Shakespeare, Webster, Ford, and many of their fellows were stimulated into writing superb poetry. If there was to be a moonlit garden on those wooden boards, Shakespeare had to create it in his lines, and he did so, superbly. In *The Merchant of Venice*, Jessica and Lorenzo enter, talking the sweet nothings which lovers traditionally exchange, but as they speak the poet is unobtrusively painting in garden, gentle breeze, moonlight, and shadow:

> LORENZO: The moon shines bright: in such a night as this,
>   When the sweet wind did gently kiss the trees
>   And they did make no noise, in such a night
>   Troilus methinks mounted the Troyan walls,
>   And sigh'd his soul toward the Grecian tents,
>   Where Cressid lay that night.
> JESSICA: In such a night
>   Did Thisbe fearfully o'ertrip the dew,
>   And saw the lion's shadow ere himself,
>   And ran dismay'd away.

Already the scene is filled with chequered moonlight and shade. And presently Lorenzo is saying:

> How sweet the moonlight sleeps upon this bank!
> Here will we sit, and let the sounds of music
> Creep in our ears: soft stillness and the night
> Become the touches of sweet harmony.
> Sit, Jessica: look how the floor of heaven
> Is thick inlaid with patines of bright gold.

And when Portia and Nerissa enter at a distance, weary from labors at court and the subsequent journey, but happy with what she has accomplished, Portia says:

> That light we see is burning in my hall.
> How far that little candle throws his beams!
> So shines a good deed in a naughty world.

There was no candle wasting its light in the actual afternoon of the Shakespearean stage, but how the whole theater must have been illuminated by those three lines!

The fact is, under proper direction, that whole passage could still be done with dazzling effect in afternoon light. The trouble with the elaborate scenic effects to which the late nineteenth century was so devoted is that scenes of that order, which now could be bathed in all sorts of enchanting lighting effects, are bound to seem like a gilded lily. Austin Dobson well understood the problem when he wrote his lines on the great actor Richard Burbage, who was Shakespeare's leading man; he called it *When Burbage Played*:

> *When Burbage played, the stage was bare*
> *Of fount and temple, tower and stair,*

Two broadwords eked a battle out;
Two supers made a rabble rout;
The Throne of Denmark was a chair!

And yet, no less the audience there
Thrilled through all changes of Despair,
Hope, Anger, Fear, Delight and Doubt,
When Burbage played.

This is the Actor's gift; to share
All moods, all passions, nor to care
One whit for scene, so he without
Can lead men's minds the roundabout.
Stirred as of old these hearers were
When Burbage played.

2

In Shakespeare's Day

It was as an actor that Shakespeare began his career in the theater, but there is little reason to assume, as has often been done, that his histrionic gifts were extraordinary. It is true that the early scant sketch of his life written by John Aubrey states that he "did act exceeding well," but Aubrey had the reputation of being given to "follies and misinformations," and, besides, wrote the better part of a century after Shakespeare's acting days were over.

In his own plays, Shakespeare appeared as old Adam in *As You Like It* and, in a role which might be described as still older, the Ghost in *Hamlet*. Neither calls for an actor of genius. A younger brother of the dramatist, interviewed when he was "stricken in years" and his memory probably "weakened by infirmities," could recollect only "the faint, general, and almost lost ideas he had of having seen him [his brother William] act a part in one of his own comedies, wherein being to personate a decrepit old man, he wore a long beard, and appeared so weak and drooping and unable to walk, that he was forced to be supported and carried by another person to a table, at which he was then seated among some company who were eating, and one of them sung a song." The description is, of course, of the charming scene in *As You Like It*, during which Orlando carries old Adam in, and the account remains the sole instance of a member of Shakespeare's family contributing to posterity what must be called a memorabile. Shakespeare's first editor, Nicholas Rowe, included in his 1709 edition of the plays a brief biography in which he said that Shakespeare was originally taken into the company "in a very mean Rank"—that is to say, his job was to help out in bit parts—and that "the top of his Performance was the Ghost in his own *Hamlet*." That is credible enough. Molière is the exception which proves what has been the rule, that great dramatists have never been leading actors. Conversely, many leading actors have at one time or another yielded to the temptation to capitalize on their popularity by writing their own plays. These creations of vanity rarely survived their authors.

At any rate, after 1603, when many of his greatest works were yet to be written, Shakespeare would seem, after fifteen years in London, to have lost all interest in appearing before audiences, for there is no reference to his acting after that date.

"All books about Shakespeare's life have to include conjecture. There is no crime in reasonable conjecture," observes that most reasonable and elegant of Shakespearean conjecturers, Ivor Brown, whose own delightful and exquisitely formulated guesses are usually molded around a solid armature of fact. I myself have long indulged in speculation as to how Shakespeare discovered his true vocation. I must reject the old deer-stealing story, despite the weight of indirect evidence which has been brought to sustain it. There seems to me a ridiculous lapse of common sense required to believe that Shakespeare became the world's greatest poet-dramatist because he was driven from his native Stratford for poaching deer and rabbits on the estate of Sir Thomas Lucy. Without underestimating the power of accident and the unexpected as forces shaping a man's life, I still ask: If he had been so driven from Stratford, why to the theater in London? If there were any logical connection between getting caught poaching and becoming a great poet-dramatist, I should certainly not labor to finish writing this page, and would lose no time directing my steps toward the nearest grounds where I might poach with the certainty of being caught.

In 1565, the year after Shakespeare's birth, his father became alderman at Stratford, and in 1571 chief alderman and justice of the peace. It would have been to the Shakespeare home that strolling companies of players would come for permission to act at Stratford. The boy William must have brushed against actors often enough, and if he found the theatrical profession a glamorous one he would not have been the first or last youth to have his head turned by it. But at eighteen, in what has all the marks of having been a shotgun marriage, he found himself married to a woman of twenty-six—in those days, therefore, well on her way, before her pregnancy, to becoming an old maid. Six months later his wife presented him with a daughter, and less than two years after that with twins. Three years later, when he was twenty-four, Shakespeare was in London and involved in the work of the theater. In other words, between the ages of twenty-one and twenty-four he left his native Stratford. If I am justified in believing that the man who became the world's greatest poet-dramatist had been stage-struck as a boy, it requires not too much imagination to suppose that his dream of becoming an actor seemed, in the years after his enforced marriage, less and less probable as he became more and more a paterfamilias. A man ten years older in all likelihood would, however reluctantly, have renounced the dream in favor of his worldly responsibilities; a youth in his early twenties married to a woman for whom, as his will and testament was to indicate, he cared little, might very well in an it's-now-or-never mood of desperation run off to the theater in London.

In the mid-eighteenth century the lads who guarded the horses for patrons of the theater were known as "Shakespeare's boys," because, the story went, when Shakespeare first arrived in London he earned his livelihood by holding the horses for members of the audience. We are to imagine that, being a genius, he held the horses so much better than anyone else that soon he was in demand, and presently had organized a group of boys under him to hold the horses, and that the boys held the horses so well that patrons of the theater would have none but Shakespeare's boys guarding their horses. One hopes the story is true; if so, it shows Shakespeare resolved to get close to the theater at any cost. It was then indeed but a step from the outside to the inside of the theater, and after a time he became an actor. A man who was at once so exceptionally and objectively observant of the human scene must eventually have realized that he had no special talent for acting and so, I like to think, in desperation again, concentrated on what early was a demonstrable gift, writing for the actors. An analogy in another art fortifies me in this conjecture. Robert Schumann's first dream was to become a professional pianist. He was forced to start a little late because of his family's insistence that he complete his studies in the law; genius that he was, he invented a mechanism for strengthening a weak finger, in order to make up for time lost. It worked so well that he managed to paralyze the finger and thus put an end to that dream. We can only be grateful that it did, for in his despair he turned to composing.

The great Shakespearean actor during the playwright's lifetime was not Shakespeare himself but Richard Burbage (?1567–1619). The son of the man who built the first theater in England, Burbage emerges in the earliest records as an athletic figure. His father had been ordered to hand over half the profits of his playhouse to the widow of John Brayne, who had supplied the money for building of the theater. When the claimants appeared for their money, they were greeted by young Richard Burbage with a broomstick in his hands. After the scuffle he held up his weapon and observed that surely he had given them their half and "sent them packing."

It was for him that Shakespeare created the roles of Richard III, Hamlet, Othello, and Lear, and in all probability Romeo, Brutus, Macbeth, Antony (in *Antony and Cleopatra*), and Coriolanus too. He was equally respected for his avocation as a painter. A woman's head painted by him can be seen today in the Dulwich Gallery, and Shakespeare and he collaborated in painting and gilding a shield for the Earl of Rutland, a task for which they were each granted forty-four shillings in gold. A second shield for the same nobleman was painted by Burbage three years later.

Burbage and his dramatist, it is clear, were close friends, and their friendship must have been an important encouragement to Shakespeare. There is one amusing anecdote that has come down to us about both of them. A woman of London had been smitten by Burbage, who at the time was enacting Richard III. Before leaving the playhouse, she invited him to come and spend the night with her. He was to seek admission under the name of Richard III. "Shakespeare overhearing their conclusion went before, was entertained, and at his game ere Burbidge came. Then message being brought that Rich. the 3d was at the dore, Shakespeare caused returne to be made that William the Conquerour was before Rich. the 3d." The prank, recorded in the diary of John Manningham under the date of March 13, 1602, though as worded referring to a much earlier date, did nothing to impair the close association of the two men. In his will Shakespeare, on March 25, 1616, left a sum to Burbage for the purchase of a ring.

It is not sufficiently remembered in discussions of Shakespeare's intentions concerning the heroes of his tragedies that he knew before he began to write that Burbage was going to enact those parts. The portrait of the great actor shows him to have had a muscular, possibly even stocky figure, and it was inevitable that Shakespeare's conception of his tragic hero would take into account Burbage's physique. Thus, that wisp of a wisp the world has so often seen impersonating Hamlet, sometimes effeminately, could not possibly have been the Prince of Denmark of whom Shakespeare had been thinking.*

Though we have no direct reference to Burbage's style of acting, there is a description of "An Excellent Actor" in the 1615 edition of Overbury's book *Characters* (an addition, after Overbury's death, probably written by Webster) in which the reference to painting makes it fairly certain that the model was Burbage. It makes it possible to gauge what Burbage's art was like:

He doth not strive to make nature monstrous, she is often seene in the same Scaene with him, but neither on Stilts nor Crutches . . . What we see him personate, we thinke truely done before us; a man of a deepe thought might apprehend the Ghosts of our ancient Heroes walk't againe . . . Hee is much affected to painting, and 'tis a question whether that make him an excellent Plaier, or his playing an exquisite painter. Hee adds grace to the Poet's labours: for what in the Poet is but ditty [i.e., a passage to be recited] in him is both ditty and musicke . . . What he doth fainedly that doe others essentially: this day one plaies a Monarch, the next a priuate person. Heere one Acts a Tyrant, on the morrow an Exile: a Parasite this man to night, to morrow a Precisian [i.e., a Puritan; doubtless Malvolio is here referred to, for in *Twelfth Night* he is called a "precision"] and so of diuers others. I obserue, of all men liuing, a worthy Actor in one kind is the strongest motiue of affection that can be; for when he dies, wee cannot be perswaded any man can doe his parts like him.

He was named with Marlowe's leading actor, Edward Alleyn, as one of the two "best actors of our time," and the same contemporary said of him that the delight of watching these two men was the "pleasure of graceful action" ever "fitted to the speech." Another praised him for "animating" the dialogue and enriching it "with action" and called him "a delightful *Proteus* so wholly transforming himself in to his Part, and putting himself off with his Cloathes,† as he never (not so much in the Tyringhouse [i.e., dressing

---

*See the present author's *The Heart of Hamlet* for abundant proof afforded by the play itself that Hamlet was an athletic, violent, and nonprocrastinating man.
†Method actors, take note!

room]) assum'd himself again until the play was done."

It is clear that he was remarkable for the musical quality of his voice, the grace of his movements, the appropriateness of his gestures to the lines, and, what was most important, the illusion of reality he imparted to his roles. He had, of course, the advantage of having Shakespeare in the company; how much the dramatist's advice and direction may have perfected his art we are free to imagine. It was, surely, one of the most creative relationships on record. We have no way of knowing to what extent Burbage's style may have been oratorical, but we may assume that he satisfied the criterion of naturalness which Hamlet (being enacted at the moment by Burbage himself) held up to the players. Enough to know that he convinced his audiences that he was indeed whatever man he was portraying.

If it was lucky for Burbage to have had Shakespeare at his side as coach (as later Molière's troupe was lucky to have him), Shakespeare was equally if not more fortunate to have had as heroic actor and comedian a man of such genius and versatility to count upon!

On June 29, 1613—some two years after Shakespeare had retired from active participation in its affairs–the Globe Theatre was destroyed by fire during a performance; luckily nobody was hurt or lost. Henry Wotton was present and tells us that the drama had to do with "some principal pieces of Henry the Eighth . . . King Henry, making a mask at the Cardinal Wolsey's house, and certain cannons being shot off at his entry, some of the paper, or other stuff wherewith one of them was stopped, did light on the thatch, where, being thought at first but an idle smoke, and their eyes more attentive to the show, it kindled inwardly, and . . . within less than an hour, the whole house burned to the very grounds. . . . Only one man had his breeches set on fire, that would perhaps have broiled him, if he had not, by the benefit of a provident wit, put it out with a bottle of ale." Ben Jonson, who was also in the audience, observed that there was a ditch filled with water surrounding the theater, so that the fire could easily have been extinguished had not the means of using it been lacking.

The Globe was rebuilt the next year, this time with a roof of tile instead of thatch.

There was more than one lament when Burbage died. London was in mourning, and the playwright Middleton wrote:

> *Astronomers and Stargazers this year*
> *Write but of four eclipses, five appear,*
> *Death interposing Burbage and there staying*
> *Hath made a veritable eclipse of playing.*

Another anonymous admirer said:

> *What a wide world was in that little space,*
> *Thyself a world, the Globe thy fittest place!*
> *Thy stature small, but every thought and mood*
> *Might thoroughly from thy face be understood.*

And his whole action he could change with ease
From ancient Lear to youthful Pericles.

Which is as good as a treatise on Burbage's distance from the present tendency to rearrange the character of a play to suit the personality of the actor!

Those ladies and gentlemen who find it intolerable that Shakespeare should have written his own plays have advanced some two dozen others working alone or in combination (e.g., Cardinal Wolsey, Francis Bacon, Queen Elizabeth, Raleigh, Oxford, Burton) as the true author (or authors) of the plays. They have often held up Shakespeare's will as proof that he had nothing to do with their composition. Is it not highly suspicious, they ask, that the man who died at Stratford was careful to dispose of his possessions, even remembering to leave his wife his "second best bed," but of his most precious possessions, his plays—if he had really written those attributed to him—made no bequest at all? Indeed, even Bardolaters were long worried about that omission, and too many are worried still. It is amusing to read how in 1795 the boy forger, William Henry Ireland, was so anxious to repair Shakespeare's oversight that he invented a document, a Deed of Gift (as well as an ancestor of his own), and wrote out that *pièce justicative* in Shakespeare's own hand! According to young Ireland, Shakespeare bequeathed to "Masterre William Henrye Irelande," good Elizabethan and friend of Shakespeare, "mye written Plays of Henrye fowrthe Henry fyfthe Kyng John Kyng Leare as allsoe mye written Playe neverr yett impryntedd whych I have named Kyng henry thyrde of Englande." (It was, no doubt, the intention of the lad to compose the last-named work and credit it to Shakespeare, who had rather carelessly forgotten to write it himself.) It might seem astonishing that such a detail in the forged Deed of Gift did not at once strike the "experts" whom the boy had taken in, were it not that our own proposers for authorship other than Shakespeare's dwell on Shakespeare's failure to mention his plays in his will. (They no longer belonged to him.) It was probably gratifying to those who accepted the Ireland forgeries as authentic that at last there was evidence that Shakespeare had not forgotten his plays in his will.

But now, with our extensive knowledge of Elizabethan theatrical conditions (a knowledge which those who object to Shakespeare's authorship seem unwilling to share), we realize that what *would* have been extraordinary was a mention of the plays in Shakespeare's will. A company of players in those days consisted of a group of men who owned shares in the company and who paid for the plays written for them, as well as for the costumes and props. Plays, costumes, and props belonged to the company. Once the dramatist had been paid for his work (up to £7 for a play), the drama no longer belonged to him but to them. At the time of his death Shakespeare's plays were not his to bestow; they were the property of the company to which he belonged and in which he owned shares. Of the thousands of plays produced during the Elizabethan and Jacobean periods, only a few hundred have come down to us. It was because of Shakespeare's popularity that as many as eighteen of his plays had been published, without his authority, before Heminge and Condell issued the first collected edition of his plays in 1623, seven years after his death. They printed the First Folio, thirty-six plays of that edition, because they were anxious to rescue them from oblivion as well as to inform the reader:

> Where [before] you were abus'd with diuerse stolne, and surreptitious copies, maimed, and deformed by the frauds and stealthes of iniurious impostors, that expos's them: even those, are now offer'd to your view cur'd, and perfect of their limbes; and all the rest, absolute in their numbers, as he conceiued them. [It cannot be conceded that the First Folio made good these promises of flawless texts; for the printing throughout is fairly deplorable.] Who, as he was a happie imitator of Nature, was a most gentle expresser of it. His mind and hand went together: And what he thought, he uttered with that easiness, that wee haue scarce receiued from him a blot in his papers.

Shakespeare's troupe, first called the Lord Chamberlain's Men and after the accession of James I the King's Men, had eight shareholders to begin with, including the playwright, Burbage, the celebrated clown, Will Kempe (?–1603), and Heminge (1556–1630). Another important figure, John Lowin, became a shareholder when the number was increased.

Of these, the most colorful character was Will Kempe, the first man to enact the incomparable Dogberry. He had played with Alleyn, and before coming to the Lord Chamberlain's Men was already famous as a clown and dubbed the "most Comical and conceited [ingenious] . . . Jestmonger." Kempe was also adored for his dancing and jigs. Along with Shakespeare and Burbage, he was an original shareholder when the Globe Theatre was bought in 1599, but he quickly sold his shares. Ivor Brown reasonably surmises that the temperamental Kempe had managed to have a row with Shakespeare, who was famous for his equable disposition. It may very well be that Shakespeare had let Kempe know he was fed up with his self-indulgence on the stage where he made ducks and drakes of a play by freely improvising his clowning merely to please the worst elements in the audience. Indisputably it was personal pique that caused Shakespeare to interject into *Hamlet* the prince's caution to the players to avoid such trumpery, for the lines have nothing to do with the action of the tragedy itself. "And let those that play your clowns speak no more than is set down for them; for there be of them that will themselves laugh, to set on some quantity of barren spectators to laugh too, though in the meantime some necessary question of the play be then to be considered; that's villainous, and shows a most pitiful ambition in the fool that uses it." It is very probably some such objection voiced to Kempe which made him quit the company.

Kempe, as he himself put it, then proceeded to dance himself "out of the world," for the next year he made a bet, which he won, that he could dance from London to Norwich. This exploit took him from February 11 to March 11, 1600. He then went to Italy and Germany, and is described as "dancing the morrice ouer the Alpes." By 1602 his funds were so low that he borrowed money from the theatrical manager, Henslowe. Thereafter, there are no records of him, though he may be the man who was buried in St. Saviour's Church in November 1603 with the ungracious inscription: "the man Kempe."

He was succeeded in the Lord Chamberlain's Men, probably in 1599, the year he left, by Robert Armin (?1568–1611), a comedian of much subtler technique, for whom, it seems, Shakespeare wrote the wonderful roles of Touchstone, Feste, and the Fool in *Lear*. He also became the second Dogberry.

John Lowin (1576–1653), who at the age of twenty-six had acted with Henslowe's company, joined the King's Men in 1603, the following year, and became one of the best-known actors in that troupe. A big man, he was acclaimed for his bluff soldiers and gruff villains, and especially for his Falstaff. During the Puritan Commonwealth, after the theaters had been officially closed (in 1642), Lowin could be caught performing at the Drury Lane Cockpit. (A theater with an interesting history: it was built in 1609 for cockfights, and converted into a theater in 1616 by Christopher Beeston. On Shrove Tuesday, 1617, while merrymaking, the London apprentices set fire to it, but Beeston rebuilt it. When the theaters were ordered closed by the Puritans, illegal performances were occasionally still given at the Cockpit.) In his old age Lowin became quite impoverished and opened The Three Pigeons, a tavern at Brentford. He died in 1653 and was buried in the churchyard of St. Martin's-in-the-Fields.

We know the names of other actors in Shakespeare's company but little of interest concerning them. Though we do know that Robert Gough (?–1625) and Richard Robinson (?–1648), as boys, played the heroines and that Richard Baxter (1593–?1666), who joined the company after Shakespeare's death to play small parts, one day accidentally hurt a member of the audience who was either on the stage or close to it with his sword; a riot very nearly resulted. When the theaters were closed in 1642, he was one of those who managed to act in secret until 1648, and may have been "Mr. Baxter," one of the earliest actors of the Restoration when the theaters were reopened. But beyond Burbage and Alleyn, actors, as such, were not considered worth memorializing. Their social status was too low.

Yet actors were once instrumental in rendering patriotic service to England. In Cornwall there was an antique theater surviving in a meadow; it went by the name of Piran Round. Here, even as late as Shakespeare's day, the Cornish mysteries were performed for several thousand spectators at a time. Around 1600, some strolling players were performing at night in Piran Round when a Spanish detachment landed by boat to plunder and set fire to the town. As the invaders were making their way across the fields, the players were representing a battle scene on the enclosed grassy plot. They "struck up a loud alarum with drum and trumpet on the stage, which the enemy hearing, thought they were discovered, made some few idle shots, and so in a hurly-burly fled to their boats. And thus the townsmen were apprized of their danger, and delivered from it at the same time."

With the growth of Puritanism the attacks on stage and players continued. In 1587, before the outset of Shakespeare's career, Stephen Gosson's *A School of Abuse* had denounced them illogically in what he called his "pleasant invective against poets, players, jesters, and such like caterpillars of a Commonwealth." Caligula thought so much of actors that he allowed them "openly to kiss his lips, when the senators might scarcely have a lick at his feet." Domitian's murder was fitting because it occurred as the emperor was returning from a play.

In the reign of Charles I, the anonymous author of *A Short Treatise against Stage Plays* attacked all drama as unchristian: tragedy is murder and comedy social vice, both bad instruction for the body politic. Moreover, he asked, in what page of Holy Writ is sanction given to the profession of player? And though actors are not mentioned in the Bible, the effects they produce are specifically condemned there. Men laugh at sins in comedy, but Ham was cursed for laughing at his father. Young men wear the clothes of women in plays, yet Deuteronomy is very clear on that subject as an abomination.

In Arles, the Church fathers decided that no actor should be allowed the sacrament. (Was anything more needed to convince men of an actor's wickedness?) Moreover, to avoid the theater was merely an act of self-preservation: how many men had been slain in a theater or on their way to or from one! How many actors had died at the conclusion of a play! How many patrons had lost their lives when theaters caught fire or stages were swept away by storms, crushing innocent spectators! (No data are given to substantiate these catastrophes.) The hand of God was evident enough in the punishments He had meted out.

In 1631 the churchwardens and constables petitioned Archbishop Laud to remove the players from Blackfriars, where a thriving theater was attracting large audiences. Shopkeepers in the parish complained that their wares were knocked off the open stalls by coaches and people hurrying to the theater; residents, for the same reasons, had difficulty getting beer or coal delivered to their houses, and in case of fire what help could penetrate the mobs of theatergoers?

In 1633 a powerful broadside aimed at the theaters was issued by William Prynne in his *Histrio-Mastix*. He had seen painters beautifying the old Fortune Theatre and the Red Bull; at Whitefriars he had noted a new theater being built. In his book, which runs over twelve hundred pages, he exclaimed, "There are five devil's chapels in London; and yet in more extensive Rome, in Nero's days, there were but three, and those were three too many!" The plays themselves were "the very pomps of the devil which we renounce in baptisms," and are "sinful, heathenish, lewd, ungodly spectacles, and most pernicious corruptions." He went on to point out the violent ends justly visited upon kings who favored plays, though he was well aware that the British king approved of them and the queen herself was not averse to appearing in court masques. For his impudence, Puritan Prynne was sentenced to imprisonment for life, the loss of both ears, and a fine of £5,000. It was not until 1640 that the Long Parliament released him and he entered London in triumph with wreaths of ivy and rosemary about his hat.

When the official closing of the theaters in 1642 still did not succeed in abolishing the profession of acting, in the spring of 1647 a Puritan Parliament disbanded all companies of players. Its decree described actors as heathens, intolerable to Christians, and vicious beyond redemption; the whip and the stocks would now compel them to obey the laws they had flouted. That plays, nevertheless, continued to be given is clear from the press of October of the same year, declaring that Parliament was taking new steps to suppress them. These measures proved effective, and all life went out of the opposition to the suppression.

During the struggle between the king and his Puritan Parliament, a great many actors enlisted as soldiers on the king's side. One such actor, Will Robinson, encountered the Puritan Harrison in battle; as Harrison ran him through with his sword, he cried, "Cursed is he that doeth the work of the Lord negligently!"

The suppression of the players was inconsistent. While Shakespeare's works were banished from Blackfriars and the Cockpit, at the foot of Holborn Bridge, owners of puppet shows were making a mint of money with their simple-minded exhibits. When an excellent troupe of players took over the Cockpit for a few days in 1648, on the fourth day, in the middle of their performance, Puritan soldiers invaded the premises, captured the actors, expelled the audience, and smashed the seats and stage to smithereens; the players were then marched through the streets in their costumes and jailed.

The execution of Charles I put an end to all hopes for a return of the theater to its days of glory. One of the last of the actors to persevere valiantly was Robert Cox. After the ban of 1642 he performed short comic roles at country fairs and appeared at the Red Bull in London, varying his comedy with feats of legerdemain and rope-dancing. His repertory was made up of passages from popular plays; he was much liked as Bottom in the broad comedy scenes from *A Midsummer Night's Dream*. Unhappily, in 1653, he was seized at the Red Bull along with fellow actors by soldiers of the Commonwealth and sent to prison where he died two years later.

3

The Restoration

Soon after the accession of Charles II to the throne in 1660, two London theaters were licensed to give plays. And of those two, only one at a time was attracting enough audience to be successful. The general public absented itself—and no wonder. Restoration plays did not interest the ordinary Londoners who had once given enthusiastic support to the many theaters the city could boast of in Shakespeare's day. Audiences now consisted of a handful of courtiers.

That age, which so prided itself on its "taste," today seems remarkably lacking in it, largely because taste evidenced itself in outward things only, while the core was fairly rotten. Charles and his entourage had spent their long exile in France; they returned to England eager to play the sedulous apes to the French manner. In Paris and Versailles, elegance, wit, classic dignity, and a satirical approach to the comic were at a premium, as were the pseduo-Aristotelian "rules." So these became indispensable for the British court and its hangers-on. Those criteria were so well suited to the French critical temper and its love of clarity that they made possible the masterpieces of Molière and Racine. Unhappily they were at war with that spacious, romantic nature of the English which had already produced such a luxurious and magnificent flourishing of poetry in Spenser and Marlowe, as well as the plays of Shakespeare and his fellows.

The elegance and wit of Molière (like that of his contemporary, La Fontaine, in his *Fables*), whatever labors he expended upon his comedies, have the effect of naturalness, of an effortless and true simplicity. His satire is rooted in his love of decency and common sense, and his faith in human kindness. The dignity of Racine which breathes through the most elegant verse ever written in France, because it gives form and shape to the violent emotions his leading characters experience, only reinforces their effect on us. His art is inseparable from the exquisitely rhymed Alexandrines of his verse and—perhaps unique to him—from those three unities which so easily have played havoc with the work of other dramatists. The secret of accomplishments like these was not granted to the Restoration dramatists.* Their tragedies work too hard at elegance and end by being pompous and stuffy —and exceedingly boring. Their comedies, at first, seem diverting because of some excellent wit; but it is fatal to read too many of them for there is in all of them a pervading heartlessness and cynicism which soon enough render the wit wearisome and, finally, distasteful.

The Shakespearean plays which these small Restoration audiences were permitted to see were more often than not, as has already been indicated, garrotted by tasteless adaptations, omissions, and additions, and irrelevant music and dancing which were interpolated by tasteless "improvers." It is worth remembering, in defense of those audiences, that the reading public was, on the whole, unacquainted with Shakespeare's plays. The collected editions, the folios, published in 1623, 1632, 1663, and 1685 were large, cumbersome books, expensive to buy. By the time the fourth folio was printed in 1685 only three thousand copies had been sold, a scant number for a sale of fifty-two years. Pepys, for all his addiction to reading, seems not to have owned Shakespeare's plays until the summer of 1664.

In Restoration matters Pepys is usually a good barometer, precisely because his preferences were so average. On March 1, 1662, he reports seeing *Romeo and Juliet* "the first time it was ever acted [i.e., since the theaters were reopened], but it is a play of itself the worst that ever I heard, and the worst acted that ever I saw these people do, and I am resolved to go no more to see the first time of acting, for they were all of them out more or less." On September 29 of the same year, he saw *A Midsummer Night's Dream*, "which I had never seen before, nor shall I ever see it again, for it is the most insipid, ridiculous play that ever I saw in my life." The next year he saw *Twelfth Night*, "a silly play, and not related at all to the name or day"; in December he expected to see "a rare play," the "story of Henry the Eighth, with all his wives." On July 7, 1664, he at last bought a volume of Shakespeare's plays, obviously one of the folios. It was his opinion that *The Adventures of Five Hours*, an adaptation of a play by Calderon, was the best play he had ever seen "or think I ever shall." Reading it, he admired it more than ever. Then he read *Othello* (which he had seen on October 11, 1660), and which he "ever heretofore esteemed a mighty good play, but having so lately read *The Adventures of Five Hours*, it seems a mean thing." On December 28, 1666, he records having been at the playhouse, where the king and courtiers were kept waiting for more than an hour for the actors, to see *Henry V*, which was well acted, "but I sat so high and far off, that I missed most of the words, and sat with a wind coming into my back and neck, which did much trouble me. The play continued till twelve at night; and then up, and a most horrid cold night it was, and frosty and moonshine."

*With the possible exception of Congreve, though it cannot be denied that he is as guilty of callousness as his fellows, for all his polished wit. Compare his Millamant (of *The Way of the World*), the most engaging of Restoration heroines, with that scintillating but warm-hearted girl upon whom she was modeled, Beatrice (of *Much Ado about Nothing*).

Of course, not everyone was so impervious to the beauties of Shakespeare. The great critic of the age, Dryden, seems to have had a lifelong struggle between his love of Shakespeare and the classic rules and "taste" to which he felt he owed allegiance, and which he, himself, had done so much to promulgate. In 1668, in his fine *Essay of Dramatick Poesy,* he obviously spoke out of the fullness of his heart: "Shakespeare was the man who of all modern, and perhaps of ancient poets, had the largest and most comprehensive soul. All the images of Nature were still present to him, and he drew them, not laboriously but luckily; when he describes anything you more than see it, you feel it too. Those who accuse him to have wanted learning, give him the greater commendation: he was naturally learned. . . . He is always great, when some great occasion is presented to him." Inevitably, Ben Jonson, the classicist battling for the classic "rules" unsuccessfully among a host of Elizabethan and Jacobean romanticists, was the predecessor whom Dryden most honored. Of him, he added, "I admire him, but I love Shakespeare." In 1672 his view was severer: "Shakespeare, who many times has written better than any poet in any language . . . writes, in many places, below the dullest writer of ours or any precedent age." In 1676 he speaks out with more becoming modesty in the third person as the author of *Aurungzebe:* "A secret shame/Intrudes his breast at Shakespeare's sacred name."

In 1693, when William and Mary were on the throne, Thomas Rymer, called by Macaulay "the worst critic who has ever lived," judged Shakespeare harshly by the neoclassical rules, and found him wanting. He denounced Shakespeare in tragedy as "quite out of his element, his brains are turned; he raves and rambles without any coherence, any spark of reason, or any rule to control him, or set bounds to his frenzy"; the tragic parts of *Othello* make "none other than a bloody farce, without salt or savor." In answer to this Dryden the next year wrote: Shakespeare had a genius for tragedy, "and we know, in spite of Mr. Rymer, that genius alone is a greater virtue . . . than all other qualifications put together." In the long run Dryden knew that a universal genius like Shakespeare could not be measured by any set of rules.

The presentation of Shakespeare was affected not only by the mauling of the plays but also by differences in the structure of Restoration theaters. The new tradition was, in many respects, quite alien to Shakespeare's original conceptions. The Theatre (1576), The Curtain (1577), The Rose (c. 1587), The Swan (c. 1596), The Fortune (1600), The Hope (1613), the converted tavern of The Red Bull, the Theatre at Newington Butts, of which not much is known, and the most celebrated of them all, The Globe (1599), where many of Shakespeare's plays were originally performed, were all "public" playhouses and had a number of features in common. They were open to the sky, had a large open stage thrust out into the center of the enclosed space, with audiences standing around that platform (the so-called groundlings). Under the enclosure were galleries, with a roof over the top one; at the back of the stage was the "tiring house" and doors for entrances and exits; above the tiring house was an open balcony (sometimes only windows) used in the plays for balconies (*Romeo and Juliet, The Merchant of Venice*), walls of a town (*Richard II, Henry V*), or upper rooms (*The Comedy of Errors*). At the back of the stage itself was a curtained space, used for eavesdropping scenes (*Much Ado about Nothing, Hamlet, Othello*), or, when the curtain was opened, to show a scene where furniture, like thrones or beds could have been made ready (*Romeo and Juliet, Othello*); on the stage itself were trapdoors for the emergence and disappearance of apparitions (*Macbeth*) or for burial scenes (*Hamlet*). The actors had their own stage door at the rear of the theater; the audience entered from outside by the only other door, on the payment of a penny; those who did not wish to mingle with the standing groundlings could pay an extra penny or two (sometimes as much as sixpence) to mount to the galleries, where there were benches and stools. During performances, it was common for the public to be eating fruit and cracking nuts, and to show their dissatisfaction by throwing the cores and hulls at actors they did not like. Performances began at 2 P.M. The furniture was scant, when there was any at all, but the costumes were magnificent. Often given as gifts by noblemen from their own wardrobes, the costumes were always contemporary and the noblest Roman of them all, like his fellow Romans, appeared as an Elizabethan gentleman, and Cleopatra as a Jacobean lady of fashion.

There were also a few "private" theaters, which were roofed and charged higher admission—the two Blackfriar Theatres (1576 and 1596), The Porter's Hall (1615), and The Cockpit (1616). These had not been built specifically as theaters, but were renovations of existing buildings. They were used mostly by the children's companies, the target of some acerbic remarks by Hamlet; but later the owners of The Globe used the second Blackfriars when the weather and temperature made it advisable. These private theaters had stages much resembling the public ones. The differences were: the necessity of using candles, when the light coming through the spacious windows was insufficient; the benches for seating the audiences in the pit (whereon the groundlings stood in the public theaters); and on the stage, as in masques presented at court, some movable furniture and scenery. They retained, however, the inner stage. In 1608 or 1609 the King's Men began to use the second Blackfriars, and it was for that playhouse that Shakespeare must have written his last three works, *Cymbeline, The Winter's Tale*, and *The Tempest*, as well as the two plays on which he collaborated after his retirement from London, *Henry VIII* and *The Two Noble Kinsmen*.

When the Puritan government banned the theaters, some players joined other professions in order to survive. But the majority of younger ones refused to submit to the prohibition. We are told that they met and "made up one Company out of all the Scatter'd Members of Several," and even "ventured to Act some plays with as much caution and privacy as cou'd be, at the Cockpit." During one such performance, foot soldiers surprised them in the middle of a play and carried them off to prison, still wearing their costumes. Despite such harassment, they were not easily discouraged. On one occasion they bribed an officer at Whitehall to let them perform at the

Red Bull for a few days during the Christmas holiday.

Sir William D'Avenant (1606–1688), returning to London after several years in exile, contrived to circumvent the Commonwealth ban by presenting instead of a "play," an "entertainment" or an "opera." In May 1656 he put together a small theater "at the back part of Rutland House," in Aldersgate Street, and there gave an "entertainment . . . after the manner of the ancients" and subsequently what has been called the first English opera, *The Siege of Rhodes,* advertised as a "representation by the art of prospective [*sic*] in scenes, and the story sung in recitative music." This performance probably introduced the first elaborate scenery into an English theater.

Shortly after his accession to the throne, Charles II, after temporary use of a new Red Bull Theatre on Vere Street and a renovated Cockpit, authorized two London theaters. To prevent the emergence of further new companies, he granted in August 1660 the right to Killigrew and D'Avenant to open their two playhouses and choose the members of their companies. He gave Killigrew his patent on April 25, 1662, and D'Avenant his on January 15, 1663. In consequence these two managers and the men who fell heir to their patents had a monopoly on London theater for one hundred eighty years. Only they could legally present "legitimate" playwrights—with the exception of the Haymarket which was opened occasionally during the summer. This was the situation until 1843. D'Avenant's company (the Duke of York's Company) began at the old theater in Salisbury Court, but the next year moved to Lincoln's Inn Fields. Killigrew's (the King's Company) moved in 1660 from the Red Bull to Vere Street, and in 1663 to a new theater in Brydges Street, Drury Lane.

For more than ten years Lincoln's Inn Fields and Drury Lane were the only theaters in London. From 1670 to 1680, D'Avenant's widow, son, and the actors Betterton and Harris operated a new house in Dorset Gardens. A second theater, designed like the one in Dorset Gardens by Sir Christopher Wren, was built, but burned to the ground on January 25, 1671/1672 the company vacated the house in Lincoln's Inn Fields. The King's Company opened its new theater in March 1674. In 1693 Christopher Rich decided to remodel it in order to provide more room for the audience at the expense of the stage. Rich was the first of a series of businessmen who took over the theater not because they loved it, but for the money they could make out of it. He himself was an autocratic lawyer, succeeded by a long line of wretches with whom the theater could well have done without. A contemporary described this new breed of managers as "Adventurers, who, though entirely ignorant of Theatrical Affairs, are still admitted to a proportionate vote in the management of them," and complained bitterly that "while the Theatrical Hive has so many drones in it, the labouring Actors are under the greatest discouragement, if not a direct state of oppression." The old profit-sharing system vanished, and actors were placed on fixed salaries. They thus lost their financial stake in the play, and the theater became a kind of battleground between businessmen and artists, and, only too often, between businessmen and businessmen. There eventually developed the custom of subletting the lease of a theater: at the time of Garrick that was already a nuisance; today Miles calls it "a positive disgrace."

The earlier Restoration theaters, being indoor playhouses, had their affinities not with the old public theaters, but with the private ones. Influenced by Italian design, their stages had a much smaller apron, curving out into the pit where there were once more benches for the audience. The stage was surmounted by a proscenium arch for the first time. In these theaters were the rudimentary beginnings of the boxed-in stage. "Doors of entrance," as they were called, opened on the forestage. The Lincoln's Inn Fields playhouse on Portugal Street measured some seventy-five feet in length and thirty feet in width. In Brydges Street, the Theatre Royal had about the same dimensions as Drury Lane which now occupies the same site. A visiting Frenchman described the Theatre Royal as the best he had ever seen among European playhouses, and praised its well-equipped stage, handsome decor, and gilded upholstery, though it was at that same theater that Pepys complained of assaulting draughts.

Mrs. Mary Meggs (?–1691), known as Orange Moll, was granted a license for thirty-nine years, at £100 outright and 6s. 8d. a day, for the right to sell oranges and other edibles in Killigrew's playhouse. This did not include the rough crowds in the galleries. They, unlike their more refined counterparts below, did not limit themselves to conversing loudly and throwing peels, but were quite ready to use the whole fruit as a weapon against the performers. Orange Moll became an indispensable adjunct to Killigrew's theater. On one occasion the actress Mrs. Knipp (?–1677) sent her to Pepys with a message that he was to come and speak to her after the play, while on another occasion she recalled that "Sir W. Pen and I had a great deal of discourse with Moll; who tells us that Nell [Gwynn (1650–1687)] is already left by my Lord Brockhurst, and that he makes sport of her, and swears she hath all she could get of him; and Hart [the actor], her great admirer, now hates her; and that she is very poor." Despite Orange Moll's gossip things began to look up for Nell Gwynn very soon, when the king made her his mistress. Orange Moll was certainly efficient, for Pepys records on November 2, 1667, that a well-dressed gentleman sitting just in front of him was eating some fruit during a performance of *Henry IV, Part I*, choked on the food, and fell down as though dead, "but with much ado Orange Moll did thrust her finger down his throat, and brought him to life again." Pepys also informs us that she was not above cheating. During a performance of *The Tempest* she came into the pit and asked to be paid for twelve oranges "which she delivered by my order at a late play, at night, in order to give to some ladies in a box, which was wholly untrue, but yet she swore it to be true. But, however, I did deny it, and did not pay her; but for quiet, did buy 4s. worth of oranges of her, at 6d. a piece." When a fire which destroyed Drury Lane in 1672 was found to have started under the stairs where Orange Moll kept her fruit she was thought to have been responsible through careless handling of her light when replenishing her supplies.

The Elizabethan private theaters had depended chiefly on their large windows for light, while the Restoration playhouses, like the Italian theaters, were illuminated mainly by chandeliers hanging over the stage. A curtain was also introduced, though not much employed. At the opening of a performance, a prologue would be spoken on the apron; then the curtain, hung from above the proscenium opening, would rise and remain unseen until the conclusion of the play. The end of a scene was indicated by the change of scenery, which was effected without lowering the curtain, and the end of an act by an empty stage.

It is a matter of some dispute as to when actresses were first on view in London. According to two dubious references, it is possible that a very few actresses had appeared in the last decades before the time of the Puritan revolution. But in 1592 Thomas Nashe could still boast that English players differed from those across the Channel "that have whores and common courtesans to play women's parts."

All of Shakespeare's women were enacted by boys, of course—just as boys have played female roles in school plays from time immemorial. (The Puritan Prynne had, indeed, accused the boy-actors of "that unnatural sodomitical sin of uncleanness." But the charge was without basis: the boy-actors had been lodged with adult actors who were family men and treated them as members of the family circle.) Several of Shakespeare's comedies effected something like total realism when the heroines (Rosalind, Viola, Imogen) throughout most of the play assumed the garb of young men. To appear as women, the boys wore a kind of platform shoe, the chopine, which elevated their height by about a foot, while the female dress of the time was so elaborate and so entirely hid the body that the illusion of femininity was not difficult to maintain, particularly if their voices were pitched high enough.

Apparently a woman was first seen on the London stage during the Restoration when on December 8, 1660, the mistress of Prince Rupert, Margaret Hughes (?–1719), enacted Desdemona at the new Red Bull Theatre on Vere Street. For that performance Thomas Jordan wrote a prologue complaining of the men who had been appearing as heroines:

> Our women are defective, and so siz'd,
> You'd think they were some of the guard disguis'd,
> For to speak truth, men act, that are between
> Forty and fifty, wenches of fifteen;
> With bones so large and nerve so incompliant,
> When you call Desdemona, enter Giant.

To introduce Margaret Hughes, Jordan said:

> Mistake me not,
> No man in gown . . .
> . . . In this reforming age,
> We have intents to civilize the stage.

With the Restoration of the Stuarts, D'Avenant brought together the first theatrical company in 1660. It included the brightest star of the age,

Thomas Betterton, as well as as Edward Kynaston and others. At the beginning, men continued to enact female roles, particularly Kynaston, William Betterton, Mosely (who was usually the bawd), and Floyd (who appeared frequently as the whore in Restoration plays), but in 1662, when Charles II granted D'Avenant a revised patent, it contained what has been called the Magna Carta of the English stage: permission that women's roles be enacted by women. Among the actresses soon to join D'Avenant's troupe were Mrs.* Davenport, Mrs. Saunderson (later Mrs. Thomas Betterton), Mrs. Davis, and Mrs. Long, all of whom were leading actresses and were lodged in D'Avenant's own house, and Mrs. Gibbs, Mrs. Norris, Mrs. Holden, and Mrs. Jennings.

At first, there were not enough actresses, and it was necessary to continue to use young men for women's roles. One of the last of these was Edward Kynaston (?1640–1706), whom Pepys thought "the loveliest lady I ever saw." He was much petted by women of fashion, and Colley Cibber tells us: "Kynaston at that time was so beautiful a youth that the ladies of quality prided themselves in taking him with them in their coaches to Hyde Park in his theatrical habit, after the play." His forte was "in moving compassion and pity," and few actresses were to do as well as he in the roles in which he had appeared. Once, when King Charles came to the theater and found the actors unready to begin, he demanded to know the reason. The manager confessed that Kynaston, who was to play the role of the queen, "was not shav'd yet."

As he grew older Kynaston gave up female parts, though when he was "past sixty his teeth were all sound, white and even, as one could wish to see in a reigning toast of twenty." But while doing his female characters he had developed a sort of whine in his speech, which he carried over later into men's parts. When George Powel, a fellow actor, had a fit of vomiting after a debauch and Kynaston inquired whether he still felt ill, Powel replied, "How is it possible to feel otherwise when I hear you speak?" Nevertheless, even in his male roles, Kynaston commanded a majestic presence. "He had," says Cibber, "something of a formal gravity in his mien, which was attributed to the stately step he had been so early confined to, in female decency." But he seems to have postponed too long retiring from the stage, and in his last years his memory constantly failed him. He died quite wealthy, and was buried in St. Paul's Churchyard.

It seems incredible that the actor who was considered the nonpareil of the Restoration should have been squat, ill-formed, and clumsy to the degree that his elegant clothes, laces, and curled periwig (for in that raiment did Shakespeare's heroes appear on the boards in that era) could not conceal his awkwardness. Yet such was the case of Thomas Betterton (1635–1710), as reported by Anthony Aston, a wild Irishman. According to Aston, Better-

*Mrs. was then also a designation for spinster, Miss for a lewd woman.

ton had an enormous head which was disproportionate to his undersized corpulent body; his legs (which in the clothes of the day were very much in evidence) were ungainly and his feet large; his face was fretted with pock-marks; his eyes, though very expressive, were small; his neck was thick and short, and his shoulders stooped. He wisely refrained from using his short fat arms for a gesture, and usually kept his left hand "lodged in his breast, between his coat and waistcoat . . . His voice was low and grumbling, yet he could tune it by an artful climax, which enforced universal attention, even from the fops and orange-girls. He was incapable of dancing, even in a country dance." To this picture must be added the fact that, since he was generally admired, he must have spoken his lines with something of that nasal twang to which Restoration acting was given as a result of the court's exile in France during the Puritan regime.

It may be that earlier in his career Betterton did not present a stooped figure and looked taller, for Aston saw him only during the last decades of his career, as did Colley Cibber, who greatly venerated him as an actor. He might even have been slender and graceful as a young man, for how could he have been cast as Mercutio in 1662, if his figure at that time had been anything like what Aston describes?

For some ten years, the two patent companies were unable to sustain themselves financially—this was before Rich entered the picture. So in 1682 they were united and their performances were given at the smaller house in Drury Lane. The Dorset Garden (after 1685 it was known as the Queen's Theatre) was used only for some grand spectacle, and was eventually torn down in 1709. With the merger some actors left the company, including the two greatest tragic actors, Charles Hart and Joseph Harris. Betterton was thus left the undisputed leader of the stage.

This single company endured for thirteen years. In 1695, Christopher Rich, the patentee, undertook to lower the salaries of the chief actors, many of whom rejected his offer and managed to win a new patent to perform from William III. With the help of a number of noblemen's subscriptions they finally opened a modest new theater on the site of a tennis court on Portugal Street and another in Lincoln's Inn Fields, a modest building. Its first performance was of Congreve's *Love for Love* on April 30, 1695.

In 1705, Sir John Vanbrugh raised a subscription to build a new theater in the Haymarket. The acoustics were bad, the interior much too large for plays, and the enterprise was doomed to failure from the beginning. By 1710 it became an opera house. Vanbrugh attempted to unite the two acting companies again, but Rich refused to cooperate, even though Vanbrugh had the backing of the government. He succeeded in "unloading" the Haymarket on Owen MacSwiney, Rich's assistant. Rich hoped to gain control of the Haymarket too, but a quarrel with MacSwiney put an end to that scheme. On October 6, 1707, Skipwith, a large shareholder in Drury Lane, gave his entire interest in it as a gift to his friend Brett, who succeeded in effecting a union between the two companies; all actors returned to Drury Lane, and operas were to be given at the Haymarket under MacSwiney. Brett retired and Rich once more began to oppress the actors at Drury Lane until the court stilled him in 1709 as the result of a petition by the players, who had begun to return to the Haymarket. Rich was dispossessed from Drury Lane in 1709. Finally during the season 1711/12 the management was subleased to three leading actors, Robert Wilks (1665–1732), Thomas Doggett (?1670–1721), and Colley Cibber (1671–1757).

As actor-manager of the single troupe, Colley Cibber developed an enthusiasm for Betterton which is contagious. Despite Aston's description of a gauche-looking Thomas Betterton, Cibber conceded: "Betterton was an actor, as Shakespeare was an author, both without competitors; formed for the mutual assistance and illustration of each other's genius. How Shakespeare wrote, all men who have a taste for nature may read and know [Shakespeare, by this time, was being published in more popular editions]—but with what higher rapture would he still be read could they conceive how Betterton played him. Then might they know the one was born alone to speak what the other only knew to write. . . . Could how Betterton spoke be as easily known as what he spoke, then might you see the Muse of Shakespeare in her triumph. . . . I therefore tell you that all the Othellos, Hamlets, Hotspurs, Macbeths, and Brutuses whom you may have seen since his time have fallen short of him." (Cibber's account was published thirty years after Betterton's death.)

To give examples of Betterton's brilliance, Cibber cites particular interpretations. Many actors doing Hamlet, in the prince's interview with the Ghost, "express rage and fury, and the house has thundered with applause." Betterton, on the contrary, opened the scene "with a pause of mute amazement; then rising slowly to a solemn, trembling voice, he made the ghost equally terrible to the spectator as to himself."* While in his reactions to the Ghost's revelations, his expostulations were always "governed by decency, manly, but not braving; his voice never rising into that seeming outrage of wild defiance of what he naturally revered." (The last comment gives us a good idea of how that scene was usually done.) Cibber comments on the actor's problem of steering between the Scylla and Charybdis of tearing a passion to tatters and conveying too little feeling, and calls the solution of it "of all the master-strokes of an actor the most difficult to reach. In this none yet have equalled Betterton."

Nevertheless, Betterton could vary the temperaments of the different characters he portrayed. His Hotspur was done with "wild impatient starts" and "fierce and flashing fire"; his Brutus with "unruffled temper" for during the dispute with Cassius "his spirit flew only to his eyes; his steady look alone supplied that terror which he disdained an intemperance in his voice should rise to."

If Cibber knew Betterton only in his maturer days, Pepys had seen him from the time the theaters had reopened, and was just as enthusiastic. In 1661 he and his wife thought Betterton "the best actor in the world," and

*Barton Booth, who played the Ghost, said that when he and Betterton acted this scene together, "instead of my awing him, he terrified me. But divinity hung around that man."

he found the player's Hamlet "beyond imagination." When he saw him two years later in the same role, he said that Betterton gave him "fresh reason never to think enough" of him.

The great actor's Othello had all the men in the audience in tears, although he himself was already an old man. Sir John Perceval wrote in 1709: "I declare that they who cannot be moved at Othello's story so artfully worked up by Shakespeare, and justly played by Betterton, are capable of marrying again before their husbands are cold, of trampling on a lover when dying at their feet, and are fit to converse with tigers only."

His versatility, all apparently within the confines of his unexaggerated and dignified style, can be gauged by his success in the role of Sir Toby Belch, as Macbeth in D'Avenant's outrageous version, Troilus, Thersites, Falstaff, Antony, and other Shakespearean roles. Some of Aston's remarks, while paying tribute to Betterton, are a corrective to Cibber's enthusiasm: "I have often wished that Mr. Betterton would have resigned the part of Hamlet to some young actor (who might have personated, though not have acted it, better), for . . . he appeared a little too grave for a young student, . . . and his repartees seemed rather as apothegms from a sage philosopher, than the sporting flashes of a young Hamlet." But Aston goes on to speak admiringly of Betterton's reserve: he "kept his passion under, and showed it most (as fume smokes most when stifled). Betterton, from the time he was dressed to the end of the play, kept his mind in the same temperament and adaptness as the present character required. If I was to write of him all day, I should still remember fresh matter in his behalf."

Steele, who saw Betterton as Hamlet when the actor was seventy, noted that he had lost none of his old vigor. Of his Othello, when Betterton was seventy-two, Steele remarked that he so well created the illusion of the Moor's passion, that it was enough to "admonish a man to be afraid of his own heart, and perfectly to convince him that it is to stab it to admit that worst of daggers, jealousy."

When Rowe published his *Shakespeare* in 1709, the first of all critical editions of the complete plays, Betterton was still on the stage, and his praise of the actor is similar to what Cibber was to write years later. No matter what the Shakespearean role, Rowe says, Betterton "does it as if it had been written on purpose for him, and that the author had exactly conceived it as he plays it."

Unlike Pepys, Betterton cherished a deep and sincere devotion for Shakespeare's works, and it is to him that a debt of thanks is owed for keeping them alive in an age so unsympathetic to everything Shakespeare stood for, even though he was far too often compelled to act in versions which horribly perverted the dramatist's intentions. That devotion led Betterton, when well advanced in years, to make a journey into Warwickshire to collect what biographical data he could find about his idol. He came back with a small stock of anecdotes, most of them sheer fiction, and it is to him that we owe the (what I consider silly) deer-stealing story. This simple man, the son of an undercook to Charles I, and so much honored by his contemporaries, had the courage in that profligate age to stand aloof from the moral viciousness which was so much à la mode, while maintaining both personal dignity and consecration to his profession.

His wife, the former Mary Saunderson (?–1712), was a leading member of his company. They were married around 1663. She was particularly admired for her Lady Macbeth, and among other roles also appeared as Juliet, Ophelia, and Queen Katharine. During her career—she retired in 1694—she was said to have had no rival in Shakespearean roles. After her retirement she continued to give instruction to the younger actresses, and Cibber said of her, "She was a woman of an unblemished and sober life."

A prominent member of Killigrew's troupe was Charles Hart (?–1683) who before the Commonwealth had been a boy-actor. He was Shakespeare's great-nephew, his father having been the son of Shakespeare's sister Joan. He fought in the civil war on the Royalist side, was one of the original company at Drury Lane, became one of Nell Gwynn's first lovers and brought her to the stage. Among his Shakespearean roles were Othello and Brutus. Audiences were eager to see him, and he acted "with such grandeur and agreeable majesty," that a courtier said of him he "might teach any king on earth how to comport himself." His manners were laudable. Once, a rogue of a player convinced a simple-minded clergyman that the actors felt the need of being reformed and desired a chaplain for the theater. He easily talked his dupe into standing behind the scenes each morning, ringing a bell, and crying out, "Players! players! Come to prayers!" While the actors were having a merry time over the minister's folly, Hart happened to come in, was incensed at the indignity to the cloth, and invited the clergyman to dinner.

Samuel Sandford, whom King Charles called "the best villain in the world," was a member of D'Avenant's company. Cibber describes him as "an excellent actor in disagreeable characters." He was a notable Iago. "Poor Sandford," Cibber tells us, did not perform the role of a villain by choice, "for having a low and crooked person, such bodily defects were too strong to be admitted into great or amiable characters, so that whenever in any new or revived play there was a hateful or mischievous person, Sandford was sure to have no competitor for it. . . . And so unusual had it been to see Sandford an innocent man in a play, that whenever he was so, the spectators would hardly give him credit in so gross an improbability."

It is open to question whether Shakespeare intended his Iago to be the misshapen or at any rate repulsive-looking man which Sandford personified, and which, indeed, most Iagos have tended to be on our own stage. The average villain of *Othello* as seen on the boards is so frightening a spectacle that, one would think, everyone who knows him would start running in the opposite direction as soon as he is in sight. The attractive, dashing young fellow (he is only twenty-eight!) which Brian Aherne made of him in 1937, in my opinion, was far closer to what Shakespeare had in mind. How else account for Iago's popularity among his fellows? His handsomeness and outward agreeableness made Aherne's Iago a far more dangerous and devilish character.

Sandford's lot was not enviable. The audience was used to seeing him "groaning upon a wheel, stuck with daggers, impaled alive, calling his executioners, with a dying voice, cruel dogs and villains." When it was his misfortune to be cast as a decent man, "The pit, after they had sate three or four acts in quiet expectation that the well-dissembled honesty of Sandford (for such of course they concluded it) would soon be discovered, . . . when, at last, finding no such matter, but that the catastrophe had taken quite another turn, and that Sandford was really an honest man to the end of the play, they fairly damned it."

He was so masterful in portraying villains that the lesser actors, attributing his success to his personal defects, made themselves up to look as monstrous as possible when called up to play villains or murderers. King Charles himself, who was of swarthy complexion, remarked upon the murderers in *Macbeth*, "Pray what is the meaning that we never see a rogue in a play, but, Godsfish! they always clap on him a black periwig when it is well known one of the greatest rogues in England always wears a fair one?" (This may have been a reference to the Earl of Shaftesbury.)

Sandford's delivery was quite distinct from that of his fellow players. His voice was piercing and his diction impeccable. It was Cibber's conviction that he was the perfect Richard III, and that Shakespeare, had Sandford been a member of his troupe, would have selected him for the role, as he had "an uncouth stateliness in his motion, a harsh and sullen pride of speech, a meditating brow, a stern aspect, occasionally changing into an almost ludicrous triumph over all goodness and virtue." He was a sort of "theatrical Martyr to poetic justice." One curious assignment Cibber does not mention: in *Macbeth* Sandford played Banquo's ghost, though not Banquo himself before his murder. Was it because it was desired to make the ghost appear as grim as possible? He also performed comic roles, like that of Sampson in *Romeo and Juliet*, doubtless bringing to them a grostequeness undreamed of by the dramatist.

Elizabeth Barry (1658–1713) was the first outstanding English actress, and is said to have performed one hundred nineteen different roles. The dramatist Otway, the one great writer of tragedy in his time, was madly in love with her all his life. The daughter of a barrister who lost his fortune as a partisan of Charles I, she was provided for by a noblewoman and a friend of her father's. She received a good education and in 1673 an opportunity to appear on the stage. But she proved so hopelessly without talent, in the opinion of the directors, that she was dismissed three times. She could neither sing nor dance and had a poor ear for the requirements of dramatic diction. But the Earl of Rochester took her under his wing, and wagered with a friend that he could make a leading actress out of her in six months. (Could this possibly have given Shaw the idea for his Professor Higgins and Eliza Doolittle?) He went over the texts of plays with her line by line, and, being intelligent, she began to develop rapidly. Though not good-looking, she had a strong and pleasant voice, and he taught her to make the most of it. He attended thirty of her rehearsals (many of them dress rehearsals), and gave her his severest criticism. He won his bet. He also fathered a daughter by her.

She later became the mistress of the dramatist Etherege, and bore him a daughter too. But Otway, who loved her hopelessly, she treated most cruelly, even though her greatest triumphs were in his plays. That she was selfish and calculating presented no obstacle to her success, and she eventually had all London at her feet. Cibber wrote that she had no equal in exciting pity. It was said that the way she exclaimed, "Ah, poor Castalio!" in Otway's *The Orphan* caused the entire audience, as well as herself, to weep, and that when appearing as Queen Elizabeth in another silly play on the Earl of Essex, her "What mean my grieving subjects?" was uttered with such grace and dignity that the audience burst into "thunders of applause." "In characters of greatness," Cibber testifies, she had an air "of elevated dignity, her mien and motion superb and gracefully majestic; . . . no violence of passion could be too much for her; and when distress or tenderness possessed her, she subsided into the most affecting melody and softness."

She was not only cruel but vindictive. Once a dispute arose with another actress, Mrs. Boutell, as to who should wear a certain veil in *The Rival Queens*. The property man decided, apparently justly, for Mrs. Boutell. During a climactic scene when it was Mrs. Barry's business to seize her enemy, "Mrs. Barry, with the exclamation of 'Die, sorceress, die! and all my wrongs die with thee!' sent her polished dagger right through the stiff armor of Mrs. Boutell's stays. The consequences were a scratch and a shriek." But no real harm was done. Mrs. Barry's excuse was simply that she had been carried away by the scene.

During Betterton's later years, she frequently appeared with him, acting Mrs. Page to his Falstaff, Calpurnia when he played Brutus, Queen Katharine to his Henry VIII, Lady Macbeth to his Macbeth, and Cordelia to his Lear. She retired the night after his last appearance on the stage, and went to live in the charming village of Acton. She was able to live in luxury as she had managed to extract a good deal of money and jewelry from her admirers, and had been the first player to profit from benefit performances. Only authors were given the privilege of such performances until James II commanded the first one in her interest.

Davies recorded that she died, at the age of fifty-five, from the bite of a favorite lap-dog, whom she did not know to have rabies. Bellchambers comments, rather quaintly, "There seems to be no grounds for disturbing his supposition."

The beauty of the Restoration stage was Anne Bracegirdle (?1663–1748), a pupil of Betterton, who along with his wife and with his characteristic kindness gave her every encouragement. She began to act as a child of six and was doing young women's parts in her early teens. She was a great favorite of the public as well as of her fellow actors, and in Betterton's advanced years played Desdemona to his Othello, Mrs. Ford to his Falstaff, Ophelia to his Hamlet, Cordelia to his Lear, Isabella to his Angelo, and Portia to his quite aged Bassanio. But she was most famous for her perfor-

mances of the heroines in Congreve's plays: she was his great Millamant in
The Way of the World. At the very pinnacle of her success, she decided to retire
because of the threat posed to her preeminence by Anne Oldfield. "Never
any woman was in such general favor of her spectators," says Cibber, "which
to the last scene of her dramatic life, she maintained by not being unguarded
in her private character." She was, he says, "the darling of the theatre.
. . . Scarce an audience saw her that were less than half of them lovers,
without a suspected favorite among them. . . . Her constancy in resisting
them served but to increase the numbers of her admirers."

She was still living when Cibber wrote this encomium, and it is possible
that he considerably exaggerated her chastity. That she was involved with
the actor William Mountfort of Drury Lane, a married man, was common
gossip. Brown, in his *Letters from the Dead to the Living,* has a passage in which
the slain Mountfort is complaining to other gentlemen whom he has met
among the shades, of a weakness in his back which makes him "bend like
a superannuated fornicator." "Some strain," says one of them, "got in the
other world, with overheaving yourself." Mountfort asks for advice on how
to ease his pain, and the other counsels, "Get a warm girdle and tie [it]
round you." Mountfort angrily scorns the suggestion with, "How can a
single girdle do me good, when a Brace was my destruction?"

The play upon her name refers to the murder for which, enamored of him
or not, Mrs. Bracegirdle was innocently the cause. In 1692, when she was
about nineteen, a Captain Richard Hill, of the same age, proposed marriage
to her but was rejected. Convinced that she had refused him because of her
love for Mountfort, he several times publicly swore to be avenged "with
some of the bitterest invectives that could spring from brutal animosity."
Among Hill's friends was Lord Mohun who, though a youth, was far gone
in dissoluteness; he schemed with Hill to help him abduct Mrs. Bracegirdle,
whom Hill was to violate, after which, according to the moral standards of
the time, she would be only too glad to marry him. They hired a coach, six
horses, and the assistance of several soldiers. On Friday, December 9, 1692,
she dined at the house of Mr. Page on Prince's Street. When she left there
at ten o'clock accompanied by her mother and Mr. Page, two of the soldiers
seized her, nearly knocked her mother down, and tried to force Mrs. Bracegirdle into the waiting carriage. Her mother held on to her firmly, while Mr.
Page shouted for help. When assistance came, Hill insisted upon taking her
home to Howard Street, and the Strand, where she lodged. Lord Mohun,
meanwhile, concealed in the carriage, dismissed the soldiers, and joined Hill
on Howard Street. Her landlady came out, scolded Hill and Mohun, and
sent her servant to warn Mountfort, who lived nearby in Norfolk Street, that
he was in danger. Mrs. Mountfort sent in search of her husband. Between
eleven and midnight, the watch found Hill and Mohun drinking in the street,
and the landlady came out seeking to have the two culprits apprehended.
At that very moment, she saw Mountfort coming in their direction, hurried
to him, but was brushed aside before she could warn him. Conversation
between him and Mohun ensued, during which he denied any amorous

attachment to the actress. Hill, approaching them, caught some of Mount-fort's remarks, gave him a blow on the ear, and challenged him to fight. They both went into the middle of the road, and after two or three passes Mount-fort was mortally wounded. He was only twenty-eight. Lord Mohun was arraigned before Parliament as an accomplice and acquitted. Hill fled from the scene of the killing, making good his escape. Mountfort, who died the next day, swore before dying that Hill had stabbed him while he was striking him with the other hand.

Among those who laid siege to her virtue were Lord Lovelace and Con-greve; it was the dramatist who was most often seen in her company. He wrote this lyric to her:

> Pious Celinda goes to pray'rs
> Whene'er I ask the favor;
> Yet, the tender fool's in tears,
> When she believes I'll leave her.
> Would I were free from this restraint,
> Or else had power to win her!
> Would she could make of me a saint,
> Or I of her a sinner!

Rumor had it that she and Congreve had married, and a contemporary versifier wrote these lines on the assumption that that was the fact:

> Since Angelica, bless'd with a singular grace,
> Has, by her fine acting, preserv'd all his plays,
> In amorous rapture, young Valentine said,
> One so fit for his plays might be fit for his bed.
> He warmly pursues her, she yielded her charms
> And bless'd the kind youngster in her kinder arms;
> But at length the poor nymph did for justice implore,
> And *he's married her now*, though he'd————her before.

A century later, Edmund Bellchambers heaped calumny on her head and ridiculed Cibber's hymn to her purity as either "dullness or dissimulation." He hinted that she had not been the injured party in the notorious Hill affair, and had simply made the most of the opportunity to figure as a heroine after Mountfort's death, which he attributed to "one of those casual encounters which mark the general violence of the times."

Drury Lane had its share of rogues, none greater than Cardell Goodman (?1649–1699). The son of a clergyman, he was expelled from Cambridge for participating in the slashing and cutting up of a portrait of the chancellor of the university, the Duke of Monmouth. But the disgrace did not disqualify him for the stage, which, as Cibber puts it, "like the sea-service refuses no man for his morals that is able-bodied." He joined Killigrew's company in 1667 and made a notable Julius Caesar. But his habits and manners were so disgusting that he was nicknamed "Scum" Goodman. His salary was so miserably low that he was forced to share his bed with the equally impecunious Captain Griffin, and share as well the one whole shirt they owned in common. One of them, who had a rendezvous with a lady, took the liberty of wearing the shirt when it was not his turn, and in consequence the roommates had a terrific fight.

To supplement his meagre income Goodman became a highwayman, but was soon taken and sent to Newgate. He escaped the rope only because James II pardoned him, it being his first offense. The late king's cast-off mistress, the Duchess of Cleveland, now middle-aged, became enamored of Goodman, apparently because of his exploits, and established him in fine quarters as her kept and much younger lover, bought him splendid clothes, and gave him an income that enabled him at last to dine well. He repaid her with so much attention that when "my duchess," as he boastfully called her, was expected to attend Drury Lane, he would refuse to appear on stage until he knew she had been seated in the audience, even though the king and queen were kept waiting.

But his success with her went to his head. Apparently her two children got on his nerves, and he suborned an Italian quack to poison them. The plot was discovered in time, and Scum Goodman was brought to trial. But good luck never deserted him. Normally he would have been tried for murder; instead he was charged merely with a misdemeanor and given a heavy fine.

Out of gratitude to King James, who had pardoned him for his crimes as a highwayman, he became a Tory, and carried his allegiance to dangerous extremes. William and Mary had come to the throne, and after the death of Queen Mary, Goodman joined a conspiracy to assassinate King William. The plot was revealed, and Scum Goodman indicated his willingness to "peach" in exchange for his life. Naturally, his fellow conspirators thought he would be better out of the way. Their agents found him in Drury Lane at the Dog, but once more his luck held out. They had planned to cut his throat, but he succeeded in talking them into allotting him £500 a year if he agreed to live abroad. He disappeared from London, and was thought to have escaped to Paris. The British ambassador there could find no trace of him. Nobody ever knew how he ended.

We are considerably indebted to the *Apology* of Colley Cibber for much of what we know about Restoration theaters and their actors; it is his sole enduring work. He was the son of a Danish sculptor, and it was against his family's wishes that he became an actor at nineteen. He was of medium height, sandy-haired, shrill-voiced, and though his exceedingly thick legs made him clumsy, he was so thin that he soon earned the name "Hatchet Face."

He never forgot Betterton's kindness to him. At the beginning, Cibber acted as a "volunteer," for the sake of the experience of being on stage. On one occasion his bungling of a line threw the older man off; Betterton, at first angered, inquired the young man's name and ordered that he be fined, but learning that Cibber was receiving no salary at all, commanded, "Put him down ten shillings a week, and forfeit him five." Young Cibber was naturally delighted.

He developed into an excellent comic actor, and he was especially appreciated in the role of a fop, which suited both his voice and personality. But, despite his subsequent success in the theater as an actor-manager, he was generally disliked for his rudeness to lesser actors and playwrights, his arrogance, his social climbing, and his snobbery. He was often pilloried by the critics, and was later the model for the protagonist of Alexander Pope's savage *The Dunciad*. Henry Fielding said of Cibber's autobiography: "How strongly doth he inculcate an absolute submission to our superiors! . . . How completely doth he arm us against so uneasy, so wretched a passion as the fear of shame! How clearly doth he expose the emptiness and vanity of that phantom, reputation!" Fielding's bitter comment was undoubtedly due to Cibber's appointment as poet laureate in 1730, a result of his assiduous cultivation of great men. Such general indignation at the appointment would be more comprehensible—for Cibber certainly had not a vestige of poetic talent—if his predecessors, such as Tate and Shadwell, had not been even worse mediocrities.

His one great success in Shakespearean acting was as Justice Shallow. Davies said of his interpretation: "No audience was ever more fixed in deep attention, at his first appearance, or more shaken with laughter in the progress of the scene." Of a later performance, the same critic said, "His manner was so perfectly simple, his look so vacant . . . that it will be impossible . . . not to smile at the remembrance of it. Cibber's transition from asking the price of bullocks, to trite, but grave reflections on mortality, was so natural, and attended with such an unmeaning roll of his small pig's-eyes, accompanied with an important utterance of tick! tick! tick! not much louder than the balance of a watch, that I question if any actor was ever superior in the conception or expression of such solemn insignificancy."

But as a tragedian, his acting was disastrous. Though he also performed the roles of Gloucester and Worcester (*Henry IV*), it was his Iago which was detested. Insufferably obvious in his portrayal of villainy, and insignificant and mean in his action, he was further accused of not seeming "to understand either what he said or what he was about" in that role. He was equally disliked in non-Shakespearean tragedy, and he was eventually fairly hissed off the stage. In a play by Thomson, he was damned two nights in a row, and the part was then assigned to the actor Williams, "but he, marching slowly, in great military distinction, from the upper part of the stage, and wearing the same dress as Cibber, was mistaken for him, and met with repeated hisses, joined to the music of cat-calls; but as soon as the audience were undeceived, they converted their groans and hisses to loud and long continued applause."

Cibber was most successful as a playwright, and was largely responsible for furthering that sentimentality which became the curse of the eighteenth and much of the nineteenth century. He wrote a series of "weeping" comedies, which introduced all the viciousness of Restoration moral standards but ended in a burst of hopelessly unconvincing reformations intended to pass as an endorsement of virtue. His first, *Love's Last Shift*—translated by a too French Frenchman as *La Dernière Chemise de l'Amour*—set the style, and perhaps the most revolting of them is *The Careless Husband*. But his name in drama will longest be remembered for the version he made of Shakespeare's *Richard III*, which Hazlitt dubbed "a vile jumble." It includes passages snipped from *Henry VI, Part 3, Richard II, Henry IV, Part 2*, and *Henry V*, plus lines of Cibber's own composition—of which the best known, "Off with his head; so much for Buckingham," and "Richard's himself again!" have often been admired as Shakespeare's. I find myself less than indignant at Cibber's cavalier way with the play for despite the fact that *Richard III* has always been one of the most popular of the plays, it has long seemed to me a melodrama rather than a genuine tragedy, and I thoroughly endorse James Agate's observation that it is "really a boy's play—a play for one boy to write and another to see." The startling thing about Cibber's version is that it held the stage right through the eighteenth and most of the nineteenth century —and, in fact, has not been abandoned yet, for actors still seem to prefer including passages from the other history plays, and to agree that the "monomaniac of crime" into which Cibber converted Richard at the expense of the subtle schemer Shakespeare invented makes a better play. This, despite the fulminations of the historian Genest: "One has no wish to disturb Cibber's own tragedies in their tranquil graves, but while our indignation continues to be excited by the frequent representation of *Richard the Third* in so disgraceful a state, there can be no peace between the friends of unsophisticated [i.e., unadulterated] Shakespeare and Cibber. . . . To the advocates for Cibber's Richard I only wish to make one request—that they would never say a syllable in favor of Shakespeare."

When his *Richard III* was first produced at Drury Lane in 1700, Cibber played the title role, and, as he himself confesses, based his performance upon his notions as to how Sandford might have done it. But he met with scant success. As a contemporary reported it: "This same mender of Shakespeare chose the principal part . . . for himself; . . . he screamed through four acts without dignity or decency. The audience, ill-pleased with the farce, accompanied him with a smile of contempt, but in the fifth act, he degenerated all at once into Sir Novelty [one of Cibber's comic roles]; and when in the heat of the battle . . . the king is dismounted, our comic-tragedian came on the stage, really breathless, and in a seeming panic, screaming out this line thus—*A harse, a harse, my kingdom for a harse.* This highly delighted some, and disgusted others of his auditors; and when he was killed by Richmond, one might plainly perceive that the good people were not better pleased that so execrable a tyrant was destroyed, than that so execrable an actor was silent."

Whether the audiences deserved better actors than Cibber or merited a great actor like Betterton is open to question. While exhibitionistic nobles did occasionally insist upon occupying space on the Elizabethan stage, the problem became a recurrent one during the Restoration. In 1664 Charles II was compelled to forbid visiting behind the scenes; in 1673 he decreed that "no person of what quality so ever presume to stand or sit on the stages or to come within any part of the scenes before the play begins, while 'tis acting, or after 'tis ended." But clearly the law was relaxed after a while. By 1696, a character in a play complains, "They spread themselves in parties all over the house; some in the pit, some in the boxes, others in the galleries, but principally on the stage; they cough, they sneeze, talk loud, and break silly jests, sometimes laughing, sometimes singing, sometimes whistling, till the house is in an uproar."

The violence to which the age was addicted intruded only too often into the theater. One example will suffice. A young gallant addressed some insulting remarks to an actress as he was sitting in a box, and she replied with utter contempt. At her next entrance onto the stage, he broke into loud cries, ridiculing her performance—"as other young men of honor have sometimes made themselves undauntedly merry with." But this fellow went further. He threw at the actress "such trash as no person can be supposed to carry about him." A champion of the young woman called him a bully, and was immediately challenged to a duel in Hyde Park. The rowdy then proved himself a coward by begging to be excused from the encounter.

4

Theater in the New World

In Restoration England, the general public was absenting itself from the theaters. It is, therefore, hardly surprising that in the American colonies there were no theaters from which the public could absent itself. Massachusetts and Philadelphia were not inclined to forget that their fellow Calvinists had branded playhouses with the responsibility for keeping places of worship empty, for lending support (one wonders how) to the hated Catholic faith, and of corrupting the innocent. They were "the bastard of Babylon" and the "chapel of Satan," and spared no talents in making attractive harlotry, rape, adultery, murder, treachery, blasphemy, flattery, and rebellion against just authority. Samuel Sewell was at great pains to frustrate every attempt to present plays, and William Penn asked what was intended to be a crushing question: "How many plays did Jesus Christ and his apostles recreate themselves at?"

It would seem that the first actor to venture upon North American shores was that youthful vagabond of whom we have already taken notice, Anthony Aston (?1682–?1749, ?1751, ?1753). He had played all over Great Britain from 1697 to 1700 before crossing the ocean to perform in Charleston. While there, he wrote a play, *The Fool's Opera: or the Taste of the Age,* which was later published in London in 1731 under the pseudonym of Mat Medley. He was a vagabond, a loose liver, and a frequenter of wine shops, and has left us this sketch of his own life: "My merry hearts, you are to know me as a gentleman, lawyer, poet, actor, soldier, sailor, exciseman, publican in England, Scotland, Ireland, New York, East and West Jersey, Maryland, Virginia (on both sides of Cheesapeek [*sic*]), North and South Carolina, South Florida, Bahamas, Jamaica and often a coaster by all the same." After an account of his mother and father, he continues: "As for my relations everywhere, I don't care a groat for 'em, which is just the price they set on me." He was first a clerk. "Instead of copying bills I was prone to making verses, reading plays, and instead of going to proper offices I went to see

Thomas Doggett, making comical faces in the last two acts."

He was seven when he wrote his first peom. Luckily it has come down to us; its title was "In Praise of Peace":

> Once, in a fight, when standing at his Ease,
> Did boldly eat a piece of Bread and Cheese;
> His Fellow asked him for a little Crumb,
> Tho' not so big as Supernaculum.
> The greedy Dog deny'd: why should he grudge it?
> He had above a Peck within his Budget:
> But while his Hand cramm'd Meat into his Gullet,
> His Mouth received a spightful leaden Bullet.
> Now Bread and Cheese lies trampled on the Ground,
> And such another Piece can ne'er be found:
> So I'm resolv'd I never War will make
> But e'er keep Peace for Bread and Cheese's sake.

Aston was proud enough of this nonsense to preserve it. Yet it is agreeable to think that the history of acting on these shores began with so flamboyant a character. He explains that having arrived in America in 1701, "after many vicissitudes at Charles-Town, full of lice, shame, poverty, nakedness and hunger," he "turned player and poet."

When he sailed from Charleston on a sloop, they ran into a "frightful Storm; we scudded with Bare Poles a-fore the Wind, when I was lash'd to the Helm to steer for twelve Hours . . . Our Vessel was knock'd all to pieces, as were all the clothes wash'd off me." He was rescued, clothed, and returned to Charleston, where he boarded a vessel for New York. "Being in November, the Nor-wester blew us from the New York coast," and the ship was glad enough to gain "the Capes of Virginia." A Quaker loaned him a horse which conveyed him to Philadelphia. From there he "rode through Elizabeth-Town and so in the Packet to New York." In New York, he occupied himself all winter with "acting, writing, courting, fighting." He must have appeared there as a kind of one-man variety show. He called his presentation a "Medley," and it was probably made up of short comic scenes from plays he knew, with a song or a monologue serving as an interval between them. It may be assumed that he was none too successful in New York, for otherwise, considering his arrogance, he would have allotted that city more than a line in his autobiographical sketch. Indeed, almost everything about him is wrapped in uncertainty. He was probably born in 1682, but the year of his death has been given as 1749 or 1751 or 1753. Indeed, as Daniel Frohman once speculated, no one can say with assurance that he died at all; "perhaps he is still walking the earth, enjoying plays, the music of laughter, anticipating the incredulity that he would cause if he played his greatest part by strutting out onto the stage of Times Square, sweeping off his hat and saying, 'I am Anthony Aston.'"

After New York he was again in Virginia and by 1704 he was back in England. His influence on the future of theatrical representations in the colonies cannot have been very significant.

While eighteenth-century English audiences were finding their way back to playhouses, in the New World the ban on theaters continued. Boston and Philadelphia remained hostile to all stage productions. So was New York by fits and starts. In 1700 the Assembly of Philadelphia forbade the giving of "stage plays, masks and revels," as being "rude and riotous sports." In New York, the Council, in May 1709, prohibited the acting of plays and the exhibition of prizefighting. Virginia was more liberal.

In Britain, Quin and soon Macklin were attracting the public to the plays of Shakespeare; in the American colonies, however, there was still no theater. Not until March 23, 1730, is there any record of a Shakespearean performance, and even then it was given in a tavern. The play was *Romeo and Juliet,* and Dr. Joachimus Bertrand advertised himself as undertaking the role of the apothecary, which he anticipated would be recognized "as a great condescension in a physician."

In 1749, Thomas Kean was manager of a troupe that acted in a converted warehouse in Philadelphia. Joined in partnership by Walter Murray, he took his company to New York in 1750, where in a theater on Nassau Street they performed Cibber's version of *Richard III.* The Theatre in Nassau Street, as it was called, was a large room in a house on that street, and the first place used for professional theatrical purposes in New York. It was there, in 1751, that Robert Upton, an English actor, performed *Othello* without mentioning Shakespeare's name in his advertisements, though he announced that following *Othello* there would be "added a dramatic entertainment by the celebrated Mr. Gasrick [sic], called *Lethe.*" His short season was a failure.

In Williamsburg, Virginia, a playhouse, which seems to have been more like a barn than a theater, had been opened in 1716. Excavations have shown that it was some 30 feet wide by 86½ feet long; it was demolished around 1770. In 1751, the year of Upton's *Othello,* another playhouse was being erected in Williamsburg, and while it was still only a shell, the Murray-Kean company presented *Richard III* again. They too omitted Shakespeare's name, though they announced that there would be presented after the play "a grand tragic dance composed by Monsier [sic] Dencier, called *The Royal Captive.*"

The Murray-Kean company had left behind them so unsavory a reputation for "loose behavior" in Williamsburg, that when Lewis Hallam (1714–1756), who had acted at Covent Garden and Drury Lane, brought his wife, children, and ten actors to Virginia in 1752, and applied to Governor Dinwiddie for permission to stage plays at Williamsburg, he was turned down and threatened with financial disaster. But, under pressure, the governor relented, and Hallam presented Granville's *Jew of Venice,** a perversion of *The Merchant of Venice.*

The advertisements said that the scenery had been painted "by the best hands in London," and was "excelled by none in beauty and elegance." The play was finally given on September 15, 1752. Patrick Malone created a farcical Shylock to great applause, while Hallam's son, Lewis, Jr., who had

*See the present author's *The Truth about Shylock* (New York: Random House, 1962), pp. 313–26, for an examination of the mayhem which Granville visited upon Shakespeare's play.

never faced an audience before, took fright before he could speak the one line allotted him, burst into tears, and ran from the stage. The troupe played to large audiences three times a week, and varied their initial offering with *King Lear, Romeo and Juliet, Henry IV, Othello,* and *Richard III.*

In 1753, Hallam renovated the Theatre in Nassau Street in New York, rechristening it the New Theatre, and against considerable opposition presented a repertory which included Shakespeare. The playhouse was not quite forty feet wide, and the management was forced to ask "the gentlemen to give us the entire use of the stage" to make room for Juliet's funeral procession. Toward the end of the season, a rowdy threw eggs at the stage and in the process ruined the clothes of box-holders.

From New York, Hallam took his company to the old warehouse in Philadelphia "at the corner of the first alley above Pine Street," where the Kean-Murray troupe had performed briefly; it was the property of William Plumsted, who had become Mayor in 1750. The Hallams' final performance was in *Hamlet,* the proceeds of which were destined for the Pennsylvania Hospital. The directors of that institution accepted the money but declared publicly that the play had been given without their sanction! Hallam died in Philadelphia, and his widow, a first-rate actress, married the company's new manager, David Douglass.

Hallam's son, Lewis, Jr. (?1740–1808), who had fled the stage on his first appearance, became leading man of the company, which now was billed as an American troupe. Douglass improvised a new theater in New York on Cruger's Warf. Unfamiliar with the regulations, he failed to obtain permission from the governor of the colony; when he did apply for the right to perform, it was at once refused. He therefore announced that his building would be opened as a "Histrionic Academy." The magistrates were offended by the evasion, and the "Academy" was not opened. Douglass printed an apology, in which he stated: "All that I proposed to do was to deliver Dissertations on Subjects, MORAL, INSTRUCTIVE, and ENTERTAINING. . . . TO SPEAK IN PUBLICK WITH PROPRIETY." He added: "I thought the Publick would treat me with greater Favour—when they were informed I was deprived of any other means of getting my Bread." He pointed out that the expenses of coming to New York and building the edifice "amounted to a sum that would swallow up the profits of a great many nights acting." Whether his plea was responsible is not known, but eventually the magistrates did permit him to open his theater on December 28, 1758. Despite his declaration that he had had no intention of presenting plays, the "MORAL, INSTRUCTIVE and ENTERTAINING Dissertations" turned out to be performances of a comedy by Farquhar, Otway's farce, *The Orphan,* and "the Comic Scenes" of *The Spanish Friar.* Boxes were eight shillings, the pit five shillings, and the gallery two shillings. In 1759, Lewis Hallam, Jr., played Romeo to his mother's Juliet! He was an excellent actor, and after the death of Douglass took over the management of the "American Company." During the Revolutionary War he went to the West Indies. After its conclusion he returned to Philadelphia, but played also in New York, Baltimore, and

Annapolis. His second wife, though a good actress, caused much trouble in the troupe because of her bad temper and alcoholism. Before he was twenty-one, young Lewis had the distinction of being the first American-born Hamlet.

The Philadelphia playhouse, "the Synagogue of Satan," as its enemies called it, was subject to continual attack. Young Hallam's Hamlet was criticized for his "method of articulating"; when he spoke he had the bad habit of "sucking in" the first letter of the words he delivered. "Fury, eagerness or passion" were no excuse, said one critic, for "destroying the least articulate beauty of language." Nevertheless, he was the leading actor of his time in the colonies.

In the meantime, legislative bodies were still active against the theaters. The Massachusetts General Court, in order to prevent "great mischiefs which arise from public stage plays," passed a law in April 1750 imposing a fine of £20 for the presentation of a play and £5 for each actor and spectator. In Rhode Island, though there were no laws against plays, feelings against the theater were strong. When Douglass arrived at Newport with his company in the spring of 1761, he met with strenuous opposition. He decided to distribute handbills saying that in the Public Room of King's Arm Tavern on June 10 there would be delivered "a series of MORAL DIA-LOGUES in five parts, depicting the evil effects of Jealousy and other bad passions, and proving that Happiness can only spring from the pursuit of Virtue. MR. DOUGLASS will represent a noble and magnanimous Moor named Othello, and after he has married her, harbors (as in too many cases) the dreadful passion of jealousy. Of jealousy our being's bane,/Mark the small cause and the most dreadful pain." The handbill went on to state that Allyn would "depict the character of a specious villain" who imposes "on his best friend." [By which who on earth is supposed to be meant? Surely, not Othello.] Of such as this Iago "there are thousands in the world," and the villain warns us: "The man that wrongs his master and his friend,/What can he come to but a shameful end?" Hallam played Cassio, who loses his position and his general's esteem: "The ill effects of drinking would you see,/Be warned and keep from evil company." Morris was Brabantio who was "foolish enough to dislike the Moor . . . because his face is not white, forgetting that we all spring from one root . . . Fathers beware what sense and love ye lack./'Tis crime, not color, makes the being black." Mrs. Morris was Desdemona: "Reader attend, and ere thou goest hence/Let fall a tear to helpless innocence." Mrs. Douglass was Emilia, "a good example to all servants . . . Obedience and gratitude/Are things as rare as they are good . . . Various other dialogues, too numerous to mention here, will be delivered at night . . . Comencement at 7. Conclusion at half past 10, in order that every spectator may go home at a sober hour, and reflect upon what he has seen, before he retires to rest." Thus, Douglass passing off *Othello* as a series of moral dialogues that vied with church services for moral edification was so able to please Newport that he had a vast success.

In New York, on December 28 of the same year, Douglass announced in the papers that he was "of good family" and had had "a genteel and liberal education." Two months later he gave a benefit performance of his "Moral Dialogues" for "such poor families as are not provided for by the publick."

In 1767, a group of Cherokee Indians came to New York from South Carolina to seek assistance in a peace treaty between themselves and the Iroquois. Before leaving for Albany, they expressed the wish to see a play. Douglass naturally chose the favorite, Cibber's *Richard III*, and a curious public bought up all available seats. The *New York Journal* reported that the Indians watched the play with complete attention, but since they could not follow the language, they seemed constantly surprised, especially at *Harlequin's Vagaries*, which followed the Shakespeare.

Despite the inadequacy of the theatrical environment and the spasmodic character of the companies' seasons, by 1773 Shakespeare, during the twenty-four years preceding the Revolutionary War, was seen in a variety of cities for a total of not less than five hundred times for the fourteen plays, all of them in their "improved" form. Moreover, his plays were given far more frequently than those of any other dramatist. The two most popular plays were Cibber's version of *Richard III* and a bastard version of *Romeo and Juliet*. Of the comedies, Garrick's distortions of them were the best liked.

Shakespeare was also being read by some of the founding fathers. When John Adams was writing against the Stamp Act, he first conceded that the colonies must acknowledge England as their mother, and then went on to compare her with Lady Macbeth. When he received a small vote for the vice-presidency because it was feared that he was too aristocratic for the young republic, he justified himself by quoting Ulysses's speech on "degrees" from *Troilus and Cressida* (I, iii, 83), and underlined Nestor's comment that the lack of respect for these "degrees" was *"the fever whereof all our power is sick."* When a friend asked Jefferson for a list of books, he included Shakespeare with the comment that "everything is useful which contributes to fix in us the principles and practices of virtue." He gave as examples the murder of Duncan which incites a great "horror of villainy" and *Lear* which will equip any young reader with a "lively and lasting sense of filial duty." Elsewhere, he recommended Shakespeare as priceless to the student of law who must master the full eloquence of the English tongue. However, it did not occur to him to include a course in Shakespeare at his new University of Virginia, nor was the playwright mentioned in the literature course. After Washington was elected president, there were private Shakespearean theatricals "in the garret of the presidential mansion before the magnates of the land and the elite of the city."

Critical taste was not altogether wanting. A certain "Clarinda" wrote indignantly that, living some miles from Annapolis, she felt entitled to some diversion for the money she was spending at the theater, and therefore strongly reprehended the "bare faced, illiberal, and very often indecent insertions" of some actor playing low comedy, "which is generally substituted for what they have either forgot, or . . . never perused." She feared that the Hamlet neglected "to tell the clowns *to speak no more than was set down for them.* " She spoke with reason. Douglass, at the end of the second act of Cibber's *Richard III*, enlivened the proceedings by "a humorous interlude" between "a painter and Lady Pentweazle of Blowbladder Street," and after the third act by a singing of the Echo Song from Milton's *Comus*. On the same program with Granville's version of *The Merchant of Venice*, Patrick Malone, now a man of advanced years, performed on the slack wire, while vaulting a rope, lying on the wire full-length, beating a drum, balancing a pyramid of tobacco pipes on the edge of a water glass, and another pyramid of thirty tumblers of jelly in each hand, and standing on his head while holding in each hand a pistol which he was ready to fire "if agreeable to the ladies." A reincarnated Bottom the Weaver, he!

Shakespearean performances, in short, were being mixed with an incipient vaudeville—good taste apart, no wonder, for the "serious" actors delivered their lines as so much oratory, and their bodily movements were wooden. In his sixties, Lewis Hallam, Jr., was still playing Hamlet to universal admiration in the colonies, but when he took his production to London, it was barely "endured"—no doubt because it must have seemed crude to a public familiar with Garrick's brilliance and who were enjoying the nobility of Kemble. Possibly, the English tradition of patronizing all that was "American" found its beginnings here—a tradition one is glad to see is at last dying out, except among lower-middle-class snobs.

A younger member of the Hallam family, Nancy, was extolled for her performance in *Cymbeline*, which Douglass presented during the same season with *Richard III* and *The Taming of the Shrew*. Exclaimed one critic: "She exceeded my utmost idea, such delicacy of manner! Such classical strictures of expression! The music of her tongue! The *vox liquida*, how melting!" Some of this may have been owing, of course, to the unwonted pleasure of seeing and hearing *Cymbeline*, which must have struck the small audience as though it were a new play. The Rev. Mr. Boucher wrote Nancy an ode:

> *To thee I owe, that Shakespeare's tale*
> *Has charmed my ears once more.*
> *. . . She speaks!—what Elocution flows!*
> *Ah! softer far her strains*
> *Than fleece of descending snows,*
> *Or gentlest vernal rains.*

Yet that same Nancy Hallam during the intermission sang "The Soldier Tired of War's Alarm," accompanied by a band of His Majesty's Regiment.

Thomas Wignell (1753–1805) had been persuaded by his cousin, Lewis Hallam, Jr. to join the American Company at the John Street Theatre which Douglass had built and opened in Washington in December 1787. George Washington came there often and was a great admirer of Wignell. After a brief period, the latter left for England to recruit his own troupe for the new Chestnut Street Theatre in Philadelphia.

Another who moved from Boston to join the American Company in New

York was Elizabeth Johnson. Tall and elegant, she made a particularly fine Rosalind, Beatrice, and Imogen. She also played Juliet. Though she was to leave New York for London, she returned later, and was one of the first actresses to play serious male roles, though, happily, not in Shakespeare.

Another leading English actor at the close of the century destined for America was Thomas Abthorpe Cooper (1776–1849), a ward and pupil of the philosopher William Godwin. He was at first employed by Stephen Kemble, a younger brother of the celebrated John Philip Kemble, in an English touring company. At Newcastle he was doing very well as Malcolm until he came to his last speech, which ends the tragedy of *Macbeth.* At that point he unfortunately forgot his lines and broke down; Stephen Kemble at once dismissed him. After playing for a while in the provinces, he was given the opportunity in 1795 to play Hamlet and Macbeth at Covent Garden, and the next year Wignell persuaded him to accompany him to Philadelphia, where Cooper first appeared as Macbeth in December 1796. Two years later he joined the New York Company at the new Park Theatre, and appeared as Hamlet. He was highly praised for his tragic heroes in the American cities which he toured. In 1803 he returned to Drury Lane in London to play Hamlet, Macbeth, Richard III, and Othello, after which he came back to the United States.

Cooper was a handsome man with a mobile face and a mellow voice, but not very good in comedy, for which he could not command the right airiness. Washington Irving thought his Macbeth better than the one he had seen in England. He was one of the earliest English actors to become an American citizen. Unhappily, he did not know when to retire. He had less acclaim in his later years, partly because of the new rage for Italian opera, and partly because Booth and Macready were displacing most popular tragic actors. Eventually, he was forced to leave the stage and accept a position with the United States Customs House, offered him through the kindness of President Tyler.

It is not to be thought that the increase in the number of Shakespearean performances had entirely altered the narrow horizons cherished by the early colonists before the new republic was born. In 1786, the wife of the future president, Mrs. John Adams, an insatiable reader of Shakespeare, was in London with her husband, then Ambassador to the Court of St. James. She was present at a performance of Desdemona by the incomparable Mrs. Siddons and wrote that she had felt no pleasure in witnessing the tragedy because of "the sooty appearance of the Moor," and was overcome with "disgust and horror" every time she saw him "touch the gentle Desdemona." When she saw Mrs. Siddons's Lady Macbeth, her greatest role, she thought the actress "too great to be put in so detestable a character."

Indeed, as late as 1792 the sheriff of Boston appeared unexpectedly upon the stage during that city's first theatrical season, and put an end to the performance and the rest of the season, the company's repertory containing such dangerous works as *Hamlet* and *Richard III.*

There is a strange paradox concerning Shakespeare in both England and the United States. His plays dominated the English stage from the eighteenth century on, while across the Atlantic, from the earliest days of the Union they were the center of theatrical attention every season though, as we have seen, the same bill would also feature the silliest sort of singing, pantomime, and dancing. Yet no college in either England or the United States offered a course in Shakespeare. It was not until 1855 that James Russell Lowell, during his lectures at Harvard on the English poets, was to introduce Shakespeare into a college curriculum. Having been emboldened thus far, in 1863 he offered one lecture on Shakespeare, though not as part of the college course, for his audience was made up chiefly of clubwomen and a few undergraduates. In 1883, he is reported as saying at the Edinburgh Philological Institute that it was impossible for him to read Shakespeare without "wishing there might be professorships established for the study of his works."

5

The Age of Barton Booth, James Quin, and Charles Macklin

Parliament invited William and Mary to come to England and take the throne in 1688, but, unlike their Stuart predecessors, the new monarchs were Puritans at heart and found the drama as written during the Restoration little to their liking. The attempt to justify the moral depravity of Restoration comedy by pointing to the bawdries of the Elizabethans was specious. As Bernard Miles has said about the coarseness of Elizabethan and Restoration plays, "if you remove it from the one, you still have a world of wonder left, while if you remove it from the other, you have nothing." Dryden, known to be "the modestest of men in conversation," was one of the worst offenders; his play *The Kind Keeper* was too filthy for even Restoration tastes and had to be withdrawn, and his *The Spanish Friar* was little better. Moreover, Elizabethan drama was, no matter where the locale of a play, profoundly English, while Restoration comedy and tragedy took their tone from the Continental stage. As the court circle of William and Mary, no longer encouraged to live only for pleasure, began to withdraw its support from the theater, the playhouses were compelled to seek a more general public among the middle class, which had small use for the cynicism or moral viciousness of the preceding period.

The growing resentment of the new public found expression in 1698 in an overstated and pedantic attack by the nonjuring Jeremy Collier in *A Short View of the Immorality and Profaneness of the English Stage.* Collier charged that no force had been more successful in "debauching the age than the stage-poets and playhouses." A few writers tried to defend Restoration theater, but most of them, including Dryden himself, acknowledged their guilt and promised to reform, though the latter thought the chief blame lay with the Stuarts and their court:

> *Perhaps the parson [i.e., Collier] stretch'd a point too far,*
> *When with our theatres he wag'd a war.*

He tells you that this very moral age
Receiv'd the first infection from the stage.
But sure, a banish'd court, with lewdness fraught,
The seeds of open vice returning brought
. . . The poets, who must live by courts or starve,
Were proud so good a government to serve.
. . . Thus did the thriving malady prevail,
The court its head, the poets but the tail.

What replaced Restoration licentiousness was not altogether an improvement. By degrees, that moral hypocrisy which is incorrectly thought of as "Victorian," but which under the sponsorship of that pernicious sentimentality cultivated during the "correct" age of Pope and Steele, was already in full bloom, and had begun a new kind of devastation of Shakespeare's plays. It is enough to mention that in *Othello,* where the whole tragedy turns upon the hero's conviction of his wife's sexual transgression, it became customary to cut out all the references to sex—as, for instance, in the dramatically powerful passage where the line occurs: "Or to be naked with her friend in bed" (IV,i,7 seq.). The "correctness" of the age was also responsible for its little villainies. By 1712, Othello was not allowed to swoon because it was held unheroic for a man to do so.

The first actor to inherit Betterton's mantle as leading man was Barton Booth (1681–1733), whose family was not related to the later famous and ill-starred Booths. Born of a good Lancashire family, he early showed histrionic talent at Westminster School. As a result, against the wishes of his family, who had destined him for the church, he ran away from home at the age of seventeen to play Oronooko in Dublin. At that debut, he nearly ended his career before it began. It was a hot night in June of 1698, and before going on in his last scene, he mopped his perspiring face and the lamp-black came off in streaks. When he entered on stage he was greeted with roars of laughter, which, not surprisingly unnerved him. But the good-natured Irish audience followed their guffaws with loud applause. Resolved to avoid a like catastrophe, the next night he appeared with a black crepe mask fitted to his face by one of the actresses. Unluckily, the mask slipped during the very first scene, and this audience was even more hilarious than the first. "I looked like a magpie," Booth recollected later, "but they lamp-blacked me for the rest of the night, and I was flayed before I could get it off again." Despite this inauspicious beginning, he was soon a great favorite in Dublin, and continued to be during the three years of his stay there.

By the time he reached London in 1701, his fame had preceded him. He had money, youth, good looks, and a confidence in his own talent. Losing no time, he went to visit the celebrated Betterton in Great Russell Street, and that ever-generous veteran welcomed him, heard him recite, offered to tutor him, and presently took him on at his Lincoln's Inn Fields Theatre. Booth's natural ease, grace, youthful fire, and charming voice immediately captivated audiences—"Booth with the silver tongue," became his designation. But he never lost his sense of proportion. As a young actor, he decided that he "had been for some time too frank a lover of the bottle," and seeing what alcoholism was doing to his fellow actor Powel, he gave up drinking to excess, and never again departed from that resolution. He thoughtfully observed that the longest of lives would not be enough to "enable an actor to perfect his art."

The actor Aaron Hill has left a vivid characterization of Booth. He knew how to elide "with an elegant negligence" the weaker passages allotted a character he was portraying, while he would "dwell with energy upon the beauties," as though he deliberately waited for them, moments to "alarm, awaken, and transport in those places which were worthy of his best exertions." He "had a talent at discovering the passions, where they lay hid in some celebrated parts, by the injudicious practice of other actors." He moreover had the extraordinary ability to make the variations in his voice perfectly match the changes in his facial expressions. It was his "peculiar felicity to be heard and seen the same . . . *The Blind might have seen him in his voice, and the Deaf have heard him in his visage.*"

Among his Shakespearean roles, the greatest was Othello. He was particularly admired for his stance while listening to other actors during crucial moments of the tragedy. But unlike the stars of a later date, Booth was always ready to play a smaller role, such as Cassio or Laertes, in order to afford an opportunity to fellow actors to play the lead. He would be Macbeth one night, Banquo the next, and Lennox a third.

A very serious change had been taking place in the theater. After the decline in attendance, for which Collier's attack was partly responsible, to draw larger audiences it was becoming the custom to follow a tragedy by ballet-pantomimes, tumblers, and trained animals. Betterton had been indifferent when the audiences dwindled; all he wished was that they be judicious. Barton Booth agreed that fame was more important than profit, but held that a full auditorium was more advantageous to both. A full house would mean "many more spectators than men of taste and judgment," but if a pantomime "could entice a greater number to partake of a good play than could be drawn in without it," he could see no harm in it.

For all that, Booth was extremely sensitive to the quality of his audiences, and seemed incapable of exerting his best talents if he found himself confronting a public he could not respect. On one such occasion, when his performance was peculiarly languid, a man in a stage box sent him a note asking whether he was acting for his own amusement or for the entertainment of the public. It was, in fact, his habit to seek out in the pit one spectator whose taste he was sure of, and play for him alone all evening.

His personal magnanimity was as great as that of his master, Betterton. After the early death of his first wife, he set up a ménage with an actress, Susan Mountfort, the younger daughter of the actor. In 1714 they jointly bought several tickets in the state lottery, agreeing to share if any of their tickets won. She did win, £5,000, but kept the entire sum. When his friends urged him to claim his half, he laughingly remarked that the agreement had only been verbal, and that he wished her full joy of the money. In 1718, she left him to become the mistress of another man, and Booth, who had carefully guarded her savings for her, gave her £3,200, which her new lover rapidly squandered. The poor woman lost her reason as a result of her new alliance, and while quite insane played an Ophelia so convincing in its madness that she rendered most of her listeners distraught. She did not long survive that performance.

Booth married Miss Santlow, formerly a ballet dancer, and later an actress who played opposite him. It was an exceedingly happy marriage, despite the fact that she had been first the mistress of Marlborough and then of Craggs, secretary of state, to whom she had borne a daughter who was to become the mother of the first Lord St. Germains. But Booth's felicitous marriage and career were not to be greatly prolonged. His health started failing before he was forty, and it was his misfortune to allow himself to be persuaded by Theobald to act in the latter's wretched forgery of a Shakespearean play, *The Double Falsehood*—aptly titled. He struggled through the miserable role of the hero for a week, and then had to give up.

The doctors fussed over him and then sent him first to Bath, then to Ostend, Antwerp, and Holland, where a great doctor's only advice was never to take off winter clothing in England until midsummer-day, and to put it on again the next day. He and his wife returned to Hampstead and London, where fever and jaundice attacked him. In May 1733, a quack prescribed crude mercury as a cure for all his ailments, and within five days the poor man had taken nearly two pounds of it. Sir Hans Sloane came to his bedside to hasten his end. Booth was bled profusely at the jugular, his scalp blistered, and he was given every sort of cathartic. After the suffering tragedian's death, his body was opened and the special examiner calmly declared, after a bill of particulars: "There was no fault in any part of his body but what is here mentioned."

Characteristically, Booth left everything to his wife. His will stated: "I have considered my circumstances, and finding, upon a strict examination, that all I am now possessed of does not amount to two-thirds of the fortune my wife brought me on the day of our marriage, together with the yearly additions and advantages since arising from her laborious employment on the stage during twelve years past, I thought myself bound by honesty, honor, and gratitude due to her constant affection, not to give away any part of the remainder of my fortune at death." He added an account of the substantial sums he had already given his sister *out of my wife's substance*, and his "undeserving brother," as well as many other gifts to them urged by his wife. "The inhuman return that has been made my wife for these obligations by my sister I forbear to mention."

In Westminster, Booth Street was named after this admirable man.

It was during Betterton's later years that Rich invaded the theater. We have already recounted that from this time dates the damnable practice of intricate leasing and subletting of playhouses, a practice partly responsible in our own time for the swift closing and financial ruin of some worthwhile productions because the leaseholder does not allow the performance to "catch on," an attitude which cooperates with that of backers, eager, for tax purposes, to invest money in ventures they hope will fail. These policies, dictated by immediate monetary considerations, also harmonize with the overbearing power of the unions (apart from that of the actors), and result in a continual rise of ticket prices to new and astronomical heights. Production costs now include a legion of persons other than the dramatist, the actors, the directors and scenery and lighting designers, who would seem entitled to the lion's share, but who more frequently can earn only a trifling percentage of the intake because of stagehands, the musician's union, clerks, backers, and all kinds of theatrical parasites.

Through the eighteenth century, theaters were getting larger and larger. Larger theaters meant larger audiences, and larger audiences meant more money for the businessman. As the auditorium grew vaster the poor actor was more and more hard put to do justice to his vocation, since neither his facial expressions nor his voice could be seen or heard except by comparatively few. By the time of Mrs. Siddons, the auditorium had become, as she put it, "a wilderness." The inevitable consequence was that most actors tended to externalize their technique—what has been dubbed the "ham" style of acting.

Audiences, too, were now made up of the families of businessmen who wanted their money's worth. Gradually the evening's fare was extended by vulgarities which followed the play proper: farces, dancing, singing, pantomimes, and acrobatics, until, by 1800, the presentations for a night extended to six hours. It is hardly surprising that the eighteenth and nineteenth centuries look like an endless desert, with a few merciful oases in some plays by Goldsmith and Sheridan in the eighteenth century, and Wilde and Shaw in the nineteenth.

The enticements to fill a playhouse during the first half of the eighteenth century were odd. The promise of the royal family's appearance naturally insured a rush for tickets. But among other devices was the invitation to attend performances at Lincoln's Inn Fields to the quack bone-setter, Mrs. Mapp. The managers counted on her to dignify the occasions, and the old woman in turn was glad to accept, for it meant so much free advertising. She, therefore, came daily from Epsom in her carriage. On October 16, 1736, her attendance was publicly announced with that of the oculist Taylor and the worm-doctor Ward. In her honor, a song was sung on the stage:

> Ye surgeons of London, who puzzle your pates,
> . . . Give over, for shame, for your pride has a fall,
> And the doctress from Epsom has outdone you all.
> . . . Dame Nature has giv'n her a doctor's degree,
> She gets all the patients and pockets the fee;
> . . . She'll loll in her chariot while you walk the street.

On the occasion of a benefit night for Bowen, the actor had stipulated that four American Indian chiefs, billed as Indian "Kings," be invited, for he knew that public curiosity would swell the audience. The four Indians were given the center box, where they could not be seen by the people in the galleries. This caused a tumult in the upper regions, and could not be quieted even when the actor Wilks assured them that the "Kings" were indeed present in the box. The gallery continued to insist that money had been paid to see the Indians, and see them they would, or else the play was not going to proceed. In the midst of much racket, and after some negotiations, the four majesties moved from their box to four chairs on the stage, to loud cheers from the erstwhile protestors.

This seating on the stage, by the way, despite continual decrees against the practice, still plagued the actors. As late as 1732, at the opening of the first theater at Covent Garden, pit and boxes cost five shillings for admission, one and two shillings for galleries, and places on the stage cost half a guinea. In 1721, a half-drunk earl at Lincoln's Inn Fields crossed the stage from where he had been sitting, during a scene between Macbeth and Lady Macbeth, to speak to a friend who was lounging on the other side. Rich, the manager, who was standing by, informed his lordship that he would never again be admitted on the stage. The earl slapped Rich's face; Rich returned the blow. In a moment, swords were unsheathed by a half dozen tipsy fellows of his lordship, all vowing to kill the manager. But the tragedian Quin and other actors rushed to Rich's aid with their own swords, and drove the troublemakers out the stage door. The offenders, however, came round the front, stormed into the theater and to the boxes, broke the sconces, slashed the draperies, and swore—a frequent oath—to burn the building. But James Quin and a body of constables seized the drunkards and brought them before the magistrates. In anger, King George ordered that both theaters must thereafter have a guard on duty throughout performances. Thus originated the custom of having soldiers present at theatrical representations, a practice which continued for more than a century. The lower orders, of course, loved a riot as much as the "quality," and it became a popular sport to pelt the guard while on duty. Paradoxically, the audience was inclined to be well-mannered when it was known that an esteemed person, like the poet Pope, was present, and he would be accorded loud applause.

A chief source of disturbance was usually the upper gallery, the regular resort of footmen. Dryden had complained of them as a nuisance with their constant noise and rough behavior. In one of his plays and in one of Rowe's it chanced that it was a character's part to speak of hunger; the occupants of the upper gallery were accustomed to supply themselves in advance for these moments with bread, which, at the crucial speech, they would rain down upon the stage to show their sympathy. In 1697, hoping to ameliorate the situation, the upper gallery was offered free of charge. But as that only made matters worse, they attempted to suspend gratis admission, with the result that three hundred footmen armed themselves and threatened a riot.

The privilege was not abolished until the end of the eighteenth century.

The masters of these menials were not much better conducted. It became a recognized signal that trouble was afoot when the ladies were formally ushered out of the pit during a performance. In January 1740, at Drury Lane, the French dancer, Mme. Chateauneuf, failed to appear for her after-piece as announced; the ladies were sent home and an exalted marquis suggested that it would be proper to pay off the management by setting fire to the house. The noblemen decided against that expedient, but took their vengeance on the musical instruments, the expensive decorations, and the panels separating the boxes, which they conscientiously destroyed. These rioters were not punished for their devastations, and the noble marquis sent the manager £100, which covered only a small portion of the damage done.

The actor who dominated the London stage before Garrick's debut was James Quin (1693–1766). His origins were dramatic enough. His mother had been married to a man by the name of Grinsell, who had abandoned her and whom she believed dead. She then married a barrister, James Quin, grandson of the mayor of Dublin. After she bore him a son, James, in London, her first husband reappeared after years of absence, and success-fully claimed her as his lawful wife. Young James Quin became, thereby, illegitimate. He was deprived of his rightful handsome inheritance, for his father was a prosperous lawyer of good family, and the estate passed on to the technically legal heir. At twenty-one, highly intelligent, but without formal education, and having no other project in view, he decided to go on the stage. He played small parts before the Dublin audience, and the next year was accepted for walk-on bits in the company that boasted Barton Booth and Cibber. For two years he was never given the opportunity to do any significant acting. In 1716 the sudden illness of an important player gave him his chance to substitute in the role, and by the second night he was famous; the sick actor quickly recovered to reassume the part. Finding himself again reduced to a minor place, Quin grew impatient and, in 1718, went to the rival theater at Lincoln's Inn Fields, where he remained for fourteen years. There he played Buckingham (in *Richard III*), Hotspur, the Ghost in *Hamlet*, Falstaff, Othello, and Brutus.

In 1732 he was welcomed back at Drury Lane, where he specialized in the great tragic roles. A new manager, the wealthy Fleetwood, offered him £500 a year; Rich, at Lincoln's Inn Fields, refused to match the sum, saying, "No actor is worth more than £300."

A fellow actor, Bowen, had disparaged Quin's success in the role in which he had originally substituted, and Quin retaliated by speaking witheringly of one of Bowen's roles as being inferior in interpretation to that of another player. Unfortunately Quin's fellow actors agreed with Quin's judgment. Bowen, already infuriated by a political quarrel with Quin, challenged him to fight. He demanded that Quin follow him, and they went from one tavern to another until they found a suitable room. It appears that young Quin had no precise idea of what Bowen intended until the older man bolted the door, stood with his back to it, drew out his sword, and threatened to run Quin through unless he drew his rapier out to defend himself. Quin's attempt to mollify Bowen was fruitless, and he drew solely to keep the other at a distance. But the older man pressed forward and fell against Quin's blade, wounding himself mortally. While he lingered for three days, Bowen decently told the facts and exonerated Quin of any blame. His account, together with the other evidence, brought an acquittal during Quin's trial for manslaughter.

Though he was a kind-hearted man, it was Quin's misfortune to cause the death of another actor. A minor Welsh player, Williams, while acting the part of Decius in Addison's *Cato*, was given to affectations and annoyed Quin so much with his frequent pronouncing of "Cato" as "Keeto," that Quin impatiently interjected, "Would he [i.e., Caesar] had sent a better messenger!" Ironically, Decius's exit speech was: "When I relate hereafter/ The tale of this unhappy embassy,/ All Rome will be in tears." Again it was ironic that two scenes later it was Quin's lot to exit on the word "death." The angered Welshman charged Quin with making him ridiculous before the audience and insisted upon satisfaction. Quin tried to treat the whole affair as a joke, but after the play Williams lay in wait in Covent Garden Piazza (the scene of much bloodletting) for the man he now considered his enemy. Quin was forced to defend himself and, after a few exchanges, Williams "lay lifeless on the flagstones." Arrested by the watch, Quin was exonerated, though it is said he never quite recovered from the horror of having unwillingly killed two men.

Theophilus Cibber (1703–1758), the son of Colley, both because of his father's connections and his own histrionic abilities, quickly won favor with the public, though he was quite short and, as one critic put it, "the features of his face were rather disgusting and his voice was particularly shrill." He was a famous Pistol, and did Casca, Cassio, Glendower, Osric, Parolles, Roderigo, and occasionally Iago, Othello, and Richard III. But his personal life was as discreditable as his face was repulsive.

He married Susannah Maria Arne (1714–1766) in 1734 after a brief period as a widower. She was the sister of the famous composer, Thomas Augustine Arne, and had a fine voice of great sweetness. Handel wrote the contralto arias of *The Messiah* for her as well as the role of Micah in *Samson*, which indicates that he could depend upon her for deep feeling and expression in their performance.

In 1736 she began her career as a dramatic stage actress. The sing-song kind of delivery was very popular at the time, but she had little use for it. Quin said of her, "That woman has a heart, and can do anything where passion is required." She developed into a leading tragic actress, performed at the Haymarket in 1732, and was widely acclaimed for her performance as Constance in *King John*. Davies said that her "sensibility despised all art," and that her features were so expressive she could create the illusion of youth even when she was in middle age: "In grief or tenderness her eyes looked as if they were in tears; in rage and despair they seemed to dart flashes of fire." Dibden said that like Garrick she was always the character she was representing. Wilkinson pronounced her Ophelia marvelous, the very best he had ever seen. It was inevitable that Mrs. Cibber (as she is known to dramatic history) should join Garrick, which she did at Drury Lane in 1753. She and Garrick were so alike that people said they could have been brother and sister. But, though she thought otherwise, she had no gift for comedy. Her sense of humor is evident only in her letters.

This remarkable woman was treated outrageously by Theophilus Cibber. Soon after her unfortunate marriage to him he wasted no time in renewing his dissolute habits. He was not only away from home more than in the company of his wife, but he made a financial arrangement with a country gentleman, William Sloper, to take his place in her bed. He made money from his cuckold and also pocketed his wife's salary as an actress. Finally, she had enough of Cibber and retired with Sloper to the country for a time.

Theophilus was very extravagant and, to avoid his creditors, fled to France in 1738, four years after his marriage. When he returned to England he brought an action against Sloper for adultery, demanding £5,000. The jury awarded him £10, for it was proved beyond doubt that it had been Cibber himself who had sold his wife to Sloper. The story became a great scandal in London, and when Cibber appeared upon the stage of Drury Lane he was greeted with a hailstorm of apples and potatoes.

The next year he again brought action against Sloper, this time for £10,000, on the charge that Sloper was detaining Mrs. Cibber in the country. For some reason, though the facts had not changed, this time he was awarded £500.

It was over Cibber's vicious treatment of Mrs. Cibber that the unlucky Quin once again came close to killing a man. A chance remark made to Cibber resulted in a quarrel, and once more swords were out in Covent Garden Piazza. The two opponents slashed each other's arms, but luckily were parted by passers-by. In 1742 Cibber fought another duel with the actor Thomas Sheridan in Dublin because Sheridan had refused to enact the title role in *Cato*, on the grounds that he could not find a suitable costume. Cibber eventually perished aboard a ship en route to Ireland.

Evidence indicates that Betterton's style had been largely exclamatory, and Quin is said to have been the last representative of that school of acting. His person was majestic but in Shakespeare's poetic roles he was more impressive than interesting. One contemporary said that he delivered his lines with "very little variation of cadence, and in a deep, full tone, accompanied by a sawing kind of action . . . He rolled out his heroics with an air of dignified indifference that seemed to disdain the plaudits that were bestowed upon him." Still another said that he "exhibited the form rather than the soul of tragedy." Another said that his sole merit in tragedy was in his declamation and his delineation of "brutal pride."

As Macbeth, Quin was cumbersome, his facial expression never varied, and he lacked—or scorned—the ability to accommodate his body to the spirit of the role. Yet he played it for years to great applause. Indeed, when Barton Booth retired on January 9, 1728, Quin led his profession until Garrick's appearance in 1741.

Quin was originally given the great comic role of Falstaff because there was no one else in the company who could undertake it, and he surprised everyone by the excellence of his performance. It became one of his most famous roles, and it was generally conceded that his Falstaff was better than the new idol Garrick's Hotspur (1746) when they performed in the history play together. But when Quin played Brutus to Garrick's Cassius, Quin was described by the Earl of Conyngham as a "solid three-decker lying quiet and scorning to fire; but with evident power, if put forth, of sending its antagonist to the bottom," while Garrick was "a frigate turning round it, attempting to grapple, and every moment threatening an explosion that would destroy both."

Quin's Othello, an imposing black man in white, wearing an English military uniform, white gloves and a large powdered wig, expressed "the least possible grief." The *Gentleman's Magazine* complained of his general lack of tenderness and his "hoarse monotony."

Quin's eminence as the leading actor of his day was all too quickly challenged by the genius of Garrick, whose style was to put an end to the classic tradition of acting. Astonished at the difference, Quin exclaimed: "If the young fellow is right, I, and the rest of the players have all been wrong." He also observed that Garrick's was "a new religion," but that the audiences "would all come to church again." To this Garrick replied in an epigram:

Pope Quin, who damns all churches but his own,
Complains that heresy infects the town . . .
Thou great Infallible, forbear to roar,
Thy bulls and errors are rever'd no more;
When doctrines meet with gen'ral approbation,
It is not Heresy, but Reformation.

When Garrick became patentee of Drury Lane in 1750/51 Quin went back to Covent Garden at the unheard-of salary of £1,000 a year. But Garrick was so popular as Richard III that, one night, Quin was actually hissed while playing that villain. In disgust, Quin gave up, and retired to Bath in 1751.

For all their rivalry, however, the two men became good friends. They met socially at "ducal Chatsworth," where, upon finding themselves alone together, Quin, an essentially kindly man, asked after Mrs. Garrick's health, and thus began their friendship. It was at Garrick's house at Hampton that Quin was stricken with his final illness, though he died at his own house in Bath, January 21, 1766.

Tobias Smollett immortalized Quin in *Humphrey Clinker*, and Garrick composed the epitaph on Quin's tomb in Westminster Abbey, a pyramid of Siennese marble with a medallion portrait of Quin, adorned with Thalia's mask and Melpomene's dagger. Garrick's epitaph reads in part:

That tongue which set the table in a roar,*
And charmed the public ear, is heard no more;
Closed are those eyes, the harbingers of wit,
Which spake, before his tongue, what Shakespeare writ . . .

It was characteristic of the man that Quin's last recorded speech, spoken the day before he died, was: "I could wish that the last tragic scene were over; and I hope I may be enabled to meet and pass through it with dignity."

Samuel Foote, an actor-dramatist most celebrated for his brilliant mimicry and merciless satirizing of fellow actors, nevertheless praised Quin for being throughout his career "natural and unaffected, his countenance expressive without the assistance of grimace," and added that to see him impersonate "the jolly, jocose Falstaff" was to become convinced that what one was viewing was not an imitation but a real person. "I can only recommend the man who wants to see a character perfectly played, to see Mr. Quin in the part of Falstaff; and if he does not express a desire of spending an evening with that merry mortal, why, I would not spend one with him, if he would pay my reckoning."

Quin was as celebrated for his kindliness as for his rough-and-ready jests. An obscure and unemployed actor, Dick Winston, was lying hungry and weary in lodgings near Covent Garden; he had irresponsibly forfeited an old position, became an itinerant, and when he had returned could not find employment. He was in despair when Quin came into his quarters, followed by a man bearing decent clothes for Winston. Said Quin: "Now, Dick, how is it with you that you are not up and at rehearsals?" Winston, bewildered, put on his new clothes, ready for his new engagement as an actor, but faintly protesting that he had had no breakfast and had no money to buy one. "What shall I do," he asked, "until Saturday?" "I've done all I can for you," said Quin; "but as for the money, you must put your hand in your own pocket!" Winston did so, and found that Quin had put a £10 note there.

When the poet Thomson was hard up, Quin bought him supper at a tavern. Thomson tried to pay his half of the bill, but Quin replied: "I estimate the pleasure I have had in perusing your works at £100 at least; and you must allow me to settle that account, by presenting you with that sum."

In his advanced years he was approached by a fop who commiserated with him for being old, and asked what Quin would give to be as young as *he* was. Quin's answer was: "I would almost be content to be as foolish!"

Not everyone won Quin's friendship. A notable animosity developed between him and Bishop Warburton, whom he chanced to meet frequently in the house of Ralph Allen at Bath. (Allen was the original of Henry Fielding's Squire Allworthy.) Warburton was notorious for his rudeness, and chose to patronize Quin in order to emphasize the social distance between them, though the truth is that by birth Quin was the better gentleman. In a discussion, Warburton was espousing royal prerogative, when Quin said: "My Lord, spare me; you are not acquainted with my principles. I am a

*Garrick's "original" poetry was ever studded with borrowings from Shakespeare.

republican; and perhaps I even think that the execution of Charles I might be justified." "By what law?" asked Warburton. "By all the laws he had left them," rejoined Quin. Horace Walpole thought his reply summed up the truth of the controversy. Angrily Warburton asked the actor, quite inaccurately, to remember that all the regicides had come to violent ends. "I would not advise your lordship," was Quin's dry rejoinder, "to make use of that inference, for, if I am not mistaken, that was the case of the twelve apostles."

One of his recorded jests was with old Hippisley, who, originally a candle-snuffer, became a popular favorite as a low comedian. His success was due largely to his talent for using a disfiguring scar on his face (incurred by a severe burn) to twist his muscles into queer shapes which made people laugh. He informed Quin that he intended to train his son for the stage. "Why, Hippy," said Quin, "you had better begin by burning him."

In his will, Quin forgot not a friend or a servant who had been loyal. He left many bequests, from £50 to a cousin who was a physician in Dublin to £500 and a share in the residue of the estate to a kind oilman in the Strand.

His one long-lived enmity was with his contemporary thespian, Charles Macklin. They loathed each other. Quin found Macklin's style far too loose, while Macklin complained bitterly of Quin's occasional abuse of fellow actors. Quin once said to Macklin: "Mr. Macklin, by the lines—I beg your pardon, sir—by the *cordage* of your face, you should be hanged."

As Quin detested all low-comedy parts, those were often allotted to the popular Thomas Doggett, one of the triumverate managing Drury Lane (and later replaced by Barton Booth). John Downes called him "the only comic original now extant." When in 1701 George Granville made a hideous adaptation of *The Merchant of Venice* and renamed it *The Jew of Venice,* Doggett played Shylock; there is every reason to believe that he made of the usurer a farcical character. On his death in 1721, the comedian Griffin, performing in the same perversion of the play, continued the tradition inaugurated by Doggett—though, unhappily, some of our own contemporary scholars argue that it was Shakespeare's intention that Shylock be comic, quite possibly because of Doggett's interpretation. In any case, Granville's outrage passed for Shakespeare's for forty years.

On February 14, 1741, Charles Macklin undertook to revive Shakespeare's own *Merchant of Venice* after a century of neglect and perversion. His colleagues greeted his proposal with derision, for they were convinced that any "serious treatment of Shylock would be only an arrogant and presumptuous display." The news that there was to be a new kind of Shylock resulted in a packed theater on opening night. By the middle of the play, Macklin was given an uproarious ovation.

Macklin's Shylock was, for all its limitations, a healthy corrective to Thomas Doggett's clowning of the role; he presented him for what Shyock is, the villain of the plot, a blood-chilling usurer. He made him rather too venomous, so much so that rumor soon had it that Macklin himself was a kind of devil. Since he had, in fact, killed a fellow actor six years earlier, it is likely that he confused the audience into identifying him with the character he was portraying. He did not make the Jew credible as a human being, as Shakespeare had done, but he performed a service by rescuing the role from farce. His Shylock established a tradition for the role that endured for sixty years. Alexander Pope was so much impressed that he wrote:

> This is the Jew
> That Shakespeare drew.

Macklin continued to enact the role for the next fifty years. After a lifetime of triumph as Shylock, his last appearance was highly pathetic. He was thought by many to be nearly one hundred years old when, on May 7, 1789, he appeared in a benefit performance in his own honor. The ancient actor prepared his costume and makeup with his usual care, and then entered the greenroom to ask Mrs. Pope, "My dear, are you to play tonight?" "Good God! to be sure I am, sir," she replied; "Why, don't you see I am dressed for Portia?" "Ah! very true," he answered absent-mindedly, "I had forgot. But who is to play Shylock?" Everyone in the greenroom was much upset at the question, and Mrs. Pope forced herself to reply, "Why, you are, to be sure; are not you dressed for the part?" He seemed to collect himself, and put his hand to his forehead, exclaiming: "God help me—my memory, I am afraid, has left me." He came on stage at the right time and at first spoke his lines as though they were without meaning. Then he roused himself and did well for a space. But presently he could not continue, and came forward to apologize to the audience, and begged them to accept the understudy as his substitute. The house, with many a tearful eye, applauded him and showed affectionate understanding. He survived another eight years, but never again attempted to act.

The talk about his age was generally exaggerated—but not by very much. He was probably the longest-lived English-speaking actor on record, for it is certain that he was not less than ninety-seven when he died. His first official biographer gave his birth as occurring in May 1690, which would have made Macklin 107 at the time of his death in 1797. But it is now pretty well established that he was born in 1699.

To sum up the theatrical situation in London from 1710 (the year of Betterton's death) until 1742 (the year of Garrick's appearance on the London stage), the Drury Lane was the leading London theater, and those thirty-two years are thought of as the Colley Cibber period during which he, Barton Booth, and Robert Wilks controlled the playhouse. But by 1732, Wilks and Booth were both gone, and Cibber soon sold his share, though he continued to reappear in favorite roles. For three seasons after Cibber and his colleagues began their impressive control of Drury Lane, it was the only theater regularly offering drama. On the accession of George I in 1714, Richard Steele had been appointed manager and changed the license for the theater into a new patent, which then fell into the hands of Cibber, Booth, and their heirs.

But the Drury Lane's monopoly of London theater lasted for only those three years. In 1714 Christopher Rich, the old unscrupulous patentee of Lincoln's Inn Fields Theatre, had his patent renewed, and elaborately (though flimsily) rebuilt the playhouse. He did not live, however, to see its opening on December 18, 1714, and his son John, later a celebrated harlequin, succeeded him (and later ran the theater in Covent Garden) until the mid-eighteenth century. Lincoln's Inn Fields then became a serious rival of Drury Lane, and though not equal to it in presenting legitimate drama, it excelled in pantomimes. But the day of Lincoln's Inn Fields Theatre was to end in 1732.

It fell into decay, and John Rich began construction of a new playhouse in Bow Street, around the corner from Drury Lane. A subscription of £6,000 was raised to build Covent Garden Theatre there. This time, Rich ordered a small theater. Until the end of Cibber's career, Covent Garden and Drury Lane were the only playhouses legally permitted to give plays.

Nevertheless, in John Rich's earlier days, attempts were made to break the monopoly of the two patent theaters. John Potter, for instance, bought the site of an old inn in the Haymarket, and built what was called the Little Theatre in the Haymarket, across the way from the opera house. Here Fielding produced (1730–1737) a series of burlesques, beginning with *Tom Thumb the Great,* but the censorship suppressed his efforts in 1737 and closed all theaters except the two patent houses.

Various Irish chroniclers have left different versions of the name with which Macklin was born in County Donegal: O'Melaghlin, Maclysaght, Maclaughlin. It was shortly after he came to England that he, himself, shortened it to Macklin. Macklin acted first in school where he astonished everyone by his excellence in the role of the heroine of Otway's *The Orphan.* A critic later satirized the performance thus: "I played the part . . . with vast success; I say vast, for the audience all agreed there was no one thing against me but my figure, my face, and my voice." We may well believe the criticism for as a youth he was called the Wild Irishman, was fond of boxing, swimming, walking, was a great lover, but jovial comrade—in short, as someone said, he was an Irishman. In appearance, he was dark, with piercing eyes, a short aquiline nose, a massive jaw, a short upper lip and a protruding lower one; it is not surprising that with such a countenance he seemed ideal for the role he often played as a young man, the First Witch in the D'Avenant version of *Macbeth.*

His first employment as an actor was in the provinces: Bath, Bristol, the Midlands, Wales. A strolling player, he was held in contempt like all his fellows who, as a satirist put it, "were got under hedges, born in barns, and brought up in houses of correction." Despite this general opprobrium, the provinces were humming with theatrical doings. Wilkinson says of his early days as a strolling player, "my appetite for acting was unsatiable." As a member of such troupes, Macklin was accustomed to turn his hand to anything required of him. "Sometimes," said his biographer, "he . . . knocked up the stage and seats in a barn, sometimes he wrote an opening prologue, or a parting epilogue; at others he wrote a song, complimentary . . . to the village they happened to play in, . . . and sung himself; and he often . . . stood forward to repress the persons who were accustomed to . . . be rude to the actors." Even after he arrived at a position of success he for many years appeared not only in heroic parts but in harlequinades and afterpieces as well.

Macklin early developed a dislike for the oratorical style which had been flourishing for so long, and which was justified as late as Goldsmith, whose hero observes that an actor ought not "to speak and act as in common life." In Bristol, the manager agreed to try him as the Friar in *Romeo and Juliet*, provided he undertook to cut several "inches more of the brogue from his tongue." When the manager himself portrayed Romeo with an exaggerated lisp, Macklin remarked that some players would improve by having no tongue at all.

He first appeared at the Lincoln's Inn Fields Theatre in London in 1725, but was soon fired for lacking authentic tragic fire, or as Macklin himself put it: he had "so little of the hoity-toity tone of the tragedy of that day, that the manager told me I had better go to grass for another year or two" (i.e., continue touring the provinces). He took the advice and remained a strolling player for a considerable time, in the meantime acquiring a thorough knowledge of the theatrical repertory, and more and more unalterable theories about the art of acting.

In London, led by Theophilus Cibber, the chief actors left Drury Lane and gave a season at the Haymarket. The Drury Lane management had at once to recruit a new band of actors, and it was thus that Macklin was engaged by them around 1733, the same year that his mistress, Anne Grace, bore him an illegitimate daughter, Maria. By all accounts, the pair were quite happy with each other. They settled in the parish of Covent Garden, a district where taverns, coffee-houses, and notorious brothels flourished, and gambling-tables were busy. To the attractions of the last-named, Macklin was by no means immune. But lodgings were cheap in the parish, and it was then, above all, the center for theatrical activity. Macklin gave his reason for the choice: "We [Anne Grace was also a member of the company] could all be mustered by beat of drum; could attend rehearsals without any inconvenience, and save coach hire."

When Charles Fleetwood, a man of some means, bought the Drury Lane patent, the important actors who had quit that playhouse soon returned. Macklin quickly found most of his roles returned to Theophilus Cibber, and he was forced for a time to appear wherever or in whatever part he could find; he was seen at the Haymarket and Lincoln's Inn Fields, as well as at Portsmouth. At Drury Lane, he proved his willingness to cooperate by accepting the most minor parts, and became a close friend of Fleetwood, who was having his troubles with Cibber and Cibber's equally impossible sister, Charlotte Charke, so that by 1735 his position at Drury Lane was secure.

However, in May of that year the greatest misfortune of his life occurred. One night a dispute arose over a stock wig between him and a young actor named Hallam. Macklin had been looking for the wig which he was to wear in the afterpiece, presently to go on, and saw that Hallam had appropriated it. Macklin demanded the wig; Hallam refused to hand it over. Other members of the company persuaded Hallam to use another wig, which he agreed to do, though in great anger. He threw the first wig at Macklin, who, overcome with rage, flung himself at Hallam, and seizing the cane he was to bear in his role, pushed it with violence into Hallam's face, unintentionally penetrating the young actor's eye. Though blood began streaming down Hallam's face, no one realized the seriousness of the accident. Hallam died the next day. Macklin, after fleeing in panic, gave himself up and spent some time in Newgate; it seems that Fleetwood was able to arrange his release on recognizance. Macklin had time to study the legal aspects of the case—and subsequently developed an interest in the law which deepened with life. Finally, on December 12, the case was brought to trial. Among the character witnesses who appeared in Macklin's behalf were Quin (who himself had been guilty of manslaughter, and who disliked Macklin), Fleetwood, and John Rich. The jury returned the verdict of "guilty of manslaughter," with the token punishment of Macklin's being branded on the hand with a cold branding-iron. (It is ironic to consider the difference between this sentence and that of eleven others who were sentenced to death at the same sessions —one for stealing a horse, one for stealing some yards of material, one for stealing some clothes, and one for stealing a guinea.) When Macklin appeared at Drury Lane in January of the next year, he was warmly applauded.

Quin, who had left Covent Garden for Drury Lane, had his quarrels with Macklin, who insisted on inserting some comic business of his own invention in Wycherley's *Plain Dealer*, in which they were performing together. Quin's warnings were to no avail. Later, in the greenroom, Quin sat savagely chewing an apple, waiting for Macklin to come in. When Macklin entered a dispute began, and Quin threw a piece of the apple into Macklin's face; Macklin at once thrust Quin into a chair and began hitting him so hard that when Quin came back on stage his face was all swollen. His speech was so much impaired that the audience began to hiss. Backstage he demanded satisfaction of Macklin. They agreed to meet outside in Covent Garden, and Quin left for the appointment. Suddenly Macklin remembered that he was due to perform in the afterpiece. By the time the pantomime ended, Fleetwood had been apprised of the quarrel; the manager coaxed Macklin into not meeting Quin and to apologize to him the next day.

When Theophilus Cibber went to France to escape his creditors, Macklin once more was given major roles, but redemoted on Cibber's return. Meanwhile, after six years of successfully living together, he and Anne Grace married; she was listed thereafter on Drury Lane playbills as Mrs. Macklin. Macklin himself continued to do all sorts of jobs and minor roles for Fleetwood until at last, in February 1741, Macklin persuaded him to let him try his version of Shylock. It was in that role that the actor at last came into his own. He was at least forty-two years old.

It was the great night of his long life. Everyone in the company, including

Fleetwood, had been worried about Macklin's new interpretation, but the audience went wild with enthusiasm, and forced him to wait between lines until their applause subsided, and he won the admiration of the whole company. As he told Cooke, "On my return to the greenroom, . . . it was crowded with nobility and critics, who all complimented me in the warmest and most unbounded manner; and the situation I felt myself in . . . was one of the most . . . intoxicating of my whole life. No money, no title, could purchase what I felt. . . . Though I was not worth fifty pounds at the time, . . . I was *Charles the Great* for that night."

Thirty years later a traveler from Germany saw his Shylock and said: "The first words he utters . . . are slowly and impressively spoken: 'Three thousand ducats.' The double 'th' . . . which Macklin lisps as lickerishly as if he were savoring the ducats . . . make so deep an impression . . . uttered thus at the outset [that they] give the keynote of his whole character."

Although he reached the height of his powers in the great trial scene, he was unlucky to have as his Portia the popular Kitty Clive (née Haftor [1711–1785]), who was the daughter of a poor though good family from Kilkenny. Colley Cibber discovered her when she was only sixteen. Soon she enchanted audiences by the magic of her voice and rapidly became the "very queen of hoidens and chambermaids." She was already famous when in 1732 she married Clive, but soon separated from him. Fielding, satirist though he was, paid this unusual tribute to her moral character: "As great a favorite as you are at present with the audience, you would be much more so . . . could they see you laying out great part of the profits which arise to you . . . in support of an aged father; did they see you who can charm them on the stage with personating the foolish and vicious characters of your sex; acting in real life the part of best wife, the best daughter, the best sister, and the best friend."

Nevertheless, Kitty had no hesitation in standing up for what she considered her rights, even against Garrick. She was the only one who dared oppose him, and he was in some awe of her because of her ready wit, which reduced him to such fits of laughter that he was incapable of reply. Besides, everyone knew she was essentially good-natured. She was an excellent mimic and very fond of ridiculing the excesses of Italian opera but, unhappily for Macklin, totally unsuited to high comedy, and her Portia, like her chambermaid parts, was played so frivolously it became vulgar, though the audience, unfamiliar with the play as Shakespeare had written it, had no objections. In the trial scene she introduced all kinds of irrelevant comedy and vividly mimicked Lord Mansfield, whose eccentric style and manner was the laughing stock of London. It is a tribute to Macklin that her silly performance did not ruin his great scene. As one critic put it: "Mrs. Clive, peculiarly happy in low humour, with a most disagreeable face, was always the joy of her audience when she kept clear of anything serious or genteel."

Kitty grew very fat with the years, and though usually a woman of good sense, she still insisted on doing Portia, Ophelia, and Desdemona, her favorite parts, making burlesque of them. Yet in low-comedy roles, Johnson considered her better than Garrick, and Goldsmith said she had "more true humour than any other actress." When Garrick leased Drury Lane in 1746, he invited her to join the company where she remained, except briefly, until her retirement in 1769. In her way, she was very fond of Garrick, and though they were forever quarreling, they did not lose respect for each other. When about to retire, she wrote to him asking what difference age could make. "They had rather see *the* Garrick and *the* Clive at 104 than any of the moderns. . . . I assure you, I am at present in such health and spirits, that, when I recollect I am an old woman, I am astonished."

In her retirement, Walpole gave her and her brother a house to share next to his own at Strawberry Hill, which he whimsically called "Clive-den." There, she gave exquisite little suppers after her card parties. The married and the unmarried, actors, authors, artists, clergymen, people of "quality," and, of course, Walpole, came often to see her. She was so full of joy that Lady Townshend said her face made Strawberry Hill sultry.

Kitty Clive did not stint in her admiration for fellow players. After seeing Garrick's Lear, she was so overcome with his power, she exclaimed that he could act "a gridiron." In 1784 she left "Clive-den" to come up to London to see Mrs. Siddons perform. When asked what she thought of the new actress's performance, the old lady exclaimed, "Think? I think it's all truth and daylight!" She died the following year.

There is an amusing story told about Macklin and Dr. Johnson. They were arguing on some literary matter, and to underline his view Johnson quoted Greek. "I do not understand Greek," Macklin protested. "A man who argues should understand every language," Johnson declared severely. "Very well," said Macklin, and quoted for him something in Gaelic.

Macklin employed his "naturalistic" technique in all the serious roles he played. Even as Iago, who too often tempts actors to make him an obvious snarling villain, he spoke his soliloquies "plainly and without ornament," though his predecessors had delivered them with "a world of unnatural contortion of face." His Iago was so convincing that the audience often cursed him. This innovative style had its influence upon others, especially the great Garrick, though the stately Quin charged all of them with seeming "afflicted with St. Vitus dance." Among Macklin's most important roles were Mercutio, the Ghost and First Gravedigger in *Hamlet*, Richard III, Polonius, Malvolio, Osric, Touchstone, Stephano, Poins, Fluellan, and Sir High Evans. One of his most significant parts was Macbeth. For the first time in the history of this play he appeared in the dress of a highlander, although that performance did not take place until October 23, 1773, when he was already an old man. Those who could not adapt themselves to this early attempt at historical accuracy were not pleased. Judge Parry said of Macklin's interpretation that it "had nothing about it to rouse the animosity of theatre-goers, unless, indeed, it was his kilt!" Macklin's predecessors had been given to wearing a periwig and regimental uniform, but he wore not only the kilt but also boots, arms at his girdle, and his hair short and tied behind. It was the beginning of authentic period costume.

But he continued to use D'Avenant's dreadful adaptation of the play. Indeed, the public was so unfamiliar with the plays as Shakespeare had written them that when Garrick announced quite truthfully that he was going to give *Macbeth* "as written by Shakespeare," Quin, in honest astonishment, asked, "Don't I play *Macbeth* as written by Shakespeare?" D'Avenant's version had held the boards so long that Quin was unaware that any other version existed. Macklin's text, although somewhat of an improvement on D'Avenant's, still omitted Lady Macduff altogether.

At the beginning of Garrick's career, he and Macklin were good friends, and the older man gave some good counsel as to means of improving Garrick's interpretations. The younger actor joined Drury Lane company during the 1741/42 season, but by 1743 Fleetwood was so deep in debt that the actors' salaries were in arrears, and they refused to perform until paid. In September, Fleetwood had collected a miscellaneous group of players, and the unemployed former members were ready to negotiate. So was Fleetwood, except that he absolutely refused to reemploy Macklin, whom he now looked upon as an ingrate. To mollify Fleetwood, Garrick offered to come back for £100 less (his salary had been £500) if the patentee would rehire Macklin. Fleetwood was still intransigent. Garrick finally came to terms with Fleetwood, obtaining a higher salary, and Macklin published an account of the affair, charging Garrick and Fleetwood with having double-crossed the company. Macklin's admirers hissed Garrick at his first performance and threw rotten eggs and apples until the actors were forced to give up the play. Garrick published an answer to Macklin's charges, and with Fleetwood he engaged thirty ruffians to prevent a recurrence of the previous incident. The sight of these roughnecks softened the tempers of Macklin's supporters and there was no disturbance. And even though Macklin soon published *Mr. Macklin's Reply to Mr. Garrick's Answer,* which included all the relevant documents, Drury Lane remained closed to him. He never forgave Garrick for his betrayal, though in 1744 they apparently settled their differences. The more obvious it became that Garrick was becoming an actor without peer, the more difficult it must have been for Macklin to excuse him.

Temporarily exiled from the theater, Macklin made the acquaintance of the irrepressible Samuel Foote (1720–1777), who became the great mimic of his time. Well born, he was a spendthrift who was soon penniless. He formed one of a group to whom Macklin began teaching his theories on the art of acting. Of these, Foote was probably the only one with some talent. Undeterred, Macklin gave a series of performances at the Haymarket and circumvented the Licensing Act by hiring musicians and publicizing the events as concerts. Foote, whose gifts were entirely comic, was sadly miscast as Othello to Macklin's Iago for the first performance. Macklin's insistence on a natural delivery no doubt rescued the enterprise from disaster. After several other "concerts" the season closed with *Hamlet,* its hero's identity still unknown to us.

It was as a mimic that Foote eventually won fame. He took over the

Haymarket in 1747 and avoided the strictures of the Licensing Act by inviting people to chocolate or tea, and then proceeding to mimic fellow actors and public figures. In 1749 he inherited a second fortune, went to Paris, and spent it. When he returned and went as a guest to Lord Mexborough's, he was mounted on an unmanageable horse; the animal threw him off and broke his leg (1766), which was amputated. In compensation the king was persuaded to grant him a patent for the little Haymarket for the period May 14 to September 14, during which the two licensed theaters were closed each year. Foote made extensive alterations and improvements in this "Cinderella" of playhouses, which, as a critic phrased it, "had hitherto been little better than a barn."

Foote's father was a gentleman from Cornwall and an M.P.; through his mother he was related to the Duke of Rutland. Even as a boy he entertained his schoolmates until they rolled with laughter over his imitations of his ducal relatives, who invited him frequently to Sunday dinner. At Oxford he made fun of the authorities and ridiculed the provost. He was forced to "retire" to his father's house, where he brilliantly mimicked a couple of justices who were his parents' guests; in consequence, it was decided that he ought to study the law. While he was at the Temple, one of his mother's brothers strangled his own elder brother, and was executed. Shortly thereafter Cooke introduced Foote to a club in Covent Garden as "the nephew of the gentleman who was lately hung in chains for murdering his brother." He did no better at the Temple than at Oxford, and financial necessity drove him to the stage.

For a few years he was engaged alternately at the Haymarket and Drury Lane. His fourteen summers at the Haymarket are unparalleled in theatrical history for its variety of remarkable satires. He mimicked orators, various celebrated noblemen, antiquaries, the pretentious vulgarians who aped gentility, medical quacks, and Anglo-East Indians. When he used puppets, he announced that they would not be so large as life, "not larger in fact than Mr. Garrick"—who was a short man.

Among Foote's pupils was Tate Wilkinson, to whom he passed on the art of mimickry. When he brought Wilkinson on the stage to do admirable imitations of Barry, Mossop, Mrs. Dancer, Mrs. Bellamy, and Garrick, Wilkinson (apparently unexpected by the master) concluded with an excellent one of Foote; the audience was immensely pleased—not so Foote.

When acting—that is, when not mimicking—Foote had a wink, and a smile at one corner of his mouth, as well as a harsh voice. His manner was very disturbing to fellow actors, for he deliberately tried to monopolize the audience's attention by speaking with his face turned full toward the spectators. While Foote was in Dublin one Christmas, as O'Keeffe tells the story, he said in the greenroom to the manager that he felt too ill to perform, "when some of the performers . . . remarked 'Ah, sir! if you will not play, we shall have no Christmas dinner.' 'Ha!' said he, 'if my playing gives you a Christmas dinner, play I will!' and he did so. With all his high comic humor, one could not help pitying him sometimes, as he stood upon his one leg, leaning against the wall, whilst his servant was putting on his stage false leg, with shoe and stocking; he looked sorrowful, but instantly resuming all his high comic humor and mirth, hobbled forward, entered the scene, and gave the audience what they expected—their plenty of laugh and delight."

Wilkinson gives us a good idea of theatrical conditions during the 1750s. Some of the gentry were sitting on the stage; some of them were crowding the one entrance on each side for the actors. The noblemen on stage, says Wilkinson, "sported their own figures to gratify self-consequence," and also impeded the actors. When Quin, at age sixty-five, was full of stuffing for the part of Falstaff, it took him several minutes to make his way through the crowd to the stage. Once, when Holland was first acting Hamlet, in his agitation at seeing the Ghost, he allowed his hat to fall from his head. A woman sitting on the stage crossed over and fastened it on his head.

The moment the curtain rose at Drury Lane and Covent Garden, all was quiet, unless some disturbance had been planned in advance. Anyone behaving in a riotous fashion was handed over to the constables; if he was of a mind to hurl things at the actors, he was at once taken before a justice to be punished. Until 1765, lighting a theater was something of a problem. On and off stage light was provided by candles, and the cost for these at Drury Lane was some £400 a year.

Fleetwood became so indebted that he left the country, and James Lacy became patentee. In December 1744 he reemployed Macklin, who presented his Shylock with Peg Woffington (1714–1760) as Portia. She is said to have been the best interpreter of that role in her time, though she was never thought of as a Shakespearean actress. Born in Dublin, the daughter of a bricklayer who died when she was very young, Peg Woffington was befriended by a famous rope-dancer, Madame Violante. At ten she was already playing children's parts in her native city, and eventually did Ophelia at the Smock Alley Theatre. Rich engaged her for Covent Garden in 1740. She was known as the most beautiful and least vain young woman of her age, though she did not get along with her fellow actresses, Mrs. Cibber and Kitty Clive. In a fit of rage, she wounded the actress George Anne Bellamy with a dagger and drove her out of the theater.

For some years she was Garrick's mistress; by 1742 they were living together, and took turns paying the household expenses. Garrick's parties were austere while hers were lavish, and all the men of fashion were delighted to accept invitations from the beauty. Johnson was often among these guests and asked once, "Is not this tea stronger than usual, madam?"* It was Peg's turn to entertain. There was a story current that Garrick intended to marry her, and he wrote a song for her which began:

> Once more I'll tune the vocal shell,
> To hills and dales my passion tell,
> A flame which time can never quell,
> Which burns for you, my Peggy!

*A reflection on Garrick's parsimony.

Despite her love for Garrick, she had many affairs, and there was little possibility that he would make her his wife. In fact, he married Eva Maria Violetta within a few years. For Peg won the hearts of boys, young men and old men alike—not excluding Owen MacSwiney and Colley Cibber, so that people spoke of them as Susannah and the Elders. She confessed that she much preferred the company of men because women talked of nothing but silks and satins. The public was wild about her and she was especially loved in her "breeches" parts.

After Garrick, she lived for a while with Lord Darnley, who made her promise that she would stop seeing Garrick. Still suspicious, he engaged someone to spy on her and accused her of breaking her promise. She replied that she had not seen him "for a long time." Darnley then faced her with the fact that she had seen Garrick on the previous evening, whereupon she exclaimed: "Is not that a long time?"

Later she lost her beauty. She did Rosalind at Covent Garden in her mid-forties under tragic circumstances. Early in the fifth act she complained, on coming off stage, of being ill. Wilkinson, who was watching her, offered her his arm; she leaned on it, rallied, and reappeared on stage after a change of costume. For a moment she felt faint, and again summoned her strength. She began to speak the epilogue, but within a few lines her tongue became paralyzed; she flung up her hands, shrieked with terror, and staggered toward the exit, falling into the arms of fellow players. It was thus that she took permanent leave of the stage. She died three years later.

During her last years she lived with General Caesar. They had agreed the survivor should possess all the property of both. But on her deathbed, during Caesar's absence, she sent for an attorney and left what was hers to her sister.

To Lacy's chagrin, Garrick after playing in Dublin accepted an engagement at Covent Garden. But Lacy was fortunate enough to find an actor of considerable ability, Spranger Barry (1719–1777), who had already made a name for himself as Othello in Dublin. The son of a well-known silversmith, he had tried following his father's trade but had gone bankrupt. He joined the Theatre Royal in Smock Alley and there, while still quite young, played Lear, Hotspur, and Henry V. When Garrick returned to Drury Lane, he alternated with Barry as Hamlet and Macbeth. His opening performance at Drury Lane was as Othello, and he seems to have received some valuable pointers from Macklin, who played opposite him as Iago; Barry challenged the best in Macklin, whose Iago became his most admired performance after Shylock. Barry's distinguished appearance, air of nobility, and beauty of voice insured his success. Like Betterton before him, he suffered torturing pains from gout (as did John Philip Kemble later), but none of these great actors would allow their pain to interfere with their acting. When Colley Cibber saw Barry do Othello he applauded loudly, which was rare for him, and said he was superior to either Betterton or Barton Booth. Between 1747 and 1758 no one could match his Othello.

In the 1749/50 season, he went over to Covent Garden, and in 1750 both

houses produced presentations of *Romeo and Juliet*. At Covent Garden he
played a highly praised Romeo to a fine Juliet by Mrs. Cibber; at Drury Lane
Garrick and Mrs. Bellamy were their rivals. Garrick evoked more applause,
but Barry more tears. (Macklin and Mrs. Bellamy both preferred Barry.) In
1758, Barry and a partner built the Crow Street Theatre in Dublin; their
losses were heavy. Eventually he went back to London to act at the Haymarket, and reappeared as Othello at Drury Lane in 1767. His personal beauty
gave him the advantage over Garrick, but Garrick's dramatic understanding
and subtlety were far superior. As Leigh Hunt said of Barry, he made his
way "more by person than by genius." Richard Kendal made this epigram
upon the respective Lears:

> A King, Ay, every inch a King—
> Such Barry doth appear;
> But Garrick's quite another thing;
> He's every inch *King Lear*.

Noblewomen pursued him for his good looks and men of distinction
sought his congenial company. He earned enough, says Doran, to live quite
as comfortably as an earl, but he died poor. There is an amusing anecdote
connected with his income: he was objecting to the drawling way an actor
in his company, Kniper, was speaking a passage, and ventured to show him
how it should go; Kniper retorted that Barry got £100 a week for speaking
like that while he got only 30 shillings. "Give me £100 and I'll speak it your
way, but I'm not going to do for 30 shillings what you get paid £100 for."

It was in evoking compassion that Barry excelled. Said one of his contemporaries: "All exquisitely tender or touching writing came mended from his
mouth. There was a pathos, a sweetness, a delicacy, in his utterance, which
stole upon the mind, and forced conviction on the memory." Although
fifty-seven and in failing health he was still a majestic figure on stage in 1776,
though between the acts he lay insensible, or struggling, or waiting for the
return of strength. Ill for many weeks, he died on January 10, 1777,
mourned by a host of friends and admirers. Many tributes were penned to
him, including this anonymous one:

> Scarcely recovered from the stroke severe,
>   When Garrick fled from our admiring eyes,
> Resolv'd no more the Drama's sons to cheer,
>   To make that stroke more fatal—Barry dies.
>
> He dies; and with him sense and taste retreat;
>   For, who can now conceive the Poet's fire?
> Express the just? the natural? the great?
>   The fervid transport? or the soft desire?

At his Crow Street Theatre in Dublin, Barry had met Mrs. Dancer, who
played Cordelia to his Lear. Born Ann Street (1734–1801), the daughter of

an apothecary at Bath, she was disappointed in her first romance and went to Yorkshire, where she fell in love with the stage. While still young, she married an actor, a hotheaded, jealous man by the name of Dancer, who helped her realize her ambitions. She had a graceful figure and rich auburn hair, but began with a small talent. Her widowed mother, as well as her friends at Bath, were scandalized, and she was to be left a very small annuity on condition that she give up acting. She refused, but luckily the man who was then to receive the inheritance rejected it, bestowed it on her, and wished her luck.

She appeared under the name Mrs. Dancer in 1756 at Portsmouth and York. In 1758, she was at the Crow Street Theatre and remained in Dublin for nine years without any public recognition, though an Irish earl attempted to woo her. Free of Dancer, she found no one to her taste but Barry. With her new husband, she went to London where Garrick saw her at the Haymarket and at once engaged her to join his company. Barry had made a fine actress of her, and she was generally considered the equal of Mrs. Cibber and Mrs. Pritchard. She was a notable Beatrice and Desdemona. The Barrys also played at Covent Garden, where she remained after Barry's death.

Two years after Barry's death, she married Crawford, a young Irish barrister and scamp who broke her heart, squandered her money, and put her deeply into debt. Because of her, he became an actor and a lessee of the theater. But the band refused to play as he could not pay them, and, one evening, dressed for the part of Othello, he was obliged to play the violin alone in the orchestra. Soon, with only a small but, fortunately, untouchable annuity left, Mrs. Crawford's health and energy deserted her, and her acting grew careless. It was only Mrs. Siddons's reappearance on the scene that provoked her jealousy and renewed her powers.

Boaden said of her that in strength of feeling she "had a transpiercing effect that seemed absolutely to wither up the hearer." She was, in fact, too fond of achieving startling effects, depended too much upon temperament, and gave too little time to study; with advancing years her performances gradually deteriorated. During her best years her Desdemona was considered without equal. Even the great Mrs. Siddons feared her rivalry. Upon her death in 1801, she was buried near Barry in the cloister of Westminster Abbey.

Having negotiated a share of the Drury Lane patent, Garrick left Covent Garden. To Rich, whose sole stars were Theophilus Cibber and Samuel Foote, Quin wrote, "I am at Bath"; Rich at once replied: "Stay there and be damned." At Drury Lane Garrick lost no time in gathering for the 1747/48 season a distinguished company including Barry, Peg Woffington, Mrs. Cibber, Kitty Clive, Macklin and his wife. He gave a series of Shakespearean revivals with something like a return to the original texts. At the end of the season Thomas Sheridan offered the Macklins £800 a year for two years if they would come to Dublin. They accepted, but hardly had Macklin arrived when new difficulties arose. Though Sheridan was twenty years younger, his was an intransigent nature; he gave unwanted advice, and insisted upon playing Shylock himself. By 1749 season's end he and Macklin were at loggerheads. Sheridan had in the meantime acquired Theophilus Cibber as well as a promising young actor named Henry Mossop. Macklin made it quite clear that he was not at all pleased and in March, Sheridan dismissed both husband and wife without payment. Macklin brought suit for his unpaid salary, finally accepting £300. By the time he returned to London, Barry and Mrs. Cibber had left Drury Lane for Covent Garden, and Rich hired him at once to strengthen his company.

Henry Mossop (1729–1774), son of an Irish clergyman, led a foolish life. He had been turned down by both Rich at Covent Garden and Garrick at Drury Lane, when Thomas Sheridan offered him his chance in Dublin at the Smock Alley Theatre. He had a good figure, fine eyes and did well in parts calling for fire and passion, was an immediate success, and was hired by Garrick. He was much addicted to the "handle and spout" position—one arm extended, the other bent and resting on his hip. For this, he was ridiculed unsparingly. He always insisted on playing young lover parts, to which he was unsuited, and Garrick's enemies kept buzzing in his ear that it was jealousy on Garrick's part that made him refuse to give Mossop lover's roles. His first quarrel was with Sheridan, who found his puckered white satin costume for Richard III too "coxcombly"; Mossop thereupon challenged his employer to a duel, which Sheridan's good humor managed to avoid. Tate Wilkinson said that Mossop "was overburdened with a quantity of combustibles, consisting of pride, insolence, arrogance, and gall." He quit Dublin and in 1751 was hired by Garrick to play Richard III at Drury Lane. The audience was enthusiastic and Garrick gave him every opportunity for exhibiting his talents, allowing him to do Macbeth, Wolsey, and Othello. In 1759, he returned to Dublin as a star at the Crow Street Theatre for Barry, to whose Othello he played Iago. But at the end of the season, rejecting the enormous salary Barry had offered him, he chose to take over the rival Smock Alley Theatre. His incompetence as manager proved ruinous to both companies, for Dublin could not support the two theaters. When Barry was forced to give up the Crow Street playhouse, Mossop managed both houses for a few years, but the opening of a small theater in Capel Street was his undoing. In 1771 he returned to London, and the next year announced bankruptcy.

Having always been jealous of Garrick, he was too proud to ask him for a job. His gambling debts brought him to ruin, and his earlier good looks were despoiled by dissipation. He was shrunken to half his former size, his voice grew hoarse and inarticulate. Destitute, he was abandoned by his former friends and died of starvation in 1774 at the age of forty-five.

Macklin, meanwhile, after the failure at the little Haymarket, joined the Covent Garden company in 1750 and remained there until 1753. He retired on December 20, 1753, to open a combined restaurant and discussion forum in the Covent Garden Piazza, where he was to officiate as headwaiter and teacher of ancient and modern drama. The venture terminated in bankruptcy, and he went to Dublin to help his friend Barry with the building of the Crow Street Theatre. From that time on, his engagements can best be described as fitful. Sometimes he was in the provinces, sometimes in Dublin, sometimes in London. In 1773, he did a Macbeth which was bitterly criticized. Among the published protests, one read: the witches were not satisfied that the devil got Macbeth's soul after his death,

> But to punish the tyrant this would not content him,
> So Macklin he sent on the stage to present him.

Macklin was not a man to avoid a fight. He identified the persons who had hissed him, and made their names public. But this did not stop his enemies and with each performance the hissing and vituperation increased. He nevertheless insisted on playing the tragedy through to the end. At the fourth performance there was general rioting between his enemies and his partisans. The fifth was even worse. Colman, unwilling to risk any more havoc, forthwith dismissed the old man. On May 12, 1774, Macklin's solicitor filed suit against six persons for conspiring to deprive Macklin of his livelihood. At the trial, seventy-four affidavits were submitted in proof of Macklin's charges. It took the jury only twenty minutes to reach a verdict: one man guilty of riot, the other five of riot and conspiracy. When the culprits were brought back into court for sentencing, Macklin revealed himself capable of unusual generosity. He admitted that he would always feel resentment against one of the offenders, who a few days earlier had said that no doubt he would be sent to prison, and that though it was against the law to hiss in court, "it is not against the law to laugh; for depend upon it, when you play tragedy you will have a merry audience!" He suggested to the court that in prosecuting the rioters money had not been in his mind, and he proposed as punishment that they pay his legal fees, buy £100 worth of tickets for his daughter's forthcoming benefit performance and another £100 of tickets for a night when he was to play in order to make up for the management's losses. The judge, Lord Mansfield, complimented Macklin on his suggestions: "I think you have done yourself great credit and great honour . . . and I think it will support you with the public."

Violent, kind, a warm friend, yet capable of jealousy—especially of Garrick, whom he suspected of instigating the conspiracy—Macklin was a mass of contradictions. Though he achieved brilliant success in certain roles, his rise to fame was inhibited by a pugnacious temperament which made him quick to take up a quarrel and caused him to change theaters frequently. Nevertheless, he left his mark upon the history of acting, and it is beyond question that his rejections of the sing-song, attitudinizing behavior of his predecessors on the stage, and the introduction of a natural manner of delivery, greatly influenced the eighteenth century's greatest actor, David Garrick.

Other less prominent actors played important minor roles in the theatrical history of the period. Lacy Ryan (1694–1760), despite a fruitless attempt to set himself up at Covent Garden as a rival to Garrick, was still admired by the latter. Garrick went to see his Richard III (the role which had started Garrick on the road to fame), expecting to laugh at it. Instead he was astonished at Ryan's power, despite his obvious lack of training, clumsy gestures, and ungainly form. A lifelong friend to Quin, whom he had befriended in earlier days, Ryan continued to play young lovers and heroes until his death. He played Seyton to Betterton's Macbeth when still a boy, and was said in that minor role to have worn a wig large enough to cover two such heads as his.

Hannah Pritchard (1711–1768) was established at Drury Lane ten years before Garrick appeared. She was a sister to Henry Vaughan, an able low-comedian, and her husband, Pritchard, held a minor post in the theater. She led an eminently respectable, hard-working life, seems to have had little education, but she was ready to enact any role assigned to her, one of her earliest being Ophelia. She later became well known for her Hermione and Lady Macbeth, as well as for a memorable Gertrude. Her acting was of Quin's school, mannered and old-fashioned, but her articulation was perfect, even in moments of passion. Francis Gentleman said that she was so good her extraordinary "corpulence was always overlooked."

Thomas Davies (?1712–1785), a Scot, made his debut at the Haymarket in 1736, quit the stage, tried bookselling (it was in Davies's shop that Boswell met Johnson), returned to the stage, again became a bookseller, but eventually went bankrupt. During his career as an actor he played both Bassanio and Antonio, Adam, Cymbeline, Angelo, Gloucester (in *King Lear*), Henry IV, and Claudius. When he was an old man, Garrick, for friendship's sake, allowed him a benefit night. Before the curtain went up, he addressed the audience: "Ladies and gentlemen, I am conscious of my inability to do justice to the character I have undertaken, but I hope you will accept of my best endeavors to please." His performance was received with "kind applause." Churchill, the poet, satirized him mercilessly during his career as an actor, and added the sarcasm:

> *Behind came mighty Davies—on my life*
> *That Davies has a very pretty wife.*

Poor Davies died in poverty, and his friends had to pay for his funeral. His widow, a very modest woman, ended in the parish workhouse.

Harry Woodward (1717–1777) was with Garrick at Drury Lane from 1738 on. He preferred comedy to tragedy, and was an excellent Mercutio, Touchstone, and Petruchio (to Kitty Clive's Katharine). The son of a tallow-chandler, he started out in a brewery, but went on to study at Merchant Tailors'. He became a first-rate classical scholar and throughout his life charmed his friends and admirers by "the aptness and beauty of his quotations." As a professional actor Woodward was punctilious about his dress and always amenable to taking on minor roles. Though Foote mimicked him, and called him a "contemptible fellow," Garrick defended Woodward by saying, "He cannot be contemptible since you are afraid of him in the very line in which you, yourself, excel." Woodward did well financially until Spranger Barry induced him to become his partner in the disastrous Dublin venture. He lost all he had saved and was forced, like Barry, to continue acting until the end of his life.

The Haymarket's John Dudley Digges (1720–1786) was a versatile actor who played Macbeth, Lear, Shylock, and Wolsey. He had a manly figure and a noble carriage. On his first appearance as a Roman, the ill-natured Foote, who was sitting in the pit, raised his voice above a wave of welcoming applause: "He looks like a Roman chimney-sweeper on May-day." An irate observer declared that Foote "deserved to be kicked out of the house for his cruelty." At one time the unpredictable Mrs. Bellamy declared that she had been married to Digges, but that was plainly a lie because Digges had one wife already.

Frances Abington (1737–1815) was born Barton in the slums of Drury Lane. Her brother was a stableman and her father a mender of shoes when not on duty as a soldier in the Guards. Who would have guessed that the little girl who sold flowers (under the nickname of "Nosegay Fan") would someday be the fashion pattern for ladies of quality, play the first and never-surpassed Lady Teazle, and be warmly welcomed by Horace Walpole at Strawberry Hill? She rose by both charm and merit. Arthur Murphy, the dramatist, remembered that at twelve she was supporting herself and her father at the Bedford and Shakespeare taverns under the Plaza in Covent Garden. She would climb on the table and recite passages from Shakespeare for a few coins at private parties. When this way of earning a living proved insufficient and boring, she turned to selling her charms. Murphy recalled an occasion when, having waited in vain for a friend at an appointed meeting place, he decided to go to a notorious bordello, where he was sure he would find him. Entering the room, he found his friend half-dressed; thinking he saw the curtains of the bed move, he asked him if he had a companion in it. His friend told him "yes" and to go ahead and chat with her, for he would be entertained. Murphy thereupon drew one of the curtains aside and immediately recognized the companion as the girl who had once recited Shakespeare on the tables of the Covent Garden taverns. She did not seem at all embarrassed, and conversed with ease and humor.

One of her clients was the scoundrel Theophilus Cibber, who had just procured the license for the Haymarket. Cibber thought he saw possibilities in the young harlot, and put her on stage when she was seventeen. She created a favorable impression and she was soon playing Desdemona. From the Haymarket she went to Bath, thence to Richmond, where Lacy, the manager, also fell in love with her, and engaged her for Drury Lane (1756/57). When next Murphy saw her on the stage she had married a Mr. Abington under whom she had studied music. They lived in the then-fashionable quarter of St. Martin's Lane. Soon after the estimable Mr. Abington fell from her grace and into obscurity.

Mrs. Abington was extremely popular, and after four seasons at Drury

Lane she accepted an invitation to play at the Cork Theatre in Ireland. Success had not altered her values and she made no attempt on arrival to conceal her intimacy with her traveling companion, Mr. Needham. Their liaison and her taste in dress became so well known that the milliners in Cork put the following sign in their windows: "Abington caps may be had here for those that *Need'em.*" John Taylor, who has recorded Murphy's confidences, in his memoirs justifies his account thus, "I should forbear to mention the preceding circumstances of her life, if they did not afford a striking evidence that people by industry, fortitude, and perseverance, may not only rise from obscurity, but from a more degrading situation."

On the stage Mrs. Abington became distinguished for her lively spirit and skill at expressing sarcasm. She was a famous Beatrice. John Taylor once dined with her at the house of the celebrated Mrs. Jordan, for years mistress of George III's son. Mrs. Abington displayed "great spirit, and enlivened the conversation with many anecdotes of theatrical history, as well as of fashionable life, with which she had been intimately connected during the zenith of her fame; but the chief part of her conversation related to Mr. Garrick. . . . In speaking of the powerful effect of his eyes, she said . . . they seemed to operate by fascination; and that . . . she never beheld eyes that had so much expression, brilliancy, and force. . . . Shakespeare was made for Garrick, and Garrick for Shakespeare."

John Henderson (1747–1785), in his short professional life, played more than one hundred roles. He was apprenticed to a silversmith when Garrick, recently retired, encouraged him to think of acting. At the age of twenty-one, he was turned down by Drury Lane because his voice was weak and his bearing unimpressive, probably due to the extreme poverty in which he had been living. But he was determined to be an actor, and gave amateur performances including first-rate imitations of Garrick. The latter provided him with an introduction to Palmer at Bath, and he was hired at a guinea a week. His first appearance as Hamlet was well received, and he worked hard at his profession. He was stout, fair-haired, with a powerful visage. In 1777 Colman hired him for the Haymarket, where he did a highly praised Shylock. Even Macklin thought highly of it. When Henderson expressed regret at never having seen the old actor in his famous role, Macklin replied that it was obvious Henderson had not, "or you would have played it differently." John Kemble said Henderson's Shylock was the "greatest effort I ever witnessed on the stage." Drury Lane, which had previously rejected him, now sought him out. He stayed there two years. He was especially lauded for his Falstaff, Othello, Hamlet, and Lear. (Gainsborough painted him as Macbeth.) He was particularly effective in his sudden transitions from one passion to another. Iago was perhaps his weakest part, his villainy so low key that the character seemed almost cordial and sincere. Early deprivations and overwork brought him to a premature death before he was forty. He is buried in Westminster near Garrick.

Henderson and two friends visited Foote who, for once, was not only very civil but in a particularly jovial mood; he let forth a veritable torrent of wit, satire, and pleasantries for a considerable time. Henderson's friends thought it was time to interrupt Foote's merriment to explain that the purpose of their visit was to allow Foote to hear Henderson do a speech from *Hamlet,* but before the young man could finish it, Foote interrupted with a jest. Henderson was then permitted to do an imitation of Garrick, and did so without caricature. Foote complimented him on his good ear, but whispered to one of the friends that Henderson would not do.

His second role in London was Hamlet. He was severely criticized for flinging away Claudius's picture in the famous passage where the prince compares his father and uncle; the next night he kept the picture in his hand and the same people ridiculed him on the grounds that if he had been right the first night, he was necessarily wrong on the second!

He was very serious by nature, though capable of much fun. One of his parlor entertainments has been preserved by O'Keeffe. It is an imagined dialogue between an Irish peer and Garrick, the nobleman recommending his fellow student Mossop, by praise of his voice, action, and literary attainments:

NOBLEMAN: Now, Mr. Garrick, Mossop's voice—what a fine voice, so clear, full, and sublime for tragedy!

GARRICK: Oh! yes, my lord: Mossop's voice is, indeed, very good—and full—and—and—But, my lord, don't you think that sometimes he is rather too loud?

NOBLEMAN: Loud? Very true, Mr. Garrick—too loud—too sonorous!—when we were in college together, he used to plague us with a spout and a rant and a bellow. Why we used to call him "Mossop the Bull!" But then, you know, Mr. Garrick, his step! so very firm and majestic—treads the boards so charmingly!

GARRICK: True, my lord: you have hit his manner very well indeed, very charming! But do you not think his step is sometimes rather too firm?—somewhat of a stamp: I mean a gentle stamp, my lord?

NOBLEMAN: Gentle, call you it, Mr. Garrick? not at all!—at college we called him "Mossop the Pavior!" But his action—his action is so very expressive!

GARRICK: Yes, my lord, I grant, indeed, his action is very fine—fine—very fine: he acted with me originally in Barbarossa, when I was the Achmet; and his actions was a—a—to be sure Barbarossa is a great tyrant—but then, Mossop, sticking his left hand on his hip, a-kimbo, and his right hand stretching out—thus! you will admit that sort of action was not very graceful.

NOBLEMAN: Graceful, Mr. Garrick! Oh, no!—not at all—everything the contrary. His one arm a-kimbo, and his other stretched out! very true—why, at college, we used to call him, "Mossop the Teapot!"

John Quick (1748–1831) was also hired by Foote for the Haymarket in 1767, but he soon joined the Covent Garden company, where he remained for the rest of his career. He had a large repertory of comic roles, and was particularly good as Polonius and Shallow. But what he really yearned to play was tragedy. In 1790 his Richard III was hooted off the stage, and so he wisely returned to the comic. A small man with a chubby face, he was rather impetuous. For some reason he was George III's favorite actor.

John Palmer (1742–1798), the second by that name, first acted for Foote at the Haymarket. When as a young man he tried to be an actor, he was told he would make a better soldier. Garrick would not have him, and Foote thought him bad in tragedy, but satisfactory in comedy. He nearly starved as a strolling player and he was willing to do anything on the London stage at the most miserable of salaries. He went again to the country and married a woman whose "expectations" came to nothing. In 1766, Garrick hired him for Drury Lane, and while at first ridiculing his alleged powers of study, soon changed his mind. Palmer made his way slowly. His career nearly ended when Mrs. Barry stabbed him on stage with a real dagger. He later built the Royalty Theatre in Wellclose Square, but was forced to close it because he had no license. His theater put him permanently in debt and he spent his life trying to elude the bailiffs. Sometimes he would spend a week hiding in the theater; at other times he would manage to get himself conveyed outside in a piece of theatrical property.

He was one of the best general actors on the London stage from 1761 to 1798. Despite an elegant figure, he made a fine Falstaff and Sir Toby Belch. He achieved some notoriety as a congenital liar. Michael Kelly records an occasion when Palmer was to travel with him, but excused himself, saying: "My best of friends, this is the most awful period of my life; I cannot leave town; my beloved wife, the partner of my sorrows and my joys, is just confined." Kelly went on alone. About two months later, Palmer was engaged to go to Reading for a benefit, but did not go. He wrote to the poor actor for whom he was to perform that he could not leave town because "Mrs. Palmer had just been brought to bed." The letter was read to the audience, and Kelly congratulated him on having a wife who could "increase his family every two months." Sheridan called him Plausible Jack. Once, when a new comedy was to be acted, and the house was crowded, Palmer sent Sheridan a letter saying he was so ill that his life would be endangered if he played that night. Sheridan's reaction was: "This is a trick of Plausible Jack's, and . . . nothing is the matter with him, except indeed not knowing a line" of his part. He asked Kelly to accompany him to Palmer's house to investigate. Sheridan was delayed, and Kelly went on alone to Palmer's, where he found him at the table in the middle of dinner. Kelly warned him to clear away the table, for Sheridan was due any minute. In an instant Palmer was in his bedroom wearing his dressing gown, a large woolen nightcap, a handkerchief tied under his jaw, stretched out on the sofa. On Sheridan's entry, he began to groan as if in the most excruciating pain. Sheridan was taken in, and Kelly never gave him away.

His careless preparation for a part was often in evidence, and he frequently went on stage trusting to his wits. Once he delivered a prologue without knowing a line of it.

He had the misfortune to lose the wife he adored and his best-loved son.

Sorrow over their deaths, and worry about the remaining children occupied his thoughts, even on stage. Finally, during a performance of a play called *The Stranger*, with his genuinely mournful air, he replied to a question regarding the wife of the character he was playing: "I love her still," and then to the question about his children: "I left them at a small town hard by." He had scarcely mumbled these words when he fell dead at his fellow actor's feet!

Sophia Baddeley (1745–1786) was a beautiful woman and excelled as Ophelia, Desdemona, and Imogen. Although her husband Robert disapproved of her dissipated life and soon left her, he later fought a duel in her behalf with Garrick's brother. The lady rushed in, crying, "Spare him!" without indicating which of the two she meant. It proved irrelevant as the two combatants fired anywhere but at each other, and afterward all three went together to have dinner. Eventually laudanum, cognac, and paralysis put an end to her career.

Robert Baddeley had been a cook in his earlier days and continued to take pride in his mastery of the culinary art. He acted for Foote and was very good in parts calling for broken English, such as Fluellen's. When he died in 1794 he bequeathed his cottage in the country for the benefit of poor actors, and a sum of money for the company in the greenroom to be spent on cake and wine each year at Twelfth Night, a custom still observed at Drury Lane.

A Miss Seal, left in difficult circumstances, was rescued by a benefactress and educated at an academy in Queen's Square, Westminster. The rogue, Lord Tyrawley, easily persuaded her to elope and live with him at Somerset House. When his lordship felt it was time for a change, he left Miss Seal with their infant son and went to Ireland to propose to an ugly heiress; he promised Miss Seal that after he married he would abandon his wife and return to share the money with her. But he soon found that his new wife had no money at her disposal. Soon thereafter the king sent him to represent him at Lisbon. He was willing to take Miss Seal with him, but she preferred to go on the stage. When she changed her mind she arrived to a warm welcome and the discovery that she had acquired a rival. In revenge, she listened to the suit of a Captain Bellamy, married him, and in an unnaturally brief time presented him with a daughter. The frightened captain ran away and never saw her again. Lord Tyrawley immediately accepted little George Anne Bellamy (1727–1788) as his daughter. He gave her a good education at a convent in Boulogne, and then brought her up in his own house. When he was sent to Russia for a brief period she received an allowance.

The young George Anne Bellamy was extraordinarily beautiful. After some amateur appearances, she was heard of by Rich, manager of Covent Garden, who decided that she had the makings of a great actress. Quin was angry at having to play opposite "such a child," but soon found her tenderness and abilities delightful. Lord Byron, ancestor of the poet, was struck by her beauty and wooed her. But as she would not settle for less than marriage he resorted to trickery and abducted her by coach to a house at the edge of some deserted fields. The affair caused a great scandal and her half-brother, convinced she had consented to the abduction, refused to have anything more to do with her. She managed to make her way to Dublin and had a triumphant time of it there (1745–1747).

In Dublin Garrick made her one of his leading ladies, and though she played Juliet to his Romeo her attitude was not as truly professional as that of Peg Woffington or Mrs. Cibber, whom she tried to rival as a tragic heroine. She was indignant with Garrick when he thought her too young to play Constance in *King John*. Thomas Sheridan wished to give her the role over Garrick's objections and she appealed for further support to her patroness, Mrs. Butler, who persuaded all her friends to boycott the performance. The house was almost empty, and Mrs. Bellamy rejoiced that it was "the first theatrical humiliation the immortal Roscius ever met with." Garrick gave in, she took over as Constance, and the house was packed; many were even turned away. But she was still of a mind to revenge herself on "this LITTLE *great man,*" as she called him. When he asked her to perform Jane Shore at a benefit she declined, "alleging the objection he had made to my playing Constance, namely my youth." Garrick wrote her a letter promising to write her "a *goody-goody* epilogue"—which would win the hearts of the audience, and he addressed the note "To my soul's idol, the beautified Ophelia." The servant who was to deliver it to her handed it to a porter in the street, who was no "soul's idol" or "beautified Ophelia," and therefore brought it to a newsman, who got it into print.

In London, while doing Juliet's potion scene, she was disturbed by a loud laugh from Lady Coventry's box. The actress would not continue until the party left the box. Her ladyship's explanation was that she had been twirling an orange, and somebody said something silly about it. Ironically, Mrs. Bellamy had loaned Lady Coventry some money just before the latter's marriage. The actress sent a note with a servant asking that the debt be paid. Infuriated, Lady Coventry sent the reply: "If she is impertinent, I will have her hissed off the stage!" Mrs. Bellamy was never repaid.

Her father wanted her to marry his friend, Mr. Crump, because he knew that his daughter was now fairly well-to-do. Rather than agree, she went to live with a Mr. Metham. Metham was eager to marry her, but she refused. Siren and courtesan though she was in private life, she maintained her prominent position on the stage for three decades. Her passionate love scenes were unequaled and she was capable of being tender and subdued if the role called for that. She had such great beauty, her eyes were of such a lovely blue, she was so exquisitely fair that the public adored her.

She continued to live recklessly, passed from one "protector" to another, until she became a wreck, bent nearly double, her skin jaundiced; she described herself as "a little dirty creature." Abandoned by all her former admirers, this imperious, queenly actress ended up hungry, pursued by bailiffs; she even tried to drown herself in the Thames. Finally some friends, who had been supplying her with trifling sums, induced the managers to give her a farewell benefit in 1784. On that occasion she had not the courage to appear before the audience at the prologue, which was spoken for her by Miss Farren:

> But see, oppressed with gratitude and tears,
> To pay her duteous tribute, she appears . . .

The curtain rose to reveal a terrified ancient-looking woman, who looked far older than her fifty-seven years, lying in an armchair without the strength to rise. The audience, out of respect for her brilliant past, rose to greet her.

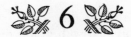

Theaters and Audiences in the Later Eighteenth Century

Garrick found Drury Lane's auditorium too small for the audiences that wished to see him perform, and its stage inadequate to accommodate the scenic elaborations he planned. So, in 1762, its seating capacity was enlarged to twenty-two hundred; when filled, the receipts could exceed £350. Then in 1775 a more drastic alteration was effected by the Adam brothers, this time not for the sake of increasing the seating capacity but to add to the elegance and comfort of the edifice itself: the boxes were made larger, new passages and entrances were added, and the exterior of the theater was rendered far more impressive; the total cost of these improvements was in the neighborhood of £4,000. Here Mrs. Siddons triumphed in 1776 and reigned from 1782 to 1793. In 1793 Drury Lane was entirely rebuilt to hold thirty-six hundred people.

George Colman did not approve of the Adams' improvements at Drury Lane; they "contrived," he wrote, "to give the interior of an old gloomy theatre a new, a gayer and even a gaudy appearance; but when the first feelings of surprise were passed, men began to reflect a little on the propriety of style adopted in the alteration, and it was generally agreed . . . the decorations were ill adopted, since the audience part of a playhouse should by no means divert the eye of the spectator from the scenic effect of the stage, and distract it by an assemblage of unnatural objects, displayed in all the glare of no-meaning painting." He preferred Covent Garden and the theater he took over in 1776, the Haymarket; the latter he described as "lightly elegant and not too extravagantly gay."

Before Garrick became manager of Drury Lane, its stage required very little scenery, for most of the acting was performed on the apron; the proscenium had on each side the entrance doors for the actors as well as the first line of the boxes for the audience. In the late 1750s he began to alter this situation; costs of productions, including scenery (which superseded the old stock sets), were as high as £1,674 during the last season when

Mrs. Siddons was a member of the company; the costs for lighting rose to £2,000. Actors, who generally wore eighteenth century dress, purchased most of their own costumes. Before 1765 the stage was lit by six moveable chandeliers, each holding twelve candles; the footlights too were provided by candles. But after 1765 the chandeliers were removed, and in imitation of the French, side-wing lights were used, so adjusted that the light could be raised or lowered for varying effects, and their brilliance augmented by the addition of reflectors. Sometimes wick oil-lamps were also employed to add to the light of the candles. But these arrangements were quite hazardous, and Drury Lane was a remarkable exception to the frequency with which theaters were burned.

The players themselves must have been far more aware of the audience than is the case today when the hall lights are extinguished. And as long as the apron still existed as part of the stage, the actors could not fail to see the occupants of the boxes to either side, as well as the audience before them. Garrick's romantic use of scenery caused the action to retreat further to the rear of the stage. The scenery itself, as Richard Southern described it, was of the "groove-sliding, wing-and-shutter" sort—that is, a system of solid wings parallel to one another, set in a series of grooves on each side of the stage, so that they could be removed off stage to make room for another set. It was possible to construct doors, arches, and gates in these moveable wings, while the background of the stage would contain one painted scene. The proscenium curtain was not yet used to divide acts and it was not until the next century that it was used to spare the audience changes of scenery. Instead, the division between acts was indicated by the playing of the musicians.

The audience did not enjoy the luxury of having individual seats, as in our modern theaters. Except for the royal family, the audience sat on long benches, where they no doubt were crushed together—even in the three levels of boxes. The worst to-do on entry was in the pit. The patrons on line outside the theater pushed and jostled each other until the doors were opened. When they were let in there was a general rushing, thrusting aside, and lack of consideration in their haste to choose the best obtainable places.

Because Drury Lane and Covent Garden were around the corner from each other, getting home after the play was a serious problem too. Tate Wilkinson gives us a vivid picture of what the exit was like on a severe winter's night: he went to the Covent Garden Piazza, hoping for a coach or chair. "No great coat, but wind, rain and tempest; pushed on all sides by the link-boys, coach-men, and crowd; hustled by the pick-pockets; and dreading every moment to be thrown down by the slippery inter-mixture of snow and rain . . . My mind suggesting fever, cold, additional broken limbs, robbery, and the being run over, I at length by the help of Providence . . . arrived at the box-lobby of Drury Lane theatre, where I was informed the performance had closed near an hour," though anyone would have thought the final curtain had just descended because the "universal outcry for 'coach' and 'chair,' was inconceivable and at any price." Some who recognized him whispered to him to be patient and that he would be assured conveyance from the theater. Suddenly someone shouted, " 'Mr. Wilkinson's carriage!' . . . I was at a loss how to act, supposing a Mr. Wilkinson's real carriage was waiting, as there are many rich Wilkinsons as well as poor; but my stupor was relieved by the box-keeper . . . bowing to me to attend me to my carriage." Wilkinson thought his troubles were over, but he was presently addressed by his cockney coachman: "Lookye, my master, I knows not whomsoever you may be, but the night is so bad it vill be the death of me and my cattle, and I don't ax you for my fare, for I was not on any stand, and you can't oblige me as to how to take you, so minds I tells you, that I von't take you into my coach, for as how to carry you to Graves-Inn Lane, without that you will give me eight shillings; and I von't because I von't, and so I tells you; but if you will give me that there price, vy I will drive you as vell as I can." Wilkinson agreed to pay the sum, was delivered to his hotel, where there were several men anxiously trying to procure a coach. But since their destination was not in that part of London where the coachman was headed, he would not take them on any terms, though he was quite satisfied he had brought "the gemman to his lodgings on so dismal a night."

As badly as audiences sometimes behaved in the early eighteenth century, they grew rather worse as the century progressed.

In 1754, discovering that despite the excellence of the company Garrick could not fill Drury Lane unless he himself was playing—which in a repertory theater was manifestly impossible—he put on the *Chinese Festival,* a magnificent ballet-pantomime. The English dancers were among the best that could be found, and he added to them some excellent foreign dancers. But by autumn, when the spectacle was shown, war had broken out with France, and many in the audience were offended that the enemy—and Roman Catholics at that!—was on display. To make matters worse, George II's presence seemed to lend countenance to the whole proceedings. The pit raised a veritable storm, which raged even more furiously when it was seen that the old king was not only enjoying himself but laughing at the disturbances in the pit. Both His Highness and performers were hissed. Garrick had been advised to withdraw the spectacle, but had dreaded losing his large investment. Instead, he lost more by repeating the performance, on which occasion the pit made an even greater to-do; only this time the occupants of the boxes, feeling it their duty to uphold the preferences of the monarch, let the pit and galleries know that they were "vulgar," which insult only raised the fever of those larger portions of the house, who hurled even greater insults at the box holders than at the dancers. The gentlemen in the boxes drew their swords, leaped into the pit, pricked members of the pit here and there, and were themselves badly knocked about. The galleries, looking on with approval, indiscriminately pelted both sides. The ladies in the boxes, beholding their defenders worsted, pointed out particular offenders to less pugnacious beaux attending them, who now felt compelled to join in, and jumped into the pit with their swords unsheathed. Nevertheless, the stronger muscles of the plebeians won the victory, and when they had routed the gentility, proceeded to break up benches, smash mirrors, destroy harpsichords, and the mob mounted the stage to cut up the scenery.

Even actors were not necessarily respecters of royalty. The youthful King of Denmark had married George III's sister, and in 1768 frequently attended the London theaters. In October, he commanded a performance of *Jane Shore* but, as the audience speedily noted, he fell asleep. Mrs. Bellamy, in a leading role, was mightily annoyed. At her line, "Oh thou false lord!" she approached the royal box and uttered the words in so piercing a tone that the young king awoke.

Actors were sometimes scarcely more polite to their royal patron, King George III. One night at a command performance at the Haymarket of *The Siege of Calais*, when the royal family was present, during the scene between two carpenters where one was supposed to say, "So, the king is coming! an the king like not my scaffold, I am no true man," the actor approached the royal box and cried instead: "An the king were here, and did not admire my scaffold, I would say, Damn him! he has not taste!" The king laughed louder and longer than anyone else in the house.

The audience was not composed entirely of admirers of royalty; some felt too strongly about liberty for that. But others (for all their love of liberty) did not object to George himself, and were pleased by his open enjoyment of the theater. He never tired of laughing at the repeated tricks of the clown, while little Queen Charlotte was clearly delighted with comedies. On one occasion, Foote was doing a caricature of an overly fashionable lady and wore a headpiece a yard high and almost as broad; by accident it fell from his head, and he stood there bald-pated; the queen's laughter could be heard throughout the theater.

But royal presence could also result in tragedy. On February 3, 1794, at a command performance at the Haymarket, the press of the mob was so great at the pit's entrance that a gentleman was thrown down the stairs; those behind him fell over him, and they in turn were trampled upon because of the numbers still pushing forward. Those who were killing their fellows by stamping on their bodies could not hold back those impelling them, and there were moans of the crushed and the dying, too horrible to hear. It was presently found that fifteen had been killed and nineteen other persons severely injured.

At Drury Lane on May 11, 1800, at another command performance, George III was standing by himself at the front of the royal box when Hatfield fired at him from below. Naturally, great excitement followed as the would-be assassin was dragged through the orchestra midst the shouts of the audience. Everyone lost his head but the king, who continued to peruse the house with his opera glass. The performance was punctuated by cries from the audience in behalf of George; the queen and the princesses (who had arrived later) were in tears, but he remained calm and cheerful.

The continued crowding of the stage must have been an outrage to Garrick, who had to perform even his great Lear surrounded by fops and their ladies. In Dublin matters were even worse. Once when he was playing

Lear there to Peg Woffington's Cordelia, an Irish gentleman advanced, put his arm around Cordelia's waist, and kept holding her while she answered her father's reproaches. Londoners never went that far, and when Garrick tried in 1762 to forbid the public to enter on the stage, his fellow actors objected: on benefit nights, they said, when places on the stage were sold at advanced prices, they would lose the most generous of their patrons if people of rank were banished. Garrick's compromise was to enlarge the house. But that turned out to be a mistake, for those too distant from the stage were bound to miss the subtleties of facial and vocal expression—even when Garrick himself was performing. And benefit nights continued to be all confusion. On one such night Wilkinson saw Mrs. Cibber lying in the tomb of the Capulets "with a couple of hundred of the audience surrounding her."

Irish gentlemen were readier than the English to use their swords in the theater, as Mossop discovered in 1769, when he was manager at Cork. One night, the attendance was unusually sparse, especially in the pit, where sat a lone little major. Mossop, to avoid a loss, since his actors were paid according to the number of their performances, announced that the play had been canceled for the night, and said that the price of admission would be refunded. But the major insisted that the play be given; Mossop could not dissuade him. The little major drew his sword; Mossop quietly put his hand on his. In one leap the major was on the stage, and both men began fighting fiercely. The audience was enjoying the sight; no attempt was made to part them until the major had run his sword through the fleshy part of Mossop's thigh, and Mossop had slightly wounded the major in the arm. Both sides won. For Mossop now unable to act could close the theater and the major, too severely wounded to be taken out at once, remained in the theater as he had sworn to do.

Once in Cork, the audience was mightily displeased. A tailor was hanged for robbery only to be resuscitated by an actor named Glover (who, it was said, was in the tailor's debt and feared the demands the executors might make). Fully recovered, the tailor went out and got drunk; inebriated, he went to the theater, told his story, and made a great point of exhibiting the mark where the rope had been, along with many a tipsy compliment to the actor for bringing him back to life. The Cork audience was not at all amused.

John Kemble, leading actor of his day, was playing Marc Antony in Dublin when his eye happened to catch a dignified old gentleman who was eagerly listening to him through an ear trumpet. Kemble smiled—at a most inappropriate moment, for he was in the presence of Octavia. He tried to suppress it but was less and less able to do so; he became agitated and the old man directed his ear trumpet ever nearer the stage, at which Kemble finally broke into a gale of laughter, and rushed in confusion from the scene. The audience laughed with him but the deaf old man, unaware of his contribution to the laughter, dropped his trumpet. His expression showed he failed to see the cause of the merriment.

Toward the close of the century the notorious Lady Hamilton attracted crowds of the curious when it was announced that she and her husband, Sir William, minister to the court at Naples, would attend a performance at Drury Lane. The audience luxuriated in watching the beautiful woman, while she remained absorbed in Mrs. Powell's performance on stage; the actress returned the compliment by paying much attention to her. Unknown to the audience, there was a reason for this mutual interest. The wife of the ambassador and the tragic actress had met long before under very different conditions—at the house of Dr. Budd, where Jane Powell was the housemaid and Emma Harte (as Lady Hamilton was then named) was an assistant maid in the nursery.

The behavior of the galleries had not much improved. At Liverpool, the short Hollingsworth, a specialist in low comedy, was looking at the house through an opening in the curtain when he was detected by a ruffian in the gallery, who seized a penknife he was about to use on an apple, and hurled it at the curtain with such deadly accuracy that it struck the poor actor within a fraction of an inch of his eye; for a while his sight was in danger. Less savage, the people in the London galleries favored throwing an orange at a lady in court dress.

At York, Mrs. Montagu, who was to play the queen in *Henry II*, refused to study the part because she wished to play the heroine, Rosamond. Pleading illness, she sent an actor on stage to announce that she would read the part. The audience insisted on her appearing to explain her own case. She stalked on stage with an imperious, "Who's afraid?" and insisted that she would read the part, since she had had no time to learn it. The house was enraged. Someone cried that they would rather hear it read by the cook-wench at the alehouse nearby than by her. Unintimidated by the shouts that she act, not read, she looked with scorn at the pit, flung her book at the crowd with a "There!—curse you all!" and proudly quit the stage to the accompaniment of hisses and laughter. She was not allowed to act again.

7

Garrick

David Garrick (1717–1779) has the reputation of having been the greatest actor to grace the English-speaking stage. The legend of his genius has been equaled only by that of Sarah Siddons. His extraordinary and natural gift for mimicry as a boy must have determined his vocation. He was a man who gave much thought and time to the study of his art. Though genuinely fond of practical jokes, he often indulged in them for the sake of learning, as the following anecdotes illustrate.

Once when he was in the company of Dr. Monsey and Mr. Windham, he left them at the top of Ludgate Hill, walked into the middle of the street, gazed toward the sky, and uttered several times to himself: "I never saw two before." Inevitably, human nature being what it is, attention was drawn to a man thus talking to himself. Several people asked him what it was he was seeing; he did not reply, but continued muttering the same words. One man decided that Garrick must have seen two storks, since storks are never to be seen in pairs. This satisfied the crowd for a while, until another man asked, "Well, but who sees *one* besides this gentleman?" Monsey, wishing to escape becoming involved, went away, but Windham held his ground, anxious to see the jest through. Garrick now assumed the stare of a madman, studied the crowd gathered about him, and presently assured Windham that he had acquired many a hint from the expressions on their faces which would be useful to him as an actor.

One day, strolling with Monsey at midday, a host of boys poured out of the school they were passing. He selected one, whom he accused of having been viciously cruel to another boy near him. The so-called victim declared that no one had ill-used him. Whereupon, Garrick laced into the supposed offender even more, observing that he was not entitled to the magnanimity of his neighbor. Garrick's awesome behavior and piercing eye left the boys agape. The actor assured Monsey that he had learned a great deal from studying their emotions.

On another occasion with the same doctor, he noted a ticket-porter ahead of them walking at a brisk pace and humming to himself. Said the actor: "I'll get a crowd around that man before he reaches Temple Bar." He rapidly passed the porter, and gave him a piercing look. The man stopped his humming at once, his eyes fixed on Garrick, who stopped at an apple stall to wait for the man to catch up with him. Then he gave him another piercing look and went on his way. The porter began to examine himself to discover whether there was anything odd about him that could have attracted such looks. Garrick continued to turn around with an accusing glance; the man took off his wig to see whether anything unusual had caught on it. By this time the curious behavior of the porter attracted the attention of the passers-by, and Garrick had effected his purpose.

Once Garrick was seriously endangered by these public pranks. He had dined with Monsey in Garrick's house in Southampton Street, and they had taken a boat for Vauxhall in the evening. At Hungerford Stairs, on the bank, stood a staunch young waterman. They had hardly taken their places in their boat when Garrick spoke to the young man: "Are you not ashamed to dress so smart and appear so gay, when you know that your poor mother is in great distress, and have not the heart to allow her more than three pence a week?" The youth looked about him to see whether there was anyone whom Garrick might be addressing; finding no one else, he seized a brickbat and threw it very close to Garrick's boat, and followed that by a succession of stones. Garrick's boatman pulled hard and with some difficulty drew out of range.

It is curious, as Edward Wagenknecht well observes, "that England's greatest actor should have had so little English in him. . . . His father was a minor army officer of French Huguenot stock, and his mother was half Irish." His French grandfather's family name was Garrigue; on the revocation of the Edict of Nantes in 1685 they had escaped with great difficulty to England from Bordeaux. Twenty-one years later the son, Peter, his name now properly anglicized, procured a commission in the army and married Arabella of Lichfield, whose mother was Irish. David was Peter's third child; his eldest son was also named Peter, and there were five other surviving brothers and sisters. The Garricks were "genteel" but poor, and tardy in paying their bills.

David Garrick was born on February 19, 1717, and raised in Lichfield. Samuel Johnson, eight years his senior, was a fellow townsman, and the two were acquainted. Johnson, the son of a bookseller, was socially inferior to the Garricks; both families were equally impoverished. When Johnson, at the age of seventeen, came home from Stourbridge Grammar School, David was beginning his studies at the Lichfield school. (Addison had attended the same school.) Native Lichfield English was quite Midland, and called for refining if one aspired to the cultural atmosphere of London. A lady asked Johnson, "Do you say 'neether' or 'nyther,' sir?" "Nayther," he replied. This happened long after the great man had left Staffordshire. Garrick no doubt improved his vowels more rapidly, for he had a fine ear. Boswell records, however, that Garrick continued to pronounce "once" as *woonse.* At the beginning of his acting career he was somewhat given to affectation in his diction, pronouncing "matron" as *metron;* "Israel" as *Iserel;* "villain" as *villin;* "Horatio" as *Horetio;* but he soon gave that up.

Garrick's schooling was interrupted at age eleven when he was sent alone to Lisbon to learn the trade of his uncle David, a wine merchant. Though his stay was brief, he had time to amuse the English merchants there with his recitations. On his return to Lichfield the same year, he had his first taste of the theater when a band of strolling players came to town, and he was given the opportunity to enact a small part in the play. (At another performance by the same company, young Samuel Johnson came back to his chair on stage after the intermission, and found it occupied by an innkeeper; when the man refused to get up, Johnson lifted man and chair as though they were of a piece, and threw them into the pit.)

Garrick's father died in 1737, and his mother three years later. Garrick later confessed that though his heart had already been set on the stage, he would not have dared indulge his ambition while his mother lived. When Johnson was twenty-four and already married to his ill-made and much older wife, he opened an academy at Edial; David and his brother George were his first pupils. David used to delight his classmates by spying on Johnson and his ugly wife through the keyhole of the bedroom door and then mimicking what he had seen.

On March 2, 1737, Johnson, with his tragedy *Irene* in his pocket, and David Garrick, twenty and intended for the bar, left Lichfield together, bound for London. When they arrived, Johnson later declared that he himself had twopence halfpenny, and David three halfpence. David entered Lincoln's Inn to study the law. A year later he inherited £1,000 from an uncle and returned to Lichfield to talk matters over with his eldest brother; they decided to become partners in the wine business, Peter to remain in Lichfield, David to station himself in London. Their stock was necessarily small, and years later Foote sneeringly said that Garrick had called himself a wine merchant with only three quarts of vinegar in the cellar.

David's chief customers were the coffeehouses in the Covent Garden neighborhood where one met chiefly the actors of the two patent theaters. He himself went constantly to the playhouses; soon he was welcome behind the scenes, and had made a particular friend of Charles Macklin. He learned all he could from his talks with the famous Shylock and his opportunities to observe the other actors. In March 1741 he went to Ipswich in Suffolk with his friend Giffard to make his first professional appearance as an actor. On returning to London he applied at both Covent Garden and Drury Lane for a position but neither Rich nor Fleetwood would have him. So he went to Giffard's theater in Goodman's Fields near Aldgate. The subterfuge necessary for the latter to circumvent the law allowing for only two patented theaters was to announce the entertainment as a two-part concert with acting in the interval, the acting "performed gratis by persons for their diversion."

And so it was that David Garrick on Monday, October 19, 1741, made his first London appearance as Richard III in Cibber's version of the play; astonishingly enough, he became a star overnight. As had his friend Macklin in the role of Shylock, he spoke naturally, without any rhetorical flourishes. He was capable of an infinite variety of feelings: fear, horror, agony, conflict, interpenetrated with the "courage of desperation." He was the first to chuckle with "sardonic delight" at the line for which Cibber was responsible: "Off with his head! So much for Buckingham."—an effect later copied by Cooke and Kean. The town went wild. No one had ever seen such a *Richard III.* William Hogarth was so much impressed that he said, "You are in your element when begrimed with dirt or up to your elbows in blood." The next day *The Daily Post* praised him for his sweet voice, his graceful face and gait, and said his reception was: "the most extraordinary and great that was ever known on such an occasion . . . When three or four are on the stage with him, he is attentive to whatever is spoke, and never drops his character when he has finished a speech." Luckily Arthur Murphy and Thomas Davies were present at that momentous debut. "He transformed himself into the very man. All was rage, fury, almost reality," commented Murphy. And of the "Off with his head!" line, Davies said that "Garrick's look and action when he pronounced the words were so significant, from his visible enjoyment of the incident, that loud shouts of approbation proclaimed the triumph of the actor."

Garrick later admitted that if behind the scenes a Mr. Leach had not recommended the juice of an orange, he would have had no voice left after the second act. This confession indicates that despite the ecstatic reception of his early performances, they must have been quite inferior to what was soon to come—even as the same Richard III.

Colley Cibber was not impressed with Garrick's initiation as an actor and criticized his Richard: "This Garrick's manner is little, like his person, it is all fuss and bustle. . . . Bustle! bustle! bustle!" Old Cibber could not accept the fact that Garrick was permanently banishing the old declamatory style of the Betterton school. Walpole, not noted for the generosity of his judgments, said seven months after Garrick's debut: "All the town is now after Garrick, a wine merchant who is turned player. . . . He plays all parts, and is a very good mimic. His acting I have seen . . . I see nothing wonderful in it." But that was a minority opinion. Lord Chesterfield invited Garrick to dinner, and the line of carriages waiting on the young actor grew daily longer and longer. Between October 1741 and May 1742, Garrick played some nineteen different characters in as many plays.

Aware of the disapproval he could expect from his family, within a month of his debut he wrote to his brother Peter at Lichfield: "My mind has been always inclined to the Stage. All my illness and lowness of Spirits was owing to my want of resolution to tell you my thoughts when here. . . . Last night, I played Richard the Third to the Surprise of Everybody, and as I shall make very near £300 per annum by it, and as it is really what I doat upon, I am resolv'd to pursue it." The reference to the £300 was doubtless to assure

Peter that he would financially do no worse as an actor than he had been doing as a wine merchant.

In 1742 he played in Dublin; the women in the audience shrieked at Richard's death, wept at Ophelia's madness as interpreted by Peg Woffington, and went into hysterics over the sufferings of Lear.

By October 5, 1742, Drury Lane was only too glad to have him. He was soon doing Richard III, Lear, and Hamlet. In January 1744 he revived *Macbeth*.

When he "restored" *Romeo and Juliet* he made a number of minor changes and some very serious ones. The last act opened with a funeral procession for Juliet inside a church with much pompous solemnity. But his chief crime was to rewrite the scene in the tomb in accordance with Otway's foolish idea of having Romeo linger, after drinking the poison, while Juliet awakens— a melodramatic notion that was used by Cibber, Kemble, many nineteenth-century actors, and is the final episode in Gounod's opera, where the lovers sing a duet before the curtain falls. In Garrick's version, Romeo drinks the poison and begins to take leave of Juliet:

> ROMEO: Soft—she breathes, and stirs! [Juliet wakes]
> JULIET: Where am I? defend me!
> ROMEO: She speaks, she lives! and we shall still be bless'd!
> 　　My kind propitious stars o'er pay me now
> 　　For all my sorrows past—rise, rise, my Juliet,
> 　　And from this cave of death, this house of horror,
> 　　Quick let me snatch thee to thy Romeo's arms,
> 　　There breathe a vital spirit in thy lips,
> 　　And call thee back to life and love. [Takes her hand.]
> JULIET: Bless me! how cold it is! who's there?
> ROMEO: 　　　　　　　　　　　　Thy husband,
> 　　'Tis thy Romeo, Juliet; rais'd from despair
> 　　To joys unutterable! quit, quit this place,
> 　　And let us fly together—[Brings her from the tomb.]
> JULIET: Why do you force me so—I'll ne'er consent—
> 　　My strength may fail me, but my will's unmov'd,—
> 　　I'll not wed Paris—Romeo is my husband.
> ROMEO: Her senses are unsettl'd—Heav'n restore 'em!
> 　　Romeo is thy husband; I am that Romeo,
> 　　Nor all the opposing pow'rs of earth or man,
> 　　Shall break our bonds, or tear thee from my heart.
> JULIET: I know that voice—Its magic sweetness wakes
> 　　My tranced soul—I now remember well
> 　　Each circumstance—Oh my lord, my husband [Going to embrace
> 　　him.]
> 　　Dost thou avoid me, Romeo? let me touch
> 　　Thy hand, and taste the cordial of thy lips—
> 　　You fright me—speak—Oh let me hear some voice
> 　　Besides my own in this drear vault of death,
> 　　Or I shall faint—support me—

ROMEO: Oh I cannot,
     I have no strength, but want thy feeble aid,
     Cruel poison!
JULIET: Poison! what means my lord; thy trembling voice!
     Pale lips! and swimming eyes! death's in thy face!
ROMEO: It is indeed—I struggle with him now—
     The transports that I felt to hear thee speak,
     And see thy op'ning eyes, stopt for a moment
     His impetuous course, and all my mind
     Was happiness and thee; but now the poison
     Rushes thro' my veins—I've no time to tell—
     Fate brought me to this place—to take a last
     Last farewell of my love, and with thee die.
JULIET: Die? Was the Friar false?
ROMEO: I know not that—
     I thought thee dead: distracted at the sight,
     (Fatal speed) drank poison, kiss'd thy cold lips.
     And found within thy arms a precious grave—
     But in that moment—Oh—
JULIET: And did I wake for this!
ROMEO: My powers are blasted,
     'Twixt death and love I am torn—I am distracted!
     But death's strongest—and must I leave thee, Juliet!
     Oh cruel, cursed fate: in sight of heav'n!
JULIET: Thou rav'st—lean on my breast—
ROMEO: Fathers have flinty hearts, no tears can melt 'em.
     Nature pleads in vain—Children must be wretched.
JULIET: Oh my breaking heart—
ROMEO: She is my wife—our hearts are twin'd together,
     Capulet forbear—Paris, loose your hold—
     Pull not our heart strings thus—they crack—they break—
     Oh Juliet, Juliet! [Dies.]

This miserable attempt to improve on Shakespeare will suffice to show what a wretched versifier Garrick was; he wrote a considerable amount of verse during his life, and none of it is any better. Yet in 1770 Francis Gentleman praised Garrick's mangling of Shakespeare in this final scene thus: "Romeo's distraction, and her tenderness, are so excellently wrought up, that we cannot suppose any heart so obdurate as not to be penetrated. . . . No play ever received greater advantage from alteration than this play, especially in the last act."

In comedy, his Benedick was greatly admired. Francis Gentleman implies that the public thought it his greatest comic part, and spoke of "the preeminence of his significant features, the distinct volubility of his expression, and his stage manoeuvres; in the scenes of repartee with Beatrice, his distinct vivacity gives uncommon satisfaction."

Of his Beatrices, special praise went to Mrs. Pritchard, who, says Gentleman, "struck out such unison with Mr. Garrick, that her uncharacteristic corpulence was always overlooked. *Mrs. Woffington we have heard receive considerable applause, which she well deserved. Much Ado about Nothing, supported by capable performers, will always please."*

It would be hasty to assume that because *The Winter's Tale* was not presented during the Restoration, it escaped the mangling received by other Shakespearean plays. In the mid-eighteenth century, Charles Kean was highly satisfied with himself for adding substance to what he considered a pretty insignificant play by having Leontes and his guests in the opening scene "crowned with Chaplets," and "discovered reclining on Couches, after the manner of the ancient Greeks." But its final vulgarization, surpassing even D'Avenant, was left to Garrick in his 1756 version which he renamed *Florizel and Perdita*. He reduced the five acts to three by the simple expedient of omitting entirely the powerful first two acts and enough of the third to make room for his own pernicious additions, including this revolting prologue:

> To various things the stage has been compar'd,
> As apt ideas strike each humourous bard;
> This night, for want of better simile,
> Let this our *Theatre* a *Tavern* be:
> The poets vintners, and the waiters we.
> So as the cant, and custom of the trade is,
> You're welcome *Gem'min;* kindly welcome, ladies.
> To draw in customers, our *bills* are spread; *[Shewing a playbill.]*
> You cannot miss the sign, 'tis *Shakespear's Head.*
> From this same head, the fountain head divine,
> For different palates, springs a different wine! . . .
> For you, my hearts of oak, for your regale *[To the upper gallery.]*
> There's good old *English stingo*, mild and stale.
> For high luxurious souls, with luscious smack,
> There's *Sir John Falstaff*, is a butt of sack:
> And if the stronger liquors more invite ye,
> *Bardolph* is gin, and *Pistol* aqua vitae . . .
> A vintner once acquir'd both praise and gain
> And sold much *perry* for the best *champaign.*
> Some rakes this precious stuff did so allure;
> They drank whole nights—what's that?—when wine is pure.
> "Come, fill a bumper, *Jack!*"—"I will, my lord."—
> "Here's cream!—damn'd fine!—immense! upon my word!" . . .
> Thus the wise critic too mistakes his wine,
> Cries out with lifted hands " 'Tis great! divine!"
> Then joggs his neighbour, as the wonders strike him;
> "This *Shakespear! Shakespear!*—Oh, there's nothing like him . . .
> The five long acts from which our three are taken
> Stretch'd out to sixteen years,* lay by, forsaken.

*The sixteen years which form an interval between Shakespeare's acts three and four are the extremest instance of Shakespeare's indifference to those spurious "Aristotelian" unities which the Italian Renaissance critics fancied they saw in *The Poetics*, and would be to Garrick's time a flagrant violation of the rules of dramatic composition, as they understood them.

> Lest then this precious liquor run to waste,
> 'Tis now confin'd and bottled for your taste.
> 'Tis my chief wish, my joy, my only plan
> To lose no drop of that immortal man!

Their "taste" and Garrick's! Such is the power of fashion that probably not one person in the audience perceived the incredible irony: Garrick wishes "to lose no drop of that immortal man" and has just announced that he has cut out two very powerful acts. As for the thinning of Shakespearean wine, the audience was too unfamiliar with *The Winter's Tale* to recognize how Garrick's additions diluted both the poetry and action which were to follow, and maybe for those few who knew the difference it was enough that the incomparable Garrick, Shakespeare's greatest lover, had done them to win their approval. Most disgraceful was the manner in which he slaughtered the magical last scene. Did space permit I would be tempted to print Shakespeare's original and Garrick's version in parallel columns. From that marvelous moment when Hermione is revealed upon her pedestal as a statue, Garrick, as earlier in his play, uses Shakespeare's lines with generous insertions of his own, so that even the beauty of what he guards is lost in his own hogwash. After Shakespeare has Perdita say, "I kneel and then implore her blessing," Garrick:

> FLORIZEL: Rise not yet;
>   I join me in the same religious duty;
>   But to the shadow of that royal dame,
>   Who, dying, gave my *Perdita* to life
>   And plead an equal right to blessing.
> LEONTES: O master-piece of art! nature's deceived
>   By thy perfection, and at every look
>   My penitence is afloat again. (*Weeps*)

Further on:

> PERDITA: Let *Perdita*
>   Put up her first request, that her dear father
>   Have pity on her father, nor let sorrow
>   Second the stroke of wonder.

Presently Shakespeare has Paulina say: "Music awake her: strike!/ 'Tis time; descend; be stone no more: approach;/Strike all that look upon with marvel. Come." Garrick:

> LEONTES [*retiring*]: Heavenly Powers! . . .
>   Support me, Gods!
>   If this be more than visionary bliss
>   My reason cannot hold: my wife! my queen!
>   But speak to me, and turn me wild with transport.

I cannot hold me longer from these arms . . .
PERDITA: O *Florizel!* [*Perdita* leans on *Florizel's* bosom.]
FLORIZEL: My princely shepherdess!
    This is too much for hearts of thy soft mold.
LEONTES: Her beating heart meets mine, and fluttering owns
    Its long-lost half: these tears that choke her voice
    Are hot and moist—it is *Hermione!* [*Embrace*]
POLIXENES: I'm turned myself to stone! where has she lived?
    Or how so stolen from the dead? . . .
LEONTES: Hark! hark! she speaks—
    O pipe, through sixteen winters dumb! then deem'd
    Harsh as the raven's note: now musical
    As nature's song, tun'd to th'according spheres . . .

In 1747 Garrick and James Lacy took over Drury Lane, and Garrick for many years was in full charge of its destiny. He worshiped Shakespeare and by 1769 their names were inextricably linked, though it is also obvious that his worship was somewhat limited by the bad taste of an age that prided itself on Taste. In May 1742 he visited Stratford-on-Avon with Macklin, and they both sat under the celebrated mulberry tree at New Place, Shakespeare's last residence, reveling in the knowledge that the great Bard himself had planted that tree. When the tree was eventually cut down, and its wood made into such a vast number of marketable objects as to have required a grove of mulberry trees, the town of Stratford delegated a committee in May 1769 to wait upon Garrick in London and present him with a rare specimen made especially for him out of that one and only mulberry tree. This particular gift to the great actor was a box on which were carved "Fame Holding the Bust of Shakespeare" and "the Three Graces Crowning Him with a Laurel"; on the sides were figures representing Comedy and Tragedy; on the back was carved a representation of "Mr. Garrick in the Character of King Lear in the Storm Scene," and the top and corners were ornamented with devices of Shakespeare's works, all curiously carved, and highly finished."

Garrick had always been a ready victim for anyone with a Shakespearean relic for sale. He had already bought a signet ring bearing the initials *W.S.*, a bad piece of Delft in the form of a salt cellar in blue and glaring yellow, and a gray leather glove with metal embroidery at the cuff. In 1762 he managed to purchase for two guineas a half-dozen pieces of the "true" hacked-up mulberry tree, and these he had made into a "Shakespeare chair," a revered object which, weather permitting, was kept in his Shakespeare Temple, a Greek-porticoed octagonal building on the banks of the Thames which had originally been erected on the grounds of his villa at Hampton; the Temple also housed a statue of Shakespeare which he had commissioned.

In tragedy, Garrick's ability to transform himself into the character he was personating seems to have been phenomenal. No doubt this unparalleled mobility of face, figure, limbs and voice, so uncharacteristic of the British, owed something to the French and Irish blood flowing in his veins. Audiences were struck by his Hamlet from the moment he first entered the stage: his deeply melancholy expressions, the look of profound reflection in his eyes, and his listless movements and postures which further indicated his depression. It is said that when the Ghost appeared, the color actually left his face. All were moved by his sensibility and melting tenderness toward Ophelia. The German traveler Lichtenberg recorded that "in the fine soliloquy, 'O that this too too solid flesh would melt,' etc. Garrick is completely overpowered by the tears of great grief for a virtuous father. . . . Of the words, 'so excellent a king,' the last word is quite inaudible, you only perceive it by the motion of the mouth. . . ." His lips trembled with agitation. "This way of shedding tears . . . shows the whole burden of inward grief . . . At the end of the soliloquy he mixed just anger with his grief; and at once, when he strikes out violently with his arm to give emphasis to a word in his indignation, the word—to the surprise of the audience—remains unuttered, choked by emotion, and only follows after a few seconds, when tears begin to flow."

This is what the eighteenth century meant when they called Garrick's style a "natural" one! *The Theatrical Review*, however, complained that he sometimes indulged in "a sort of theatrical parade in tragedy" to please the multitude, that he too often used a "hesitating stammering" for no particular reason, but conceded that though he occasionally employed them without warrant, his pauses were highly effective, and that his gifts totally eclipsed his defects.

His Macbeth provoked various reactions. Said one spectator: "Every sentiment rose in his mind and showed itself in his countenance before he uttered a word." Mrs. Pritchard played Lady Macbeth, and though she had never read the play, was praised for her dignity and her final wretched desolation, though Samuel Johnson called her "a vulgar idiot." Here again Garrick wrote a long speech to keep him on stage for the final curtain.

But of the same play Francis Gentleman said that Garrick's "matchless genius not only captivates our sportive senses, but also furnishes high relished substantial food for our minds to strengthen by." He is Shakespeare's "greatest and best commentator." He was particularly fine when he saw the imaginary dagger; the "low but piercing notes of his voice when the deed is done," the guilty "distraction" of his features when Banquo's ghost appears have never been equaled. However, another critic was less kind, claiming that in the fourth act he "looked like a Beau who had unfortunately slipped his Foot, and tumbled into a Night Cellar, where a parcel of old Women were boiling Tripe for their Supper."

Garrick's age had no regard for historical accuracy (neither did Shakespeare's!), and Garrick's Scottish thane wore the scarlet coat of an officer in George II's army, a wig, a silver-laced waistcoat, and fashionable breeches very much in the contemporary mode. What mattered was the actor's interpretation and Garrick was greatly admired for his dagger scene; transfixed by his hallucination, Garrick's face grew white and gaunt with horror; the audience believed in the apparition. After the murder, with the actual dagger in his bloody hands, he appeared spectral with his face growing paler by the moment; you knew his conscience had been stabbed, and witnessed his wild despair at the realization his hands would never again be clean. It is said that during a performance of the banquet scene he said to the First Murderer with such conviction, "There's blood upon thy face," and looked at him with such intensity that the other actor raised his hand to his face and murmured, "Is there, by God?"

When Garrick died on stage, he astounded the French dancer, Noverre, who recorded it: "At each instant the approach of death revealed itself upon his face; the eyes became dim; the voice was not equal to the effort he made to speak. Without once losing their expressiveness, his gestures showed the nearing of the last moment; his legs gave way, his face became elongated, his pale and livid features gave sign of suffering and repentance." When at length he fell, he clawed the ground, as though digging his grave. At the final moment "his death rattle and the convulsive movements of his features, arms and chest finished off this awesome picture."

None of his roles won more unstinting praise than Lear. Henry Bate said: "We never saw before so exquisite a theatrical performance, or one so loudly and universally applauded." Hazlitt tells us that at one performance "the spectators in the front row of the pit, not being able to see him well in the kneeling scene, where he utters the curse, rose up, when those behind them . . . immediately rose up too, and in this manner, the whole pit rose up, without uttering a syllable . . . At another time, the crown of straw which he wore in the same character fell off, or was discomposed, which could have produced a burst of laughter at any common actor to whom such an accident had happened; but . . . not the slightest note was taken of the circumstance, but the whole audience remained bathed in silent tears." As James Boaden expressed it, Garrick as Lear preserved "the damp of age in the fire of insanity." He excelled in the quick transitions, as the old man is hurried on by a whirlwind of feelings. Charles James Fox, the statesman, was completely overwhelmed with admiration at his interpretation.

But Johnson thought Garrick lacked feeling; he accused him of being all head and no heart. Once, when he was playing Lear, Garrick noticed Johnson and Murphy conversing in the wings. As he passed by them he said: "You two talk so loud, you destroy my feelings"; Johnson countered: "Punch has no feelings."

Johnson also employed his pen to attack his old student and friend. While it is clear from Boswell that the cannonade did not make an enemy of Garrick, it is hard to imagine his ever forgetting it. He had just done all he could to make a success of Johnson's tragedy, *Irene*, which turned out to be if not a financial success, a *succès d'estime*. On February 13, 1752, Johnson wrote a paper for the *Rambler* where Garrick figures under the recognizable name of Prospero; in it Johnson described his own and Garrick's coming up to London together to seek a fortune; in that hope one of them had been successful; not so the other, who when he comes to visit Prospero was "too little polished by thought and conversation to enjoy it with elegance and decency." The visiting friend is conducted into a back room, obviously intended only for inferior company and is treated with too much condescension. When the visitor was shown the magnificent furnishings he did "not gratify Prospero's folly with any outcries of admiration," but made no comment. Prospero served his friend quite inferior tea, spoke of his silversmith and jeweller, boasted of his intimacy with Lord Lofty, showed off his celebrated Dresden china. "When I had examined them a little, Prospero desired me to set them down, for they who were accustomed only to common dishes seldom handled china with much care." Finally, the visitor left in disgust. It is likely that this attack was as undeserved as it was unjust. Johnson never allowed anyone else to attack Garrick, and he always said that David "was the most liberal man of his day."

That was, however, not quite true. Garrick was a contradictory combination of extravagance and miserliness. Whenever a beggar approached him for a coin, his pockets always happened to be empty. Once when he was giving a dinner to Henry Fielding, Mrs. Cibber, Macklin, and others, most of the guests gave Garrick's man, a Welshman named Davy, a shilling or so, but Fielding formally slipped a piece of paper into Davy's hand. Something was obviously folded within the paper, and when the guests had gone, Davy was in high spirits. Garrick asked him how much he had received in the way of tips. Davy replied that he wasn't quite sure; he recounted the shillings and half-crowns he had received, and began to unfold the piece of paper Fielding had handed him. When opened, Davy was astounded to see that it contained only one penny. Annoyed, Garrick asked Fielding the next day why he had played such a jest on Davy. "Jesting!" cried Fielding, assuming surprise. "I was not jesting! I intended to do the fellow a real service. Had I given him a shilling or a half-crown, I know you would have taken it away from him. When I gave him a penny, I knew he had a chance of keeping it as his own!"

In an old copy of Davies's *Memoirs* of Garrick, Daniel Frohman found an unidentified clipping, already disintegrating, entitled "Account of Garrick to his Friend in Germany," and dated from London in 1768. What was still legible is worth recording, as a counterbalance to Johnson's *Rambler* essay.

I yesterday spent one of the pleasantest days of my life at Garrick's country-house . . . a little palace, and built in good proportion . . . on the banks of the Thames, which there winds through a well-inhabited and richly cultivated country; but what is called his garden, is nothing more than a large grass-plat, kept in good order, on which are scattered without symmetry, various bushes and interwoven trees . . . Near the water stands the temple of Shakespeare, a sanctuary to every Briton. . . . The statue, erected to the memory of the immortal bard, is of white marble, and as large as life. The sculptor has . . . given him a look of enchantment, as if he were . . . listening to the song of Ariel. In the house neither magnificence nor fashion are to be discovered;

but, instead of these, a pleasing, noble simplicity, which seems to belong to country life. . . . All the rooms are light and agreeable to the eye; they are ornamented with pictures of celebrated actors and actresses, in principal scenes. . . . There are four remarkable pictures, by Hogarth, the originals of his selection; but a fifth is still more so; it is meant as a counterpart to his *Marriage à la Mode*. . . . In a society of artists, the conversation turned on the expression of the passions, when Garrick rose, and exhibited them, individually, with dreadful exactness. I have myself seen something of this kind, in his repetition of a short piece, wherein he had no character, yet represented every part, even those of the women, to the performers, with incredible minuteness. It is unaccountable how a texture of nerves, so finely woven, can bear so constant a distension, without a total destruction of his health. . . . I saw him once, after having played the part of Richard, stretched . . . on a sofa, panting, pale, speechless, covered with perspiration, and unable to raise his arm. In the country Garrick regains his exhausted faculties, and he flies from town whenever he can catch an open day. "Then," he says, "I enjoy an hour or two of my life; in town, I belong to the nation." . . . The government of the theatre, often robs him of peace and comfort. . . . At one time, a storm arises in the House of Commons, or Green Room; at another, their lordships, the authors are dissatisfied . . . The voice of the people is terrible; for, as in Athens, when out of humour, the greatest cannot escape its censure. Garrick, indeed, is a great favorite, and generally suits the taste of rigid judges; yet he acknowledges their dominion with humility, and knows that they never forgive a fault—or even a neglect. Nor is he insensible to the sarcasm of solitary critics. . . . He described his sensations . . . in the following lines:

> The looking up fatigues the sight,
>   And mortals, when they soar,
> Should they once reach a certain height,
>   All wish to have them low'r.
> And friends there are in this good town,
>   Will lend a hand to help them down.

Garrick does not deserve such treatment. He has never been an enemy to genius; never humbled opening talent by contempt. . . . He still speaks of the memorable Mrs. Cibber, . . . "She felt," says he, "and made all others feel. Since her death I have not been able to perform the part of a lover." True it is, his services are most bounteously rewarded. His fortune is valued at £100,000, and the theatre produces for him, as performer and joint proprietor, £4,000 more per annum. . . . His wife is an amiable, charming woman, who retains nothing of her former situation, except—grace; but they are not blessed with children . . . Garrick's fortune will, therefore, fall to the lot of his brother's family. As he is to play next week, his desk was covered with petitions for places from ladies and gentlemen of all ranks . . . It is impossible that a picture of Garrick, in one character, can be like him in another; for the soul of this Proteus always clothes itself in a new body. He who has seen him in Lear and Richard, does not know the individual Garrick.

As for his personal defects, Goldsmith has very well summed them up in his well-known *Retaliation:*

> *On the stage he was natural, simple, affecting;*
> *'Twas only that when he was off he was acting . . .*
> *Of praise a mere glutton, he swallowed what came,*
> *And the puff of a dunce, he mistook it for fame,*
> *Till the relish grown callous, almost to disease,*
> *Who pepper'd the highest was surest to please.*

He was indeed far too sensitive to his press, and never knew when to be silent if attacked. He was a wonderful husband and a kind master to his servants, yet his vanity was such, says Colman the Younger, that at a duke's table, "he would steal a side-long look . . . to ascertain whether he had made a hit upon the butler and the footmen."

Eva Maria Violette, whose family name was Veigel until she Frenchified it, was born in Vienne, began dancing professionally when quite young, and came to London at the age of twenty-one with letters to the Earl and Countess of Burlington. She became their pet as well as the governess-companion of their daughter, later the Duchess of Devonshire. She was engaged by the Opera House and Drury Lane; even Walpole said she danced to perfection. She became popular, though in private life she was modest and quiet. The first record we have connecting her with Garrick is an occasion when dressed in women's clothes, to avoid compromising her, he slipped a love letter into her sedan, some two years after his break with Peg Woffington. Having seen him at the theater, she was already in love with him. On June 22, 1749, they were married and took up residence in Southampton Street, where they lived until 1772. Amusingly enough, his first reappearance on the stage was in what became his greatest comic role, Benedick. Mrs. Garrick was generally referred to as "sweet," and it is clear that she was an excellent hostess. Mrs. Piozzi wrote of her: "That woman has lived a *very wise life,* regular and steady in her conduct, attentive to every word she speaks and every step she treads; decorous in her manners and graceful in her person." She and Garrick had a very happy marriage.

Nevertheless, the accepted coarseness of the age may be gauged by the following anecdote. Garrick's friend Dr. Monsey had heard that the Duke of Argyle and several ladies of distinction were to sup with the Garricks; Monsey upbraided the actor for not having invited him too. "I would have asked you," said Garrick, as John Taylor tells the story, "but you are too great a blackguard." "Why you little scoundrel," said Monsey, and proceeded to quote his friendship with some of the best-bred men in England, and added that he behaved as well as the politest of their visitors. Garrick agreed to Monsey's joining his party provided he promised to behave properly. Everything went well at the supper until Mrs. Garrick began to serve her noble guests; every now and then, while she was thus occupied, Monsey tried to hand her his plate without success. Having presented and withdrawn his plate in vain several times, he could restrain his vexation no longer and cried, "Will you help me, you bitch, or not?" Garrick began to roar with laughter; the duke was struck with surprise, and everybody else was thrown into confusion.

Garrick once played a most unusual practical joke on his friend Dr. Monsey, whom he asked to come to see him on a night when the actor was scheduled to do his famous Lear. To his surprise Monsey found him in bed, and asked whether the performance had been canceled. Garrick was abed with a nightcap on and the quilt drawn up to his chin; but beneath the bedclothes he was already attired in the costume of the old king. Monsey reminded him that he ought that minute to be at the theater dressing for his role, but Garrick said he felt too ill to get up, and in a whining voice told the doctor that since he could not act that night he had arranged that a player much like him in figure, face, and voice, one Marr, be entrusted with the role, and that he doubted that the audience would be able to tell the difference. Monsey warned him of the anger of the audience if they should discover a hoax had been played on them—How could anyone succeed in pretending to be Garrick on the stage? Garrick complained of feeling worse and worse, and asked Monsey to leave so that he could go to sleep, but asked him to go to the theater and return later to report what happened. As soon as the doctor departed, Garrick jumped out of bed and hastened to the theater. There, Monsey, believing Garrick still in bed, was astonished at the resemblance between Marr and Garrick, and noted that the audience was convinced it was seeing and hearing Garrick. At the end, Monsey began to suspect that he had been tricked, and hurried back to Garrick's house. But the actor, quicker than he, removed only his outer theatrical garments, rushed home, resumed his position in bed with the quilt concealing what he still wore of stage attire, and, accompanied by friends, awaited the arrival of the doctor, who found Garrick still apparently ill. The joke was not exposed until the next day, when Monsey joined in the laughter at his own expense.

Garrick's least successful role was Othello. He was a small man, and Moorish attire made his figure look still smaller. Quin was of the opinion that he seemed to be "Desdemona's little black boy that attends her kettle," though Garrick's intention was to paint jealousy "in all its violence," for had not Shakespeare selected an African "in whose being circulates fire instead of blood"? But doubtless the chief cause of his failure was that the blacking of his face rendered it impossible to catch the wonderful expressiveness of his mobile features. Murphy said of him that their mobility would normally have made his meaning clear to a deaf man.

Garrick had his enemies. He quarreled early with Macklin. His early rise to fame infuriated the envious Foote, who accused him excessively of being stingy and prophesied that when Garrick retired he would be bound to begin again as a banker's clerk, he loved counting money so much.

Garrick gave Shakespeare's *Antony and Cleopatra* its first performance since 1660. Though much better in tragedy than in comedy, his carefully studied Benedick became one of his most notable parts. He was airy and mirthful; the ladies said he looked a "dream" in the role, and Mrs. Pritchard was "most capitally great" as Beatrice. Among his other roles were Iago, Hotspur, King John, Macbeth, Leontes, Antony, Mercutio, and Posthumus. He played Shylock, unlike Macklin, for sympathy.

It was Garrick who after a long struggle established the principle that audiences, whatever their rank, should not sit on the stage, around it, or above it. Before his reform he complained that he could hardly "step his foot" with safety because of the people around him while Mrs. Cibber as Juliet, dressed in a full white satin dress with the inevitable hoop, could barely turn she was "so encompassed around." Not only was it very often difficult for the actors, but the audience on stage obstructed the view of people in the boxes, and amused themselves by annoying the galleries. Things were worst on benefit nights, when the actors erected a "building" at the back of the stage for the holders of five-shilling seats. Juliet, reposing in the Capulet monument, was forced to have two hundred people behind her, in that "background . . . where the heads of her buried ancestors were packed."

In 1760 he also tried to abolish the old practice of permitting latecomers to see the last two acts of a five-act play at half-price. The announcement of this new policy was greeted with an uproar from the audience. One drunkard carried a torch to the stage and tried to burn up the scenery. The racket was so deafening that Garrick had to ring down the curtain and refund the price of admission to the audience.

One of his wittier effusions was in answer to Dr. Hill, who accused him of pronouncing the *i* in *mirth* and *birth* as if it were a *u.* Garrick wrote:

> If 'tis true, as you say, that I've injured a letter,
> I'll change my note soon, and I hope, for the better.
> May the just rights of letters as well as of men,
> Hereafter be fixed by the tongue and the pen;
> Most devoutly I wish that they both have their due,
> And that I may be never mistaken for U.

Lord Lyttleton suggested to him that his eloquence qualified him as a Member of Parliament; Garrick replied:

> More than content with what my labors gain;
> Of public favours, though a little vain;
> Yet not so vain my mind, so madly bent,
> To wish to play the fool in Parliament;
> In each dramatic unity to err,
> Mistaking TIME, and PLACE, and CHARACTER! . . .

Burke, who admitted his debt to Garrick, said he was the greatest of actors because he was the most acute observer of human nature he had ever known. No doubt this was the secret of his meteoric rise to success despite his lack of professional training. Grimm agreed with Burke when he said that Garrick's "studio" was in the crowded streets. "He is always there," Grimm added, and appended that he "is naturally *monkeyish*, imitating all he sees; and he is always graceful."

The great fiasco of Garrick's life was the Shakespeare Jubilee of 1769, the very date of which was five years too late. I have elsewhere dealt with the details of that disaster when the rain and the mud at Stratford, aided and abetted by the sarcasms of Foote, were ruinous to the whole rather ridiculous undertaking.

In 1776 Garrick decided to retire from the stage, and between March 7 and June 10 of that year gave some dozen performances of his leading roles. Seats were difficult to get; the house was jammed far beyond its capacity. Garrick received many letters pleading for places. Mrs. Cholmondeley wrote to request a seat also for Miss Flower, "who, poor thing, seems to be very far gone in love with you." This same Miss Flower, sitting beside Mrs. Cholmondeley said: "O, madam, he is an angel! was there ever such a man! What a voice, O what a heavenly voice, and surely there never was such a countenance, madam. There was a look of his in Lear just as he runs mad that I thought would have deprived me of my senses. Pray, Mrs. Cholmondeley, did you ever see him in his scratch wig?" (Garrick loved to wear the wig when fussing about his property at Hampton.) Mrs. Cholmondeley went on to say to Garrick: "Poor thing, I pity her! I wish and indeed I think you ought to give her a place, I ask but for two places for the Bunburys, three for myself, and one for Miss Fisher, who never saw you in Tragedy, one for the undone Miss Flower, and one for myself, who must chaperon them. . . . Do, my dear Sir, give me the places, and let me know as soon as possible that I may make the poor things happy. My best compliments to Mrs. Garrick. I wish she would use her interest with you. I wish she would."

On the next to last night, he performed tragedy for the last time, playing Lear to Miss Younge's Cordelia. When the curtain descended they lay on the stage, hand in hand, and hand in hand they rose, Garrick silently leading her to his dressing room, with many of the company following them. There he stood with her, both silent, until at last he exclaimed: "Ah Bessie, this is the last time I shall ever be your father; the *last time!*" and he let go of her hand. Miss Younge sighed, and replied with affection that she hoped before they finally parted he would kindly give her a father's blessing. Garrick took her request most seriously; she bent her head, and he raised his hands and prayed that God would bless her. Then slowly he turned around to the others and murmured, "May God bless you all!" And with his shedding of Lear's garments he took leave of tragedy forever, for he wished his last performance to be in comedy.

He died on January 20, 1779. His funeral was a public pageant, and he was buried in Westminster Abbey. On his tombstone one reads:

> Shakespeare and Garrick like twin stars shall shine
> And earth irradiate with a beam sublime—

This passage infuriated Charles Lamb.

Garrick had presented twenty-eight of Shakespeare's plays in 1,448 performances during his twenty years at Drury Lane, and he himself had appeared in eighteen different roles. It is not surprising that his name was closely identified with Shakespeare, of whom he declared that he was the "God of my Idolatry—Shakespeare—*Him him! He is the Him!* there is no Other." In his mind Drury Lane was the "House of Shakespeare," and he once wrote that he doubted he had ever written a single letter "without bringing him in, head and shoulders." It was his ambition *"To lose no drop of that immortal man!"* yet he persisted in keeping to the Restoration perversions of certain plays, and contributed some of his own. Yet if Theophilus Cibber felt he had "minced and fricasseed" *A Midsummer Night's Dream*, the truth is that the Garrick version was no further from Shakespeare's intention than Peter Brooks's wildly acclaimed mangling of the same play in 1971, and much less in bad taste than the latter.

Despite all that, due as much as anything else to the limited taste of the time and the general ignorance of Shakespeare's works in printed form, Garrick's services to Shakespeare were enormous when compared with the work of his predecessors. He left behind him a school of acting that was known for its "rapidity and passion." Kemble, who was to come later in the century, founded what Mrs. Barry called the school of "paw and pause," which often left the audience wondering whether those "actors had either lost their cues, or forgotten their parts."

It is important to remember that in Garrick's time the function of director, which when properly exercised today is similar to that of the director of a symphony orchestra controlling the players until the finished performance is unified in style and meaning, did not yet exist. I like to think that Shakespeare himself may have acted in that capacity, but there is no evidence to prove that he did. In Garrick's day, actors who had enough self-confidence were at liberty to choose their own style and manner of delivery. But Garrick brought the concept of director closer to what obtains today, when it is inconceivable to mount a play without a director. He rehearsed often and for longer hours than had been the case before him, and did not hesitate either to fine or dismiss from the cast anyone who did not show up for rehearsals.

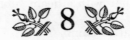

Some Other Eighteenth-Century Actors

It will be interesting to those familiar with the enormous influence Shakespeare had in Germany on Schiller's generation to say a word *en passant* about Friedrich Ludwig Schröder (1744–1816), a fine actor who was the first to introduce Shakespeare on the German stage. He began acting at the age of three, and at thirteen was befriended by an English rope-dancer and acrobat, Michael Stuart, and his wife. All the young people in Germany were reading Shakespeare, and they now were able to see him in Schröder's adaptations. To cite just one of his liberties: he kept Lear and Cordelia (Tate had already done that in his version) alive at the end of the play. Still, Schröder's audiences were transported with excitement—no doubt having suffered too many clumsy imitations of plays written in the rigid style of the three unities. Somehow or other, Schröder began to perform Shakespeare in 1776 with *Hamlet* and managed to enact the Ghost, Laertes, and the First Gravedigger as well as Hamlet. By 1780 he had given eleven of the plays. His greatest success was *King Lear* and his one failure was *Othello*.

Among the names which have peppered preceding pages of this book is that of "Gentleman" Smith, born William Smith (1730–1819). He gained the epithet from the elegance of his figure and the polish of his manners. He made his debut at Covent Garden in 1753 and remained there until he went over to Drury Lane in 1774. Besides comic roles, he also was admired in tragedy. Among the parts he played were Shylock, Richard III, Henry V, Hamlet, Cassius, Coriolanus, Edgar, Edmund, Faulconbridge, Hotspur, Macbeth, Iago, Leontes, Romeo, Iachimo, and Antony (in *Julius Caesar*).

His Hotspur and Henry V were particularly famous. Mrs. Siddons describes the adulation of Garrick's actors for him as "fulsome"; her charge is somewhat borne out by a letter from Gentleman Smith to the great actor saying in part, "Your letter has given me such spirits, that I have eat two rolls this morning, and swam a league at sea." When Macklin joined the Covent Garden company in 1773, anticipating that he would challenge Garrick at

Drury Lane, he did not attempt to match his Richard III, in which part both Garrick and Smith had won the highest praise. And when he undertook to do Macbeth, even the manager Colman objected; it was considered an affront to Smith. It was Garrick's partisans who fomented the campaign against Macklin. After the repeated routing of Macklin off the stage in his performance of Macbeth, Colman discharged him. On Monday, November 22, Macklin's friends circulated a handbill which stated that Macklin's enemies had "succeeded so far in their cursed designs" as to get him discharged from Covent Garden, "and thereby have deprived him of the means of all livelihood. Therefore, if the Public have any spirit, they will not suffer the new Play to begin till Mr. Colman promises that Mr. Macklin shall be engaged again." It was perhaps not coincidental that the star of the new play was Gentleman Smith. During his performance he was hissed, and when it was announced that the play would be given again the following week, the audience rioted until a substitute play was promised. In a letter published on November 15, Macklin charged that Smith had collected friends to do the hissing of his Macbeth. In a rage, Smith, accompanied by Henry Bate, went at once to Macklin's house, stormed into his room, and demanded whether or not he in fact had written the anonymous letter. Before Macklin could reply Smith was calling him a villain and a liar, and insisting on satisfaction. To his astonishment, despite Macklin's advanced years, the old man agreed. He went on to give Smith a sermon on his lack of breeding. As Smith prided himself particularly on his elegance, his spirits much softened, he left and the duel never took place.

Gentleman Smith retired in his eighties and published his personal letters in 1814. He was fascinated by the great stir being made over the remarkable Edmund Kean, who he trusted would rescue drama from the pedantry and bombast of John Philip Kemble's style and "restore Nature" to the boards. But it bothered him that in his Hamlet Kean was "almost *rude*" to Claudius and Ophelia—which conduct he found all wrong for "an elegant Figure. Deportment, Habit & Manners are *native*" to Denmark's prince; a "very great part" of Hamlet's role ought not be *"acted* but *be—Ease & simplicity* are absolutely necessary."

Yet one wonders precisely what the eighteenth century understood by the concepts of "natural" and achieving "simplicity," especially when one remembers the raiment of both men and women actors. Smith belonged to the Garrick school, of course, and would never have approved of Kemble's lack of variety and quickness.

Elizabeth Hartley (née White [1751–1824]) was so remarkably beautiful that she became Sir Joshua Reynolds's favorite model. She was best in pathetic parts, and therefore not too successful in Shakespeare; her Lady Macbeth, Desdemona, and Cleopatra were without distinction. Walpole wrote that she would do well as an actress "if beauty and figure would suffice . . . but she has no one symptom of genius. Still, it is very affecting, and does admirably for the stage. . . . The tears came into my eyes, and streamed down the Duchess of Richmond's lovely cheeks." There seems to have been a brief love affair between her and Smith. When he was living in retirement at Bury St. Edmunds, he remarked to a friend about his lifelong fidelity to his wife, when she suddenly looked up. He blushed, murmured that he had forgotten *"one* slip," and let the subject drop.

Mrs. Elizabeth Inchbald (née Simpson [1753–1821]) left the home of her parents at the age of seventeen determined, despite a chronic stutter, to go on the stage. In London she managed to get an engagement as Cordelia, but made no impression. She married the elderly Mr. Inchbald, who for a season or two had played at Drury Lane under Garrick. She played both at the Haymarket and Covent Garden. Harris, proprietor of the latter house, was well known as a lady's man, and had little difficulty in making bedmates of many actresses engaged by him. The pretty Mrs. Inchbald was called to consult with him one morning at his house in Knightsbridge concerning one of her plays soon to be performed. At the conclusion of their meeting Harris, a handsome fellow, accustomed to compliant actresses, tried to take the lady by storm. Her only defense was to grasp his hair with such violence that he released her. She rushed from his house and went to the greenroom of the theater where the company was rehearsing. Her fellow actors, noting her great agitation, were alarmed. She rapidly related what had occurred and concluded: "Oh! if he had wo-wo-worn a wig, I had been ru-ruined."

Realizing that she had no talent for acting, she turned to the writing of plays and novels, in both of which endeavors she became very popular.

Joseph Shepherd Munden (1758–1832) said of himself: "I never read any book but a play, no play but one in which I myself acted, and no portion of that play but my own scenes." Lamb, who loved him, said that this was probably the truth. It is hard to believe, but then you never can tell about actors!

He first acted Polonius on December 27, 1792, and made of him a dignified and venerable man (quite incorrectly, I believe). Up until that date Ophelia's father had always been presented as a buffoon. Byron said that Polonius would die with him—which, unhappily has not been the case, for he is often given Munden's sympathetic interpretation.

Munden's chief talent was for comedy. Doran says of him that he "was the most wonderful of grimacers. He created laughter on the London stage, from 1790, when he appeared at Covent Garden . . . to 1823, when he quitted it." Charles Lamb reflected that actors generally have one face, but "Munden has none that you can properly pin down and call *his*. When you think he has exhausted his battery of looks . . . suddenly he spouts out an entirely new set of features, like Hydra. He is not . . . so much a comedian as a company . . . I should not be surprised to see him some day put out the head of a river-horse."

Perhaps the most unusual tragedian and comedian between Garrick and Kemble was George Frederick Cooke (1756–1812), a man of extraordinary talents who was a number of times hissed off the stage because of his drunkenness, somewhat in the fashion of our own vastly talented John Barrymore (by whose time hissing had gone out of fashion). On one occasion he could not remember the beginning of Richard III's first speech. He tottered forward, with the object of diverting the resentment of the spectators, and placing his hand on his chest to convey the idea that he was ill, he turned up his eyes and coughed out: "My old complaint!" Laughs and hisses drove him from the stage.

Once in Liverpool, inarticulate with drink, the hisses restored him to comprehensibility. He glared at the audience fiercely and cried: "What! do you hiss me—*me*, George Frederick Cooke? *You contemptible money-getters.* You shall never again have *the honor* of hissing me! Farewell. I banish *you. There's not a brick in your dirty town but what is cemented by the blood of a negro.*"

Another time he was asked by a theatrical architect to dine with him and a manager of Covent Garden. The party was pleasant until it became evident that Cooke was going to drink far too much. His host, anxious to be relieved of him before he became offensive, suggested politely that Cooke had better go, and escorted him downstairs. When they reached the door, Cooke suddenly seized the architect by the ear and shouted that he had disgraced himself "by dining with bricklayers to meet box-keepers," and flung the man to the ground.

In a drunken fit of jealousy Cooke locked his wife up in a garret and then sauntered out for a long debauch, totally forgetting her. She might have starved to death if neighbors had not heard her cries. This incident gave her grounds for a separation from him.

He was square-faced, hook-nosed, wide-mouthed, and wore a smile which easily turned malignant. He could vary his voice from harshness to sweetness, and he knew how to make good use of his heavy eyebrows. But his gestures were awkward; he was in the habit of waving his arms and extending his forefinger too much. Still, it is enough that Edmund Kean, the greatest actor of *his* age, worshipped him, and thought that during Cooke's brief career in London, no contemporary equalled him.

No one knows where he was born, though it is said to have been in the barracks; his father was an English sergeant and his mother came from Scotland. At about the age of twenty he made his first appearance on the boards in the little town of Brentford. It was twenty years before he reached London, during which period he was a strolling player in the provinces; on occasions he performed in smaller towns with Mrs. Siddons, John Philip Kemble, Mrs. Jordan, and others. Sometimes he was able to eat well enough, sometimes he did without food. By degrees he became a split personality: Cooke sober, "scholarly, thoughtful gentleman," and Cooke drunk, "a maniac and sot." He read the classics, studied for his profession, composed moral maxims for his diary, and spent "weeks in debauchery with the lowest companions." He was not only his own worst enemy, but the enemy of a great many decent men and women who were unfortunate enough to cross his path.

His intellect was brilliant but discordant, and he himself suspected that he possessed a streak of insanity. "I am sometimes in a kind of mental intoxication," he said of himself. "Some, I believe, would call it insanity.

. . . This humor, whatever it is, comes uninvited."

On October 31, 1800, at the age of forty-five, he at last was seen in London at Covent Garden, in the role of Richard III. He instantly became famous as one of the best actors of his day. In that part he so completely eclipsed John Philip Kemble, the idol of the epoch, that Kemble never played it again. His second performance was as Shylock, to be followed by Iago and Macbeth. During his first season he entirely won the respect of the audience, and it is probable that it was his best season. His second season was announced as opening on September 14, 1801, with him again in the role of Richard III. A great crowd collected very early at the door. But when he did not appear and could not be found, they were told that an accident had befallen him and the play was changed. He turned up five weeks later.

He did Angelo (in *Measure for Measure*), Falstaff, Hubert (in *King John*), and the Ghost (in *Hamlet*), Iachimo, as well as Richard III, Shylock, Macbeth, and Iago. He held his place for a few seasons, though with increasing difficulty. It was said of him that those parts which he played well, he played better than anyone else then acting. But his debauched life weakened his powers and reduced him to dire straits. For instance, after receiving £400 in bank-notes at a benefit at Manchester during a summer tour, he got into a row in a pothouse. When the man with whom he was quarreling said Cooke was picking a fight only because he was rich and knew his victim was poor, Cooke threw the £400 into the fire so he could fight him as an equal.

Cooke was lucky in his biographer, William Dunlap. As Lord Byron said, there were two remarkable things about Cooke, "first, that a man should have so long drunk, and next, that he should have found a sober biographer." Yet, despite his dipsomania, Cooke was an actor to reckon with when he was doing himself justice.

"When sober," said Michael Kelly, no man "was better conducted, or possessed more affability of manners, blended with sound sense and good nature, than Cooke; he had a fine memory, and was extremely well informed. I asked him, when he was acting at Brighton . . . to dine with me and Mrs. Crouch; and we were delighted with his conversation and gentleman-like deportment. He took his wine cheerfully; and as he was going away, I urged him to have another bottle; his reply was, 'Not one drop more. I have taken as much as I ought to take; I have passed a delightful evening, and should I drink any more wine, I might prove a disagreeable companion.' "

Cooke was called by F. W. Hawkins "the first actor who dared to introduce the familiarities of daily life into tragedy." (But once again, we are faced with the question of what these "familiarities" may have been like at the opening of the nineteenth century. Consider the revolution that has taken place within our own decade as to what we ought to accept as "natural.") He certainly furthered Macklin's hope to put an end to the sing-song school of delivery, which Kemble had revived with greater success than ever. To insure a "natural" form of delivery, he used to write out his own parts in Shakespeare as prose in order to avoid the lilt of verse. His biographer saw a study copy in which, according to the importance of the expression, Cooke had underlined words with one, two, or three lines.

His Shylock came close to Macklin's, and kept most of the same pieces of business. The two were often compared because of a certain similarity of physical makeup. But Macklin's style was free of tricks, and Cooke's was full of them; he had a habit of "anticipating, extending, and improving the conception of his author." A good example is afforded by a scene in *Othello*, where the Moor asks Iago to kill Cassio:

> Within these three days let me hear thee say
> That Cassio's not alive.

"Mr. Cooke [as Iago] used then to start, and the spectator might read plainly in his expressive face, 'What! murder my friend and companion?'—he then covered his face with his hands, and gradually lifting his head, when he withdrew his hands, his face and eyes were turned upward—he then started again . . . and after a second mental struggle, said as if submitting to necessity . . .

> 'My friend is dead!' "

His business in the temptation scene is also interesting. Kemble, who was playing the Moor, called Cooke to rehearsal, but Cooke refused to come. "Let *Black Jack*"—as he called Kemble—"come to me." So they presented the play without having rehearsed it together. "In the scene in which Iago instills his suspicion, Cooke grasped Kemble's left hand with his own, and then fixed his right, like a claw, on his shoulder. In this position, drawing himself up to him with his short arm, he breathed his poisonous whispers. Kemble coiled and twisted his hand, writhing to get away—his right hand clasping his brow, and darting his eye back on Iago."

Cooke's transitions were "natural" and "rapid" as Iago, writes his biographer. If Cooke lacked Kemble's nobility, refinement, and grace as an actor, he was more flexible and more energetic. He spent little time in study, relied largely on intuition, and if he did not consistently keep in mind the nature of the character he was portraying, nevertheless, he had moments of powerful effectiveness, such as the exchange between Shylock and Tubal:

> TUBAL: Yes, other men have ill luck too. Antonio, as I heard in Genoa—
> SHYLOCK: What, what, what! Ill luck, ill luck?

"The impatience of a ravening appetite for the blood of the merchant" was eloquent in the way Cooke spoke the words and in "the significant eagerness of his ghastly looks and the clawing of his fingers."

Charles Lamb's admiration for Cooke's celebrated Richard III had its reservations: "We attended the first appearance of Mr. Cooke in the character of Richard the Third, last winter [1801]. We thought that he 'bustled' through the scenes with at least as much spirit and effect as any of his predecessors. . . . Now that Mr. Cooke is no longer a novitiate candidate for public favour, we propose to enter into the question—whether that popular actor is right or wrong in his conception of the great outlines of the character; those strong essential differences which separate Richard from all the other creations of Shakespeare. We say of Shakespeare; for though the Play, which passes for his upon the Stage, materially differs from that which he wrote under the same title," being a compilation of all kinds of additions, "producing an inevitable inconsistency of character, sufficient to puzzle and confound the best Actor," yet an actor is wise to adhere as much as possible to the "intention of the original Author . . . Upon these principles we . . . censure Mr. Cooke, while we are ready to acknowledge that this Actor presents us with a very original and very forcible portrait" not of the man Shakespeare drew but "of the monster Richard as he exists in the popular idea." But Lamb could not understand how Richard's deceit succeeds. "The hypocrisy is too glaring and visible."

Cooke excelled in those roles which showed human nature at its worst. During his first season he gave sixty-six performances, twenty-two as Richard. In his second season, when he finally reappeared, he made a public apology for his absence. But he was already in some disfavor for his conduct. When it was announced that he would play Hamlet, George III said, "Won't do. Won't do." His last appearance in London was on June 5, 1809, after only seven years in the capital.

Suddenly, on impulse and without notice he left for New York in 1810. When he appeared there as Richard III at the Park Theater, the house was full and hundreds were turned away. He played in New York for seventeen nights and the receipts were a staggering $21,500. In the United States during his second season he proved as undependable as he had in London, and began to lose his audience. His arrogance was insufferable. On one occasion he refused to act until the orchestra had played, "God Save the King," and the audience remained standing while it was being played. (Yet after one performance in the same city he scattered $400 among the needy.) When he was informed that President Madison was coming to see him perform, Cooke's reaction was "Then if he does, I'll be damned if I play before him. What, I, George Frederick Cooke, who have acted before the Majesty of Britain, play before your Yankee President! No! I'll go forward to the audience and I'll say, 'Ladies and Gentlemen, the King of the Yankee-doodles has come to see me act; *me*, George Frederick Cooke, who have stood before my royal master, George III, and received his imperial approbation. . . . It is degradation enough to go on before rebels; but I'll not go on for the amusement of a king of rebels, the contemptible King of the Yankee-doodles!' "

His tour of northern American cities was part triumph, part failure, depending on his drinking. Dissipation led to his death two years after his coming to New York. He was buried in the "strangers' vault" of St. Paul's

Church, New York. In a gruesome footnote, his physician, Dr. Francis (we do not know that he was responsible for dismembering Cooke's corpse), had occasion to confess that for a benefit performance of *Hamlet,* a subordinate of the Park Theater came to him in great need of a skull. "I was compelled to loan the head of my old friend, George Frederick Cooke. . . . It was returned in the morning." But the next night, at the meeting of the Cooper Club, several of the members, having heard of what Dr. Francis had done, wished to make a phrenological investigation of Cooke's head, and the skull was released again. Daniel Webster was among those present.

When Edmund Kean, Cooke's profound admirer, was in the United States (1820/21) he had the body removed to another spot in the same cemetery, and erected a monument to Cooke. While the transference of the headless remains was taking place, he took off one of the toe bones, which he thereafter kept as a sacred relic in his home until Mrs. Kean, who had had enough of it, managed to spirit it off.

William Hazlitt, who had no superior as a critic of the theater, said of Cooke that in the death scenes of *Macbeth* and *Richard III* he proved that he was a great actor: "He fell like the ruin of a state, like a king with his regalia about him."

Elizabeth Farren (1759–1829) was celebrated for her performance of fine ladies in eighteenth-century plays. She was quite tall, dignified and graceful, but thin, and had an agreeable refined voice. She was criticized for being too much given to grimaces. She enacted Olivia, Portia, Juliet, Mrs. Ford, Beatrice, Hermione, and Helena (in *All's Well That Ends Well*). Lord Derby fell in love with her, but, as he was married, she refused to see him without her mother present as chaperone. She waited until the wife died and less than two months later, on May 1, 1797, became Lady Derby.

William Farren (1725–1795) became the head of a famous theatrical family. He was at Drury Lane (1776–1784) and Covent Garden (1784–1795), playing Hotspur, the Ghost (in *Hamlet*), and Buckingham (in *Henry VIII*). His sons Percival (1784–1843) and William (1786–1861) were also on the stage. His son William, as friend and tutor, prepared Helen Faucit for her first appearance in 1833. He did Aguecheek, Shallow, Malvolio, Polonius, and Dogberry, which was his best role. He was highly regarded by the critics. George Henry Lewes found his elegance comparable to that of the best French actors. *His* family, sons and daughters, were also actors.

John Edwin "the Elder" (1749–1790) became popular first at Bath, and later at the Haymarket. He was a good, dependable actor, and knew how to make his handsome face look ridiculous, though he was not a buffoon, and his acting was subtle. But he drank too much. His best roles were Dogberry, the First Gravedigger, Launcelot Gobbo, and Sir Hugh Evans. His son John "the Younger" (1768–1803) began acting as a boy, played for a while at Covent Garden, and died young from dissipation.

The family of Robert William Elliston (1744–1831) intended him for the

Church, but amateur theatricals decided him on the stage. He was encouraged by John Philip Kemble, and made his London debut in 1796 at the Haymarket. Often seen at Drury Lane, he enjoyed considerable popularity; Leigh Hunt went so far as to say he was second only to Garrick in tragedy and without peer as a stage lover. He performed Hamlet, Romeo, Hotspur, and, later in life, Falstaff. He too drank too much. He eventually became manager of Drury Lane, and it was he who engaged Kean, and was a friend of Byron's. He had a fine voice, and a noble face and stance.

Extravagant beyond calculation, no one was particularly surprised to hear him announce (what was impossible in those days, but is common enough now) that the Prince Regent was going to confer knighthood upon him, and that the next playbill would read: "Sir John Falstaff by Sir Robert Elliston." On one occasion a drunken sailor kept interrupting the play by various shouts and imprecations. There followed this scene:

ELLISTON: May I know the cause of this unseemly clamor?
VOICE FROM THE GALLERY: It's this here sailor what makes the row.
ELLISTON: A British sailor!—the glory of our country's annals!—the safeguard of our homes and families. What is it he asks?
SAILOR [roaring]: Rule Britannia!
ELLISTON: You shall have it! Of what ship, comrade?
SAILOR [still roaring]: The *Haggermemnon!*
ELLISTON: Ladies and gentlemen, on Monday next, a nautical, national, allegorical sketch will be presented at this theatre, entitled, "The British Flag!" . . . Give 'em "Rule Britannia,"

he added to the musicians. "Rule Britannia" was now sung by the whole company and the audience, and the play proceeded.

Once when he expected the king at the theater, he went out into the royal box, found a man sleeping in the king's chair, was about to scold him, when he noted that it was the king himself. The play was about to begin. What was Elliston to do? He took a violin from the orchestra, stood just below the royal box, and began "God Save the King." At that the king awoke.

Elliston was very fond of placing his hand on his heart and addressing the spectators on any trifling pretext. He also was fond of his practical jokes. A famous one he played upon Dowton, doing the Ghost in *Hamlet,* was made the subject of an illustration by George Cruikshank; Elliston and a friend, armed with rattan canes, concealed themselves beneath the stage, and as the Ghost descended slowly kept battering Dowton's unprotected calves.

When Elliston first came to London, Kemble advised him to study Romeo, and he first charmed the audience at Bath in that part. For a brief time at Drury Lane it was thought he would excel Kemble in truth and inspiration; it was said that he captured more effectively the humor and youth of the Prince of Denmark. But his soliloquies were oratorical, rather than those of a hero revealing his inner thoughts, while his tone tended to be pompous. He had the bad habit of catching his breath at the end of words of power, which made him appear to be sobbing. Nevertheless, in his prime he was one of the great actors of his day. He awed the minor actors of the company, chiefly because he seemed so sure of his self-importance. In the coronation procession of George IV, Elliston, having drunk too much, cried out, "Bless you, my people!" "He would have believed," says Doran, "in the efficacy of a sober benediction of the pit!"

Leigh Hunt adored his art and wrote a fine piece on Elliston's death: "The death of a comic actor," he said in part, "is felt more than that of a tragedian. He has sympathized more with us in our every-day feelings, and has given us more amusement. Death with a tragedian seems all in the way of business. Tragedians have been dying all their lives. . . . Mr. Elliston was the best comedian, in the highest sense of the word, that we have seen. . . . There was no gentleman comedian who comprised so many qualities of his art as he did." Hunt was of the opinion that he became "even the best Macbeth of any comedian who excelled in comedy."

Charles Lamb, with equal affection, wrote that Elliston was always acting, off stage as well as on. "This was the charm of Elliston's private deportment. You had spirited performance always going on before your eyes, with nothing to pay. . . . Wherever Elliston walked, sat, or stood still, there was the theatre. . . . One proud day to me he took his roast mutton with us in the Temple, to which I had super-added a preliminary haddock . . . I made a sort of apology for the humility of the fare, observing that . . . I never ate but one dish for dinner. 'I too never eat but one thing at dinner,' was his reply then, after a pause, 'reckoning fish as nothing.' The manner was all. It was as if by one peremptory sentence he had decreed the annihilation of all the savoury esculents which the pleasant and nutritious-food-giving Ocean pours forth upon poor humans from her watery bosom. This was *greatness,* tempered with considerate tenderness to the feelings of his scanty but welcoming entertainer."

Finally there was John Emery (1777–1822), who began as a boy very skillfully playing old men's roles. As a grown man he went to Covent Garden and became a specialist in comic parts: Sir Toby, Dogberry, old Gobbo, the First Gravedigger, Caliban, and Barnardine (in Kemble's production of *Measure for Measure*). Hazlitt praised him as a very good mimic of country characters, but disliked his Caliban because Caliban is "a creation," and Emery could not create; he made of him a "provincial." But in a "Memoir of the Late Mr. Emery," in *The Drama,* it is said of him at the beginning of the second scene in Act II of *The Tempest* that he approached "terrific tragedy when he described the various tortures inflicted on him by the magician, and the surrounding snakes that *'snare and hiss him into madness.'* " The idea was presented to the spectators "with all the loathing and violence of desperate wretchedness; the monster, hugged and shrunk into himself, . . . glared with his eyes, and gnashed his teeth." Robson the actor speaks of his Barnardine: "When I saw Emery crawl from his den with the straws sticking in his clotted hair and filthy garments, growling out his remonstrance at being disturbed from his sleep, I absolutely started!"

Meanwhile in the United States there were several prominent actors. Owen Morris (dates unknown), with the American Company from 1759 to 1790, was noted for low comedy, particularly as Dogberry and Polonius. His first wife did Ophelia in the first New York *Hamlet*. In 1767, she was drowned in a ferry accident in New York. His second wife, known as Mrs. Owen Morris (1753–1826), did Ophelia and Beatrice and was the toast of New York.

Charlotte Melmoth (1749–1820) was a fine tragic actress, and played an important part in the history of the theater in the United States. Born in England, she eloped with Samuel Jackson Pratt, who called himself Courtney Melmoth. They separated soon. She became well known in the English provinces, appeared at Covent Garden in 1784 and at Drury Lane the next year. In 1793 she appeared in New York, but got into trouble by refusing to recite a patriotic American epilogue. She was greatly admired as an actress at the Park Theater and also in Philadelphia. Her last appearance on the stage was in New York in 1812. She later opened a school of diction and elocution.

James Fennell, an eccentric Englishman, was at the Park Theater in New York in 1806. He had been educated for the church, but instead became an actor in the English provinces, a teacher of declamation in Paris, a journalist in London, a bridge builder, a lecturer, an editor, a schoolteacher, and once more an actor in the United States. He was criticized in Philadelphia for looking upward at the line, "My father—methinks I see my father" in *Hamlet* because "the mind oppressed by grief naturally directs the orbs of vision earthward, and 'the mind's eye' never seeks in vacant space the object of its contemplation." In the same city he was congratulated when as Othello he played down the suffocating of Desdemona, for "this would be a frightful scene, indeed, were it fully represented. . . . If anything like a real *smothering* were to be exhibited, the audience, unable to contain themselves, would rush upon the stage to stop the murder." John Bernard spoke of Fennell as a "whirligig-weather-cock fellow" and "the maddest madman I ever knew."

John Howard Payne, to whom we are indebted for "Home, Sweet Home," was the first American-born Hamlet, and he played the role when he was but seventeen at the Park Theater in New York. Two years later he played it again in Albany. His performance was both immature and amateurish.

Between 1810 and 1821 New Yorkers had the opportunity to hear three great tragedians, Cooke, Kean, and Booth, though Cooke never did Hamlet there. Kean's Hamlet was at the Park in 1812 and Junius B. Booth's in 1821.

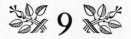

John Philip Kemble

Hazlitt revealed the worship of a whole generation when he commented wistfully, "We wish we had never seen Mr. Kean. He has destroyed the Kemble religion in which we were brought up."

John Philip Kemble (1757–1823) was the son of a Roman Catholic strolling actor-manager who had many children, the eldest of whom was Sarah, the future incomparable Sarah Siddons. John, the eldest son, after a childhood acting in his father's company, was sent to Douai to study for the priesthood. Though he already possessed a certain gelidity and an ascetic nature, he returned to the theater where as an actor he was best in very dramatic roles which he peformed with stateliness and a certain formality. After several years in the provinces, he made his London debut as Hamlet at Drury Lane on September 30, 1783. Some criticisms were favorable, others were less so. One objection made was his pronouncing the word "lisp" as *lithp*.

Throughout his brilliant career Kemble was called to account for a certain affection in his pronunciation, which he, on the contrary, seemed to feel was a refinement. Leigh Hunt lists among his consistent alterations: *airth* for "earth," *bird* for "beard," *vartue* for "virtue," *maircy* for "mercy," *marchants* for "merchants," *furful* for "fearful," *etairnally* for "eternally." The list no doubt could have been made much longer. Despite what must have been an irritation to the ears of purists, Kemble reigned for a long time until Edmund Kean deposed him.

The initial bewilderment of audiences at his interpretation of Hamlet soon gave way to enthusiastic acceptance, for they were charmed by his converting the prince into a philosopher and a man of gentleness. It was in that role that Thomas Lawrence painted Kemble.

His figure, though not notably elegant, was manly and dignified, while his features were more or less Roman. Hunt, who was not his kindest critic, said that he had a wonderful sense for small details, but that he sometimes gave "importance to minutenesses that mean nothing." He was clearly interested in maintaining an air of the "grand," which made comedy difficult for him. He could not stoop so low. Nor was he very good in love scenes. He was very effective, said Hunt, "in characters that are occupied with themselves and with their own importance," and it is not surprising that he excelled in Othello's "indignant jealousy" and the "desperate ambition of King John." Sometimes his effects were not what he had counted upon. He could let out "an eternal groan upon the interjection *Oh!* as if he were determined to show that his misery had not affected his lungs." Or he would jerk and nod his head, hoping to appear energetic, only to seem to be suffering a nervous affliction. Hunt summed up: "No actor in his declamation pleases more at times or more offends at others."

Hazlitt's view is not more admiring: Kemble's Hamlet "is like a man in armour, with a determined inveteracy of purpose, in one undeviating strait [*sic*] line, which is . . . remote from the natural grace and easy susceptibility of the character." Nevertheless, his was the first great popular Hamlet since Garrick's. To show assumed madness he disheveled his hair, and he emphasized the prince's loneliness and filial love. When he said "father" in the scene with the Ghost, he moved the spectators to tears by sinking to his knees. In the scene where the mouse trap is set for Claudius, he sat gnawing at the manuscript while *The Murder of Gonzago* was on, and when the king fled from the room, he tore the manuscript to pieces, angrily scattered them in the air, and threw himself into Horatio's arms. Salvini and Fechter used this same piece of business.

During his career he played 172 different roles. Perhaps his greatest achievement was as Coriolanus, a character fairly consonant with Kemble's own sense of personal dignity. The version of the play he gave was (with a number of excisions) all Shakespeare until the end of Act III. In Act IV he began to substitute passages from a play James Thomson had written on the same subject beginning by omitting Coriolanus's farewell to his wife, mother, and Menenius, and inserting in its place the first scene of Thomson's play. More Thomson was brought in as the play proceeded, notably in the great scene of "supplication," where the admixture was ruinous; the powerful effect of the first half of this scene, all Shakespeare, was annihilated by the total lack of dignity in Thomson's melodramatics:

> VOLUMNIA: Hear me, proud man! I have
> A heart as stout as thine; I came not hither,
> To be sent back rejected, baffled, sham'd,
> Hateful to Rome, because I am thy mother:
> A Roman matron knows, in such extremes,
> What part to take.—
> Go, barb'rous son; go, double parricide;
> Rush o'er my corse to thy belov'd revenge!
> Tread on the bleeding breast of her, to whom
> Thou ow'st thy life! Lo, thy first victim.

[She draws a dagger]
CORIOLANUS: [Seizing her hand] Ha! What dost thou mean?
VOLUMNIA: To die, while Rome is free.

It is dreadful to remember that the great Sarah Siddons had to speak these silly lines and other borrowings from Thomson, made, probably, to please the worst elements in the gallery. But his performance was wonderful.

When he entered in the opening scene with the line,

What is the matter, you dissentious rogues?

"the crowd of mob-Romans fell back as though they had run against a mad bull, and he dashed in amongst them in scarlet pride, and looked, even in the eyes of the audience, sufficient 'to beat forty of them.' . . . It was impossible not to admire the noble proportions and majestic contour of his figure, the expression of his face." In the wonderful scene in which Coriolanus is banished, and the hero has the lines,

You common cry of ours, whose breath I hate
As reek o' th' rotten fens—

it is recorded that Kemble "exhibited stately scorn, indignation, and high anger." And he accompanied his

I banish you!

"with a stately sweep of lifted arm."

The London *Times* was profoundly impressed with the play as given by Kemble in 1811: "The scenery, which we believe altogether new, exhibits a succession of Roman architecture, which exceeds any we have witnessed: the triumphal arch scene in particular . . . the costume, for attention to which the manager has long deserved credit, is here better preserved, upon the whole, than in any other play. The ceremony of Caius Marcius's triumphant return from Corioli is superb."

Sir Walter Scott highly praised Kemble as Macbeth, particularly his attempts to "appear composed" during the dialogue with Lennox, while the latter is giving an account of the "external terrors of the night, while in fact he is expecting the alarm to rise within the royal apartment." Scott called it "a most astonishing piece of playing," because "when Macbeth felt himself obliged" to listen to Lennox and turn toward him, you saw Kemble "like a man awaking from a fit of absence, endeavour to recollect at least the general tenor of what had been said."

Leigh Hunt admitted: "For the expression of the loftier emotions no actor is gifted by nature with greater external means." Kemble's head, he said, "is the heroic head of the antiquary and the artist. This tragic form assumes excellently well the gait of royalty, the vigorous majesty of the warrior."

John Taylor, who was appointed oculist first to George IV when Prince of Wales and the next year to his father, George III, became a journalist devoted to everything related to the theater. He has left us a full account of Kemble which is worth quoting extensively:

"I became acquainted with this gentleman in the first season of his performance at Drury Lane Theatre. I attended his first appearance, which was in the character of Hamlet. It was impossible to avoid being struck with his person and demeanor, though the latter was in general too stately and formal; but, perhaps, it only appeared so to me, as I had seen Garrick perform the same character several times a few years before, and had a vivid recollection of his excellence. There was some novelty in Mr. Kemble's delivery of certain passages, but they appeared to me to be rather the refinements of critical research, than the sympathetic ardor of congenial feelings with the author." Taylor was sitting in the third row of the pit next to the father of Mrs. Crouch. "When Kemble had dismissed one of the court spies sent to watch him, and kept back the other," his neighbor exclaimed, " 'Oh! fine, fine.' 'It may be very fine,' said I, 'but what does it mean, my friend?' 'Oh!' he answered, "I know not what it means, but it is fine and grand.'

"I was, at first, so little an admirer of John Kemble's performance of *Hamlet,* that considering it stiff, conceited, and unnatural, I wrote four epigrams in ironical commendation of it, and inserted them in a public print I then conducted." Taylor was introduced to Kemble in Drury Lane's lobby as the author of the epigrams, and "I was, therefore, not prepared for the unaffected civility with which he addressed me. We immediately fell into conversation, and I remember Mr. Kemble very soon began a defence of declamation, stating it as originally constituting one of the chief features of theatrical excellence on the Grecian stage; whence, on reflection, I inferred that he thought I was disposed to require too much of the manners of familiar life in dramatic representations. From that time we often met in company, became well acquainted," and eventually became friends.

Taylor was convinced that Kemble could have taken an important role in political life. "Mr. Kemble's classic and general knowledge, and the courtesy of his manners, as well as his improving theatrical powers, soon procured him high and extensive connections. He kept a hospitable and elegant table. . . .

"I found him generally [on Taylor's regular Sunday morning visits] with some book or manuscript before him relative to his art. . . . He was fond of Dryden, and sometimes read me passages. . . . I do not think he was a good reader, for he generally read in a tone either too low or too high." The only tone which is right in reading or acting is the one "which feeling suggests and expresses; and such was the charm of Garrick . . . There were many of Kemble's visitors who made court to him by telling him of faults in Garrick's acting . . . Kemble generally told me what was said to him of this kind, not as appearing to believe such remarks, but to know whether they received a confirmation from me. On such occasions I never abated in my reverence

for Garrick. . . . Kemble always listened to my panegyric on his great predecessor with apparent conviction, but I cannot help believing that he would
have liked me much better if I had never seen Garrick. . . .

"Kemble certainly believed that he possessed some comic talents," and
having a great enjoyment of jocularity, "he might naturally yield to self-
deception. My lively friend, George Colman, whose exuberant gaiety spares
nobody, . . . being asked his opinion of Kemble's Don Felix, said that it
displayed too much of the Don and too little of the Felix. Kemble could bear
jocular remarks on his acting with unaffected good-humor. . . . He had
determined to act Falstaff, . . . [but said that when] he came to the point [of
doing it], his heart would fail him. . . .

"I remember once, in compliance with his request, I told him I thought
that in one passage of *Hamlet* Garrick as well as himself, and all others, were
[sic] wrong in delivering it. The passage was where Horatio tells Hamlet that
he came to see his father's funeral, and Hamlet says it was rather to see his
mother's marriage, when Horatio observes 'it followed hard upon,' Hamlet
replies:

> Thrift, thrift, Horatio, the funeral baked meats
> Did coldly furnish forth the marriage table.

I observed that this passage was always given in anger, whereas in my
opinion it ought to be delivered with ironical praise. He immediately took
down a Polyglot Dictionary, and examined . . . the word thrift in all the
languages, and finding that it was always given in a commendatory sense,
he thanked me, and always after gave the passage in the manner I had
suggested."

Taylor pays tribute to the entire Kemble family by declaring that they
studied so thoroughly and "were all so perfect in their parts that the
prompter never was appealed to in their acting."

The manager of Drury Lane from June 1776 until the burning of the
theater in 1809 was Richard Brinsley Sheridan, who used his position socially and politically and nearly ruined it by his basic indifference. It was his
policy to leave the unpleasant part of directing the theater to an actor-
manager, and after 1788 Kemble fulfilled this unrewarding function. It was
doubtless Sheridan's ruthlessness which drove Kemble finally to negotiate
and obtain a share in Covent Garden.

As Odell well phrases it, "From 1788, when he became acting director at
Drury Lane, until 1817, when he retired, laden with honours, from public
life, John Kemble is to be reckoned with as the leading man in English
theatricals, the brains, as Mrs. Siddons was the heart, of the machine."
Moreover his adaptations of the plays were passed on to the age of Kean.

In 1788 he revived *Henry VIII*, which had not been played for twenty years;
on February 7 of the next year he gave *Coriolanus;* on October 1 *Henry V*,
which had also lain unperformed for twenty years; on October 13, *The
Tempest*, with Dryden's additions; on January 15, 1790, *The Two Gentlemen of*

Verona, another play which had not been acted for twenty years. These revivals prove how seriously Kemble accepted his responsibilities as actor-manager. In the 1791/92 season he revived *Henry IV, Part I* and *King John.*

In 1791 he appointed William Capon (1757–1827) scenic director. The new Drury Lane was too large for the scenery left over from Garrick's day, and Capon introduced some important innovations. He did away with the old flats and wings. A careful antiquarian, he tried to be historically correct in representing ancient houses and streets. The new Drury Lane opened in April 1794. The banquet scene in *Macbeth* was thought worth going to see just for itself. In 1799 he reproduced the interior of a fourteenth-century cathedral; it was 37 feet high and measured 56 feet by 52 feet, though scenery like that was actually too heavy to shift. But he won universal admiration. When the theater burned in 1809 he lost a fortune because much of the scenery was still unpaid for. Later he went to work for Kemble at Covent Garden, where his Shakespearean settings were highly appreciated for their splendor. Many of his sets were still in use in the time of Macready.

Before Kemble's time matters were quite different. Even in Garrick's day, says Boaden, "a hall, a castle, or a chamber, or a cut-wood of which the verdure seemed to have been washed away" were all set up "without selection or propriety." Kemble's appointment of Capon transformed all that. Whether it might have been better if the changes had been in the opposite direction—that is, to use as little scenery as possible and approximate the conditions of the Elizabethan boards—is another question, but then, it took the development of modern electric lighting in our own century to make scenic design of less and less consequence so that the sets would not impede the play, but permit it to proceed with rapidity, as it did in Shakespeare's day, when there were no intermissions at all between acts.

Costuming was still another matter. In 1787 the manager of the Theatre Royal, Edinburgh, furnished James Fennell for his first performance as Othello with a coat, a waistcoat and trousers of white cloth decorated with silver lace, a black wig with a tail a yard long attached to it, white silk stockings, and dancing pumps. Kemble was less revolutionary with costume and did not follow Macklin's lead in reforming it. Kemble's Othello was still a scarlet-coated British general with Turkish trousers and a turban, his Richard III wore silk knee breeches, and his Lear defied the storm in a dressing gown. He himself always preferred a Roman part, partly because he loved and wore what the late eighteenth century thought was authentically Roman. The last time he played with Young, which was in *Julius Caesar,* he entered Young's dressing room and gave him some of the props he had worn in his favorite characters, and begged him to keep them as mementos. "Well," said Kemble, referring to the beautiful scene between Brutus and Cassius, "we've often had high words together on the stage, but never off." Young's thanks touched him so much that he shook his hand and hurried from the room saying:

For this present
I would not, so with love I might entreat you,
Be any further moved.

In 1787 Kemble married Priscilla Hopkins (1755–1845), an actress and the widow of an Irish actor. She lived to a great age. When young, she had been in Garrick's company. The quality of dignity he brought to his own private life did much to elevate his profession in the public eye, especially when compared with his predecessor, George Frederick Cooke and his successor, Edmund Kean.

Like all great men, he had his detractors, who called him "the Euclid of the stage," and someone penned an epigram concluding:

Who moves in given angles, squares a start,
And blows his Roman beak by rules of art.

He was further accused of galloping "half an octave in a groan." He sometimes revived the "teapot school" of gesticulation (one hand on hip, one extended), which was not out of keeping with his Roman roles. But his Othello was pronounced too "heroic" (i.e., Roman) to be effective. His Iago was "open, frank, without the restlessness." He lacked the "material agitation" consistent with the "plottings of a treacherous" villain.

Hazlitt was quite capable of rising to his defense. Once when the London *Times* suggested that Kemble's powers were waning, Hazlitt wrote: "In that prodigious prosing paper, the *Times*, which seems to be written as well as printed by a steam-engine, Mr. Kemble is compared to the ruin of a magnificent temple, in which the divinity still resides. This is not the case. The temple is unimpaired: but the divinity is sometimes from home."

Hazlitt's phrase that Kemble played Hamlet like a man in armor has often been misunderstood to mean that Kemble's playing was stiff, when all that Hazlitt meant was that Kemble seized upon one line of his interpretation of Hamlet's character and never deviated from it, while the truth is that Kemble could be very agile, and there were even critics who considered his agility beneath the dignity of a tragic actor. But, unlike Garrick who was perpetually in motion, Kemble preferred to use his pantomimic movements sparingly. As Hotspur, for instance, he was full of enthusiasm and quickness, so that Scott observed that one would have imagined that "the grave, studious, contemplative actor, who personated Hamlet to the life, could scarcely have assumed the rapidity and energy, and hurry, and reckless indulgence of his humour, which are the chief ingredients of Henry Percy's character." The energy he displayed as Henry V inspired a caricature in which the actor is shown with "robes acting like a windmill."

In the new Drury Lane of 1794, he revived *All's Well That Ends Well* and *Measure for Measure.*

As manager of Drury Lane, Kemble complained to Sheridan that it was imperative to find some kind of novelty to please the audience, or "else the

theatre will sink." "Then," replied Sheridan sarcastically, "if you want novelty, act *Hamlet* and have music played between your pauses." Sheridan was
not exaggerating. Kemble's tempo as the prince had been proved a few
nights earlier when a gentleman came to the pit door and laid down half the
price for a place. The money-taker told him that Act III had only just begun.
The man, looking at his watch, said that was impossible: it was half-past
nine. "True," said the money-taker, "but recollect, Mr. Kemble plays Hamlet tonight."

One evening in 1783 when the company was at Limerick, some drunken
officers of the military insisted they would take Miss Phillips (later Mrs.
Crouch) home, and forced their way behind the scenes, while she in terror
ran into her dressing room and locked the door. The officers started to
break it open. Miss Phillips's father was ill at home at the time and had
asked Kemble to escort his daughter after the play. When Kemble heard
the commotion and understood what was happening, he asked the soldiers
to desist and go away. They refused. Kemble took his sword and said that
having been commissioned by her father to escort Miss Phillips home he
was prepared to do so at the peril of his life. He asked her to open the
door to him, but Kemble had taken only a few steps when one of the
officers came up behind him and cut him on the head with a sabre. Kemble might very well have been killed on the spot had not a hairdresser,
who came upon the situation, seized the officer's arm and wrested the
sword from him. Not at all terrified, Kemble turned, thanked his pre-
server, and led Miss Phillips home. He was plainly no coward.

Some of the people one would least have expected to admire him, did so.
George Frederick Cooke, obviously in a sober mood, was being tempted by
a group to disparage Kemble as an actor; Cooke certainly had nothing in
common with Kemble in his method of acting, and they had their disagree-
ments. But Cooke said that he considered Kemble "a very great" actor and
added that "those who say the contrary are envious men, and not worthy
to wipe his shoes."

When Kemble finally retired, Hazlitt atoned for his earlier judgments.
Moreover with the passage of time Kemble undoubtedly had become more
and more a master of his style. Hazlitt wrote:

> Mr. Kemble took his leave of the Stage on Monday night, in the charac-
> ter of Coriolanus. On his first coming forward to pronounce his Fare-
> well address, he was received with a shout like thunder: on his retiring
> after it, the applause was long before it subsided entirely away. . . . We
> forget numberless things that have happened to ourselves . . . but not
> the first time of our seeing Mr. Kemble, nor shall we easily forget the
> last! Coriolanus, the character in which he took his leave of the Stage,
> was one of the first in which we remember to have seen him; and it was
> one in which we were not sorry to part with him, for we wished to see
> him appear like himself to the last. . . . He played the part as well as
> he ever did—with as much freshness and vigour. There was no abate-

ment of spirit and energy—none of grace and dignity; his look, his action, his expression of the character, were the same as they ever were: they could not be finer . . .

We may on this occasion be expected to say a few words on the general merits of Mr. Kemble as an actor and on the principal characters he performed. . . . It has always appeared to us, that the range of characters in which Mr. Kemble more particularly shone, and was superior to every other actor, were those which consisted in the development of some one solitary sentiment or exclusive passion. . . . So in Coriolanus, he exhibited the ruling passion with the same unshaken firmness, he preserved the same haughty dignity of demeanour, the same energy of will, and unbending sternness of temper throughout. . . . In Leontes, also, in *The Winter's Tale* [a character he at one time played often], the growing jealousy of the King, and the exclusive possession which this passion gradually obtains over his mind, were marked by him in the finest manner. . . . In Hamlet, on the contrary, Mr. Kemble in our judgment unavoidably failed from want of flexibility, of that quick sensibility which yields to every motive, and is borne away with every breath of fancy. . . . There is a perpetual undulation of feeling in the character of Hamlet; but in Mr. Kemble's acting "there was neither variableness nor shadow of turning." He played one undeviating line. . . . In Macbeth, Mr. Kemble was unequal to "the tug and war" of the passions which assail him: he stood as it were at bay with fortune, and maintained his ground too steadily against "fate and metaphysical aid"; instead of staggering and reeling under the appalling visions of the preternatural world. . . . In the latter scenes, however, he displayed great energy and spirit; and there was a fine melancholy retrospective tone in his manner of delivering the lines, *"My way of life has fallen into the sear, the yellow leaf,"* which smote upon the heart, and remained there ever after. His Richard III wanted that tempest and whirlwind of the soul, that life and spirit, and dazzling rapidity of motion, which fills the stage, and burns in every part of it, when Mr. Kean performs the character. . . . Mr. Kemble's manner, on the contrary, had always something dry, hard, and pedantic in it. "You shall relish him more in the scholar than the soldier"; but his monotony did not fatigue, his formality did not displease; because there was always sense and meaning in what he did. The fineness of Mr. Kemble's figure may be supposed to have led to that statue-like appearance . . . as the diminutiveness of Mr. Kean's person has probably compelled him to bustle about too much, and to make up for the want of dignity of form, by the violence and contrast of his attutides. If Mr. Kemble were to remain in the same posture for half an hour, his figure would only excite admiration: if Mr. Kean were to stand still only for a moment, the contrary effect would be apparent . . .

It has been suggested that Mr. Kemble chiefly excelled in his Roman characters, and among others in Brutus. If it be meant that he excelled in those which imply a certain stoicism of feeling, and energy of will, this we have already granted: but Brutus is not a character of this kind . . . not a stoic, but a humane enthusiast . . . [with] a lofty inflexibility of purpose, mingled with an effeminate abstractedness of thought, which Mr. Kemble did not give.

In short, we think the distinguishing excellence of his acting may be summed up in one word—intensity. . . . If he had not the unexpected bursts of nature and genius, he had all the regularity of art; if he did not display the tumult and conflict of opposite passions in the soul, he gave the deepest and most permanent interest to the uninterrupted progress of individual feeling; and in embodying a high idea of certain characters . . . he was the most excellent actor of his time.

Unfortunately, it was Kemble's fate to play a crucial rule in the career of the youthful forger, William Henry Ireland. To please the bumbling semi-antiquarian, the semicollector of junk, the Shakespeare idolater who was forever misquoting his idol, Samuel Ireland, who the boy suspected was not in actuality his father and who treated him with lack of affection and patience, young William Henry (1777–1835) began a rapid career as forger of Shakespeareana, beginning with a clumsy legal document containing what purported to be Shakespeare's own signature. Chatterton, the boy wonder, who might have turned into a good poet had anyone had the decency to point out to him that it was not necessary to win fame by gauche, if talented, forgeries, was William Henry's hero. Chatterton's early death made him an irresistible idol, and when Samuel Ireland gleefully accepted the Shakespearean signature as authentic, William Henry was launched on his career as forger while still in his teens. Samuel not only swallowed hook, line, and sinker the preposterous story accounting for Henry's possession of the document, but never gave up pressing the lad for more and still more.

Henry worked for a lawyer and so had access to old parchments and seals; he later bought up a supply of paper with Elizabethan watermarks, found a way to convert ink so it would look brown with age, invented a scrawl that had not the slightest resemblance to Elizabethan writing, and a spelling (modeled on Chatterton's but far more outrageous) such as was in use at no time in English history. Growing bolder, he invented various other legal documents and financial receipts for Shakespeare, a few pages from the "original manuscripts" of *Hamlet* and *King Lear,* a love letter and love poem to Anna Hatherrewaye, and a profession of faith which made a good Protestant of Shakespeare dispelling forever the rumor that he might have been a Catholic. As for the last document, the nineteen-year-old boy must indeed have been shocked to hear the celebrated educator Samuel Parr say, when he had read to him the Profession of Faith: "Sir, we have many very fine passages in our church service, and our litanies abound with beauties; but here, sir, here is a man who has distanced us all!" The learned Joseph Warton was present on the occasion and did not dissent. "When I heard these words pronounced," William Henry recorded, "I could scarcely credit my own senses." These were praises "lavished by a person so avowedly erudite on the unstudied production of one so green in years as myself," that William Henry left the room ruminating on the words, "fired with the idea of possessing genius to which I had never aspired." What was the boy to think but that he surpassed even Chatterton?

When the word was out that these miraculously "rediscovered" examples of Shakespeare's own script together with all sorts of new documents and compositions by the Bard himself were to be seen at the Ireland house, nothing naturally would have succeeded in keeping the ever-curious James Boswell away. He came on February 20, 1795, examined the papers for a long time, "constantly speaking," as William Henry tells us, "in favor of the internal as well as external proofs of the validity of the manuscripts." He asked for brandy and water, and having drunk his glass, "redoubled his praises of the manuscripts; and at length arising from his chair, he made use of the following expression: 'Well, I shall now die contented, since I have lived to witness the present day.' Mr. Boswell then kneeling down before the volume containing a portion of the papers, continued, 'I now kiss the invaluable relics of our Bard: and thanks to God, that I have lived to see them!' Having kissed the volume with every token of reverence, Mr. Boswell shortly after quitted Mr. Ireland's house."

Today it seems to us inconceivable that the rot which William Henry passed off as Shakespeare's creation—I mean not the idiotic handwriting or spelling, but the inanity of the writings as such—could have deceived so many people. But is this unique? It is true that very few persons knew anything about Elizabethan handwriting, and the paper and ink did, superficially, appear authentic. I should like to quote a passage I have already published, for after a lifetime spent as a Shakespeare scholar, it is a subject on which I feel most strongly:

> There is little reason to doubt, I fear, that if there appeared among us today a new William Henry Ireland, more expert in procuring his materials and in imitating the Elizabethan hand, more knowledgeable in keeping within the confines of Elizabethan spelling and vocabulary, and cunning enough to have his "discoveries" emanate from acceptable archives (all of which would have to meet a more highly informed criticism today), with forgeries as poetically contemptible and dramatically ridiculous as William Henry's, his finds would be hailed by innumerable scholars as authentic. For while Ireland's century made a great fuss about taste (exhibiting little of it in its poetry or drama), our modern professional scholars, for all practical purposes, deny the existence of taste altogether. For them esthetic judgment is too subjective to figure in literary evaluations. And for that reason their discussions of literature must be riveted to matters of dates and editions and sources (not that these are unimportant, but merely that they are quite secondary to the business of literature)—matters which never approach the literary quintessence itself.

Like the "authorities" who were fooled by the boy, modern scholars feel secure only under the umbrella of fact. If the dates, manuscript, and handwriting seemed acceptable, many modern scholars would agree that Shakespeare could have written anything from an Elizabethan equivalent of Edgar Guest to Dorothy Dix.

It is not surprising that, thus encouraged, William Henry should have decided to write a play for Shakespeare (he, in fact, wrote two plays that the Bard had overlooked writing). On a wall of his father's house hung a large drawing after Mortimer's painting of Rowena offering wine to Vortigern. In February 1795, William Henry announced that he had discovered a complete play by Shakespeare, entitled *Vortigern.* He had found the outlines of the story in Holinshed's *Chronicles* taken from his father's shelves.

The various documents he "discovered" were being published by his father, and found many subscribers. One of them was Richard Brinsley Sheridan. Sheridan, as titular manager of Drury Lane, claimed first rights as subscriber to *Vortigern,* and the right to produce it there. Samuel Ireland, by no means loath, allowed him to see the manuscript of the play as it was delivered to him by William Henry sheet by sheet. Sheridan agreed to a production in advance of the publication scheduled for December 1795.

But the more Sheridan read of *Vortigern* the less he liked it. He was no lover of Shakespeare to begin with, and he decided that this must have been a very early work, and he became vague about committing himself. At last he signed an agreement: Samuel was to receive £250 plus half of all profits exceeding £350 a performance. These terms were very low, but Samuel Ireland expected a long run.

Sheridan did not live up to his agreement to produce the play before December 1795. He haggled over the terms and thus prevented Covent Garden from bidding for a production. Finally, on September 9, he signed a contract that the play was to be given not later than December 15. Time passed and no one was making the new scenery promised for the "lost" play. As usual, Sheridan shifted his responsibilities to Kemble, and arranged a meeting between him and Samuel Ireland, to take place on November 17. When father and son appeared at the appointed hour, they were told that Kemble had already left the premises. (During this year Kemble was having his own emotional problems, which resulted, at the close of 1795, in his publishing a rather astonishing apology for having made violent amorous, though unencouraged, attacks upon Miss De Camp, a member of the company who later married his brother Charles.)

Suddenly Kemble's sister, Mrs. Siddons, announced that the delicate condition of her health would prevent her appearing in *Vortigern.*

It is evident enough that Kemble had made up his mind to ruin *Vortigern.* It is one of his few spurious acts; for the honest thing would have been to refuse to present it at all. Surely, with all his experience, he ought to have known that not a line of it could have been written by Shakespeare. His wicked intentions were manifest when he announced that on the same bill he would present a musical farce, *My Grandmother,* which had to do with the gullibility of an art collector. Moreover, *Vortigern* was not advertised as written by Shakespeare; to add insult to injury, he planned to present it for the first time on April 1, April Fools' Day, but the opening was postponed a day. The Ireland partisans were glad that the expected attack of Malone, the one outstanding Shakespeare scholar of his day, had yet to appear. Malone had printed a public announcement labeling the papers as "spurious," and said that he hoped to have his book out exposing the whole fraud by the end of the month. But it was not until March 31, 1796, that Malone's *Inquiry into the Authenticity of Certain Miscellaneous Papers* appeared, on the very eve of the production of *Vortigern.*

In the most heavy-handed manner but with sound scholarship, Malone made mincemeat of the published forgeries and their pretensions. But his dislike of the Irelands went beyond scholarship. Samuel Ireland's friends were sympathetic to the principles of the French Revolution, and in Malone's eyes that was sheer treason. He claimed that the Ireland versions of Shakespeare advocated revolutionary principles.

On April 2, 1796, the London *Times* advertised a performance of *Vortigern* for that same night, omitting any mention of Shakespeare but accusing Malone of a "malevolent and unmanly" attack. It appealed to the public to judge the tragedy impartially.

By opening night public contention between the Believers and non-Believers was raging. Sheridan's first guess had been correct: more than three hours before curtain-time (6:30 P.M.) there was a long line outside Drury Lane; an hour later the surrounding streets were packed with an expectant audience. Soon some noisy boys were distributing among them a handbill of Samuel Ireland's asking "that the play of *Vortigern* may be heard with that *candor* that has ever distinguished a *British Audience.*" Every place in Drury Lane was taken and more than twenty-five hundred people paid to get in. Sheridan had assured Kemble that "the pride of having to decide whether a piece was actually written by Shakespeare or not, would fill the house . . . for you know very well, Kemble, that an Englishman considers himself as good a judge of Shakespeare as of his pint of porter."

When the prologue was spoken by Whitfield (it was written by Burgess, who undertook it when Pye, the worst poet laureate England has ever had, failed to make good his promise to write it) at the concluding passage beginning:

> Unbias'd then pronounce your dread decree,
> Alike from prejudice and favor free.
> If, the fierce ordeal pass'd, you chance to find
> Rich sterling ore, tho' rude and unrefin'd,
> Stamp it your own, assert your poet's fame,
> And add fresh wreaths to Shakespeare's honor'd name,

Whitfield was shouted down by the rowdy, and as he tried to continue he began to forget his lines. Now the volatile spectators drowned him in sympathy and urged him to proceed. At the prologue's end he was tumultuously applauded, an encouraging sign for the play itself.

The first act consisted of eight scenes, some of them over before they had hardly begun, and at its conclusion the audience was still attentive. They were so used to hearing mangled versions of Shakespeare, that although every line was balderdash they were not familiar enough with the true Shakespearean style to see this was trash. The second act was even something of a hit, and was vigorously applauded.

It was in the third act that the mischief began. Kemble had appointed the role of the Second Baron to Dignum, a bad performer with a high tenor voice, and it was he who had to speak the lines (the trumpet having sounded):

> Nay; stop not there, but let them bellow on,
> Till with their clamorous noise they shame the thunder . . .

As William Henry recorded that moment: "The idea of beholding that gentleman strut forth in tragedy is quite sufficient to excite risibility even in Melpomene herself." Dignum managed by his pronunciation "to set the whole house in a convulsive peal of laughter." That was the beginning of the end.

In the fourth act Horsus falls. His role was enacted by the comedian Phillimore, whose nose was so enormous that today he might perform Cyrano without altering his proboscis; Kemble's casting him in the role must have been pure malice. In all events, Phillimore overextended himself in the death scene. "On receiving the deadly wound," William Henry reports, either deliberately or by chance he "so placed his unfortunate carcass that on the falling of the drop-curtain he was literally divided between the audience and his brethren of the sock and buskin; his legs & c., being towards the spectators, and his head, & c., inside the curtain." The roller at the bottom of the curtain was heavy, and Phillimore, dead, began to groan beneath its weight; finding his colleagues slow in rescuing him, he extricated himself behind the curtain—which piece of buffoonery brought hurricanes of laughter and loud applause.

In the second scene of the last act there is one line which brought down the house. Ironically, the speech in which the line occurs is easily the best and perhaps the closest to poetry in the play. Kemble deliberately grimaced and strutted, unfairly overemphasizing Vortigern's apostrophe to death in order to provoke an uproar. At the line

> And when this solemn mockery is ended . . .

he somehow contrived to make it sound like a résumé of the entire play. In fact, as William Henry says, Kemble "laid such a peculiar stress" on the line ("in the most sepulchral tone of voice possible") as made it "the *watchword* for the general howl." The shouting continued for at least ten minutes. Then Kemble, having waited for silence, "instead of proceeding with the speech at the ensuing line, very politely, and in order to amuse the audience still more, redelivered the very line . . . with even more solemn grimace than he had in the first instance displayed."

Having done his worst, Kemble now assumed the role of a gentleman mediator. After the second and louder outburst at the line, he advanced to ask the audience for quiet and requested a "fair" hearing for what was to follow. But there was nothing but laughter for the rest of the last act.

When Mrs. Jordan, whom the audience adored, came out to deliver the epilogue, she was granted an ovation—but it was for herself, not the play. When, next, the actor Barrymore tried to announce *Vortigern* as the play for the next bill, violent yells of protest were heard from every corner of the theater, followed by a series of brawls which could not be stopped for twenty minutes. Finally, Kemble appeared and stated that on Monday night *The School for Scandal* would be given instead.

Although William Henry's confession of the truth was to follow not long after, Kemble's shabby conduct as actor-manager of *Vortigern* remains the most unpleasant part of his record—for surely, once he had agreed to present and act in the play, it was his bounden duty to do his best by it. He must have been aware of this, for he tried to rationalize that night of April 2, 1796. Years later he related to Charles Marsh, the chatty author of *The Clubs of London,* an account of the night's events. It was a mishmash of the actual facts, in which he held everyone responsible but himself; he even confused the parts assigned to various actors, and quoted, in order to be funny, lines which were not in the text.

That may have been somewhat owing to his complete abandonment of his stage presence once a play was over. William Jerdan remembered him "as different from John Kemble on the stage as it is possible to remember" when "in his convivial hours and conversation."

One night Jerdan was in the front seat of the stage box to see his Coriolanus, a performance which "fixed and transported me from beginning to end." The next day, he happened to call, and Jerdan said that although he had often seen him in that role, "I had never thought that he played it to such absolute perfection. 'And I will tell you the secret,' he responded. 'I caught your eye, on my entering the stage; I knew I had got you, and I performed Coriolanus to you, as if quite insensible of any other audience.' " Kemble went on to explain, what many of the best interpreters in all the arts must feel, "that the performer was curiously sensible of the sympathies or the negligence of his hearers, and that . . . the slightest symptom of having failed in producing a desired effect, was enough to damp his efforts for a whole evening." Among his friends he had a lively sense of the comic in theatrical criticism.

Leigh Hunt was his most relentlessly adverse critic and conducted what amounted to a war against Kemble's domination of the London theater. He objected to his Hamlet as "not the man, but his mask; a trophy, a consul's robe; or, if you please, a rhetorician," and dismissed him as "a teacher of elocution rather than an actor and not a good teacher, on that account." Though Kemble's stipulation for dignity naturally narrowed his range, Leigh Hunt must be taken as too great a partisan of Kean's romantic style to appreciate the classic. "Mr. Kemble," he wrote, "is a peculiar instance of almost all these essentials to good acting, and at the same time an example

[of] how much they may be injured by an indiscriminate application of study. His conceptions of character are strong where the characters themselves are strong, his attention to passions is fixed by large objects." He "exhibits little of the enthusiasm of genius . . . It is no small praise to say of an actor that he excels in soliloquies; . . . [which] require great judgment because the speaker has no assistance from others, and because the audience, always awake to action, is inclined during a soliloquy to seek repose in inattention."

On the other hand, he objected that Kemble's voice was "hollow and monotonous from the malformation, as it said, of his organs of utterance," even though his speech "is confident and exact," and "at all times carefully distinct." What Hunt may not have known was that Kemble struggled all his life with a very advanced case of asthma, which may very well have been the reason for his deliberately slow delivery. Hunt went on to state how Kemble would improve on the following poem:

> Varchue [*Virtue*], the [*thy*] happy wisdom's known
> In making what we wish our own; . . .
> For since the soul that purses [*pierces*] mine,
> Sweet Myra's soul, is full of thine,
> In my breast too thy spirit stares [*stirs*],
> Since all my soul is full of hairs [*hers*]!

Nevertheless, Hunt had in all honesty to pay this deserved tribute to Kemble: "Were it not for Mr. Kemble's exertions the tragedies of our glorious bard would almost be in danger of dismissal from the stage; and it does him infinite credit to have persevered in his exertions in spite of comparatively thin houses; to have added to the attractions of his poet by a splendour of scene as seasonable as well-deserved; and to have evinced so noble an attachment, and helped to keep up so noble a taste, in an age of mawkishness and buffoonery."

As manager, Kemble had his troubles. He fought a duel with one actor as a result of a quarrel over rehearsals; Kemble with characteristic lofty contempt fired his pistol into the air and no one was hurt. His leading ladies harassed him with their rivalries, unannounced absences from scheduled performances, and cabals. He frequently castigated audiences for their rowdiness or for the apples and bottles they hurled on the stage. On September 20, 1808, Covent Garden burned to the ground, at a loss of more than £150,000; the new theater cost an outrageous £300,000.

A week before the grand opening, it was announced that boxes would be raised from six to seven shillings, and the pit from three shillings sixpence to four shillings. A special attraction was to be the celebrated soprano, Mme. Catalani, who was to be paid £50 a night. There ensued an outburst of popular fury, the Old Price Riots, protesting against an increase in prices whose sole aim was to pay the salary of a foreign opera singer. When Kemble stepped proudly on stage opening night, hisses, shouts, and whistles drowned out his prologue. The tumult continued throughout *Macbeth*, with intermittent yells of "Old Prices" and "No Catalani," and he and Mrs. Siddons were particular objects of the abuse. Rioters stood with their backs to the stage while the actors conscientiously continued with the tragedy. Hardly a word of it or of the musical farce which followed it could be heard. When the performance was over, the audience would not depart, and Kemble sent for the police. The sight of two officers of the law on the stage only provoked the mob to greater anger; the constables retreated, and fire engines appeared. The theater did not begin to empty until 2 A.M. when a chorus of "God Save the King" was struck up.

The riot continued every night for many weeks, though the playhouse suffered no damage. Some nights the audience danced, pounding their feet during the play, wore "Old Prices" hats and "Old Prices" brooches, and supplemented their antics with bells, horns, rattles, gongs, and howlings. Oddly enough, the journals took their part, not excluding the *Times,* and poor Kemble was the chief victim, as though it were all his fault. He was monstrously accused of personal profiteering and corruption; and every kind of manufactured slander was levelled against his personal life. Outside his house in Great Russell Street crowds gathered to smash his windows. It has been suggested that in the minds of these people he had become identified with his famous role of Coriolanus. London now claimed him as theirs. After three months he was forced to bring back the old prices and make a public apology from the boards.

When he retired on June 23, 1817, although the heat was intense, the house was jammed. He, of course, performed his famous Coriolanus, and every passage which might seem to apply to his retiring was seized upon with deep emotion. When he came to the lines,

> As soon in battle
> I would before thee fly, and howl for mercy,
> As quit the station they've assigned me here . . .

there were great shouts and cries of "No! No! Do not quit!" from most of the spectators.

One takes no pleasure in recounting that Kemble's retirement from the stage was both brief and unhappy. While he was manager at Covent Garden his company was a financial failure. He not only suffered much pain from gout during his last days, but was forced to sell his fine collection of old plays to the Duke of Devonshire.

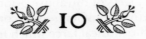

Sarah Siddons

Garrick will probably always be spoken of as the greatest actor known to the English stage; just so, Kemble's sister, Sarah Siddons, is likely to be remembered as the greatest English actress. Endless panegyrics have been bestowed upon her, Reynolds painted her as the Muse of Tragedy, and there are portraits of her by Lawrence and Gainsborough.

"She was Tragedy personified," wrote Hazlitt. "She was the stateliest ornament of the public mind. She was not only the idol of the people, she not only hushed the tumultuous shouts of the public in breathless expectation, and quenched the blaze of surrounding beauty in silent tears, but to the retired and lonely student, through long years of solitude, her face has shone as if an eye had appeared from heaven; her name has been as if a voice had opened the chambers of the human heart, or as if a trumpet had awakened the sleeping and the dead."

Again he wrote: "Grandeur was the cradle in which her genius was rocked: for *her* to be, was to be sublime! She did the greatest things with child-like ease; her powers seemed never tasked to the reserve. . . . The least motion of her hand seemed to command awe and obedience." She sat "majestic in the throne of tragedy—a Goddess, a prophetess and a Muse." She caused tragedy to "stand with its feet upon the earth, and its head above the stars, weeping tears and blood. . . . While the stage lasts, there will never be another Mrs. Siddons! Tragedy seemed to set with her; and the rest are but blazing comets." He further said: "The enthusiasm she excited had something idolatrous about it; we can conceive nothing grander. She embodied to our imaginations the fables of mythology of the heroic and the deified mortals of elder time. She was not less than a goddess or a prophetess inspired by the Gods. Power was seated on her brow; passion radiated from her breast as from a shrine." Thomas Holcroft compared her to Garrick. "Even Garrick couldn't awaken more public admiration than she."

She was over medium height, muscular but not too much so; her movements were graceful rather than angular. However, Gainsborough found her nose far too long. Her personality was captivating, her features were strong, very expressive, and flexible. Her voice could be plaintive, firm, or powerful, according to her wishes. Her eyes were large and she had expressive brows which she raised or rapidly lowered to show disdain, sympathy, or pity. Her articulation was ever clear and penetrating; her stage presence was completely self-assured.

Dr. John Doran sums up his account of her by saying: "Those who knew her best have recorded her beauty and her grace, her noble carriage, divine elocution, and solemn earnestness; her grandeur and her pathos, her correct judgment, her identification of whatever she assumed, and her abnegation of self. " [He means, of course, of her own personality while on the stage.] According to Campbell, she "increased the heart's capacity for tender, intense, and lofty feelings, and seemed something above humanity, in presence of which, humanity was moved, exalted, or depressed, according as she willed. Her countenance was the interpreter of her mind, and that mind was of the loftiest, never stooping to trickery, but depending on nature to produce effect."

But she was too aloof and avaricious to be liked by her fellow actors. She detested publicity of any sort. Despite the feelings of those in her profession, she numbered among her friends Samuel Johnson and Horace Walpole.

The London public eventually treated her like a queen. It is a matter of record that when, in her sedan chair, she came upon a mob, she had only to say, "Good people, let me pass. I am Sarah Siddons," and a path would at once open for her to go by.

Toward the end of her career, she grew stout, and her acting began to be considered out of date. (Kean had by then fairly demolished the vogue of the Kemble school.) She had been prudish since girlhood, and in the part of Rosalind absolutely refused to appear in breeches, wearing a costume which was absurd in the extreme, a cross between the masculine and feminine.

Sarah Kemble (1755–1831) came of an acting family. Her grandfather had acted under Betterton and Barton Booth; her parents had played with Quin. Her father, Roger Kemble, was the head of a troupe of strolling players. His eldest child was Sarah, the next John; both of them and Stephen and Elizabeth, who followed, were made part of the acting company almost as soon as they could speak. Later Roger Kemble did what he could to dissuade his children from entering his profession because of the privations he had endured, but it was by then too late.

Sarah's first audience hissed her off the stage as too young, but she quickly won applause by reciting a fable. At thirteen she played at Worcester as Ariel, with her father, mother, brother John, and sister Elizabeth participating in the play. For the next four or five years the company wandered through many towns and villages. By the time she was eighteen, she found herself performing in the same piece by the dramatist Nathaniel Lee with a Mr. Siddons; he had also acted with her in *The Tempest.* It was inevitable that she should have begun to attract men behind the scenes as well as on the stage; these included the Earl of Coventry and a number of squires. But Sarah and Siddons had already fallen in love, though her parents objected to the match. Siddons introduced his plight to the audience by writing a comic song, which won their sympathy. As he left the stage, Sarah's mother gave him a sound box on the ears.

The result was that the lovers both left the company, Siddons to continue his wandering career, Sarah to enter the family of Mr. Greathead of Guy's Cliff, Warwickshire. She hired herself as a lady's maid at £10 a year; she was not exactly in a servile position for her chief duties were to read to the elder Mr. Greathead. Despite her place, Sarah had not at all relinquished the idea of going on stage. Likewise, Siddons had not given up his hope of marrying her, and her father at length agreed. They were wed on November 6, 1773. They both rejoined her father's company for a short while, until they left for Chamberlain and Crump's company in Cheltenham. There Mrs. Siddons at once established a reputation.

Lord Ailesbury mentioned her to Garrick, who sent an emissary to see her, and on receiving a highly favorable report Garrick engaged her at £5 a week for the Drury Lane company. Her first appearance was as Portia opposite King. In the following months she appeared several times in unimportant pieces, once with Garrick, but the impression she made was slight. Her second appearance with Garrick was as Lady Anne to his Richard, which she repeated twice, the second time in the presence of the royal family. Five nights later Garrick made his final appearance as an actor, and her engagement at Drury Lane was over. Garrick had been very kind to her, but the actresses accustomed to playing the leading roles were not eager to share them with anyone else. Sheridan gave as an excuse for not engaging her that Garrick had not thought much of her ability—which was probably a lie. Mrs. Abington, by exception, defended her, to no avail, and said to the others, "You are all fools!"

Back she went to the provinces, where she grew in power and assurance at York and Bath, winning increasing praise and self-assurance. Meanwhile she had given birth, by 1782, to four children. When she left the Bath stage she gave her children as her chief reason for trying London again. Henderson, who had seen her act, said, "She is an actress who has never had an equal, and will never have a superior." Instead of giving him the credit, she attributed "the enthusiastic accounts" of her which made her now welcome in the metropolis to the Duchess of Devonshire.

On October 10, 1782, she had her first real opportunity to show London how great an actress she now was. It was at Drury Lane in a play then much admired, Southerne's *Isabella.* Her father, now sixty-one, came to town to be with her, and he accompanied her to the theater, while she held her son, Henry, by his hand. She was twenty-eight, but, remembering her earlier

London failures, very timorous. It proved to be a night comparable to Garrick's taking London by storm with his Richard III. "I never heard," she reported, "such peals of applause in all my life." During the next three weeks she appeared in the same role eight times, and after that, sixteen times until the season was over in June 1783. The *Morning Chronicle* spoke of her natural simplicity in depicting sorrow, and the *Morning Post* lauded the "minute beauties" of her interpretation and concluded: she is "beyond all comparison . . . the first tragic actress now on the English stage." Even Sheridan sat in his box with his eyes overflowing.

There is an interesting piece of irony connected with this play. The hero's name was Biron. It soon became downright fashionable for the ladies in the audience to become so much affected by the play that they were often "led out in a fit of hysterics." It was still an epoch in which excessive "sensibility" was distinctly à la mode. When Mrs. Siddons played Isabella in Edinburgh, Sir Walter Scott remembers seeing Catherine Gordon of Gight, a young Scottish heiress, plain and gauche, making something of a spectacle of herself even among all those swooning ladies by falling "into violent fits" and being "carried out of the theatre, screaming loudly" Isabella's words, "O my Biron! My Biron!" At the time she had no knowledge that the dangerous Captain Jack Byron, a rogue if ever there was one, existed. The next year, 1784, she was sent to Bath to escape the Scottish adventurers who were after her money. In the same season Captain Byron came to Bath to find an heiress, managed to meet the same Miss Gordon, married the unattractive girl for her money, and fathered her son, the famous poet-to-be. Poor Mrs. Byron was to have many an occasion to cry, "O my Byron! My Byron!" both concerning her husband, who quickly spent all her money, and her intractable son.

When Mrs. Siddons first performed Isabella in Dublin, a newspaper of that city reported:

Last night Mrs. Siddons, about whom all the world has been talking, exposed her beautiful, adamantine, soft and lovely person for the first time in the Theatre Royal, Smock-Alley, in the bewitching, melting, and all tearful character of Isabella. From the repeated panegyrics in the London newspapers, we were taught to expect the sight of an heavenly angel: but how were we supernaturally surprised into the most awful joy, on beholding an earthly goddess! The house was crowded with hundreds more than it could hold, with thousands of admiring spectators, that went away without a sight. This extraordinary phenomenon of tragi-excellence, this star of Melpomene, this comet of the stage, this sun of the firmament of the muses, this moon of blank verse, this Queen and Princess of tears, this Donellan of the poisoned bowl, this Empress Rusty-fusty of the pistol and dagger, this chaos of Shakespeare, this world of weeping clouds, this Juno of commanding aspect, this Terpsichore of the curtains and scenes, this Proserine of fire and earthquake, this Katterfelto of wonders, exceeded expectations, went beyond belief, and soared above all the powers of description. She was nature itself. In short, she was the most exquisite work of wit.* Where expectations were raised so high, it was thought she would be injured by her appearance; but it was the audience who were injured. Several fainted even before the curtain drew up;† but when she came to the scene of parting with her wedding ring, ah, what a sight was there! The very fiddlers in the orchestra blubbered like hungry children for their bread and butter! and when the bell rang for music between the acts, the tears ran in such plentiful streams from the bassoon player's eyes, that they choked the finger-stops, and making a spout of the instrument, poured such a torrent on the first fiddler's book, that, not seeing the overture was in two sharps, the leader of the band actually played it in one flat: but the sobs and sighs of the groaning audience and the noise of corks from the smelling bottles, prevented the mistakes between the flats and sharps being perceived. One hundred and nine ladies fainted, forty-six went into fits, ninety-five had strong hysterics. The world will credit the assertion, when they are told, fourteen children, five old women, a one-handed sailor, and six common-councilmen, were actually drowned in the inundation of tears that flowed from the boxes and galleries, to increase the briny flood in the pit. The water was three feet deep; and the people that were obliged to stand upon the benches, were, in that situation, up to their ankles in tears.

King George had little taste for tragedy; what he wanted to do in the theater was laugh. But the royal family came to see her in 1783 five times during the month of January. In consequence she was invited to Buckingham House. Sarah remembers: "The King was often moved to tears which he so vainly endeavoured to conceal . . . and Her Majesty the Queen at one time told me . . . that her only refuge from me was actually turning her back upon the stage." At Buckingham House she was several times summoned to read to the king and queen. The king "graciously commended the propriety of my action, particularly my total repose in certain situations. 'This is,' he said, 'a quality in which Garrick faild [sic]. He could never stand still; he was a great fidget.' . . . Her Majesty was extremely gracious and more than once during the reading desired me to take some refreshment in the next room. I declined the honour, however, altho' I had stood reading till I was ready to drop." Her Majesty expressed astonishment to find Mrs. Siddons so collected in a new position, as though she had been used to a royal court. "At any rate, I had frequently personated Queens."

Of course, this sudden burst of fame brought her enemies. There was one newspaper which slandered her daily. Dublin was now anxious to see her, and she crossed the Irish Sea during a storm, landing in Dublin in the middle of a wet night. She played with success both there and at Cork. She returned to England richer by £1,000, but with an antipathy for the Irish people.

At last, on her return to Drury Lane during the 1783/84 season, she had

*In eighteenth-century usage "wit" meant intellect.
†The power of fashion!

two opportunities to play Shakespeare, once opposite Smith in *Measure for Measure* and once as Constance opposite her brother, John Philip Kemble, in *King John*. Leigh Hunt said of her in the latter role, that in the "passage in which Constance wildly seats herself upon the ground, and exclaims, 'Here I and sorrow sit: let kings come bow to me,' [Mrs. Siddons performed with] the electrical effect, and . . . marvellously . . . reconciled the mad impulse of it, with habitual dignity." In her grief she paced up and down "as the eddying gust of her impatience drove her."

She became a great favorite of the ladies of fashion and was often "entrapped" into parties where there were hosts of well-bred people, some of whom even stood on chairs to stare at her. One invalided lady from Scotland, whose physician had forbidden her going to the theater, without introduction went to Mrs. Siddons's lodgings in Gower Street, calmly sat down, gazed at her for a while, and then without a word walked out.

Edinburgh was anxious to see her, but characteristically took its time to make up its mind about her abilities until the signal was given by Lady Randolph, who uttered aloud, "That's nae bad"—whereat the whole house shook with applause. People in that city during her first engagement of three weeks massed in crowds hours before the opening of the doors. As soon as the play was over, servants and porters took up their places for the next day, lying or standing, until the box office opened.

She was the constant talk of the town in London, and in 1782 one journalist gave a detailed description of her:

Her height was above the middle size, but not at all inclined to the *embonpoint*. There is . . . nothing sharp or angular in the frame, [her attitudes are] distinguished equally by energy and grace . . . Her face is peculiarly happy, the features being finely formed, though strong, and never for an instant seeming . . . coarse and unfeminine under whatever impulse. On the contrary, it is so thoroughly harmonized when quiescent, and so expressive when impassioned, that most people think her more beautiful than she is. So great, too, is the flexibility of her countenance, that the rapid transitions of passion are given with variety and effect that never tire . . . Her voice is naturally plaintive, and a tender melancholy in her level speaking denotes a being devoted to tragedy; yet this seemingly settled quality of voice becomes at will sonorous or piercing, overwhelms with rage, or, in its wild shriek, absolutely harrows up the soul. . . . Her lamentation has a dignity which belongs, I think, to no other woman; it claims your respect with your tears . . . She is sparing in her action, because English nature does not act much; . . . it arises immediately from the sentiments and feeling, and is not seen to prepare itself before it begins. . . . No laborious strainings at false climax . . . is ever heard; no artificial heaving of the breasts . . . none of those arts by which the actress is seen . . . can be found in Mrs. Siddons . . . She must be seen to be known. What is still more delightful, she is an original; she copies no one, living or dead, but acts from Nature and herself.

(Oh that word *Nature!* and how throughout the history of our language it has meant whatever the age chose to have it mean!)

As has been said, her brother, John Philip Kemble, made his London debut as Hamlet in 1783, the year after Sarah's great triumph. It was not until the two were in a position to act opposite each other that each came truly into his own. But that took some time, for the actors who then monopolized leading parts at Drury Lane were unwilling to surrender them.

It was during the 1783/84 season that Sir Joshua Reynolds painted her as The Tragic Muse. Sarah wrote, without much modesty: "About this time he produced what is reported to be the finest female Picture in the world, his glorious Tragedy. . . . When I attended him for the first sitting, after many more gratifying encomiums than I dare repeat, he took me by the hand, saying, 'Ascend your undisputed throne, and graciously bestow upon me some grand Idea of the Tragic Muse.' I walked up the steps & seated myself instantly in the attitude in which She now appears . . . When I attended on him for the last sitting, . . . he said, 'No, I will meerly [*sic*] add a little more colour to the face.' I then beged [*sic*] him . . . that he would not hieghten [*sic*] that tone of complexion so exquisitely accordant with the chilling and deeply concentered musing of Pale Melancholy." He agreed and later thanked her for the suggestion. He was flattered to note that many people seeing the finished work wept, and added, "You yourself, you know, can do no more than bring forth tears which, tho' you do not see, and sighs and sobs which, tho' you do not hear, you make us all so severely feel." Reynolds often came to see her at the theater and "always sat in the Orchestra, and in that place were to be seen (glorious constellation!) Burke, Gibbon, Sheridan . . . and, 'though last not least,' the illustrious Fox of whom it was frequently observed that 'Iron tears were drawn down Plutos [*sic*] cheek'; and these great men" would often visit her in her dressing room after the play "to make thier [*sic*] bows." The Prince of Wales was among them, and said, "Garrick's conduct toward me" was sheer jealousy [poor Garrick] and G. A. Steevens said about the great success of her first performance, "If Garrick could hear this, it would turn him upon his face in his Coffin." Yet Garrick had certainly done his best for her toward the end of his life.

Perhaps the oddest thing about Sarah Siddons's career is that once she had her first season in 1782 at Drury Lane, she immediately came into her own. She was great, and never became greater. Unlike her, her brother, John Philip Kemble, continued to develop through the years until he became by degrees a better and better actor.

Among the valuable changes Mrs. Siddons effected in the theater was a minor revolution in costume and makeup. Before she came to dominate the stage, actresses, whether appearing as Lady Macbeth or Cleopatra, were all dressed alike, in court skirts over huge hoops, and trains tucked up to the waist, their hair powdered and surmounted by a forest of feathers. They moreover used reddish-brown *marischal* powder, then in fashion, and worn with an "abundance of pomatum in the tubular curls of the ladies' headdresses."

Sarah Siddons changed all that. She abandoned the huge hoops under the dresses, thereby making movement easier, did away with the towering wigs, refused to use the brownish powder in her hair, and explained, "My locks were generally braided into a small compass so as to ascertain the size and shape of my head." Reynolds approved.

Before coming to London her favorite roles were Juliet, Cordelia, Portia, Imogen, and Rosalind. But in her maturity no character was more identified with her than that of Lady Macbeth, which she first presented at Drury Lane when she was thirty. (She had performed it in her earlier days at Bath, and had studied the part for years.) Once London had seen her do it, the public never seemed to have enough of it, and she continued to play it until her retirement. So much has she become legendary as the Lady Macbeth of all time that I used to think, before I knew the facts, that Reynolds had her Lady Macbeth in mind when he painted his famous portrait of her. But of course when he painted it he had not yet had the opportunity to see her in the role.

Leigh Hunt spoke of the grandeur of her gesture when we first encounter Lady Macbeth, reading the letter from her husband, at the conclusion of which she "used to elevate her stature, to smile with a lofty and uncontrollable expectation, and, with an arm raised beautifully in the air, *to draw the very circle she was speaking of*, in the *air about her head*, as if she ran her finger round the gold." This gesture very powerfully exhibited *her* ambition to be queen, which I thoroughly doubt Shakespeare had in mind at all. When Macbeth came in, she was plainly such a malevolent force that Kemble "hung his head as if he could not withstand her penetrating gaze or the language which interpreted aright the ambitious whisperings of his own heart."

Boaden said of the same scene, "She read the whole letter with the greatest skill and, after an instant of reflection, exclaimed—

> Glamis thou art, and Cawdor—and shalt be
> What thou art promised.

The amazing burst of energy upon the words 'shalt be' perfectly electrified the house."

At the beginning of the second scene of Act II, when Lady Macbeth is waiting to hear that Duncan has been killed, Mrs. Siddons bent down to the door, her ear against it. As Macbeth, having joined her, speaks of the muttering sleepers and the prayer in which he could not join, she listened, "her arms about her neck, shuddering." Once at Brighton during a performance in which her younger brother Charles was playing Macbeth, she had a narrow escape. "Macbeth threw the cup from him in the Banquet Scene with such violence, that it broke the arm of a glass chandelier which stood on the table, and sent it very near to Mrs. Siddons's face. She nonetheless remained unruffled as though "made of marble." The great actress herself has written her idea as to how Lady Macbeth ought to behave during that scene: she has "tottered to her throne"; she endeavors to entertain her startled guests "with frightful smiles, with over-acted attention, and with fitful graciousness; painfully, yet incessantly, labouring to divert their attention from her husband." Yet this interpretation strikes me at odd variance with one of Mrs. Siddons's strangest ideas. Having acted Lady Macbeth up to this point as a woman, to quote her, "in whose bosom the passion of ambition has almost obliterated all the characteristics of human nature," "a perfectly savage creature," the "evil genius" of her husband, and a wife who wields "unbounded influence" over him, it is perhaps not too astonishing that she should say: "I have imagined that the last appearance of Banquo's ghost became no less visible to her eyes than it became to those of her husband. Yes, the spirit of the noble Banquo has smilingly filled up, even to overflowing, and now commends to her own lips the ingredients of her poisoned chalice." It was doubtless unfair enough that Shakespeare had allotted the magnificent metaphor to Kemble's role instead of to hers; but fond as she was of Philip, she was not going to allow him to be the only one to see the ghost!

The sleepwalking scene is, of course, the part of the play that most actresses, with good reason, set great store by. She introduced an innovation which caused much comment. Professor Bell noted that on her entrance in this scene Mrs. Siddons "advances rapidly to the table, sets down the light, and rubs her hand, making the action of lifting up water in one hand at intervals." He also recorded that while she spoke the words "One, two," she was "listening eagerly." It was her setting down of the candle which particularly struck the critics. That she should do so clearly shows her intention "that her hands may be more at liberty to imitate the process of ablution," said *The European Magazine*, yet the next month the same periodical called it "an error, which would be inexcusable in the youngest performer." Even before the performance itself, Sheridan came into her dressing room to argue against what she proposed doing, but she pointed out to him, as she says, "the impracticability of washing out that *'damned spot'* with the vehemence that was certainly implied by both her own words, and by those of her gentlewoman," if still retained the candle. She convinced him, and later he congratulated her for being obstinate. Even her walk was different from that of her predecessors, who, writes Boaden, "rather *glided* than walked . . . Their figure, too, was kept perpendicularly *erect*, and the eye, though open, studiously avoided motion." But Mrs. Siddons poured imaginary water from an imaginary ewer over her hands, "bent her body to listen to the sounds presented by her fancy, and hurried to resume the taper where she had left it, that she might with all speed drag her pallid husband to their chamber." Leigh Hunt was less satisfied: "Mrs. Siddons's refinement was not on a par with her loftiness. . . . When she could not get the blood off, she made a 'face' " and passed her hands before her nose, "as if she perceived *a foul smell.*" Hunt thought she would have done better to recognize *"the stain on her soul."*

As she left the stage she seemed "to *feel* for the light; that is, while stalking backwards, and keeping her eyes glaring on the house."

Once, during a short season at Leeds, a ridiculous moment occurred which no one could have foreseen. It was an exceedingly hot night and Sarah was plagued by thirst. Between scenes, therefore, her dresser sent a boy in haste to "fetch a pint of beer for Mrs. Siddons," and urged him to be quick. The play proceeded and the boy returned with a frothing pitcher, looking about for the dresser who had sent him. Not being able to find her, he asked a scene-shifter, "Where is Mrs. Siddons?" The scene-shifter pointed her out to the boy; she was at the time on stage doing the sleepwalking scene. "To the surprise and horror of all the performers," Charles Mathews remembers, "the boy promptly walked on the stage close up to Mrs. Siddons, and with a total unconsciousness of the impropriety he was committing, presented the porter! Her distress may be imagined; she waved the boy away in her grand manner several times, without effect; at last the people behind the scenes, by dint of beckoning, stamping, and calling in half-audible whispers, succeeded in getting him off with the beer, part of which in his exit he spilled on the stage; while the audience were in an uproar of laughter." After the performance was over, Winter said to the boy, "Ma bairn, let me gi' thee a piece of advice: Niver go upon t' stage, Moses, ma lad, without thy name's i' t' bill."

Mrs. Siddons was, for the public, Lady Macbeth, but it is strange indeed that after her retirement she should have informed the world that all during her long career she had played her famous role with an interpretation utterly different from her own convictions as to what Shakespeare had intended. Far from being the quintessence of evil, Lady Macbeth is, she said "fair, feminine, nay, perhaps fragile." She possesses "every fascination of mind and person," and yet is herself "of a temper . . . so irresolute and fluctuating," that the actress should stress her remorse; her love is so protective of Macbeth that she should show "tenderness and sympathy," and "she devotes herself entirely to the effort of supporting him." Her mind is "naturally higher toned" than his. This is certainly not the "evil genius" which she had been playing for nearly three decades. It may be that the popular notion of Lady Macbeth as a sort of tigress is owed to the tradition set by Mrs. Siddons's performances, but neither that nor her later comments on the lady's character seem to me to be what Shakespeare had in mind. Despite her florid style, Mrs. Jameson's ideas are much closer to the facts.

One naturally wonders about her relations with William Siddons, who was so romantic a wooer, and who fathered her considerable brood of children, though they never interfered with her career. As an actor he made a mediocre impression at Bath, but later devoted himself to doing an inferior job as manager of his wife's accounts. He won the reputation of being a hard bargainer—the laws of the time declared that her earnings belonged to him. He was eleven years older than she, and his position was not an easy one. As Roger Manvell well states it, from a supporting actor who might have got along well enough in the provinces, "he had declined into the unexciting and unwanted husband of a woman of genius." He lacked the imagination to maintain the increasingly important figure she was making in the best social circles, or even the skill to manage her finances well. He seems to have been devoted enough to her and their children, but as he grew older his temper does not appear to have improved. He allotted his wife an allowance out of the money she had earned and was earning. It is a relief to think how much the world has improved since then—though not yet in all parts of the globe. In 1804 the two finally parted; by this time he was suffering from an advanced case of lumbago and could not walk without canes; he spent most of the rest of his days at Bath. From late December 1807 to February 1808, Sarah came to visit him there. He died the following month, on March 11.

She, of course, played many Shakespearean parts during her lifetime. Of her Volumnia, the actor Young said that when her son returned to Rome, "instead of dropping each foot . . . in cadence subservient to the orchestra —with head erect, and hands clasped firmly to her bosom, as if to repress by manual force its triumphant swellings, she towered above all around her, and almost reeled across the stage; her very soul . . . dilating and rioting in its exultation, until her action lost all grace, and . . . became so true to nature, so picturesque and so descriptive, that pit and gallery sprang to their feet, electrified by the transcendent execution of the conception." Her Desdemona was widely admired, though one would have thought that it was not within her range. Campbell was absolutely astounded by the simple, "I had almost said playful persuasiveness, with which she won over the Moor to Cassio's interest. In that scene, it is my belief that no other actress ever softened and sweetened tragedy so originally." Her Hermione in Pauline's chapel, says Boaden, was like one of the noblest of Greek statues, "like one of the Muses in profile." While standing for the statue, one night, her drapery flew over the lamp which was behind the pedestal, and caught fire; one of the scene-men crept on his knees and put it out without her knowing it. Since she was clothed entirely in muslin she could have been burned to death.

As is so often the case with members of her profession, she, who was incomparable in tragedy, fancied herself equally expert in comedy, but she was unsuited to the comic spirit. In *As You Like It* her Rosalind was agreeable only in the passages containing sentiment, but she was utterly devoid of the ability to project the humor which is part of all good comedies. Someone said her Rosalind was too much like Lady Macbeth! And her dress in that role was perhaps the strangest ever seen on a stage. She wore "hussar boots with a gardener's apron and a petticoat behind." (She must have looked something like a twentieth-century hippy.) Orlando's failure to recognize her as a woman was totally incomprehensible.

But in tragedy, she was infallible. She was great, said Macready, when rising to scenes of violent agitation which seemed "beyond her power to endure"; she could express emotion in a sort of pantomime in which her whole body participated. She admits being unlike her brother John, who "in his most impetuous bursts is always careful to avoid any discomposure of his dress." She paid no heed to such matters.

She tells us that, before her triumph in London, at the age of twenty, she was preparing a performance of Lady Macbeth, and stayed up long after everyone else in the house went to bed. The thoughts of Duncan's murder brought on a "paroxysm of terror," and when she finally ran to her room, the very rustling of her dress seemed "like the movement of a spectre pursuing me." As a girl she believed "that little more was necessary than to get the words into my head" and that once on stage one would know what to do; she gave no thought to detail or character development. But as she matured, she learned not to depend on the inspiration of the moment, and there was no noticeable difference between the various performances of the same play, once she had mastered her role. (I am of the opinion that this ought to be true of all great interpreters. It was certainly true of Toscanini as conductor of an orchestra.) Like her brother John, she first carefully analyzed the character; both of them then built up consistency of characterization. But there was an important difference here. His was a consistency imposed by him on the role, while hers emanated from what the dramatist had written, and therefore allowed a greater variety.

Though Garrick was quick and John Philip Kemble slow, both indulged in carefully planned "tricks" and "starts" during the action. Not so Mrs. Siddons. She never permitted her audience to remember that she was acting. Boaden observed that she never allowed her eye to "wander from the business of the scene—no recognizance of the most noble of her friends," which was not true of John. "On stage I never felt the least indication that she had a private existence." She was equally superb in the art of listening to the other characters of the play; "she heard a narrative at all times better than it was ever told."

Grandeur was her "natural" element, or, as Campbell the poet phrased it, "the sublime and energetic." She made you feel "as if you were witnessing some god-like soul from the heroic world pouring forth its sensibility," though at the same time it was "a true and perfect picture of a human being in pathetic or terrific situations." What he especially admired was the absolute control she maintained over everything she did, the way she sustained a role, "her self-devotion to it."

When her brother John moved to Covent Garden during the 1801/02 season, she, of course, went with him, chiefly because Sheridan had become totally impossible to work with. On September 20, 1808, at four o'clock in the morning, Covent Garden, the edifice erected in 1733 and greatly altered in 1792, was in flames. In three hours the entire auditorium, the scenery, costumes, musical and drama libraries were but ashes. Not exempt from destruction were the organ which Handel had left to the house, and unpublished manuscripts of important composers. A number of firemen and some of the on-lookers were killed by falling rafters or scalded to death by the steam. The Kembles lost everything that had been left in the theater as well as their investment. But they bravely presented a season at the Opera House, where Sarah did her Lady Macbeth many times again.

A new theater was built on the site of the ruins in an amazingly short time, and opened for the 1809/10 season with *Macbeth*. The prices of admission were raised and that resulted in constant rioting. On opening night the house was full, but three times as many as were admitted remained in the lobbies and entrances, and when Kemble appeared there was so much hissing and hooting that it was impossible to hear him. As the play proceeded, it was a sort of pantomime, for not a word was to be heard. He was greatly unnerved, but his sister retained her composure through the dumbshow. The experience must have decided her to retire in 1812. Her last performance was on June 22, 1812, as Lady Macbeth.

Like far too many singers and actors, Mrs. Siddons retired none too soon (she had become stout and had lost a great deal of her innate dignity on stage), but was unfortunately urged to come out of retirement. Many influential people organized attempts in 1813 and 1815 (the latter headed by Lord Byron), both of which she rejected. However, she finally consented to appear on June 7, 1815, as Lady Macbeth, and gave several other performances, including one for her brother John's farewell performances in 1817. Hazlitt, who had idolized her, saw her then as well as the years before. What he wrote on June 16, 1816, must have been written with anguish:

> Players should be immortal, if their own wishes or ours could make them so . . . They not only die like other people, but like other people they cease to be young, and are no longer themselves, even while living. Their health, strength, beauty, voice, fails them. . . . Mrs. Siddons retired once from the stage; why should she return to it again? She cannot retire from it twice with dignity. . . . Any loss of reputation to her, is a loss to the world. Has she not had enough of glory? The homage she has received is greater than that which is paid to queens. . . . She was regarded less with admiration than with wonder, as if a being of a superior order had dropped from another sphere to awe the world with the majesty of her appearance. . . . To have seen Mrs. Siddons was an event in every one's life; and does she think we have forgotten her? Or would she remind us of herself by shewing us what *she was not*? Or is she to continue on the stage to the very last, till all her grace and all her grandeur are gone? . . . If it was reasonable that Mrs. Siddons should retire from the stage three years ago, certainly these reasons have not diminished since. . . . Mrs. Siddons always spoke as slow as she ought: she now speaks slower than she did. . . . The machinery of the voice seems too ponderous for the power that wields it. There is too long a pause between each sentence, and between each word in each sentence.

Her brief reemergences from retirement were like the deliberate vandalizing of a great masterpiece.

On May 6, 1828, Tom Moore dined at Samuel Rogers's and among the party was Sarah Siddons, with whom he had a great deal of conversation, "and was, for the first time in my life, interested by her off stage." She spoke of the loss of friends, of whom she had lost twenty-six during the last six years; he reflected that "it is something to *have had* so many." She gave a number of reasons for her regret at leaving the stage; her chief being that "she always found in it a vent for her private sorrows, which enabled her to bear them better; and often she got credit for the truth and feeling of her acting when she was doing nothing more than relieving her own heart of its grief . . . Rogers has told me that she often complained to him of the great *ennui* she has felt since she quitted her profession, particularly of an evening. When sitting drearily alone, she has remembered what a moment of excitement it used to be when she was in the midst of preparing her *toilette* to meet a crowded house and exercise all the sovereignty of her talents over them."

Other Kembles and Mrs. Jordan

Stephen Kemble (1758–1822), a younger brother of Sarah and John Philip, was very nearly born on the stage, for he came into this world right after his mother had played Anne Boleyn. His debut in Othello at Covent Garden, which was moderately successful, was a trifle earlier than John Philip's first appearance at Drury Lane. Stephen was a man of enormous girth, and the current joke was that Covent Garden had the *big* Kemble while Drury Lane had the *great* Kemble.

Everyone thought it remarkable that he was able to perform Falstaff without any stuffing because he was so fat, to which Hazlitt remarked, "We see no more reason why Mr. Stephen Kemble should play Falstaff, than why Louis XVIII is qualified to fill a throne, because he is fat, and belongs to a particular family"; Falstaff was no mere paunch; his mind was the man and he "had guts in his brains." Nevertheless, one innovation of Stephen Kemble's became traditional, and that was the notion of discovering Falstaff in his first scene on a couch, as if awaking, which makes good sense of his opening line, addressed to the prince: "Now Hal! what time of day is it, lad?" He has also been credited with an even more important improvement: he is believed to have suggested that it would be much better for ghosts simply to walk off stage than to have them rise and lower themselves through squeaking trap doors.

John Taylor was very fond of him, and married one of his wife's sisters. Stephen had many a story to relate about his experiences as a strolling player. In a Yorkshire town their theater was a hideous sort of barn, and the attendance so poor that the company had not enough money to pay even for their lodgings, not to mention the purchase of food. He was occupying a wretched garret, where the landlady daily demanded why he did not pay her. In order to conceal the fact that he could not buy any food, he remained in bed two days, pretending to be sick. On the third day he ventured out, and three miles off discovered a field of turnips. He treated himself to a cold, hard, but welcome enough meal. The next day, on his way to have the same dinner, he met Davenport, member of the same company of actors, who explained that he was famished and begged for help. Stephen Kemble, a man of unfailing good humor, told him that luckily he was enroute to dine with a friend and invited Davenport to accompany him. Poor Davenport protested that his shoes were in so deplorable a condition that he was ashamed to be seen in them. Kemble assured him that the friend was not one to stand on ceremony, and that the condition of the shoes did not matter. All the way, Davenport, nearly exhausted from long hunger, heavily complained, while Kemble tried to lift his spirits with the prospects of a rewarding feast. When they at last reached the turnip field and Kemble said they had arrived, Davenport looked around for the house that was not there, and reproached Kemble for the deception. Kemble triumphantly indicated the field of turnips and said, "This is my friend. It afforded me dinner yesterday, and I suppose I shall be obliged to trespass on the same kindness till the end of the week." Davenport had enough sense to be thankful for what lay before them.

One of his whimsical stories was of a time when he was manager of a theater at Portsmouth, which opened only twice or thrice a week. A sailor approached him on one of the other nights and asked him to open the house. The manager said that since the town did not expect a performance, he could not afford to oblige. The sailor protested that he was leaving the country the next day, and asked what it would cost to open the house. "Five guineas," answered Kemble. The sailor agreed on condition that he be the sole audience, and asked for *Richard III*. The house was lighted, the company collected, and the sailor took up a position in the front row of the pit. Kemble played Richard, and the sailor was very attentive, applauding and laughing at the right places—but turning around every once in a while to be sure that no one else was in the audience. When the piece was over, he declared himself thoroughly satisfied, and thanked Kemble profusely.

A story he told indicates only too well the inferior position actors held in the provinces. Once in some town in Ireland he was walking with the mayor who *"honored"* him by taking his arm. One of the lesser actors bowed to the mayor "with the most obsequious humility," but the politico paid no attention. The actor then ran ahead of them, and at another convenient spot "repeated his humiliating obeisance." Still, however, the mayor gave him no heed. Again the man ran to a place where he felt sure he would be noticed, but was again unsuccessful. Determined to exhibit his respect for the official, he tried another time at another post, showing, if that were possible, "a more obsequious courtesy." At length the mayor wearied of the game. He turned his head to gaze at the undaunted actor, though without even a nod of recognition, and muttered, "I see you, I see you," which the poor actor accepted as an act of gracious condescension.

Charles Kemble (1775–1854) was the eleventh child of the parents of John Philip, Sarah, and Stephen Kemble. He first entered the civil service, but then left it for the stage. After his debut at Sheffield at the age of seventeen as Orlando, he went to London and did Malcolm to his brother's and sister's Macbeth and Lady Macbeth at the new Drury Lane. At the beginning he was very awkward, and he did not know how to project his voice, which was found too weak. But he learned, and later became a celebrated Romeo, a fine Mercutio, Orlando, Laertes, Benedick, Cassio, Macduff, Falconbridge, Marc Antony (to his brother's Brutus), and managed to make himself a valuable part of the company. Of course, when his brother Philip and his sister Sarah moved over to Covent Garden, he went with them. Hazlitt admired his Edgar, which he said was perfect, "and his fine face and figure admirably relieved the horror of the situation." He was a poetical actor, though not particularly an emotional one. He therefore largely avoided tragic roles. He visited the United States in 1806, and was a great success there.

His brother John Philip, though often inconsistent in his costuming, had produced some of the history plays with much emphasis upon "ancient habits and manners." Charles carried this tendency much further, and began a tradition which, depending on your point of view, for good or bad, was responsible for the considerable attention given to historical accuracy in later productions of Shakespeare. The crucial production was his *King John* in 1823, which boasted costumes designed by Planché and which were historically correct. The event took place at Covent Garden. This was probably the first time that any Shakespearean play was given "with the utmost possible accuracy of costume, every detail being worked out with patient and loving care." The playbill itself read: "KING JOHN. With an attention to Costume Never equalled on the English Stage. Every Character will appear in the precise HABIT OF THE PERIOD. The whole of the Dresses and Decorations being executed from indisputable Authorities, such as Monumental Effigies, Seals, Illuminated MSS., & c." There followed on the bill a circumstantial account of who and what these authorities were, such as "King John's Effigy in Worcester Cathedral, and his great Seals. Queen Elinor's Effigy in the Abbey of Fonteveraud. Effigy of the Earl of Salisbury in Salisbury Cathedral, Effigy of the Earl of Pembroke in the Temple Church, London, King John's Silver Cup" at Norfolk, "Illuminated MSS in the British Museum, Bodleian and Bennet College Libraries" and so on.

It is an open question whether the insistence on historical accuracy in costume and settings, which became more and more of an obsession in Shakespearean productions right through the nineteenth century, was a blessing or a curse. As for the costuming, even in the twentieth century I have seen many a production of Shakespeare in which the costuming was so beautiful (even when the play was deliberately set in a period either non-Shakespearean or not of the epoch of the play itself) that the play was totally smothered by aesthetic charm, and as for the settings being historically accurate (luckily, this is a tendency which we have gradually abolished in our time), the cumbersomeness and imposing quality of the scenery can very easily dwarf the play. And the play *is* the thing we go to see and hear.

Charles Kemble gradually became a most graceful and refined actor, and that field of comedy which neither John Philip nor Sarah Siddons was truly at home in he made as much his own as secondary parts like Laertes. Although he tried more passionate roles, his voice was ill-suited for them. He was a wonderful Mercutio and a very bad Falstaff. His wife, the former Miss De Camp, retired from the stage, having played ably with her husband, to return ten years later for one performance, as Lady Capulet to the Juliet of her daughter at her debut on October 5, 1829. Their daughter, Fanny, by the way, nearly ruined her father's carefully planned and executed settings suggestive of medieval Verona; despite his pleas and those of Mrs. Jameson, Juliet refused to renounce the traditional white satin ball gown. She was firm on the recommendation of her mother who had assured her, she said, that one ought to use on the stage nothing that was in itself "ungraceful or even curiously antiquated or singular, however correct it might be."

Charles Kemble introduced an interesting innovation as Benedick, in whose soliloquy, "This can be no trick," it had been traditional for Benedick to walk about the stage much agitated, and at "She's a fair lady!" to take off his hat, pie it, and adjust his dress. Hunt speaks of what Charles did at this point. "His utterance of his grand final reason for marrying—'The world must be peopled'—with his hands linked behind him, a general elevation of his aspect, and a sort of look at the whole universe before him, as if he saw all the future generations that might depend upon his verdict, was a bit of the right masterly gusto."

As he got older he began to take on heavier roles—Othello, Shylock, Macbeth, and Hamlet. He came to New York with his daughter Fanny in 1832, playing a crazed Prince of Denmark, and when he returned to England he left Fanny in the United States.

He became by degrees so deaf that he could not hear the most powerful peals of thunder, and he retired to devote himself to public readings.

Frances Anne Kemble (1809–1893), daughter of Charles Kemble, had a career belonging to the next century, but may be spoken of further, since we have already mentioned her, in this place. She had no wish to become an actress, but agreed to do so to help her father, who was then managing Covent Garden, and whose lavish expenditures were bringing him close to bankruptcy. Her Juliet (despite the dress) was an instantaneous success, and for three years she was able to fill the theater with that role, as well as Portia, Beatrice, and a good many non-Shakespearean parts. She appeared many times with her aunt, Sarah Siddons, and, unlike the other Kembles, was equally at home in comedy or tragedy, though not actually a great performer. She seems to have excelled as Desdemona, making of her an important figure by emphasizing (quite accurately) both her femininity and strength of character—the latter trait, though clear in the play was still overlooked by most women who performed the role. Macready was not pleased with her in that interpretation. Fanny felt that the Desdemonas she had seen seemed too ready victims, whereas on the Italian stage they ran for their lives.

She gave up acting in 1834 to marry Pierce Butler of Philadelphia, but her marriage was unhappy, and she divorced him in 1845. In 1857 she began to give readings in England and the United States, and continued doing so until 1868. She finally settled in London with her daughter, and died there.

When young she was extremely beautiful, with a graceful figure and a wistful expression, which she retained all her life. At her first Juliet, Leigh Hunt was charmed in her early scenes because he found her very "natural," but as she began to express feelings, he found her completely artificial. She expressed no real passion; her emotion was too loud, her gravity excessive. In fact, he declared, he had never seen a good Juliet on the English stage. Perhaps, he added, that was because the English are not by nature passionate. When he saw Fanny's second performance his opinion remained unchanged. He thought her Beatrice very clever, but lacking that necessary "giddy grace," and on the whole thought her inferior to Mrs. Jordan.

Dorothy Jordan (1761–1816) was the darling of her age. Her popularity resembles that enjoyed by Mae West for at least two decades. It is not that their styles are similar—we are dealing with the era of John Philip Kemble and Sarah Siddons!—but that the public adored each for always being, as Hazlitt says, no matter what the role, "herself." Dorothy Jordan's humor, he says, was prodigal, and she played the same person in all her characters. (In a tragic actress that might easily be a damnable trait, but not at all so in a comedienne.) She was, he added, always inimitable. "Her face, her tones, her manner were irresistible. Her smile had the effect of sunshine, and her laugh did one good to hear. Her voice was eloquence itself. . . . She was all gaiety, openness, and good-nature. She rioted in her fine animal spirits, and gave more pleasure than any other actress, because she had the greatest spirit of enjoyment in herself."

Clearly she won the hearts of her critics. Hazlitt calls her elsewhere "the child of nature, whose voice was a cordial to the heart, because it came from it, rich, full, like the luscious juice of the ripe grape; to hear whose laugh was to drink nectar; whose smile 'made a sunshine' . . . who talked far above singing, and whose singing was like the twang of Cupid's bow. Her person was large, soft, generous like her soul." Leigh Hunt said that her voice was "pregnant with melody"; Lamb that "her voice sank, with her steady melting eye, into the heart." Sir Joshua Reynolds thought her Viola was "tender and exquisite," and her Rosalind far superior to Mrs. Siddons's; William Robson agreed no one could possibly equal her in that part, and was convinced she would be incapable of playing any role which was ill-natured. Lamb found her equally marvelous as Ophelia.

When one considers her life, one may very well wonder how she managed her career so well, although the answer probably lies in her biographies: she was a woman of endless good humor, generosity, quickness of sympathy, and kindliness. She was the illegitimate daughter of an unimportant actress, Grace Phillips, and a Mr. Francis Bland. She first appeared in Dublin when she was sixteen, and was seduced by Daly, the manager of the Crow Street Theatre in Dublin. She played for him a number of sentimental heroines in wretched plays, and finally yielded to him when he threatened her with prison because she did not have the money he advanced to her to repay him. She secretly escaped from Dublin with her mother and sister and went to Leeds, where her mother changed Dora's name from Bland to Jordan. She met Tate Wilkinson, who befriended her, and with whose company she played for a short engagement in several towns. Daly found out her whereabouts, and while she was gaining popularity he appeared with a warrant for her arrest. A gallant Yorkshireman named Swan paid £250 for her debt, and Daly was compelled to leave.

While playing at York to enthusiastic audiences, she was heard of by the Drury Lane management in London. They sent various emissaries to watch her, including Gentleman Smith, who was so impressed that he urged London to engage her. She left the provinces but retained Swan as a disinterested friend for life. Mrs. Siddons, who also had seen her, thought it "unthinkable" that she appear before London audiences. Nonetheless, the same Sheridan hired Dora Jordan, and she was soon playing secondary roles with Mrs. Siddons.

It did not take her long to realize that she had a special gift for comedy. She made her London debut in 1785 and was soon appearing as Viola. Her ability to combine gaiety and pathos was irresistible.

Richard Ford, good-looking, well-mannered, of easy grace, was the son of a Bow Street magistrate. He easily persuaded her that he wished to marry her. Later he told her his family objected to the marriage. Nevertheless, she allowed herself to become involved with him and bore him four children. (She had already given birth to Daly's child.) For a while she took the name of Ford and was everywhere introduced as Ford's loving wife. Her popularity at Drury Lane was ever on the increase, as was her salary. For all Mrs. Siddons's disparagement and the jealousy of the veteran Kitty Clive, Dora's Rosalind was a tremendous hit. Covent Garden now began making inviting offers to her, so that Sheridan and Kemble had to meet the competition by giving her a salary equal to Mrs. Siddons's. Peter Pindar wrote this epigram:

> Had Shakespeare's self at Drury been
> While Jordan played each varied scene,
> He would have started from his seat,
> And cried, "That's ROSALIND complete!"

It is likely that all this unlimited enthusiasm was not actually justified. There was an element of coarseness in her acting which made it difficult to conceive of her capturing the poetical nature of Shakespeare's girls. Instead she carried the public through the sheer force of her personal magnetism. Though she probably missed the tenderness and delicacy of Viola and Rosalind, she established a style which was much copied.

In 1791 she left Richard Ford to become the mistress of the Duke of Clarence, later William IV, to whom she bore ten children, all of whom were given the name of Fitzclarence. There is an amusing story told of a retort she made to King George III. Hearing that his son was giving Dorothy Jordan an allowance of £1,000 a year, the king wrote her a letter reducing the amount to £500. On the bottom of a playbill she sent His Majesty was written: "No money returned after the raising of the curtain." Daly appeared again from Dublin to see the child he had fathered, but had to leave frustrated. Ford, to whom she had continually appealed to marry her, was furiously jealous when the Duke of Clarence began to court her, but with such competition there was nothing he could do but disappear from the picture.

John Philip Kemble, after playing opposite Dora, exclaimed: "I could have taken her in my arms and cherished her, though it was in the open street, without blushing." But naturally, as the birth of Fitzclarences continued, she was compelled to absent herself more and more from the stage, too frequently having to cancel appearances at the last minute. She was slowly losing her hold on the public, and was growing fat. When Drury Lane burned to the ground she lost as much as the Kembles, and all her costumes and jewels were gone. "This ends it all," she said, "I shall act no more." She did make a few appearances outside London, but was tired of the profession. The more vulgar newsprints were filled with caricatures of her and with calumnious allegations against her; every imaginable vicious lie was broadcast. Eventually the Duke of Clarence broke the relationship between them.

She lived five more years, and for want of funds left for France. Her children, all of whom married into the nobility, seem to have done nothing for her. She died in France on July 3, 1816, at the age of fifty. But rumors continued to haunt her memory, and word had it that she was subsequently seen in England. It is ironic that thirty years after her death the *Manchester Courier* should have said that her laugh "made the listener doubt if such a woman could ever be unhappy."

But even when she grew fat, Hazlitt's enthusiasm was unabated. Her best quality, he said, was her heartiness; she still made a wonderful Rosalind though she was "very fat" and looked forty, for she still contrived to communicate a sense of frank and lively youth, and "her laughter is the happiest and most natural on the stage."

She was once sitting with John Taylor in the greenroom before going on stage in *As You Like It*. He happened to express his surprise at the great success an actor had recently achieved on the stage, and confessed being astounded at the lack of public taste in this instance. "Oh, Mr. Taylor," she exclaimed, "don't mention public taste, for if the public had any taste, how could they bear me in the part which I play to-night, and which is far above my habits and pretensions?"

A signal example of her kindliness was her behavior toward William Henry Ireland during the negotiations and performance of his forged *Vortigern*. Whether she too had so little judgment as to have been taken in by his miserable piece of pseudo-Shakespeare, or simply felt sorry for the boy, it is impossible to guess; but she certainly proved herself a friend to him at a time when she was at the height of her popularity, and the hostile forces were gathering against him.

On November 18, 1795, the very day after Kemble snubbed the Irelands at the theater, she arranged a meeting between them and the Duke of Clarence. They brought with them the manuscript of *Vortigern*; Clarence, as a prince of the realm, probably felt that he was an authority on all matters. He pronounced the play to be Shakespeare's very own, and counseled Ireland not to surrender a copy of it to Drury Lane until work had begun on the promised scenery. He also added some words of disparagement of Sheridan and Kemble, and then and there subscribed to seven copies of the forthcoming publication of young William Henry's forgeries. When the book appeared, Samuel Ireland was summoned by the Prince of Wales for a visit to Carlton House. The prince listened while Samuel Ireland read several of the documents, declared that the external appearance of the papers assuredly proved their validity, but asked for more time to come to a final decision.

When after every sort of delay *Vortigern* was presented on April 2, 1796, Mrs. Jordan not only generously played the leading female role (such as it was) but the Duke of Clarence was in the royal box to lend his moral support, and William Henry reports that he was so nervous "I did not enter the theatre till a very short period previous to the rising of the curtain . . . I soon retired from observation behind the scenes; where I continued the greater part of the time . . . engaged in conversation with Mrs. Jordan." That generous woman was doing all she could to tranquilize and reassure the boy.

Dorothy Jordan's daughter, Mrs. Alsop, tried the stage too, and performed Rosalind at Covent Garden in October 1815. Hazlitt said that she was "a very nice little woman," who possessed none of her mother's genius.

🌿 12 🌿

Master Betty and Other Phenomena

There is nothing new about the public's losing its head over infant prodigies. Shakespeare himself had reason to complain of the serious competition from which his company suffered because of the popularity of the boy actors referred to in *Hamlet:* "An aery of children, little eyases, that cry out on the top of the question."* In my own lifetime I have heard infant pianists, infant violinists, and infant orchestra conductors whom the critics praised as simply incredibly gifted, and who before very long were never heard of again. There have been in our century, of course, a very few notable exceptions, such as Josef Hoffman and Heifetz, but such are rare.

Among actors the signal example of the child prodigy is William Henry West Betty (1791–1874). He was a Shropshire boy, born near Shrewsbury of Irish descent. In 1802 he was taken to Belfast and saw Mrs. Siddons. On the spot he developed a passion for the acting profession. His father was a man of means who had taught him fencing and elocution, but was astounded to hear his son declare: "I shall certainly die, if I do not become an actor!" Although only ten, he had a strong will and the next year made his first appearance on stage at Belfast in a leading role. The manager declared that this was an "infant Garrick." Although only eleven, he had shown neither nervousness nor confusion on the boards. The applause was deafening. After playing several other parts, he went up to Dublin with the commendation of the Belfast ladies that he was "a darling."

At Dublin, besides other roles, he did Romeo and Hamlet! He is said to have learned the lines of the Prince of Denmark in three days. Opinion was divided in Dublin, largely, as usual, because of political division, and one curious playbill, inviting the public to come and see him, read, "The public are respectfully informed that no person coming from the theatre will be stopped till after eleven o'clock." The idea here was that it was advisable to

*A nest of young hawks, unfledged hawks, who cry out the dialogue in a shrill voice.

get home early if you did not wish to be taken for a traitor; those were the days of the United Irishmen. But on the whole, the Dublin public worshipped the eleven-year-old.

So did Cork, Waterford, Londonderry, and other Irish cities. When he continued his triumphant progress to Scotland, a critic in Glasgow who was ill-natured enough to criticize Master Betty adversely "was compelled to leave the city." The worship was more lavish at Edinburgh. Home, the author of the popular *Douglas,* sat sobbing in his box and declared he had never before seen his hero acted exactly as he had conceived him. Duchesses and countesses caressed the child; some critics said that he excelled Kemble. Lords of the Court of Sessions presented him with books and gave him their blessings. Birmingham next exalted him, and at the end of a dozen performances a Bromwicham poet celebrated the "Infant Roscius" as having crushed the pride of all his predecessors, and was "Cooke, Kemble, Garrick, all in one!" Theatrical coaches to carry six within brought an eager public from the Doncaster Races to Sheffield, where crowds from London fought the local people for admission to the theater. One bard indited a long poem containing the lines:

> Would Sculpture form APOLLO BELVEDERE,
> She need not roam to France, the model's here!

The fever was caught by Liverpool, Chester, Manchester, and Stockport. Sometimes Master Betty played twice a day. His earnings were in excess of £500 a week. Royal dukes were flattered with his company; managers gave him silver cups, and John Philip Kemble wrote to Master Betty's father to express the pleasure he would experience if he could welcome Master Betty to the Covent Garden stage at £50 a night, benefit performances not included.

On December 1, 1804, the public was already crowding the Covent Garden Piazza at ten in the morning; by two o'clock every avenue was thick pressed with people. When the doors were opened, once again a number of people lost their lives rushing for places. "The pit was two-thirds filled from the boxes. Gentlemen who knew that there were no places untaken in the boxes, and who could not get into the pit avenues, paid for admission into the lower boxes, and poured from them into the pit, in twenties and thirties at a time. . . . Upwards of twenty men who had fainted, were dragged up into the boxes." So read the contemporary accounts.

The play was an inferior one. But when Master Betty appeared in the second act, he was greeted by an uproar of applause before which he remained self-possessed. He was thought "a perfect master." Said one journalist: "The oldest actor is not equal to him. . . . Nature has endowed him with genius which we shall vainly attempt to find in any of the actors of the present day."

Their Majesties were delighted with him and led the applause. They invited him to the Royal Palace for an audience. Parliament adjourned so that they all might see him act, and excel Garrick in Garrick's own roles. He played Hamlet, Romeo, Richard III, and non-Shakespearean parts. When he was performing, Kemble, Mrs. Siddons, Mrs. Jordan, Cooke, and Kean played to empty houses, and he appeared at both Drury Lane and Covent Garden. In twenty-three nights he drew £17,000 at Drury Lane alone.

At the end of the season he toured the provinces. But when he returned to Drury Lane the next year he found "garlick among the flowers," and was even hissed. He managed, however, to overcome the opposition and again carried off heaps of money. But the craze in London was over. He continued to play for a time in the provinces, but soon retired to Bath on March 26, 1808, before his seventeenth birthday. That year he entered Christ's College, Cambridge, and became Captain Betty of the North Shropshire Yeomanry Cavalry.

But after his father's death in 1812, he began to pine once more for the stage. Again he went through the provinces, ending with a month at Covent Garden, only to find the public no longer interested in seeing him. He was twenty-one and no longer a prodigy! He was able from time to time to collect country audiences, to whom his name still meant something.

His success was, of course, ridiculous. The very fact that he could "learn" the role of Hamlet in three days speaks for itself. Betterton acted it for fifty years and admitted that he had not yet plumbed its depths. Betty's feelings were inevitably those of a child during his reigning years. He quit acting finally in 1824, by which time he was an actor of no distinction. He died after having outlived his fame by some 70 years!

Yet, when he was a child and a prominent family was on its way to Coventry the lady begged the landlord of a hotel for a sight of him. The landlord said that the lad and his parents were having dinner, and the lady could see him only if she would agree to carry in one of the dishes and serve it. She was only too happy to do so. Only Campbell was not taken in by his precocity, and said he had "not even the elements of a good actor," that all the fuss being made over him was "an hallucination in the public mind, and a disgrace to our theatrical history."

Master Betty was the most sensational example of the child prodigy in his time, but not the only prodigy. Master Burke made his debut at Cork at the age of five! At the age of twelve he was making his first appearances in New York. He did Richard III and Shylock, and also led the orchestra in operatic overtures, played violin solos, sang his own songs. But he grew into a good violinist, good enough to play at concerts with Jenny Lind and Thalberg.

The most amazing and successful of the "infant phenomena" in the United States were the Bateman children. On December 10, 1849, E. A. Marshall, manager of the Broadway Theater, introduced them. Ellen Bateman, aged four, enacted Richard III and her sister Kate, aged six, Richmond. The Broadway Theater by that time had built a reputation as a house of legitimate drama, and the announcement of the coming of these prodigies was treated with scorn. "But those who came to scoff on the first night returned to praise during their one week's engagement. Four-year-old Ellen next did Shylock and Lady Macbeth, and six-year-old Kate played Portia and Macbeth! They were praised for "the correctness of elocution, . . . the proper comprehension of the language and the business" they displayed. "The simple task of committing to memory the text of so many parts was in itself a marvellous effort for children of their tender age. . . . Every fresh character they undertook was a surprise. . . . Lady Macbeth was, perhaps, the most successful of Ellen's assumptions, while Kate read Portia with amazing skill and propriety." One is glad not to have been there to see them.

They appeared in Boston, Baltimore, Philadelphia, and other American cities, and were then taken to England by P. T. Barnum in 1851. In London they first appeared at the St. James's Theatre in August. They were well liked. They returned to the Old Broadway in November 1852, and opened in a comedy written especially for them. Before they left New York, Mayor Kingsland presented each child with a tiny gold watch "on behalf of a committee of leading citizens." In 1856 they retired from the stage; they were eleven and thirteen, already too old to continue their profession! Kate returned later to the stage with some success.

13

Kean

Ever since Macklin had transformed Shylock from a comic figure to a fiendish one, until well past the first decade of the nineteenth century the character was presented as blood chilling, a villain intended to provoke the hatred and animosity of audiences. (Garrick never attempted him.)

A new tradition was introduced when Edmund Kean (1787–1833) appeared in the role at Drury Lane on January 26, 1814. He was only twenty-seven at the time, and although he had been acting since childhood, he was unknown to the London public. In the provinces he had already performed a fiendish Shylock, in keeping with Macklin's style.

When he arrived in London he was still grieving over the death of his beloved five-year-old son. He stood in the chilly hall of Drury Lane, a little "pale, restless man," with dark eyes in a coat with two or three capes. Nobody paid any attention to him. His family was living on Cecil Street on little more than air. He stood waiting in that cold hall of Drury Lane day after day, hoping for an interview with the manager, and sneered at by the actors who passed him. Even the players with whom he had performed in the provinces ignored him. No one was willing to grant him the opportunity to show what he could do with Shylock. While he was still waiting several other players were given the part, and failed. Finally, the management agreed to let him play not Shylock, but Richard III. He boldly replied, "Shylock or nothing!" It was later said that he was afraid of the smallness of his figure and trusted to Shylock's gown to hide it.

At last he was granted what he had been requesting. There was but one rehearsal, the morning of the performance. Watching it, the manager and his fellow actors were panicked by his originality; the manager exclaimed: "Sir, this will never do! It is quite an innovation; it cannot be permitted." "Sir," said Kean, despite his desperate need, "I wish it to be so." Up to the very performance he was studiously avoided. That night on the way to the theater he thought, "I wish I was going to be shot!"

He put on his costume and went down to the wing. The house was half empty. He had already created a sensation among his fellow actors by wearing a black wig instead of the traditional red one. But during his very first scene (the third in Act I), he was interrupted several times by applause each time louder and more enthusiastic. By the third act and despite the many empty seats there was a veritable "whirlwind of approbation." From that night on Edmund Kean was for his time the undisputed genius of the London stage.

Hazlitt never forgot that first night. "The boxes were empty, and the pit not half full. . . . The whole presented a dreary, hopeless object. I was in considerable apprehension for the result. From the first scene in which Mr. Kean came on, my doubts were at an end. . . . Mr. Kean's appearance was the first gleam of genius breaking athwart the gloom of the Stage, and the public have since gladly basked in its ray, in spite of actors, managers, and critics." Kean was to remain Hazlitt's most cherished actor.

As Hazlitt described his predecessors, Shylock had been "a decrepit old man, bent with age and ugly with mental deformity, grinning with deadly malice, with the venom of his heart congealed in the expression of his countenance, sullen, morose, gloomy, inflexible, brooding over one idea, that of his hatred, and fixed on one unalterable purpose, that of his revenge." Kean's Shylock was vigorous, handsome, and a man of intellect. At the conclusion of the trial scene his very appearance seemed to change, and he was able by brilliantly controlling his voice to transform the audience's feelings from hatred to pity. He contrived to leave the stage with such dignity that he even made the spectators sympathetic toward him. Though some critics objected, the public liked it very much. As the part grew on him Kean portrayed Shylock more and more as "a persecuted martyr who, through the forces of circumstances, finally becomes the avenger."

Though I have shown elsewhere that I very much doubt that this is what Shakespeare meant, this is the Shylock we still see today.

The day after Kean's first appearance, Hazlitt wrote in the *Morning Chronicle* that "for voice, eye, action, and expression, no actor has come out for many years at all equal to him. The applause, from the first scene to the last, was general, loud, and uninterrupted. Indeed, the very first scene in which he comes on with Bassanio and Antonio, shewed the master in his art, and at once decided the opinion of the audience. . . . Notwithstanding the complete success of Mr. Kean in the part of Shylock, we question whether he will not become a greater favourite in other parts. There was a lightness and vigour in his tread, a buoyancy and elasticity of spirit, a fire and animation, which would accord better with almost any other character." Hazlitt then went on to describe the Shylock London had known since Macklin, concluding that the usurer is "a man brooding over one idea . . . and bent . . . [on] revenge." Other actors have been more successful in showing a man "proof against every sentiment of humanity. . . . But in giving varied vehemence of declaration, in keenness of sarcasm, in the rapidity of his transitions from one tone and feeling to another, in propriety and novelty of action, presenting a succession of striking pictures, and giving perpetually fresh shocks of delight and surprise, it would be difficult to single out a competitor. . . . It would be endless to point out individual beauties, where almost every passage was received with equal and deserved applause."

With considerable justification, Edward Wagenknecht said that in his private life "Kean represents the stock caricature of the dissipated, profligate actor whose power carries within itself the seeds of its own ruin." According to Macaulay, Kean was ultimately descended from George Savile, Marquis of Halifax, through a natural son, Henry Carey, who won fame as a composer of songs, and was responsible among other works for "Sally in our Alley"; he also gained some notice as a writer of farces. He married and became the father of a son whom he named George, after the marquis. But he fell upon evil days, sank into extreme poverty and eventually hanged himself. George Savile Carey, grandfather of our actor, had been trained as a printer, but turned to acting, in which his talents showed themselves so feeble that at the end of his one season at Covent Garden he was dismissed. He began to lecture in various towns on the art of mimicry, wrote a ballad opera, a burlesque, a comedy, and several songs—but without any recognition. He was also cursed with a wayward daughter, Anne, the mother of our actor. She joined a company of strolling players and became intimate with a Kean, one of three brothers: Aaron, Moses, and Edmund. Aaron was a tailor, Edmund a builder, and Moses (the only well-known of the three, who strangely reminds one of Samuel Foote), who was a tailor, a successful mimic, and, like Foote, had a wooden leg. For some years Moses was employed during the summers at the Haymarket. It is not known which of these three fathered Anne's child, though his being named Edmund somewhat strengthens the case for the builder. It has been said that the family was of Irish descent, though there was a rumor, because of the actor's rather Semitic face, that the Keans were originally Cohens.

The exact birthplace of the great actor is disputed: an empty room, or an equally poor room in Castle Street, Leicester Square, or a wretched garret in Southwark. Had it not been for Charlotte Tidswell, a minor actress, who was Moses's mistress, the child might very well have been born in the street.

There is nothing but uncertainty about his next years. Miss Tidswell seems to have taken charge of him—his mother being utterly indifferent to his fate, so that Kean often thought that Miss Tidswell must have actually been his mother (Why, he asked, did she "take such good care of me if she was not my mother?"). As for the elder Edmund Kean, he committed suicide in his early twenties. Among the things our Edmund inherited must certainly have been a streak of insanity. He also had some trouble with his legs in early boyhood and had to wear a pair of iron braces. Miss Tidswell taught him elocution, though her methods were a little severe; she tied him to a bedpost to rivet his attention. He danced and tumbled at fairs and taverns, jumped through hoops of fire, tightrope walked, and was generally knocked about and undernourished; just when he was finding ways to survive, his mother appeared on the scene.

Still a stroller, still a doxy, still a vagabond, she went about the country peddling perfumes and pomatums, obliging her son to act as her "pack-horse." Though he resented it furiously, he gained self-confidence, learned soliloquies from the plays, and recited them at gentlemen's houses. Whatever he managed to earn, his mother appropriated. Once in a while Miss Tidswell would be there to feed him or render him some service. He finally decided to run off to sea as a cabin boy on a ship bound for Madeira, but returned disgusted with sea life, and went back to playing at fairs, as before, alternating feasts with famine. At Windsor Fair he made enough of a stir for George III to send for him to hear his recitations; he was rewarded with two guineas, which either his manager or mother took from him.

He seized the opportunity to deliver an occasional passage from a play on benefit nights in London theaters. He joined a company of strolling players, starved much, began to find solace in drinking. He was at Belfast when Mrs. Siddons was acting there, and she heard him; her verdict was that he performed "well, *very* well, but there was too little of him to make a great actor!" At the Haymarket it was remarked that in those minimal parts allotted him, he did his utmost. But he felt that these insignificant bits were leading him nowhere—certainly not to London, where he was sure he belonged. So he returned to the country and opportunities for bigger parts, even if it was only two days each week, with the risk of starving the other days.

His earnings were so scant that he could not afford conveyance from one engagement to another, but had to walk from place to place; or on occasion swim a river. Sometimes he was applauded, sometimes he was hissed. In Guernsey he was severely criticized for turning his back on the audience at certain moments (a "natural" stance they were unaccustomed to in the provinces) and when the pit hissed his Richard III, he addressed the line, "Unmannerly dogs!" pointedly at them. They were silenced. Years later when the pit at Drury Lane hissed him, not for poor acting, but for personal immorality, he tried the same trick in that play with the same result.

The year before his sensational victory in London, he received this notice in March 1813 from a Guernsey paper:

His vanity has repeatedly prompted him to endeavour to procure an engagement at one of the theatres in the metropolis. The difficulties he has met with have, however, proved insurmountable, and the managers of Drury Lane and Covent Garden have saved themselves the disgrace to which they would be subject by countenancing such impudence and incompetency. [Kean has] one of the vilest figures that has been seen either on or off the stage. And if his mind was half so qualified for the representation of Richard III, which he is shortly to appear in, as his person is suited to the deformities with which the tyrant is supposed to have been distinguished from his fellows, his success would be most unequivocal. As to his Hamlet—it is one of the most terrible representations to which Shakespeare has ever been subjected. Without grace or dignity he comes forward—he shows unconsciousness that anyone is before him, and is often so forgetful of the respect due to an audience that he turns his back on them, in some of the scenes in which contemplation is to be indulged. . . . His voice is harsh and monotonous, but as it is deep answers well enough the idea he entertains of impressing terror by a tone which seems to proceed from a charnel-house.

One of the reasons that Guernsey turned on him so savagely is that he was supposed to do Charles I in some ridiculous melodrama. Kean loathed the play and the role, went out and got drunk, and sent the theater a message that Charles "had been beheaded on his way to the theatre." He sat in the audience hurling insults at his substitute.

A young Waterford girl who was a commencing actress at Gloucester was upset because Kean kept forgetting his lines. "Who is that shabby little man?" she asked. After giving him a dressing down, she heard him ask, "Who the devil is she?" She was Mary Chambers, and they soon fell in love, got married, and were forthwith dismissed from the company. There followed years of struggle, privation, during which she was a good wife and he was valiantly preparing himself for London. "If I could only get there, and succeed! If I *succeed* I shall go mad!" Patience, patience! Success was less than a year away.

They walked the two hundred miles from Birmingham to Swansea, she carrying within her their first child. The son was born, but they were a failure at Swansea. Then they crossed from Wales to Waterford, where they met young Sheridan Knowles, cousin to Sheridan of Drury Lane, and friend of Hazlitt, Coleridge, and Lamb. But he was still in his twenties and trying his luck at acting. One evening he watched Kean do Richard III, and then follow it as Harlequin in a pantomime. Knowles became his friend, and wrote a melodrama for Kean to act in.

At Waterford Kean was working steadily and hard; we have an account of his acting in Hannah More's tragedy, *Percy,* a benefit performance for himself, and after the tragedy his giving "a specimen of tight-rope dancing, and another of sparring with a professional pugilist. He then played the leading part in a musical interlude, and finished with Chimpanzee, the monkey . . . and in this *character* he showed agility . . . and touches of deep tragedy in the monkey's death scene, which made the audience shed tears." It is said that he one night came home in his ill-smelling chimpanzee skins, and refused to take them off. He slept in them, and drove his poor wife to the sofa.

Mrs. Kean bore a second son, and they were presently on the road again. His inability to achieve anything resembling a stable income, no matter how small, drove him into fits of fury and drink. Somehow or other, despite utter poverty, they survived. At Exeter, where he was acclaimed but made almost no money, he flung an overcoat on his costume and at the tavern near the theater added trifles to his earnings by teaching dancing and fencing, elocution and boxing. Thence they went to Dorchester on foot, he carrying his son Charles on his back, Mrs. Kean leading the increasingly ill elder son Howard. In the boxes at Dorchester Kean observed a man deeply intent upon his acting, and acted for him alone; the man turned out to be Arnold, the stage manager of Drury Lane, and before the night ended he began to negotiate with Kean. Kean rushed home in a hysteria of happiness, and cried, "If Howard only get well, we shall all be happy yet!"

Howard died, but his father had no time to grieve; he had to continue acting and dancing, as the time approached when they were to come to London.

When the 1813/14 season opened, the condition of Drury Lane was such as "could be relieved only by a genius." And there stood the needed man, night after night, in the cold hall of Drury Lane, ignored, sneered at, ridiculous in his rags and smallness of stature—until in sheer desperation the management yielded to his insistence upon doing *his* Shylock.

That was on January 26, 1814. A few days later he repeated the performance. Hazlitt said the next day that "by his admirable and expressive manner of giving the part," he had "fully sustained the reputation he had acquired" the first time. "His style of acting is . . . more significant, more pregnant with meaning, more varied and alive in every part, than any we have almost ever witnessed. The character never stands still; there is no vacant pause in the action; the eye is never silent"; and Hazlitt conceded that "for depth and force of conception" he had seen others he preferred in the role, but "for brilliant and masterly execution, none."

On February 12 he did Richard III and on March 12 Hamlet. By that time he was the leading actor in London. The London *Times* ignored Kean at first, but was soon admitting that no one has often "seen a much better Shylock."

Hazlitt pronounced Kean's Richard entirely his own. It was admirable in its distinctness, precision, and perfect articulation. But Kean, he felt, risked dissipating the impression of his character by the very variety of his resources. He was more refined than Cooke, and much bolder and more original than John Philip Kemble. Sometimes, however, he lacked the requisite dignity in scenes of state business. His concluding scene was his most brilliant. "He fought like one drunk with wounds."

Having witnessed Kean's first Hamlet, Hazlitt admitted that he had thought highly of the new actor before, but now thought more highly of him than ever. As a whole, the performance was perhaps less perfect than Shylock or Richard, but there were parts excellent beyond anything he had already done. Hazlitt made the objection that Kean's Hamlet was too strongly and pointedly delineated (which, of course, was the right thing to do!), for Hazlitt thought of the prince as "wrapped up in the clouds of his reflection"; he ought to be an amiable misanthrope. Kean was remarkable in his first scene with the Ghost in his surprise, eagerness, and filial confidence. The closet scene and scene with Ophelia were marvelous.

Against the counsel of Drury Lane, Kean headed for the provinces again, once the season was over. In May 1814 he performed Othello at Drury Lane. Hazlitt said the farewell to arms speech was like "the swelling of some divine music." The latter part of Act III "was a masterpiece of profound pathos." In the same month he acted Iago to a miserable Othello by Sowerby. Hazlitt considered this "the most faultless" of his performances to date. The "accomplished hypocrite" was never before so adroitly enacted—a gay, lighthearted, cordial monster.

He had saved Drury Lane and the shareholders of the theater showed their gratitude by presenting Kean with £500, and four of the committee each gave him a £100 share in the theater. Wroughton gave him a point-of-lace collar which Garrick had worn as Richard III, Lord Essex a handsome sword, and the poet Byron a gold snuff box.

Byron had met Kean at Holland House, for the great actor was now sought out by the most distinguished members of society. In the Holland House circle were Tom Moore, Count D'Orsay, Lady Blessington, Samuel Rogers, the painter Lawrence, and Byron. Byron wrote in his journal: "An invitation to dine at Holland House to meet Kean. He is worth meeting, and I hope, by getting into good society, he will be prevented from falling like Cooke. [Though being *born* into good society did nothing to help Byron from falling, and into some of Kean's very own vices!] He is greater now on the stage, and off he should never be less. There is a stupid and underrating criticism upon him in one of the newspapers. I thought that last night, though great, he rather underacted more than the first time. This may be the effect of these cavils, but I hope that he has more sense than to mind them." Byron and he soon became good friends, dined together, and had more than a little in common in their sense of fun and the ludicrous.

Byron made Kean a number of presents, including a valuable snuff box and a sword. The box had on it a representation of a boar hunt and Byron thought it a fitting gift to Kean after seeing his Richard III.

But the friendship was interrupted for a while. Byron had arranged a dinner especially in the actor's honor, and had among his guests his good friend Kinnaird. Kean feigned illness and made that the excuse for his leaving early, but it was not long before the poet discovered that Kean had gone off to preside at a dinner for pugilists. Offended, Byron would not speak to Kean for some time. However, when he saw him in his celebrated role of Sir Giles Overreach, Byron forgave him, and immediately made him the gift of a very handsome sword with a Damascus blade, and at a benefit for the actor sent him £50.

On one occasion Kean entertained Byron and his friends at home by sketching the face and body of a dancer at the opera with a piece of burnt cork upon the back of his hand; he then used his two middle fingers to represent thighs and legs, and his nails the shoes. He wrapped a handkerchief about his wrist to serve as a turban. The dancer he had thus fabricated began to dance with great abandon, and assumed one absurd attitude after another. Byron was hysterical with laughter and pleaded for an encore.

During Kean's first season, Leigh Hunt had been imprisoned and was not able to see the actor until the next year, during the month of February 1815. He confessed to being quite disappointed with Kean's Richard III. Perhaps that was because "his expectations had been raised to a very high pitch by the reports"; he had been very eager to see him just because he had sickened at "the artificial style of the actors lately in vogue," and he anticipated finding Kean "natural." He thought it fair to mention, however, that "thanks to the magnificent inconvenience of these fine theatres," he was fairly distant from the stage. On the other hand, "many of the most . . . ardent admirers of this gentleman think him much fallen off from what he was last season." Hunt found Kean still far from "natural" as Richard, though Hunt considered him "to be equal, at all times, to the best actors in vogue; but in particular passages, he undoubtedly goes far beyond them."

Leigh Hunt may have seen Kean in an off night. For two and a half years later Hazlitt was saying about his Othello: "Mr. Kean's Othello is, we suppose, the finest piece of acting in the world. It is impossible either to describe or praise it adequately. We have never seen an actor so wrought upon, so 'perplexed in the extreme.' The energy of passion, as it expresses itself in action, is not the most terrific part; it is the agony of his soul, showing itself in looks and tones of voice. . . . His lips might be said less to utter words, than to bleed drops of blood gushing from his heart. . . . In fact, [it was so in] almost every scene or sentence in this extraordinary exhibition of natural passion. The convulsed motion of the hands, and the involuntary swellings of the veins of the forehead in some of the most painful situations, should not only suggest topics of critical panegyric, but might furnish studies to the painter or anatomist,"

In March of 1816 Kean was thrown out of his gig, dislocated an arm, and was badly bruised. He naturally was forced to give up playing that night. A morning newspaper was quite facetious about the accident, hinting that his nonappearance might have been due to other causes. Kean was indignant. He had never missed a rehearsal or a performance.

When he appeared upon the stage again in April, it was to present his Shylock once more. He was greeted with an ovation. Hazlitt again lauded him: "For voice, eye, action, and expression, no actor has come out for many years at all equal to him." He possessed, Hazlitt added, all that John Philip Kemble lacked of perfection.

Naturally, his mother, having heard of his triumphs, turned up again with one Henry Darnley, who insisted on calling him, "dear brother." She demanded an allowance of £50 a year, which he of course gave her.

In the seasons which followed Kean, besides repeating the roles he had already introduced into the repertory, did Macbeth, Romeo, Richard II, Timon of Athens, King John, Hotspur, Coriolanus, Wolsey, Lear, Posthumus, and Henry V. He also did an amalgamation of the three *Henry VI* plays, and on July 19, 1830, presented a formidable program at the Haymarket in a performance made up of the fourth act of *Richard III*, the fourth act of *The Merchant of Venice*, the fifth act of Massinger's *A New Way to Pay Old Debts* (some critics thought his Sir Giles Overreach in that play was the top of his performances), the second act of *Macbeth*, and the third act of *Othello*.

Hazlitt, whose enthusiasm for him exceeded that toward any other actor alive or dead, was not blind to the fact that Kean had an "insignificant figure" and "a hoarseness of voice" which necessarily diminished the character he was portraying. Nevertheless Kean was equal to the greatest in "truth of nature and force of passion, in discrimination and originality." He was "all violence, all extreme passion"; he was "possessed with a fury, a demon" that left him "no repose, no time for thought, or room for imagination." His Othello was superb, and compared to him Cooke "had only the *slang and bravado* of tragedy." Even Kemble, with "all his study, his grace, and classic dignity of form," could not be compared with Kean, for Kemble had "the external requisites . . . without the internal workings of the soul." Kean was proof of "the triumph of genius over physical defects, of nature over art." When Coleridge saw Kean's Richard III during the second season, he said, "Seeing him act was like reading Shakespeare by flashes of lightning."

Now at the height of his powers, Kean used to meet his friends at a public house called the Coal-Hole, off the Strand, and they called their club The Wolves. Kean, as chairman, spoke hoping "no one would enter this circle of good fellows without a pride that ranks him with the courtier, or philosophy that levels him with the peasant." The members were actors and those connected with the theater, as well as those who loved a merry tale and a good drink. He had once said he would go mad if he ever attained success in London; what he did do was lose all sense of restraint and begin a life of such eccentricity that stories about him multiplied by the hour. He bought a carriage and several fine horses. One of these, whom he named Shylock, he was fond of mounting when leaving the theater or tavern, and going tearing through the night recklessly without a destination, down streets, along country roads, and often not returning home until daybreak, exhausted and covered with mud. An admirer gave him a tame lion from America as a pet, and visitors, who shrank from approaching the animal, often found him teaching the creature tricks in the drawing room; he was also fond of rowing up and down the Thames in a wherry with the lion seated in the stern. He made great friends of various boxers and frequently attended the matches.

When Grattan, the officer to whom he had once taught fencing in Waterford, came to London in 1816, Kean received him like a long-lost brother. One night, when the actor was not performing, Grattan invited him to dinner in Leicester Square to meet a couple of friends. At six o'clock Kean arrived in his carriage, dressed in a silk-lined coat, white breeches, and buckled shoes, and said that he had an engagement for a party at nine. The dinner was good, the company excellent, but he did not stir to leave. Messengers arrived to summon him, but the decanters were still passing around, stories were still being told and songs sung, and he did not get up to leave until midnight. Still unwilling to part with such good fellows, he insisted that they accompany him, without mentioning his destination. They all entered his carriage, the horses were driven rapidly, and they stopped at a passage leading from the Strand. Fairly drunk, they staggered along the narrow passage to the Coal-Hole. Kean, followed by his friends, staggered up the stairs, entered a room and was greeted with wild applause. There were some sixty men present, but when Kean's uninvited guests were seen, those present accused him of a great outrage on The Wolves in admitting strangers, and agreed that amends could be made only by enlisting the newcomers as members. Scarcely knowing what they were doing, the strangers took an oath, signed their names in a register, and paid a few guineas as initiation fees. Kean took his place as Head, made a florid speech; bottles were passed around until at last the new Wolves left with the others, more than a little confused by the whole evening.

Much sought after now as a social lion by ladies of the nobility, he usually refused their invitations and had small respect for their patronage. Byron was the only nobleman whom he admired, and the feelings were reciprocal. But Kean was ill at ease among men of rank or intellect, and felt much more at home among actors or tavern friends. Byron tried again and again to introduce Kean to men of talent, for he feared that Kean's weaknesses would bring him down as had been the case with Cooke. Shortly before going into exile, Byron invited Kean to dinner to meet his old friend Lord Kinnaird and a few other men of distinction. Kean had already accepted an invitation to join friends at a tavern, and tried to excuse himself from Byron's party. The poet, however, insisted, and Kean came. But he paid no attention to the lively conversation, and remained silent. As soon as dessert was over, he slipped quietly from the room, without being noticed by Byron, who learned from the servants that Kean had kept his carriage waiting from the time he had entered, and had just driven away.

On another night, several noblemen and friends invited him, and to put him more at ease asked also a fellow player. They all knew Kean could be very witty when he wished to be; they toasted him and loaded him with compliments. But as soon as the servants removed the cloth Kean said to his fellow actor, "A couple of years ago, not one of these lords would have noted the poor stroller. Now their admiration is unbounded. Pshaw! I prefer a quiet glass with a friend like you to all their champagne, effervescent like themselves—let us go." They left unobserved, and made for a tavern.

At the close of the season in 1818, Kean and his wife went abroad. In Paris he met the great Talma, who had seen him act in London. "He is a magnificent uncut gem," the French actor declared. "Polish him and round him off, and he will be a perfect tragedian." In honor of Kean, Talma gave a banquet to which the leading members of the Théâtre Français were invited, and Kean was presented with a gold snuff box. The pair then went on to Geneva, climbed Mont Blanc, and visited the hospice of St. Bernard. He sang to the monks, accompanying himself on the spinet, told them anecdotes of his early life, and left them with regret.

On returning to London, he decided that he would visit the United States, where his old idol, Cooke, was buried. He made his first appearance in New York at the end of November 1820. The chief theater in New York had just burned down, and temporary quarters were found in a small house in

Anthony Street. His reputation had long ago crossed the Atlantic and many people came all the way from Philadelphia to see him. The building was much overcrowded. In the preceding years certain American actors had been more or less imitating his style. The *National Gazette* admitted that it had not expected much, having seen these imitators who had the reputation of being "good copies"—but he had not yet finished his first soliloquy as Hamlet before "we saw the most complete actor, in our judgment, that ever appeared on our boards. The imitations we had seen were indeed likenesses, but it was the resemblance of copper to gold." The demand for tickets continued night after night; the press of people was a recurring hazard to life and limb, and the management was forced to issue a statement that "to prevent the riotous scenes which have disturbed the peace of the town . . . the managers have directed that the box-tickets and the whole lower tier, and fourteen of the second row next to the stage, shall be sold by public auction." The theater which had up to then grossed $1,000 a week was making that much every night.

Of course there was adverse criticism. One writer objected that his "pronunciation does him an injury in the country where we have the pure English." On the other hand, there were some who deeply appreciated him; one such was Dr. Francis, who came to know him, and said with insight: "His little but well-wrought strong frame seemed made up of a tissue of nerves. Every sense appeared capable of immediate impression, and such impression having within itself a flexibility truly wondrous. The drudgery of his early life had given a pliability to his muscular powers that rendered him the most dexterous harlequin, the most graceful fencer, the most finished gentleman, the most insidious lover, the most terrific tragedian." Dr. Francis was deeply impressed with the fact that all the lines of the Shakespearean tragedies were firmly fixed in Kean's mind, and that he saw him consult the text only once, that being when he was about to do King John. He himself considered the third act of *Othello* his greatest achievement. Just the same he admitted that he detested being an actor!

Nevertheless, he was profoundly touched by the admiration and kindliness he evoked in New York, and at a farewell banquet given him he spoke with genuine emotion and openness: "There are hearts conjoined to mind by ties of affection and alliance, which are at this moment, perhaps, anticipating with joy my professional success in this country, and in which will arise a permanent sentiment of gratitude for the favour I have here experienced."

His next venture was to Philadelphia, where again the press seemed hostile in advance. The *Literary Gazette* indicated little friendliness toward "the foreign tragedian," an actor who "though sufficiently distinguished at home, is to be magnified and glorified here." Again, as seems luckily to be a tradition in the United States in politics as well as the arts, the public decided for itself, and his performances was greeted with many a *Bravo!*, and another critic spoke of the "wondrous powers of this extraordinary man." Kean himself wrote: "Both on and off the stage, in this country," everything "has exceeded my most sanguine expectations. I am getting a great deal of money . . . I am living in the best style, travelling magnificently, and transmitting to England £1,000 each month."

A strange thing happened at Philadelphia, according to the personal recollections of the manager of the theater there. There were "some determined critics" who felt that no one could fill the place of Cooke, and who "were on the first night loud in condemnation of the new actor, whom they honoured with the names of quack, mountebank, and vulgar impostor. . . . His second appearance at once converted these judges into his most enthusiastic admirers." Kean's presence began a tradition that has never since died, but was then entirely novel, "the habit of calling out performers, dead or alive, after the curtain has dropped, to receive a tribute of extra applause. The absurdity of dragging out before the curtain a deceased Hamlet, Macbeth, or Richard, merely to make a bow . . . is one which we date from this time."

Stories by the hundreds about the Wolves club, the tame lion, his midnight rides, his eccentricities, his fondness for taverns had preceded him, and people were anticipating an arrogant and offensive man; instead, they found him unassuming, mild, and utterly devoid of affectation. He was most delicate in his suggestions to the minor actors, and they did all they could to please him. However, he was the easy prey of parasites who waited at the stage door to carry him off to a late supper when he was in a state of extreme exhaustion. His idol Cooke could drink wine, bottle after bottle; Kean could be undone by three glasses of port. The manager, Wood, who perceived this danger, got into the habit of delaying him after the performance merely to tire out these dangerous idlers; once "we stayed inside the building until nearly three o'clock in the morning before the rumbling of the carriages announced the departure of his persecutors."

From Philadelphia he went to Boston, where he was billed to play for nine evenings. Again, because of the demand, tickets had to be auctioned off. He began with Richard III, was at once the talk of the town for his remarkable acting, and eagerly sought after by society. For the nine nights he received more than £630; his popularity was so great that he was engaged for another six nights, and earned another £440. When he appeared before the curtain after his last performance, there were loud demands that he prolong his stay. He thanked them but explained that his engagements in the South prevented his staying on.

Three months later, in early May, he decided to visit Boston again. One of the managers at once wrote him advising against it because this was the season when the majority of those who made up the audiences were out of town. He urged him to wait until autumn. But Kean was sure he could attract a full house and appeared on May 23 as Lear. The first two nights receipts and audience were sparse. On the third night he was to play Richard III; peering through the curtains, he saw there were but some twenty persons in the house. He told the manager that he was unwilling to play for "bare walls." He was urged to go on just the same, but refused, saying he would leave Boston the next morning. He had scarcely left the theater (unfortunately he had come to this decision before putting on his costume) when the boxes began to fill and a fair-sized audience had taken their seats. Word was quickly sent to him, but he would not come back. Meanwhile the audience grew impatient at the delay; the manager came out to say that Mr. Kean refused to perform that night. They demanded to know why, and he told them that Kean's reason was an uncrowded house. A substitute Richard acted instead, and the play proceeded, but Bostonians considered themselves insulted, and general fury began to ferment against him. The following paragraph printed in a leading paper speaks for itself:

ONE CENT REWARD

Run away from the "Literary emporium of the New World," a stage player calling himself Kean. He may be easily recognized by his misshapen trunk, and his coxcomical Cockney manners. His face is as white as his own froth, and his eyes are as dark as indigo. All persons are cautioned against harbouring the aforesaid vagrant, as the undersigned pays no more debts of his contracting after this date. As he has violated his pledged faith to me, I deem it my duty to put my neighbours on their guard against him.

"PETER PUBLIC."

The New York papers also took up the attack on Kean, and abused him violently. He found it necessary to write a long letter to various periodicals. But he felt their full wrath only on reaching New York. Stunned by the change in mood after his previous triumphs, he gave a frank and full explanation of what had happened, and promised to return to Boston during the regular season personally to vindicate his action by his performances. The managers of the Boston Theater published a protest saying they had suffered enough mortification and heavy financial losses from Kean's failure to fulfill his obligations, and rejected Kean's assertion that they had understood why he had refused to perform that night. The attacks on him increased in violence. Kean's last words on leaving the United States in a letter to the press, disclaiming any intention to offend the Bostonians, were: "It is with reluctance and regret I leave my friends in America."

Before his departure, and with the help of his friend Dr. Francis, he made good his desire to have erected a monument to his old idol, George Frederick Cooke; Cooke's remains were removed from the strangers' vault to a suitable spot in the adjacent cemetery. When at Kean's desire the lid of Cooke's box was raised, there were left only a few bones. Deeply moved at the vanity of all human life, he removed a bone (some authorities claim it to have been from the foot, others the forefinger of the right hand). Above the place where the remains now lay were set (on June 4, 1821) a pedestal and an urn, with the inscription: "ERECTED TO THE MEMORY OF GEORGE FREDERICK COOKE by EDMUND KEAN, of the THEATRE ROYAL, DRURY LANE. 1821.

> Three kingdoms claimed his birth;
> Both hemispheres pronounce his worth."

The next day Kean was on his way to England.

On arriving at Liverpool on July 19, 1821, he at once wrote to Elliston, manager of Drury Lane, announcing: "I shall be at the stage-door of Drury at noon on Monday next. . . . I am full of health and ambition, both of which are at your service, or they will run riot." Elliston concluded that Kean was prepared to act on Monday night, and at once had enormous playbills printed and posted all over London, informing the public that "this eminent actor will re-appear as Richard III on Monday." Considerable ceremony greeted him. On Monday a procession made its way through London: first six liveried outriders, next Elliston in his carriage drawn by four gray horses, next Kean in a carriage drawn by four black horses. As he descended from the vehicle Kean was given an ovation by the mob which had followed in the rear. He was, naturally, delighted, and although he was surprised to find himself billed for that night, and was weary from his journey, he went on before a packed house which greeted him with cheers and shouts of pleasure. On Wednesday he did Shylock, on Thursday Othello, and the following Monday Richard III again. Poor health prevented his performing again that season. By November he was well again.

In the summer of 1822, while Drury Lane was closed, Elliston had the whole interior reconstructed; the boxes were brought five feet nearer the stage, the pit made smaller, the ceiling lowered fourteen feet, in addition to added decor in the great salon; the cost was £22,000.

George IV was crowned the day Kean landed at Liverpool, so a brass plate was placed in the center of the pit, reading: "GEORGE IV. KING. THEATRE ROYAL, DRURY LANE." An important event occurred on February 10, 1823, when Elliston announced that the original fifth act of *King Lear* would be restored in Kean's performance that night. At last Tate's absurd perversion, which had held the stage for over a century and a half, was on its way out. (Kean had already appeared in what was more or less the Tate version.) His audience, Kean now felt, could have no idea of his power until they saw him over the dead body of Cordelia. (In Tate's version neither Lear nor Cordelia were other than felicitously happy at the end.) I have said that Kean's experiment with the restoration of Shakespeare's tragic end helped usher Tate's version out. Still it was not actually Shakespeare's play that Kean now gave, despite this important reinstatement, for he retained Tate's foolish love story between Cordelia and Edgar and continued to omit the Fool. The public was not pleased with the tragic ending and this version was given up after three performances. Three years later the American actor James H. Hackett was surprised to see Kean return to the Tate version in the last act. Kean admitted that when he discovered that the public liked Tate better than Shakespeare, "I fell back on his corruption; though in my soul I was ashamed." It was not until 1838 that Macready would restore the play as it was written by Shakespeare.

Though he had achieved the dizzy heights of success that he had not dared dream of a decade and a half earlier, Kean was still insecure about his hold upon the public, and his thoughts often turned toward death. He began to drink more heavily than ever before, and was subject to sudden fits of melancholy and depression.

One night his wife informed him that their son Charles knew how to act; she asked the boy to repeat the speeches he had delivered to her; at last the father broke in and sent the lad to bed, warning him: "Remember, we will have no more acting." When the boy, confused, left the room Kean said to his wife that their son might succeed as an actor; "but if he tries, I will cut his throat." Pacing the room with agitation, and ignoring his wife's disapproval of what he had said, he cried: "I am the first and shall be the last tragedian of my name." At three o'clock that next morning, he sent for a hackney-coach, placed in it their spaniel Portia, a case of pistols, two lighted candles, and a bottle of brandy. He told his dresser to mount the box beside the driver, who asked where they were going. "To Hell," Kean replied. They drove to the neighborhood of Waterloo Place, where Kean told the coachman to stop and wait for his return; then he himself disappeared. Hours passed, daylight broke, but Kean did not show up. The coachman drove back to the Kean house.

· Increasing eccentricity became a way of life with him. Once, after the theater, he decided to take a drive in order to recover from his exhaustion. At Brixton he noted a crowd around a tavern, and joined the mob, made up chiefly of drovers, all fairly drunk; one of them was arguing with a rat catcher, and Kean immediately offered to act as judge. At this the drover said some insulting words; Kean answered by flinging a pint mug in his face. The drover rushed at the actor, a fight took place, and Kean came out of it the worse for bruises and a bleeding face.

The reason for his increasing dissipations became clear soon enough. Alderman Cox was suing him for £2,000 for the loss of the love and company of Mrs. Cox. On January 17, 1825, the case was heard in the Court of King's Bench. The affair had started eight years earlier when Kean was playing Othello at the Taunton Theatre. A good-looking, lavishly dressed woman in a box caught his attention; it was obvious that she was paying the narrowest attention to his every move and word; toward the close of the fourth act she fainted. There was confusion, of course; the play was halted while the lady was lifted across the stage and placed in the star's dressing room. When the curtain fell, she apologized for the interruption she had caused, expressed her profound admiration for him, and introduced her husband, Robert Cox, an alderman of London, who was twelve years older than she. Cox had been a widower when he married her and her fortune in 1805. During the trial, Cox's counsel spoke of her as a woman of intellect with an admiration for Shakespeare, and of Cox as "tender" and "unsuspicious."

At first Cox was delighted to make the acquaintance of the famous actor, and invited him to visit them in London. Kean and his wife did so, and a friendship developed between the two couples. But presently Mrs. Kean understood that her husband's feelings for Mrs. Cox were of a different order from those of friendship, and when all four were present she suggested that it would be best if they ceased seeing one another. Though she refused to visit the Coxes again, they continued to entertain Kean frequently. Cox indeed kept coming to a box to see the actor, either alone or with Mrs. Cox's niece. At the trial Kean's dresser testified that Kean had refused to allow Mrs. Cox into his dressing room, but Cox himself often waited for the actor after a performance, brought him home with him for supper, and persuaded him many times to stay there overnight. He was indeed tender and unsuspicious!

The comedian Cowell told a story that during Lent when the theater was closed Cox was one of a party dining at a tavern. It was remarked that contrary to custom, Kean was drinking very little; Cox, who was guest of honor spoke up: "I have excused Mr. Kean. The fact is, I have made a promise for him that he shall spend the evening with my wife, and if he takes too much wine, I don't know what may be the consequences." Cox laughed boisterously, Kean left early, and Cox remained with his hosts until three in the morning. The letters exchanged between Kean and Mrs. Cox left little doubt as to their relationship. He called her "my heart-strings," and declared they were made for each other. When he was playing outside London, he wrote in the same strain. ("Fly swift, ye hours, until we meet once more.") It would appear the lady's motives were not strictly amatory; she and her husband benefited from the large sums he was constantly giving her—as their correspondence indicated. No one ever exceeded Kean in generosity when his emotions were involved.

Kean's counsel brought in plenty of evidence that Kean was not the only recipient of Mrs. Cox's favors. Through it all Cox continued, it would seem, to express tenderness and lack of suspicion. When Kean left for America, Mrs. Cox offered to go with him, but he refused. Her letters to him betrayed considerable concern as to how much money he was making. On his return, their intimacy was resumed, Mrs. Kean attempting to bear it with patience. When out of London, he wrote Mrs. Cox his fear that his wife might be following him or appear unannounced. "I am watched more closely than Bonaparte at St. Helena," he wrote his "heart-strings." Again: "The eyes of Argus may be eluded, but those of a jealous wife—impossible."

The love affair ended when Mrs. Cox became enamored of a youth, a clerk in her husband's office, though Kean's passion was as hectic as ever. Suddenly Cox's financial situation had become desperate; he was in need of a large sum, when this unsuspecting husband came upon a large bundle of Kean's letters to his wife. He was shocked. The only recourse open to his outraged honor was a suit for £2,000. He continued to be tender, however; he took lodgings for her in Norfolk Street, where, oddly enough, Cox's clerk also took up residence. The alderman sought neither divorce nor separation from his erring wife; all he wished was £2,000.

During the trial Kean refused to use his "heart-strings'" letters. The jury took ten minutes to award £800 to the tender husband.

Kean suddenly became the chief butt of laughter in London, was estranged from his family, and avoided by many friends. Elliston was afraid that it would be advisable for Kean to cease acting for a time until the scandal died down. But one week after the hearing, Kean insisted on playing Richard III (January 24, 1825). He was, he said, "ready for war." On that day immense crowds were at the theater, and the streets leading to it were clogged with people. When the doors opened, there was a tremendous rush, and pit and galleries were filled at once. Many, without the right to be there, took over the boxes and first circle. There was a great deal of shouting for and against Kean, quotations from the letters he had sent his beloved, jeers, and much talk of heart-strings. The noise was so great that the musicians playing the overture could not hear themselves. When the curtain rose, the actors were engulfed in cries for "Kean! Kean!" When Kean at length entered and came to the center of the stage, as was his usual entrance in this role, the pit rose, and there were hootings, shrieks, cheers, uproars—all increasing in volume. Bewildered, he stood still. Then he bowed, expecting to be heard; his gesture only increased the fury of the mob. He decided to begin his part, but the din completely drowned out his voice, so that the scene was performed in pantomime. In the pit blows were interchanged; in the boxes, cards were exchanged as preliminaries to duels. Kean made another attempt to address the audience, but this only exasperated them the more. He tried to continue the play as usual, and his valor only caused his enemies to shout the most offensive and shameful names at him; oranges were thrown at him by the virtuous. He went on to the end. At the fall of the curtain when he and Elliston were called for, neither appeared.

Four days later Kean bravely performed Othello. The audience was smaller but the confusion just as great. A man in a box, during the first scene, began to abuse Kean by name; Kean's friends pelted the offender with oranges until he left the theater. In the pit, one brave man mounted his bench and declared that an actor's private life was not for an audience to judge; he was rebuffed by the rejoinder that Kean's appearing so soon after the trial was an expression of contempt for the public. Cheers, hisses, and fights ensued again, while not a line of the play was heard. After the play Elliston was summoned. He stated that his engagement of Kean had been made before anyone knew there was going to be a law suit. He ended by asking them to hear Kean, and came back with him. After cheers and hisses the actor was allowed to speak. He told the audience that they were going to be disappointed if they thought that he intended "explaining or justifying" his "private conduct . . . I stand before you . . . as the representative of Shakespeare's heroes." His private conduct had been judged by legal tribunal, he added, "and decency forbade my publishing letters and giving evidence that would inculpate others . . . I will not submit to be trampled upon by a hostile press; but if the public is of opinion that my conduct merits exclusion from the stage, I am ready to . . . take my farewell." The speech was followed by cries of "No, no! Kean for ever!"

Though confusion continued on his next appearances, the opposition was getting weaker and weaker, and eventually was heard from no more. The newspapers had been largely responsible for the violence against him. The worst of these was the London *Times,* which set itself up as the guardian of chastity—a situation all the more revolting since the editor of that journal was well known to be living in adultery. Just the same the *Times* declared that Kean's supporters were bullies, prize fighters, Jews, and, in sum, vermin. What Englishwoman of character, it asked, would "after the filthy exposure of Mr. Kean" ever think of going to a theater where he was playing? And who were the actresses and whence came they—these women whom Elliston brought on the stage "to be fawned upon and caressed by this obscene animal?"

It did not take long for all this to be forgotten by most people—except Kean. For the next months he was near madness in his personal distress. When his engagement ended in March, the theater was filled, and at the conclusion of the play he was called for. The hearty welcome accorded him gave him a few minutes pause before he could collect himself, and then he spoke: "I have been able to overcome one of the most powerful and most malignant attacks to which a professional man has ever been subjected." There were cries from the audience: "The rascally *Times!*" He thanked the public for saving him from that base plan for his destruction. "My gratitude is indelible, and my endeavours to merit your favours shall be unceasing."

But he was thoroughly disillusioned. He had been betrayed by the woman he loved and obviously used for the basest of motives, he had lost his family, and he decided to go to live in the United States. He thought he would first make a tour of the British provinces. At Edinburgh he was hissed, and one man rose from a box to declare that the theater would never see him or any member of his family again, and that he would persuade his friends to do likewise as long as the playhouse was so indifferent to morality.

It is not surprising that Kean's brain was affected. He would mix the lines of the character he was playing with an account of his private affairs (as poor John Barrymore was to do during his last years on the stage). Sometimes in playing his tragic roles he would turn somersaults and handsprings, with the explanation, "I may as well practice, for I suppose I must come back to this." At Cheltenham, as a result of an attack in a local paper which brought up the trial, he kept a horsewhip in his hand, and told the spectators, "I keep this little instrument to punish cheating aldermen and lying editors." At Greenock the audience was so hostile that he left the theater before he had finished *Richard III,* and in his costume went down to the harbor and boarded a boat sailing for Bute. At Manchester and Dublin he was greeted with the old enthusiasm. In June he was back in London for what he thought would be his last performances there; there was no opposition, but the audience remained cold.

Grattan said that before Kean left for America, he had never seen a man so changed. "He had an air of desperation about him." He had suffered too much.

When he arrived in New York to play the Park Theater, it was to find admirers and enemies ready to create a disturbance on his very first night. He made his entrance as Richard but the booing and the cheering made it impossible for him to speak. The manager came forward and asked the audience to give Kean a fair hearing; the bedlam began all over again. The play proceeded, nothing being audible because of the shouts of "Cox" and "Mrs. Cox," mingled with every sort of low epithet hurled at the actor himself. Then oranges began to fly; one hit him in the chest. He picked it up and with elaborate disdain threw it in the wings. This action for some reason vastly augmented the mob's fury. A member of the orchestra leaped on the stage to rescue his wife, an actress, and led her off stage.

The next day a letter by the actor appeared in the *New York Advocate.* The voice of the public, he said, proves only too clearly his having been in error, and he promised to go to Boston to atone for his mistake; but he was in the country this time under far different circumstances. "Then I was an ambitious man . . . now the spark of ambition is extinct, and I merely ask a shelter in which to close my professional and mortal career." The letter was followed by editorial comment which stated that offended virtue could best show itself by not going to the theater to cause a riot. A few nights later, he did Othello; this time word had got around to his supporters not to cheer, the hissing grew less, and by the third act his superb acting silenced even his enemies. At the end he was thunderously applauded, and recalled by an audience now anxious to atone for its misconduct. From that night on, all his performances were enthusiastically applauded at the Park.

At Albany his reception was more than gratifying. But matters were far different in Boston. The day before his first performance he inserted a letter in a newspaper admitting his former error and adding that he had suffered for errors and indiscretions. But the press reacted to this letter with bitter hostility, calling for vengeance for the insult visited upon the city, and bringing up the recent trial. By the afternoon of his opening night, there was already an uproar around the theater. All tickets had been sold, and only minutes after the doors were opened, all places were taken by men; women had wisely stayed away. Kean appeared before the curtain, not yet in his costume, to make public apology and explanation. A wild howl silenced him, and he was showered with cabbages, oranges, brass buttons, water squirted from syringes, and bottles of ill-smelling drugs. A great many of these hit him, and he left the stage. He tried a second time, with like result. When *Richard III* at last began with a substitute for Kean, the audience shouted that they wanted Kean on stage. One actor announced that he had already left the premises. The play stopped, but not the violence. The hundreds outside who had not been able to enter broke the bolted doors open and forced their way into the boxes; battles were fought, windows broken, and those who wished to escape injury were forced to jump through the windows. The battle now continued in the pit, from there to the stage, and thence behind the scenes, with insistent calls for Kean. His pursuers, like a pack of wolves, searched everywhere, including the wardrobes. They donned helmets, seized halberds and swords, rushed back on stage, wrenched brackets from the chandeliers, and broke the glass. The mob outside hurled bricks in the windows; the curtains were torn to shreds, and the gas put out. About one o'clock that morning Kean, disguised, set out for Providence, from there to Worcester, and thence to New York, where he arrived prostrate. The Boston *Courier*'s comment was: "We did not believe that so worthless a fellow, such a double-faced beggar for 'an asylum in which to end his professional and mortal career' would have confidence enough to raise so much feeling on his account."

In New York he played Lear to an enthusiastic audience, and when he was called for he said a few words about his reception in Boston. He was persuaded, after declining, to go next to Philadelphia, where he was pelted in the same manner as at Boston. For the first half of the play he could not be heard, but seizing a favorable moment he stepped forward and said: "This is your quarrel, not mine." The effect of the remark and his brilliant performance brought silence, and after the play a large crowd gathered around the stage door, cheering him loudly. For the next two weeks of his stay in Philadelphia his audiences were wild in their applause. After returning to New York, he went to Charleston, where Joe Cowell, who had emigrated there from England and greatly admired Kean, hastened to greet him. What he found was "this wreck of better days feeble in body, and that brilliant pale face a Raphael might have envied for a study" sickly looking. But Baltimore turned out to be another Boston for the first part of the play; when Cowell, the manager, came on the empty stage and picked up all the missiles which had been thrown, Kean was allowed to proceed and ended by receiving great applause. The next day leading citizens left their cards, dinner parties were given him, carriages placed at his disposal, and while he was in that city he earned more than £50 a night.

He did well at Montreal and Quebec. At Quebec a number of Indians came to see him; Kean wished to make their acquaintance, entertained them, sang for them, tumbled for them, and asked to become a member of their tribe. Ceremoniously they invested him with their costume and gave him the name of Alanienouidet. He suddenly disappeared with them, and left their encampment only when a few friends sought him out there. On his return to New York he sent an invitation to Dr. Francis to come and visit the famous Indian chief Alanienouidet. The doctor, having no idea who this strange Indian was, came, and found Kean seated on a great throne in his Indian garb; thick gold rings hung from his nose and ears, his face was streaked with yellow and red paint; he wore a collar of bear skins, and buffalo hides on his body. A tomahawk also dangled from a broad belt, and in his hands he held a bow and arrow. He was as delighted as a child with the impression he had made on Francis.

His performances during his final week in New York were a triumph again. He left for England on December 5, 1826, a man much depleted in health.

Meanwhile in London, Elliston had become bankrupt, and Stephen Price was the new manager. Kean received a letter purporting to have come from

Price asking him to return to Drury Lane. He hastened home, only to learn that the letter was a hoax. However, he was offered an opportunity to play there for twelve nights at £50 a night. He opened as Shylock, and although he was not due to appear until the third scene, the crowded house was shouting for him before the curtain rose; the cries continued during the first scene of the play, until he at last appeared. The cheering was deafening; the pit rose, handkerchiefs were waved all over the house. It is said he gave one of the best performances of his career to an audience that had last treated him with disdain. When called for at the fall of the curtain, he took his time, and appeared without costume or makeup. He looked worn and haggard. They asked for a speech, but he merely bowed, and left. His Othello was also well received; still, it was obvious that some of the old fire was gone. But in a performance of *Richard III* he showed himself indisputably to be only a wreck of his former self. He was now so used to squandering his money that he was forced to work when he should have been resting.

He therefore accepted an engagement for Dublin, where his fatigue was only too obvious; he was, moreover, suffering from a sore leg. In his honor, the committee and actors commissioned a portrait of him to be painted, and he insisted on posing in the costume of the Indian chief. He made his farewell speech before the curtain in that same outfit.

Back at Drury Lane, his health was rapidly declining. Asked to appear in a new play, he missed many rehearsals, including the final one, but spent many days memorizing his lines. When the play was presented and he was due on the stage, he failed to appear and was found in his dressing room weeping and in total despair: he could not remember his part. Forced to appear, he spoke, said the dramatist, "two or three sentences, but not six consecutive words" of the nine lines written for him. His looks and tone were appalling, and he continued almost motionless and with glazed eye. It was obvious to all, as the play went on, that not only did he not know his lines but he had lost his dramatic power. There was not a spark left of that genius which had carried him through so many triumphs. A morning paper said the sight of "the wreck of great energies" had proved "afflicting."

On his way to his dressing room the dramatist found him being supported by two men. Hanging his head, he murmured, "I have ruined a fine play and myself; I cannot look you in the face."

Mrs. Kean was living alone in retirement on an allowance; their son was at Eton. Kean intended his son for the navy. But a few months before he was to leave Eton, Mrs. Kean sent for him and implored him not to take up a profession that would remove him from her during her illness. He gave his word, met his father, told him he could not leave his mother sick and helpless, and when asked by him what he would do when thrown upon his own resources, said he would go on the stage. Kean was in a rage.

"Mr. Kean, Junior" appeared at Drury Lane October 1, 1827, in an old non-Shakespearean play; a mere stripling somewhat resembling his father, though totally lacking his expressiveness, he was nevertheless well greeted. But *The Times*, once so malicious about his father, continued the attack

against the son, and advised him to quit the stage. In subsequent performances the audiences became smaller and smaller for the boy. At Dublin he
fared better and was very much liked.

Meanwhile his father agreed to act at Covent Garden, where he did Shylock to great applause. He acted in that theater throughout the winter,
though illness several times prevented his appearance. In the spring of 1828
he went to Paris with his *Richard III,* but the Parisians, used to the declamatory style, did not particularly appreciate his energetic acting. His second
appearance was to be as Othello; the house was crowded, but Kean was not
to be found; messengers traced him to a café, where he was quietly drinking
cognac. He was already drunk. Upon being informed that a full house
awaited him, including the Duchess de Beri, he disclaimed any interest: "I
am not a servant of the Duchess de Beri." At length persuaded to leave his
drinking, he went to the theater—but it was only too obvious that he had
had too much to drink. The next night the audience was so thin that he
returned to England.

During the autumn a friend offered to make peace between him and his
son. The latter came to see his father in the country and Kean not only
warmly welcomed him, but offered to do a benefit night for him at Glasgow.
They both appeared together and the receipts were over £300.

In November, Kean was again at Covent Garden in his most celebrated
roles. But his health was bad and his performances uneven. He forgot lines,
but then would gather his spirits together and be something like the old
Kean. In December his son, now seventeen, was at Drury Lane; and father
and son were at rival houses. The boy's acting was still highly immature.

In January 1829, Kean retired to Bute because of his health and embel-
lished the furnishings of his cottage. But he now had a liaison with a notorious woman known as Ophelia, a degraded and unprincipled doxy, who
squeezed out of him every shilling he earned. His son was touring the
provinces, learning his profession, and was engaged in October for the
Haymarket in London with success. In December Kean returned to Drury
Lane though his contract with Covent Garden had not expired. The management of that theater tried to procure an injunction against his acting at
the rival house, but failed.

After repeating his repertory of great tragic heroes at Drury Lane, Kean
wished to introduce new roles. *Henry V* was announced for February 22,
1830, but on that evening he was seized with an attack of illness while
dressing for the part. His dresser called for help, and when the manager
came in poor Kean did not even recognize him. Under the rouge his face
was haggard and ghastly, and he seemed unable to move. The performance
was canceled before the doors had been opened. His health somewhat
recovered, he was ready for the new role on March 8. But he kept the
audience, a full house, waiting a long time. When he came on stage he was
wildly applauded. He began, spoke a few lines, hesitated, looked to the
prompter, added words not in the text, omitted others, finally mangled his
part completely. The audience was amazed but filled with pity for the fall

of such greatness. There were long waits between acts, with Kean, when on stage, hesitating, mumbling, confusing the lines and throwing the other actors off. When the audience was forced to wait a half-hour after the fourth act, they began to hiss and shout. Kean came on stage, a beaten, solitary figure, to address them. When he was able to procure silence, a most distressing colloquy ensued:

KEAN: Ladies and gentlemen, it is now many years since I have had the honor to enjoy a large share of your approbation. You may conceive, therefore, how deeply I deplore this moment when for the first time I incur your displeasure.

CRIES FROM THE AUDIENCE: No, no, not the first time.

KEAN: If you wish that I should proceed, I must request your silence. For many years, give me leave to say, I have worked hard for your entertainment.

A VOICE: You have been well paid for it.

KEAN: That very labor and the lapse of time and circumstances have no doubt had their effects upon my mind.

ANOTHER VOICE: Why do you drink so hard?

KEAN [*hesitant*]: Ladies and gentlemen, I feel that I stand before you in a most degraded situation.

VARIOUS VOICES: No, no. Why did you put yourself into it?

KEAN: You are my countrymen, and I appeal with confidence to that liberality which has always distinguished Englishmen.

He put his hand on his heart, bowed, took his place among the actors, tried to continue the last act, botched and so abbreviated it that it did not last ten minutes.

Two days later he wrote to the manager of Drury Lane, admitting that the unlimited enthusiasm he had once received had given him a false sense of his invulnerablity, and that his memory was now deserting him. One can only conjecture on what violent dissipation must have preceded his fiasco in *Henry V*, for in a few weeks he was playing Richard III with a great deal of his old spirit and was warmly applauded. One paper went so far as to say: "It is a matter of doubt if he ever played Richard better." His next role, Hamlet, was begun with his old vigor, but soon he began to omit and confuse passages. Between scenes he went neither to his room nor the greenroom, but sat in the wings panting, with his dresser beside him to provide hot brandy punch.

Offered £100 for two nights at the Victoria Theatre, his first night as Richard was all that he could desire, but on the second night when he played Othello to Cobham's Iago, he was constantly put off by cries of "Bravo, Cobham!" Applause for him was much weaker. After the play, when he was called for, saturated with alcohol he asked the audience: "What do you want?" "You, you!" some cried. "Well then, here I am. I have acted in every theatre in the United Kingdom of Great Britain and Ireland, and in all the principal towns throughout the United States of America, but in my life I never acted to such a set of ignorant, unmitigated brutes as I now see before me," and made his exit.

From then on he acted irregularly, sometimes at the Haymarket, sometimes at Drury Lane. Doran saw him in 1832 "for the last of many times as Richard. The sight was pitiable. Genius was not traceable in that bloated face; intellect was all but quenched in those once matchless eyes; and the power seemed gone, despite the will that would recall it. . . . By bursts he was as grand as he had ever been, . . . he moved with difficulty, using his sword as a stick." There were moments of marvelous effectiveness. "But he was exhausted before the fifth act, and when, after a short fight, Richmond gave him his death blow, he grasped Kean by the hand, and let him gently down, lest he should be injured by a fall."

His last appearance on the stage was Othello, with his son, Charles, playing Iago, on March 25, 1833. His nerves were shattered, he begged his son to remain close by. He got as far as: "Villain, be sure thou prove my love a whore . . ." when he fell into his son's arms and cried: "Oh God! I am dying . . . speak to them for me." He was carried out.

He sent a note to his wife to come see and forgive him; she went and forgave. He lingered a while, and died on May 15. As Doran says in extenuation of his vices, the other great actors who had been his predecessors had known no such privation, no such disappointments, no such lack of affection, care, education, and lack of the barest needs as Kean in his youth. "Kean was trained upon blows, and curses, and starvation, and the charity of strangers." Yet he cherished his ambition and never ceased to prepare himself to be ready when the moment struck. He had "said that success would drive him mad. I believe it did."

Hazlitt wrote of his Othello that though his voice and person were "not altogether in consonance with the character," there were "repeated bursts of feeling and energy which we have never seen surpassed." The latter part of Act III "was a masterpiece of profound pathos and exquisite conception, and its effect on the house was electrical." This was at Kean's first season in the theater. When he soon undertook Iago, Hazlitt called it "the most faultless of his performances, the most consistent and active . . . A gay, light-hearted monster, or careless, cordial complete villain." As Macbeth later that year, his playing of the scene after Duncan's murder was perhaps his greatest performance: "the hesitation, the bewildered look, the coming to himself when he sees his hands bloody, the manner in which his voice clung to his throat and choked [sic] his utterance . . . beggared description." It was unforgettable. His Hamlet raised him even higher in Hazlitt's estimation, though he felt he made the prince too strong. Hazlitt thought his Coriolanus not sufficiently patrician: "he is one of the people." The critic blamed the early detractors who could not see that though an actor might have an insignificant body and the voice of a raven, and lack grace and dignity (all of which Kemble had), he might "yet have enough nature and passion . . . to set up a whole corps of regular stagers," for Kean's "merits far exceeded his defects."

Lewes wisely said:

> It is not by his faults, but by his excellences, that we measure a great man. . . . Thus estimated, Edmund Kean was incomparably the greatest actor I have seen, although even warm admirers must admit that he had many and serious defects. . . . His miming power, though admirable within a certain range, was singularly limited in its range. . . . But he was an actor of such splendid endowments in the highest departments of the art, that no one in our day can be named of equal rank. . . . Critics who had formed their ideal on the Kemble school were shocked at Kean's want of dignity. . . . He stirred the general heart with such a rush of mighty power, impressed himself so vividly by accent, look and gesture, that it was vain to protest against his defects. . . . His physical aptitudes were such as confined him to the strictly tragic passions; and for these he was magnificently endowed. . . . I remember the last time I saw him play Othello, how puny he seemed beside Macready, until the third act, when roused by Iago's taunts and insinuations he moved toward him with a gouty hobble, seized him by the throat, and . . . seemed to swell in stature which made Macready appear small. On that very evening, when gout made it difficult for him to display his accustomed grace, when a drunken hoarseness had ruined the once matchless voice, such was the irresistible pathos— manly, not tearful—which vibrated in his tones and expressed itself in look and gestures, that old men leaned their heads upon their arms and fairly sobbed.

Keats said of Kean: "The sensual life of verse springs from his lips. His tongue seems to have robbed the Hybla bees and left them honeyless." Byron wrote of him:

> The shrine thou worshipest is nature's self,
> The only altar genius deigns to seek.

His contemporary, Booth, Sr., said that Kean's farewell to arms speech "sounded like the moan of ocean or the soughing of wind through cedars." People were forever comparing him with Kemble, to Kean's annoyance; there was no need of it, he felt. "However," he would add smilingly, "I can do one thing he could not do!"—and then he would cut a somersault.

14

Contemporaries of Kean

William August Conway (1789–1828), whose real name was Rugg, was born in London. At Bath he fell in love with the stage and, despite parental objections, decided to become an actor. He did so well at Chester that Macready, manager of the theater, engaged him; after playing Macbeth and other non-Shakespearean roles, he accepted an offer from the Crow Street Theatre in Dublin in a number of parts. He was probably the tallest actor then in the profession, being six feet two inches, and also one of the best-looking. His nickname was Handsome Conway. For all his good looks, he was pathologically sensitive. In Dublin he fell in love with Miss O'Neill, with whom he acted, but she proved immune to him.

Covent Garden heard of him and he appeared there in 1813, playing Romeo, Henry V, Coriolanus, Petruchio, Orlando, Richmond (in *Richard III*), Prince Hal, and Antony (in *Julius Caesar*). He assumed other important roles, but often had to do secondary ones in support of Kemble. In 1819 Mrs. Piozzi, then a woman of eighty, fell madly in love with him and, though he was young enough to be her grandson, proposed marriage. He, naturally, did what he could to evade her advances.

The press was untiring in its attacks on him because he was clearly ill at ease and self-conscious on stage. "Mr. Conway must always be tracing a circle with one leg, while with the other he acts the part of a pivot," was a characteristic comment. Hazlitt, speaking of his Romeo, said, "He bestrides the stage like a Colossus, throws his arms like the sails of a windmill, and his motion is as unwieldy as that of a young elephant; his voice breaks as thunder on the ear like Gargantua's, but when he pleases to be soft, he is 'the very beadle to an amorous sigh.' "

Unable to bear these banterings longer, he refused any further offers from London or the provinces, saying he would rather break stones on the road than accept the most attractive engagement on the stage. At the end of 1823 he started out for America, and in January played successfully in New York as Coriolanus and Petruchio among others. Four years later, on January 24, 1828, wearing summer apparel on a boat bound for Charleston, as the passengers were going down to dinner, he committed suicide by jumping overboard. His body was never found.

Ira Aldridge (1807–1867) was the first prominent black actor to emerge from the United States, and also the first black man from America to become a naturalized British citizen. He is said to have been born on the west coast of Africa.

In 1787 the earliest Afro-American Free School was founded in New York by the Society for the Manumission of Slaves. It opened with forty pupils; Cornelius Davis, who gave up his white classes, was teacher. In 1815 a comfortable building was erected on William Street as African Free School Number 1. Number 2 was opened in 1820 on Mulberry Street, near Grand. Ira was a student at Number 2. The schools were producing future distinguished citizens. The teaching was first-rate and the students eager. From boyhood Ira was ambitious to be an actor. The gallery at the Park Theater (which opened facing City Hall Park in 1798) was reserved for blacks; the third tier of boxes was set aside for prostitutes. Doors opened at six-thirty and the performances began at seven o'clock. Thomas Abthorp Cooper had emigrated from England and in 1805 became manager of the Park. At the age of eleven Ira could have seen Wallack as Macbeth, Richard III, Romeo, Hamlet, Coriolanus, Henry V, and Brutus. In 1820 Kean came to do Richard III, Othello, Hamlet, Lear, and Shylock.

A Mr. Brown, steward on a Liverpool liner, hired a house on Thomas Street and opened a tea shop much patronized by the blacks of the city. James Hewlett started out there as a singer, and then began to do scenes from plays. A native of the West Indies, Hewlett also went with the world of fashion to Saratoga. There he advertised himself as "Vocalist, and Shakespeare's proud Representative." Brown soon built a theater on Mercer Street seating about three hundred fifty. This was the first playhouse for blacks in the United States; white people began to attend—and places were set apart for *them!* Hewlett continued with his imitations of Kean's Richard III and parts taken by other actors. The last one hears of him is in New York during 1830/31 at the Chatham Theater, where he was billed as "the celebrated tragedian."

Aldridge was probably acting in a similar capacity at Brown's theater while Hewlett was the star. Charles Mathews, the actor, came to the United States in 1822, and visited the theater for blacks where a tragedian was doing speeches of Hamlet; Mathews reports that the soliloquy went in this manner: "To be or not to be, dat is him question, whether him nobler in de mind to suffer or lift up him arms against a sea of hubble bubble and by oppossum end 'em." At the word "opossum," the whole audience burst forth with the cry "Opossum, opossum!"—a reference to a popular song, "Opossum up a Gum Tree." The tragedian (who was definitely not Aldridge) stepped forward and said he would be happy to oblige by singing the song, which he did.

We know that Aldridge got a job behind scenes with the Wallack brothers. James Wallack took him to England, but made the mistake of saying that Aldridge was his servant. A quarrel and a rupture followed. Aldridge was then seventeen. The next year, 1825, he was engaged at the Coburg Theatre in London. Apparently he attended the University of Glasgow for a while.

At the Coburg he was presented as "MR. KEENE, TRAGEDIAN OF COLOUR." By 1827 he was being called "The Celebrated Mr. Keene, the African Roscius." By 1831 this had changed to "I. W. Keene Aldridge, the African Roscius." He did Othello at Brighton in 1825, but was not well received. He was chiefly criticized for lacking passion and dignity.

During his first year in England he married a white woman, an admirer, and he never returned to the United States. In 1827 the government of Haiti gave him a commission in the 17th Grenadier Guards of its army as "the first man of colour in the theater." But he must have concentrated on his art for he was later lauded for the very qualities which the critics first said he lacked. Later he played Shylock, Lear, and Aaron (in *Titus Andronicus*). At Belfast he played with Charles Kean, whose father was deeply impressed by his abilities.

In 1833, Edmund Kean retired and Laporte, manager of Covent Garden, engaged him to do Othello. Except for the dying Kean the cast remained the same. Aldridge was blamed for lack of spirit and feeling, his "drawling" manner and vulgar accent. But the audience liked him. He was also charged by the critics with ranting too much. He was twenty-six, but the critical verdict was: "he has no genius, but is not without talent." His second Othello was canceled.

It looked as though he were doomed to play in the provinces. He made one appearance at the Royal Shakespeare Theatre at Stratford as Othello on April 28, 1851. On July 14, 1852, he left England for Brussels, Cologne, Bonn, Leipzig. After six months he began to act in English with local casts speaking German. Leopold I of Belgium became his patron. Royalty at Leipzig was enthusiastic over his Macbeth. He played at Berlin and Potsdam; one German critic wrote: "After this Othello it would be an anti-climax to have seen an ordinary Othello again." They loved him just as much as Macbeth, and for it King Frederick IV of Prussia awarded him the Prussian Gold Medal of the First Class for Art and Science—an award that had also been given to Franz Liszt. At Dresden Jenny Lind called him the greatest Othello of them all.

After three years he was back in England playing the provinces. He now tried Hamlet and was highly praised for it. In 1857 he was invited to Stockholm, and the next year to Serbia, where he did Richard III. It was the first time Shakespeare was acted in that country.

He was made a knight of Saxony; he visited Moscow; there is a plaque to him at the National Theater in Belgrade. At last he was invited again to the West End in London in July 1858. He was now praised for the sweetness of his voice, and it was noted that he changed many words to make them less "offensive." In the same year he was feted at St. Petersburg. His Othello was compared to a tiger—and this may have been a just description, for in London Madge Kendal, who played Desdemona opposite him, has recorded that in the last scene "he used to take Desdemona out of bed by her hair and drag her round the stage before he smothered her." The Haymarket audience, she added, thought the business too brutal and hissed him.

It was generally agreed that he avoided attitudinizing. Wherever he played in Europe the rest of the company always spoke German, and he would throw in an occasional German phrase—probably to give fellow actors their cues. His Shylock was praised too; he made him greedy, firm, and proud. St. Petersburg saw his first Lear, and it has been affirmed that he exerted a great influence on the Russian actors. He made a second tour of Russia in 1862. The next year, at the age of fifty-six, he became a British citizen. His wife, who was nine years his senior, died in 1864. His second wife was twenty-seven years younger than he; she was a young Swedish woman whom he married in 1865. He had had a child by her five years before the marriage.

He died in Lodz, Poland, where he is buried. During his lifetime he amassed a considerable fortune. Sometimes he had been advertised as descended from "Princes of Senegal." It is believed that the great spur to his ambition was given him by the ever generous Edmund Kean. From what we know of his style it was fairly solemn and gloomy—except for the concluding scene with Desdemona, as already described.

Charles Mayne Young (1777–1856), when he did *Antony and Cleopatra* at Covent Garden in 1813, incorporated much of Dryden's version (*All for Love*), but he must be credited with having introduced for the first time an historically accurate toga when he performed Coriolanus and Brutus. Alas, it was generally thought that his toga did not in any way match the costumes of his fellow actors in the cast. It was the great François-Joseph Talma who had taught him how to wear a senatorial robe, and Young, in turn, taught Charles Kemble how to wear one. He was himself an actor of the John Philip Kemble school and in that style won considerable respect at the Haymarket. His Iago was "jocular and sarcastic," but little more than that, and made Othello seem, as did José Ferrer in our own time, "an object of contempt for his credulity."

Young's father was an eminent London surgeon, but profligate, selfish, tyrannical, and utterly callous toward his family. He made life at the Young home intolerable, going so far as to propose bringing his mistress to live with them. The three boys took their mother away. The doctor was one of those hypocrites who though beastly at home could charm strangers; he was much admired for the melody of his speech and his good looks.

One night two ruffians were discovered in the act of laying a corpse at his door. They had been employed by Dr. Young, who, when they were arrested and committed for trial, came to their rescue; he avowed himself responsible for the offense, since they were his instruments, and insisted that their malfeasance had been done in the interest of science with the object of saving human life. His eloquence so moved judge and jury that not only were the culprits acquitted but the judge declared that after Young's extraordinary display of forensic powers, "if you had bent the powers of your mind to the study and practice of the law, there are no heights in the legal profession to which you might not have aspired."

Before young Charles left home, it was his father's practice to give dinners frequently to friends and acquaintances; Charles was allowed to appear when the dessert was being served. It was on one such occasion that while descending the stairs to the dining room in his best clothes he saw a sluttish woman on one of the hall chairs and a boy, fantastically dressed and with "the blackest and most penetrating eyes" he had ever beheld, standing by her side. He thought them strolling gypsies. But he had no sooner entered the dining room than the doctor, with a smirk and a smile, asked the butler to "bring in the boy." On the child's entry he was asked to furnish an example of his histrionic ability. With incredible self-assurance the lad advanced, knitted his brow, hunched up a shoulder blade, and with a sardonic grin and husky voice recited Gloucester's opening soliloquy in *Richard III*. After that he went on to serious and light verses from the poets, danced a hornpipe, sang comic and pathetic songs, and for a full hour kept the company vociferously applauding. A napkin was opened on the floor and a shower of crowns and shillings was thrown on it for him. Having stuffed his treasure into his gaping pockets with an expression of gratitude, he joined his ragged companion in the hall. The doctor remarked that it was not the first time he had had the boy in to amuse friends, and that all he knew about the lad was that his name was Edmund Kean.

While still a clerk, Charles Young began studying for the stage, and acted among other towns at Liverpool, Manchester, and Glasgow. In 1805 he married the beautiful Julia Ann Grimani. They were very happy, but she died the following year after the birth of their son Julian. Young was in such a state of shock that he could not look at the boy for six years.

Young appeared as Hamlet at the Haymarket in London on June 22, 1807. When that theater burned to the ground the next year, he moved with the company to the Opera House, where his popularity grew. He was at Covent Garden for the 1809/10 season, and stayed there for twelve years.

In July 1810 it was announced that there had arrived the largest elephant ever seen in England. The manager of Covent Garden thought it would be a fine idea to use it in a pantomime he was planning, and he bought the beast for nine hundred guineas. Mrs. Henry Johnston was to ride it, and Miss Parker, the Columbine, was to "play up to it." Young was passing the Covent Garden box office when his ears were assailed by a great and inexplicable uproar within the theater. One of the carpenters told him that "it was something going wrong with the elephant," though he could not tell what the trouble was. It had been arranged that Mrs. Johnston, seated in a howdah on the elephant's back, should pass over a bridge in the center of numerous followers, and they were testing the monster's tractability. But the wise animal, having tried the bridge, understood it was too slight, and refused to budge. Nothing would induce it to move on. It was in the midst of this that Young came on the stage.

He was indignant. There stood the great animal, its ears flapping, its eyes lowered, submitting to blow after blow from a sharp iron goad which the keeper was thrusting angrily into its neck at the base of the ear. The floor was already covered with blood. Worse yet, the keeper was being urged to strike severer blows. Young upbraided them all, went to the poor creature and began to pat and caress him. When the keeper was about to renew his blows, Young caught him by the wrist and made him stop. Luckily at this point, the captain of the ship which had brought over the elephant and who had given him much attention on the voyage, came in and demanded to know what was the matter. The elephant needed no advocate. As soon as he saw the captain, he waddled over to him, caught his hand with his proboscis, plunged it into his bleeding wound, and then thrust it before his friend's eyes to behold. Even the hardest hearts of those present were touched, including the manager who had been urging more extreme measures. In fact, the latter rushed into the street, bought a few apples at a stall, and offered them to the elephant. The wounded animal eyed the fruit askance, then took them and threw them to the ground, where he crushed them to a pulp as evidence of his scorn. Young, who had also gone out to bring some fruit for the poor beast, astonished everyone when they all saw the elephant accept the gift and eat every bit of what was given him. After that, he gently twined his trunk about Young's waist, proving that if he did not forget a wrong, he could appreciate a kindness.

In the year 1814 the elephant, whose name was Chuny, was given to the menagerie at Exeter Change, and Young was fond of paying him a visit, when passing through the Strand, thus keeping alive their friendship. Poor Chuny had a tragic end. For causes unknown, he went mad, and it took 152 shots to dispatch him.

In 1822 Young accepted an offer to play opposite Kean at Drury Lane. While Covent Garden, because of its bad financial situation, wished to reduce his salary from £25 to £20 a week, Drury Lane was offering him £50 a night, for a nine-month season during which he was to perform three times a week. He and Kean were to alternate in the roles of Othello and Iago; both men were receiving the same salary. On their first night of playing together, while Young was in his dressing room receiving congratulations from many friends, Kean was storming about the premises looking for the manager, Price, and swearing he would not give up the role of Othello to Young the next night. When Price explained that the terms of the contract required this interchange, Kean violently cried: "I don't care! if he plays after me the part I have just played, I will throw up my engagement, and you may seek your redress in a court of law." Price wished to know what had caused Kean to change his mind so radically in the evening since he had taken the opposite position in the morning. Kean replied: "I had never seen Young act. Everyone about me for several years has told me he could not hold a farthing rushlight to me; but he can! He *is* an actor; and though I flatter myself he could not act Othello as I do, yet what chance should I have in Iago after him, with his personal advantages and his damned musical voice? . . . I tell you what. Young is not only an actor, such as I did not dream him to have been, but he is a gentleman. Go to him, then, from me, and say that, if he will allow me to retain Othello . . . I shall esteem it as a personal obligation conferred upon me. Tell him he has just made as great a hit in Iago as I ever did in Othello." Young at once agreed to refrain from doing Othello to Kean's Iago.

Young's son Julian compared the equipment of the two actors:

> Young had a small, keen, brown, penetrating eye, overshadowed by a strongly-defined and bushy eyebrow. Kean's eye was infinitely finer; it was fuller, blacker and more intense. When kindled by real passion off the stage, or by simulated passion on, it gleamed with such scorching lustre as literally to make those who stood beneath its rays quail. In this feature . . . he had an immense superiority over Young. In figure, stature and deportment, Young had the advantage . . . for he had height, which Kean had not; . . . he moved [his limbs] gracefully: and his head and throat and bust were classically molded. Kean in his gait shuffled. Young trod the boards with freedom. Young's countenance was equally well adapted for the expression of pathos or of pride; thus in such parts as Hamlet . . . [and] Cassius he looked the men he represented. Kean's variable and expressive countenance, and even the insignificance of his person, rendered him the very type of a Shylock, a Richard, or a Sir Giles Overreach. Even his voice, which was harsh and husky (except in low and pathetic passages such as the "farewell" in *Othello* . . .) so far from detracting from its impressiveness, rather added to it. Young's voice, on the other hand, was full bodied, rich, powerful, and capable of every variety of modulation, and therefore in declamatory power he was greatly superior to Kean, and Kemble too . . . Young's happiest hits were the result of natural sensibility, quickness of apprehension and study. Kean dazzled his audience by coruscations of fancy, and the vivid light he shed on passages of which the meaning was obscure. Young hardly ever astonished; but . . . rarely failed to please. Kean's acting, as a rule, was unequal, negligent, and slipshod. . . . I have heard my father say that the passages on which Kean had bestowed most pains, and which were chastely and beautifully delivered, he never got a hand for; while his delivery of those which, to use his own phrase, caused "the house to rise to him," were in bad taste and meretricious.

Young's judgment of Kean's "bad taste" must be modified by the recognition that he himself belonged to Kemble's school, not Kean's, and his son's lauding his "declamatory" abilities has more significance than a casual reading might suggest. It was generally recognized that Young had learned much from Kemble, a fact that was memorialized in *The Thespiad:*

> To copy nature is by Kemble tried,
> To copy Kemble, Young is satisfied.

At any rate Young's success at Drury Lane was so great that Covent Garden invited him back with a tempting raise in salary.

He gave his farewell performance as Hamlet in 1832, and lived quietly among a large circle of cultivated friends. His personal character was impeccable; he was a great favorite in society, and mourned his wife until the end of his days.

A declaimer rather than a tragic actor, happily devoid of tricks, he performed many roles including Romeo, Petruchio, Othello, Iago, Ford, Macbeth, Cassius, Falstaff, King John, Lear, Shylock, Jaques, and Coriolanus. Hazlitt perhaps summed up his talents by saying that in *The Tempest*, which as a production was a travesty and caricature, modernized and loaded with all sorts of claptrap situations, Young as Prospero was "a respectable actor . . . who seldom gratifies and who seldom offends us, who never disappoints us because we do not expect anything from him." His Prospero was "grave without solemnity, stately without dignity, pompous without being impressive."

The Wallack family is not without interest. Henry John (1790–1870) played in London, New York, and the English provinces, and was well known for his Falstaff; he managed the Wallack Theater in New York from 1837. His brother James William (1791–1864) played at Drury Lane as Laertes and Iago, and came to New York in 1818. He was very handsome and distinguished looking, and introduced a repertory of Shakespeare's plays in 1852 at the second Wallack's Theater for some ten years. James's nephew, John Johnstone (1820–1888), known as Lester, performed in London and New York. He had a powerful physique, and did Macbeth, Othello, Iago, Richard III, but was not suited to comedy, except as Mercutio and Jaques; he acted with Helen Faucit and Charlotte Cushman. Wallack's Theater flourished under him until 1882.

Edmund Shaw Simpson (1784–1848) was an American actor and manager. His first appearances were in the English provinces and Dublin. Then he was engaged to come to the Park Theater in New York in 1809, where he remained for thirty-eight years. He played Richmond to the Richard III of Cooke, Kean, and the elder Booth, and became a great favorite until forced to retire because of an accident which made him lame. He was highly esteemed by the public for his long period of activity in drama, and his valiant struggle against adversity in his final years.

An interesting note is the appearance of the first Yiddish Shylock. At the Rochester Theatre, England, Sherenbeck, a Jew from Chatham, gave a performance of the role with a pronounced Yiddish intonation and accent, and was a great success, particularly in the trial scene. He was the first but by no means the last to attempt this.

John E. Harwood (1771–1809) was an American actor who married Benjamin Franklin's granddaughter. He became a famous Falstaff at the Park Theater in 1806 with Cooper acting as Hotspur. He had been with Thomas Wignell for some time in Philadelphia at the Chestnut Theater, but came to New York in 1797 to do low comedy parts. Dunlap, historian of the American stage, said he delivered some of the "richest pieces of comic acting ever witnessed." But later he changed his style, and preferred to act the polished gentleman. He remained at the Park Theater until his death.

James H. Hackett (1800–1871) was a fine Shakespearean scholar and a favorite comedian in the United States. His great roles were Falstaff and Dromio. But he also undertook tragedy, performing Richard III, Othello, Iago, and Gloucester. He did much to increase the prestige of American histrionic talent. He began to act in 1816 and continued throughout the Civil War, seen as frequently in England as in his own country. He was familiar with the Shakespearean criticism of Goethe and Schlegel, as well as that of Coleridge, and exchanged letters with John Quincy Adams on matters of Shakespearean interpretation. He was perhaps the first American to become a star in England, and was celebrated abroad for his Falstaff. He was handsome, hard working, and became manager of the Astor Place Theater though he had the misfortune to occupy that position during the riot which occurred there when Macready was appearing.

He showed early his extraordinary gift for mimicry and when he was nineteen married a popular actress of the day, Catharine Lee Sugg. Shortly after their wedding they settled, in April 1820, in Utica, New York, in the grocery business, and also sold crockery, then in demand. By 1825 he had enough money to think of returning to New York. His wife had already made a reputation (she was two years his elder) in comedy. "Her merry, romping lasses have never since been equalled, and her chambermaids were almost as meritorious," said a contemporary critic. We have some verses describing her:

> There's sweet Miss Lee Sugg—by-the-by, she's not pretty;
>   She's a little too large, and has not much grace;
> Yet there's something about her so witching and witty,
>   'Tis pleasure to gaze on her good-humored face.

On marrying she left the stage, but returned to it occasionally to help out her husband when he was in financial difficulties. When Hackett came back to New York he invested all his money unwisely, and was left almost penniless. But his friends rescued him, and it was then that Mr. and Mrs. Hackett turned to the stage (she for the second time).

Junius Brutus Booth (1796–1832) was the first of an acting family which became famous and notorious. He was born in a fairly well-to-do family with strong republican sympathies—hence his given name. It was a line that had no connection with Barton Booth. Junius Brutus was sent to Eton where he developed an enthusiasm for the classics and languages. But we find him at thirteen already the villain in a real life drama. He was accused by a neighbor's maid of seducing her and getting her with child. His father, a respected attorney, pleaded that his son's youth made the charge impossible, but young Junius Brutus was found guilty of fathering the baby.

The haphazardness of the following years was perhaps a first indication that his sanity would be questioned. He tried the navy, printing, the law, and sculpture by turns as a vocation, but soon hated each. Against his family's wishes he became an actor. At seventeen he was with a company of strolling players, and he soon was doing only bit parts; next he joined a troupe bound for Amsterdam. One of his early biographers gives us this picture of the lad in the hold of the vessel: a handsome, intelligent-looking youth, "seated astride a barrel eating a meat pie and shouting: 'By Holy Paul, I will not dine until his head be brought before me!' " In this traveling company he eventually was given the opportunity to enact Richard III.

In the midst of Napoleon's campaigns, Junius managed to elope with Marie Christine Delannoy and marry her, despite her mother's watchfulness. That year, 1815, they returned to England, nearly penniless. The marriage proved disastrous.

Like many another actor who rose to fame, he was rejected by Covent Garden, and accepted an offer at the Worthing Theatre for a miserable thirty shillings per week. But when Covent Garden heard how well he was being received, they called him, and he came for all of £2 a week as salary —luckily without breaking with Worthing. Luckily, because one night when Kean failed to appear at Worthing in *A New Way to Pay Old Debts*, which contained one of his most celebrated roles, Booth took his place. That night his own following began to increase until during his second season at Covent Garden he was given the chance to do Richard III. A contest immediately arose between followers of Kean and those of Booth. That contest had an odd quality because there was a marked physical resemblance between the two men. Booth was only twenty and Kean was at the very pinnacle of his fame—but the challenge certainly must have been discomforting to Kean. It was on February 12, 1817, that Booth gave his performance, which was at first accused of being an "ingenious fac-simile" of Kean's. Hazlitt wrote that "a gentleman of the name of Booth," who has acted "with considerable applause at Worthing and Brighton," has just done Richard III; "We do not know well what to think of his powers till we see him in some part in which he is more himself. His face is adapted to tragic characters, and his voice wants neither strength nor musical expression. But almost the whole of his performance was an exact copy or parody of Mr. Kean's . . . It was . . . at the same time a successful piece of plagiarism." Hazlitt went on to say that he did not blame Booth for his plagiarism "upon a first and trying occasion," but now he had better "come forward in his own person."

Success went to the young man's head and he began to squabble with the management. They offered an increase to £5 a week; he demanded more. One is strongly tempted to believe that what followed was a clever scheme hit upon by Kean to put the lad in his place. At this juncture Edmund Kean drove over to Covent Garden and carried off Booth to Drury Lane, where he found that a contract awaited him. Flattered, Booth agreed to play such parts as were assigned him for £8 the first year, with an increase to follow each year. It was at once announced that Booth would play Iago to Kean's Othello. It was a full house that watched them that night. There was plenty of sympathy for Booth against the Covent Garden management, and when

Iago said, early in the play, "I know my price," a voice from the pit cried out, "And you didn't get it at Covent Garden."

Molloy gives a graphic account of that night: "Booth at first seemed nervously to shrink from the contest, but overcoming his dread, went through his part with courage, and was ever and anon warmly applauded. Kean's self-possession was, as usual [at this time of his life], undisturbed. It was noticed that there was a greater firmness in his tread, that his voice was more clear, rapid, and decisive, but only the light flashing in his eyes indicated the emotions passing in his soul. His peculiar habit of walking diagonally from the middle of the stage into a corner, and then going half-way across the footlights, was adopted by Booth, and two persons moving in this way . . . had a somewhat ludicrous effect. As the tragedy advanced Kean's power was gradually felt, whilst Booth's declined in proportion. . . . Yet when he delivered his speeches he regained his position, and was warmly applauded." Barry Cornwall, who was present, remarked that Kean was reserving his strength during the first two acts, but once the jealousy was awakened in the third act, "he seemed to expand from the small, quick, resolute figure . . . and to assume the vigour and dimensions of a giant. He glared down at the now diminutive Iago; he seized and tossed him aside, with frightful and irresistible vehemence. Till then we had seen Othello and Iago . . . together; now the Moor seemed to occupy the stage alone . . . It seemed dangerous to cross his path, and death to assault him. There is no doubt but that Kean was excited on this occasion in a most extraordinary degree. . . . The impression which he made upon the audience has, perhaps, never been equalled in theatrical annals."

At the end of the play, Kean brought Booth out and, said John Howard Payne, who was present, "seemed to enjoy Booth's success just as much as the audience did . . . a sort of fatherly feeling, as if dragging an over-modest son to receive the honours of his success." The excitement engendered that night resulted in the announcement that the performance would be repeated two nights later. But Booth did not show up.

He had made enough inquiries and had enough time to think the situation over to realize that the parts he felt particularly able to do would never be given to him, and he wrote a letter saying as much to the Drury Lane committee: "I have since found . . . that every character which I was either desirous or capable of playing was already in possession, and that there was no chance of my appearing in the same. What occasion, therefore, could you have for me, unless to crush any talent I may possess in its infancy?" There can be little doubt that this statement was an exaggeration or that Kean's cordiality had been a trick to suppress a conceivably dangerous and young rival. Indeed, it has been reliably reported that Kean's Othello that night had been better than ever—it was one of his greatest roles—and that he did all he could to relegate Iago to a minor position in the play.

The Covent Garden management apparently saw through Kean's ingenious plot, and was ready to welcome back the prodigal son. Public announcements at once informed London that Booth would appear as Richard

III. On February 25, 1817, he had to endure just such conditions as Kean was later to know after he had fallen into disgrace. The playhouse was jammed for hours before the curtain. Cheers, hisses, shouting, insults—from pit and gallery—drowned the voices of the actors. It was rumored that Drury Lane had sent its hangers-on to ruin the production, for among the cries were: "Liar! Pretender! Imitator of Kean!" Booth tried to speak to the audience but was greeted with shrieks of derision. Placards on poles were brought out saying: GRANT SILENCE TO EXPLAIN; MR. BOOTH IS WILLING TO APOLOGIZE; CAN ENGLISHMEN CONDEMN UNHEARD? It was all of no use.

At the performance of *Richard III* the next night matters did not improve. This time two placards were shown the spectators: HE HAS BEEN PUNISHED ENOUGH and LET US FORGIVE HIM; they were answered by jeers and boos. That was March 1; the pandemonium continued on March 3 and 6. The necessity of addressing the audience after the play, so that after a while the hostility ended, nevertheless engendered in Booth a lifelong hatred of curtain calls.

The resemblance of the two tragedians operated only to Booth's disadvantage. To finish the charges of plagiarism once and for all, he attempted a role Kean had never performed, Posthumus (with Charles Kemble as Polydore) in *Cymbeline.* He was praised for his naturalness and reserve. Unfortunately he was bandy-legged, and one night a ruffian in the gallery called out: "Ah, ha! you're a pretty fellow to stop a pig!"

He spent three more years in England, ever increasing his triumphs. He went on tour and in a single day sometimes played in three different places, at 11 A.M., 4 P.M., and 8 P.M. Once he made an effort to master Hebrew and played Shylock in that language—an exploit which may be responsible for the story that he himself was Jewish. According to some the family name was originally Beth and of Spanish extraction. But he had always been fascinated by foreign languages, and to perfect his version of Shylock he conversed, his daughter Mrs. Clarke tells us, with learned rabbis, joining them in their worship. Booth could read the Talmud, but for that matter he also knew the Koran, and was fond of arguing points of doctrine with Roman Catholic clergy. All of which means no more than would an argument to prove Kean an Indian because he had been made a chief and liked to wear the headdress.

In 1820 Harris persuaded him to do Lear, which had not been played for years because of George III's madness. But now George III was dead, and on April 13 Booth had as his supporting cast Charles Kemble as Edgar, Macready as Edmund, and Sally Booth (no relative of his) as Cordelia.

In 1821 he deserted his wife and ran off to America with Mary Anne Holmes. After forty days on the ocean they landed at Norfolk on June 30, and a few nights later Booth began his career all over again in Richmond with *Richard III*. His reputation as a star had reached the United States, and during the early acts the audience showed little enthusiasm. He seemed to be playing without interest; that was doubtless due to the fatigue of his long sea journey. But suddenly in the fourth act his old passion returned, and the audience was "electrified." The final judgment was that Richmond had never seen any acting so overwhelming as that of this little man.

Four nights later he accepted an offer from Petersburg. A member of that town's company, Ludlow, described his first impressions of Booth. When rehearsals were to begin at 10 A.M., Booth had not appeared. The manager decided to proceed without him. They were at the fourth act when Booth arrived. "A small man whom I took to be a well-grown boy of about sixteen years came running up the stairs wearing a roundabout jacket and a cheap straw hat, both covered with dust, and inquired for the manager." Recognizing him, the manager exclaimed: "Ah! Mr. Booth, I am glad you have arrived. We were fearful something serious had happened to you!" Ludlow, unable to credit this "boy" with being the famous Booth, thought the manager "was trying to put off some joke upon us." Booth went through the rehearsal carelessly, and explained that having missed the stage coach, he had been forced to walk all the twenty-five miles to Petersburg.

By October 2, he was playing in New York, where his power and energies were so great and he seemed "so much in earnest on the stage, that when there was any fighting to be done, actors and actresses were afraid of him," is one report. But his son, Edwin, said that if his "expression of terror and remorse were painful in the extreme, his tenderness was exquisitely human." His playing was certainly uneven; sometimes he performed absent-mindedly; then suddenly he was able to gather his forces together and hurl himself into a fierce, almost crazed, turbulence of tragic action—overwhelming actors and audience alike.

After New York he toured the South, and it was at Charleston that Junius Brutus II was born. Mary Holmes was to bear him ten children, of whom three became actors.

Privately, when sober, Booth was a reticent and modest man: his Richard was therefore all the more astonishing for its force and violence. When doing Shylock he emphasized (however incorrectly) the man's religious austerity: he broke completely with Macklin's tradition of a blood-chilling villain. He made him, said a contemporary, "the representative Hebrew."* Whether or not Booth's premise be granted, his representation was impressive enough, for he was right in the respect that he made the money-lender a man of "pride and intellect."

In 1822 he purchased the Bel Air Farm in Harford County, Maryland, not far from Baltimore. For the rest of his life, whenever opportunity afforded, he went there to find peace; the house contained a rich library in many languages. But over the years, the death of a number of his children, all illegitimate, gradually further unsettled a mind never too firm in its grip on reality.

His stay in the United States was broken in 1825 when he crossed the ocean again to do Brutus. For two seasons he was acclaimed in Britain,

*See the present author's *The Truth about Shylock*, which undertakes to prove that Shylock is not a representative Jew, that the play is neither an attack upon nor a defense of Jews, but is concerned with a question totally different from that of anti-Semitism or special pleading for Jews.

Ireland, and the Netherlands, but on March 27 he was back in New York, in the country he had adopted as his own.

Now began the most erratic period of his life. It took very little to make him drunk, and he indulged in all manner of sprees with nefarious companions; too often, when billed to perform at the theater, he would disappear for days, after which he would play with renewed and almost frenetic energy, or else so gently one could believe he had been living quite normally. It was even true that he was often unable to account for his missing days.

He became very superstitious. He insisted upon having Moorish coins to jingle in his pocket when playing Othello, with a crescent pin attached to his scarf—or an antique dagger for Richard III. For Shylock he would wear a breast ornament usually worn by the rabbi in a synagogue, always keeping it under his gabardine. These things were talismen of good fortune for him, and he often carried them in his pocket all day according to the character he was to portray that night.

His hold on sanity weakened. One day on a voyage to an engagement in the South, he was talking to a friend of William Conway, an actor who had killed himself by jumping overboard; as the boat neared the place where this act had taken place, Booth hurried out on deck, crying that he had a message from Conway, and leaped into the ocean. With great difficulty he was saved by men in a boat lowered to rescue him. Yet, as he was being hauled into that boat, he called to his friend and bade him watch out: "You're a heavy man: if the boat upsets we'll all be drowned."

This same close friend, Tom Flynn, was attacked by Booth after a night's debauch in Charleston. Booth had crawled through the window and was beating Flynn's head hard with an iron fire-dog. Luckily for Flynn, he avoided death by a punch which broke Booth's nose and disfigured him for the rest of his life.

Such mad exploits would be followed by intervals of peaceful living at his farm, which in turn were succeeded by long intervals of acting and management. At Annapolis, the company waited day after day for him to appear, as announced; performance after performance was canceled; his mistress-wife was able to tell them only that he had left the farm days ago. After a week of this, the manager was accosted by a ragged urchin, who informed him: "We've got one of your playing chaps aboard our sloop raising hell with the captain. You'd better come and take him away." When the manager reached the sloop, he found Booth with a musket leveled at the captain, who was on his knees with a bowl in his hands as Booth was exclaiming in a tragic voice: "Drink, sir, drink. You're bilious and require physic. I know it by your eyes—your skin. Drink or I'll send you to another and a better world." The captain had already been forced to drink six such bowls, and was sure this one would be the death of him.

On a Sunday morning shortly after this Annapolis engagement, citizens of Philadelphia on their way to church were overcome by the spectacle of a man dressed as Hamlet, mounted on a circus horse, and addressing them as follows: "Ladies and gentlemen, I intend to perform *Hamlet* tonight for the benefit of the poor, and a good play is worth forty sermons both for morals, and reformation." Then he shouted: "Join in chorus, citizens," as he sang:

> O, 'tis my delight
> Of a shiny night
> In the season of the year.

At another time, he seriously thought of giving up the stage to take on a job as the lighthouse keeper at Cape Hatteras. Again, he wrote a note to the young Rev. James Freeman Clarke, to inquire about "a place of interment for his friend(s) in the churchyard, and also the expense attendant." Clarke came to the actor's hotel, and found Booth a "short man, but one of those who seem tall when they choose to do so. He had a clear blue eye and fair complexion. . . . When excited his expression was so animated, his eyes so brilliant and his figure so full of life that he became another man." After offering wine and cigars to the clergyman, Booth read aloud the entire text of *The Rime of the Ancient Mariner.* "He actually thought himself the mariner—so I am persuaded—while he was reading," commented Clarke. Booth went on to discuss Coleridge, Shelley, Keats, conceptions of passages in the Bible, and concluded with a recitation of Byron's poem to his dog. After this entertainment, he rose, took a candle, and asked, "Would you like to see the remains?" Clarke asked if the death had been sudden. "Very." "Was he a relative?" "Distant." They went to an adjoining room, but there was no corpse on the bed. Booth proceeded to a corner where there were spread out on a large sheet "about a bushel of wild pigeons." Clarke refused to perform the ceremony, but Booth actually bought a plot in the cemetery, and gave a regular performance of a funeral service at the grave. "For several days he continued to visit the grave of his little friends and mourned over them with a grief which did not seem at all theatrical." The Rev. Mr. Clarke may have been closer to the truth than he suspected. For three years Booth had been living strictly on a vegetable diet; he loved animals, and the great havoc wrought on pigeons at that season incurred his great wrath.

His madness sometimes even intruded upon his performances of *Richard III.* It was as though he suddenly became unbalanced. On several occasions while playing Richard he simply refused to die and attacked Richmond so savagely on Bosworth Field as to back him off the stage, and out of the stage door of the Bowery Theater, chasing him up the alley, sword still in hand, into the street. At the Boston Theater one night when he had been announced as Lear, the full house was kept waiting and waiting for him. Messengers were sent all over town to find him, and were about to give up when he was discovered among a circle of drunkards who were listening to him reciting poetry, passages from Shakespeare and from the Bible. He fought the men who tried to get him to the theater until he suddenly came to his senses. When he arrived at the playhouse and heard the din in the audience, he pushed aside friends who tried to restrain him, opened the curtains, thrust forward his head and shoulders, shook his fist at them, and cried: "Shut up!" That had the effect of stunning them for a moment and he continued, "Keep quiet! You just keep still and in ten minutes I'll give you the God damnest King Lear you ever saw in your life." And he did.

But he was fundamentally a gentle and kind man. When a sailor came to his door to beg for bread, he not only fed him, but noting that the man had a wounded leg, Booth went down on his knees, and washed and bandaged the leg. Visiting a Louisville jail, he had pointed out to him a notorious horse thief, Fontaine; Booth was told that he had no lawyer and that anyhow his case was hopeless; yet the actor sent him an attorney and paid the bill. Grateful, Fontaine willed his skull to Booth with the request that it be given him after the execution so that he might use it in the fifth act of *Hamlet*. For a time Booth did as Fontaine had wished.

Once he announced playing on April 1, and then thought it a good April Fools' joke to go off instead into the country. When the angry manager told the audience what Booth had done and added that he would never again be permitted to act in that house, the manager was hissed, and the audience stayed away until Booth returned to its stage.

On his way home from a tour abroad in 1837 his life was threatened when a lunatic rushed at him with an axe; somehow the actor was able to make the man stop dead in his tracks by holding him with his eye.

Most of his life was spent in the United States. His knowledge of foreign languages was amazing; in New Orleans he acted Racine in perfect French much to everyone's astonishment. Assuredly, he was a fine actor, probably rough and unpolished, but full of grandeur and eloquence. His voice was resonant and his gestures "ample." He used to play Othello in a yellow dressing gown; once, having at hand no black stockings, he blackened his legs and during the performance soiled Desdemona's white gown.

He had his own way of preparing for a role. His son Edwin said that when he was to do Othello he would mumble verses from the Koran all day; if Shylock he would be a Jew all day. Only too well aware of the limitations of his height, he refused to do such roles as Coriolanus, which, he felt, called for a tall man.

When he visited England, his family there knew nothing of the ten illegitimate children living in Maryland with their mother, Mary Holmes. Many years later his English son, Richard, came to America to see his father, and Booth's abandoned wife followed. She then learned the facts, but was unable to persuade him to return to her. She divorced him in 1851. As soon as the divorce had been granted, Booth married Mary, whom he had loved constantly ever since their elopement. She was a loyal, devoted wife, a good mother, and did what she could to establish balance in the family.

He had a certain black humor. At one time he resolved to become a vegetarian, and while he was rigidly conforming to this notion and traveling on a steamboat in the West, he found himself at table opposite a very solemn-looking Quaker. They had had an agreeable conversation for a time, when courteously the Quaker said, "Friend, shall I not help thee to the breast of this chicken?" Booth declined with thanks. "Then," persisted the Quaker, "thee must take a bit of the mutton, for thy plate is empty." Once more Booth declined, and the Quaker suggested a slice of ham. "Friend," Booth boomed in his best declamatory style, "I never eat any flesh but human flesh, and that I prefer raw!" It is understandable that the astounded Quaker quickly moved to another table.

Booth never encouraged his son Edwin, destined to be the most famous American actor of all times, to go on the stage. When the boy accompanied him on tours it was exclusively to act as guardian and save him, as much as possible, from his weaknesses. In 1852 they went to California together. When the time came for the elder Booth to return home, Edwin stayed on in the West—which engendered the first of the many tragedies in his life. On the Mississippi steamboat carrying Junius Brutus Booth back East, the elder Booth died. When Edwin heard the news he was overwhelmed with sorrow, and he never forgave himself for not having been on that boat with his father.

Walt Whitman said of Junius Brutus Booth that he "illustrated Plato's rule that to the forming of an artist of the very highest rank a dash of insanity (or what the world calls insanity) is indispensable. Without question Booth was a royal heir and legitimate representative of the Garrick-Kemble-Siddons dramatic traditions but he vitalized and gave an unnameable *race* to those traditions with his own electric idiosyncracy. As in all art-utterance it was the subtle and powerful something *special to the individual* that really conquered."

Whitman's concluding observations are indisputable enough, but his lumping Kemble and Siddons with Garrick, and Booth with all three, indicates that he knew nothing about the history of acting in England during the preceding century.

Junius Brutus Booth II (1821–1883), the eldest of Mary's sons, acted with his father and played Iago to his Othello. He was married three times and two of his sons became actors; the elder of these two shot his wife and himself in a London hotel. The other son, Sydney Barton Booth (1873–1937) was quite successful, and played opposite many prominent actresses.

✤ 15 ✤

William Macready, Edwin Forrest, and the Astor Place Riot

We have already dealt with riots and near-riots in the theater. The most notorious one in the United States was the Astor Place Riot, which occurred on Thursday, May 10, 1849.

The Astor Place Opera House (or Theater) occupied the south side of East Eighth Street where it converged with Astor Place east of Broadway, and on its east side faced Cooper Square. The riot began with the eruption of an old feud between an American actor, Edwin Forrest, and an English one, William C. Macready. Both at the time were leading actors in their respective countries.

At 11 A.M. of that morning, Mayor Woodhull of New York called a conference. He had been informed that "there was likely to be a disturbance" at the theater, but its proprietors, Niblo and Hackett, dismissed the idea. They added that it was Mayor Woodhull's job to keep order.

The "Bowery B'hoys" were busy distributing and posting handbills, urging all New Yorkers to show up at the "English Aristocratic Opera House." The "B'hoys" were hoodlums and incendiaries from the Bowery district (which was not in those days, of course, either the neighborhood of flophouses, which it later became, nor the costly SoHo area of artists' studios, which it is now). When the esteemed Macready arrived at 5:40 P.M. at the theater, the house was filling. Niblo and Hackett were unwise enough to sell more tickets than there were places for the audience.

The anti-Macready ruffians had bought up all the tickets they could well in advance. They were the first to gather before the doors of the playhouse. They came streaming up Broadway to Astor Place and Eighth Street and some came down from Harlem. During the afternoon the windows of the theater were barricaded. Almost all the policemen of the city were on duty and placed so they surrounded the theater. When the house was full, they refused to allow the louts who had no tickets to enter.

When the curtain rose on *Macbeth*, those outside began to shout: "Down with Macready!" "Burn the damned den of the aristocracy!" As Macready came on stage he was greeted with cheers and boos. This was not the first appearance of his New York season, nor his first season in the city. His first tour in America had been in 1826; that autumn both he and Forrest were appearing in New York—Forrest the chief attraction of the "democratic" Bowery Theater, Macready of the "aristocratic" Park Theater. Macready at the time went to see Forrest as Antony in *Julius Caesar* in December 1826, and spoke of him as having "vehemence and rude force," but doubted that he understood some of the passages he delivered; with "careful discipline" Forrest might make a good enough actor, he thought, but he had no conviction that Forrest was equal to discipline; "the injudicious and ignorant flattery . . . of his supporters, the 'Bowery lads' . . . would fill his purse, would blind him to his deficiency of taste and judgment, and satisfy his vanity, confirming his self-opinion of attained perfection."

Perhaps resentment against Macready, who was rather too stiff-necked for his own good, began in Philadelphia that same season when he had upbraided a property man for supplying arrows of "inferior American quality" for a production of *William Tell;* an avalanche of letters to the papers denounced Macready's insult, and he was compelled to apologize.

Forrest, who numbered among his admirers Washington Irving, James Fenimore Cooper, and Mayor Cornelius Lawrence, had triumphed in New York. In 1836 he had gone to London and appeared at Drury Lane, which Macready had just quit after a quarrel with the manager, Bunn, to go to Covent Garden. As a challenge to Macready, Forrest during his first week had given *Othello.* The critics accorded him rave reviews. On Macready's invitation, Forrest had come to meet him a few days later, on Sunday, October 30, and had been presented to Macready's friends, who included Browning. Forrest had been impressed with Macready's breeding and courtesy, and the next June had married the nineteen-year-old daughter of a friend of Macready's.

Macready's second tour of the United States began in September 1843 and ended in Boston in October 1844. Forrest entertained Macready in New York during October. Macready was pleased with his host, but blamed him as an actor for conditioning American audiences to "exaggeration in all its forms." American papers praised their native son as the Englishman's superior. Annoyed, Macready at once answered that Forrest was *"not an artist. Let him be an American actor . . . but keep on this side of the Atlantic, and no one will gainsay his comparative excellence."* From this time on Macready began to speak ill of Americans for their uncouthness (a self-congratulatory predeliction very common among Britishers in the nineteenth and early twentieth centuries, but which has happily disappeared in Britain except among the lower orders and university pedants). When he returned to England in November of 1844 he had earned £5,500 in the United States.

It may have been during this second engagement in New York that a cowboy, confident of his histrionic abilities, pleaded so unremittingly with Macready for the opportunity to prove himself that at last the tragedian succumbed, and gave him a minor role as king. The cowboy walked and scowled in a manner befitting a monarch. However, the direction had determined the spots on stage where each of the combatants in a duel was to fall; the spot in the center was naturally allotted to the star. But the cowboy wished to be more prominent, since he was king, and fell in the center of the stage. "Move over!" Macready whispered fiercely, giving him a kick. The cowboy would not budge. "Confound you!" growled the tragedian, "move over! You're on my spot, I tell you!" He added another kick to reinforce the argument. Angered, the cowboy raised himself on his elbow and roared, "Look here, Macready. I'm king in this here drammer, and I'll die where I darn please!"

In February of the next year Forrest came to England once more and opened in *Othello* at the Princess Theatre. He was hissed by some members of the audience, but praised by the journalists. Macready's diary reveals that he was not pleased with Forrest's critical success; Forrest was apparently mistaken when he blamed Macready as the instigator of the hissing. Macready despised provincial audiences for their vulgarity, but Forrest was extraordinarily popular with them. While in Edinburgh he went to see Macready in *Hamlet*. Macready's own judgment was that it was the finest *Hamlet* he had ever given. But Coleman, the manager, who was playing Marcellus, thus described the prince's stage business just before the *Murder of Gonzago* in the mousetrap: Macready "would strut from side to side ... extravagantly flirting his handkerchief above his head, and behaving less like Hamlet than Osric." Forster, Macready's friend, interpreted this waving of the handkerchief as "ill concealing ... the sense of approaching triumph." At any rate, at that moment a man in the upper boxes hissed. Macready wrote: "The audience took it up, and I waved the more, and bowed derisively and contemptuously to the individual." Macready, convinced that it had been Forrest who started the hissing and originated the disturbance, collected all available evidence to prove himself right, and wrote in his diary: "No Englishman would have done a thing so base ... The low-minded ruffian! That man would commit a murder, if he dare." Forrest himself called Macready's use of the handkerchief, *"pas de mouchoir"* (i.e., dance of the handkerchief). Colemen definitely identified Forrest as the man who started the hissing. In March 1846, in a letter to the London *Times*, the American player defended his right to hiss as a traditional method of registering disapproval. Bitterly in his journal Macready wrote: "I cannot *stomach* the United States ... No more America for me!"

Nevertheless in 1849 he was there again. On May 7, three days before the Astor Place Riot, during the first scene, C. W. Clarke, an American actor, was loudly applauded. Before entering in the third scene, Macready's first line was heard off stage; it was greeted by cheers, groans, and hisses. Though the majority was supporting him its numbers were outshouted by the Bowery B'hoys, who when he entered assaulted the English actor with rotten eggs, potatoes, asafoetida, old shoes, and a copper coin. He picked up the coin and "placed it in his bosom." For fifteen minutes there was no

1. Jane Cowl as Juliet. When I was a boy and saw her in some movie or other, I realized for the first time that human beings could be beautiful. *(Courtesy of Frank Lockwood)*

2. Richard Burbage, for whom Shakespeare wrote the roles of Richard III, Hamlet, Othello, Lear, Malvolio, and doubtless most of the other leading parts in his plays. He was an actor of grace and musical voice as well as physical stamina. *(Courtesy of the Dulwich Gallery and Frank Lockwood)*

4. Will Kempe, the original Dogberry. He is seen here dancing himself "out of the world," when he danced from London to Norwich. From an old engraving.

Tartlon, celebrated Elizabethan own. From an old engraving.

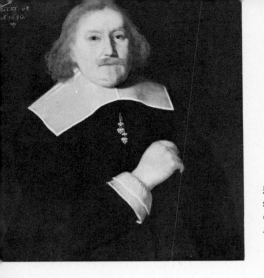

5. John Lowin, especially admired for his Falstaff in Shakespeare's company. He survived the closing of the theaters in 1642. *(Courtesy of the Ashmolean Museum, Oxford)*

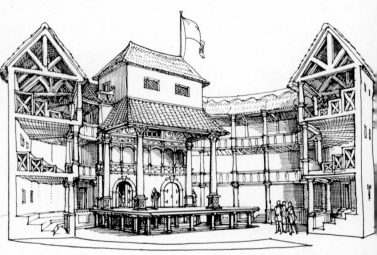

6. Sketch of an Elizabethan playhouse, modeled on The Swan. *(Courtes of Frank Lockwood)*

7. The Duke of York's Theat in Dorset Gardens, one of t two patented theaters appoi ed during the Restoration; t one was opened by D'A nant's widow, son, and the tor Thomas Betterton. *(Co tesy of the Walter Hampd Memorial Library, The Pl ers)*

8. Thomas Betterton, the leading actor of the Restoration, from a mezzotint after the painting by Sir Godfrey Kneller. *(Courtesy of Frank Lockwood)*

9. Edward Kynaston, who enacted feminine roles during the Restoration. A youth of great beauty, much pampered by the ladies, he kept Charles II waiting while he shaved before appearing as a queen. From an engraving by Harding. *(Courtesy of Frank Lockwood)*

10. Colley Cibber, actor, playwright, and historian of the Restoration stage. A portrait in painted plaster. *(Courtesy of the National Portrait Gallery, London)*

11. Anne Bracegirdle, a pupil of Betterton's, and the leading beauty of the Restoration stage. She played opposite her teacher as Desdemona, Ophelia, Mrs. Ford, Cordelia, and Isabella. She was also Congreve's Millamant. *(Courtesy of Frank Lockwood)*

12. Barton Booth, who succeeded Betterton as the leading actor of his day. "The Blind might have seen him in his voice, and the Deaf have heard him in his visage." (*Courtesy of the Walter Hampden Memorial Library, The Players*)

13. James Quin, leading actor before Macklin and Garrick, as Falstaff, one of his great roles. (*Courtesy of Frank Lockwood*)

14. Samuel Foote, celebrated for his brilliant mimicry and merciless satirizing of fellow actors. (*Courtesy of Frank Lockwood*)

15. Charles Macklin, who revived Shakespeare' *Merchant of Venice* after a century of neglect and whose Shylock was, as Shakespeare had in tended, a blood-chilling usurer. Portrait by Zo fany. (*Courtesy of the National Gallery of Ir land*)

16. Frances Abington as Beatrice in the "over-hearing" scene of *Much Ado*. Garrick thought her the wickedest woman alive. From an engraving. *(Courtesy of the Victoria & Albert Museum, London)*

17. "Snug in the Gallery." The cheaper seats were a constant source of disturbance and brutal interference with performances. *(Courtesy of Victoria & Albert Museum, London)*

18. David Garrick as Richard III, the role in which he took London by storm. *(Courtesy of the Walter Hampden Memorial Library, The Players)*

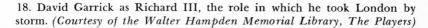

21. Garrick as King Lear, from a mezzotint by McArdell after a painting by Wilson. Lear was probably his greatest role. (*Courtesy of Frank Lockwood*)

19. Portrait of Garrick by Robert Edge Pine. (*Courtesy of the Walter Hampden Memorial Library, The Players*)

20. Garrick "Between Comedy and Tragedy," an engraving from a painting by Sir Joshua Reynolds. (*Courtesy of the Walter Hampden Memorial Library, The Players*)

22. Garrick in 1745, from an engraving by McArdell after a painting by Pond. *(Courtesy of Frank Lockwood)*

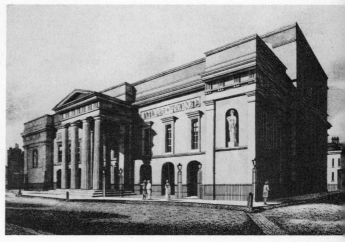

23. Covent Garden Theatre, London. *(Courtesy the Walter Hampden Memorial Library, The Players)*

24. John Philip Kemble as Coriolanus—an actor at his best in roles which required stateliness and a certain formality. *(Courtesy of Frank Lockwood)*

25. Catastrophe at the Haymarket, February 3, 1974. From a contemporary print. *(Courtesy of Frank Lockwood)*

26. John Philip Kemble as Hotspur in *Henry IV. (Courtesy of the Walter Hampden Memorial Library, The Players)*

27. Sarah Siddons, portrait by Gainsborough, who despite his complaint that there was no end to he nose, did justice to a beauty which everyone acclaime As a woman she was to the London stage what Garric had been as a man. "She was," said Hazlitt, "Traged personified," and was "the idol of the people." *(Cou tesy of the National Gallery, London)*

28. Sarah Siddons as Lady Macbeth by Henry Fuseli. To the public she *was* Lady Macbeth, although privately she did not approve of the interpretation she gave audiences. *(Courtesy of Frank Lockwood)*

29. Master William Henry West Betty, child prodigy and vast success at the age of eleven. As an adult he no longer interested the public. *(Courtesy of the Victoria & Albert Museum, London)*

30. "The Extinguisher," in which Fame is shown lifting aloft Master Betty to extinguish the light of his most celebrated contemporaries. *(Courtesy of the New York Public Library)*

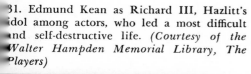

31. Edmund Kean as Richard III, Hazlitt's idol among actors, who led a most difficult and self-destructive life. *(Courtesy of the Walter Hampden Memorial Library, The Players)*

32. Another view of Kean's Richard III by the Cruikshanks. *(Courtesy of the Museum of the City of New York, Theatre and Music Collection)*

33. Ira Aldridge as Aaron in *Titus Androni-cus*. Aldridge, said to have been born in Africa, was raised in the United States, immigrated to England, where he married a white woman, and was phenomenally successful in many European countries in a number of Shakespearean roles, including Macbeth. *(Courtesy of the Museum of the City of New York, Theatre and Music Collection)*

34. James William Wallack as Gloucester in *Richard III*. He played Laertes and Iago in London and came to New York; he introduced a repertory of Shakespeare's plays for some ten years. *(Courtesy of the Museum of the City of New York, Theatre and Music Collection)*

35. Interior of Covent Garden, 1815. *(Courtesy of Frank Lockwood)*

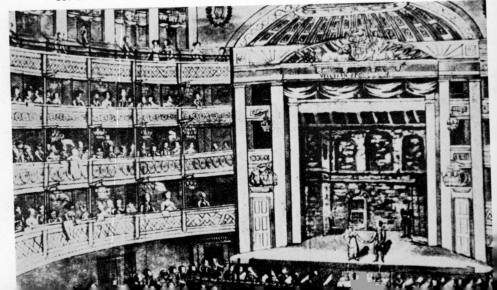

37. Junius Brutus Booth (the Elder) as Richard III, the first of an acting family which became famous and notorious; his sons were Junius Brutus II, Edwin, and John Wilkes. Touched with genius himself, he was unreliable in his profession, and undeniably the victim of a streak of insanity. *(Courtesy of the Walter Hampden Memorial Library, The Players)*

36. Interior of the Park Theater, New York. *(Courtesy of the Museum of the City of New York, Theatre and Music Collection)*

38. The Astor Place Riot, New York, the product of a feud between the American actor Edwin Forrest, and William Macready, the visiting English actor, who was performing Macbeth at the Astor Place Theater at the time. *(Courtesy of the Harvard Theatre Collection)*

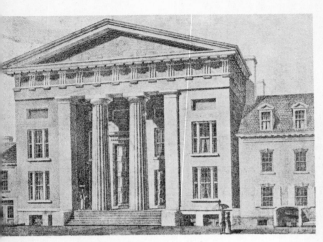

40. William Charles Macready as Macbeth, a portrait by the American artist Henry Inman. Macready's disdain for fellow actors left him almost without a friend in his profession. (*Courtesy of the Metropolitan Museum of New York, Rogers Fund*)

41. Macready as Hotspur in *Henry IV*. (*Courtesy of the Museum of the City of New York, Theatre and Music Collection*)

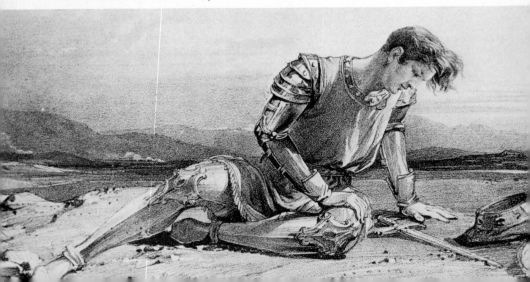

42. Macready as King Lear with Helen Faucit as Cordelia at Covent Garden, 1838. *(Courtesy of the Walter Hampden Memorial Library, The Players)*

43. Edwin Forrest, 300 percent American in his patriotism and the idol of the Bowery Boys. *(Courtesy of Frank Lockwood)*

44. Forrest as Macbeth, after an engraving by . Thew in 1859. Winter found his interpretation "robust" but lacking any hint of petry. *(Courtesy of the Museum of the City New York, Theatre and Music Collection)*

45. Forrest as King Lear. Among his many admirers was Walt Whitman, who delighted in his vigorous style and his abandoning the classic mood of Kemble and Siddons. *(Courtesy of the Walter Hampden Memorial Library, The Players)*

46. Edwin Booth as Hamlet, his most celebrated role, his sentimentalizing of which made it the model for the whole century and after. (*Courtesy of the Museum of the City of New York, Theatre and Music Collection*)

47. Another view of Edwin Booth as Ham (*Courtesy of the Walter Hampden Memo Library, The Players*)

48. Edwin Booth as Iago. In London he alternated this role with that of Othello opposite Henry Irving. Both were better as the villain. An engraving of 1879. (*Courtesy of the Museum of the City of New York, Theatre and Music Collection*)

49. John Wilkes Booth, the handsome member of the family, a fierce partisan of the Confederacy during the Civil War, who assassinated Lincoln because he was convinced that the president intended making himself king. *(Courtesy of the Walter Hampden Memorial Library, The Players)*

51. Laura Keane, noted American actress, who was starring in *Our American Cousin* at Ford's Theater, Washington, on Good Friday, April 14, 1865, the night John Wilkes Booth killed Lincoln. He collided with her in the wings as he was escaping. *(Courtesy of the Museum of the City of New York, Theatre and Music Collection)*

50. The three Booth brothers in *Julius Caesar,* Edwin as Brutus, John Wilkes as Mark Antony, and Junius Brutus II as Cassius. *(Courtesy of the Harvard Theatre Collection)*

52. Interior of Booth's Theater at its opening, February 3, 1869; the set is for Act I of *Romeo and Juliet.* From a watercolor by C. W. Witham. *(Courtesy of the Museum of the City of New York, Theatre and Music Collection)*

53. Sarah Bernhardt in her suite at the Hoffman House with Mlle. Saylor, 1896. (Courtesy of the Museum of the City of New York, Theatre and Music Collection)

54. Bernhardt as Hamlet. Max Beerbohm, though he adored her as an actress, said her Prince of Denmark was "from first to last très grande dame." (Courtesy of the New York Public Library)

55. Another view of Bernhardt as Hamlet. The performance was in French prose, which Beerbohm declared doomed to failure. The "Rest, rest, perturbed spirit," which came out as "Paix, paix, âme troublée," reminded him of the music hall ditty, "Loo, Loo, I love you!" (Courtesy of the Victoria & Albert Museum, London)

action on stage; he was waiting to address the audience, but it proved in vain. The actors went on with the play, but it was all dumb-show because of the shouting. During the intermission the other actors wished to stop the performance, but he insisted they continue. The second act was like the first; during the third act men in the upper tier threw four chairs at the stage. At this Macready brought down the curtain. The audience was informed that he had left the theater, but the shouting continued. Clarke appeared to repeat the assurance that Macready was no longer in the theater, after which announcement there were cheers for Forrest and "native talent," and jeers for the "English bulldog" and the "codfish aristocracy."

The next day Macready was promised by forty-seven prominent citizens, including Washington Irving and Herman Melville, that should he agree to continue his engagement he could count on the respect and good will of New York audiences.

When on May 10, 1849, he was greeted with cheers and jeers Macready felt, upon his entrance, that he could subdue the rowdies by his haughty bearing. "Looking at the wretched creatures in the parquet who shook their fists violently at me, and called out to me in savage fury, I laughed at them, pointing them out with my truncheon to the police." The first three scenes were unheard because of the noise and movement among the spectators. At the conclusion of the fourth scene, the police rushed in, closed in upon the louts in the center, and began to carry them out of the theater."

As though it were a signal, the arrest of the inside rioters began an attack on the theater from the outside. Stones were hurled like hail at the windows. During the banquet scene, one of Macready's fellow actors urged him to cut it short and end the play as swiftly as possible. He refused: the audience had paid to see *Macbeth* and *Macbeth* they should see.

Between the acts he found that his dressing room was flooded because the stones had broken the pipes. As the melee continued outside, he recorded that in the last act "I flung my whole soul into every word I uttered, acting my best." At the end he was called for and loudly cheered.

He was now well aware that all that had happened was but a prologue to a personal attack on him. His friends insisted that he disguise himself in Malcolm's surtout. They could not go out through the stage door and therefore joined the departing audience into Eighth Street. Two lines of police kept the front clear. The actor and his friends crossed Broadway through the crowd, and thus escaped injury. Three hours later Macready was hurried off to New Rochelle, and from there to Boston. Twelve days later, after living in seclusion, he went back to England.

In the meantime, on the day of the riot, General Sandford's militia showed up (around 9 P.M., some time after Act III had begun), and marched from Broadway into Astor Place. The rabble at once hurled stones at them, and a number of soldiers were badly injured. The troops were ordered to fire above the heads of the mob, when someone started the rumor that the cartridges were blank, and the stone-throwing began again. (The scene reminds one of certain events at American colleges during recent years.)

The command was now given to fire point-blank at the mob. Two men fell, one of them dead. The fight commenced once more; six more were killed and six injured. The fighting and firing did not end until after midnight, by which time twenty-two had been killed and one hundred wounded. Macready and Forrest never met again.

William Charles Macready (1793–1873) was the son of an actor-manager and an actress. He was first seen at the Birmingham Theatre, which his father managed, as Romeo at the age of seventeen, a chubby-faced lad wearing a flowered sash that reached to his armpits, a ruff, white kid gloves, white stockings of silk, dancing pumps, and a large black hat with white plumes. He was a great success.

On September 16, 1816, he appeared at Covent Garden for the first time to begin a five-year contract at a salary of £16. Kean, who was in the audience, applauded him loudly. He played Othello, which Hazlitt found "effeminate" and too "whimpering and lachrymose," as well as Iago, whom Hazlitt described as a "mischievous boy" whipping a top. Edinburgh in 1819 did not give him much encouragement. But his Richard III of 1819 impressed the spectators and began a dangerous rivalry with Kean.

He did Coriolanus, Jaques, Edmund, and discarded Cibber's version of *Richard III*, which, more or less, was the only one the public had seen in that strangely popular play since the Restoration, and gave the play Shakespeare wrote. Soon thereafter he did King Henry IV, Prospero, Iachimo, and Hamlet. In 1821 he was doing Hamlet, King John, and Shylock. In 1823 he challenged Kean by bringing back a harsh Shylock in the Macklin tradition, but it was one of his least successful roles.

His temper was far from amiable. He managed to make his relations with Covent Garden so disagreeable that his second five-year contract was canceled. From there he moved to Drury Lane at a salary of £20 a night, and remained there, with certain intermissions, for some thirteen years. He added to his repertory Macbeth, Leontes, and Vincentio the Duke in *Measure for Measure*.

On June 24, 1823, he married the actress Frances Atkins.

In 1835 while at the Drury Lane under Bunn's management, he became furious when asked to do the first three acts of *Richard III* as an afterpiece. On April 29, still fuming over it, he was passing in his Richard III costume to his dressing room when he noted that the door to Bunn's office was open. He walked in, and abandoning all self-control, called the frightened Bunn a "damned scoundrel," and knocked him down. Terrified, Bunn asked whether he intended murdering him, and Macready shouted that that was what he intended to do. They were separated by actors; Bunn sued him, and was granted £150 in damages. Twelve days later he was back at Covent Garden as Macbeth, and enthusiastically welcomed. He later publicly apologized for his assault on Bunn and inscribed in his diary: "I can never never during my life, forgive myself."

Though less popular than Kean or Young, Macready was the favorite of the educated. He loved great drama, but loathed the theater. He would have been far more contented as a clergyman or a schoolmaster. Wagenknecht has put it aptly: "Temperamentally Macready was the Perfect Victorian Gentleman raised to the *n*th power. . . . He was a lofty-minded idealist, but he could also be an unconscionable prig." He lacked Kean's fire or passion; his face was ugly, but his figure and voice were very good. He was best at "character acting." Few have equalled his Lear, in the opinion of J. K. Knight. Talfourd, who called Kean "the most intensely human," Kemble "the most classical," thought Macready the "most romantic of actors." Hazlitt praised him for being natural and easy, Leigh Hunt for his "tenderness, passion" and sensibility. Macbeth was Macready's favorite role and it was generally agreed in his day no one equaled him in that character—which in itself would indicate that he must have been wonderful in his delivery of great poetry, for surely *Macbeth* is Shakespeare's greatest poem—though Hunt complained that Macready failed to make one feel much for Macbeth, and preferred him as King John, because he was at his best when he had to give way to "soft or overwhelming emotions." Hunt thought Macready's King John the best he had ever seen, for he made the king "petulant and a bully." According to Hunt, he absolutely refused to try King Lear "in obstinate despair of doing it justice." If Hunt was right, Macready was wise in that decision, for his performances were those which required "sensibility"; that was "his forte." His Othello was quieter than Kean's—a "troubled person," and too "intellectual" (which Shakespeare's naïf Moor certainly is not), and though he worked at the part for years, the public never cared for him in it. On the other hand, he made a fine Iago.

Though he had a good life at home, he had few friends among actors. "Coldly ceremonious when in good temper, fiercely abusive when in a bad one, always on the watch for slights, and morbidly alert to conjure up affronts, his existence in the theatre was little better than a long-drawn ordeal to himself and a frequent source of exasperation to his colleagues." This egotism revealed itself in his Iago, with its tendency to dwarf Othello, but aware of the flaw he worked on it until Iago incarnated a villain of intellect and passion masquerading as a plain honest soldier. At the same time he managed to project his feeling that the audience hardly deserved the subtlety of his performances. He was tall enough for a heroic part, but had no sweep, "no massy movements in his action"; not surprisingly, therefore, he left out always the "Like to the Pontic" speech, with its amazing swell and surge like that of the ocean itself.

When Fanny Kemble was his Lady Macbeth, in one of his characteristic "lashing-abouts" he broke her finger. She was afraid of his damaging her further in the last scene of *Othello*, though she did play it with him. He could not understand why she wished to do it, as he considered Desdemona's role absolutely *"nothing,"* of less consequence even than Emilia's. She vowed to be even with him because in long speeches he was prone to take hold of an actress's head, hold it under his arm (perhaps in the way I have seen men in the streets of Venice take similarly a strangle-hold of their sweethearts to show their affection), and release her at the end "more dead than alive." She found a way to escape the choking embrace by placing pins in her hair in such a way that if he took her by the head he would be compelled to let go instantly.

He eventually did Lear, and his Hamlet was widely acclaimed; in the end, critics generally, despite earlier criticisms, declared him the best tragic actor after Kean.

G. H. Lewes wrote a long essay on him. He said that while Kean was a man of genius, "in Macready I see only a man of talent, but of talent so marked and individual that it approaches very near to genius." He conceded that Kean, though capable of the "highest reaches" of his art, "was inferior to Macready in that general flexibility of talent and in that range of intellectual sympathy which are necessary to many and various parts. In this sense Macready was the better actor." Macready was superior in another respect: Kean was incapable of doing justice to or often trying new plays—he "seemed to require the wide range of Shakespearean passion for his arena," while Macready did better in other plays than the Shakespearean masterpieces. He had "a voice powerful, extensive in compass, capable of delicate modulation in quiet passages . . . and having tones that thrilled and tones that stirred tears. His declamation was mannered and unmusical; yet his intelligence always made you follow the winding meanings through the involutions of the verse, and never allowed you to feel, as you feel in the declamation of Charles Kean and many other actors, that he was speaking words which he did not thoroughly understand." In *Macbeth* "nothing could be finer" than his interpretation of "a conscience wavering, . . . superstitious, and weakly cherishing the suggestions of superstition." His Hamlet "I thought bad, due allowance being made for the intelligence it displayed. He was lachrymose and fretful." "In King John, Richard II, Iago and Cassius all his great qualities were displayed. . . . In tenderness Macready had few rivals. . . . You lost all sense of his sixty years in the fervour and resilient buoyancy of his manner." As Lear "the fretful irritability of the senile king was admirably rendered." "He was a thorough artist, very conscientious, very much in earnest, and very careful about all the resources of his art. Hence he was always picturesque in his costume. Often, indeed, his 'get up' was such that . . . he seemed to have stepped from the canvas of one of the old masters . . . He did not belong to the stately declamatory school of Kemble, but in all parts strove to introduce as much familiarity of detail as was consistent with ideal presentation . . . Whenever he had an emotion to depict, he depicted it sympathetically and not artificially; . . . he felt himself to be the person, and . . . identified himself with the character." It has been related of him that in the scene of the third act when Shylock came on in a state of "intense rage and grief" at his daughter's elopement—unlike most actors who "come in bawling and gesticulating, but leaving us unmoved because they are not moved themselves," Macready "used to spend some minutes behind the scenes, lashing himself into an imaginative rage by cursing *sotto voce,* and shaking violently a ladder fixed against the wall. . . . He had worked himself up to the proper pitch of excitement which would enable him to express the rage of Shylock."

His last appearance was as Macbeth at the Drury Lane on February 26, 1851. In his final scene he was given an immense ovation. He was insistently called for, and when he appeared it was in his own clothes. He stood there "waiting till the thunderous reverberations of applause should be hushed." Then he spoke:

"My last theatrical part is played . . . As I look back on my long professional career, I see in it but one continuous record of indulgence and support extended to me . . . and upholding me in most trying emergencies." He thanked them for "a life made happy by your favour," which with time "seemed to grow; and undisturbed in my hold on your opinion, from year to year I found friends more closely and thickly clustering round me." (One of his greatest services to Shakespeare was to discard all of the perversions of the plays in vogue since the Restoration, and often preserved by Kean or added to by Garrick.) He could therefore add: "We have assurance that the corrupt editions and unseemly presentations of past days will never be restored, but that the purity of our great poet's text will henceforth be held on our English stage in the reverence it should ever command." (Luckily for him he was no clairvoyant and could not foresee the violence done, in the name of modernity, from which the plays would suffer during the last few decades of our own time!) His final words were characteristically dignified: "With sentiments of deepest gratitude I take my leave, bidding you . . . with regret and most respectfully farewell."

Lewes complained that "a less deliberate speech would have suited the occasion better"—as though any undeliberated speech might have been anticipated from Macready!—but he respected him for his "calm, grave, sad, and dignified" manner.

In Macready's favor we ought to remember that he encouraged Browning (mistakenly, of course) to write for the stage; however unplayable they proved, we are glad to have those plays to read. Macready was so much disliked by his colleagues in the profession that it is not surprising that he found his friends outside the playhouses, and they included Dickens and Bulwer-Lytton. While such actors as Kean had only intensified the low opinion held by society of his vocation, Macready was regarded a gentleman, and had an income large enough to live like one. His marriage was very happy, and he was a most devoted father to his numerous children. Yet he never got over his condescension for everything theatrical or altered his view that his fellow actors were "miserable wretches" and "beasts." He went so far as to say that all of them—"I know no exception—are either utter blackguards or most ignorant empirics," and that he would prefer to see one of his children "dead than on the stage." No one "who had the power of doing anything better" than becoming an actor, "would, unless deluded into it," enter that profession.

The most popular of his leading ladies was Helen Saville Faucit (1817–1898), a woman of great beauty and charm who, because of these and the real scarcity of gifted actresses during the 1830s, stood out as being more talented than may have been the case. Some critics thought her manner exaggerated. She appeared in three plays of Browning, but was at her best in Shakespeare. She was greatly admired in Paris. She married in 1851, and became Lady Martin in 1880 when her husband was knighted.

Hazlitt complained that her Cleopatra (1813) "bordered too much on the affected levity of a modern fine lady," and lacked all dignity and passion. Her repertory was large, and she did Juliet, Ophelia, Portia, Imogen, Lady Macbeth, Beatrice, Rosalind, Constance, Hermione, Miranda, and Desdemona. As Desdemona she managed to convince the stubborn Macready that a staunch heroine, worthy of being a hero's bride, would not diminish his Othello. Eventually she became tired of always being subordinated to him—even in the comedies—and went off on her own. *Punch* once said that Macready "thought Miss Faucit had a very handsome back, for when on the stage with him, he always managed that the audience should see it and little else."

Decades before Ellen Terry she had the good sense to understand Lady Macbeth as a woman impelled entirely by her love for her husband and her desire to see him wear the "golden round." But she disliked the role and hated to play it.

She became well known for her Beatrice. In 1846 the Manchester *Courier* called hers "a performance of rare beauty," though totally differing from any familiar to the public. She was "less buoyant, less boisterous." She had not the "hearty laugh of Mrs. Jordan," nor the biting sarcasm of others, but was always refined and delicate. Twenty years later the same periodical praised "the artistic care bestowed even upon those trifles which go to sum up the whole conception, but would be unheeded by a less consummate mistress of art. But far more gratifying is it to listen to the beautifully modulated voice, and observe even critically each studied gesture. . . . Throughout there was exhibited a degree of culture and refinement of manner such as one might naturally look for in a lady so circumstanced." Clearly, Helen Faucit was long ready to take up the social graces required of Lady Martin.

In the same year of that second Manchester performance of *Much Ado* a rival paper, the Manchester *Guardian*, lauded her "beautiful display of delicate irony which runs throughout the part," and her "vivacious acting" in the scene in which she and Benedick wear masks. But it was when "Beatrice was left in the Chapel with Benedick, MISS FAUCIT rose to the greatest height of her acting; her alternations of grief for Hero, of indignation at the treatment her cousin had received, her eagerness to have Claudio killed, and her wish that she were a man to execute the immediate vengeance she desired, were rendered with great force."

On the same occasion the Manchester *Examiner and Times* declared that there never has "been a better Beatrice than MISS HELEN FAUCIT'S.

. . . A second-rate Beatrice is a misfortune which must be borne with a Christian spirit, but a Beatrice such as *MISS* HELEN FAUCIT'S is an enjoyment which Shakespeare himself might envy us. . . . Nothing escapes her eye, though her back be turned; and nothing her ear. . . . She is moved and stirred by everything around her, and nothing controls her but the grace which is her second nature."

Since *Much Ado* is my particular favorite among the comedies, I cannot resist recording Macready's own absurd understanding of Benedick—in which, I regret to say, he is at one with most commentators, who are superficial in their view of Shakespeare. "His great peculiarity," reports Halliwell-Phillipps, "consists of the ludicrous manner in which he seizes on the distress of Benedick on finding the theory of a whole life knocked down by one slight blow. His chief scene is the soliloquy after he has heard Don Pedro and his companions narrate the story of Beatrice's love. The blank amazement depicted in his countenance and expressive of a thorough change in his internal condition, is surpassingly droll. The man is evidently in a state of puzzle, and a series of the quaintest attitudes of reflection evince his perplexity." It is my profound conviction that one must be something of an idiot to believe that Don Pedro and the others *make* Benedick fall in love with Beatrice or that Hero and Ursula *make* Beatrice fall in love with him. To read the play with any attention is to realize that these two have been in love with each other before Act I opens, and that it is their pride and public stance which constitute the wall between them; what their friends do is to make it easy to demolish the wall. To credit Shakespeare, the man who knew all about psychology centuries before it became a "science," with being capable of anything so infantile as the idea that others can make a pair fall in love, is an insult to his genius and delicate perceptions of the human comedy.

When she became Lady Martin, Helen Faucit discoursed at some length on *The Winter's Tale*.

I was called upon to play Hermione very soon after my *début*. I was still very young, and by my years and looks most unfit even to appear as the mother of young Mamillius. Why Mr. Macready selected me for the task I could not imagine, and most gladly would I have declined it. But his will was law . . . You were so earnestly reminded of your duty to sacrifice yourself to the . . . effort he was making to regenerate the drama—that there was nothing left but to give way. . . . Therefore play Hermione I must, even as I had not long after to play Constance of Bretagne, a still severer trial, and a much greater strain upon my young shoulders. . . . My first appearance as Hermione is indelibly imprinted on my memory . . . Mrs. Warner [the Paulina] had rather jokingly told me . . . to be *prepared* for something extraordinary in his [Macready's] manner, when Hermione returned to life. But prepared I was not . . . for such a display of uncontrollable rapture. . . . It was the finest burst of passionate speechless emotion I ever saw. . . . I naturally lost something of my self-command, and as Perdita and Florizel knelt at my feet I looked, as the gifted Sarah Adams afterwards told me, "like

Niobe, all tears." . . . Mr. Macready's passion was so real, that I could never [thereafter] help being moved by it, and feeling much exhausted afterwards.

She was always aware, when enacting this role, of the sympathy of the audience. The great moment came, of course, during the statue scene. "In Edinburgh, upon one occasion, I have been told by a friend . . . that, as I descended from the pedestal and advanced toward Leontes, the audience simultaneously rose from their seats, as if drawn out of them by surprise and reverential awe. . . . As 'there is a pleasure in poetic pains, which only poets know,' so there is a pleasure in the actor's pains, which only actors know, who have to deal with the 'high actions and high passions' of which Milton speaks. Unless they know these pains, and feel a joy in knowing them, their vocation can never rise to the level of an art."

The press in London, Edinburgh, Dublin, and Glasgow were rapturous in 1847 and 1848 at the perfection and sublimity of her Hermione.

Edwin Forrest (1806–1872) might be described as three hundred percent American in his patriotism. In 1828 he offered a substantial prize for the best five-act tragedy on an American theme, and continued that practice for many years. In 1834 he was aboard an American warship in Europe; before greeting the commander, he dropped to his knees and kissed the American flag. Back in New York after two years he was welcomed as a conquering hero, and appeared at last at the *fashionable* playhouse, the Park. When he publicly announced that he was going to play in London, he confessed that he preferred playing for an American audience.

Walt Whitman, not more deficient than he in love of country, gives us a quite different picture of Forrest's earlier audiences at the Old Bowery Theater. The house was crammed with "alert, well-dress'd, full-blooded young and middle-aged men, the best of average American born mechanics . . . bursting forth in one of those long kept-up tempests of hand-clapping peculiar to the Bowery—no dainty kid-glove business, but electric force and *muscle* from perhaps two thousand full-sinew'd men."

Forrest was born on March 9 in Philadelphia of Scottish and German-American parents. His father died when the boy was thirteen, leaving little beyond honorable debts to be paid; the mother opened a small millinery shop, where she had the assistance of her two elder daughters, while the boys went to work elsewhere. Edwin tried a printing, then a cooper's and a ship-chandler's firm, and finally took a position with importers. In his spare time the brilliant lad was devouring Shakespeare. This love of theater began when he was ten, when with his brother William he joined a thespian club, performances being given in barns and the price of admission anything from an apple to five pins, or, best of all, a handful of marbles. The shows must have been well attended for the boys soon had a splendid collection of marbles.

Edwin also loved to visit the old South Street Theater, which had an enormous pit and a double row of boxes. And it was there that he made his first appearance on a legitimate stage. He was eleven and it was sheer luck. Edwin was playing marbles in front of the theater with other lads when the manager, Charles Porter, strolled by and watched the game. For some reason he asked Edwin whether he thought he could perform the part of a girl in a play. The boy of course cried, "Yes, sir!" Doubtless he would have agreed to play the part of an octogenerian. The fact was that the little girl who was to enact the role was ill, and the play was to open the following night. Mr. Porter gave Edwin his lines to study. The lad, hastening home, had little trouble memorizing his part. To help out with the costume, one of his sisters gave him some cloth for a bodice, another an old turban for a hat; he made do with some material for a skirt.

He lost his security the next night in anticipation of his appearance as Rosalia di Borgia in the melodrama *Rudolph; or The Robbers of Calabria;* a mirror informed him that he required more curves, so he thrust some pieces of tapestry into the bodice. But he had forgotten to examine his feet; his skirt was much too short (for those days!) and his shoes were still a boy's. When he came on stage, a boy in the gallery shouted: "The heels and the big shoes! Hi yi! Hi yi!" Oblivious of the play, Edwin became so enraged that, forgetting he was Rosalia, he yelled back, "You wait till this play is done, and I'll lick the stuffin's out of you!"

The audience roared with laughter and the curtain descended. Edwin was thrust from the stage. But he kept his word with the boy, sought him out, and in the alley gave him a sound thrashing.

At the age of thirteen he was given another chance at the Tivoli Garden but failed; the next year, with like result, at the Walnut Street Theater. In December 1820 he applied by letter to a manager at New Orleans, but received no reply. In September 1822, when he was sixteen, he was at last enrolled in a traveling troupe; there were short but successful engagements in Pittsburgh and Maysville, Kentucky; and after that Lexington, where they had a longer stay—until February 1823. Thence they made the hazardous trip to Cincinnati, the women in covered wagons, the men on horseback. On March 6, 1823, Forrest had his first public chance to do Shakespeare, as Richard III. Moses Dawson, editor of a paper in Cincinnati, wrote: "Edwin Forrest has a finely-formed and expressive countenance, expressing all the passions and marvelous exactness and power, and he looks the character of Richard much better than could be expected from a person of his years. He assumes a stately majesty of demeanor, passes suddenly to wheedling hypocrisy, and then returns to the haughty strut of towering ambition, with a facility which sufficiently evidences that he has not only deeply studied but also well understood the immortal bard. The scene with Lady Anne appeared to us unique, and superior to everything we have ever seen not excepting Kemble or Cooke. . . . We consider Mr. Forrest's natural talents of the highest grade, and we hope his good sense will prevent him from being so intoxicated with success as to neglect study and industry."

After a few other towns, the company, having had less success, disbanded at Dayton. Unexpectedly James H. Caldwell, to whom he had written in New Orleans, offered him a job at $18 per week. It was not, however, that Caldwell had remembered the letter of a juvenile but that he had chanced to see Forrest at Lexington. Caldwell was something of a father of drama in New Orleans, for he had erected Amory Hall there in 1823. The next year, Edwin joined his troupe, and it was with them that he achieved his first real fame. He performed an admirable Iago. In fact, his success was so immediate and so vast in that gay city that Caldwell became jealous and began casting him in old men's parts; the ambitious Forrest made no objections and felt his theatrical education was thereby broadening. He even went for a time to live with the Indians so that he could do an Indian role more effectively on stage.

But Caldwell could not abide the young man's success, and expressed dissatisfaction no matter how valiantly Forrest tried to please him. At length they fell into a bitter dispute over a girl, and Forrest challenged his employer to a duel; Caldwell refused to accept the challenge. That put an end to his triumphs in New Orleans. But his reputation was made and was traveling ahead of him. He repeated his Iago in Albany, 1825/26, and enacted Richmond and other parts with Edmund Kean who much influenced his style.

His early days of poverty remind one of Kean's: he sang, danced, did somersaults at the circus, yet before he was through he became the nation's favorite actor, and remained so for thirty years. Of course, he had his detractors. William Winter's harsh judgment of him was that he was "utterly selfish," and motivated by "vanity, pride, self-assertion, and avarice of power, praise and wealth," though admitting that if Forrest was a "vast animal," he was nevertheless "bewildered by a grain of genius."

One of his friends, an actor, Andrew Jackson Allen (1776–1853), had a patent for ornamenting leather with gold and silver. When Forrest was doing a "burly, loud and violent" Richard III, Allen said bluntly during an altercation with him: "What in hell would your Richard be without *my spangles?*"—which would seem to indicate that at the beginning of his career Forrest was mostly exterior show.

He thought himself a fine Hamlet, in which role he wore his own hair, curled, with black side whiskers and a tuft under his lower lip; he also wore a small mustache. His figure was stalwart and he had huge calves. This should have made him quite fit for the part—if one discounts the side-whiskers, the tuft, and the matching mustache—but the critics would not have appreciated that, for Hamlet unfortunately had already been typecast as a frail, delicate creature, which is belied by the play itself. So not surprisingly Winter said: "He was as little like Hamlet as it would be possible for any person to be." According to Alfred Ayres, he took six minutes to get through the "To be or not to be" speech instead of the traditional three. Ayres therefore admired his "deliberation."

The Bowery Theater was to usher in a new era in the theatrical annals of New York; its history, though the playhouse was to be located in several different buildings, was long. Its significance was that, unlike the aristocratic Park, it was a theater largely for the lower classes. The project had been planned in 1823, and since the city now had grown to a population of 125,000 a new playhouse was in requisition, particularly since many fashionable and well-to-do citizens were now living on the East Side. On the site of the old Tavern and Cattle Market (known as the Bull's Head), a very elegant structure was erected, its façade simulating white marble, with lofty columns and spacious portico. Stage and auditorium were larger than any other in the country, and the seating capacity was three thousand. At first it was called The New York Theater, Bowery; but Hackett and Hamblin, into whose hands it came, redubbed it The Bowery Theater, though in an excess of patriotism it was for a few years known as the American Theater. The prices of admission were first fixed at 50 cents for the boxes and pit, and 25 cents for the gallery. But a few nights' experience proved it wiser to make a distinction between boxes and pit for the sake of the more refined members of the audience, and admission to the boxes was now 75 cents and only 37½ cents for the pit, to everyone's satisfaction.

The opening occurred on Monday evening, October 23, 1826, and the theater was the first to make the daring experiment of lighting the stage with gas. The *New York Mirror* pronounced the playhouse inside and out to be "splendid . . . A Frenchman would declare, 'It was *grand*—it was *magnific* [*sic*]—it was *very well.*'"

Edwin had been seen in Albany by a man connected with the new Bowery Theater; he, having received no salary, was so destitute that he had to pawn his costumes to procure money enough for the trip to New York when he was offered the engagement. When he arrived in the city, the new theater was still in the process of being built. He took rooms in a tavern on Cortlandt Street. Miserable, penniless, without friends, and homesick, he was lucky enough one day to meet on the street an actor named Woodhull, who was to be given a benefit at the Park. Edwin offered to help out without a fee, and suggested he play Othello. Though the house was half-filled, the audience was enthusiastic. Among those present was Charles Gilfert, new manager of the Bowery-to-be. He had managed the Albany company and run out of funds, but admired Forrest and congratulated him. Edwin confessed his poverty, and the next day Gilfert gave him enough money to pay all his debts—enough, indeed, to enable Forrest to go to Albany to redeem his costumes.

On the Monday following the Bowery's opening, Forrest appeared as Othello. The place was crowded and Forrest was cheered. The stockholders met him in the greenroom, tore up his contract calling for $28 a week, and gave him a new one for $40. When, a few months later, his contract with Gilfert expired, Forrest was playing elsewhere at a salary of $200 a night! He was just twenty-one. From then on he met success and acclaim everywhere. In the meantime Gilfert was doing very well at the Bowery until it was destroyed by fire in 1828. His losses were tremendous, and he died of a broken heart. That same year the house was rebuilt, but in 1836 it was again burned to the ground. The third Bowery was not a success, and it too was destroyed by fire in 1839, only to be rebuilt again. In 1846 it burned again and was rebuilt in eighty-four days.

In 1829 Forrest returned to the Park, and remained there for seven years. In 1836 he went to Europe and made his first appearance at Drury Lane on October 17; then he toured the provinces. He came back to America with his new wife, and made long tours, including New York and Philadelphia, with great financial returns. We have already discussed the beginnings of his bitter rivalry with Macready and their growing enmity in 1845, when Forrest made his second visit to Britain.

Winter, ever his adverse critic, called his Macbeth a "robust warrior" without distinction or imagination, clumsy and prosaic. According to this critic, he was good only when violence and sonority were called for; in London in 1845, Winter observed that Charlotte Cushman's Lady Macbeth cast Forrest into the shade. He did make one addition which Winter liked: after Macbeth entered Duncan's room to murder him, the three witches were seen above the battlements at the back, slowly rising, as though they had come to "preside" over the crime. (But this touch is, of course, entirely wrong, for it makes the witches responsible for Macbeth's acts, which was certainly not what Shakespeare had in mind!)

His later Othello is said to have been shaped by intense personal grief. The fact that his four babies were either stillborn or had died shortly after birth had turned him against his wife. He sought comfort as well as pleasure with actresses and prostitutes, but it was another matter when he discovered that his wife had been deceiving *him!*

George Jamieson had played Iago to his Othello the previous spring at the Park, and was now with the Cincinnati company. Forrest went to a local artist to sit for a portrait, but finding the artist not at home, returned to the City Hotel. He found, as he has stated it, "Mrs. Forrest standing between the knees of Mr. Jamieson, who was sitting on the sofa, with his hands upon her person. I was amazed and confounded." She replied "with considerable perturbation, that Mr. Jamieson had been pointing out her phrenological developments." He accepted the explanation.

But he began to lose patience when, while he was on tour, she kept open house until all hours. On Thursday evening, January 18, 1849, his wife had gone to a party at her sister's. While she was away, Forrest remained at home, as the housekeeper noted, in a state of great agitation. When she returned, Mrs. Forrest found her husband still in the library, and for four hours he ranted and raved himself into a wild fury, and stated that she was no longer his wife. He rushed from the room leaving her to a night spent weeping. The next morning after he left the house, she went to her bureau, opened the bottom drawer with a key, and cried to the housekeeper, "Oh God! . . . Forrest has opened my drawer and gotten all my letters!" These letters were mostly from her sister, but they included "a foolish letter from

Jamieson" that "I didn't want him to see." She then went upstairs, brought down another bundle of letters and spent all day burning them.

The letter which had broken Forrest was one Jamieson had written to her in Cincinnati some three weeks before they had been found together at the hotel. It became the center of contention at the trial. Jamieson had addressed her as "Consuelo." It read:

> Our brief dream is over, and such a dream! . . . A doubt of thee can no more find harbor in my brain, than the opened rose would cease to be the hum-bird's harbor. . . . Dearest, write to me, and tell me you are happy. Think of the time when we shall meet again, . . . my heart's altar . . .

> Adieu! adieu! and when thou art gone,
> My joy shall be made up alone
> Of calling back with fancy's charm,
> Those halcyon hours when in my arm
>   Clasped Consuelo! . . .
> Adieu! adieu! when next we meet,
> Will not all sadness then retreat,
> And yield the conquered time to bliss,
> And seal the triumph with a kiss:
>   Say Consuelo?

Forrest was the more undone because her parents were drunkards and her sister had an illegitimate child. Brooding over the matter in his misery, he ordered her from the house. This was just about the time that the Astor House riots were to take place.

At first he promised to keep their separation secret, but soon was suing for divorce. She replied with a countersuit. She had many friends because of her beauty and elegance of speech: he had many enemies. He spied on her and made a dreadful scene involving a man who was totally innocent.

In the divorce court she was exonerated and he was found guilty. He appealed the case five times in eighteen years, and lost each time. In 1868 he was forced to pay her $64,000 alimony, of which the lawyers got $59,000!

Unfortunately he lost his head and began making speeches from the stage on how she had dishonored his house, in public he always referred to her as a whore and drunkard, while through it all she kept her dignity.

He was a sullen, sulky man, and kept these traits when he played Othello —"a bull of a man, with great bulging muscles," as he has been described. He was the only actor then alive who had the right physique for the role. His movement at times was that "of a boulder that has been set rolling; he beat his breast and ranted in over-powering tones," and "thrust his fist into the face of the audience—by way of showing animation or passion." Yet in the earlier scenes he was admired for the romantic fervor of his voice, while his love scenes were full of mellowness.

When he appeared as Lear in 1846 at the Park, he was highly praised by the critics for having achieved a dignified style. At a banquet given him the next month to celebrate his return from England, William Cullen Bryant presiding, Forrest said that American actors would bear "successful comparison with any of the 'stars' that twinkle on us from abroad."

That fidelity to nature for which he was being forever praised sometimes greatly disturbed the audiences in death scenes. He would hang out his tongue, contort his features, and writhe on the stage floor. His defense was that a man of his physique could not die without a demonstration of extreme agony.

As his voice began to go, he gave up acting for readings. In December 2, 1872, he read *Othello;* two days later it was *Hamlet,* and three afternoons later *Othello* again, at the Tremont Temple in Boston. He started out for New York that night, arrived early Sunday morning and spent the day in bed. A few days later, when the servant had breakfast ready, she rang for him. Receiving no response, she went to his room and found him moaning and twisting on the bed. He looked utterly desperate but could not speak. When she came back with a doctor, Forrest was dead. He was fully dressed; beside him were the eight-pound dumbbells with which he exercised every morning, and a copy of *Hamlet* with the page he had been reading face down on the night table.

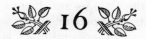

16

Edwin Thomas Booth

The tragic actor whose fame is as legendary in the United States as that of Garrick in England, Edwin Thomas Booth (1833–1893), was the second eldest surviving son of Junius Brutus Booth. Born at the Maryland farm on November 13, 1833, he was named Edwin after Edwin Forrest and Thomas after his father's close friend, Flynn. His education was astonishingly casual, considering his father's devotion to literature, and he himself spoke bitterly of it in a letter to his daughter, Edwina: "When I was at Eton (I don't refer now to the dinner-table) my Greek and Latin were of such a superior quality that had it not been for an unforeseen accident, I would have carried off all the honors. The accident lay in this—I never went to school there except in dreams . . . I have suffered so much from the lack of that which my father could easily have given me in youth, and which he himself possessed."

As has already been indicated, he found himself while still very young his father's guardian. If, as he grew older, everyone who knew him remarked on the melancholy to which he was prone, the causes for it were rooted in the circumstances of his life, and started early. Like all his brothers and sisters, he was born illegitimate, and when as an adolescent he traveled with his father, it was often necessary to keep careful watch over him through many a midnight and into the early hours of the morning. The vigil ended sometimes with having to lock Junius Brutus in his hotel room. He was doomed to lose his first wife within a few years of their marriage, to have as brother the man who killed Lincoln, and to marry for the second time a woman who became insane. For a man of his gentle nature it is remarkable that he was not crushed by his adversity, and that he could rise in his profession to heights which make him inevitably the first to come to mind when speaking of great American actors.

Although Junius Brutus had given him names of men associated with the theater, he did not wish his son to follow in his footsteps. Yet he was still a boy at school when he and his friend John S. Clarke (who later married

Edwin's sister, Asia) did the Cassius and Brutus scene from *Julius Caesar,* during which Junius Brutus slipped in, unknown to the lads, who were performing "in white linen trousers and black jackets before the school." Edwin made his first public appearance in his father's company at the age of sixteen. He was given the role of Tressil in *Richard III* in Boston, and at eighteen was playing in New York, when his father suddenly refused to go on stage as Richard III, and his son was compelled unexpectedly to take his place.

In California he served an apprenticeship as actor in San Francisco, Sacramento, as well as in mountain and mining towns. On occasion he even blackened his face to sing Negro songs. With other actors he toured Hawaii, Australia, and the South Seas. In the company for a while was Laura Keene, (?1820–1873), born Mary Moss in England where she acted until 1851, when she came to the United States; in 1852 she was in New York en route to Australia. She spent most of the remainder of her life in America and opened her own theater in New York on November 18, 1856, playing Rosalind in *As You Like It.* Since the Civil War was on, hers was the only playhouse open in 1861. Her company was playing *Our American Cousin* at Ford's Theater in Washington the night that Edwin's brother, John Wilkes Booth, assassinated President Lincoln, on April 15, 1865.

Edwin first began to attract notice in San Francisco. Mrs. Catherine Sinclair, the woman whom Forrest had sued for divorce because of adultery, established herself in that city, and managed to defeat the yellow journalism which damned her for her adultery and breaking her husband's heart; she managed it with such grace that opinion soon cast him in the role of villain. At San Francisco Hall she did Katherine to Edwin's Petruchio; in May he performed his first Benedick, in June Romeo, and in September Shylock. In July they set out for Australia, but did not fare well there.

Matters were different in Hawaii. The new king there, Kamehameha IV, was most anxious to see *Richard III,* which Booth, now manager of the troupe, was willing to give. But since the monarch was in mourning for his father, he could not appear publicly. Instead, an armchair was placed in the wings of the playhouse, and he watched from his chair. When it came to the coronation scene, Booth had to ask the king whether they might borrow his chair; he graciously consented and watched standing up. After a fierce quarrel with Booth Miss Keene had left the company; for the part of Lady Anne it was necessary now to call upon the services of a white man, who had been only a stagehand in the United States, had a Dutch accent, was under five feet, and was cross-eyed and bow-legged. One can imagine *that* Lady Anne, especially when Richard addressed her as "Divine perfection of woman." Offstage the other actors were rolling on the floor with laughter. When the play was over, the king in an English strongly British, complimented Booth and told him that he had seen his great father play the same role in New York.

Edwin did not come back East until 1856, where his position as a leading actor was established at the Boston Theater on April 20, 1857, in *A New Way to Pay Old Debts.* On May 14 he played Richard III in New York at the Metropolitan Theater, which was on lower Broadway, at that time the center of the theatrical district. As he drove down the street lined with trees, he saw his name advertised everywhere on the sides of buildings and in shop windows:

SON OF THE GREAT TRAGEDIAN. HOPE OF THE LIVING DRAMA. RICHARD'S HIMSELF AGAIN.

He is said to have ground his teeth, clutched his forehead, and groaned to his companion: "I'm ruined!"

In the cast at the Metropolitan was another beginner, Lawrence Barrett, who had contrived to reach New York by a devious and difficult route; along with his fellow actors he was prepared to detest Booth as an upstart. But once they met Booth, all hatred vanished. Barrett describes him as a "slight, pale youth with black, flowing hair and soft brown eyes. He took his place with no air of . . . self-assertion, and gave his directions with a grace and courtesy which have never left him."

The next day the critics said Booth's Richard III was an imitation of his father's; like Junius Brutus I, he walked through early scenes too tamely, and when he wished, said the *New York Tribune,* he "renders the passage with a vigorous truthfulness which startles his audience into wild enthusiasm." Still inexperienced, he had not yet learned to control his voice or his walk, which was too youthful for the roles he played. Two critics became his devotees: William Winter, later a power on the *Tribune*—who at the age of *twenty-one* prophesied that Booth's name would "eclipse any which has adorned the stage within the memory of living man!"—and Adam Badeau, who had come to scoff at the "Hope of the Living Drama," and was so deeply moved that he came backstage to make Booth's acquaintance. He and Winter soon were good friends of the actor. Badeau could not understand Booth's omnipresent depression, since he seemed to have before him all that any man could wish, nor his outburst of conviction "that evil is hanging over me, that I can't come to good."

In this time of his life Booth was wont to go on sprees until early hours of the morning. He was sent all sorts of poems, flowers, scarves, and ostrich feathers by adoring young women, as well as expensive rings and brooches accompanied by delicately scented notes. Badeau testifies: "More than once Booth saved some foolish child from what might have been disgrace, and sent her home to her family. And he never injured a pure woman in his life" —whatever that may imply!

One of Booth's earliest managers, William Stuart, was fond of telling the story of a strange *Othello* he had arranged. Davison, a famous German tragedian, played the Moor in his native German, Edwin Booth played Iago in English, and Methea Schiller, who was something of a linguist, played Desdemona in German when the dialogue was directed to Davison, and in English when the lines were intended for Booth. Stuart paid Davison $3,000 for three such performances; he had enjoyed himself so much that he was only too eager to continue for $250 a performance, "and on departing," observed Stuart wryly, "like most of these great German tragedians, he would have recited a soliloquy on the clock for ten dollars. He shortly after, as might be expected, went mad, and Schiller, poor girl, died of cholera at Pittsburgh on the same day as her husband and two children were on their way East from Salt Lake City."

Once, during Edwin Booth's early struggles, he was barnstorming in Virginia at a place called Lee's Landing where the theater was a tobacco warehouse, crowded with planters from miles around. The troupe was scheduled to take the weekly steamer, due late at night, and between acts of *The Merchant of Venice* they busied themselves with their packing. They were in the middle of the trial scene when they heard a whistle; the manager conveyed to them from the wings that the steamer was there and would leave in ten minutes. If they missed it they would have to wait a week for another departure. He also indicated that they were not to explain matters to the audience: a fight would surely ensue. Edwin, playing Bassanio, resolved to capitalize on the innocence of the planters, and so when the Shylock began to sharpen his knife on his shoe, Booth walked up to him and with a solemn face asked: "You are bound to have the flesh, are you?" "You bet your life," said George Ruggles, the Shylock. "Now, I'll make you one more offer," Bassanio continued, "in addition to this big bag of ducats. I'll throw in two kegs of nigger-head terback, a shotgun and two of the best coon-dogs in the state." "I'm blamed if I don't do it!" cried Shylock hastily. The audience, tobacco raisers and coon hunters all, were mightily pleased. "And to show there's no hard feelings," put in the Portia, "we'll wind up with a Virginia reel." When they got aboard, the captain of the steamer, who had seen the play's conclusion, said, "I'd like to see the whole of the play sometime. I'm blamed if I thought that fellow Shakespeare had so much snap in him."

There are various well-known stories about the little old lady who said she was so fond of *Hamlet* because it was full of quotations. There is one, not well known, apparently connected with Edwin Booth when he was doing that play in the West. This dear little old lady was sitting in a good seat, and at the end of the second act said to the man next to her, "Would you mind telling me who that man in black was?" "That was Hamlet," he informed her. "Oh, thank you most kindly," said the little old lady, picking up her bag and umbrella, and rising to leave the theater. "You're not going, are you?" asked her neighbor, "there are three more acts." "I know," she replied, "that's why I'm going."

Edwin Booth had acted on occasion with "little Mary Devlin," after their meeting in Baltimore, not one of his numerous infatuations but a woman he was to love for the rest of his life, even more after he had lost her. As popular as he became with the ladies, they were even more infatuated with his brother, John Wilkes, who was very handsome and by far the best looking of the Booth brothers. John Wilkes played Richmond to Edwin's Richard in Charlotte Cushman's company. Unlike his gentle brother, John Wilkes was a passionate man, something of a dandy, and a great favorite among waiters in restaurants and maids in hotels; by the time he was twenty he had had several narrow escapes arising from his involvement with women, but his innate grace enabled him to extract himself. Clara Morris, the actress, observed the manager's wife in another company, a woman advanced in years, shake a finger at John Wilkes for an impudence; John seized the woman's hand, made a profound bow, and kissed her fingers. Though he later became a very good actor, John Wilkes was, at first, a fumbler; Edwin tried to help him and give him every advantage, but the younger man resisted Edwin's corrections.

In October 1858, in Boston, Edwin was again playing with Mary Devlin in *Romeo and Juliet*. Perhaps because they were in love, the performance proved very exciting. "The two lovers were at their best," said Julia Ward Howe, "ideally young, beautiful, and identified with their parts." Whatever impression he made on stage, privately Edwin could not have been called handsome, except for his remarkable eyes and very musical voice; his figure was slight and therefore a constant challenge to the heroic roles he liked best.

Julia Ward Howe became very fond of Mary, whom she called "this exquisite little woman," and also saw Edwin in *Hamlet*, a performance which inspired her to pen a tribute to him, printed in the *Atlantic Monthly:*

> And, beautiful as dreams of maidenhood
> That doubt defy,
> Young Hamlet, with his forehead grief-subdued,
> And visioning eye.

Booth's temperament was such as to make him the most convincing Hamlet of his age—to those who were ready to accept the notion (not Shakespeare's!) of an oversensitive, melancholy, overthoughtful prince. Even Mary called him "my Hamlet." Undoubtedly he gave a very moving performance in that role and became identified with it, and therefore may very well be more responsible than anyone for the continuing misconception of the prince as a man whom Shakespeare portrayed as violent, highly philosophical, but exceedingly impetuous.

Though in love with Mary, Booth was in principle averse to marrying an actress, and had not become engaged to her. When a Boston lawyer proposed to her, Booth left town, and she asked Charlotte Cushman's advice —which was to accept the lawyer. Mary wrote Edwin to tell him of the proposal, and he sought escape from his misery in gallons of alcohol, which landed him in bed in a very sick condition. When friends apprised her of his state, she came at once to him, and they agreed to marry as soon as it should be feasible.

It was characteristic of him that he should have felt it necessary to confess to her, even though it made her weep bitterly, the blackest side of his past life, withholding nothing: "Before I was eighteen I was a drunkard, at twenty a libertine. I knew no better. I was born *good,* I do believe, for there are sparks of goodness flashing out from among the cinders." In his childhood, he told her, he was neglected and exposed to "all sorts of temptations and evil society." He had been allowed "to roam at large, and at an early age and in a wild and almost barbarous country where boys become old men in vice."

Without chiding, without judging, she did all she could to strengthen his fight against drink; the strength of his love for her seems to have cured him. She disliked the salacious works for the stage imported from France, which were crowding out tragedy, and helped build up his morale by writing to him: "You can, if you will, change the perverted taste of the public by your truth and sublimity, and you must study for this."

Adam Badeau was now writing for *The New York Sunday Times,* and praised his friend Booth as the sole representative of pure poetic tragedy. The two had many an argument over the interpretation of Booth's roles; in the end Badeau had to yield his analyses to Booth's histrionic instinct. "This marvelous inspiration," he wrote, "that comes down on a man as suddenly and strangely and unaccountably to the actor as to the audience . . . this surpasses in strangeness any other gift vouchsafed to the race." He was probably thinking of that native incandescence of which we have spoken in the first chapter.

On July 7, 1860, Edwin and Mary Devlin were married in New York. For the event John Wilkes traveled north, and after the ceremony flung his arms around his brother's neck and kissed him. The honeymoon, shared with his mother and his brother Joe, was in a cottage on the Canadian side of Niagara Falls. His sister Asia, who had disapproved of Mary from the beginning, made it plain that she had no intention of seeing her sister-in-law. As it was, the newlyweds were happiest when left alone.

That year he played with Charlotte Cushman in *Henry VIII, Macbeth,* and *The Merchant of Venice.* In her brusque way, Miss Cushman criticized Booth's Macbeth as too "polished and very intellectual," and she begged him to remember "that Macbeth was the grandfather of all the Bowery villains."

At the Winter Garden that autumn Booth for the first time as his father before him found himself a rival of Edwin Forrest. But now even Walt Whitman, once Forrest's great admirer, asked whether the older actor's style was not too blustering to serve as a model for young players. Forrest, after an absence of three years because of rheumatism, returned to enact Hamlet. His reputation was still great and his old supporters were eager to see him put down young Edwin Booth, who had made such rapid strides toward fame. Forrest opened in September 1860, at Niblo's Garden, and followed his Hamlet with Lear, Othello, Macbeth, and Richard III. Booth opened as Hamlet in November at the Winter Garden; he was twenty-seven.

This was the season in which Booth established himself as the chief American tragic actor. He had improved enormously, departing more and more from his father's noisy delivery; he refined his style and began to be recognized as the founder of a new school of acting. The *Tribune* compli-

mented him on the "gigantic strides he has taken" in his art. For reasons
to be revealed in the next chapter, Charlotte Cushman, however, assured
him that he did "not know anything at all" about Hamlet. (She may have
been right!) Forrest, naturally, was not pleased by his rival's performance.
As Booth walked the stage moodily contemplating the ground, Forrest
sneered. "What's the damned fool doing? He looks like a super hunting for
a sixpence."

Now Booth felt the need of a change—to be seen outside of his native
land. In the spring of 1861 he received an offer to appear in England. While
he was terminating his season at the Winter Garden, Lincoln was inaugurated, and the next month Fort Sumter was fired upon. Among the men who
enlisted were his friends Cary and Badeau. One prominent New Yorker
remarked: "In the first year of our war, when we were profoundly miserable
and frightened, what a relief it was to go and see Booth in *Hamlet.*"

The war caused some division in allegiance, though not in affection, in the
Booth family. Edwin and Junius and eventually Asia were for the North;
Joseph, a medical student at Charleston, served as a doctor with the Confederates; and John Wilkes, who at the time was in Albany, spoke so witheringly
of the Union that he was ordered either to be quiet or quit the town.

Edwin's hopes for acting in England seemed about to be realized when
he received an invitation from the Haymarket in London. Though loath to
leave the country at a time of crisis, particularly when his wife was expecting
a child, he felt that a London appearance would be "the grand turning-point
of my career." Mary, of course, went with him. What they apparently did not
know was that the Haymarket was a playhouse specializing in comedy, and
that on their arrival its manager, Buckstone, would admit that he was "rather
afraid of tragedy." It was for this reason that Booth allowed himself to open
in one of his weakest roles, Shylock, on September 30, 1861. It was a
performance without life. His second appearance was before a half-empty
house. The political situation may have contributed to his failure. The
British newspapers that year were all supporting the secessionists.

Mary's confinement was near, and he left her in London to act in Liverpool and Manchester, in which latter town Laertes, Cassio, and Bassanio
were played by a young man, John Henry Brodribb, who was to become the
leading English actor under the name of Henry Irving. Attendance was as
bad as in London. He rushed back to the metropolis to be with his wife when
the baby was born, December 9, right after the Trent affair, when England
was within an inch of entering the Civil War on the side of the South. He
did not attempt to act in England again at this time, and returned to the
United States with Mary and their little daughter, Edwina.

Nevertheless, when he played again at the Winter Garden the fact of his
having had an engagement in London had improved his eminent position.

When his brother, John Wilkes, read in the journals that Edwin had made
$5,000 for one month's performances in Boston, he decided to become a
star himself, and in October 1860 he had so billed himself in Alabama. In
February of the next year he was in Albany, and it is said that the power,

horror, and fury he communicated (in a play called *The Apostate*) were so uncannily reminiscent of his father—except for the fact that he was exceedingly handsome—that a group of spiritualists in the city announced that Junius Brutus's spirit had probably been invisibly on stage, inspiring his son. John Wilkes, though fond of his family, was now anxious to excel Edwin. Although a bitter antiabolitionist, with patriotism only for the South, he was, in a way, challenging Edwin's supremacy in the North. The Confederates were piling up victories, but when Edwin went to England, John Wilkes had decided to make the most of his opportunity and in St. Louis, Chicago, and Baltimore he starred himself; in Baltimore, near their old home, he advertised: I AM MYSELF ALONE!

Though some critics found him bombastic, there were those who thought him better than Edwin. One called him "the best of living Romeos," and it is said his passionate embrace of Juliet lifted her out of her shoes; his Desdemona's face was contorted by the clang of his scimitar as he flung himself upon her body. His Hamlet, unlike the sensitive prince of his brother, was hot-blooded and clearly insane. After a *Richard III* he was put to bed to nurse the bruises sustained in the all too realistic battle scenes he had fought.

The Edwin Booths now made friends with Richard and Elizabeth Stoddard, and through them became acquainted with a number of writers and artists. Both Stoddards published their poems in the *Atlantic Monthly* and *Harper's*. Unlike most members of his profession, Edwin avoided the stellar role off stage. Instead, he was taciturn and retiring. Louisa May Alcott, who could sympathize with such an attitude, wrote in her diary, "Saw Booth at the Goulds, a handsome, shy man, glooming in a corner." Those who knew him longest realized that Mary's influence had somewhat relaxed him in company, and he was learning to be sociable. He had given up most drinking for two years. Now that they went to dinner parties, it was more difficult; he began by accepting only one glass. But the temptation was too great and the old habit was back, as he drank glass after glass. Inevitably, Mary, observing his regression, began to lose that expansive gaiety for which she was well known.

She began to dread the idea that she might die before him. When asked why, her answer was, "He needs me so." Once friends heard her sob out a prayer, as her arms were flung around him, "Almighty God, Merciful Father, spare him the cross! Take him first, I do beseech Thee!" For now there occurred too frequently those mornings when sick at heart and in body, Edwin would sob in her arms his promise to give up drinking.

In Boston Edwin always did particularly well. One season he made $5,000 in two weeks. Nevertheless, Booth was absolutely hopeless in financial matters, and no matter how much he earned he never seemed to be able to hold on to any of it. While he was away Mary took a house in the country at Dorchester for herself, the year-old Edwina, and a nurse. He joined her before beginning his new season at the Winter Garden, and they were both supremely happy. Nevertheless, she wrote to Elizabeth Stoddard: "I look

with dread and horror upon the four weeks' separation that must ensue.
. . . Well you know the demon that pursues a noble, ungoverned spirit like
Edwin's. He is so gentle, so yielding, so *abstemious* now & I advise with him
& he promises that the victory shall be his."

During January 1863, despite her growing illness, she drove into Boston
with Edwin to see John Wilkes act at the Museum. Edwin's engagement had
been an extraordinary success, John Wilkes's in Boston was fabulous, and
broke all records.

Edwin's personal problems evidently blinded him to what was clear to
everyone else, that Mary's health was rapidly failing. She herself made no
mention of it to him. When Booth was back in New York his friends perceived that something was gnawing at him. However, he opened with a very
successful *Hamlet*, Lawrence Barrett being his Laertes. Then as the week
progressed his acting grew clumsy. He was drunk regularly now, exaggerated Hamlet's melancholy, sentimentalized Othello, and made Richard
III far too savage. His friends tried to help him temper his drinking by
emptying out the window glasses that were brought to his dressing room.
They took turns following him after the theater—just as he had done with
his own father.

During his second week in New York, his brother John Wilkes arrived with
the news that Mary was ill with a fever. She had ventured out into the snow
to call on a friend in Boston, the horse-car had been delayed because of the
heavy fall of snow, and waiting for the car on an exposed street corner she
had caught a severe chill. She was very ill for the next few days but insisted
to John Wilkes that Edwin must not be disturbed, for it might break the run
of his performances. His brother's message encouraged Edwin to slip away
from his friends; he was so drunk when he came on stage next day that he
was a keen source of embarrassment to them. Elizabeth Stoddard wrote to
Mary: "Sick or well, you must come." The night before they had even
debated bringing down the curtain before the play was half over. Booth has
recorded that as he lay awake in New York in the earliest hours of the
morning with a dizzy head, he felt a blast of cold air twice hit his right cheek;
he rolled over and felt the same on his left cheek, then distinctly heard his
wife's voice whispering, "Come to me, darling. I'm almost frozen." Mary
was forced to answer Elizabeth that she could not stand up, much less make
the trip to New York. On that night, February 20, she suddenly became so
much worse that her doctor called in one of his colleagues. She demanded
to know the truth, and was told she could live only a few hours.

Booth had been getting bad notices. The *Herald* stated flatly that it would
have been better to close the Winter Garden than allow the public to see
"Mr. Booth when he was really unfit to act." On that same night of February
20, three telegrams—at least one from Mary's doctor—lay unopened in his
dressing room. After he had staggered through *Richard III*, the manager
came in with a torn envelope, and read the message aloud: "This is the
fourth telegram. Why does not Mr. Booth answer? He must come at once."

It was too late for a train to Boston. The next morning Edwin and Stoddard took the first to leave and he sent a telegram from the station saying that he was on his way. But Mary died a few minutes after seven, while Edwin's train was just leaving New York. He later insisted that at that hour he had seen his wife's face beside him in the train. When a friend met him at the Boston station with a carriage, he said: "Don't tell me. I know."

At the funeral, as Edwin walked with John Wilkes beside him, Julia Ward Howe thought at once of his acting during the scene of Ophelia's burial, so similarly grief stricken were his eyes. Poor "little Mary" was only twenty-two.

The clergyman who had married them hoped that Edwin would find consolation in his art. Booth's reply was that his art had become hateful to him; "it has become a trade." Because of his reticence off stage no one guessed his suffering, but he admitted to Stoddard, "My grief *eats* me." Naturally he was stricken with remorse, and he blamed himself and his conduct for her death. To the attempts of his friends to lighten the burden, he had one answer: "They tell me that time and use will soften the blow, that I shall grow to forget her. God forbid!"

He gave up the bottle, and in compensation began to smoke as many as fifteen cigars a day. The smoking habit became in its turn a lifelong addiction. He told Elizabeth that "all the accumulated vices I had acquired in the wilds of California and Australia" had been raging "until the angel quenched" them and made him "if not a *man,* at least a little worthier than I was." He admitted that only the temptation to drink had remained with him.

He chose May 19, the day on which Mary would have been twenty-three, to visit Laura Edmonds, the spiritualist. He came away from his first experience exalted at the prospect of further communication with his wife. But his joy was short-lived. After four or five séances, he felt that nothing was being accomplished. Yet he persisted in believing that Mary's spirit continued to seek him out. He could not, however, bear to go anywhere that had associations with her.

Unhappily, at this time he somehow learned that Elizabeth Stoddard had been Mary's informant about his drunkenness. He felt betrayed, and at once broke his friendship with her and her husband.

Some months later he bought a house on East Nineteenth Street and brought his mother and his sister Rosalie to live with him and look after Edwina. Everything about his daughter reminded him of Mary.

Six months after his wife's death, Edwin's sister Asia relented, and he and his sister once again became friends. En route between performances in the North and South John Wilkes would stay with his brother in New York. As an actor he was allowed to pass across the lines of battle; everyone seemed to know him, not only because of his personal beauty and very black mustache, but also because of his picturesque dress, flowing cape, and broad hat worn low at an angle. In the spring he had been taken into custody at St. Louis for remarking that he hoped "the whole damn government would go to hell." He was fined and set free, after taking an oath of allegiance to the North.

Adam Badeau was wounded and went to convalesce at Edwin's house. Both brothers carried him upstairs and dressed his wounds. "Imagine me," said John Wilkes, "helping that wounded Yankee with my rebel sinews." "If the North conquer us, it will be by numbers only," he added to Asia. She cried: *"If the North conquer us? We are of the North."* "Not I, not I," he exclaimed. "So help me holy God! my soul, life, and possessions are for the South!"

At first, after Mary's death, certain passages in the plays brought Edwin close to breaking down. But by degrees, much of the significance of lines which had escaped him took on deeper meaning and his art became stronger —for it seems to be a law of life that suffering either destroys or creates us anew. In the autumn of 1863 Forrest was his rival again, but when he did Hamlet, it became clear from the empty houses that audiences preferred to see Booth, even John Wilkes (in Philadelphia), when the play was *Macbeth.*

Edwin began a tour after his season ended, and at Ford's Theater in Washington President Lincoln saw his Shylock, liked it, but said, "I'd a thousand times rather read it at home if it were not for Booth's playing." Back in New York, where his brothers visited him whenever they were in town, he finally grew tired of John Wilkes's cursing of the North, and asked him why he did not fight for the South if his prejudices were so violent. "I promised mother to keep out of the quarrel and I'm sorry I promised," was his answer. His charming voice and manners, personal beauty, and bright eyes were making a favorite of him among the women of Washington in governmental circles. He was doing little acting, except in his private life. Habitually he would turn up late at Asia's house in Philadelphia, covered with red mud, not bothering to wake her, and going to sleep on the couch in his riding clothes and boots.

Edwin paid far less attention to the war, but John Wilkes was convinced that if Lincoln were reelected, the president would declare himself king. Asia objected that such a thing could never happen, and her brother would respond with imprecations against Lincoln's appearance, "his pedigree, his coarse jokes and anecdotes, his vulgar similes and his frivolity"—all of which he held a disgrace to his office.

On November 25, 1864, Edwin gave *Julius Caesar* at the Winter Garden, himself Brutus, Junius as Cassius, and John Wilkes as Antony. They had never played together before and the advertisements read:

> THE THREE SONS OF THE GREAT BOOTH
> JUNIUS BRUTUS
> EDWIN AND
> JOHN WILKES
> FILII PATRI DIGNO DIGNIORES

Though up to this night the name Booth in New York had meant Edwin, Junius was establishing himself in the city and was sometimes called *the* Booth—he most resembled his father—and he rather unkindly said of Edwin that though the public was wild over Edwin, in "a thousand years" he would "never be able to approach father." But John Wilkes was even thirstier for recognition: "I must have fame, fame."

On the next night Edwin gave *Hamlet*, the first of his "perfect productions." He had been working hard at it, and the materials and scenery were spectacular. Moreover, he never had identified himself more with the prince. All Shakespearean companies being repertory in practice, to have the same play run for three weeks indicated remarkable success. Edwin's *Hamlet* made theatrical history and ran for an unheard-of one hundred nights, concluding March 26, 1865. He soon went to Boston.

On April 3, General Grant marched into Richmond. In Washington, John Wilkes was conspiring with two schoolmates, one stupid youth, a German, and a Confederate deserter to kidnap Lincoln and exchange him for some much-needed Confederate prisoner-soldiers; they met on H Street at the boardinghouse of Mary Surratt, a widow whose son was also involved in the scheme. Two kidnapping attempts failed, and John Wilkes was gradually lashing himself into a fury. He had always been able to hold his liquor well; now he would drink a quart of brandy within two hours.

Good Friday fell that year on April 14. When John Wilkes went to Ford's Theater to collect his mail, he heard that President Lincoln, his wife, and General and Mrs. Grant were going to attend the performance that night of *Our American Cousin*, with Laura Keene as star. Four hours later when a friend met him on Pennsylvania Avenue he was riding a mare, "sitting on his horse like a Centaur," faultlessly dressed, and elegantly—the "handsomest man in Washington," as Ford's brother called him.

At the last minute Grant found he could not be present at the theater. John Wilkes stopped at the saloon next to Ford's Theater, and called for brandy. Someone twitted him on his father's superiority as an actor. Booth answered, "When I leave the stage I'll be the most famous man in America." Making sure that, as an actor well known in town, he would require no ticket, he went back for another brandy, strolled leisurely into the theater, singing softly, and went up to the balcony, where he leaned against the wall. Without a sound, he moved down the side aisle. The soldier who was supposed to be guarding the president's seat had disappeared to take a seat in the balcony. Booth quietly entered the box's anteroom, and through a hole in the door (which he is thought to have bored earlier in the day) saw Lincoln in his rocking chair, Mrs. Lincoln beside her husband, and their two guests. At the moment there was but one actor on the stage. John Wilkes stepped into the box, aimed a small derringer at the president, shouted, *"Sic semper tyrannis!"* and fired. The president's head dropped, his guests jumped to grasp Booth, who made his way to the front of the box, seized the railing and jumped over, landing on the stage with his left leg folded under. He had broken a bone above the ankle. Forcing himself to his feet, he hopped past the astonished actor, Harry Hawk, collided with Laura Keene and an actor, Ferguson, in the wings, pushed Miss Keene aside, and made for a passageway. Dragging his damaged leg, he slashed with his dagger at two men who tried to block his way, and burst through a door into the back alley, where his mare awaited him. The sound of the hooves was the only one heard in the theater until Mrs. Lincoln cried, "He has shot the president!" The audience rose in confusion, many of them waving guns, until the word went around from those who had recognized him that it had been John Wilkes Booth.

He proudly identified himself at the Navy Yard Bridge to the sergeant there. In the theater there were faintings, screams, tramplings on one another, while six soldiers carried Lincoln out into Tenth Street across the way into the house occupied by Charles Warwick. The president died the next morning.

Edwin Booth was in Boston. In the autumn of 1864 he had cast his first and only vote during his life, and it had been for Abraham Lincoln. On the night of April 14, he was acting the role of Edward Mortimer; he had just come from New York and his triumphant one hundred nights as Hamlet, then a record. On his last night a committee told him that they had ordered a medal struck in his honor to commemorate the event. On the morning of April 15, he awoke to a nightmare. The manager informed him that he was going to close the playhouse. Asia in Philadelphia, and Junius in Cincinnati heard the woeful news of their brother's crime too; Junius had to be smuggled out of his hotel to escape a menacing mob. When their mother learned what her son had done, she cried, "O God, if this be true, let him shoot himself. Let him not live to be hanged."

Edwin's trunks were searched in Boston and he had to answer many questions before he was allowed to go back to New York to join his mother. There, his devoted friends did all they could to convince him that his own character and reputation had not altered in the public's opinion. But their kindness was unavailing. Overwhelmed by grief and shame, he felt there was no alternative but to give up his life's work, the stage. In the ensuing months his health became worse, and he longed for death.

Clergymen did not refrain from capitalizing on the fact that Lincoln had met his end in a theater. No good man, was their general agreement, ought to be seen in a playhouse, whence thousands pass "into the embrace of gaiety and folly, intemperance and lewdness, infamy and ruin."

A considerable portion of the American mob, Edwin's friends notwithstanding, screamed for the arrest of *all* actors, but the particular target was the Booth family. Edwin received many vile and threatening letters. During the last few days before John Wilkes's capture, the assassin's favorite mistress tried to kill herself with chloroform, his photograph under her pillow. Because one great-grandfather of the Booths had been a Portuguese Jew, a new wave of anti-Semitism threatened to engulf the entire family; much was made of their technical illegitimacy. Asia heard from Edwin, who tried to console her by writing, "Think no more of John . . . He is dead to us now. . . . Imagine the boy you loved to be in that better part of his spirit in another world." The War Department offered $50,000 for the apprehension of the murderer. Even the defeated South washed its hands of him; he has "struck himself from existence . . . He has the brand of Cain upon his brow." When in September 1865 Asia wrote a book, *Passages, Incidents and Anecdotes, in the Life of Junius Brutus Booth by His Daughter*, the volume bore this tragic dedication: "MOTHER: that name, so Hallowed and Revered, is but a synonym of sorrow; To you the very patient and long suffering, I dedicate these pages," and opened with these words: "A calamity without precedent has fallen on our country. We, of all families, secure in domestic love and retirement, are stricken desolate!"

These were the unanticipated reversals of fortune of the beautiful John Wilkes Booth who had been so certain he would be hailed as a hero. In the marshes of Maryland, where he lay hiding, he wrote that he could not repent his deed. "God's will be done. I have too great a soul to die like a criminal."

At two in the morning of April 26, Colonel Baker and Lieutenant Conger surrounded a tobacco barn near Port Royal, Virginia, and ordered John Wilkes Booth to surrender. John Wilkes first asked for the right to fight them singly. When they denied, he called out gaily, "You can prepare a stretcher for me."

Conger threw a lit torch into the barn and as the flames leapt, he saw Booth distinctly. "His eyes were lustrous like fever, and swelled and rolled in terrible beauty."

Calmly, as though on a battlefield, John Wilkes shifted his carbine to his left hand, drew his revolver, pulled the trigger, and fell headlong forward. His body was dragged outside, and water was given him. "Tell mother," were among his last halting words, "I died for my country." Then he pleaded with his captors to put him out of his agony by killing him. Baker coldly replied that Booth must live. The soldiers went through his pockets and passed around a pipe, a nail file, a compass, a knife, a diamond pin, a pocket diary with the photographs of John Wilkes's fiancée and four pretty actresses. His final words were, "Useless, useless," and with them he died.

Edwin received a number of letters from women claiming to be John Wilkes's wife and demanding money, and his sister Rosalie allowed herself to be swindled out of the little she had by one such claimant. Junius and John Clarke, Asia's husband, who had been imprisoned, were released. Clarke was indignant that Edwin had not been arrested, said he loathed the whole hypocritical family, and demanded a divorce from Asia, though in the end, for his own advantage, he decided not to pursue that line. Asia was about to give birth, and the nurse attending her refused to stay on. Even the family doctor could barely be induced to help her. On July 7 several of the conspirators, including Mrs. Surratt, were hanged.

Aware that acting was the one profession he was fit for, Edwin came out of retirement and reappeared as Hamlet at the Winter Garden on January 3, 1866. The *New York Herald* screamed, "Is the Assassination of Caesar to be Performed? Will Booth appear as the assassin of Caesar? That would be, perhaps, the most suitable character." But other papers defended him, and promised—accurately—that the theater would be crowded with delighted audiences. It was evident that among the packed audience were men who obviously never went to the theater, and might be prepared for violence. But the sight of Booth's slender figure clothed in black amidst the splendor of the Danish court, caused everyone present to rise and cheer him again and again, with an occasional curse upon the *New York Herald.* Booth bowed his head in thanks for what amounted to a public acknowledgment of his innocence in Lincoln's murder.

Years later, when he received a letter about his brother, he replied to his correspondent that he could give "very little information regarding my brother John. I seldom saw him since his early boyhood in Baltimore . . . We regarded him as a good-hearted, harmless, though wild-brained boy, and used to laugh at his patriotic froth whenever secession was discussed. That he was insane on that one point no one who knew him well can doubt . . . [He] declared his belief that Lincoln would be made King of America . . . Knowing my sentiments, he avoided me, rarely visiting my house, except to see my mother. . . . He was of a gentle, loving disposition, very boyish and full of fun. . . . He possessed rare dramatic talent, and would have made a brilliant mark in the theatrical world." (Montrose J. Moses says of John Wilkes that had he led a normal life, "it is believed he would have surpassed Edwin in the power and scope of his acting.")

Edwin could never be persuaded to perform in Washington again.

At the Winter Garden New Yorkers saw revivals such as *The Merchant of Venice* of peerless splendor; Shylock, for instance, was to be seen moving in the midst of scenes accurately depicting St. Mark's and the senate chamber of Venice. In January 1866 the citizens of New York presented Edwin with a "Hamlet medal," in recognition of his superb art.

But it is important to remember that even though Edwin's own sensitive melancholy nature made him particularly attuned to his interpretation of the Prince of Denmark, and that, like modern Method actors, he converted Hamlet into himself, still, as all great interpreters do, he always held sufficiently aloof to control the performance. He was even known in the very midst of tragic moments to whisper little jokes to fellow actors on stage with him.

Nor was opinion unanimous on this most famous of his roles. *The Nation,* never hostile to him, said that though his characterization in the part was "beautiful, elegant, graceful, exquisitely refined and delicate," it was "neither intellectually nor morally strong. It is a romantic and sentimental Hamlet, pensive but not deeply reflective; sad, with the low-spiritness of the morbid temperament . . . not the settled sorrow of a great soul steeped in thought and agony. He is vacillating [as Coleridge falsely described Hamlet to be]. . . . His gesticulation is feeble; his declamation smooth, easy, balanced as if no profound emotion was in him. He is distinguished from those about him by the finish of his artistic elaboration [the minor members of Booth's cast were notoriously second-rate, but this situation remains as true today in Shakespearean performances featuring stars as it was then], rather than by the grandeur of the traits which he impersonates." Mrs. Bowers, who later acted with him, thought his Hamlet not a particularly superior one, but that he was remarkable "as an embodiment of a noble yet complex soul environed by a body of singular charm and comeliness." On the other hand, Augustin Daly said that Booth was "the greatest tragic actor of his time, and beyond dispute, the noblest figure, as man and actor, our stage has known this century." Otis Skinner remarked that no other actor of those days "so completely filled the eye, the ear and the mind with an ideal of romantic tragedy," and that he was never extravagant in his work. E. H. Sothern regarded his light as "so steady and pure" and his acting "so free from exaggeration that he baffled imitation."

In March of 1866, the Winter Garden burned to the ground. Booth at once started the construction of a playhouse to cost a million dollars on Sixth Avenue and Twenty-third Street. The horseshoe-shaped auditorium seated nearly two thousand people. While it was being built, Booth made the catastrophic mistake of becoming engaged to marry Mary McVicker, daughter of a Chicagoan who was a power in matters theatrical in the Windy City. Uppermost in his mind was to supply a mother for Edwina.

The first play given at the new theater was *Romeo and Juliet,* on February 3, 1869, with Mary McVicker as Juliet. The next day the *Herald* ridiculed him: "Mr. Booth knows as well as we do that he can't play Romeo . . . It is almost funny to see his struggles . . . Miss Mary McVicker, for whom Mr. Booth thus gallantly sacrificed himself . . . is in no way worthy of the sacrifice. She is . . . a strong, practical Western woman, with . . . a good deal of raw vigor and rude force." This critic was more observant of the McVicker nature than Booth, who made the tragic error of marrying her on June 7 of that year.

On July 4, 1870, his new wife bore him a son, Edgar, whose life was over in a few hours. That death, no doubt, was the beginning of Mary's burning hatred of Edwina and Edward. By 1880 she was hopelessly insane, and though her step-father had liked Edwin and had helped him with his new theater, the McVickers chose to believe every mad invention of Mary's distorted mind.

At his theater Booth continued his well-attended repertory, playing many roles—for instance, different nights, Brutus, Cassius, and Antony in *Julius Caesar.* It could have been presumed that the theater was prospering, but Booth was hopelessly impractical in business matters; in 1873 he gave up the management, and in 1874 declared bankruptcy. The theater itself continued to star many an important actor and actress: McCullough, Clara Morris, E. L. Davenport, Lawrence Barrett, Dion Boucicault, Charlotte Cushman, and Modjeska. It finally closed its doors in April 1883.

Booth was forty when bankrupt, though he wrote a friend that this was far from the heaviest blow he had sustained in life. His enemies leaped at the chance to attack him. Said the *Philadelphia Press:* "Booth's Theater has been the tomb of his fortunes and his renown. Mr. Booth did, it is true, shine in it to advantage, but it was as a brass tack does on an old-fashioned hair trunk. His company was one of the worst ever gathered together in this country."

He spent the summer of 1874 with Mary and Edwina at Cos Cob; but his wife's odd behavior made it a far from peaceful time. The chief victim of her attacks was Edwina.

In 1875 Mary's father paid Booth's debts, but Edwin was now under the terrible burden of repaying him. Booth did his best to humor his wife in her fancied wrongs—to no avail. She appointed 10 P.M. as Edwina's bedtime, and sent her husband to his room a half-hour later.

When he appeared at Augustin Daly's Theater in 1875, his arm, broken that August, in a sling, it was a full and enthusiastic house that greeted him. In the cast of his *Hamlet* were two new players, Maurice Barrymore (Laertes) and John Drew (Rosencrantz). Barrymore soon after married Drew's sister, and they had three children, all to become famous—Lionel, Ethel, and John. Booth now gave *Richard II* for the first time, delighting audiences by making that weak king, this time with good reason, a sort of cousin to Booth's Hamlet. His Lear was depicted as touched with madness from the very first scene.

The next January he went on an elaborate tour of the South. His wife, though in no condition to travel, refused to let her husband out of her sight and went along. As the brother of Lincoln's assassin, he provoked a great deal of curiosity. In Mobile he received a plea for free tickets from Sergeant Corbett, who was sure that Edwin would not refuse "when I tell you that I am the United States soldier that shot and killed your brother." Booth sent the free passes. There were crowds everywhere eager to see him.

That tour over, he received an offer from John McCullough to come to the new California Theater in San Francisco. His stay there lasted for eight weeks and broke all existing theatrical records in the United States. David Belasco, who lived there, got a job as a super in Booth's company.

Booth was back in the East again, still refining his art—too much so, in the opinion of some, including the critic of the *New York Sun*. Walt Whitman, a fanatical admirer of Booth's father and the heavy-handed style of Forrest and Salvini, objected that "Edwin had everything but guts: if he had had a little more that was absolutely gross in his composition he would have been altogether first class."

Edwin had at last paid off his debts to the McVickers, was making money, and decided that he ought to try England again. Across the Atlantic Henry Irving had become the great star, as actor-manager of the Lyceum, with Ellen Terry as his leading lady. Booth admired Irving, believing that he succeeded where he had failed, winning a public that was willing to see the first-rate plays which he produced and in which he himself starred. (Truth to tell, some of Irving's greatest hits were in second-rate melodramas, though he gave a great deal of Shakespeare.)

On April 23 (the day of Shakespeare's birth), 1879, Booth was acting the role of Richard II in Chicago. He had reached the final soliloquy and was sitting with a calcium light centered on him. For some reason, he could never later explain, he altered his usual posture and suddenly stood up. That instant the crack of pistol-fire was heard, and he saw a second shot's flash directed at him. He quickly moved to the footlights and pointed up to the balcony where a moving figure was about to shoot again. "Arrest that man!" he cried.

The would-be assassin turned out to be a clerk from St. Louis who told a new story each time he was questioned: Booth had violated his sister's honor; he was Booth's illegitimate son; he had himself a native talent which his "father," Edwin Booth, had thwarted. His last explanation was the maddest of all: his name was Mark Gray and a few nights before Booth mocked at him in *Richelieu*, and during the course of the play Booth had said, "Mark where she stands!" with particular emphasis on "Mark." Gray added, "He said it sneeringly, and I know he meant me." The poor lunatic was confined to an asylum.

From England Asia wrote that her husband was in a fury that Booth not only was unhurt but now had given the public reasons for sympathizing with him. Then he raged against all the Booths "who get all the notoriety without *suffering!!*" Gray meanwhile bragged from his cell that he had been planning to kill Edwin for three years.

His wife's condition was steadily worsening. On some days she would not permit anyone, not even his dresser, to speak to him or approach him. She would follow him to the wings and hold on to his robes until it was his cue to enter upon the stage.

In June of 1880 Booth carried out his plan, long meditated, to return to England, and was accompanied by his wife and Edwina. They did not remain long in London because Walter Gooch, manager of the Princess Theatre, was busy renovating it, and it was here that Booth hoped to make his mark. They went to the continent for a while, and when Booth returned to London his heart sank. The scenery was trashy; the company had only two decent actors, one of whom was killed in a train wreck and the other prevented from participating because of complications in his contract—in both cases before the opening. Moreover, the theater had had too long a history of presenting wretched plays to banish in a night.

At his wife's insistence he began with *Hamlet* on November 6, 1880 (his friend, the critic William Winter, had wisely urged *Richelieu*), and the audience was filled with well-wishing Americans, who kept insisting upon Booth's superiority to Irving. Booth's disillusionment, his negative feeling about the theater, were bound to project themselves into his role. It was as if he walked through the part. The newspapers pronounced him "Artificial," "Uninspired," "Cold and classical," "A disappointment." Not all the reviews were bad, but none of them was inspiriting. Even though his performances improved each night, the impression evoked by the opening could not be eradicated. Clement Scott ridiculed Booth's "poor and unattractive dress, his tangled black hair hanging in feminine disorder," though he admitted it was "impossible to keep the attention off that remarkable face, that strange power of expression, those eyes that rolled and changed." Passages which in the United States had evoked thunderous applause, left London audiences unimpressed. Soon the house was nearly empty.

E. H. House wrote the truth when he said: "An actor's position among his fellows is apt to be measured by the amount of money he can earn in a season; and no matter to what eminence a 'star' has been exalted, the habit of applying the same criterion to his own reputation will always cling to him. No one who was acquainted with Booth will suppose that questions of profit or loss entered largely into his calculations while in London; yet with the remembrance that for a single performance in America he was accustomed to receive from $500 to $1,000, it was natural and inevitable that he should feel chagrined to know that he was playing night after night to bare expenses."

He tried *Richelieu* and receipts were better, but only for a few days. Queen Victoria and the Prince of Wales ignored him, and he declared them "too stuck up." On November 23 he wrote to House: "If I can continue here through the Spring season I feel pretty certain that I shall get all I came for —an unequivocal English endorsement." But by December 22 he was less sanguine: "My work is harder than I have been used to, and I do not receive the support I need from the company. If I get no other benefit here, I shall learn to appreciate the good will that has always stood by me in the American theatres. . . . Though the newspapers are not cordial, the public is. Financial success, as we reckon it, is a thing unknown in this country."

Socially the Booths were welcomed among the most distinguished literary people in London; but his wife's illness was now so bad that he began to dread going out with her. Charles Reade, whose novels Booth greatly admired, had been living in seclusion. House, who was now in England, induced him to see Booth's Lear early in March 1881; the actor wrote his friend: "A very, very sick wife, and the wear and tear of my nightly strain . . . make it impossible, just now, for me to appoint a day [to make Reade's personal acquaintance] . . . I'm sorry that Friday was the night that Mr. Reade saw me, for I was unusually disturbed then." On that night Mary had been seized in his dressing room with such violent convulsions that the physician who was summoned for a while doubted that she could survive the night. Nevertheless, Reade was "deeply impressed" and he felt that Booth had given a superb performance, even after the curtain fell he was still identifying the actor with Lear. "Poor old man," he said to House as Booth was taking his curtain calls, "they have broken his mind, but see how he holds his dignity."

Reade, despite forbidding weather, went back to see *The Merchant of Venice*. "I would not have missed *Shylock* on any account," he declared; "the scene with Tubal is the biggest thing I have seen on the London stage in this many a year." He added: "The London press is an ass!" Though delighted at Reade's reactions, Booth admitted that he would not have chosen *The Merchant of Venice* at the end of his engagement, and made another "selection but for the miserable poverty of Gooch's resources."

When his season ended in March, Booth had a free month, and at last visited Reade, who spoke with warmth and enthusiasm of Booth's father. "They called Kean impetuous," he said, "but Booth was more so. He never waited for effects, not he, but sprang upon them the moment they were in his reach. Very few things escaped him. If his body was not moving, his eye was always busy. It went to its aim like a dart. . . . He did not trifle with Shakespeare's lines. Blank verse came from his lips like music. You have the art too . . . I wish you could restore it on our stage. Give our actors a metrical speech to deliver, and —endure it if you can. They either gabble away the sense or hammer the melody out of it." Reade also defended Forrest against Macready, who, he felt, was equally guilty in the case of the Astor Place riot: "If the Englishman who bragged of his cultivation had kept his arrogance and vanity in hand, in the first place, the catastrophe would not have occurred."

Booth had had enough of the Princess Theatre's limitations, and asked Henry Irving whether he might not give some matinée performances at the Lyceum. Instead, Irving proposed that they should star together in one of the Lyceum's elaborate productions of *Othello*, with the suggestion that they take turns in doing Othello and Iago. Reade suspected Irving's motives.

While the rehearsals for *Othello* were in progress, Edwin received a letter from Irving's wife, from whom he had been separated for ten years and who had borne him two sons: "Dear Mr. Booth, can you spare me a box? I should like to have my sons see what good acting is."

Irving was doing Iago to begin with, Ellen Terry was Desdemona, and Booth Othello. Irving was masterful as a director, particularly in scenes calling for crowds; he was also remorseless in making everyone, including Ellen Terry, go over and over again any lines or business which did not satisfy him. With Booth, however, he was uniformly considerate and would ask him his preferences. Booth would reply that he left the matter to Irving. Once in a while he would show the way "I usually do it"—to the dissatisfaction of the whole company because of his casual manner. He was too much accustomed to be the "star" in an uncoordinated company.

The Lyceum, unlike Booth's Theater, was not vast, but intimate. Irving's costumes were splendid—too much so, thought devotees of Booth. In the second scene, when Iago and Othello both appear, both actors were wildly applauded. After a week both stars exchanged roles; the consensus of the critics was that both were first-rate Iagos and second-rate Othellos. Irving's frame was too lean for the Moor; Booth was too short. Both men made very good villains, and Iago was one of Booth's best roles. Irving, as usual, as *Macmillan's Magazine* said, was "never content to do as others have done, to find the same meaning in words that others have found, to read human nature as others have read it." As Iago he picked his teeth with a dagger, then wiped it on his sleeve; as he overheard Cassio's speech with Desdemona, he ate a cluster of grapes and spat out the seeds one at a time. All these tricks, the magazine thought, were "much less really natural to the character than Mr. Booth's still, respectful attitude, leaning against the sun-dial . . . ever watching his prey."

Irving's rapid rise to stardom during the previous years had made him many enemies; whatever his project he could always count on savage opposition. Such proved the case when he and Booth costarred. There was also that slow-to-die snobbery of the lower classes to everything American. Yet fairness to Irving obliges one to acknowledge that his conduct toward Booth was impeccable, even though, as House phrased it, "the small army of detractors" insisted that Irving "was bent upon turning the personal misfortunes of the stranger to his own professional account, and exalting himself to the detriment of a foreign rival." The manifest injustice of the accusation needs no more proof than the simple fact that when Irving invited Booth to act with him he was taking a very real risk at a time when the Lyceum was at the very pinnacle of its financial success. Moreover, in order to give his guest a fair share of the proceeds, Irving doubled the prices for tickets in every part of the house except the pit and gallery. (It may be remembered how Covent Garden had been wrecked at the beginning of the nineteenth century when it raised the price of seats.) Irving met with a storm of protests at the rise, but he did not give in.

House put it very well: "Irving risked more . . . than he himself took into full reckoning . . . As to his hope of gain, what was it?" At best, public approval for lending "a consoling hand to a distinguished brother actor, and helping him to recover some of the equanimity he had lost." He may have thought—without discredit to himself—that his cordiality to Booth would make an American tour for himself welcome to Americans. Irving was determined to maintain the supremacy of his theater, and it is to be doubted that any other motive took precedence over that one.

In any case, Booth's reception at the Lyceum was a great victory for him after his previous experiences in London. "It carried everything before it," says House, who was there; "noisier welcomes I have heard, but never one more eloquent." The Lyceum audiences were entirely with him and for him, as often as he appeared.

Throughout his brief engagement at the Lyceum "the tide of his triumph rose steadily, until at the close," says House, he could honestly enjoy what he had come for, "an unequivocal endorsement."

During this triumph his wife grew madder as she approached death; insisting that Edwina was the cause of all her trouble—that Edwina, as she told Asia, pinched her while she was asleep and often "woke her roughly," frightened her, and *"dared* her" to tell Edwin of it. "I mention this," Asia added "to show you how she may talk to a stranger—who would believe her." The McVickers were in London too, crediting every insane report of Mary. Despite all this tragic unrest, Booth was negotiating with managers in Germany for performances there. The Lyceum season ended on June 10, and on June 18 the whole family sailed to New York though it seemed impossible that Mary could survive the voyage.

Besieged by reporters on his arrival, Booth had only the highest praise for Irving both as an actor and a man. Three days after his landing, the nation was shocked by the shooting of President Garfield. Naturally, the newspapers drew analogies with John Wilkes's murder of Lincoln. Booth despaired of ever hearing the end of his brother's deed; it was for the same reason that Asia had gone to live in England. Mary sometimes seemed better, sometimes worse. He could only wish for the death that was inevitable "or for my own."

On October 3 he began an engagement at Booth's Theater. His success in London quickened interest in him again. But the newspapers fed upon the credulity of the McVickers, and some went so far as to accuse Booth of two falsehoods—that he was a drunkard (he had not touched liquor for years) and that he had married Mary for the McVickers's money. Others dwelt on his cruelty as a husband; his wife cringed every time he approached her!

He was in Philadelphia with Edwina on his forty-eighth birthday, November 13, when he received a telegram that Mary had died at five o'clock. At the funeral the Reverend Mr. Robert Collyer intoned praises of Mary in which were implicit Edwin's brutal mistreatment of her.

In June of 1882, with Edwina, he went back to London to play at the Adelphi. He was a much changed man. No longer young-looking, his face was stronger, his features had hardened, even a little coarsened, his hair had thinned on his forehead, and he had begun to look a great deal like his father. He was smoking much too much, and began to suffer spells of vertigo. After six weeks his profits were, as he put it, quite "English"—some $500.

He had arranged to open in January 1883 at the Victoria; but there was a comedy hit running there, and the manager refused to end it. In some despair Booth signed in Berlin with the smaller Residenz. He was to perform in English; the rest of the company, who had never acted Shakespeare, would speak the lines in German. When they were given their parts of *Hamlet, Prinz von Dänemark,* he noted that the First Player in the acting troupe whom he was to hire to play before Claudius was a very old man with a white beard that reached his waist. Booth objected that that character was always played as much younger a man. The German, waving his copy, indignantly replied that Shakespeare had specified an old man; does not Hamlet address him as "old friend?"

Booth was an enormous hit. The audience, though mostly German, was deeply moved by Booth's sensitivity. They were not used to such intensity, but rather to a traditional loud declamatory manner. Ophelia was so absurd that the spectators laughed at her. But that did not take away any laurels from the visiting American. When the performance was over, the stage director ran out upon the stage, kneeled, and kissed Booth's hand. The fellow actors began to weep too. The audience had their handkerchiefs out and were wiping moist eyes. Booth was called for bravos twenty-four times. The other actors kissed him and thanked him profusely. The newspapers next day were rapturous in their praise.

After Berlin came triumphs in other German cities and in Vienna. He was in demand everywhere and back in the United States he did a considerable amount of touring.

He heard from a young man who nurtured ambitions to go on the stage. On July 27, 1884, he answered him from Newport:

I was indeed "startled," and I must confess, pained by your letter announcing your determination to abandon your profession for that of the stage, and in sincere frankness I beg you to reconsider the matter, for I really have no hope for a satisfactory result from such a change. The feelings which prompt you to take this step—I mean your "love, enthusiasm and natural inclination"—do *not* imply an ability for the art. There are hundreds of disappointed lives wasting on the stage where they felt—as you do—that a brilliant destiny awaited them. You may be able to recite in private with perfect ease and propriety, even with excellence, and yet have no other qualification for the highest form of dramatic expression. It is a life of wearisome drudgery; and requires years of toil, and bitter disappointment, to achieve a position worth having. [He continued with the explanation that he had already applied in vain to his manager for acting posts for friends.] You can form no idea of the many who solicit my influence—every season; professionals and amateurs; friends and strangers, of all qualities, male and female. It is very seldom that I can serve them, for managers prefer to judge for themselves, and as my "support," no matter how capable it may be, has been abused by the press for many years past, and will always be 'til the end of my career, my recommendation is not re-garded by managers whose judgments are greatly influenced by what the critics say. I have known many who, like you, gave up home, friends and respected positions for the glitter of the actor's callings and who now are fixed for life in subordinate positions, unworthy their breed-ing, education and natural refinement. I beg you, as your friend and sincere well-wisher, to abandon the mistaken resolve, and enjoy the drama as a spectator, which pleasure, as an actor, you would never know, and retain family, friends and happy home that now are yours. Had nature fitted me for any other calling I should never have chosen the stage; were I able to employ my thoughts and labor in any other field I would gladly turn my back on the theatre forever. An art whose professors and followers should be of the very highest culture, is the mere make-shift of every speculator and bore that can hire a theatre or get hold of some sensational rubbish to cull the public. I am not very much in love with my calling as it now is (and, I fear, will ever be), therefore you see how loth I am to encourage anyone to adopt it. I think you will take my advice as it is meant—in sincere friendship and believe that my only wish is to spare you sorrow that must follow the course you would pursue. With cordial regards for yourself and family, I am truly yours, Edwin Booth.

One could wish that every boy or girl who has "starred" in high school or college theatricals could be forced to study this kind and deeply felt letter.

In September 1886 Booth sent an old friend who lived in Charleston, South Carolina, a check for $1,000, with a note: "The earthquake horror reminds me that I have (or had) many dear friends in Charleston. I can't help all of 'em, but if the enclosed can relieve you and the dear ones, use it—would to God I could offer more. Bad as it is, it might be worse. The Almighty loves us, despite his chastisements. Be true to him. He will not desert you. My life has been a chapter of tragedies, as you know, but I have never despaired—never lost my 'grip' of the 'eternal truth.' The worst is not so long that we can say, this is the worst. Give my love to all old friends of mine, and assure them that though I may never see them again in the flesh, they are vivid in my memory, 'wreathed with roses and red ribbons.' Your old friend, Ned."

Thoughts of his death were not alone in Booth's mind. Lawrence Barrett in 1886 wrote to the editor of the *Louisville Times:* "I don't know what is to happen when Mr. Booth dies. I do not see a single gleam of promise in the skies for the elevation and ennobling of the stage. It is rapidly falling into the hands of common, vulgar people who are as incapable of playing the great parts which the dramatic geniuses of England and America have kept aloft for two hundred years as was the Gravedigger of personating Hamlet." His next words sound as though they were written today. The chief trouble with young American actors, he said, is "their contempt for industry. Most of them come to the stage ill-prepared . . . Genius itself must labor to accomplish great ends, and how much more, then, must mere talent exert itself. . . . In one place a man who was *Harlequin* today essays *Benedict* or *Jacques* tomorrow, and in another the man who was a heavy villain yesterday starts out to star as *Hamlet* or *Iago.* [To bring this up-to-date, substitute for "Harlequin" and "heavy villain" a role in any of the naturalistic or avant-garde plays today.] Crop after crop of these aspirants are withered by the frost of failure, but they seem to have plenty of successors, undeterred by the fate of those who have gone before."

In 1887 Booth suggested to friends a plan upon which he had been meditating for some time: to start in New York a quality club mostly for actors, where they could meet and enjoy the company of men distinguished in other fields—as he put it, "a beacon to incite emulation in the 'poor player' to lift up *himself* to a higher grade than the Bohemian level." On January 7 of the next year The Players, as the club was named, was incorporated by Booth and thirteen others including, besides fellow actors, Mark Twain and General Sherman.

He bought a house for The Players at 16 Gramercy Park—where it still thrives, now under the presidency of the untiring Alfred Drake—and kept the top floor for himself as his home. The great architect, Stanford White, remodeled the beautiful old building. The visitor to the lavatory now will find there Booth's motto for it: "Nature her custom holds, let shame say what it will." The house was opened on New Year's Eve, 1888, and the deed to the property handed over to the vice-president, Daly.

Booth's tours continued. In Rochester in early April 1889, he suffered a slight stroke. By the middle of the month he was in San Francisco. In September in Louisville he celebrated his fortieth year on the stage.

The distinguished actress, Modjeska, joined him and they came to New York to open at the Broadway Theater. Suddenly the *Herald* published what he called "a load of filth out of the clear sky." The vicious article said that Modjeska was asking for a release from her contract, and that her reason was the "ungentlemanly and unchivalrous" advances Booth had been making to her, a married woman. The article was rendered the spicier by such sub-headings as: MR. BOOTH DENIES IT. TOO OLD FOR LOVE MAKING. The writer had asked Booth if there were any truth in the rumors; he responded, " 'My dear fellow, Madame Modjeska and I are old enough to have grandchildren. My love-making days off the stage are over.' " Booth had agreed to see the reporter only to shield the actress' name. The truth was simply that she was too old now to play either Ophelia or any other role requiring a young woman. The two met only on stage, and never off it.

In January 1890, The Players asked Booth to sit for a portrait by Sargent. The great painter portrayed his subject just as he had seen him at The Players, and the painting was hung over the mantel.

His last performance was as Hamlet in a matinée at the Brooklyn Academy, on April 4, 1891. Booth himself had not planned it as his farewell. He simply expected to rest for a year. But he got into the habit of confining himself to his rooms on the third floor of The Players, looking over Gramercy Park's verdure. In his rooms were portraits of John Wilkes, his first wife, and his father.

He died in the early morning of June 7, 1893, and the funeral was held at the Little Church Around the Corner. He was buried in Mount Auburn Cemetery in Cambridge, where lay his first wife and his second wife's infant son.

It is not strange that a life so filled with disaster should have led him to an unusual view of death. He wrote to William Winter: "I cannot grieve at death. [One of Winter's sons had just died.] It seems to me the greatest boon the Almighty has granted us." He felt that men who died young were lucky to "go early from this hell of misery to which we have been doomed." He was not fond of companionship, and outside of his family, his first wife, and Edwina, other close relationships seemed superfluous. "I love those best who let me alone," he said; and a friend explained, "He had stage-fright everywhere but on the stage." He had no interest in music or the fine arts, cared nothing for sports, and he never got over his shame of his inadequate education.

He ended the long vogue for Cibber's *Richard III* by restoring the original version with cuts (1876). He was remarkable for his projection of "hypocritical goodness," which was diabolically effective when contrasted with Richard's open malignity. Winter says Booth "was the only actor I ever saw who made absolutely credible the winning of Lady Anne." (One would say that that was an almost impossible feat.) That critic thought Forrest, in comparison, "ludicrous." Booth was in full control of his performances, after he had given up drinking. Once, Winter entered the theater after the play had started and took a seat in the front row, when Booth saw him he stood "so that one side of his face was not visible to others in the audience," and winked and grimaced at his friend, "then instantly flashed toward the center, exclaiming, 'Stay, you that bear the corse, and set it down.' "

Lacking Forrest and Salvini's excellent outbursts of violent physical power (Booth Senior, Kean, and even Irving were notable at such moments), Booth presented Shylock as an injured, insulted (Shakespeare did not!), and resentful man, and, oddly enough, closed the play with the trial scene, thus leaving it suspended between tragedy and comedy.

Winter thought his performance in the last act of *Othello* perfection itself. When he played Iago (by general consent a far superior performance) he played the villain as "frank and not only plausible, but winning. The gay, light-hearted, good-humored soldier whom he thus presented would have deceived anybody." (This clearly *is* what Shakespeare intended.)

Booth was never quite successful in comedy—his nature was too reserved and melancholy, and socially he was a silent man. When John Wilkes killed Lincoln, Edwin said: "All my life I have thought of dreadful things that might happen to me, and I believe there was no horror that I had not imagined, but I never dreamed of such a dreadful thing as *that!*" Believing with Edwin (quite unreasonably!) that Hamlet was insane, Winter thought that no other actor had "more completely entered into and expressed the soul of Hamlet." His version of the play excluded all "offensive words and passages." Winter reports that Booth would transpose a few lines as well as "a few words" in that play, which "were changed, but without alteration of the sense,"—as though that were possible! His Gertrude usually wore Claudius's portrait in miniature, as he himself wore that of his father. Sometimes he had both portraits on the wall, sometimes he left them to the imagination—which I believe the best method. In most modern productions of the play, there is positively an epidemic of miniature-wearing (always, with Hamlet's exception, of the king). To indicate that the skull was Yorick's, Booth usually had a fragment of the jester's cap still clinging to it.

In his hands, Macbeth metamorphosed from year to year until "majesty and martial heroism" became the chief outlines of the character—a considerable feat when one remembers the slightness of his form. No one, Winter says, ever spoke the lines of anguish better than he ("Had I died an hour before this chance" etc. and "She should have died hereafter.") When defeated at the end, without a sword, he still fought wildly, "stabbing the air with his hand."

Though his Othello was limited by his unheroic frame, it was poetic—as it should be, for Shakespeare gave the Moor some of the most exquisite lines he ever wrote. He touched audiences most by his sweetness and tenderness, and was tireless in his study to identify himself (Hamlet always excepted) with the characters he portrayed—quite unlike the Method actors of our time. Ellen Terry, who was his most famous Desdemona, said that it was impossible to convey the idea that she was blind to her husband's suspicions "if her lord is raging and stamping under her nose!" Booth kept his wrath until the scene where Othello "overwhelms her with the foul word and destroys her fool's paradise." He underplayed the violence and omitted the slapping of her before Lodovico.

But he was the best Victorian Iago, dispensing with superfluous business and making him totally unvillainlike (quite unlike José Ferrer's Iago when performed with Paul Robeson). His secret was to make Iago *think* the villain, but never speak it.

In his old age he played Iago to Salvini's Othello. Because he was lonely he had once more taken to drink. On one occasion he stumbled on the stage, broke the guardrail and almost fell over the footlights. Salvini was splendid in defending him and praised Booth's Iago as "absolutely admirable."

Since it was as Hamlet that Booth is still best remembered, a few insights as to how he produced it would not be amiss. As the houselights dimmed (we are speaking of 1871, when he was the height of his fame here), the orchestra was playing Gluck's beautiful overture to *Iphigenia*. For the second scene the change of setting was made before the eyes of the audience: a chamber wall rose out of a long slit across the stage with an easy gliding motion; this flat was met by side wings, enclosing it at right angles, through the use of hydraulic machinery. The miniature Hamlet wore about his neck was actually the portrait of Booth's own father. When Hamlet answered Claudius with: "I am *too much* i' the *sun*," Booth raised his left hand with the palm toward the king as if shutting out the king's light. (There are, of course, several other meanings in that line.) When the Ghost in the fifth scene began to disappear, Hamlet was on his knees with both hands stretched out as if begging it to stay. (The dramatic suitability of this gesture is dubious.) And when the Ghost was at last gone, Hamlet fell flat on his back, his head toward the spectators, and tossed and writhed a moment; he began his next speech lying upon his side, his hands covering his face. One imagines that Booth's falling flat on his back inspired Olivier to do the same thing in his dreadful movie—except that Olivier fell back so often in that scene that one wondered how he avoided cracking his skull on those stone pavings of the battlements. On the entry of Horatio and Marcellus, at "There's ne'er a villain dwelling in all Denmark . . ." Booth was (quite correctly) about to add "greater than the king," but the reason Booth gave for refraining was certainly a silly one—that Hamlet suddenly remembered that such a phrase would be treason—as though that would have bothered Hamlet! The reason he refrained, of course, is that he suddenly realized that to impart what the Ghost had told him would, perhaps, be rashly ruining his case before he had had a minute to think over the Ghost's terrible revelations. In the "get thee to a nunnery" scene, Hamlet saw the king and Polonius eavesdropping very early in the scene, in order, said Booth, to allow him to "act out" the rest of the scene for their benefit. If he did that too early in the scene—i.e., before "Where's your father?"—it would have robbed all that preceded of sense and deprived the play of the dramatic impact of Hamlet's sudden change of tone toward Ophelia.

When Irving brought over six of his best Lyceum productions to New York, Booth was embittered at being unable to return Irving's hospitality as he no longer had a theater of his own. He also felt it wrong to act in the same cities when Irving went on tour, for that would have appeared as though he were competing with the man who had treated him so well. So Booth went to Boston when Irving played in New York, and when Irving moved to Boston, Booth quickly left for New York. The situation made him feel like a lost beggar, and his acting suffered in consequence. He wrote to a friend: "I am not very much in love with my calling as it now is." During his last year of acting his performances became more and more perfunctory.

17

Princesses of Denmark
and Other Vagaries

Perhaps the strangest chapter in the history of Shakespearean acting is the inexplicable obsession which has driven some women to assume men's roles, an obsession not to be construed as a kind of avant-garde for the women's liberation movement of our times, for it has had nothing to do with women's rights. It may be that because female roles had in Shakespeare's day been enacted by males this inversion was conceived, but I am of the opinion that the common notion that Hamlet, the hero of the most popular of the plays, is a kind of milk-sop too sensitive to act—although the tragedy throughout shows the prince in action on land and sea—encouraged the dears to think of him, quite incorrectly, as a sister under the skin. Certainly those women who did Hamlet never abandoned their womanliness—with the exception, as we shall see, of Charlotte Cushman.

After all, the males who took on female parts in Shakespeare's theater were mere boys whose voices had probably not yet changed; in any case, no adolescent is so firmly masculine that, with talent and aided by woman's garb, he could not pass as a woman. There was little doubt that this was what Richard Strauss had in mind when he created the lovely and romantic music for Octavian in the *Rosenkavalier*. A man in his thirties, unless nature had made the sort of error she sometimes makes, would be far too old to act the parts Shakespeare wrote for women with any show of femininity without causing acute distaste. (The witches in *Macbeth* are perhaps an exception, though there are enough women in the world who seem cast for those roles without preparation.) We were given positive experience of that disgust when a touring English company starring Ronald Pickup presented a revolting version of *As You Like It* in the late 1960s; the Rosalind moved with the grace of a robot which was about to fall apart, and the Celia seemed a twin of Hermione Gingold at her most extravagant.

To date there are more than half a hundred female Hamlets on record. If Hamlet was thought of as a wilting, indecisive figure—and men have only too often so interpreted him—that was no doubt an invitation to these ladies to make him even more effeminate, and thus portray him in a way even more remote from Shakespeare's conception of him as a rash and violent man.*

The roll call of women Hamlets includes, besides many others, Sarah Siddons, Kitty Clive, Mrs. Inchbald, Mrs. Bartley, Mrs. Battersby, Eliza Marian Treway (best known as a comic), Mrs. Powell, Ellen Bateman, Fanny Wallack, Charlotte Cushman, Charlotte Crampton, Charlotte Barnes (of frail and languishing physique in a Van Dyck garb), Clara Fisher, Alice Marriott, Julia Glover, Emma Waller, Susan Denin, Mrs. Conway, Julia Seaman, Marie Seebach, Winetta Montague, Mrs. Minot, Adela Belgarde, Louise Pomeroy, Anne Dickinson, Nellie Holbrook, Sarah Bernhardt, Mrs. Bandmann-Palmer, Clara Howard, Esmé Beringer, Eva Le Gallienne, and Judith Anderson.

Nor is that the whole story. There have been female Romeos, Falstaffs, Iagos, Hotspurs, and Shylocks too. There is, however, no account of any woman attempting Macbeth, Brutus, or Coriolanus.

Most of the ladies in question have made an impression by their talents in enacting female Shakespearean roles, a fact which makes the obsession only the odder. I propose to deal with only a few of these actresses.

Sarah Siddons seems to have been the first woman to perform Hamlet; she appeared as the prince at Worcester in 1775 when she was twenty, and again in 1777; she was still doing it in Dublin in 1802. Self-conscious about her figure, she wore a shawllike garment. Strangely enough, no one seemed surprised, for she kept the play in her repertoire, though she never acted it in London. What tempted her to do it at all? Was it, conceivably, her desire to capitalize on that interminable nose of which Gainsborough complained?

Kitty Clive, who played opposite Garrick with notable popularity as a heroine, once essayed Shylock with a Jewish accent. Mrs. Inchbald, friend of Mrs. Siddons and a bad stammerer, was Hamlet in 1780 at the Theatre Royal.

Charlotte Crampton, a squat brunette, and one of the finest fencers of her day, did not only Hamlet but Romeo, Iago, Richard III, Shylock, and Hotspur as well. Macready said that if she "were only a foot taller, she would startle the world." When she was about fifty she visited Omaha in 1867/68. Her husband was then younger than her thirty-year-old dissipated son. Milton Nobles said that she was "indescribable. In each male character she looked a guy, but we soon forgot her looks. Her intensity and vitality were wonderful. In the big scenes the largest man in the company grew small beside her. . . . As Shylock she wore an old (borrowed) gray dressing gown." She tied a rope about her waist and looked "like a bag of old clothes." For a beard she used blackening, and her face was a "comedy mask."

Mrs. Macready, lessee of the Prince of Wales's Theatre, Birmingham, in 1866, also appeared as Shylock.

Alice Marriott, broad of hip and heavy of breast, played Hamlet for the

*See the author's *The Heart of Hamlet.*

first time at Marylebone Theatre in 1861. In 1863 she took over the management of Sadler's Wells and the next year did Hamlet again. In 1869 she
made her New York debut in that role. Winter said she was "gloomily
comic."

In London Mrs. Powell seems to have been the earliest woman to perform
Hamlet; that took place at Drury Lane in 1802. First known as Mrs. Farmer,
then as Mrs. Renaud, she had been seen at both the Haymarket and Drury
Lane in 1787 in female roles. She supported Mrs. Siddons in the company
and became Mrs. Powell when playing opposite Kemble as Lady Anne in
Richard III. For a number of seasons she remained at Drury Lane, and was
considered very good in the roles she took. It was she who substituted for
Mrs. Siddons when she declined the role, in William Henry Ireland's forged
Shakespearean play, *Vortigern.* When she did Hamlet at the age of forty-two,
Mrs. Jordan was her Ophelia.

Not astonishingly, the record indicates that only two women have appeared as Falstaff. In July 1786, at the Haymarket, in *Henry IV, Part I*, Mrs.
Webb's Falstaff was "a huge hill of flesh, surmounted by a front of a fiery
fretful expression." Her voice was "as deep as a well." She was thought to
have exhibited execrable taste.

Julia Glover also needed no padding to play the fat knight in *The Merry
Wives of Windsor* at the Haymarket, for she was not only one of the cleverest
but also the fattest woman then on the stage. She played Hamlet in 1822
at the Lyceum. After the first act Kean came behind the scenes and congratulated her: "Excellent! Excellent!" as he grasped her hands. Her response was: "Away, you flatterer! You come in mocking to scorn at our
solemnity." As a child she played the Duke of York to Frederick Cooke's
Richard III. Later she did Lady Macbeth and Desdemona, but by then, we
are told, she was "monstrously fat" and only of "middle height." She came
to Covent Garden in 1797, much to the displeasure of Mrs. Abington and
Mrs. Pope. Against her will she had to enact the queen in *Richard III.* During
a considerable portion of her career her father, a Betterton (perhaps a
distant relative of the famous actor), had been appropriating all her salary
and treating her with exceptional brutality. Eventually he sold her to Samuel
Glover, who was expected to inherit a large fortune, for £1,000, which was
never paid. She was married to Glover in 1800. In 1810 she appeared at the
Lyceum with the company from Drury Lane, which had been driven from
their playhouse by fire. When it was newly rebuilt in 1812/13, she returned
with them, performing opposite Kean in *Richard III* and *Othello.* She was
especially good in comic roles, where her enormous bulk was not disadvantageous. *The Stage* described her as a "violent actress," yet, despite her
rotundity, she was generally praised for possessing a polished style.

In 1881/82 during a world tour Mrs. John Jack performed Hal to her
husband's Falstaff. Julia Marlowe, perhaps encouraged by the fact that she
had first appeared on the stage as a child in the role of Sir Joseph Porter
in a juvenile performance of the Gilbert and Sullivan operetta, later did Hal
as well. In June 1837 at the Walnut Street Theater in Philadelphia, Mrs.

Harry Lewis enacted Richard III and Othello. Rebecca Deering, an American actress, was Richard III at Birmingham in 1883, and proceeded to repeat the role at least two hundred times; she had a flexible voice and could, a critic said, "lower it to sweetness or lift it to an impulsive shout."

By 1901 at least twenty-one women had appeared as Romeo. In July 1810 Mrs. Freeman played him to her daughter's Juliet. Indeed, it became not uncommon for a woman Romeo to appear opposite some female member of her family. The most famous of these, Charlotte Cushman, was at her best when her sister Susan was her Juliet. In July 1853 Emma and Ellen Feist followed the same pattern at Richmond, Surrey; four years later Melinda Jones at Albany, New York, had her daughter Avonia as the Capulet heir. When Esmé Beringer appeared in her "picturesque" Romeo at the Prince of Wales Theatre in May 1896, she too played opposite her sister. (In 1938 she also performed Hamlet at the Arts Theatre.) Ellen Tree played Romeo at Covent Garden in 1829; Mrs. J. M. Wallack did the role for a week at the Marylebone in 1854, and Felicita Vestvali created a sensation at the Lyceum by appearing as Romeo in doublet and hose.

Mrs. John Drew enacted the role in 1846 and on one occasion attempted Marc Antony in *Julius Caesar;* she is said to have been unique in her ability to make her audience forget her sex. On the other hand, Anna Dickinson, in March 1882, dressed in purple as Hamlet, according to Winter, was obviously female, though a little "resembling a boy."

In the mid-nineteenth century, Mrs. Nunn was a popular actress in the West York circuit, and was seen as Romeo, Hamlet, and Othello. Mrs. Charles Whitley also did the Moor at the Avenue Theatre, London, in February 1897. But there have been more female Iagos than Othellos. (Let us hope that there is nothing in the female character which made that role seem the more congenial.) The list of female Iagos includes Mrs. Waller, at Albany, New York, in 1857; at around the same time Charlotte Crampton; Rebecca Deering in England, 1883, and thereafter frequently in the provinces; in Scotland Emilie Burke, playing opposite her uncle, Henry Talbot. Miss Burke was also one of two female Petruchios on record, the second being Dorothea Baird in 1893 in a cast made up entirely of women! Another all-female cast appeared at Copley Hall in *A Winter's Tale,* of which W. J. Lawrence said: "An Adamless Eden! how dull it must have been for the dear creatures!"

Beginning with 1895 Mrs. Bandmann-Palmer gave over a thousand performances as Hamlet. In 1899 Clara Howard played the prince at the Imperial and at the Pavilion, the play itself being reduced to melodrama, quite literally, with a continual background of music.

Of all the ladies who chose to impersonate Shakespeare's heroes the most interesting is Charlotte Cushman (1816–1876), who has generally been named as the first great American-born actress. A descendant of the Pilgrim fathers, she made her debut at her native Boston at the age of nineteen as a singer in *The Marriage of Figaro,* and was well thought of. In New Orleans the vastness of the theater impelled her to overstrain her voice, and she succeeded in ruining it.

Low in funds and with the responsibility of supporting her mother, brothers and sister, and totally without any training, she turned to acting. Thus began a career which was to last forty years; she acquired great wealth and the unique position of being America's earliest native actress. Still nineteen, she made her debut in the city where she had lost her voice, as Lady Macbeth. She came north and played stock for eight years, and learned what she could from actual experience on the stage. The actors whose technique she was studying were performing in the stately Kemble tradition.

When she was about twenty-seven, Macready, whom she had seen and admired, sent word to her that he wished her to play Lady Macbeth opposite him in Philadelphia, thus liberating her from the drudgery she had endured in stock. She was to act with him in 1842, 1843, and 1849. Knowing full well that he despised both his own profession and Americans in general, Charlotte was nervous at their first encounter. He admitted to her that he was not especially effective in gesture; "facial expression is what I principally depend upon," he told her. He was accustomed to practice with his hands tied behind him, before a mirror, his aim being to keep "the muscles of the face undisturbed, whilst intense passion would speak from the eye alone." Charlotte realized that such devices were not for her.

When she first appeared with him the audience quickly noted the extraordinary similarity of their features, the same depressed nose, the prominent chin, and broad brow. They might have been brother and sister, they looked so much alike—or as Forrest might have said, brother and brother. She was tall, with square shoulders and a sturdy frame; her blue-gray eyes were her best feature; otherwise her face was unattractive. She never in her life managed to act with grace of movement, but she projected strength and dignity with her commanding presence. She was amazed at Macready's polish and realized the crudity and lack of discipline in her performances before she had worked with him. It was from him that she learned to study texts with care, analyze characters, and look for nuances. She never ceased to feel grateful to him for, she said, she had been groping in darkness until she acted with him. She went with him to the Park Theater in New York, where she supported him in several important roles. And that required what was then a fatiguing train ride between New York and Philadelphia every other day.

Lady Macbeth became one of her best-liked roles for many years and she herself loved the part. But she played that much-misunderstood woman as basically masculine, an interpretation which is, of course, thoroughly wrong. (In our own time Judith Anderson did full justice to Lady Macbeth and made her, as Shakespeare created her, entirely feminine.) Until Duncan was murdered, Charlotte was a hard and powerful wife. When she played the role later with Booth, as he felt her powerful hands upon his shoulders, and heard her baritone, "He that's coming must be provided for," he felt like retorting, "Well, why don't you kill him yourself? You're a great deal bigger than I am!" After Duncan's murder she became the horror-filled sleep-walker. Regal and "darkly tragic," she was fierce and implacable. Privately she held an odd theory: that Macbeth and his lady throughout the play were more or less drunk! She also thought that the tragedy should evoke "a barbaric atmosphere." However, it was conceded by the critics that her Lady Macbeth, for all its ferocity, was highly poetic.

She later expressed the regret that so many Macbeths were "little men." She was referring, doubtless to Edwin Booth and Lawrence Barrett, with both of whom she was to perform the part, though in an earlier era she might with as much reason have complained of Garrick and Kean.

Indeed, she was not in the least impressed with Booth. When Mary Devlin was hesitating between accepting the hand of Booth or that of a lawyer, Charlotte advised her to accept the lawyer. When she played Lady Macbeth to Booth's Macbeth she found his style effete, and informed him that as regards his celebrated Hamlet, he did not understand the first thing about the Prince of Denmark. (She probably was right, but she might have said as much to most of the actors who have performed the role.) And she called his Macbeth "a mere willow." Once she shouted at him, "Dear boy, don't be afraid of overdoing it. Remember that Macbeth was the great-grandfather of all the Bowery ruffians." She played his wife as though Lady Macbeth were the boss of the castle. One spectator said that she bullied her spouse, cornered him, and "pitched into him" with a manlike fist.

While admiring Macready's remarkable shadings, she became more and more aware of his shortcomings; the contempt with which he treated his fellows, his mannerisms—such as his keeping his mouth wide open as he listened to the witches so that she felt like throwing "something into it"— his pauses to suggest thinking which broke up lines and communicated the effect of stuttering, and his hacking the poetry into prose. But she found more to learn than to criticize in him, and considered herself vastly in his debt.

In Boston, in addition to Macbeth's lady she played Gertrude, Goneril, and Emilia. She was particularly praised for Emilia, who, with Charlotte's "grandeur of tone," was proclaimed a new revelation, a performance which came near to diminishing Macready's Othello.

Contemptuous of Americans, Macready urged her to go to London and perfect her art by playing with an English company. (The truth is that this advice might be given with profit today to a great many American actors who aspire to Shakespeare.) She borrowed the money to go and remained in England for five years, enacting Rosalind, Queen Katharine, and Romeo. Her first appearance in England was in Milman's *Fazio;* the London *Herald* praised her and said, "It may be that her career in this country will be a brilliant one." The *Sun* declared that since Kean there had not been such a debut, and hailed her as a genius.

When next she did Rosalind, she was not only lauded for a perfect characterization, but credited with inspiring the whole company to do its best. She was to do the same role in New York in 1850; *The Spirit of the Times* was to call it a "martial" characterization, the most perfect Rosalind possible. (Martial one can imagine Charlotte as being, but Rosalind?)

In America she had formed a most intimate friendship with a woman painter two years her junior, Rosalie Sully, a submissive girl, whom she habitually called "beloved"; her diary is full of references to their intimacy. In London she cultivated another such friend, Eliza Cook, a poet also two years younger than herself; Eliza wore her hair cut short like a man's, and often struck manly attitudes. Unpleasant rumors began to circulate in Philadelphia.

One critic said of her that she was best in roles in which "the woman, for the time being, assumes all the power of manhood." The truth is that she more and more came to love playing men's roles—especially Romeo, Hamlet, and Wolsey. She had been a tomboy as a child, and had tyrannized her brothers and sister. Considering her career and conduct as a whole, one is tempted to yield to the conclusion that there were at least strong tendencies in her makeup toward lesbianism. It is of some significance that she confessed to Mary Devlin that she sincerely wished "that she had been a man."

During her lifetime she enacted 188 different roles, including Portia, Viola, and Rosalind—all of whom appear as men in major portions of their comedies—Hamlet, and Romeo. Romeo was the most famous of these. She had first attempted him in Albany, New York, in 1837, and now gave it in London (1845), where it ran for eighty nights—in those days of repertory an almost unheard-of run. The acclaim was wide. The critics agreed that in gait, voice, and bearing she was a convincing young man. Her sister Susan (1822–1857) played Juliet. The London *Times* was rapturous and summed up its opinion: "It is enough to say that Miss Cushman is far superior to any Romeo we have ever had." Madame Ponisi later said: "She was the best Romeo I ever saw or ever shall see. She may not have been an ideal Romeo, so far as her looks or her costume were concerned, but she simply *lived* the character. When I played Juliet to her, she hypnotized me as the snake does the bird. I became oblivious of her sex." Westland Marston thought her more virile than any male he had seen as young Montague. Another critic was so much delighted at her being so "ardently masculine" and Susan so "tenderly feminine," that he thought the least Charlotte could do was to marry her sister. Browning, however, thought the performance hideous, and complained about the way this Romeo was forever "whining" in Verona.

In Boston when she did the part at the National Theater, a man in the audience sneezed in a fashion plainly meant to be derisive, right in the middle of a romantic passage. Cushman stopped at once, led her Juliet off, as might a cavalier, returned to the stage, and said in a loud voice, "Some man must put that person out, or I shall be obliged to do it myself!" The man was evicted—luckily for him, not by Charlotte—and the audience gave her three cheers. She proceeded with the scene as though nothing had occurred to interrupt it.

Inevitably there were objections to a woman's "unsexing of the mind and heart," but the dissidents were in a minority. Sheridan Knowles compared her Romeo to Kean's unsurpassable Othello during the Moor's third act; he had never expected to see anything like that again, "and yet I saw as great a thing in Romeo's scene with the Friar . . . My mind and heart are full of this most extraordinary performance."

Upon her return to the United States her success as Romeo was as great, though there were those who were scandalized that a woman in men's clothing should make love to another woman. Walt Whitman was one of her most passionate admirers. He resented it when her Lady Macbeth was compared to that of Mrs. Siddons. "She is *herself,*" he protested, "and that is far, far better . . . [She] is ahead of any player that ever trod the stage,"—better than the Kembles, Kean, Macready, each of whom had, he conceded, "merits," but she "assuredly bears away the palm."

When her sister Susan married in 1849, she found a replacement in Matilda Hays, a very feminine creature. The two soon became so intimate that Elizabeth Barrett Browning called their relationship a "female marriage." With Matilda and a young British actor, C. W. Couldock, she set out for America and arrived in New York in September 1849. It was altogether a triumphal return, though after the Astor Place riot she had feared the worst, because of her known resemblance to and association with Macready. The embittered Forrest did attack her in Philadelphia as "anti-American" for bringing along Couldock, and accused her of aping Macready's mannerisms, but her receipts still far exceeded what Kean's had been—or, for that matter, Forrest's or Macready's. She played twenty-seven nights, the longest run every known in New Orleans and went on to electrify Washington. When she did her Romeo in New York, with Couldock as Mercutio, the papers expressed great pride that an American had surpassed her English male rivals. She toured many American cities and, having amassed a fortune, planned to retire early from the stage.

Like the pianist De Pachmann in the twentieth century, Charlotte gave many "farewell" performances. The first of these was in 1852, but she was still saying her farewells in 1875. During her last years she devoted herself mostly to Shakespearean readings.

Sarah Bernhardt (1845–1923) explained her rare interpretation of male roles by saying that she preferred "not male parts but male brains," and that "generally speaking, male parts are more intellectual than female parts." It was also her opinion that the female temperament was more at home in the acting profession than the male. Acting is the only art "where women may sometimes prove superior to men." However, "a woman can only interpret a male part when it represents a mind in a feeble body." Nevertheless, and despite her description of Hamlet and L'Aiglon as "unsexed beings," more suitable for women to play than men, when she came to doing Hamlet, she enacted him quite otherwise.

There was no resemblance between her and Charlotte Cushman. Bernhardt had not a touch of the masculine in her makeup. "No one," said James Agate, "ever accused Sarah of masculinity." (He considered her the first of all contemporary actresses.) She had a slim figure, dark eyes, and her voice was likened to a "golden bell," and also to "the silver sound of running water."

In 1872 she played Cordelia in a French translation of *King Lear*. Her first

London appearance (1879) was in her most famous and greatest role, probably the greatest role ever written for the French stage, as Racine's Phèdre; she came the next year to New York, and returned to both cities often.

Her debut as Hamlet was in Paris in 1899 at the Théâtre des Nations, in a French prose translation by Marcel Schwob and Eugène Morand. It was considered a success; some critics even called it superb. Catulle Mendès fought a duel with a journalist friend who disliked her performance. (Actually the quarrel seems to have been over the color of her wig.) Her wig was blond, and she wore black clothes. Maurice Baring was of two minds about her interpretation. He declared that this was the first time that Hamlet had been done correctly, adding that "the rendering, tradition, the language, the authorship went to the winds; you knew only that something which had been invented by one great genius was being interpreted by another great genius."

The same year she took her production over to London. *Punch* affirmed that all it lacked to make it perfect was Irving as Ophelia. The incomparable Max Beerbohm, though he adored her as an actress, could not believe in her as a man and wondered whether she would next play Othello to Monsieur Mounet-Sully's Desdemona.

His critique in the *Saturday Review* was entitled, "Hamlet, Princess of Denmark." He regretted that he could not take the performance seriously. Sarah, of course, never laughed, but Max, not to be disruptive, "kept an iron control" on the corners of his lips. He found the serious devotional air of the audience at the Adelphi ludicrous: no one dared even smile. A smile might have become a laugh, and "one laugh in that dangerous atmosphere and the whole structure of polite solemnity would have toppled down."

First of all, he said, it is impossible to translate Shakespeare either into French or into prose—a declaration with which one must entirely agree. An example was "Rest, rest, perturbed spirit," which came out, *"Paix, paix, âme troublée,"* reminding him of the music hall ditty, "Loo, Loo, I love you!" The French version was "thin, dry, cold—in a word, excruciating."

In England, he continued, *Hamlet* "has long since ceased to be treated as a play. It has become simply" a hoop through which every eminent actor must sooner or later jump. He hoped that Sarah's example would not establish a precedent for actresses. (He was quite young himself, and evidently unaware of her many predecessors who, though women, had attempted the prince.) He thought her no more qualified to play Hamlet than Othello. "Her friends ought to have restrained her . . . The custom-house officials at Charing Cross ought to have confiscated her sable doublet and hose." He concluded with a masterstroke of wit: the "only compliment one can conscientiously pay her is that her Hamlet was, from first to last, *très grande dame.*"

She brought the play to the Garden Theater in New York; her first performance was on Christmas night, 1900. The house was only half-filled. "It was a performance," said Winter, "well calculated to commend itself to persons interested in freaks." Despite all the rough treatment accorded Hamlet,

Winter could not remember a time when the prince was "more effectively crucified." She padded her figure to fill it out, but Sarah still looked like what she was, a thin, elderly woman. Many novelties were introduced: knocking together the heads of Rosencrantz and Guildenstern; kicking Polonius in the shins and catching a fly off his nose; the First Player's handing Hamlet the text of the mousetrap, which he "conveniently carried"—presumably with his whole repertory, in his belt; Hamlet's using Ophelia's hair as a screen while he watched the king during the mousetrap scene; the dying prince standing up, his falling body caught by Horatio, and then borne away upon great shields, "to the general relief" of the audience.

The *New York Dramatic Mirror*, moreover, found Sarah very boyish, very Gallic, very volatile, very nervous, and on the whole very superficial. It objected to the buffoonery introduced as well as Sarah's squeal when Claudius identified himself with the murderer in the mousetrap; on the king's quitting the scene, she seized a torch and continued squealing all the way as she followed him out. At Ophelia's grave, Sarah fell beside it, calling, "Ophelia, Ophelia!" The whole thing came close to farce. Throughout her American tour in 1901 the general reaction was that it was indeed a farce.

Agate, who worshipped her, sought to justify her by saying that the theory of acting of this greatest of all actresses, as he deemed her, was that an actor imposes a single personality on all the roles he plays, whether it be Hamlet, Richard III, Othello, Iago, Shylock, or Lear. To this, I imagine, our own Actors Studio would emphatically, and quite outrageously, agree. George Bernard Shaw was less than an admirer of Sarah and accused her of working up a "head of steam" to produce "explosions with the requisite regularity." He too, but not admiringly, charged her with not entering "into the leading character; she substitutes herself for it."

In 1957 Siobhan McKenna tried an experimental Hamlet, Irish inflection and all, at the Theater de Lys in New York. It was not a notable success.

A more publicized Hamlet, a total failure, was as recent as 1971 when at the age of seventy-three Judith Anderson undertook a considerably cut—it ran under two hours—version of the play, in which her voice was as beautiful as ever. But the undertaking was a strange one for a woman who for a great part of her career on the stage has brilliantly projected feminine voluptuousness (e.g., in *As You Desire Me, Medea, Macbeth*, and many other plays). Indeed, her Lady Macbeth was one of the finest ever presented in its understanding of the essential womanliness of the character. Consciously or unconsciously, as Hamlet she was mimicking Sarah Bernhardt's view when she announced that she did not think of the prince as being a man, but saw him as "asexual." As she acted him, she said, he could be "a daughter torn by anguish for a murdered father and a loved mother who desecrated the father's memory." Despite her age she was quite boyish (wrong, of course, for Hamlet), and was completely dwarfed by all the other members of the cast who towered over her. The performance was largely oratorical and full of ineptitudes. The less than two hours seemed endless to me, and I was forced to quit Carnegie Hall before the disaster was all over. But Dame Judith thoroughly enjoyed playing the role in a tour of college campuses, and was much gratified by a three-page letter sent her by a girl who thanked her and thanked God "you exist, thank God I saw you." That girl, for all her prolixity of thankfulness, never saw Shakespeare's play, as Dame Judith presented it, and I have been tempted to wonder whether or not the college girl had not already been enlisted in that branch of the woman's lib movement which would like to see men unsexed.

Since we have here been speaking of Shakespearean curiosa, this seems a place as fitting as any, without any insult intended to the ladies, of appending two pieces of curious Shakespeareana. The first of them suggests itself, as allied to Miss McKenna's unfailing Irish intonation. It was a handbill announcing, in 1793, a performance of Hamlet by a Mr. Kearns. The bill read:

KILKENNY THEATRE ROYAL

By his Majesty's Company of Comedians.
(The last night because the Company go tomorrow to Waterford)
On Saturday, May 14, 1793
Will be performed by command of several respectable people in this learned metropolis, for the benefit of Mr. Kearns,

THE TRAGEDY OF HAMLET

Originally written and composed by the celebrated Dan. Hayes of Limerick, and inserted in Shakespeare's works.
Hamlet by Mr. Kearns, (being his first appearance in that character) who, between the acts, will perform several solos on the patent bagpipes, which play two tunes at the same time.
Ophelia by Mrs. Prior, who will introduce several favourite airs in character, particularly, "The Lass of Richmond Hill" and "We'll all be unhappy together," from the reverend Mr. Dibdin's oddities.

It would also be a pity not to take some note of the "Dog Hamlet." At Standard, Shoreditch, and the City of London, Tom Matthews, the clown, and W. W. Lacy played this condensed canine version. The dog followed Hamlet around throughout the course of the play, and in the last scene would be let loose on guilty Claudius, pinning him to the floor of the stage while Hamlet killed his father's murderer. This extraordinary piece of nonsense was given in the early nineteenth century, when well-trained dogs were much in demand upon the boards.

❀ 18 ❀

Samuel Phelps and Barry Sullivan

Samuel Phelps (1804–1878) came of an affluent family, but was orphaned at sixteen. The next year he came to London to work on newspapers, but he had already fallen in love with the stage. He became a member of an amateur group which performed frequently at a private theater. At twenty-two, still an amateur, he appeared at the Olympic successfully enough to convince him that he should quit journalism, and he accepted an offer of eighteen shillings a week on the York circuit. In the following years, he covered a great deal of territory in the provinces and was seen at Belfast, Preston, Dundee, Aberdeen, Perth, Inverness, Worthing, Exeter, and Plymouth in a great many roles, including Richard III, Macbeth, Shylock, Othello, and Lear. At Exeter, where he did his first Hamlet, the *Devonshire Chronicle and Exeter News* reported that the audience, as was by then usual with favored actors , often punctuated his passages with applause, "but they were too deeply engaged in catching the tones and manner of the performer to allow them to interfere with the current of his vivid declamation, and a single 'hush' repressed what all were most willing to award." (Actors of reputation were so accustomed to these interruptions that Macready confessed in his diary that he required the stimulation of these outbursts to encourage him to do his best.)

What was new about Phelps's acting was that he was clearly so much identified with the character he was portraying that he could not tolerate these interruptions. The *Western Times* understood this, and when Phelps gave, as had been the rule since the Restoration, Cibber's version of *Richard III*, which was especially conceived to give the actor these "points" where applause might be anticipated, the critic confessed himself "astonished" at Phelps's indifference to these "points"; "the spectators were constantly turning and greeting each other with exclamations of wonder and delight. . . . There was nothing of Kean, nothing of Macready, nothing like the following after old 'points,' nothing like a desire to make new. The chief beauty of the delineation was in its evenness." The Plymouth *Herald* eulogized his Richard the next year (1837) and described it as "illumined by the steady light of a pervading intelligence, and not by the flickerings of occasional intelligence . . . Breaking, as he does, through all the commonplaces of precedent—not with an idle aim at novelty, but with the simple impulse of an original and energetic mind—he throws himself at once upon the chance of finding an unprejudiced recipient in his critic, and being measured solely by the standard of the poet's meaning." (Oh, for the emergence in our own gimmick-ridden times of a Shakespearean actor or director with just those objectives!) Before long Phelps was being hailed as the best tragic actor since Kean.

He did well enough to receive offers from Drury Lane, the Haymarket, and Covent Garden. Macready saw him at Southampton, and Phelps decided to sign with him for the autumn of 1837 at Covent Garden. In the meantime he had his first London appearance at the Haymarket as Shylock in August of that year. It seemed like a challenge to the memory of Kean's debut, and the audience greeted him with wild enthusiasm. Next morning the reviews were favorable, though failed to echo the audience's enthusiasm. Most of them recognized his attempt to end the "point" system but the *Sunday Times* charged him with *missing* every point. Macready, reading of Phelps's success, recorded his conflicting feelings: "If he is greatly successful, I shall reap the profits . . . But an actor's fame and his dependent income is so precarious, that we start at every shadow of an actor." At the Haymarket, Shylock was followed by Hamlet, Othello, and Richard III.

Macready took over the management of Covent Garden in September 1837, and he was greeted with high hopes, for since the fading of Kean's powers, the London theater had been in a bad way. But the literary world which admired him was unaware of his arrogance and jealousy toward fellow actors, and his ungovernable temper. Beyond that was another dangerous fault: his insistence on dominating the new playwrights, whose work he habitually revised in order to strengthen the importance of the roles he was to play. Indeed, since there were only two legal autumn and winter theaters his power over contemporary dramatists was virtually unlimited.

It was with the greatest veneration that Phelps came to Macready's Covent Garden in October. But Macready was already in debt and the audiences were poor. He was, moreover, dissatisfied with the members of his company, and he did not allow time to see Phelps's work immediately. When he did, he offered him £12 a week; small as that salary was, it exceeded that of the other members with the exception of Helen Faucit.

In his first roles at Covent Garden, Phelps was at once a success. Macready was more fearful of competition than pleased at the improved prospects for his company. His Othello earlier in the season had not been well received; the unrestrained applause for Phelps in that role caused Macready to rage with envy. In November he began rehearsals on the most admired of his Shakespearean roles, Macbeth, and relegated Phelps to the part of Macduff. The night the play opened, during the fight with Macduff in the last act, he lost his temper and attacked Phelps with unwonted violence. He said in his diary: "I had drunk much wine, and was very vehement, swearing rather loudly . . . at Mr. Phelps in the fight." The next day he apologized to Phelps, who had taken no offense. Nevertheless, for the entire month he assigned no other role to the innocent object of his resentment than Macduff. This was foolish indeed, for he needed any star material he could get for his supporting players were poor, and the presence of another star would only have added interest. Drury Lane was doing well, but by mid-December Covent Garden's expenses were £2,200 in excess of its intake.

Phelps could hardly have failed to understand that his manager was deliberately withholding opportunities for him to show his abilities, and Macready is even said to have informed him that he had every intention of keeping him out of the contest—as he imagined it to be—just as Kean had suppressed Macready. The manager's conduct became clear enough for the *Sunday Times* to observe, "Mr. Phelps would be a serious loss to Covent Garden." As a matter of fact, Phelps did protest to Macready against his being held back, and was reminded that their contract had specified salary but not the allotment of roles. He asked Macready to release him from his contract; Macready refused to do so unless Phelps agreed to leave London. Nevertheless, the critics took note of Phelps's excellence as Macduff, and to that limited extent Macready's malice did not entirely succeed.

Despite his failures, Macready undertook to manage Covent Garden for another season. Anxious as he was to escape from Macready, Phelps could not apply to Drury Lane, for the manager of that theater had been finding opera so profitable that he intended to devote the 1838 season to it; Macready was going to the Haymarket for the summer interval; moreover, the manager there was still angry with Phelps for having left it for Covent Garden. Phelps was therefore forced to renew his contract at Covent Garden on the same terms.

He found himself worse off than ever. In 1838 he was playing such minor roles as Antonio in *The Tempest,* the First Lord in *As You Like It* and the High Constable of France in *Henry V.* Macready had engaged John Vandenhoff to play the parts Phelps had anticipated but soon confided to his diary that Vandenhoff's Iago was the poorest and most "unmeaning, slouching, ungainly, mindless, unimaginative performance" he had ever seen. The second year of management proved as unsuccessful as the first, and the theater was rarely full.

Only a furious quarrel with the proprietors prevented Macready from leasing Covent Garden for a third year. He was forced to leave without his costumes because they were held for unpaid claims. He had no choice but to accept the offer of Webster, manager of the Haymarket, at the excellent salary of £100 a week, to begin in August. Because of its summer patent, it was the only theater then open in London presenting legitimate drama. The theater was small, and was regularly attracting full houses. Unlike Macready, Webster was perfectly willing to play minor roles and engage the most popular actors for leading parts. Though he had specialized in presenting comedy, he now anticipated a long season extending into the winter with the presentation of tragedy as well. He had no competition to fear.

Ignoring Macready's suggestions, Webster engaged Phelps to come to the Haymarket as Macready's chief supporting actor. Macready must have been distinctly less than delighted at Webster's advertisement:

> First appearance this season of the eminent tragedian
> Mr. MACREADY
> First appearance of
> Mr. PHELPS
> and
> Miss HELEN FAUCIT.

Webster proposed alternating the two men as Othello and Iago. Miss Faucit was to be Desdemona and Mrs. Warner, Emilia. It was a strong cast and opened to full houses. The audience's preference for Phelps and the reviewers' agreement with that judgment displeased Macready, who did his best to upstage his rival during the second performance. Its reception was the same. He now transferred his anger to the Haymarket theater itself, dubbing it "a doghole," in which the audience "is so close upon me, and yet I cannot feel their sympathy." What he was really missing, because Phelps's technique annihilated the artificial effects traditional on the stage, was the audience's failure to respond to the "points" he habitually made.

When their roles were reversed, Phelps's Othello was an even greater triumph than his Iago had been; his tenderness was subtler and more convincing toward Desdemona than Macready's and in retrospect caused Macready's to appear affected. At the end of the play the applause for the new Othello was thunderous. As Iago, Macready was much better than his interpretation of the Moor, and this time he was highly praised. Phelps was called the most "natural" Othello since Kean; "though he wanted dignity, he was always true to nature," said the *Weekly Dispatch,* and added that in the role he was "much superior to Macready." As might have been expected, Macready was fairly enraged at this judgment, which was quite general; the second time Phelps took the part of the Moor, Macready was so furious at the audience's reaction that he could not conceal his feelings on the stage. He himself wrote in his diary: "Acted Iago very unsatisfactorily, and *quite lost my temper—an inexcusable fault."* After the final curtain, he refused to appear for the spectators' approval. Two days later he told the manager that he would not act in the play again.

He insisted on doing Shylock himself, and it was a complete failure; the *Weekly Dispatch's* critic went so far as to say it was the worst piece of acting he had ever seen. However, Macready was able to achieve his chief purpose: Phelps had been cast as Antonio, and was thus removed as competition in the play. In turn, Phelps showed his resentment by walking, as the *Spectator* said, "undertaker-fashion" throughout his performance.

During the summer of 1840 Charles Kean was engaged as a star performer at the Haymarket. He had always played leading roles because of his name, though he was not the brilliant actor his father had been. He was now scheduled to do Macbeth, Richard III, Shylock, and Hamlet. Macready left at once for the provinces. Phelps, who had played three of these roles to the audiences' admiration, now was reduced to the Ghost in *Hamlet*, Henry VI in *Richard III*, and once more Macduff. This situation was even more disturbing than his subjugation to Macready, for Charles Kean had neither the prestige nor the talent of Macready; he was far more interested in achieving vulgar theatrical effects than in understanding Shakespeare. His severer critics called him inadequate, complaining that he was willing to ruin the play for theatricalisms, gave the wrong emphasis to lines, was often grotesque, hurried, and careless. The *Morning Herald* summed up his acting: "Mr. Charles Kean's vigorous and most elaborate misrepresentation of Macbeth . . . [is like] all his Shakespearean parts, and our strengthened conviction is, that he is merely a noisy, yet most tricky commonplace."

In 1841 Macready took over the management of Drury Lane; the season proved so unsuccessful that he was forced to close after six months. The Haymarket was now the only legitimate theater in London. Macready left again for the provinces, because of a quarrel with Webster, who now engaged Phelps as leading support to Charles Kean. When Macready reopened Drury Lane in 1842, Phelps had won a wider reputation than ever, for Webster had given him leading roles in several non-Shakespearean comedies. At Drury Lane Macready, even though the critics complained of his preference for actors inferior to Phelps, assigned him to play old Adam in *As You Like It* and Hubert in the most important production of the season, *King John*. A characteristic criticism was that "boisterousness" was the quality of all the actors "save Phelps." The *Morning Post* said that he "is one of the few living men who touch our hearts, and this, not by loud words and hurried delivery and strong tones (although his strength is plentiful), but by the genial undercurrent of living feeling . . . He calls forth a tear by . . . the strong persuasion that his grief or passion is actually grappling with the very roots of his own heart." The queen was so much moved when she saw Phelps's Hubert that she ordered a portrait of him in costume by Sir William Ross.

Phelps played Iago again to Macready's Othello. His audiences' approval was so evident that Macready withdrew the play after three performances. In January 1843 Macready at last looked at the manuscript of Browning's *A Blot in the 'Scutcheon*, which had been in his possession for a year. He was in the habit of asking a dramatist to read his work to the actors, or, failing that, to ask the stage manager to do so. This time he assigned the job to his prompter and then left the room; the stage manager, knowing that Macready did not much care for the play, read the script in low-comedy fashion and provoked a great deal of laughter. The following day, Macready informed Browning that since the actors had laughed at his work the poet had better revise it. Browning agreed, came back with the alterations, was kept waiting, and treated rudely by Macready. He was ready to ask for further revisions, but was not prepared for Browning's resistance. "I fear he is a very conceited man," Macready wrote in his diary. He himself attempted further cuts, gave up the task, and decided to allow Phelps to do the part of Tresham instead of himself, as originally planned. Phelps was eager to do it. At one of the late rehearsals, Macready, his diary informs us, "offered to give to Browning and Mr. Phelps the benefit of my considerations and study in the cuts . . . Browning, however, in the worst taste, manner, and spirit, declined any further alterations, expressing himself perfectly satisfied with the manner in which Mr. Phelps executed Lord Tresham. I had no more to say. I could only think Mr. Browning a very disagreeable and offensively mannered person."

The audience responded to the performance with great enthusiasm, applauded Phelps wildly, and the stage manager announced the play would be given three nights a week. Macready recorded: "I was *angry* after the play about the call being directed without me." The *Morning Post* gave the drama a lengthy review, full of praise, and said: "Phelps took the part which Macready would otherwise have acted, and if we missed a little of the refinement which carries the latter actor so triumphantly through his blotchy mannerisms, it is due to Mr. Phelps to say that in other respects he gave a singular passion and power to the proud brother, which we believe could have been shown by no other actor than himself. . . . The actor was forgotten in the terrible truth of his fiery utterance." After three highly acclaimed performances, which led London to expect a long run for the play, Macready withdrew it. Browning, who had looked upon Macready as a friend with whom he had had warm associations, was so shocked at this treatment of his play that thereafter when they met in the street the poet turned away.

The deficits at Drury Lane were piling up because of Macready's inability to be objective as a manager. The proprietors refused to lease the theater to him for another season. There was a great deal of argument, and out of spite Macready used his influence to draw up a petition asking that there be an end to the exclusive licensing of the patent theaters. His vindictiveness resulted in a step that affected the entire future of London's theaters.

On August 22, 1843, the monopoly which had been operating for two hundred years was abolished by the Theatres Regulation Bill, passed by both Houses of Parliament, and freedom to give plays was granted to all the theaters which were licensed in London.

Phelps refused Macready's offer to accompany him to the United States. But the disbanding of the Drury Lane company worked great hardship on the actors. Worse yet, one of them, Elton, lost his life in a shipwreck, en route from Edinburgh; his former fellow actors, most of whom were without employment, were anxious to give a benefit for Elton's widow and impoverished family, but could find no theater until the lessee of Sadler's Wells, a playhouse at a considerable distance from the theatrical center, offered it for the purpose. On August 5, *Othello* was presented, with Phelps and Mrs. Warner as Othello and Desdemona. Despite the inconvenient location of the theater, the audience was large—people who lived within easy reach of

Sadler's Wells were not the sort who could be expected to come to see Shakespeare—and the Elton family was richer by £70.

After that Phelps and his colleagues were forced to travel in the provinces again. Suddenly Thomas Greenwood, who had the lease of Sadler's Wells, asked Phelps to become colessee and manager of that suburban playhouse. The offer was startling. First of all, the theater was miles away from the twenty theaters in London's West End. Moreover, for a long time it had housed cheap amusement with a succession of melodrama, clowns, acrobats, and an audience known to be uncouth. If the educated and well-to-do Londoner would not patronize any of the many available West End theaters which might have been expected to produce Shakespeare, now that the patent theaters had lost their exclusivity, what could be hoped for from untutored and rough laborers? But Phelps was in a desperate situation, did not wish to be exiled from his wife in London, and agreed to Greenwood's proposal.

It was a decision that was to have far-reaching consequences on Shakespearean productions.

Sadler's Wells had one of the longest histories in English theatrical annals. It was built in the 1680s by a man named Sadler, on whose land was discovered a medieval well said to have remarkable medicinal powers. For the sake of that well he built a place where multitudes of people flocked to see dancers, fighting cocks, and to hear musicians. The house soon became notorious for its rowdy pleasures. A grand jury indicted it in 1744 as a site harmful to morals. Rosomon, a new owner, changed the fare to harlequinade, burletta, and pantomime, and achieved a long success as manager. He took down the old wooden structure and replaced it with a good-looking stone building in 1765, with a seating capacity of twenty-five hundred—as many as both patent theaters in the West End. During the performances wine was served, and there were specail ledges for the bottles at the back of the seats. He also introduced tightrope walkers, trained dogs, racing ponies; the famous clown, Grimaldi, came every year. In the early 1800s an immense water tank 90 feet long, 25 feet wide, and 5 feet deep was placed under the stage for aquatic spectaculars; a second tank was installed above the stage to create an artificial waterfall, the water itself being supplied by the river which ran beside the theater. Sea stories could now be given with such realistic effects that for thirty years Sadler's Wells became the home for "nautical drama." When the audiences gave sign of wearying of these maritime adventures, the management began to present, in the 1840s, silly melodramas, such as *Intemperance, The Outcast Woman,* and *Woman's Love.* There were also dramatizations of Dickens and Scott in pirated versions, and innumerable farces. It was generally understood that "respectable persons" did not take their families to Sadler's Wells.

What recommended the theater to Phelps was that its rent was much lower than any theater in the West End. Once Drury Lane and Covent Garden had been enlarged, during the first half of the nineteenth century, managers in those playhouses who might have wished to present Shakespeare had become more and more dependent on the patrons of the boxes for support, since those in the pit, once the chief source of income, much preferred dancing and pantomimes. It was naturally with some misgivings that Phelps, Mrs. Warner, and Greenwood took over the distant theater with the object of dignifying the stage. Greenwood was acting manager and Phelps what we now call director.

Phelps issued handbills warning the old patrons to anticipate a change of fare, and expressed his and Mrs. Warner's hope "of constantly rendering it what a Theatre ought to be; a place for justly representing the works of our great dramatic poets." Because of his failure to advertise, Phelps was astonished at the size of his audience on opening night, May 27, 1844, to see *Macbeth*. He was even more astounded at the cheers which erupted at the following lines—

> MACBETH: If we should fail?
> LADY MACBETH: We fail?
> But screw your courage to the sticking place
> And we'll not fail.

—until he understood that the ovation was intended to assure the new management that it had the backing of the spectators and that *it* would not fail.

Unlike Macready, whose Macbeth was very gentlemanly, Phelps's Thane was a self-confident soldier, vigorous and commanding on his first entry. He spoke the great lines with a close approach to naturalness, with subtle shadings, and a complete avoidance of theatricalism. Mrs. Warner, already familiar to London audiences as Lady Macbeth, seemed better than ever. On May 29 the *Times* observed that playing a Shakespearean tragedy "at this place is a bold undertaking." Phelps allowed the play to run for six nights while he was preparing *Othello*. Gradually other plays were added to the repertory.

It was not until July 29 that several London critics made the journey to see Phelps's opening Hamlet. They were amazed at the acting and the magnificence of the scenery. By September Sadler's Wells had taken its place as an important theater, despite the pilgrimage necessary to attend it, and Phelps had the satisfaction of reading about himself that he "has more real genius in him than any actor of our time, and it is now making itself manifest. He was kept down by the overbearing power of Macready."

It is unfair that whereas the names of Garrick, Kean, and even Macready are famous today, that of Phelps is almost unknown. For his accomplishment was prodigious. At Sadler's Wells he produced thirty-one of Shakespeare's plays, a total of sixteen hundred nights, depending solely on the patronage of his audiences and making the adventure a profitable one. His contemporaries justly appraised him as a great actor, and recognized the originality of his interpretations. His Hamlet was as noble and spiritual as Macready's, but, as one critic said, though Macready was great in the role, "particular passages stood out too much: you thought too frequently of Shakespeare's beautiful language, and too rarely of the character he had conceived." It would seem, however, that unlike Edmund Kean, Phelps understated Hamlet's anguish and preferred to see the Prince as a man of philosophic bent whose trust in the world had been undermined.

He was the first actor since the Restoration to give a *Macbeth* shorn of D'Avenant's "improvements"; he made the hero less a victim of the witches, and presented Macbeth as bold and commanding, even in his encounters with the three. It was a performance of scope and power, and differed in that respect from both that of Macready and Edwin Booth.

Again, he restored the full text of *King Lear* and at last allowed the public to see the Fool, whose part had been either omitted or ruthlessly cut (as a character whose very presence had been considered in bad taste!), for what he is, an indispensable part of the tragedy as Shakespeare had conceived it. Phelps was at pains to make Lear seem eighty years of age both in voice and movement. Macready had made the king arrogant in Act I, Phelps as the victim of a bad temper—which was surely what Shakespeare had intended. What Phelps emphasized throughout the play was Lear's inability to forget that his daughters had rejected him. It has been said that while Macready used the language to explain the king's suffering, Phelps used the suffering to illuminate the language. One critic described his "indignant and convulsive grief as harrowing," but felt that though his Lear provoked pity it was not tragic because it was not awesome. In November of 1845 both he and Macready were appearing in the play; the *Court Journal* compared them: some of Phelps's "bursts of passionate anger" no one has ever "seen exceeded"; in the last two acts he proved himself "not merely an excellent and admirable, but a great actor"; he made one feel "a greater depth, simplicity and unity of purpose, and a more perfect embodiment of that purpose than even in the great performance of Macready." Acting with total abandonment, Phelps in tragic parts sometimes trembled from head to foot on stage.

With the exception of Hamlet, Phelps, during his extended management of Sadler's Wells, played Leontes more often than any other hero. Until by his acting he made *The Winter's Tale* a favorite that play had long been considered better in the library than on the stage. Earlier Leontes had been presented as a kind of less significant Othello—that is, as a man of honor and trust led into unjust suspicion of his wife; Phelps followed Coleridge's interpretation that this is a man jealous by nature, and he portrayed him from the beginning as too violent in his love and too eager to torment both himself and Hermione. In his portraiture Phelps was master at showing a gradual transition from one state of mind to another (as in Leontes's devastation at the loss of Hermione) and the underlying war of emotions in the process; Macready, on the other hand, dealt in rapid shifts of emotional reactions. Phelps used the same technique with Brutus; at the beginning the hero was calm and firm, in contrast to Cassius's excitability. By degrees one saw Brutus becoming more involved emotionally; after Caesar's murder he resumed his placidity, now varied with flashes of tenderness. This is certainly the character as Shakespeare depicted it. It was in that role that Phelps took his farewell of Sadler's Wells.

He knew himself unequal to the demands of a passionate lover on stage, and therefore never willingly did Romeo; in *Antony and Cleopatra* he did himself justice only in the political scenes and those in which he was trying to escape from Cleopoatra's power over him.

Essentially a tragic actor, he was not at his best in comedy. His Falstaff was only fair, though his Henry V was greatly praised. But he revolutionized the role of Malvolio; by tradition Malvolio was performed with strut and sneering; Malvolio, as Phelps conceived him, was the personification of megalomania. He played him with icy calm, heavy tread, and vacuity of expression. He so transformed himself that Phelps was not recognized by the audience until they heard his voice. He played him less for laughs than for quintessential comic effect.

It has been said that "in the range and variety of his acting only Garrick approached him." He certainly broke with preceding techniques by his avoidance of "points," his willingness to lose his own personality in the role he was interpreting, as well as his voice, gait, and even his physique. No one ever involved his audience more in the emotions portrayed. If equally consistent in characterization as Macready, he was perhaps not as subtle psychologically. Possessed of a passionate force similar to Kean's he did not work up to the thrilling climaxes of the latter.

In addition to his valuable contribution to the future of Shakespearean performances, Phelps is an important figure in the history of the theater. Within a year of his management of Sadler's Wells, he instituted a systematic method of training the members of his company. Macready had drilled his actors at rehearsals, but Phelps became the first real director, in the sense that he exerted himself to see that individual performances took their right and proportionate place in the work as a whole. Unlike his predecessors he was constantly attentive to the meaning and tone of the drama as a unity, and was tireless in going over with his troupe again and again their interpretations to see that they harmonized with the totality of the work.

He left Sadler's Wells in November of 1862, and accepted an offer by Charles Fechter to join him at the Lyceum. He signed a contract calling for three performances a week at the ridiculously low salary of £40 a week. Though warned by friends that this was a trick to humble him, Phelps was unwilling to believe that Fechter had mean ulterior motives. However, when after three months he had not been asked to make a single public appearance, he realized that the £40 were a pay-off to keep him from acting. When Fechter asked him to do the Ghost in *Hamlet* Phelps balked and a quarrel resulted. Both men agreed to submit the case to their friend, Charles Dickens. The novelist suggested that Fechter either allow Phelps major roles or else cancel the contract. Fechter preferred the latter expedient.

Soon Phelps was playing and directing for Drury Lane. His opening drama was *Manfred*, the romantic poetic drama by the long-dead Byron, Phelps himself taking the title role. It had a long run. Its success cannot have been due to the play itself, which is not a good one, but to Phelps's fine reading of Byron's lines. After *Manfred* (1864) came many Shakespearean plays, and an elaborate production of Goethe's *Faust* (1866).

He continued to play short engagements in the provinces. His last years were embittered by the loss of his wife, to whom he had been intensely devoted; she died in 1867 after a long illness. A few months later he was stricken again by the loss of his thirty-nine-year-old son.

In October 1876 at a banquet given by the lord mayor to members of his profession, Phelps, giving as proof his eighteen years' success at Sadler's Wells, proposed that the government ought to subsidize a Shakespearean theater for the general public: "If that could be done by me as a humble individual, why could it not be done by the Government of this country? . . . If I could find any member of Parliament (which I fear is hopeless), I would willingly devote what little of life remains to me, to point out the way in which this could be done."

He died at the age of seventy-four on November 6, 1878. Gissing said: "We have none left like him. He had the interest of the legitimate drama at heart, and I can imagine with what scorn he thought of the trash which now occupies our boards. He had lived to see the days when *Our Boys* could run for fifteen hundred nights, and *Pink Dominoes* bid fair to run still longer."

Thomas Barry Sullivan (1821–1891), though considered in London an outsider, was, according to Winter, an actor of "exceptional ability." He was particularly impressive in presenting the "grim, sarcastic, pitiless" humor of Richard III.

Born in Ireland, he joined a touring company after seeing Macready, and performed in Ireland, the English provinces, and Scotland. In London he was first seen as Hamlet at the Haymarket. He had a season at Sadler's Wells, and in 1858 came to New York, where he enacted a variety of roles. After touring Australia he returned to England, and played Benedick to Helen Faucit's Beatrice at the Shakespeare Memorial Theatre in 1879. After that he was rarely seen in London, but acted often in Ireland and the provinces. Though never first-rate, he had a vigorous forcible delivery in the old Shakespearean traditions which made him popular with audiences more naive than those of the metropolis. A sturdy man whose face was disfigured by smallpox, his natural roughness made him shy away from most romantic or comic parts.

His Hamlet was intellectual rather than poetic, and evoked no pathos; however, he certainly seems to have been on the right track by portraying him as a man of action, as Shakespeare had created him. Nevertheless, he adopted Macready's twirling of the handkerchief routine and was hissed by Forrest in Philadelphia just as the older actor had hissed Macready in Edinburgh. But Sullivan retorted by pointing at him in the stage box, as he spoke the line, "That great baby you see there is not yet out of his swaddling clouts." (Either Winter is in error in reporting this, for the *"I must be idle"* passage which accompanied the twirling of the handkerchief occurs *after* the the *"great baby"* line, or else Sullivan may have, like countless actors, distorted the play by transposing the two passages.)

In 1875 with well-intentioned patriotism, the band of the 69th Regiment was stationed at the theater to greet the Irish actor, but most inappropriately and prematurely blasted out its welcome with "Lo! the Conquering Hero Comes!" on the Ghost's first entrance!

When Irving, in 1876, opened in Dublin with *Hamlet,* the students of Trinity College invited him the next morning to address them in their dining hall, much to Irving's gratification. The students of Belfast University, not to be outdone, escorted Sullivan in a torchlight procession before he opened in *Richard III* and after the performance a student mounted the stage to deliver an address effusively praising Sullivan. In 1877 Irving seemed bent on following in Sullivan's heels in making the round of the provinces, and challenged the Irishman by performing those roles in which Sullivan had been acclaimed. Even in his rival's strongholds, Irving was generally successful. But in Manchester, the audiences remained stalwartly faithful to Sullivan. It was there, in fact, that the two met, and Irving invited Sullivan to a Sunday supper.

George Bernard Shaw had some interesting things to say about his compatriot. In July 1895 he said that those who recalled the late Barry Sullivan in his physical prime would remember "not an obsolete provincial tragedian, trading on the wreck of an unaccountable reputation, but an actor who possessed in an extraordinary degree just the imposing grace, the sensitive personal dignity of style." "A touch of stateliness and sonority" in his lines would cause him to "abandon his part, and become for the moment a sort of majestic incarnation of abstract solemnity and magnificence. His skill and intense belief in himself gave him the dangerous power of doing so without making himself ridiculous; and it was by this power, and by the fascination, the grace, and the force which are implied by it, that he gave life to old-fashioned and mutilated representations of Shakespeare's plays, poorly acted and ignorantly mounted." However, when with age he lost grace and resilience, "there was nothing left but a mannered, elderly, truculent and . . . rather absurd tragedian of the palmy school."

In December of the same year, Shaw wrote of him again that "his utter aloofness from his fellows gave him an almost supernatural distinction" which made him the perfect Hamlet "in his best days." He had—luckily, Shaw felt—no talent for expressing love, but it was that aloofness "which carried him over parts he could not play at all, such as Othello, through which he walked as if the only line in the play that conveyed any idea to him" was that Othello was "perplexed in the extreme." He "represented the grandiose and the violent on its last legs."

Sullivan was the one actor who kept Cibber's Richard on the stage during the second half of the nineteenth century. But, said Shaw, in December 1896, "it was an exhibition, not a play. Barry Sullivan was full of force, and very clever; if his power had been less exclusively of the infernal order, or if he had devoted himself to the drama instead of devoting the drama to himself as a mere means of self-assertion, one might have said more for him."

19

Henry Irving and Ellen Terry

The man who dominated the London stage for the last thirty years of Queen Victoria's reign was born John Henry Brodribb (1838–1905) in Somerset. As a boy of eleven he was tall and lanky and dubbed with the nickname of Spindleshanks; he also suffered from a pronounced impediment of speech. His mother consoled herself for his interest in actors with the conviction that nature had obviously disqualified him for the profession. During Phelps's seventh winter season at Sadler's Wells, young Brodribb was in the audience, brimming with excitement at the prospect of witnessing *Hamlet*. The lad could have had few more fortunate experiences as an introduction to the Shakespearean stage in London. He has recorded that it took him weeks to digest the encounter.

Beginning in life as a clerk, he nevertheless attended the city elocution class led by Henry Thomas and his wife. The teacher and his pupils offered semipublic performances, to which journalists were invited. Young Brodribb first appeared as Captain Absolute in *The Rivals,* and was praised for his "intelligent tact."

When his uncle gave him £100, the sum of a paid-up insurance policy, the lad decided to excape from his desk to the stage. He bought a collection of wigs and theatrical properties at various costumers; hearing of an amateur *Romeo and Juliet* planned at the Soho Theatre, he paid three guineas for the role of Romeo, and, reasoning that the name of Brodribb would never do for an actor, he adopted that of Henry Irving. His debut occurred on Monday night, August 11, 1856, when he was eighteen. His mother never managed to forgive her son, or to alter her conviction that as an actor he was destined to be damned.

The next step, of course, was to learn his profession in the provinces, and the example of Barry Sullivan's success outside of London was encouragement enough. At Edinburgh he had his first great opportunity in 1857. The Edinburgh stock company had already established a tradition of excellence, and Irving was quickly promoted from walk-on parts to juvenile lead. It was his good fortune to be allotted the role of Pisanio to the Imogen of Helen Faucit in *Cymbeline*. She had been widely admired as an actress ever since 1837, when she had joined Macready as a leading lady. Still rather awkward, Irving hit upon an original piece of business in the scene where Imogen kneels before Pisanio, drawing his sword and forcing it into his hand with the cry that he do her husband's bidding and kill her; he flung the sword away into the wings. At this the large audience applauded him wildly. Soon he was playing Horatio in *Hamlet*. His continued success at Edinburgh decided him to try London in 1859.

At twenty-one he was a youth of unusual pallor, with coal-black hair, dark brows, and radiant eyes, but on no account could he have been considered good-looking. In the cast of two mediocre plays at the Princess Theatre, he and the rest of the troupe failed because of the inferiority of the vehicles. Next he did Osric to a very poor Hamlet, whom the critics roasted; Irving quickly realized that he was in the wrong pew, and asked to be released from his contract. On December 19, 1859, he gave a reading of *The Lady of Lyons* in which, despite its length, he held his audience's attention unwaveringly and indeed reduced them to sobs; one critic declared that there was a "finer and indefinite something which proved incontestably and instantaneously that the fire of genius was in the artist." (I venture to suggest this is a long-winded way of saying what we discussed in our first chapter, that rare and precious possession, luminosity.)

To anticipate a little, he was twenty-nine when he first acted with his greatest leading lady, Ellen Terry, on, as she put it, a

"very foggy night in December . . . Until I went to the Lyceum Theatre, Henry Irving was nothing to me and I was nothing to him. I never consciously thought that he would become a great actor. He had no high opinion of *my* acting! He has said since that he thought me at the Queen's Theatre charming and individual as a woman, but as an actress *hoydenish!* I believe that he hardly spared me even so much definite thought as this. His soul was not more surely in his body than in the theatre, and I, a woman who was at this time caring more about love and life than the theatre, must have been to him more or less unsympathetic. He thought of nothing else, cared for nothing else; worked day and night; went without his dinner to buy a book that might be helpful in studying, or a stage jewel that might be helpful to wear. I remember his telling me that he once bought a sword with a jewelled hilt, and hung it at the foot of his bed. All night he kept getting up and striking matches to see it, shifting its position, rapt in admiration of it.

He had it all in him when we acted together that foggy night, but he could express very little. Many of his defects sprang from his not having been on the stage as a child. He was stiff with self-consciousness; his eyes were dull and his face heavy. The piece we played was Garrick's boiled-down version of *The Taming of the Shrew*, and he, as

Petruchio, appreciated the humour and everything else far more than I did, as Katherine; yet he played badly, nearly as badly as I did; and . . . I was at this time much more easy and skillful from a purely technical point of view.

Was Henry Irving impressive in those days? Yes, and no. His fierce and indomitable will showed itself in his application to his work. Quite unconsciously I learned from watching him that to do work well, the artist must spend his life in incessant labour, and deny himself everything for that purpose . . .

Henry Irving, when he played Petruchio, had been toiling in the provinces for eleven solid years . . . [with but trifling success.] Even that was forgotten in his failure as Petruchio. What a trouncing he received from the critics who have since heaped praises on many worse men!

What trouncings he continued to receive—as well as acclaim—during his career! While no one denied his intensity, some always found his mannerisms revolting, even ludicrous. Perhaps because of his tall, slight figure, the weakness of his voice, and the delicacy of his features, he could not well express noble passions. Certain roles were beyond him. His attempts at tender love-making appeared effeminate. Agate, who admired him more than any other actor of his time, pronounced his Romeo "abominable," and said it had "not a redeeming feature in his whole performance." Othello also eluded him; he was neither noble nor passionate enough for the Moor; Ellen Terry accused him of screaming and ranting incoherently in the role.

Concluding her earliest impressions of him, Ellen Terry wrote, "I think this was the peculiar quality in his acting afterwards—a kind of fine temper, like the purest steel, produced by the perpetual fight against difficulties. . . . Henry Irving at first had everything against him as an actor. He could not speak, he could not walk, he could not *look*. He wanted to do things in a part, and he could not do them. His amazing power was imprisoned, and only after long and weary years did he succeed in setting it free."

The focus of his acting was movement. "He drew a character," said A. V. Cookman, "in sharp, sudden, delicate, superb movements, each guided by a craftsmanship on which he had worked with what seemed to his associates almost inhuman concentration." His characterizations were not so much natural as a challenge to nature—they had the "splendid madness of a dream." His height, his intensity of expression, the ascetic and angular look of his face rendered him more than equipped for some parts, and were perfect for projecting horror, pride or the sardonic. He was able to cast a spell more often than not over his audience, a spell which made his strange pronunciations, his unmusical speech, his odd intonations, his unbeautiful voice seem right. Agate said that he was the greatest male actor he had ever seen; though his legs and voice were weak, his faults became him better than the virtues of any other actor.

He was frequently criticized for not being able to project his voice. Once, after the curtain had fallen and Irving came forward to thank the audience in words that for once reached the back of the gallery, one person up there shouted at him: "Why didn't you speak like that before?"

It is interesting to contrast Ellen Terry's first impressions of him with her final estimate. Once she described his face as noble, his brow as superb, his Roman nose as refined, strong and delicate. She said that in 1867 his hair had been a beautiful blue-black, and that in 1891 it was even more beautiful when streaked with white. He had more distinction of bearing, she thought, than any man alive. She never recovered from her astonishment at his capacity for work; it always came first with him, and she was sure that he would die only when he was all tired out. After a performance "he looked like a corpse."

But she also deplored his taste in non-Shakespearean plays; "oddly enough Henry was always attracted by fustian." It is true that he remained out of touch with the best of contemporary playwrights. He never did Henry Arthur Jones, Pinero, Ibsen, or Shaw. (Shaw sent Ellen Terry *The Man of Destiny,* hoping that Irving would play Napoleon and she the Strange Lady. Irving didn't like either Shaw or his play, and usually referred to him as "Your Mr. Pshaw!") When Shaw was invited in 1905 to attend Irving's funeral, he replied: "Irving would turn in his coffin if I came, just as Shakespear will turn in his coffin when Irving comes."

After nine years in various stock companies as a youth, Irving was offered a role at the St. James's Theatre in 1866 by Dion Boucicault in the latter's new play, *Hunted Down.* Among the audience were such notables as George Eliot and G. H. Lewes. The novelist asked Lewes what he thought of Irving. "In twenty years," was the reply, "he will be at the head of the English stage." "He is there," Eliot rejoined, "I think, already."

This success meant that Irving could remain in London. At the Queen's Theatre, as we have seen, he was to play opposite Ellen Terry in Garrick's version of *The Taming of the Shrew;* at this time neither of them particularly admired the histrionic talents of the other. It was only after their names became inseparable because of their long partnership at the Lyceum that legendary stories grew around their early devotion to each other as performers. Ellen Terry has an amusing account of one such myth: "Ever anxious to improve on the truth . . . people have told a story of Henry Irving promising that if he ever were in a position to offer me an engagement I should be his leading lady . . . The newest tale of my first meeting [with him said in print] that on that famous night when I was playing Puck [she was all of ten at the time!] . . . and caught my toe in the trap, 'a young man with dark hair and a white face rushed forward from the crowd and said: "Never mind, darling. Don't cry! One day you will be queen of the stage." It was Henry Irving.' "

For some time Great Britain had been going through one of its recurrent visitations of hysteria over the "phenomena" of spiritualism. Two American brothers, William and Ira Davenport, arrived with a novel sort of séance. They had themselves placed in a jerry-built cabinet, and were firmly tied with ropes so that they could not reach a tambourine and a guitar resting on the floor. The lights were extinguished and shortly there were heard thumpings on the tambourine and strummings on the guitar. The rapt audience was only too ready to conceive those to be deliverances of a heavenly music. When the lights were on again the brothers were still bound as they had been and the instruments were lying on the floor just where they had been placed. The accepted implication was that some musically inclined spirit had left the other world to visit the glimpses of the moon with this assurance that life in the hereafter had its own diversions. The Davenport Brothers came to Manchester while Irving was playing there at the Theatre Royal. They were accompanied by a man who called himself the Reverend Dr. Ferguson, and his saponaceous commentaries on the proceedings reduced the audience to investing them with an aura of religiosity.

With two fellow actors Irving went to experience this demonstration of the occult, and was, of course, outraged at what to him was vulgar blasphemy. He and his friends decided to unmask the trickery. Dr. Ferguson had impetuously offered £100 to anyone who could with equal success summon the spirits. The three actors, after a private dress rehearsal, were ready to expose the hoax publicly. On the afternoon of February 5, 1865, they rented the library hall of the Manchester Athenaeum, and were rewarded with a large audience who had not the vaguest idea of what they were to expect. They had merely been informed that they were to witness a display of "preternatural philosophy" in a "private Séance à la Davenport," by members of the Theatre Royal troupe.

Irving made the opening address. He explained that he and his friends, unlike other members of the Davenport audience "were neither astonished, perplexed, nor bewildered." They had reasoned that "there is no effect without a cause; these things are done somehow." If the cause were indeed supernatural, then they of course could not reproduce the effects. Convinced that what had been done was not supernatural, they bore in mind "the first axiom of Euclid, that the nearest way from one given point to another is by a straight line"; they therefore found the line. Before some friends they had been able "to reproduce all the phenomena," and Irving himself had had "rather the equivocal honour of impersonating a certain reverend gentleman." Their performance had so faithfully reproduced the Davenport phenomena that they felt encouraged to undo what "in their own words" Davenport and Ferguson pretended was "a new hope for mankind." If, he added, he and his friends "can succeed in destroying the blasphemous pretensions of the unlicensed spirit dealers, our object will be attained." His last words were: "I will assume, as well as I am able, the appearance and manner of the doctor, and endeavour as hastily as possible to introduce him to you as our 'media'."

With great rapidity Irving put on a wig and a beard, made a few touches on his face, assumed the right neckerchief and tightly buttoned surtout, and in a minute was the renowned Dr. Ferguson. He was so perfect a copy of the man he was mimicking that the audience roared with amusement. Now imitating the gravity, as well as the unctuousness, of his original, he stepped forward to make his address:

> Ladies and gentlemen,—In introducing to your notice the remarkable phenomena which have attended the gentlemen, who are not brothers [*Laughter*] . . . I shall therefore at once commence a long rigmarole [*Laughter*] for the purpose of distracting your attention . . .[*Laughter*] I need not tell this enlightened audience of the gigantic discoveries that have and are being made in the unfathomable abyss of science . . . (because if I did they would not believe me). [*Laughter*] . . . Concerning the early life of these gentlemen, columns of the most uninteresting description could be written. [*Laughter*] I will mention one or two interesting facts . . . In early life one of them . . . was constantly and most unconsciously floating about his peaceful dwelling in the arms of his amiable nurse [*Laughter*] while, on other occasions, he was frequently tied with invisible hands to his mother's apron strings. [*Renewed laughter*] Peculiarities of a like nature were exhibited by his companion, whose acquaintance with various spirits commenced many years ago . . . [*Roars of laughter*] Many really sensible and intelligible individuals seem to think that the requirement of darkness seems to infer trickery. [*Laughter*] So it does. [*Cheers*] But I will strive to convince you that it does not. [*Hear, hear*] Is not a dark chamber essential to the process of photography? and what would we reply to him who would say "I believe photography is a humbug". . . But we don't want them [i.e., scientific men] to find—we want them to avoid a common-sense view of the mystery. [*Laughter*] We want them to be blinded by our puzzle, and to believe with implicit faith in the greatest humbug of the nineteenth century. [*Loud applause and laughter*]

Throughout this discourse and in the midst of ever increasing laughter Irving never abandoned his gravity or assumed dignity. He then introduced his two friends, Frederick Maccabe and Phillip Day, well known to the patrons of the Theatre Royal. They were both quietly bound on each side of a cabinet, tied securely hand and foot. On the floor were placed a trumpet, a bell, a tambourine, and a guitar. As soon as the cabinet doors were closed, the "manifestations" began. Discordant sounds were heard within the cabinet, and hands appeared at its opening. Dogs barked, cats meowed, a confusion of noises resounded through the hall; Doctor Irving-Ferguson asserted that these could not possibly emanate from human voices. Every now and again the trumpet was thrown out of the cabinet; a man near the platform asked Irving to be careful that the instrument did not hurt anyone. Irving replied that he could not be responsible for any tricks the spirits chose to play, but politely asked the man whether he had been hit. When the man said no, Irving remarked that this was proof enough that the manifestations were being directed by a higher power. Finally, the doors of the cabinet were opened and the "brothers" appeared bound as before. They walked out, freed of their fetters, rebound themselves, and the whole

Davenport program proceeded in the dark with vast success. Everything the impostors had done was repeated by the actors in the minutest detail, while Irving-Ferguson kept up a running stream of witticisms. He insisted, like Ferguson, on an unbroken chain of contacts in the audience, "else," he announced, "you may be touched in places you least expect." "In the pocket!" cried one man. "Yes," Irving answered, "in the pocket, or in the head, or in any other empty receptacle."

At the end of the performance, the delighted audience unanimously voted their thanks and the "Doctor" was called for again and again.

By public demand the performance was repeated the following Saturday in the Free Trade Hall, and once again at the Theatre Royal. Irving, who at the time was doing stage roles (though of little consequence), nevertheless refused, protesting that his mission having been accomplished, to prolong the farce was too undignified an undertaking for a profession he so esteemed. The immediate consequence of his declining to repeat nightly his success in the two halls was that he lost his engagement at the Theatre Royal!

In London, after Petruchio he played three different villains in non-Shakespearean plays, one of them being Sikes in a dramatization of *Oliver Twist*. He played at the Queen's Theatre, until March 1869, and in August of that same year he was still playing the villain at Drury Lane.

In July he married Florence O'Callaghan, the daughter of the surgeon-general for the East India Company. Irving was heavily in debt, accumulated during many lean years, and was struggling to liquidate them. Mrs. O'Callaghan did what she could to cure her infatuated daughter on the grounds of Irving's inability to support a wife, but, naturally, these objections only fortified the girl's resolution to marry him. Even when his debts had been cashiered, he was well aware he lacked the means for matrimony, but Florence was still eager to marry without further delay; they had agreed to marry in July, a time he was fairly sure of unemployment. After he had left for London, Florence, too, seemed suddenly apprehensive about the future. That July he wrote to her: "On Sunday night your manner I thought was unsurmountably cold . . . Nothing I think could so soon dull affection in man or woman as indifference. You at first lavished on me such love that if I become spoiled—the fault is all your own. But you still love me as you did —don't you my darling? *Answer this.*" They were married on the fifteenth of the month. Within the next two years they had two children, Henry, born on August 5, 1870, and Laurence Sidney, born on December 21, 1871.

Before the birth of the elder son, Florence already showed herself to be temperamental; although during their engagement he had noted her moodiness, he now preferred to ascribe it to her pregnancy. She had come from a home of some elegance and did not conceal her displeasure at her new and more modest situation. Moreover, she showed quite openly her dislike for his professional friends. He had anticipated being able to invite them to an after-performance supper (he was now acting in a light comedy) and sit up chatting with them until they had dissipated the tensions of the night—innocent enough pleasures which she called "debaucheries." She considered the naturalness of their laughter and hearty talk barbaric after the artificial exchanges she was used to at her parents' table. Her nagging became unendurable, so he rented a cheap lodging in Drury Lane where he might go and study without annoyance.

When Henry was born, though Irving's joy at becoming a father was great, Florence and the infant went off to the seashore. He suddenly had a taste of the freedom he had lost with bachelorhood. He wrote to a friend that wife and child were at Southend, and invited him to come and "have long chats," and then quoted Othello, " 'Why did I marry?' . . . I'm going to dine with three jolly people . . . three of the jolliest old busybodies you can conceive." When speaking of the refreshments he intended for his friend's visit, he made the depraved suggestion of having cocoa!

He and his wife now arranged an amicable, but not a legal, separation; he was to see his son once a fortnight. Early the next year Florence pleaded with Irving to return to her; she promised to change her ways. He agreed, warning her of the conditions of life which she had found unbearable, and which, in the very nature of things, must remain the same. In the meantime he was on tour, and soon bound for Ireland. From there he wrote her: "We (Montague, English and other members of the company) made up a party amongst which were three natives, driven by a Dr. Shaw of Trinity College, Dublin, to the Dardle—a divine spot—where we dined al fresco. A delightful day we had of it, and you'll be surprised to hear (accusing me, dear, as you sometimes do, of chronic dullness) that I was the life and soul of the party. I astonished myself, I frankly tell you—but I really was in great form. You dislike practical joking, I know, so do I—sometimes—but Montague and I yesterday concocted and carried out with genuine success the rarest and best acted little plot that has ever been conceived."

It is not known whether or not Florence was ever apprised of the details of this rarest and best acted little plot. If she was, it requires little imagination to be certain that she would not have approved of it.

During the picnic it was remarked that Irving and Montague were unwontedly cool toward each other. Suddenly they separated themselves from the others and were observed to be indulging in an acrimonious quarrel. When they rejoined the group Montague said something quite insulting to Irving, who reacted furiously. In the dark as to what this was all about, their friends could only be embarrassed and puzzled. Again, without warning, the two went off, and this time had soon completely vanished. Fearing that they might come to blows, the party went in search of them. Below some rocks they found Irving extremely pale, a bloody hand clasping a knife, and muttering: "I've done it! I told him I would! He provoked me!" When one of the others tried to approach him, Irving waved him off with the bloody blade. "Back!" he cried fiercely. The other demanded to know where Montague was. "There he is—the scoundrel—the false friend!" was Irving's answer as he pointed a long finger to where the victim was lying on his belly among the rocks. Actually, Montague had stuffed a handkerchief into his mouth to stifle the convulsions of laughter he was undergoing. He was, of course, not even scratched. Irving, with his characteristic care for makeup, had cut his own wrist to provide the blood.

The prank illustrated fairly well that Ellen Terry would not unjustly accuse him of loving fustian.

Florence, expecting another baby, was probably not receptive to his practical jokes or his reported successes in the provinces. When he rejoined her in August 1871 it was with the hope of making a new start in their relationship.

At this juncture Bateman took over the management of the Lyceum, the theater which was to become associated with Irving's name for most of his life. It was a structure that had already had a long and complicated history.

It was built almost parallel to the Strand on Exeter Street near Catherine Street, which has since become part of Aldwych. The first Lyceum was designed by James Paine, the architect of many bridges and noble houses throughout London and the country. Its foundation stone was laid in 1771. The first public exhibition held in the building was given by "the noted Flockton" with his puppet shows and sleight-of-hand tricks. By 1789 he was advertising his "inimitable Dexterity of Hand, Different from all pretenders to the said Art. To which will be perform'd an ingenious and Spirited opera called The Padlock. Principal vocal performers, Signor Giovanni Orsi and Signora Vidina. The whole to conclude with his grand and inimitable Musical Clock, at first view, a curious organ, exhibited three times before their Majesties." This marvelous clock had no less than nine hundred figures working each at various trades.

The Lyceum next became an exchange, a place where debating societies held forth, and where was held a "scientific" exhibition of Count Zambeccari's air balloon (102 feet in circumference, 33 feet in diameter; it was said to hold 18,200 cubic feet of "inflammable air"). Next came "A majestic Diana in a car of gold, drawn by two beautiful reindeer"; a waxwork exhibition reported to have come direct from Constantinople and to be "an exact Representation of the Seraglio," and included "the grand Signior, and many of the most beautiful Turkish and Armenian Ladies; . . . also the Empress of Germany, Empress of Russia, the French King and Queen, the the Kings of Spain, Prussia, Portugal, and Naples . . . A Sleeping Venus, of exquisite beauty—A most beautiful Venus, in full length, being the exactest imitation of nature ever seen . . .—Voltaire, that justly admired French genius, who died in Paris in the year 1778, aged 85." The charge for admission was 1s.

Next, there was an exhibition for the sale of paintings by the Old Masters, including "the celebrated Madonna and Child by Murillo," and works by Van Dyck, Rembrandt, Teniers, Hobbema, and others. The waxworks returned with figures including George III, his queen and the Duke of York, as well as Franklin and John Wesley. Presently the Lyceum had an entertainment of Philosophical Fireworks and Musical Glasses, which proved very popular and was often revived. The Philosophical Fireworks included "a Sun turning round," "a Star varying—a Triangle—a Dragon pursuing a

Serpent—a Star of Knighthood—a Flame proper for Lighthouses." The music performed on the glasses was described in the advertisement as "a very difficult and much-admired Selection."

Robert Palmer, brother of John Palmer, an actor celebrated for his Joseph Surface, gave a lecture on heads, followed by the musical glasses. In June 1789 there was an exciting display of an "Aeropyric Branch," illuminating the building during the interval. This was suspended by a chain from the cupola, and "a light is produced in an instant, changes its colour, and is extinguished without any visible means whatever." The stunt was made possible by illuminating gas, still unknown to public buildings.

A description by the *Gazetteer* gives a vivid picture of what the Lyceum was like in those days: "The room is fitted up with peculiar taste and elegance; and like the House of Commons, on which it seems to be modelled, has a gallery for strangers, while the body of the room is appropriated solely for members who are subscribers to the institution. The gallery runs along each side of the room . . . and from the top of each of the eighteen pillars that support it, hangs a glass lustre, from which the room is illuminated. At the end of the room . . . stands a throne, with a canopy covered with green, fringed with gold." This arrangement was doubtless prompted by the needs of the debating society, and hence, too, the recurrent analogy in descriptions of this Lyceum with the House of Commons.

There were also: "Theatrical Imitations" by George Saville Carey of Garrick, Barry, Mossop, Foote, Henderson, and others; and, on the same program, "Madame Mara and her Mouse; the African Slave's Appeal to Liberty; a Poetical, Tropical, and Whimsical Delineation of a Methodist Preacher." Admission three shillings to the house and two shillings to the gallery. This Carey, who returned often to the Lyceum, was thought by many, Macaulay among them, to have fathered illegitimately Henry Carey, from whom was descended Edmund Kean.

In 1789 an Irish giant was entertaining at the Lyceum. His advertisement said of O'Brien that he was "indisputably the tallest man ever shown," that he was "a lineal descendant" of "puissant King Brian Boreau," that he measured "eight feet four inches" in height, although the average in his family was nine feet, "which he hopes to attain by the time he is of age."

For a time the Lyceum became known as Mendoza's Academy because of the boxing that flourished there between the hours of 1 and 3 P.M.; admission one shilling sixpence to the boxes and one shilling to the gallery. Mendoza found it necessary to announce in the papers that he "has divested his Exhibition of every degree of Brutality and rendered the Art of Boxing equally neat with Fencing," and hence ladies were more than welcome.

In March 1790 the Lyceum was announced for auction by Christies. It apparently did not change hands. In August the sensation was that "most Wonderful of all Animals . . . the Rhinoceros." The next year the attraction of that object of "the attention of Naturalists for ages past" was strengthened by the addition of "a most beautiful Zebra" and "a stupendous Ostrich," and, later, several dwarfs ("Lilliputians Alive"), a heifer with two heads, and "a wonderful American Elk." The Lyceum had become "a place of first resort for every admirer of the wonderful works of Creation."

In the autumn of 1790 Charles Dibdin (1745–1814) began to change the history of the Lyceum. He was a famous songwriter, and performed for 108 nights. When the first amphitheater in Westminster Bridge Road burned down Philip Astley transferred his circus, or as much of it as the building could accommodate, to the Lyceum in 1794. After him Handy's circus took over, featuring equestrian performances. For a while the Lyceum was in a bad way; a Mr. Crook on a particular Thursday at midnight offered "A Valuable Collection of Unredeemed Pledges." In 1798 an astronomical lecture with the appalling title of Diostrodoxon was held. Cartwright and his Aeropyric Branch were there again in 1800. In the meantime Samuel Arnold, the composer (1740–1802), had bought the lease of the Lyceum and converted it into a theater, but when he applied for a license the managers of the two patent theaters, Drury Lane and Covent Garden, successfully blocked it. So the poor man had to forfeit not only the improvements he had made but his lease as well; it passed into the hands of Lingham, a breeches maker.

In 1800 Robert Ker Porter (1777–1842), a not negligible figure in the arts, diplomacy, and literature, exhibited at the Lyceum his earliest great panorama. The Storming of Seringapatam, mounted on rollers, and 120 feet long; that was followed by similar large paintings, the Siege of Acre, the Battle of Lodi, the Battle of Alexandria, and the Battle of Agincourt. In 1804 Frederick Albert Winsor (1763–1830) gave his lectures on the new means of illumination. His remarks were illustrated by a burner shaped "with much taste" in the form of a "cupid grasping a torch with one hand" and holding a long, flexible tube with the other. (Gas was not to be used in a London street until 1807, when Winsor lit up part of Pall Mall with it; but he was so little encouraged that gas was not in general use in the throughfares until 1812.)

Other painting exhibitions followed. Madame Tussaud's now famous exhibition came to the Lyceum from Paris in 1802. But the history of the Lyceum as a regular theater dates from 1809. On February 24 of that year the third Drury Lane was destroyed by fire, and the actors found a temporary home at the much-abused Lyceum until Drury Lane should be ready again in 1812. This in no way impinged on the powerful monopoly of Drury Lane and Covent Garden, and when Samuel James Arnold, Dr. Arnold's son, applied for a license at the Lyceum in 1809 he was given one from June 3 to October 3, and then only for light musical works; the name of the theater was altered to the English Opera House.

In the summer of 1810 ballad operas, burlettas, and other musical trivia were presented there. A year later the use of horses at Covent Garden was burlesqued in the Quadrupeds. In 1811 Tom Moore's only dramatic effort, *M. P.*, a comic opera in three acts, was seen, and the same year at last Shakespeare was presented, *Much Ado* and *As You Like It*, both for benefit performances. During these years there was a great deal of confusion about the name of the theater; one night it would be called The Theatre Royal, Lyceum, and the next Theatre Royal English Opera.

Arnold obtained a ninety-nine-year lease of the property in 1815, acquired some of the adjoining property, and the first truly substantial theatrical building was erected on the site at a cost of £ 80,000. The new Lyceum was opened on June 17, 1816, with an opera by Arnold. This building remained until it was destroyed by fire in 1830. Musical pieces continued to be the order of the day. In 1818 Charles Mathews began to give his recitations and songs. Washington Irving saw and enjoyed him vastly. During the 1820 season *The Vampire, or the Bride of the Isles* was given thirty-seven times and frequently thereafter. Its success provoked new hostilities from the two patent theaters. In 1821 the Lyceum began to give fancy dress balls (later imitated by Harris at Covent Garden); they were called Carnivals—admission one guinea, supper tickets one-half guinea.

And now we pass again to Shakespeare at the Lyceum, even though the ban against giving him at the "minor" theaters had not been lifted. It required a special occasion. Mrs. Glover (1781–1850) played Hamlet for her benefit to a crowded house. As the actor Walter Donaldson recorded it, without any reference to Mrs. Glover's phenomenal *embonpoint*, he said that her "noble figure, handsome and expressive face, rich and powerful voice, all contributed to rivet the attention of the *élite* assembled." Bursts of applause "greeted her finished elocution as she delivered the soliloquies." In the stage box were Edmund Kean, Munden, and Douglas Kinnaird.

After this special occasion, matters were dull again at the Lyceum; *The Vampire* reappeared and comic operas were revived. In the following years these were varied with farces and burlettas—largely because permission was lacking to compete in serious drama with the two patent houses. In 1828 there were *Soirées Françaises* during which Molière's *Les Fourberies de Scapin*, *Le Médecin Malgré Lui*, *Tartuffe*, *L'Avare*, and *Le Misanthrope* were presented to enthusiastic audiences, as well as Beaumarchais's *Le Mariage de Figaro*.

Edmund Kean, already in his decline, that same year found himself acting at the Lyceum with the Covent Garden company, whose theater had been damaged by a gas explosion. He did Richard III, and Charles Kemble Orlando; then Kean did Shylock and Sir Giles Overreach; Kean did Othello to Charles Kemble's Cassio. According to Doran, those who saw Kean "from the front" perceived "not a trace of weakening of any power in him. But, oh, ye few who stood between the wings where a chair was placed for him, do you not remember the saddening spectacle of that wrecked genius—a man in his very prime, with not merely the attributes of age about him, but with some of the infirmities of it. . . ?"

In 1830 the Lyceum, which had endured since 1772, was entirely destroyed by fire between 1 and 2 A.M. on February 16.

The Lyceum with which Irving was to be familiar was reconstructed and opened on July 14, 1834, with opera. Its builder was Samuel Beazley (1786–1851), playwright as well as architect. He built the St. James's Theatre, the colonnade of Drury Lane, the old part of the Adelphi, the South Eastern

Railway and its London Bridge station, and also the well-known Hotel Lord Warden at Dover. He was the author of over a hundred farces and other pieces which attracted the public in the 1830s and 40s. He was a very generous man; no one ever came to him for a loan and went away empty-handed, though he was always short himself. While driving with a friend who envied him his never requiring public conveyances, Beazley agreed: "I have a carriage, and a cabriolet, and three horses, and a coachman and a footman, and a large house, and a cook, and three maid-servants, and a mother and a sister, and—half a crown."

He was never known to speak ill of anyone and was admired for his considerateness; nevertheless, in his plans for his new Lyceum he did commit a serious blunder. He forgot to include a gallery staircase, which therefore had to be added after the theater had been built. The playhouse's boast was that it was cool in summer and warm in winter; in June 1835 he announced: "The PUBLIC are most respectfully informed that, in consequence of its complete ventilation, the TEMPERATURE OF THIS THEATRE is many degrees cooler than that of the external atmosphere!" The program further quoted from *Measure for Measure:* "To reside in thrilling region of thick-ribbed ice." No doubt, more convincing was the promise of "AN EXCELLENT ICED CREAM OR WATER ICE GRATIS."

Nothing worthy of our notice among the ensuing years of various blood-and-thunder pieces, French plays, and Italian opera was presented at the Lyceum with the exception of Mozart's *Marriage of Figaro* and Donizetti's *The Elixir of Love*. But during the summer of 1838 there emerged a man unfortunately named William Shakespeare, who claimed descent from the great poet, with the additional impertinence of "What's in a name?" He appeared in a "dramatic sketch," himself playing Shakespeare, as well as Richard Burbage, Leicester, and Queen Elizabeth. He quickly returned to the oblivion which suited him better.

On January 29, 1844, the licensing law favoring the two patent theaters was altered in favor of the "minor" playhouses, which were now allowed to present the works of Shakespeare, if they chose. At the Lyceum dramatizations of Dickens became immensely popular, especially his *Martin Chuzzlewit*. In 1847 Madame Vestris, who was married to Charles Mathews, took over the management. She was born in London (1707–1856), the granddaughter of the engraver, Bartolozzi, and married a ballet dancer, Auguste Vestris, in 1813. He deserted her, and in 1838 she married the actor, Charles James Mathews. She played mostly in light comedies and burlettas, but when she and Mathews took over Covent Garden in 1839 she performed in Shakespearean comedy, as Rosaline in *Love's Labour's Lost*, which was beautifully mounted, although omitting many lines from the text and transposing certain scenes (nevertheless, she deserves credit for being the first to give the play since the closing of the theaters in 1642). She also performed in a splendid revival *A Midsummer Night's Dream;** and *Romeo and Juliet*.

*In *A Midsummer Night's Dream,* though the acting was pronounced "miserable," the version Mme. Vestris used was closer to Shakespeare's original than it had been in all the years from

In 1845 she gave *The Merry Wives of Windsor*, with herself as Mrs. Ford. (Bishop and Reynolds had worked the play into an opera in which Mme. Vestris had made herself popular as Mistress Page years before. This version lasted for something like a century.) At the Lyceum no less than seven songs from the other plays were introduced, such as "Blow, blow, thou winter wind," and "I know a bank where the wild thyme grows."

When the balance is struck she must be thanked for doing her best for Shakespeare at a time when her courage was much needed. She was not strictly speaking beautiful but won over audiences by her engaging and informal manner. She "possessed lustrous eyes, a flexible mouth . . . and a forehead arched by abundant dark hair that fell in thick tresses upon her well-formed neck and sloping shoulders . . . In her rich contralto voice she had sung . . . Don Giovanni in *Don Giovanni* in London, [been] Captain Macheath . . . as well as Lydia Languish . . . she was confessedly irresistible . . . She was charmingly arch and vivacious . . . She never failed to give her personal attraction the advantage of rich and tasteful costume, and . . . was such a votary of elegance in dress, that she would display it in rustic or humble characters," wrote Dr. Westland Marston.

When in March 1856 Covent Garden again burned down after a masquerade ball, the Lyceum once more provided shelter for its company, who had been chiefly engaged in giving opera. The interior of the Lyceum was repainted in pale blue, white, and gold throughout, except for the ceiling, which was washed so "that the cupids and other mythological" figures could "assume a dim and shadowy appearance. A new and elegant chandelier" was hung from the center of the roof so that no other gas appliances were needed. The private boxes were augumented to sixty-eight; there was a grand tier and a tier above, and eight boxes in line with the gallery. On opening night in April 1856, Queen Victoria and Prince Albert appeared in the Royal Box. Italian opera did not, however, monopolize the season. Adelaide Ristori (1822–1906) was making a tour of Europe and the Italian tragedienne made her debut at the Lyceum on June 4, 1856, as Medea in a version by Scribe and Legouvé. She was warmly received despite her acting in her native Italian. At the Lyceum she later became a celebrated Lady Macbeth in 1857.

On September 15, 1856, Charles Dillon (1819–1881) took over the management of the Lyceum. He had first appeared at Sadler's Wells only five months before appearing in the same part of Belphegor at his new theater, this time with Marie Wilton (the future Lady Bancroft). Most of the cast was unknown, and Miss Wilton recounted: "I had little or nothing to say on my first appearance. . . . At the end of the act, where my best scene occurred

---

D'Avenant to her performance of 1841. The play had been converted into an opera, *The Fairy Queen* (1692), *The Fairies* (1755) and the two dreadful adaptations of Garrick (1763) and Reynolds (1816). Leveridge (1716) and Lampe (1745) had attempted operas too on the play, and there was *The Fairy Tale* of 1763. To this list of ignominious perversions of an exquisite work should be added prominently Peter Brook's ecstatically praised three-ring-circus version of 1972. As for *Romeo and Juliet* Mme. Vestris tried valiantly to restore Shakespeare's text, but Garrick's still-popular watering-down of that tragedy drove it from the boards.

with Mr. Dillon, the applause was tremendous, and there was a great call. I waited, hoping and expecting to be taken before the curtain by Mr. Dillon; but my friend the stage manager turned round to me sharply, saying, 'Now then, Miss Wilton, go to your room; you are not wanted.' " She walked slowly to her dressing room as Dillon was called again and again. In her room she concealed her distress from her mother, who kept asking whether she had received a curtain call. Suddenly she heard the call-boy crying, "Miss Wilton! Mr. Dillon says you must go before the curtain." She went on alone, savoring the public's acclaim. The calls for her continued, and she was about to appear a second time when the stage manager said, "That will do; we shall never get the piece over if this be allowed to go on."

In March Dillon performed Hamlet and the following December Othello. His performances were in great contrast to Phelps's, whose style now leaned toward the declamatory side, though his "perception of poetry and recital of blank verse" were brilliant; Dillon was more the actor, and he was praised for his "naturalness"; his voice was clear, flexible "and of sufficient compass, wanting no sustainment from artificial elocution"; his style was "free, flowing and easy." But his Hamlet, though clever, was superficial and lacked "any clear conception of the chief character," or "any exhibition of his mental development." Helen Faucit played his Lady Macbeth, a character for her new to London, and soon after Beatrice to his Benedick. In the same year Ira Aldridge, "The African Roscius" of whom we have already spoken, appeared at the Lyceum as Othello. After him came more melodramas and burlesques, dramatizations of Dickens—then in January 1863 Charles Albert Fechter took over the management of the Lyceum until November 1867. Of him we shall have to speak in our next chapter.

Hezekiah Linthicum Bateman (1812–1875) was born in Baltimore, educated to be an engineer, but, like Irving, disappointed his parents' expectations and instead became a theatrical manager. At twenty-one he left home to become an actor, and played juvenile parts with Booth and Charles Kean, though he made no impression. Handsome, tall, his sympathies, like those of John Wilkes Booth, were with the South, and though never a soldier he had the courtesy title of colonel bestowed upon him later in life. Undeterred by his failure as an actor, he determined to become a manager. He married Miss Cowell, the daughter of an English comedian living in the United States, and in so doing made a wise choice. She was not only a devoted wife but also a perfect partner for his ambitions. She bore him eight children, managing in the interims to write plays, and with him concentrated her theatrical hopes on three of their girls, Kate, Isabel, and Virginia. They all lived in Brooklyn during the Civil War and Hezekiah had some difficulty keeping from his neighbors his fury over Southern losses; when he gave expression to his wrath, it was explosive, and his rages became so little forgotten that on both sides of the Atlantic he was dubbed "Chained Lightning."

After some success as an impresario, he eventually realized that Isabel and

Virginia had no love for the theater so he and his wife concentrated on training Kate, whose ambition made her fully cooperative, and eventually she became famous both in America and Europe. For her sake they made many a trip to and from Europe, sometimes spending all the money they had. It was Hezekiah's boast that he was so accomplished a poker player that he could always win enough to pay his passage.

Kate married George Crow, who took over the management of her affairs and thus left her parents free to launch Isabel and Virginia on the London stage. Virginia made her first appearance with Kate at the Haymarket and it was for Isabel's sake that the Batemans engaged Irving and took over the Lyceum.

Their opening night was September 11, 1871. Their first venture, Mrs. Bateman's adaptation from the German of a French tale, in which Irving played a love-sick sentimental peasant to Isabel's gauche heroine, was a dismal failure. That was soon withdrawn in favor of a dramatization of the *Pickwick Papers*, casting Irving as Alfred Jingle, and that fared no better. For at least four years before the Batemans took over, the Lyceum had fallen on evil days and several preceding managers had been ruined there. Generally it was conceded that the Lyceum was unlucky and the Batemans were further proof of it. Blanchard, the dramatic critic, pronounced the Dickens as "very bad indeed; and I think Bateman must soon give up."

It was at this juncture that Irving reminded Bateman of an earlier promise that given the proper circumstances he should be allowed to play the lead in a play eventually called *The Bells*, an adaptation from the French of *Le Juif Polonais* by Erckmann-Chatrian. As the promise had been given before the opening of the Lyceum, Bateman felt neither eager nor obliged to fulfill it. One can hardly blame him. The action was set in an Alsatian village where the respected burgomaster (Irving) is about to marry his daughter to the chief of police; the burgomaster had once been an innkeeper, and he knew very well that his prosperity had its foundation in the murder he had committed fifteen years earlier of a Jewish traveler. He appropriated the traveler's gold, disposed of his body, and the whole affair had been forgotten— except by him. Yet as he grew older and more venerated, he became more and more haunted by the sound of the sleigh bells for which he had waited so attentively on the night of the murder. One day at a fair he comes upon a mesmerist who can made his subject reveal his innermost secrets; the possibility preys upon the burgomaster's mind, and he dreams that in a court of law the mesmerist forces him to reenact the deed; in his dream he is condemned to be hanged; in the morning when his family comes to summon him to his daughter's wedding, they find him clawing at an imaginary rope about his neck; he staggers from his bed and dies in their arms.

Bateman, an essentially good-natured man, gave in, and once having agreed, yielded to all that Irving insisted he needed for the play, though the rest of the company was convinced that this third venture would be a greater failure than the other two. *The Bells* was destined to make the fortunes of Irving, Bateman, and the Lyceum, though when first presented on November 25, 1871, the house was half-empty. But by the final curtain it had made up in volume of applause for the poor attendance. Irving's performance as Mathias, the burgomaster, became the talk of London. The Pall Mall *Gazette* said: "Acting at once so intelligent and so intense has not been seen on the London stage for many years." John Oxenford, whose judgments in *The Times* were something like the final authority, wrote: "As a valuable actor, especially of bad men in good society, Mr. Irving has for some years been recognized by the London public. But when he appears as a tragic artist, with the duty of sustaining a serious drama single-handed, he may almost be said to make a *début.* Decidedly the full measure of his deserts was never known till Saturday last." Oxenford realized that it was more or less a one-man play; "the part . . . would crush an aspirant whose ambition was disproportionate to his talent." He above all admired Irving's handling of the dream sequence. "The outer world is gone, and conscience is all triumphant, assisted by an imagination which violently brings together the anticipated horrors of a criminal court and the mesmeric feats he has recently witnessed. The struggles of the miserable culprit . . . protesting against the clairvoyant who wrings his secret from him, are depicted by Mr. Irving with a degree of energy that . . . seemed to hold the audience in suspense. It was not until the curtain fell, and they summoned the actor before it with a shower of acclamations, that they seemed to recover their self-possession." Henry Irving's reputation was made.

All London rushed to see *The Bells* "and the Lyceum became the playgoing resort of the literary and artistic world, for it was recognized that a new force in the theatre had arisen."

It is a choice piece of irony that the leading Shakespearean actor of his day should have established himself with this sort of dross. But Irving remained devoted to *The Bells* and continued to play it during his final tour of 1905. The poor taste in drama (outside of Shakespeare) was all his own, as Ellen Terry was to remark; yet the age must be held accountable too. Today it would be impossible to revive *The Bells* except with tongue in cheek, as Helen Freeman did so admirably (when I was young) in *Fashion,* or as those brilliant performers did with *Neither Maid, Wife Nor Widow* and *Ten Nights in a Barroom* when it was fashionable—and highly rewarding—to take the Hudson Tube to Hoboken to see those heart-breaking melodramas done in a style that had everyone rolling in the aisles with mirth, with the added attraction that one could adjourn afterwards to one of the places where the forbidden beer was generously served up to the foreigners from New York.

After his great triumph on the first night of *The Bells,* Irving and his wife went to a small supper party that had been arranged for them by the Hain Friswells. The great success called for champagne. Exhilarated by the congratulations and delight of his friends, he still could not help noticing how Florence dampened their spirits by aloofness and ill-humor. She kept needling her husband with the likelihood that he was boring everybody, and insisted on leaving early. He was still in high spirits as they drove home in a brougham, and laying his hand on her arm he said, "Well, my dear, we too shall soon have our own carriage and pair!" Smoldering with rage, she cried, "Are you going on making a fool of yourself like this all your life?"

Just then they were crossing Hyde Park Corner. Irving told the driver to stop. Without a word he got out of the brougham and allowed his wife to continue her journey home. He never came back to it, and he never spoke to her again during his life.

Irving was now past thirty-three. He was performing nightly, and *The Bells* ran till the middle of May. Other melodramas followed during subsequent years; then Irving planned a bold stroke, very much against Bateman's wishes. On October 31, 1874, he appeared as Hamlet; by this time his reputation was so great that within a few minutes of the opening of the doors the house was packed.

The audience at first was stunned. He did not wear a flaxen wig, as did Fechter, or any elaborate princely garb. He wore unostentatious black with a loose cloak trimmed with fur; his mourning raiment was relieved only by a heavy gold chain. "His face bore a troubled, wearied expression; the disordered black hair was thrown carelessly over the forehead, and the marvelous eye of the actor told of the distracted mind." His interpretation was so original that the audience kept breathless silence for the first two acts. One spectator wrote: "Silence also ushered in the third act. All was new in this Hamlet—the speech, the dress, the manner. Nothing called to mind the effect-snatching expedients of his predecessors. No wonder the audience was held fast by a spell expressed in silent astonishment . . . Scarcely had the dialogue with Ophelia in the third act reached its termination when the spell was broken; a hurricane of applause shook the benches, and everyone felt that the tall, seemingly nervous actor, who, with ruthless nonchalance, had thrown overboard the conventional, pathetically puffed-up prince, to make of him an unconstrained gentleman with a tinge of melancholy upon him—that this actor was the new Hamlet, the Hamlet of the future." It has been thought that this conception was influenced by Goethe's absurd analysis of Hamlet and his problem: "We have here an oak planted in a costly vase, fit only to receive lovely flowers within its bosom; the roots expand, the vase is shivered." (This the Hamlet who says, after he has killed Polonius, "I'll lug the guts into the neighbor room," the Hamlet who boards alone a pirate ship and single-handedly subdues the crew, the Hamlet who grapples with Laertes in Ophelia's grave.) Irving's Hamlet had one great shortcoming: "the lack of cruelty in his nature."

Throughout his long career he had, of course, his bitter critics as well as his staunch defenders. We have already seen how some of the very greatest Shakespearean actors overcame formidable physical disadvantages: Betterton his clumsy figure, Garrick his shortness, many of the actresses their rotundity, Kean his hoarse voice and insignificant figure, but surely none who made a name for himself as the leading actor of his age started out with greater disabilities. Irving, as Harold Hannyngton Child, a great admirer, wrote of him: "was tall and very thin . . . a voice monotonous and not powerful, a peculiar pronunciation, a stamping gait, and a tendency to drag his leg behind him, angular and excessive gesture, and a slowness of speech which became more marked when powerful emotion choked his utterance . . . It has been said that in all his parts he was 'always Irving' [James Agate, who thought him the greatest actor of his time, admits that too]; this is true inasmuch as his physical characteristics . . . could not be disguised . . . He has been called an intellectual actor," and his detractors said of him that he could not express great passion. Yet Child says he was "unsurpassed in the portrayal of fear, horror, scorn, or malignity, and he could draw tears as freely as any 'emotional' actor . . . Irving's bent led him towards the bizarre and fantastic, and touches of these appeared in all his work." On the positive side Child has this to say, "His personal magnetism was very strong; he inspired devotion in those who worked with him and adulation in his admirers."

George Bernard Shaw conducted a long war against him. "I sometimes wonder," he wrote, "where Mr. Irving will go to when he dies—whether he will dare to claim, as a master artist, to walk where he may any day meet Shakespear whom he has mutilated." Concerning a *Cymbeline* Shaw wrote again, "In a true republic of art Sir Henry Irving would ere this have expiated his acting versions on the scaffold. . . . A prodigious deal of nonsense has been written about Sir Henry Irving's conception of this, that, and the other Shakespearean character. The truth is that he has never in his life conceived or interpreted the characters of any author except himself. He is really as incapable of acting another man's play as Wagner was of setting another man's libretto. . . . He was compelled to use other men's plays as the framework for his own creations. His first great success in this sort of adaptation was with *The Merchant of Venice*. There was no question then of a bad Shylock or a good Shylock: he was simply not Shylock at all; and when his own creation came into conflict with Shakespear's as it did quite openly in the Trial Scene, he . . . positively acted Shakespear off the stage. This was an original policy . . . Shakespear at his highest pitch cannot be set aside by any mortal actor, however gifted." On the other hand, Shaw observed, when Irving was acting works by others, works of "the merest trash, his creative activity is unhampered . . . and the author's futility is the opportunity for the actor's masterpiece."

He also attacked Irving's pronunciation, whose "pure vowel method" would cause him to deliver the line "One absorbing thought which makes a slave of me" as "One ap-sorbing thot which mĕks a slĕv of me (the *p* in absorbing being a German *b*, and the italic letters pronounced as in the French fidèle)."

Agate makes an arresting addition to his "Irving was always Irving" by reminding the world "that there were at least twenty Irvings, and all of them different." Nevertheless, he complained that though there were differences between his Shylock, Wolsey, and other Shakespearean characters, "you felt that they were superficial, and that each character had only just missed being Mr. Gladstone," and that his Shylock was intelligent as a man but lacked the "characteristic temperament. He was not noticeably Jewish,"* though he had the grandeur, mysticism, the authority and poetry of the race. But because he made Shylock pathetic, he "turned the play into a tragedy," and made the last act seem like an "irrelevant epilogue."

As a matter of fact, I have reason to believe that ever since 1879, when Irving portrayed Shylock as a man victimized, that has been the axiomatic conception of the role for actors. People seemed no more bothered then than now at some unpardonable additions introduced into the play to fortify an actor's or director's, not Shakespeare's, meaning. Only Shaw was well aware of what Irving was up to. Despite the almost universal praise bestowed upon the idol of the age, Shaw said that Irving "has never thought much of the immortal William, and has given him more than one notable lesson— for instance, in *The Merchant of Venice*, where he gave us not 'the Jew that Shakespeare drew,' but the one he ought to have drawn if he had been up to the Lyceum mark."

Irving made Shylock "a patriarch of Israel, wronged in his most sacred affections." Further distorting what was not meant to be a tragedy, he introduced a scene showing Shylock returning to his house "by light of lantern" to knock "on the door of an empty house." Ellen Terry, his Portia, speaking with the tongue of actors, wrote that "for absolute pathos," she had never seen anything to compare with that scene. What does it matter that Shakespeare wrote no such scene, and that its intrusion is in violation of everything he tells us about Shylock's relationship to his daughter? (For example, she has already said, "Our house is hell," and soon Shylock himself will be wishing her dead at his feet with the ducats in her coffin.) William Winter also paid tribute to that "image of the father convulsed with grief."

To be fair, Irving was actually preceded in his sentimental interpretation of Shylock by an English girl in the audience at one of the play's performances. "When I saw this Play at Drury Lane," the poet Heine (d. 1856) reported, "there stood behind me in the box a pale, fair Briton, who at the end of the Fourth Act, fell to weeping passionately, several times exclaiming. 'The poor man is wronged!' It was a face of the noblest Grecian style, and the eyes were large and black. I have never been able to forget those large and black eyes that wept for Shylock! When I think of those tears I have to rank *The Merchant of Venice* with the Tragedies." Of course, despite the largeness and blackness of her eyes, the lovely Briton was not responsible for Irving's Shylock!

A fairly lively idea of his presentation can be had from an account in *The Theatre* for December 1879: The fierceness associated with Shylock since Macklin was not Irving's.

> "The bearing of this Shylock is distinguished by a comparatively quiet and tranquil dignity . . . He feels and acts as one of a noble but long-oppressed nation . . . In point of intelligence and culture he is far above the Christians . . . and the fact that as a Jew he is deemed far

*As I understand the play, he was to that degree carrying out Shakespeare's intentions.

below them in the social scale is gall and wormwood to his proud and sensitive spirit . . . A picturesque background is at the outset provided for this striking figure by a view of the Palace of St. Mark with a quay on which porters are landing bales of merchandise. Mr. Irving's acting here is studiously quiet in tone, but full expression is given to the religious fervor of the Jew, the sense of wrong which rankles in his bosom. . . . In the Scene where the loan is agreed upon we have a fine illustration of the text; the Jew touches Antonio on the heart [!] and, seeing Antonio recoil from him [as well he might!], apologizes for his error by a bow. . . . The background of the Scene of Jessica's elopement is formed of Shylock's house at night, with a bridge over the canal which flows by it, and with a votive lamp to the Virgin on the wall. There a barcarolle is sung by some Venetians in a gondola, and a number of masqueraders rush merrily past. The noise having subsided, the curtain drops, to be raised a few moments afterwards—a pleasing innovation—to exhibit Shylock returning without any suspicion of Jessica's treachery to his plundered and deserted home . . . The Scene which follows . . . [shows] his reason seem[ing] to reel under the heavy blow it has received, and the brief allusion to his dead wife is full of pathos and tenderness.* The father is here more visible than the usurer.† . . . In the Duke's Court—a fine mediaeval chamber, with portraits of Venetian dignitaries of times gone by on the walls, and with a crowd of deeply-interested spectators, including Tubal and other Jews, at the back—he slowly and gravely comes in . . . He stands like a figure of Fate. . . . Nor is this superb calm less conspicuous when the cause turns against him. The scales drop from his hands, but that is all. . . . Eventually, crushed by the conditions on which his life is spared, he stalks with a heavy sigh from the Court, only stopping to cast a look of deep pity at the ribald youth [i.e., Gratiano] who is barking like a cur at his heels.

Now, all this, with the possible exception of the description of Gratiano, is sheer tommy-rot: the tragic pathos, the elaborate decor of Venice, the moving husband and father, etc. And, since in these superficial times when almost everyone is in haste to prove himself what is at the moment held to be markedly "liberal" without regard to the facts and at everyone else's expense, lest my preceding observations give such good folk the temptation to rush in and construe what I have said as having anti-Semitic "implications," allow me to state at once that I do not intend to discuss in this place at length and with all the proofs what my convictions are as to what Shakespeare meant Shylock to be. In 1962 I published a book in which I took 369

*The *entire* "brief allusion" to his wife, when Tubal tells Shylock that Jessica had given a ring for a monkey, is : "I had it of Leah when I was a bachelor. I would not have given it for a wilderness of monkeys." It is hard to see how any actor could make less than two lines in a five-act play stand out as "full of pathos and tenderness."

†The father who "is here more visible than the usurer" has just said—and with more meaning to the drama than actors of Irving's persuasion care to note: "A diamond gone, cost me two thousand ducats in Frankfort! *The curse never fell upon our nation till now; I never felt it till now . . . I would my daughter were dead at my foot, and the jewels in her ear! would she were hearsed at my foot, and the ducats in her coffin!*" (Italics mine.)

pages to go into that matter exhaustively, and I should need as much space to do it all over again. I, however, owe it to these good folk (and to myself) to declare this much:

1. When Heminge and Condell, good friends of Shakespeare and members of his company, published what they intended to be the complete works, they divided the plays into three groups: comedies, histories, and tragedies, and *The Merchant of Venice* was included, as it should be, not as a tragedy, but a comedy—a serious enough comedy, but a true comedy in the sense that it has, as a comedy must have, "a happy ending."

2. In that comedy Shylock, a man of considerable parts, is nevertheless the villain.

3. I do not believe that *The Merchant of Venice* was written to degrade the Jews—even though Jew-haters have seized upon Shylock *later* as though Shakespeare had so intended. That would be like blaming the horrifying acts of Christians upon Christ.

4. I do not believe that *The Merchant of Venice* was written in defense of Jews. I do not believe that Shylock's being a Jew is a main issue of the play.

5. I do not believe that Shakespeare has portrayed Shylock as a very good Jew, or as a representative of his people.

6. I do not believe that Shylock had any tenderness for his daughter or for anything else except his money.

7. I *do* believe that *The Merchant of Venice* is no more concerned with "the Jewish question" than *Othello* is concerned with "the Negro question," but that it is concerned primarily with two other important matters:

    a. Like *Measure for Measure* one of its chief issues is Mercy versus Justice-by-the-Letter-of-the-Law and

    b. The question about the future of money: Is money to be used to make life more beautiful by putting it to the use that is possible— i.e., spending it beautifully, as do Portia, Bassanio, and Antonio? Or is to become a rank poison that will constrict and make hateful the man to whom it becomes an end in itself and wishes only to accumulate it—like Shylock, a man equipped otherwise with qualities that might make up a human being of heroic mold?

I confess to holding one grudge against Irving. Everything we know about him shows that he was above all interested in being "original." It is a kind of outrage that he should have admitted as late as 1901 to J. H. Barnes, while he was still acting his pathetic-tragic Shylock, that he agreed that Shylock, as conceived by Shakespeare, "was not a man for whom we feel mostly sympathy because of his wrongs." This sort of "originality" which flies in the face of the creation itself in order to think up a "new interpretation," which began with Irving, has become the curse of several decades of the English and American theater. It makes the interpreter not the man or woman who is anxious to serve the creator's intentions (like great interpreters such as Toscanini and Arrau), but rather renders the creator as a kind of slave to the vanity of the director or actor. It has given us decades of revolting Shakespearean performances. Such "originality" does not illuminate the creation; it destroys it.

I object, too, to Irving's emphasis on lavish settings, which his contemporaries so much adored. More than anyone else it was he who helped transform Shakespearean productions into spectacles, suffocating the sublimities of dialogue and characterization by massed crowds and luxurious scenery. This tendency became worse and worse as the century advanced, but it is luckily one upon which the twentieth century eventually turned its back.

Why should Irving have transformed Shylock into a creature he apparently did not himself believe in? Barnes was of the opinion that to have played the role differently would have required "a greater amount of physical power" than the frail Irving possessed. In other words, some of Irving's "originality" was an attempt to compensate for his own physical lacks.

He was infinitely painstaking with his costumes. For example, a friend of his owned an old cardinal's robe of the precise hue Irving thought right for Wolsey. Irving borrowed it and sent it to Rome along with the robe he was to wear, with instructions that his robe be dyed the same color. However, that tint was no longer obtainable in Rome, so he was forced to try—and succeeded in—having the match made in London. His explanation was: "When you are getting into the skin of a character, you need not neglect his wardrobe." He never economized on his costumes. On his production of *Henry VIII* he spent £300,000, which in those days was a fantastic sum for a production. One of the deplorable results of this tendency was the distinction long made on Broadway between plays and "costume plays" (in which latter category Shakespeare's works were, of course, included). By definition an audience was to anticipate being interested not in the play itself, but in the pretty (or hideous) pictures the *mise-en-scène* would exhibit. Even today it has become traditional first to applaud the set when the curtain goes up; and everything gets applauded these days—bad settings, bad acting, bad singing, bad piano or violin playing, bad musical composing (for some reason everything connected with music now not only gets applauded but is hailed with shouts of *Bravo!*—even when the singer is female).

Irving's 1874 Hamlet ran for an unprecedented two hundred nights. In September 1875 he enacted Macbeth, which was given for eighty nights. His Thane of Cawdor was not the perennial robust soldier but a man of disordered nerves. Irving was accused of showing a hero without courage, another Mathias of *The Bells. Hamlet* was revived and then in February 1876 Irving took on *Othello*, which the great Italian actor Salvini had given in London only the year before. Irving's Moor was even more hotly attacked than his Macbeth; the comparison with Salvini was inevitable. "However sound may be Dogberry's opinion as to the unsavoury nature of comparisons, one in the present case is unavoidable," wrote a critic, "and we proceed to draw it in an impartial spirit. Signor Salvini's Othello, then, was a splendid example of the capabilities of histrionic art, but gave undue, at times offensive, prominence to the sensual side of the character. By reason of his majestic presence and the beauty of his voice, he seemed to have been expressly designed by nature to represent Othello. These physical advantages Mr. Irving does not possess, but he gains a point against the Italian tragedian by exhibiting Othello as an intellectual and romantic rather than a sensual personage, and, in the most trying scenes of the play, his acting could hardly be surpassed for depth and genuineness of feeling." But his Othello was never one of his most popular roles. Dutton Cook said of the 1876 performance that when Irving stood aghast at his murder of Desdemona, "as he folds round him his robe," he resembled "one of the late Mr. Fenimore Cooper's Mohawk braves draped in his blanket."

On January 29, 1877, Irving did Richard III at the Lyceum, but did not until the 1896 revival get rid of Cibber's version of the play. Again the spectacle was of primary importance. The opening scene was a street of old London "with many quaint buildings and the Tower in the background"; it was brilliantly lit as if by the sun of summer. The buildings represented were "gaily decorated." The air was filled with the "melodious clangor of many silver chimes." It "was received with acclamation by the public and press alike." The *Morning Post* called it "a fine performance, brilliant, energetic, impassioned and full of life and character." One of the most agreeable results of his personating Richard was that on the first night William Henry Chippendale (1801–1888), who had acted with Edmund Kean, presented him with the sword Kean had used in the role. Not long afterward he was given a particularly valuable ring by the Baroness Burdett-Coutts; it was a ring which had long been worn by Garrick, who on his deathbed bequeathed it to his butler; after passing through various hands Baroness Burdett-Coutts procured it in 1865. This memento bore the following inscription: "THIS RING ONCE MR. GARRICK'S is presented by the BARONESS BURDETT-COUTTS TO MR. HENRY IRVING in recognition of the gratification derived from his Shakespearian Representations, uniting . . . the charm of original thought, giving delineations of new forms of dramatic interest, power and beauty, JULY 1876." Understandably he became a friend of the baroness, and through her became a familiar in the Dickens circle.

Richard was one of Irving's favorite roles, and Shaw had his explanation for that. The play itself, said Shaw, is *Punch and Judy* at its best. "It has abundant devilry, humor, and character . . . Richard is the prince of Punches; he delights Man by provoking God, and dies unrepentant and game to the last. His incongruous conventional appendages, such as the Punch hump . . . [leave] nothing lacking to the fun of the entertainment . . . Punch . . . [as] Richard has always been a favorite part with Sir Henry Irving. The crafty mischievous, the sardonically impudent, tickle him immensely, besides providing him with a welcome relief from the gravity of his serious impersonations."

That Shaw was not exaggerating is made clear by Irving's devoted biographer, Brereton.

He recognized that the Richard of history and of Shakespeare is a man who dominates by the sheer force of his intellect. His misshapen body is compensated for by the alertness and penetration of his brain, and by the strength of will which enables him to stifle heart and conscience while he marches steadily, relentlessly, without fear or remorse, through a sea of crime to the throne, his innate cunning and deadly, biting humour becoming more emphasized . . . His best scenes . . . are those in which Richard woos Lady Anne . . . The malignant humour of Richard's opening soliloquy is one of Henry Irving's finest bits of acting, and the wooing scene is played by him so . . . plausible and finally convincing to Lady Anne, he makes the audience feel the cleverness, the trick, the scorn, the mockery, of the entire scene . . . The depth of Richard's cunning, his supreme contempt for the men around and beneath him, and, above all, his wicked, satisfied delight in gulling the easily-led fools, his fiendish glee at cheating them to his own purposes, and the splendid sarcasm of the actor—in face, voice, and gesture . . . will long be remembered.

After Richard came revivals of his non-Shakespearean successes—notably *The Bells.* By June 1875 Mr. Bateman had died, and the Lyceum had been under the management of his widow, who continued to retain her daughter Isabel as leading lady. Irving felt that it was high time that he had a company of his own choosing, and when he suggested leaving the Lyceum to Mrs. Bateman, she allowed him to take over the management in August 1878. He was then forty years old. Henceforth, until his retirement many years later, the name Lyceum would be synonymous with Irving and his productions.

While he toured during the autumn, the theater was altered for improvements.

With Bateman out of the picture Irving was no longer obliged to play opposite their ungifted daughter Isabel and she was free to leave the theater which she had never cared for. She followed her strongly religious cast of mind and eventually became a nun. Upon Irving's return to London one of his first moves was to engage Ellen Terry (1847–1928) as his leading lady.

Ellen Terry was born at Coventry, the daughter of minor actors. Her paternal grandfather, according to her, had been "an Irish builder," although authorities say he was an innkeeper at Portsmouth; her mother was the daughter of a Scottish minister, also of Portsmouth. Eleven children were the fruit of that marriage; two of them died in infancy. Ellen and three of her sisters, Kate, Marion, and Florence, and a brother, Fred, were trained by their parents for the theatrical profession. Ellen's first opportunity came at the age of nine when she was chosen by Mrs. Charles Kean out of a half dozen aspirants to play the part of Mamillius in *The Winter's Tale* at the Princess Theatre. The same year she was also Puck in the Charles Kean company and was described as "a downright intolerable, precocious, genuine English ill-bred, unchildlike child." Through the use of machinery, her

Puck grew "out of the ground on a toadstool," was made to disappear when necessary and flew through the air—wonderful effects in which Charles Kean specialized, After playing a fairy in a pantomime and various other children's roles, she did Fleance in *Macbeth* three years later.

During her childhood she was kept busy in the theater, and the career upon which her parents had been counting was proceeding very well. When sixteen she appeared at Bath as Titania; her costume was designed by a man who was to figure importantly in her life, Edward William Godwin, architect. That same year, 1863, she was at the Haymarket playing, among other roles. Desdemona, Hero, and Nerissa. But she was not happy in the theater, and shortly after Tom Taylor, the dramatist, introduced her to the painter, George Frederic Watts (1817–1904), who, bewitched by her beauty, married her in 1864. She was seventeen and he was some thirty-one years her senior, a recluse and a semi-invalid. It was her dream that she would be living "in Heaven" to dwell with Watt's pictures—forever, she thought; she pictured herself as serving as his model, cleaning his brushes, "and [playing] my idiotic piano to him"—a veritable Wonderland, she fancied his studio would be. He, however, had different views, and wrote that "to make the poor child what I wish her to be will take a long time, and most likely cost a great deal of trouble, and I shall want the sympathy of all my friends." She could find nothing to do for him but pose, and that she did until she fainted. Watts and his friends did, in fact, treat her as "the poor child," probably induced to do so by her irrepressible high spirits. When Tennyson visited she was not encouraged to talk with him but play with his children. When great or interesting people called, "I sat," she said, "shrinking and timid, in a corner —the girl-wife of a famous painter. I was, if I was anything at all, more of a curiosity, a side-show, than hostess to these distinguished visitors." Yet, she confessed that while she was with Watts, "I never had one single pang of regret for the theatre." Possibly she proved too much for Watts, and it seems most likely that for this very feminine young woman life with him was one of great frustration. At any rate, when the marriage "suddenly came to an end, I was thunderstruck." The separation was Watts's desire, and "the whole thing was managed by those kind friends whose chief business in life seems to be the care of others." The legal phrase given as the reason was "incompatibility of temper." As she said, it *"more* than covered the ground."

The marriage had lasted only a year. She returned briefly to the stage and it was during this period, in 1867, that she first acted with Irving in Garrick's version of *The Taming of the Shrew,* neither of them making a signal success of the venture. Irving found her charming, as everyone else always did, but saw in her only a frivolous girl who had married an elderly husband, had parted from him, returned to the stage for a year or two, and was about to leave it again to live (in sin) with an architect.

Still dissatisfied with acting, she took Edward William Godwin, the architect, as her lover and they went to live together in 1868. For six years she gave up the theater, and bore Godwin two children whom she adored: a daughter, Edith, and a son, Edward Gordon Craig, himself to become internationally famous as a theatrical designer. (If you read her autobiography,

The Story of My Life, you get the impression that Godwin was simply the man who designed her costumes, and that Edith and Edward must have been born without benefit of a male parent.)

The clichés of history are not always dependable. Not only did Ellen have these two children illegitimately, but it also seems beyond question that she later was physically intimate with Irving. It was the Victorian Age, notorious for its intolerance of any relationship less than the "respectable." Even a divorce was then considered a social stain. Yet no word of opprobrium was ever breathed against Ellen Terry's character. One friend testified that during a lifelong acquaintance, "I have never known a woman with a purer mind or a more stainless heart." Said another: "for unadulterated goodness" there was no one equal to her. And still a third: her character "would do credit to a saint." During the "wicked 1920s" such sexual attachments as she formed during her life would very likely have written *finis* to a theatrical career, as it did with several Hollywood stars. But throughout her lifetime Ellen Terry was the darling and the delight of her age. She herself insisted that if it be a characteristic of a true artist to give up everything for his art, then she could not honestly call herself an artist; she admitted to being first of all a woman, and declared that the greatest happiness proceeds from "absolute devotion to another human being."

For six years she had been lost to all her old admirers—in fact she had been so lost to the world that her father had been willing to identify the corpse of a suicide as that of his own daughter. Then one day Charles Reade, best known as a novelist, became the instrument to the beginnings of a glorious career. Let her tell the story:

> One day I was driving in a narrow lane [in Hertfordshire, where she, Godwin, and the children lived], when the wheel of the pony-cart came off. I was standing there, thinking what I should do next, when a whole crowd of horsemen in "pink" came leaping over the hedge into the lane. One of them stopped and asked if he could do anything. Then he looked hard at me and exclaimed: "Good God! it's Nelly!"
>
> The man was Charles Reade.
>
> "Where have you been all these years?" he asked.
>
> "I have been having a very happy time," I answered.
>
> "Well, you've had it long enough. Come back to the stage!"
>
> "No, never!"
>
> "You're a fool! You ought to come back."
>
> Suddenly I remembered the bailiff in the house a few miles away, and I said laughingly: "Well, perhaps I would think of it if some one would give me forty pounds a week!" [She had deliberately mentioned what she considered a preposterous sum just to put him off.]
>
> "Done!" said Charles Reade. "I'll give you that, and more, if you'll come and play Philippa Chester in *The Wandering Heir* [a play by Reade]."

It was a shock to her that he had agreed to the sum.

Since it seemed the only way of giving the bailiff his walking papers and of salvaging the few pieces of furniture that they still had, she unwillingly accepted. The whole Godwin ménage removed to London to settle in Bloomsbury.

But Godwin deserted her when she returned to the stage, leaving her with their two children to support. There can be no question that she had loved him dearly until the day he revealed himself for the egocentric creature he was. She was in the process of harnessing the pony to take Godwin to the station while she was pregnant with Edward. Godwin exclaimed: "Haven't you cost me enough money already, without obliging me to fetch a doctor for you?" She nearly left him then, for she no longer had any faith in him. However, their affair ended when he left her for another woman.

Her serious theatrical career began on April 17, 1875, when she appeared at the old Prince of Wales's Theatre as Portia in the Bancrofts' production of *The Merchant of Venice*. The undertaking was a failure for the Bancrofts— it ran only three weeks, but Ellen Terry's Portia became the talk of the town. She stayed with the Bancrofts another year, after which she joined John Hare at the Royal Court Theatre, where she won great acclaim in the title role of *Olivia*, a dramatization of *The Vicar of Wakefield*.

Irving had not yet seen her in the part, but Lady Pollock told him that in Ellen Terry he would find the leading lady he sought. He went to see her.

At last Watts agreed to divorce her. She had met him once after the separation in a street at Brighton, "and he told me that I had grown!" She was never to speak to him again. But once, years later, when she was famous, she was visiting at a house next to a new one he occupied; he saw her through the hedge. He thereupon wrote her a letter asking her to "shake hands with him in spirit." He said it was very important to him. "If you cannot, keep silence. If you can, one word, 'Yes,' will be enough." She answered only, "Yes."

While she was at the Royal Court Theatre she married Charles Wardell, a young officer of the 66th Regiment forced to retire because of wounds, who now acted under the name of Kelly. He had had no training, but his bluff manner occasionally stood him in good stead. They were married in November 1877—and were separated in 1881. Her reason for marrying was to give her "poor children" a father, and her brother has said that she put the names of the dozens of suitors who were after her (Forbes-Robertson included) into a hat and drew out Kelly's.

When she saw Irving in 1878 she found the actor to be quite different from the awkward young Petruchio she had known; she saw that in the intervening years he had lost "much of that stiff, ugly, self-consciousness which had encased him as the shell encases the lobster." His very forehead and features had altered. "He was a man of the world, whose strenuous fighting was to be done as a general." But his "manner was very quiet and gentle."

Although he was soon writing to his old headmaster that he had "engaged Ellen Terry—not a bad start—eh?" he had somehow not done more than hint to her that such was his purpose on taking over the management of the

Lyceum, so that she was forced to write him from Liverpool, where she was touring with her new husband, "I think I understand, you wd like me to be with you at the Lyceum next season and will you be good enough to understand that I on my part most earnestly desire to be with you. I hope we shall be able to arrange."

By mail it was satisfactorily arranged that she was to be given forty guineas a week plus "a half clear benefit." Up to the time she began to act at the Lyceum she had been under constant pressure to provide the necessities of life for her children, herself, and frequently her husband.

For the opening night of the Lyceum under his own management, December 30, 1878, Irving revived *Hamlet*, with Ellen Terry as Ophelia. It was enthusiastically applauded. Said the *Athenaeum:* "The chief grace in the new representation consisted in the delivery of the speeches to Ophelia in the third act." *The Saturday Review* welcomed Ellen to the first rank of actresses, praised her for her "power of conception . . . and execution so perfect that every word seems to be spoken, every gesture to be made, from the emotion of the moment." Her mad scene was described as wonderfully moving, and it was noted that in the scene during which Laertes takes leave of Polonius, she relieved its possible tedium "by exhibiting . . . the interest which a sister would naturally feel in her brother's prospects" while the old man was delivering his celebrated platitudes (not that *The Saturday Review* thought of them as that!). In the mad scene "instead of the incoherent outpouring of imbecile unconnected phrases which has too often passed for Shakespeare's representation of Ophelia's madness, Miss Terry shows us an intelligible, and . . . consistent state of dementia . . . Her power of facial expression, her action, and her intonation, combine to show us the origin in her disordered state of mind of each wild and whirling word she utters."

This was the beginning of a partnership between Terry and Irving that continued until 1896 and was still unbroken in 1902. Unquestionably an egoist, he nevertheless was too able a manager to deprive the Lyceum of her genius; he often gave a play for her sake rather than his own. Her admiration for him was boundless, though she was not blind to his failings, and her respect was endless. She went so far as to say that the improvement of his Hamlet over his earlier performance and its triumph when they both opened the Lyceum with the play was not owing to her Ophelia. "He was," she said, "always independent of the people with whom he acted." It was true enough that Irving remained to the end his own man.

In November 1879 he gave that unfortunately influential Shylock of which we have already spoken, a Shylock "which was considered by many Jewish writers as a vindication of their race." The eulogies he received in the press would fill a bulky volume. As for Ellen Terry's Portia, it remained her most celebrated role, and when she first gave it it came as a surprise. Earlier portrayals of Portia had emphasized her morals and her mind. Hazlitt, so often fine on Shakespeare's characters, had stigmatized this heroine as affected and pedantic. Ellen Terry's Portia for the first time emphasized her womanliness: it was all grace, sparkle, piquancy, ardor, sweetness and passion. Odell says she never has had a rival in that part.

This *Merchant of Venice* established an almost incredible record of running for two hundred fifty consecutive nights. Winter did make the objection that she "occasionally disfigured her performance of Portia by irrelevant and farcical interjections," but he ended by conceding that hers was "the most spontaneously feminine, completely symmetrical and absolutely enchanting embodiment of that part." In a lecture, the actress, instead of claiming (as, for instance, do Margaret Webster and innumerable directors and actresses) that Portia saves Antonio's life by a lightning flash of inspiration during the trial—a perfectly idiotic idea—said that Portia hit on a plan for saving him as soon as she learned of his trouble. But she added something else, which I find hard to accept, that she saved him by a quibble, a quibble being "not a man's idea" but "a woman's." Ellen Terry was clearly unfamiliar with the practices of barristers and attorneys, and could never have read Dickens's great novel, *Bleak House.*

Naturally, the difficult-to-please Shaw spoke of Ellen Terry's art in terms less than superlative.

Miss Terry, as we all know, went on the stage in her childhood, and not only "picked up" her profession, but was systematically taught it by Mrs. Charles Kean, with the result that to this day her business is always thoroughly well done, and her part gets over the footlights to the ends of the house without the loss of a syllable [more than can be said of many of her compatriots in London today] or the waste of a stroke. But if Mrs. Charles Kean qualified her to be the heroine of a play, Nature presently qualified her to be the heroine of a picture by making her grow up quite unlike anybody that had ever been seen on the earth before. I trust Nature has not broken the mould. . . . The great painters promptly pounced on her. . . . She added what she learned in the studio to what she had already learnt on the stage so successfully that when I first saw her in *Hamlet* it was exactly as if the powers of a beautiful picture of Ophelia had been extended to speaking and singing . . . When she came to the "touches of nature" . . . she seized on them with an enjoyment and a tender solicitude for them that shewed the born actress; but after each of them she dropped back into the pictorial . . . And here you have the whole secret of the Lyceum; a drama worn by age into great holes, and the holes filled up with the art of the picture gallery. . . .

The most advanced audiences today, taught by Wagner and Ibsen . . . cannot stand the drop back into decoration after the moment of earnest life . . . Even the second-class public, though it still likes plenty of pictorial beauty and distinction (meaning mostly expensiveness and gentility) in the setting. . . . nevertheless needs far more continuous drama to bind the whole together and compel sustained attention and interest. Consequently the woman who now comes on the stage with carefully cultivated qualifications as an artist's model . . . no longer finds herself fitting exactly into leading parts . . . and automatically driving the real actresses off the stage. Miss Ellen Terry innocently created a whole school of such pictorial leading ladies. They went to the Lyceum, where, not being skilled critics, they recognized the heroine's pictorial triumphs as art, whilst taking such occasional sallies of acting as the Shakespearean "touches of nature" admitted of as the spontaneous operation of Miss Terry's own charming individuality. I am not sure that I have not detected that simple-minded Terry theory in more critical quarters. The art, of course, lay on the side where it was least suspected. The nervous athleticism and trained expertness which have enabled Miss Terry, without the least appearance of violence to hold her audiences with an unfailing grip in a house which is no bandbox, and where really weak acting . . . drifts away under the stage door and leaves the audience coughing.

As a corollary to this criticism Shaw admitted that every famous man of the last quarter of the century was in love with her. At Dublin it was pronounced that criticism was nearly impossible because her "genius . . . transforms critics into lovers." When she was fifty, the eighteen-year-old Channing Pollock, future playwright, saw her Portia in one of the English provinces, and without a card spent one-twentieth of all the money he had for the flowers he sent her—and that night had twelve cents left for dinner. At the Lyceum itself the young Oscar Wilde wrote a sonnet to her Portia:

> *I marvel not Bassanio was so bold*
> *To peril all he had upon the lead*
> *Or that proud Aragon bent low his head*
> *Or that Morocco's fiery heart grew cold;*
> *For in that gorgeous dress of beaten gold*
> *Which is more golden than the golden sun,*
> *No woman Veronese looked upon*
> *Was half so fair as thou whom I behold.*
> *Yet fairer when with wisdom as your shield*
> *The sober-suited lawyer's gown you donned,*
> *And would not let the laws of Venice yield*
> *Antonio's heart to that accursèd Jew—*
> *O Portia! take my heart: it is thy due:*
> *I think I will not quarrel with the Bond.*

It is, of course, a wretched sonnet, but it is interesting as unintentionally bearing out Shaw's contention. The octave of the poem clearly implies that Bassanio, Aragon, and Morocco all fell in love with Portia's clothes—or at least, the better-than-a-Veronese picture she presented.

Clement Scott said that she was "a poem that lived and breathed," and brought into being "the girl heroines that we most adored in poetry and the fine arts generally."

Yet even Sir Johnston Forbes-Robertson, an erstwhile suitor, admitted that the everyday Londoner did not consider her beautiful and thought her voice "hoarse and broken, and her movements uncouth."

Shaw was right to this extent: she could work her effects up to a climax, but could not sustain them. She herself admitted as much: "On the stage, I can pass swiftly from one effect to another, but I cannot fix *one,* and dwell on it, with that superb concentration which seems to me the special attribute of the tragic actress." Her friends have testified that she was the same off stage, racing brilliantly from one subject or idea to another, without any necessary connection.

In May 1881 Irving played a series of twenty-two performances of *Othello,* in which, at his invitation, he and Edwin Booth alternated the roles of the Moor and Iago. Ellen Terry found Booth at rehearsals very gentle and considerate, as, for example, when he said to her: "I shall never make you black. When I take your hand I shall have a corner of my drapery in my hand —that will protect you." Acting with Irving was a revelation in two respects to Booth. First of all, he was unused to Shakespearean productions in which the leading actor or manager insisted on having even the most minor characters acted by men and women of real ability. This was one of Irving's great contributions to Shakespearean productions which—alas!—was already extinct by the twentieth century!* Secondly, in view of his own laissez faire attitude toward his own American companies he was naturally astonished at Irving's behaving as a good director should. "Mr. Irving," he observed, "is despotic on the stage. At rehearsal his will is absolute law, whether it concern the entry of a messenger with a letter, or the reading of a letter by Miss Terry. From first to last he rules the stage with a will of iron, but also with a patience that is marvelous. He sits among his players watching every movement, listening to every word, constantly stopping anyone—Miss Terry as well as the messenger—who does not do exactly right. He rises, explains the fault, and that part of the scene is immediately repeated . . . Over and over again the line is recited or a bit of action done, until all is perfect."

With Ellen Terry as Desdemona and Arthur Wing Pinero as the Roderigo, and Booth and Irving, mutually respecting each other, the cast was more than interesting, though, as we have seen, the time was one of the most distressing in Booth's life. While the critics considered both men better as Iago, the general verdict was that Booth's Othello was rather better than Irving's. Booth later said, "My engagement with Irving was one of the most agreeable that I have ever played. He is one of the most delightful men I have ever met; always obliging, and always kind in every possible way." Nevertheless, when he was playing the Moor Booth was probably the only actor to play opposite Irving at the Lyceum who failed to be overborne by Irving, despite the theatrics of his Iago. Irving gave his villain a veneer of gaiety to make him the more horrifying; he also would knock his hand

*Some years ago I told a prominent actor, a man with a strong virile personality, who had admired my book on *Hamlet,* that I thought him perfect for the prince as I conceive him. "I will *never* do Shakespeare!" he said to me fiercely. "I will never do him, much as I love him. Did you ever see a Shakespeare production which did not look as though it had been put on by a college sorority?"

against his breast to show how hard his heart was, would twist his thin mustache and play various stunts with his dagger. (Too many Iagos have since imitated that sort of thing.) Ellen Terry rejected the all-too-popular conception of Desdemona as "a ninny, a pathetic figure chiefly because she is half-baked"; she understood that Shakespeare had given his heroine a vein of strength, and so Ellen Terry portrayed her.

In March 1882 Irving revived *Romeo and Juliet*, bringing back into the text Romeo's callow infatuation for Rosaline. This was his most extravagant production to date, and it demonstrated his mastery in handling large crowds. However, he did not make a good Romeo; such romantic roles were not for him. But Ellen Terry made a fetching Juliet, full of charm and simple grace, as well as adding a delicately comic touch in the scene where the Nurse delays bringing the news about her forthcoming marriage with Romeo. With only a break for the summer, *Romeo and Juliet* ran for 161 performances—no doubt because of its spectacular production.

In January 1880 Irving extended invitations to some three hundred persons to a "Supper in the Theatre at Half past Eleven O'clock on the Evening of Saturday, February the Fourteenth, 1880, to commemorate the One Hundredth representation of *The Merchant of Venice*." There were many distinguished people at the supper and, says Laurence Irving, "the youngest but by no means the least conspicuous guest was an exquisite young graduate of Oxford who for the first time was shedding his effulgence on a London season—Oscar Wilde."

It would be absurd to attribute Irving's attempting Romeo or later Lear to a sonnet Oscar Wilde, not long down from Oxford, rather pompously addressed "To My Friend Henry Irving," who hardly knew the young man at the time. The verses were written apparently in 1881, the same year as the sonnet addressed to Ellen Terry, and while it is no better as a poem, it is more interesting because it affords a good idea of the kind of "fustian" to which Irving was addicted when he was not giving Shakespeare:

> *The silent room, the heavy creeping shade,*
> *The dead that travel fast, the opening door,*
> *The murdered brother rising through the floor,*
> *The ghost's white fingers on thy shoulders laid,*
> *And then the lonely duel in the glade,*
> *The broken swords, the stifled scream, the gore,*
> *Thy grand revengeful eyes when all is o'er,—*
> *These things are well enough,—but thou wert made*
> *For more august creation! frenzied Lear*
> *Should at thy bidding wander on the heath*
> *With the shrill fool to mock him, Romeo*
> *For thee should lure his love, and desperate fear*
> *Pluck Richard's recreant dagger from its sheath—*
> *Thou trumpet set for Shakespeare's lips to blow!*

The same year, 1881, on the opening night of the Booth-Irving *Othello*, the audience was entertained before the curtain rose "by the ubiquity of

Oscar Wilde who, combining elegance and agility, was seen now leaning languidly from a box, now chatting in the stalls, and a moment later figuring prominently in a box opposite to the first." Though Irving did not know Wilde very well, "his sons," says Laurence Irving, "delighted in his company and in his gentle wit." It was an odd coincidence that on the same day in 1895 that Wilde was convicted at the Old Bailey, his knighthood was announced. Irving had only contempt for those members of his profession who joined in the hue and cry against Wilde. Ellen Terry left a bouquet of flowers from herself and Irving with a message of sympathy at Wilde's home where, desolate, he awaited his second trial. When, two years later, Charles Ricketts went to meet Wilde on his release from Reading Gaol, among a few messages of words to bolster his courage was one from Irving.

After *Romeo and Juliet* came *Much Ado,* which was an immense success from its opening production in October 1882 until it was withdrawn for the summer in June 1883. "A series of harmonious pictures brought to the spectator the very atmosphere of Messina." The church scene had "massive pillars, decorated roof and costly altar." But it was the acting which enraptured the audience. Max Beerbohm was ecstatic: "There never has been, nor ever will be, so perfect a Beatrice as Miss Terry, and . . . Miss Terry never will be, nor ever has been more perfect than as Beatrice. Beatrice, in all her sunniness and jollity; a tease, a romp; a woman with something beyond her generous womanhood—some touch of fairydom in her—here is she incarnate and unrivalled." But he was less happy about Irving. "A pity that she has missed a Benedick to match her. Sir Henry Irving, as I remember him, was too sardonic, too spiritual, not human enough." One critic thought Irving's Benedick was too clownish.

But most criticism was as enthusiastic about him as about his Beatrice. Frederick Wedmore in *The Academy* for October 21, 1882, wrote that Irving had never "done anything more complete than his Benedick. He plays it with the keenest sense of enjoyment and appreciation, and with . . . authority of interpretation . . . The element of satire in the part . . . is much in his own humour. The chivalry of the character suits him, and so does the graciousness of the character, and so does its quiet and self-analytical wit. . . . If Beatrice 'speaks poniards,' this newest Benedick can look them. In a word MR IRVING was made for Benedick, or Benedick for MR IRVING. It is seldom that a success is so unmistakeable . . . Nearly all that MISS ELLEN TERRY can do quite perfectly she can do in Beatrice . . . Beatrice's seriousness is permitted to be half a jest. The sorrows she deals with are the sorrows of comedy. . . . At other times due leisure is allowed her to form a whimsical attachment, and to say defiant things brilliantly, and with the utmost good-nature. . . . Not one point of importance is lost by either of them."

The Saturday Review of the same date is no less rapturous. After paying tribute to the magnificence of the scenes and costumes and to the perfection with which, for a change, Hero, Claudio, Don Pedro, and Don John are performed, it goes on to speak of Ellen Terry's being "in the earlier scenes, the incarnation of light-hearted mirth, which is never heartless, and of gay coquetry, which never loses the charm of spontaneity. In the Cathedral scene she arrives at a pitch of emotion which is both tender and deep," and in her denunciation of Claudio "she attained a force that was perhaps not expected by some of her hearers." Irving's Benedick is "a singularly harmonious combination of the mixed qualities which go up to make the part. He is, before all things, well-bred and chivalrous; he is gay, with a fund of poetry beneath the gaiety. . . . His scenes of pure Comedy are given with infinite grace."

Shaw, with his public stance against romantic love, detested *Much Ado,* and the diatribe he wrote against it proves a total want of any sense of poetic spirit (strange in a man who loved music so much!)—a want which, in the long run, has already dated most of his plays. Of Beatrice he says, "In her character of professed wit she has only one subject which a really witty woman never jests about . . . Beatrice jests about it for the sake of indelicacy. There is only one thing worse than the Elizabethan 'merry gentleman,' and that is the Elizabethan 'merry lady.' . . . When a flower-girl tells a coster to hold his jaw, for nobody is listening to him, and he retorts, 'Oh, you're there, are you, my beauty?' they reproduce the wit of Beatrice and Benedick exactly. . . . When I tell you that Benedick and the coster are equally poor in thought, Beatrice and the flower-girl equally vulgar in repartee, you reply that I might as well tell you that a nightingale's love is no higher than a cat's. Which is exactly what I do tell you." I will never forgive Shaw for this obstinacy and perversity.

And yet Shaw had a long drawn-out Platonic love affair (the question raised in my mind has always been whether he was capable of any other kind) with Ellen Terry. They exchanged about two hundred fifty letters which read like the wild love letters of two adolescents. They began when he was forty-six and continued for two decades!

In October 1883 Irving's company set out for the United States for the first of eight tours he was to give there. This one lasted until March 1884 and in addition to New York included fifteen other cities. Public and press alike responded with the greatest possible enthusiasm. An example from *The Philadelphia Inquirer* of March 19, 1884, is characteristic: "In the church scene, MR IRVING made one of the happiest displays of his art. When Beatrice told him she loved him, his change from the mocking, railing Benedick to the jubilant, conquering lover, his quick, fervent seizing and clasping her in his arms . . . were all admirably done." In other portions of the play "there shone the strong light of intellectuality, . . . a wondrous courtesy and patience of voice and manner . . . As Beatrice, MISS TERRY was dazzling in the fascination of her manner, enchanting in her tenderness, full of admirable vivacity, never once playing the shrew, and though her words were sharp as steel, they seemed always sheathed in velvet and to convey the idea that she loved Benedick [bless her for being one of the few who have understood this!]; she softened the wordy blow she struck him and turned it to nought by the tender light of her eyes . . . Her eyes, full of all changing expressions, as the heart of Beatrice was full of varying emotions, never rose higher than Benedick's, her tone was ever sweet and low in all her banterings. . . . The entire impersonation was perfect in its grasp of the character, in its faultless execution, in its sweet and tender grace."

When I was a very young man I had as a good friend John Macy, the pioneer critic of American literature—a man of the rarest culture and most exquisite taste in books—and I shall never forget how he mimicked for us a curtain speech of Irving's. His voice had Irving's famous hoarse croak, and he held in his hand a crumpled handkerchief. "Ladies and gentlemen," Macy said, "I cannot thank my American audiences enough for their gracious appreciation of our efforts. I should like to announce that tomorrow night we present *The Merchant of Venice*. I—er—shall present Shylock of course, and Miss Terry will present Portia, and I—er—shall, that is to say, I—er—shall present Shylock. Thank you." And with a bow he swept out of the room. Agate, Irving's profoundest admirer, said that though he was the greatest actor he had ever seen, Irving had a "staccato, raven croak" of a voice and that his speech was "a mass of slurred consonants and unintelligible vowels"—though perhaps Agate was not thinking of Irving's Shakespeare. Ellen Terry remarked that in *Richard III* his voice was vocally unequal to the last act, but that he made up for it by looking "like a great famished wolf." O. Henry must have heard him on one of his American tours, for in a short story, "The Song and the Sergeant," he writes of a character, " 'Mr. Sergeant,' said he, out of his throat, like Actor Irving."

Some years later when *Much Ado* was once more revived, *The Saturday Review*'s enthusiastic criticism gives us a glimpse of a further refinement in the distortion of Shakespeare: Irving habitually thrust into his Shakespearean productions unnecessary business. Said the periodical: "How full of thought and appreciation all of MR IRVING's productions are, we see by comparing them with what is done at other houses. Where else should we have seen such a charming little episode as that of Beatrice catching sight of the pretty child in the masked dance scene [What was the pretty child doing there?], kissing him, and catching him up playfully in her arms?" The invention was harmless enough and not so superfluous as having Shylock return tragically to an empty house, but it is again the sort of Irving addition which established a new tradition for improving on Shakespeare the twentieth century has perpetuated with unwarranted interpolations which often kill the play. Thus, for instance, was Piscator's notion of beginning *King Lear* with a half-naked Cain and Abel struggling on a mound until Abel was killed. (Very subtle, eh?) Thus was a recent Stratford (Connecticut) *Merchant of Venice* made up of a cast in which most of Bassanio's friends were flagrantly homosexual and Antonio left heartbroken at the success of Bassanio's marriage to Portia. Thus was this same notion of the Antonio-Bassanio relationship carried to extremes at Lincoln Center in 1973, so that during the suspense of the trial scene Bassanio made such physical love to comfort Antonio that all that was lacking was a bed for them to complete the act. This search for novel ideas has been the curse of twentieth-century Shake-spearean productions, and it may all be said to have started with Irving, whose "originality" everyone (but Shaw) cherished.

At the Lyceum Irving produced *Twelfth Night* (1884), *Macbeth*—this time with Ellen Terry—(1888), *Henry VIII* (1892), *King Lear* (1892), *Cymbeline* (1896), *Coriolanus* (1901). His last performance at the Lyceum was on July 19, 1902, as Shylock, and in his last year of acting, 1905, he was content, besides playing his non-Shakespearean dramas, to limit himself to *The Merchant of Venice.*

He felt that Macbeth "was a poet with his brain and a villain with his heart," and he called him a "hypocrite, traitor and regicide" (the last-named epithet is hardly a discovery!) who concealed his crimes with the glamour of poetic thought—which is to say that Macbeth's sufferings had nothing to do with his conscience, and without Macbeth's conscience it is fair to say that the play degenerates into melodrama. Fanny Kemble was certainly closer to the fact when she said that Macbeth's "soul writhes and cries and groans over its own deterioration." Irving's Macbeth suffered, too, because his figure was insufficiently robust to be convincing. (For that matter, remem-bering that the roles were originally written for Burbage, Irving's figure was insufficiently robust for Hamlet, Shylock, Brutus, Othello, or Coriolanus.)

Twelfth Night was not a success; it was too rollicking, with an excess of animal spirits; and again (as with Shylock) Irving created too much sympathy for Malvolio (certainly against Shakespeare's intentions), approaching tragedy too closely for the health of the play. Ellen Terry's Viola, however, was tender, graceful, very light in humor, and "consistently picturesque." But she became ill shortly after the opening, and her place was taken (less satisfactorily) by her sister Marion.

As Lady Macbeth her impersonation was that of an affectionate, if deter-mined, woman, who believes that encouraging her husband in his ambition will bring him peace. *The Daily Chronicle* said that she had never acted with more intensity, and her Lady Macbeth "has no outward resemblance to any other character she has played." The high point of her performance was the scene in which she realizes the futility of all they have done ("Nought's had, all's spent . . .), and her surrender to despair makes itself deeply felt. Oddly enough, it was in this role that Sargent chose to paint her.

King Lear, says Brereton, perhaps in extenuation of his hero's shortcom-ings, "can never be popular." He might have said, with more propriety, that the title role is assuredly the most difficult male part Shakespeare ever created: it begins *fortissimo* and the actor must go on from there. Very few (Garrick, whose Lear was considered his greatest interpretation, was a nota-ble exception) have been equal to it. Shaw had a point when he said that because "Irving tried to interpolate a most singular and fantastic notion of an old man between the lines of a fearfully mutilated version of King Lear, he was smashed." Of course, as spectacle *King Lear* was not wanting. Said the London *Times*: "The new Lear . . . appears in rich, flowing robes which might have graced a Roman emperor . . . The storm which rages at the

Lyceum" is a veritable storm, the desolate heath being swept "by furious blasts and beating rain and illumined by coruscating lightning as dazzling in its brilliancy as the rolling thunder that accompanies it is terrifying."

Max Beerbohm, who revered Irving, considered Coriolanus a role which Irving should never have attempted, not so much because of his age and the limitations of his voice, but because, as usual, he made of the Roman hero an intellectual. "As a schemer (in the large sense of the word) Sir Henry . . . is seen at his best. As a passive, stubborn monster, with the strength and insentience of a rock, he is seen at his very worst; indeed *he* is not seen at all." As Volumnia Ellen Terry "was not less disastrously wasted . . . She is always, whatever she do, the merry, bonny, English creature . . . always reminds me of a Christmas-tree decorated by a Pre-Raphaelite. To see her thus when she ought to have been a typical Roman matron, was rather more than I could bear."

It was in April 1889 at a command performance at Sandringham that Queen Victoria saw Irving and Ellen Terry for the first time; the program consisted of *The Bells* and the trial scene from *The Merchant of Venice*. He had already been approached on the subject of a knighthood but had rejected it. However, he changed his mind and in 1895 he became Sir Henry Irving, the first actor to be knighted for his services to the profession. (Naturally, the wife he had not seen all these years, and whose unwillingness to divorce him forced him into only he knew what compromises, automatically became Lady Irving.) His elevation to knighthood was perhaps less important to him than to all the members of the theatrical world, for it suddenly made them eligible as human beings whose respectability was as great as anyone else's. As we know, many actors since Irving have been knighted.

To estimate objectively his influence on his contemporaries as a producer and actor it is necessary to remember that although he came to look on Shakespeare as his particular property, he actually acted in many more non-Shakespearean plays. Most of these were trash. But it is also fair to observe that such has been the practice of a number of great actors— Garrick, for one; and the great Sarah Bernhardt and the equally great Eleanora Duse almost seemed to prefer to act in inferior plays, their point of view apparently being that what they wanted above all else was a "vehicle."

Irving had been ill for some time, and on October 13, 1905, he played *Becket* at Bradford, and when he returned to his hotel he collapsed and died. He was sixty-seven. After cremation, his ashes were buried in Westminster Abbey.

Ellen Terry, at the end of Irving's seventh American tour in 1902, left Irving's company, though she appeared with him a few times at the Lyceum and elsewhere.

She had intermittently acted with other companies. In April 1902, for instance, she went to Stratford-on-Avon to do Queen Katharine with Frank Benson's company. In June of the same year she was very successful as Mrs. Page in Herbert Beerbohm Tree's *The Merry Wives of Windsor*. In 1903 she even went into management, taking the Imperial Theatre to produce Ibsen's *The Vikings at Helgeland*, staged by her son Gordon Craig, and his first large-scale piece of work. It was a *succès d'estime* but the cost had been heavy, the public proved only mildly interested, and the play was withdrawn. After her last performance as Portia with Irving in 1903, she began to appear in prose drama, taking the lead in plays by Barrie and Shaw. In September 1906 she appeared as Hermione in *The Winter's Tale* at His Majesty's Theatre. In March 1907 she was married legally for the third time to James Usselmann, a young American, who was acting in her company under the name of James Carew; she lived with him until 1910.

She continued to act, though her memory and her eyesight were both failing her. In 1925 she became Dame Ellen Terry, and she died on July 21, 1928, at her house in Kent. Her remains, too, were cremated, and her ashes were placed in a casket on the wall of St. Paul's Church, Covent Garden. Her little house at Small Hythe, Kent, was converted by public subscription into an Ellen Terry museum.

John Gielgud, whose mother was the daughter of Ellen's elder sister Kate, did not see much of Ellen Terry when a boy because Ellen was rather unwelcome at his parents' on account of having borne two illegitimate children; but he remembers her distinctly as a "charming, vague, benevolent old lady, always fumbling in an enormous bag for things she couldn't find."

Irving's two sons, Henry Brodribb Irving (1870–1919) and Laurence (1872–1900, born after Irving had parted from his wife) both went on the stage. While anxious to help Henry, Irving did what he could to discourage him and wrote seriously of the necessity of learning the rudiments of his profession. "Supposing, now, you were at the Lyceum, and I anxious to push you on. What could I do? How could you begin? By playing a small part in London—a bad beginning. You must learn the A.B.C. of your work first. . . . And I am obliged to tell you this—and also I am sorry—that my name will be a hindrance to you and not a help . . . Nothing can help you but your own, your talent, perseverance and conduct in life."

In 1903, when Henry was thirty-one, he had the chance to act with his father at Drury Lane in the role of Salerio. In 1905 he was playing Hamlet at the Adelphi, and his father saw him in it, and was not pleased with what he saw. "Harry," as his family called him, thereafter wisely avoided Shakespeare, and appeared in contemporary plays and pot-boilers. He first made a name for himself as a polished villain, but was a sensation when Frohman engaged him to play the title role in Barrie's *The Admirable Crichton*, which ran for three hundred nights. Irving said of it, "Barrie—M'yes—charming piece, fantastic comedy," and then added, after a pause, "Do you—er—*like* acting, me boy?"

Of the acting of Laurence Irving, James Agate said, when he saw him as Hamlet, "superficially intolerable," for there was no poetry, no philosophy, no pathos, and, moreover, Laurence's voice was uncontrolled. He also botched his lines. But it was a great Hamlet because "the inner fires of imagination" showed he had something of his father in him. Crosse reports that his Iago was brilliant because the villainy was never obvious. In 1898 he became engaged to Ethel Barrymore. He is his father's most important and, all things considered, impartial biographer.

20

Foreign Actors Play for English-Speaking Audiences

During the nineteenth century a number of actors and actresses from the Continent came to England and the United States to perform Shakespeare. Some are particularly interesting.

Bogumil Dawison (1818–1872), a tall, slender man with a leonine head, came to the United States and delivered his lines exclusively in German. His voice was sweet (certainly an advantage when German is the language you are speaking!) but not very strong. He was one of the best tragedians in Germany. He did Hamlet on December 10, 1866, and played the prince with no fire or inspiration, made of him a sentimental yet robust enough character. The chief weakness was perhaps an excess of stage business; his Hamlet seemed incapable either of grief or introspection.

A little over two weeks later he was playing Othello to Edwin Booth's Iago at the Winter Garden; he spoke in German, Booth in English, and the Desdemona, Mme. Schiller, in German to Othello and in English to the rest of the cast. This was the first of the polyglot Shakespearean performances during the century, but unhappily not the last. The experience of the audience could not have been enviable.

I should like to introduce a few words here on the translation of Shakespeare. It ought to be no news that the greater the poet, the more impossible the task of rendering him in another language. What should be expected, then, of translations of the world's greatest poet? The mystery, therefore, is: How does it happen that Shakespeare is well known all over the world, loved and read by people with very little education in the versions made in their own tongue? I have studied carefully many translations in German, French, and Italian, and have been simply horrified at how the beauty and magnificence of sound, image and thought have been either totally lost or else transmogrified. It must be that the masterful handling of plot, the incomparable comprehension of the human condition and of human psychology are enough for the non-English-speaking world. One-half of

Shakespeare, his uniqueness, his greatness as a poet, is lost in translation. In French some of his most sublime passages sound to me like French pastry; in German like so many loaves of substantial bread baking in an oven; and in Italian like those saccharine Neapolitan songs which are sung nightly on the Grand Canal in Venice and which give the tourist the illusion that he is hearing old Venetian music.

So far as the English-speaking audiences go, to account for their tolerance of these polyglot monstrosities, we must remember that in the nineteenth century bad taste was rampant, especially in the United States. As late as 1911, the famous critic Winter could say of *Othello* that the last parts of the tragedy contain "such foulness and such excess of agony" that those passages are, quite justifiably, usually omitted. "Many lines of *Othello* must, indeed, be discarded that it may be made endurable, not to say decent, in a public representation, and . . . the community, perhaps, would not suffer an irreparable loss if it were altogether relegated from the stage to the library." (!)

Adelaide Ristori (1822–1906), a celebrated Italian tragedienne, was the daughter of actors, and was already a success as a child. At eighteen she became famous as Mary Stuart in Schiller's tragedy. In 1855 she appeared in Paris, and soon threatened the preeminence of the famous Rachel (1821–1858). She went to London, where she made her debut at the Lyceum in 1856 as Medea in the play by Scribe and Legouvé; she was so much admired that she appeared there in other plays, all Italian, that year and the following. The one Shakespearean role in which she made a great impression was as Lady Macbeth, at the Lyceum in Italian in July 1857. Her performance was so powerful that she made the Thane of Cawdor's wife "the entire play," said Henry Morley. But as Odell amusingly reflects, "Who cares when it is a matter of subordinating Duncano, Re di Scozia, and Macbetto?" The Macbeth, Vitaliani, allowed her to dominate him throughout, and after the sleepwalking scene and the announcement to Macbeth of his wife's death, "short work is made" of the rest of the play, "which is condensed into a single page." One of her innovations was at the end of the banquet scene, to take off her now too heavy to bear crown and throw it on the table; then, as if to find some relief from her mental and physical exhaustion, she took up the goblet, "and drank, and drank, and drank." She seems to have adopted Sarah Siddons's absurd conviction (which Ristori probably had no way of knowing) that Lady Macbeth also sees Banquo's ghost. She made her as ambitious as her husband, and equally desirous to share the throne. Nevertheless, despite all these errors, it was said that she provided "one of the great pictures of the contemporary stage."

After leaving London she made a tour of the world, and returned to London twenty-five years later to play Lady Macbeth in English, which she had learned especially so she could deliver the lines in their original language. During her final American tour in 1885 (she had performed there in Italian in 1866) she played Lady Macbeth opposite Edwin Booth.

In her memoirs, Ristori wrote that a close study of Lady Macbeth's character had convinced her that "affection for her husband was the last factor actuating her deeds . . . Knowing his inferiority of mind, his weak nature . . . she used her affection for him as a means to satisfy her [own] ambition." In the third act, "I did not allow to pass unobserved the entrance of the hired assassin" to tell Macbeth of Banquo's murder and Fleance's escape. . . . "At the end of the act, at the moment of leaving, I make it apparent that I am penetrated with a deep sense of pity for Macbeth who *for my sake* [italics mine] has become the most miserable of men."

One gathers that she must have given an overwhelming performance, but it was not Shakespeare's Lady Macbeth. It would be hard to have more incorrect ideas than she nurtured about the play.

The attentive student of literature must be well aware that no word has had more varying and opposing connotations than the word *nature*. It is clear that when Edmund cries, "Thou, Nature, art my goddess," he is not addressing the divinity whom Rousseau worshipped, or that when Addison praises an object for its truthfullness to nature ("like the ancients"), he did not have in mind the qualities which Wordsworth would have entertained had he used the expression. It would have struck no one as odd in the eighteenth century that a woman wearing a white wig a foot high, with beauty patches on her face, a dress whose stiff armature gave her skirt an enormous circumference which completely concealed the outlines of the human form, and whose practice had made her perfect in the exquisite use of a fan—it would have struck no one, I say, as odd to hear that woman being praised for her "naturalness." Even today we are being asked to accept the uniform of a goodly part of the younger (and older!) generation, a uniform which includes dirty hair, dirty clothes, dirty shoes, and dirty face (as much of it as can be seen through the men's growth of hair on lip and around the face) as being right because it is not "artificial" in the way of the despised Establishment, and is therefore "natural." We have seen that periodically since Shakespeare's time actors have been praised for their "natural" style, even though it is obvious to us that that "natural" style was either declamatory or made up of all sorts of stagey tricks.

One is therefore a little cautious in accepting the verdict that Charles Albert Fechter (1824–1879) should be credited with pushing the art of acting further toward the realistic—i.e., natural—than any of his predecessors. Born of French parents, he started out in Paris as a sculptor, but in 1846 went on the stage there, and was soon a success. He was tall, handsome, and had an uncontrollable temper. In 1852 he had advanced so far that he was cast as the first Armand in *La Dame aux Camélias*. He went to London, and in November 1860 appeared at the Princess Theatre in *Ruy Blas*, the blood-chilling *The Corsican Brothers*, and other plays. Then, unexpectedly he suddenly played Hamlet in March 1861, speaking what he would have called the English language. His broken accent caused much adverse comment; he was the first actor to play the part in a fair wig ("a cross between golden and ginger"). At first his prince was clean-shaven, but in later revivals he wore a small beard and moustache. Winter says his pronunciation of English was "execrable," and that he delivered the "To be or not to be" soliloquy so rapidly that the audience was made to feel it ought to be omitted altogether from the text, as slowing the action too much. Indeed, he normally spoke everything as French actors still do in modern plays, with great rapidity. Ellen Terry meditated on the fact: "English cannot be phrased as rapidly as the French. But I have heard foreign actors, playing in the English tongue, show us this rapidity, this warmth, this fury—call it what you will—and have just wondered why we are, most of us, so deficient in it. Fechter had it, so had Edwin Forrest. When strongly moved, their passions and their fervour made them swift. The more Henry Irving felt, the more deliberate he became. I said to him once, 'You seem to be hampered in the vehemence of passion.' 'I *am*,' he answered. This is what crippled his Othello."

Winter also considered Fechter's blank verse abominable, and his Hamlet gross, unattractive, an impetuous, tearful, explosive Frenchman. His eyelids were reddened as though from constant weeping. His delivery, even with the Ghost, was colloquial. The description, at least, fortifies the notion that Fechter was struggling for a realistic approach to the role.

Despite all the criticism of his pronunciation and manner his Hamlet was the rage of London at the time. The very controversy kept the houses filled for five months nightly. His triumph was attributed by Dickens, Clement Scott, and Justin McCarthy to the unconventionality of his performance, because he had broken with all the old traditions of "measured stride and measured pause . . . the statuesque attitudes of portentous . . . melancholy." What Fechter really did was to convert *Hamlet* into the "gentlemanly melodrama" then very much in style, and add the ingredient of his realistic acting. The public agreed that Fechter's Hamlet proved that the realism of French melodrama, which had been thought "vulgar, degenerate, and un-English," was in fact exactly what "English literary drama most needed."

Before the Batemans had taken over the Lyceum or Irving had acted there, Fechter managed the theater from 1863 until 1867, featuring a number of melodramas. In 1869 he went to the United States and opened the old Globe Theater as Fechter's Theater.

After Hamlet he tried Othello (1861) with no success whatever. Lewes, who had been loud in his praise of the Hamlet, said that the Othello was one of the worst ever seen. Fechter then tried Iago, but the production was quickly withdrawn. As Othello, Lewes said, Fechter's naturalism, largely the product of his personality, emerged as mere feebleness; his sinking into "the *familiar*" only vulgarized the Moor, and in his eagerness to use a great many small details of "business" Fechter "entirely fritted away the great effects of the drama." Instead of an heroic, impassioned Moor, he gave the audience "an excitable creole of our own day." Lewes had had time to think the matter over, and with considerable insight remarked that an effort to achieve realism can work like a poison. "It is not consistent with the nature of tragedy to obtrude the details of daily life. All the lounging on tables and lolling against chairs," which give a sense of everyday realism are "unnatural in tragedy." And when on the stage Fechter takes out his door key to let himself into his house, and on going out again relocks the door, "the *intention* is doubtless to give an air of reality; the *effect* is to make us forget the 'noble Moor' and to think of a sepoy." When he leans on the shoulder of Iago [as later did Robeson on the shoulder of.Ferrer] . . . and when he employs that favorite gesticulation which reminds us but too forcibly of a *gamin* threatening to throw a stone, he is certainly *natural*—but according to whose nature?" George Eliot thought his Othello "lamentably bad . . . positively demoralizing."

Ernesto Fortunato Giovanni Rossi (1829–1890) was the first Italian actor to play Othello, following it with Hamlet and other Shakespearean roles, always in Italian. He traveled through a great deal of Europe, playing the tragedies of Alfieri and Shakespeare. His great contemporary Salvini praised him for his fine intellect and untiring study which enabled him to perform his parts so that they had the polish of a diamond. But Salvini deplored the fact that too often audiences lost touch with the character being portrayed and were only aware of Rossi's study of his inflections and design of his motions.

He was born in Livorno, and left school to become a strolling player. In 1852 he joined Ristori's Royal Sardinian Company and went with them to Paris. Five years later he was in Vienna with his own troupe, and was taking on the roles of Richard III, Othello, Hamlet, Shylock, Coriolanus, Macbeth, and Lear, and was acclaimed in many European countries. When the King of Holland heard him recite Dante in his melodious but unflexible voice, he paid him the compliment of offering him his throne on the grounds that the throne of the Netherlands was of a small kingdom, while Rossi was the "Emperor of all hearts." He eventually came to the United States, to the public's displeasure. In London (1876) opinion was more divided. A Parisian critic wrote of his last scene in *King Lear* that when he was sobbing out his life over the dead Cordelia, the audience, most of whom understood not a word of Italian, wept floods of tears, and it was almost a relief to them when Lear himself died and the curtain fell. His death was "thrillingly natural." Stanislavski saw him when he was creating a furor in Russia (1877/78) and thought Romeo one of his best roles; "In lyric passages" and the love scenes he found him "inimitable."

But the American audience in the nineteenth century could not stomach his Othello—and, one feels, with reason. Winter said his Moor was a common man, "infuriated by demoniac jealousy." Rossi was large, stout, and moon-faced; he was authoritative enough, and lacked no animation, until in Act I he suddenly turned operatic, with his face full front to the audience and his back to the senators he was supposedly addressing. His conduct with Desdemona throughout most of the play was far too sensual, and his Othello had no dignity. Like Salvini he raised his foot over Iago's head as if to stamp out his brains; his killing of Desdemona was far too brutal. When he committed suicide, he emitted "spasmodic gurgling sounds" (the new realism!) as though he were being choked by blood. Henry James was sickened at this "bestial fury" and his bellowing "in his pain." But Charlotte Cushman, as one might have expected, admired his Hamlet as the best she had seen in a foreign language.

Rossi left his views on the art of interpretation. He began by distinguishing the artist from the mere actor. The true artist, he said, must have personal beauty and dignity, perfect diction and pronunciation (this would have disqualified most of the great actors of whom we have already taken notice), be the possessor of a wide education and knowledgeable in history, be perfect in his native tongue, have a large acquaintance with literature, especially that of the theater, an ear for the melody of verse, and a well-developed sense of the aesthetic. (I can think of no great actor who could have met all of these "requirements.")

What he says next, however, shows greater insight than any other theoretician on record. An artist, he says, is one who, above all, must be able to take possession "bodily, physically and morally" of the character he is portraying; he must make the thoughts, feelings, virtues, and shortcomings of that character his own while he is portraying him; he must make that character come to the life as the dramatist intended him to. He must obliterate his own personality absolutely, just as the greatest dramatists have obliterated their own characters in creating their plays. Only the actor who can do this merits the title of artist.

That much is so good that it ought to be the credo of every actor, even though Rossi did not impress American audiences as meeting his own qualifications for the histrionic art. He played King Lear at Her Majesty's Theatre in June 1882. Again he spoke Italian while his supporting company used English. On one evening during this engagement he played the first three acts in Italian and the last two in a wretchedly broken English. The results were so appalling that when he shortly left the country, the *Athenaeum* remarked: "Signor Rossi quits our stage with a promise to return when he is able to act in English. For the performance of that promise we shall wait with resignation."

The male foreigner who made the greatest impact upon the English-speaking world with his Italian performances of Shakespeare was Tommaso Salvini (1829–1915). He was born in Milan, it is always said, of actor parents. But he himself tells us that while his mother was indeed an actress, his father was a professor of literature. At fourteen he was already performing in the comedies of Goldoni, and by 1847 he was a leading member of Ristori's Royal Sardinian Company. In 1849 he temporarily left the stage to enlist as a soldier in the war for Italian independence, and became a friend of Mazzini and Garibaldi. In Florence he devoted himself to the classics and prepared himself for various roles, including Othello and Hamlet, before resuming his career as actor. His theatrical career was a continual series of triumphs. He first played Othello in 1856, and although this remained his most celebrated role, he was also frequently seen as Hamlet, Macbeth, Coriolanus, and Lear. His appearances in England were frequent, and he was five times in the United States; on the fourth of these tours he did Othello to Edwin Booth's Iago.

He first appeared in New York on September 16, 1873, as Othello, at the Academy of Music. Winter, conceding that when he acted Italian drama he was without peer, labelled his Othello as "radically and ruinously false in ideal." (One should remember that to Winter there was no one equal to Edwin Booth.) Salvini made the mistake, according to Winter, of showing his jealousy far too early in the play—when Brabantio warns Othello, "She has deceived her father and may thee, " and demonstrated his jealousy with a tigerish glare. I have seen *most* Othellos in my lifetime make a similar mistake, entering upon the third scene of the third act already suffocating from jealousy of Cassio *before* Iago has even begun to poison his mind. If Othello were by nature a jealous man, there would be no tragedy at all.

Winter further objected that the performance was "all prose." If true, that would have been a most serious flaw, for Shakespeare has given none of his heroes more exquisite poetry to deliver. Winter describes Salvini as rushing in to beat down the naked swords of the night brawlers *with his own hands,* and, when dismissing Cassio, shaking his fist in Cassio's face. (That would surely belie Othello's love for Cassio as well as his sorrow at having to demote him.) Winter said that as the drama proceeded, the Moor became less and less noble. After his "Farewell" speech, he hurled Iago to the floor and lifted his right foot to step on his head (as Rossi had done). He was an "incarnation of animal fury, huge, wild, dangerous, and horrible, but he was consistently common and bestial." In the last scene of the play he prowled to and fro like "an enraged tiger." Desdemona tried to escape from him: he dragged her to the bed and killed her there "in the most extreme violence of snorting fury." When he struck at Iago, the thrust was enough to have killed the villain instantly. The whole conception, Winter insisted, was wrong, for he was all sensuality with no mitigating admixture of spirituality. If Winter's account was truthful, Salvini was assuredly not Shakespeare's Othello.

Yet he was praised for his performances of the role throughout Europe and America. Henry James considered him the perfect Moor, and said that he won your sympathy from the moment he came upon the stage. James was aware that others had called Salvini's Othello an Italian bandit and butcher, but he countered that nothing could be more convincing, "more tragic, more suggestive of a tortured soul and of a generous" beneficent strength "changed to a purpose of destruction . . . It is magnificently quiet, and from the beginning to the end has not a touch of rant or crudity." James further wrote: "It may seem to many observers that Salvini's rendering of the part is too simple, too much on two or three notes—frank tenderness, quick suspicion, passionate rage. . . . I have heard this performance called ugly, repulsive, bestial. . . . What an immense impression—simply as an impression—the actor makes upon the spectator who sees him for the first time as the turbaned and deep-voiced Moor!"

Salvini's delicacy in the earlier scenes with Desdemona was described by E. T. Mason as having "exquisite high-comedy effects," and in them the actor "gives more of the essential spirit of high comedy than could be found in the Mercutio of some noted actors." (If Salvini did find elements of comedy in the earlier scenes—especially with Brabantio—then he was perceptive to a rare degree, for they are there, though very much understated, and I have never seen an actor who was aware of them. But "high comedy"? That is going too far.)

Other critics found his love scenes in bad taste and out of keeping with "the chastity of the hero's love."

James Agate, on the other hand, agreed with James. He never saw a finer performance of Othello (April 26, 1875) and found Salvini easy and graceful in movement, his voice full, rich, and melodious. He thought him calm until passion was required of the role, and then he was terrifying. His face was very flexible in showing passing emotions, and most expressive of all were his eyes. He was as great in portraying love as hate. The early scenes were charming, the later ones horrifying. Agate's summary: "A great artist."

Daniel Frohman considered him the "greatest foreign artist" to visit the United States. He made of his art "a religion." He never undertook to play a role until he had studied it for years. Frohman says he refused to play Lear until he had pondered and worked over it "for a decade." On the evening of any performance he would go to his dressing room at five o'clock so that he might have hours to prepare. For lighting he preferred candles since their illumination was more natural than the pale effect of gas. Step by step, as he made up, "he hypnotized himself" into the role he was to personate. His incarnation of Othello was so complete, says Frohman, and he himself was so racked by hatred and jealousy during the performance, that his nervous system was severely taxed by each performance. For that reason, he required intervals during his enactment of that part.

Salvini, Frohman said, "could do as much with his eyes as with his lips, and would stand for what seemed like endless periods of time in silence "while he looked the whole gamut of emotions—hatred, contempt, humor."

He toured Italy, Spain, Portugal, and South America. Everywhere he went he was decorated. King Victor Emmanuel gave him a ring from his own finger. At Montevideo Salvini lost the ring, and by popular subscription the citizens had one just like it made for him.

He came to the United States in 1873 during a season of commercial depression, but he was well received—so well, that he decided on a second American tour, which, despite the inferiority of his English-speaking support, caused a furor. In between these two visits he had acted in England, Scotland, Ireland, Germany, Austria, and Hungary with unvarying success.

Winter found his Hamlet powerful, dominant, and a man of action, robust and master of every situation—exactly opposite to the Hamlet Shakespeare had created, Winter thought. But Salvini was right and Winter (whose *beau idéal* was Booth's Hamlet) was entirely wrong. The one exception I must take to Salvini's Hamlet, as reported by Winter, is that his prince was not haunted by sorrow or stricken with shock. That, of course, is at variance with the very basis of the play. Salvini, as Hamlet, was Italian enough to attempt, as he was dying, drawing Horatio's head close to his own as if to kiss him —but he lacked the strength to do it.

His Macbeth had very long red hair, with a thick tangled beard that almost hid his face. His huge frame was massively armed; he was a barbaric chief living among barbarians. He was marvelous at such moments as "Methought I heard a voice cry, 'Sleep no more!' " His attitude toward Lady Macbeth was domestic and colloquial. At the end of the cauldron scene he fell into a swoon, headlong, while the witches reappeared and hovered over him with hideous gestures.

In 1875 while in England Salvini married an Englishwoman. He loved her dearly, and it was a great personal tragedy when she died three years later. He said, "With her the large part of my inspiration has vanished. I fear I must now always remain . . . without the hope of improving in my art."

In private life he was a genial and affable man, magnificent to behold, majestic, and of easy grace. Emma Lazarus said, "Criticism of Salvini is an impossibility . . . His genius is so transcendent, his art so perfect."

One objection I should register to his handling of the text of Othello is that he entirely omitted the Moor's eavesdropping while Cassio holds Desdemona's handkerchief. He thought it too crude. But that scene is the turning point of the play, for although Othello has already determined to have Cassio put to death, it is the sight of Othello's gift to his wife being thrown back at Cassio by a whore, which convinces him that Desdemona must die too.

Coquelin (1841–1909), the great French actor, once said concerning the art of acting: "The actor must carry self-restraint so far that where the creature he simulates would burn, he must be cold as ice." This is another way of phrasing Hamlet's advice to the players: "In the very torrent, tempest, and—as I may say—whirlwind of passion, you must acquire and beget a temperance, that may give it smoothness." This is counsel which all interpreters, whether on the stage or in the concert hall, would be wise never to forget. Salvini found himself in some agreement with this except that he would add that this impassivity is right up to a point. For, in addition, the actor must also feel, though "he must guide and check his feelings as a skillfull rider curbs and guides a fiery horse." The actor has a double task: he must feel himself and he must make others feel, "and this he cannot do without the exercise of restraint."

I cannot leave Salvini without recording an anecdote, one of the most amusing I have ever heard, told me, as was that flashing view of an Irving curtain speech, by my old and distinguished friend, John Macy. As a young man John had been invited to attend a banquet given at the Papyrus Club in Boston for Salvini, when the famous Italian actor was in that city. And while I cannot write it as well as John told it, I feel I have a duty to see to it that it is not lost. One of the reasons that John's version was funnier than mine can be is that he did not know a word of Italian, and the pseudo-Italian he invented for Salvini's utterances was excruciatingly ludicrous, a sort of equivalent in Italian of the "pig Latin" we used to invent as kids. But to *write* an Italian for the great Salvini that is to be printed in a book is another matter, and I freely confess that there is only a very vague resemblance between what I have him say and the general drift of John's phraseology. One thing I guarantee: the interpreter's remarks are *precisely* the ones John recounted to me. Those I have never forgotten.

On that occasion Salvini, who apparently could speak no English, was accompanied by an interpreter, a little man about half the size of Salvini's noble figure, and equipped with a thin, whining voice.

There were many eloquent tributes to Salvini at the banquet, which his interpreter translated for him by whispering in his ear, and the great man showed his pleasure and gratitude in that highly expressive face of his. Finally, he was called upon to make some remarks himself. What follows is my attempt to give the gist of what happened, with the reminder that the interpreter is made to say exactly what John told me he did say:

SALVINI [rising, bowing that magnificent figure, and speaking in the gentlest and warmest tones]: *Amici dilettissimi, reco a Voi l'omaggio ed il saluto dell'italica nazione, che, per essere anch'essa amante della libertà, é amante della nazione americana e del sommo poeta che scrisse nell'anglico idioma, Shakespeare.*

INTERPRETER [rising, figure dwarfed, in a wheezing voice]: Mr. Salvini he say he like very much play Shakespeare for de American peoples. [He sits.]

SALVINI [smiling radiantly and speaking with energy]: *Di più dirò: che del suo sommo poeta, Dante, non é men caro al cor dell'italica schiatta quel grande scrutatore d'ogni umano sentire, Shakespeare, l'incomparabile.*

INTERPRETER [rising again, in whining tones]: Mr. Salvini he say he like very much play Shakespeare for de American peoples. [He sits.]

SALVINI [by degrees raising his powerful voice to a dramatic *fortissimo*]: *Intendo, concludere, amici dilettissimi, dando Vi pegno e garanzia che, quando l'ora della morta scocchi per Salvini, egli serberà ancora come tesoro inestimabile la sua affezione per la grande nazione americana, una nazione che ha tenuto la fiaccola della libertà alta nanti il mondo, un'affezione che morte rinverrà radicata nell'imo del mio core.* [He pauses, and then with an expansive gesture of both arms:] *Prego, dov'é il cesso?*

INTERPRETER [rising again, more plaintive than ever]: Mr. Salvini he say he like very much play Shakespeare for de American peoples. And where, please, is de piss house?

Jean Mounet-Sully (1841–1916) was one of the leading actors at the Comédie Francaise in Paris, and celebrated for his enactment of the great classic roles in French drama. He had a fine physique, a beautiful voice, and was a fiery actor who depended on his much-lauded penetrating gaze. He was, they say, capable of considerable originality in the traditional roles. In April 1894, he came to New York to do Hamlet in French, and portrayed the prince as "an amiable young man who loved his father, grieved for his father's death, saw his father's ghost, and thereafter pretended to be a grinning, skipping lunatic," said Winter. His expression of awe was sometimes picturesque despite "a peculiar obliquity in his eyes." In the closet scene, he followed the Ghost offstage out of the queen's antechamber and screamed, out of sight of the audience, in the passageway. He did himself small justice in Shakespeare, for in France his Oedipus was glorious, and he was as skillful in comedy as in tragedy.

Helena Modrzejewska, better known as Modjeska (1844–1909), hardly belongs among these foreigners who came to visit the English-speaking world, for she is thought of, quite correctly, as essentially an American actress. She was born in Poland, the daughter of a musician named Opido. She did not act until after her marriage in 1861, when she and her husband formed a traveling company. After his death she married again, and for ten years played many roles in Warsaw, including Shakespearean parts. She was a remarkably fine actress, equally admired in tragedy and comedy.

In 1876 she and her husband moved to California, intending to try their luck at ranching. They made a complete failure of it, and she returned to the stage, playing at the California Theater, San Francisco, in 1877. Despite her poor command of English she was a vast success, and thereafter toured the United States extensively, as well as England and the Continent. She eventually was looked upon as one of the leading actresses of her day, and was especially famous for her sleepwalking scene in *Macbeth*. She was a woman of great charm, but on the English-speaking stage she also demonstrated great power and was most in demand for tragedy and strongly emotional roles. She retired in 1905 after a farewell appearance at the Metropolitan Opera House in New York.

We have already mentioned the fact that she played Lady Macbeth to Edwin Booth's Thane of Cawdor. Her interpretation was highly intelligent and similar to Helen Faucit's. She so played the part that the audience felt her power over her husband was due to her own beauty and charm, and she took the (correct) position that she wished him to kill Duncan because, out of love for Macbeth, she wished him alone to have the crown. There was no hint of malice and no show of energy in her interpretation.

There were, of course, a number of people who, admiring her skill as an actress, could not overlook her Polish accent. Odell was such a critic. He admired her Juliet (to the Romeo of Forbes-Robertson) and thought the meeting of the lovers and the balcony scene "in spite of her maturity . . . sweetly and sympathetically played [in London at the Court Theatre in 1881] by the Polish actress, but . . . there was always the accent to forget or to try to forget . . . I saw Modjeska in many Shakespearian parts," admiring her brilliance in acting and her charm "but forever and forever there was Shakespeare spoken with an accent that I could not for one moment put out of my consciousness. One simply had to accept Modjeska's Shakespearian impersonations despite this severe drawback." Nevertheless, Daniel Frohman wrote: "One of the greatest Juliets who played the part under my management, was Madame Modjeska who was over sixty years old when she enacted the role. But she was so appealing, so effective and so dramatic that nobody questioned the matter of age."

Shaw affords a possible clue as to her style. He says that hers was "the best manufactured acting I ever saw," and adds that it was strict, adroit, fine, clever, elaborate, and erudite, but "not genial."

I wish that I could find some excuse for devoting a chapter to Eleanora Duse (1859–1924). In 1923, after her return to the stage, she came to the United States to tour—and to die of pneumonia in Pittsburgh. I like to think that one of the few truly intelligent things I have done during my life I did that year although I was very young: I dropped everything to which I was committed during her stay in New York and went to see her in each of the five plays she gave at the old, vast Century Theater. The company acted in Italian, a language of which at that time I had no knowledge, though I had in advance read through several times translations of the dramas, which included *Ghosts, The Lady from the Sea, Cosi Sia, La Porta Chiusa,* and D'Annuzio's *Dead City.* I sat in the gallery, but could hear and see everything. The atmosphere was so tense that I think if someone had dropped a pin, everyone would have jumped. I had never seen such acting before and I have never seen anything approaching it since. She was sixty-five at the time, and I watched her in roles varying from girlhood through young maturity to old age, and she was always completely the character. And her means were so economical! (I had already seen Bernhardt managing, wooden leg and all, to cover the entire stage and move her arms about like windmills.) Duse would sit in a chair for half an hour, and use her beautiful voice and endlessly expressive face to deliver all the meanings; and I remember that once when she got up to walk a few steps to a table, the suspense was almost unendurable. It has been very difficult to be satisfied with other performances since I saw her.

If I have not given her more space in this book, it is because she was not a Shakespearean actress—except in her youth. Her first great performance was as Juliet when she was a mere slip of a girl in her father's wretched touring company. Of course, she did the part in Italian. When she came to Verona with the troupe and saw the tombs of the Scaligeri, she cried, "There's Juliet's grave!" and burst into tears. She completely identified herself with Juliet when she was playing the role. This was her first experience in that kind. Years later she said: "On a Sunday in May in the ancient amphitheatre [of Verona] under the open sky . . . I was Juliet . . . No triumph ever gave me the intoxication and the fullness of that great hour. Truly, when I heard Romeo say, 'Oh, she doth teach the torches to burn bright,' I was on fire, I became a flame. With my small savings I had bought a bunch of roses in the Piazza delle Erbe . . . The roses were my only ornament. I blended them with my words, my gestures."

Years later, in November of 1888, she created the role of Cleopatra in Boito's adaptation of Shakespeare (that enormously gifted composer and dramatist made two Shakespearean librettos for Verdi: *Otello* and *Falstaff*) and toured with it. Lucien Guitry, the great French actor, saw her do the part in St. Petersburg in 1891, and declared that in the last act she was sublime. With one hand she took the asp, with the other opened her dress, then flung the serpent into her bosom, and with both hands fastened the smock. Guitry wrote: "What's happening? . . . Is it going to bite? Is that her release? Then suddenly the sting, a flash of anguish, a contraction . . . It is over, she is dead."

Shaw, who, of course, never saw her do Shakespeare, was in raptures over her acting. He said, "I should say without qualification that it is the best modern acting I have ever seen." He further wrote: "Duse, *with* her genius, is so fascinating that it is positively difficult to attend to the play instead of attending wholly to her." He often compared her to Bernhardt to the French actress's disparagement. He knew that there were "years of work, bodily and mental, behind every instant" of Duse's performances, and he said that it was the "rarity of the gigantic energy needed to sustain this work which makes Duse so exceptional; for . . . [it] so requires energy of a quality altogether superior to the mere head of steam needed to produce Bern-hardtian explosions with the requisite regularity . . . Sarah Bernhardt has nothing but her own charm . . . Duse's own private charm has not . . . been given to the public." She gave you the charm of the character she is portraying.

Arthur Symons thought she reached "a supremacy in art, so divine in her pure humanity, so mystic in the spiritual sense of the word, and so pathetic in her humility, which has rarely, if ever been equalled, and which could never be surpassed."

But James Agate was a faithful Bernhardtian. He concedes about actresses, "Either you are a Duse or a Bernhardt; either you sit still and are, or move about and pretend." Obviously he felt that the business of the theater is to pretend, for he said that being a Bernhardt takes more out of you than being a Duse. After all, he remarked, Duse can mope while she "is calculating her income tax." The observation is more clever than in good taste.

Herbert Beerbohm Tree
and Johnston Forbes-Robertson

Herbert Draper Beerbohm Tree (1853–1917) was the second son of Julius Beerbohm and Constance Draper, and was also a much older half-brother of the "incomparable Max" Beerbohm. Julius Beerbohm was of German, Dutch, and Lithuanian extraction, and was himself a grain merchant. Herbert at the age of seventeen became a clerk in his father's office, for diversion participated in amateur theatricals, and before long had made something of a name for himself in them. At the age of twenty-five he went on the stage and took as his professional name Beerbohm Tree. He won success so quickly that by 1887 he had leased and was managing the Haymarket. There in 1889 he directed *The Merry Wives of Windsor,* himself playing Falstaff; his wife, Maud Holt, was Anne Page. He did so well with this production that his career was launched as a leading actor-manager of the day. His Falstaff was less remarkable histrionically than from the point of view of makeup, but his production did well enough for him so that he lost interest in confining himself to the modern plays which had earned him a reputation at the Haymarket, and began concentrating on Shakespearean revivals. Eventually he was looked upon as the true successor of Henry Irving. The important part of his career began in 1897 with a series of Shakespeare's plays at Her Majesty's Theatre that continued until his death.

Meanwhile in January 1892 he had appeared as Hamlet at the Haymarket. W. S. Gilbert said that it was funny without being vulgar. Winter, who saw the 1895 performance, said that Tree was fluent of speech, with a slight lisp, but shallow and insensitive to real poetry, "metallic" in his readings, and excessive in his gesticulations. His prince was sometimes mad, sometimes sane, always near the borderline between the two—which is tantamount to what J. Dover Wilson was preposterously to say of Hamlet in his influential *What Happens in Hamlet.* What Tree stressed was that the prince was a *student.* But of real terror, grief, pathos, or passion there was nothing. He concluded the tragedy, apparently inspired by Horatio's "And flights of angels sing thee to thy rest!" by employing a chorus of distant angels!

That crowning touch of vulgarity is the key to Tree's approach to Shakespeare. Max Beerbohm, who was devoted to his older half-brother, confided to S. N. Behrman that Herbert had a passion for the huge and monumental. "'Big' is a word that attaches itself in my mind to so much concerning Herbert. His body was big, and his nature big, and he did so love big things! Mountains, cathedrals, frescoes, Shakespeare, summer skies, Wagnerian opera . . . Things on a small scale, however exquisite, did not satisfy him."

A good example is what *he* did to *The Merchant of Venice.* Irving had been outrageous enough with his introduction of a pathetic Shylock returning to an empty house, with the bridge over the canal, the barcarolle being sung by a passing gondolier, etc. Tree far overshadowed Irving with his elaborateness. His production featured the Jewish quarter of Venice, with linen hanging on lines to increase the realism. Jews were seen going into their synagogue in Act II, and their prayers were heard. And he not only followed Irving in having Shylock return to an empty house, but he actually tore into the house and raged through its rooms, "appearing now at this window and now at that" until he collapsed. Then he dashed into the street again and began tearing his garb to ribbons. Then, in case any of the spectators were missing the point, he sprinkled ashes upon his head. His roars and shrieks were much admired.

Nobody in the history of Shakespearean production had carried the element of spectacle to the extravagant extremes which were to make Tree's productions so well liked by the undiscriminating. No one knew better how to lose the play in a welter of scenic effects and interpolated tricks. Never were there such diametric opposites as Herbert's love for lavish display and his half-brother Max's exquisite delicacy and preference for the dainty and economically shaped. With Herbert's talent for exaggeration the Falstaff in *Henry IV, Part I* degenerated into a low clown full of horseplay (the sort of thing that is still done whenever Verdi's *Falstaff* is presented at the Metropolitan Opera House these days). Nevertheless, it would be unfair to him to doubt his love for Shakespeare, however ill-advised that love was. He managed to produce seventeen of his plays, more than any other West End manager ever attempted after him.

Loving display for its own sake, his scenery was always overelaborate. He encouraged his actors to take curtain calls after every scene! Those constant interruptions were only tedious. He also lacked completely any sense of his own limitations, and often tried roles beyond his powers. Though now and then he was capable of delicate strokes of characterization, as a whole his tragic acting was very weak. So was his judgment. In *Macbeth,* for example, there was an elaborate scene of Duncan's being escorted to bed; to make time for it, huge chunks (of what is one of Shakespeare's shortest plays) had to be omitted. But, of course, he has not been alone in perpetrating that sort of crime. Olivier, in his movie of *Hamlet,* in order to allow the camera to play lovingly with all that stonework at Elsinore, all those staircases, the raging sea, and—especially, and oh, so subtly! Gertrude's bed—had to omit about

a third of the play (including the characters of Rosencrantz and Guildenstern). In *A Midsummer Night's Dream,* in order to emphasize the forest, Tree
let loose many live rabbits to scamper across the stage—a detail which
successfully distracted the attention of the audience from the actors.

It is not surprising that a friend of Agate's never liked to see Tree's
performances in Shakespeare because Tree "frequently made himself
ridiculous." An instance which might be cited as proof is that, according to
Max, when Herbert went to Harvard, he read to the students "Hamlet's
fourth soliloquy in the voice of Falstaff, and Falstaff's 'honor' speech in the
voice of Hamlet." (Characteristically, the chief thing that Max remembered
about the occasion was that all the Harvard boys parted their hair in the
middle.) Agate said that Tree's bearded makeup for King John was like the
picture in *Little Arthur's "History of England,"* showing John granting the
Magna Carta.

Shaw had nothing kind to say of Tree's Falstaff in *Henry IV, Part I:* "Mr.
Tree only wants one thing to make him an excellent Falstaff, and that is to
get born over again as unlike himself as possible. . . . He will never be even
a moderately good Falstaff. . . . Mr. Tree might as well try to play Juliet."
He saw that Tree's *"tours de force* in the art of makeup do not impose" on
the perspicacious; "any man can get into a wicker barrel and pretend to be
Falstaff, or put on a false nose and call himself Svengali." Archer thought
that Shaw had been unfair to Tree, to which Shaw responded: "Mr. Tree
is infinitely obliged to me; for all London, it appears, is flocking to the
Haymarket to see whether Henry IV is really so bad as I think it."

In his production of *Julius Caesar,* Tree decided to "give special prominence" to the character of Caesar, and therefore he himself enacted not
Brutus, but Antony. "Mr. Tree's memory failed him as usual," said Shaw,
and he noted that the actor-manager had introduced the business of "bringing Calpurnia on the stage to attitudinize over Caesar's body" after the
assassination.

In September 1882, when he was twenty-nine, after a long and assiduous
courtship, he married Helen Maud Holt, who was ten years younger than
he. She was a versatile actress and quite remarkable in high comedy; for fifty
years she was seen in a variety of roles, and she played the majority of
Shakespearean heroines. Their daughter, Viola Tree (1884–1938), played
her namesake in her father's *Twelfth Night,* Beatrice to his Benedick, and
Perdita to Ellen Terry's Hermione.

From all accounts Tree must have been a very engaging human being,
witty, always in high spirits, and big-hearted. His brother Max recalled how
one day, when he was standing on the doorstep of his mother's house in
Upper Berkeley Street saying goodbye to a friend, Herbert stepped out of
a taxi "in the dreamy yet ample and energetic way that he had of stepping
out of taxis." Max's friend said politely, "Oh, how are you, Mr. Tree?"
Herbert gazed around the street and replied, "I? Oh, I'm radiant." A few
days later Max's friend said that if any ordinary man had described himself
as radiant, it would seem absurd, but that Herbert's use of the expression

was right: "he looked radiant, it was obvious that he felt radiant, and he told the simple truth in saying that he *was* radiant." Max said that no man had more zest than his brother. "The gigantic risks of His Majesty's Theatre never . . . caused him to turn a hair. He was glad if things were going well; if they weren't, he had a plan for making them do so within a few weeks. He could look Ruin in the face and say, 'Oh, I'm radiant'; whereat Ruin always slunk away . . . foiled again."

And gigantic risks there were in the taking over of His Majesty's Theatre. He had been using the Haymarket and directly opposite was a deteriorating opera house, Her Majesty's, which there was talk of demolishing. Tree decided to procure the site and build a theater in which he could better realize his elaborate hopes. He assumed the risk without the necessary funds, and he spent a considerable amount of time trying to raise them. His wife was worried, but he told her that she was upsetting herself about trifles. Luckily the remarkable success of *Trilby* (in which he played Svengali)—it ran for six months and more—and the financing which came to his aid enabled him to start the new building. His Majesty's Theatre opened in April 1897: the poet laureate, Alfred Austin, wrote an ode for the occasion, rhymed, patriotic, and pompous; and the play, *The Seats of the Mighty,* was given to an audience which had in its midst much of the aristocracy and the Prince of Wales. After all his frantic efforts before and on that opening night, all the postperformance conversations of congratulation, all the receptions and ceremonial feasting, Tree went with two friends up to Piccadilly to the Junior Turf Club, the "cabmen's shelter," at 3 A.M. and remained there drinking coffee and playing dominoes with the cabbies for three hours.

It was his excess of good health and animal spirits, his vitality, which made him so attractive to everyone. Nevertheless, and perhaps naturally enough with such a nature, he did what he could to avoid the company of unhappy people: he wished to see everyone happy. If circumstances made it impossible for them to be so, he did not want to be near them. He bore no one malice and easily forgave outbursts of wrath such as he himself was never subject to, but he had little use for those who would not enjoy life.

Max said that Herbert too had considerable skill in drawing with a pencil; he especially enjoyed drawing Irving. Max remembered that Herbert talked excitedly, "and used to pass his hands through his [red] hair, and leave it all standing up on end." His "necktie was often on one side, and his top-hat always lustreless, and he never had a flower in his buttonhole." Max never saw him read a newspaper, yet he seemed "to know just what was going on all the world round." He read very few books, yet he had excellent literary taste. One of his most obvious traits was that he bore a deceptively "unperceiving manner," a radiant but "abstracted and roving regard." It was this, Max concluded, which threw people off their guard and made his brother so acute a judge of human character. This cultivated vagueness was extremely useful to him during the days of his management, when he was constantly beset by hordes of people pushing themselves; the vagueness helped him escape from having to utter "the dangerous word *yes* or the unpleasant word *no.*" He was actually quite unworldly, and cared little for money. His head was never turned by fame; indeed, he seemed unaware that he had it. Without affectation, he nurtured a strong dislike of slang.

Tree paid his first visit to the United States in January 1895: Max accompanied him as a private secretary (a not very useful one, as he himself admits, because of the time he expended in polishing the prose of the letters he was required to write) on a salary. They stayed at the luxurious Waldorf on Fifth Avenue and Thirty-third Street (where the Empire State Building now stands). Tree found New York magical. "He was not the sort of tourist," says Max, "who takes a home-made tuning-fork about with him" to condemn the discords. He liked what to a Britisher were the excessively overheated rooms at the hotel, he liked the ice on the streets, the "slow, low voices" of male New Yorkers and the "piercing voices" of the women, the "fabulous expensiveness of cabs." He had nothing against the grimness of Chicago or the primness of Boston. All the rest of his company "had brought over a tuning-fork." They were forever grumbling, while Tree kept up his sunny cheerfulness.

After three months they sailed home, and Tree was "the life and soul of the liner." On the last evening he organized a concert with his usual unlimited vitality, though his efforts had their rewarding moments of amusement. Max has left us a vivid account of one of these: "I shall never forget the conversation between him and a very earnest, a very 'ahr-nest,' actor who had volunteered to recite Mark Antony's funeral speech." The rehearsal took place the day before in the dining saloon. The actor stood at the end of the room before the organ screen, folded his arms, and for some minutes somberly looked at Herbert and Max before suddenly breaking out in a voice of thunder with "Friends, Romans, countrymen—" when Herbert cried, "One instant! . . . An idea has just struck me. Didn't Antony address the crowd from *above?*" The actor agreed that it had been from the "rostrum." "Rostrum, yes—rostrum. My idea is this: How would it be if you spoke your speech from that little place up there?" Tree pointed to the organist's gallery. The actor nodded, and was about to ascend the circular staircase, when Tree interrupted with: "One instant, Mr———! Another idea! What did Antony *wear?*" "A toga, Mr. Tree." "Toga, yes—toga." Tree had already seized a tablecloth from a table. He was as solemn as the actor while he draped him. The following night, when the performance was given, the actor recited the funeral oration up in the organ gallery, but when he came down the winding staircase, "Major-General Sir Somebody Something," the chairman, sprang up from the front row to shake the actor's hand, but was "warded off with a fierce gesture. The end was not yet. Antony had but . . . come down among us to read Caesar's will. 'If you have tee-arrs, prepare to shed them now.' "

Tree continued to lavish fortunes on scenery and costumes, and employed leading painters for the sets. Alma-Tadema, for instance, designed sets and costumes for *Julius Caesar.* Shaw accused Tree of surrounding himself "with counter-attractions and lets them play him off the stage." In the opening scene of *The Tempest* (an exceedingly brief scene, by the way), on Tree's stage a ship was rocking on a very real-looking sea, waves splashed, wind roared. In *Antony and Cleopatra* he rearranged the text for the sake of the spectacle: the return of Antony to Alexandria (which in Shakespeare provides a speech in the text) was adorned with a tableau of excited crowds, dancing girls, music, and then the arrival first of Cleopatra, then of Antony. In *Richard II* real horses were used in the Coventry lists, and Richard (Tree) entered London on a horse instead of using the speech in which the Duke of York only describes the occurrence.

In 1916, the tercentenary celebration of Shakespeare's death, Tree (now Sir Herbert) was in the United States again, with far more success than his earlier visit; he gave *The Merchant of Venice* with Elsie Ferguson as his Portia, and *Henry VIII* with Lyn Harding, Edith Wynne Matthison, and Willette Kershaw.

His daughter, Viola, thought of Herbert as bearing no resemblance "to fathers as a race." His voice was always to be heard before he appeared in a room or the garden, for he would call out loudly "and penetratingly from wherever he was, 'Viola!' or 'Children!' This had the effect of a flourish of trumpets; we all dropped our game or our lesson and ran to find him. I remember him best standing on the stairs or in the hall, always leaning on something; sometimes he leaned on my head—always with his hat on, and wearing a flamboyant coat, and carrying some very tall walking-stick . . . in his hand."

It must not be forgotten that Tree, unlike Irving, did not ignore the major playwrights of his day. He was the first Professor Higgins to Mrs. Patrick Campbell's Eliza Doolittle in Shaw's *Pygmalion*, probably the best play Shaw ever wrote; it opened April 11, 1914. Tree also produced and performed Oscar Wilde's *A Woman of No Importance*. Tree was very fond of Wilde's company, and even jotted down some of Wilde's stories in his notebooks. One of these related how when Oscar went to America he had one secretary for autographs and one for locks of hair; in six months one had died of writer's cramp and the other was completely bald. Another gave Oscar's rejoinder to a New Yorker who was praising Columbus for discovering America; said Wilde: "It had often been discovered before, but it was always hushed up." Tree proved quietly his tolerance for human frailty; when Wilde, out of prison, was in bad straits financially in early 1900, Tree at once sent him money with a letter reflecting on the "distinguished work" Wilde had accomplished in the past, said that he "most sincerely" hoped that Wilde's "splendid talents may shine forth again," and that he would not allow "misfortune" to "submerge" him.

It was characteristic of Shaw that, being asked to contribute an article to a memorial volume on Tree after the latter's death, he should have written that "Tree was the despair of authors . . . With his restless imagination," Tree thought "he needed nothing from an author but a literary scaffold on which to exhibit his own creations." When Tree did Shakespeare, he turned to him "as to a forest out of which such scaffolding could be hewn without remonstrance from the landlord . . . The author, whether Shakespeare or Shaw, was a lame dog to be helped over the stile" by Tree's ingenuity.

Johnston Forbes-Robertson (1853–1937) was the offspring of a highly romantic marriage. One day his father saw a woman in the street with whom he at once fell madly in love. He wrote to her and asked her to marry him. The actor was their son. His parents were both cultivated people and quite well-to-do. Thus Forbes-Robertson started out in life in a home of advantages far superior to most actors of his day. His father was an art critic for the *Sunday Times,* and his mother was a highly talented painter; their friends included some of the most notable members of contemporary artistic circles. While still a child, Johnston already exhibited an interest in acting; still in school, he presented *Hamlet* for his parents and their friends in which he played the prince (in the future to be his most celebrated role) and his sister Ida was both Ophelia and the First Gravedigger; the guests included Charles Dante Gabriel Rossetti, Mr. and Mrs. Ford Madox Brown, Richard Garnett, the famous painter Alma-Tadema, and, lying on the floor in front of them all, Swinburne, who somewhat upset the youthful Hamlet by chanting the lines in "his melodious voice" along with the hero. It was also the boy's privilege to hear on various nights Swinburne recite all of Webster's *The Duchess of Malfi* and a reading, before its publication, of *Atlanta in Calydon.* One of his mother's friends even gave him some valuable exercises in the use of his voice, which extended its range and gave it a highly valuable flexibility for long passages.

His boyhood was spent in an artistic and literary milieu. Rossetti used him as a model for the head of Eros in his painting, *Dante's Dream.* Summers were spent in France with a priest who taught him French and the mysteries of Gothic architecture. Rossetti, viewing some of the lad's work, advised that he be trained as a painter. He was sent at the age of sixteen to an art school, and there made friends with another student who had just published a book, *Erewhon.* The student was, of course, Samuel Butler. Young Johnston was readily admitted into the school of the Royal Academy, for which he had been preparing, and at the academy he came to know Millais, Leighton, and Landseer.

It would seem that a mere accident turned him from painting to the stage. The dramatist Wills had seen him act as a child, and asked his parents whether they would permit their son to take part in his play *Mary Queen o' Scots* at the Princess Theatre. Forbes-Robertson later said that he actually had had no wish to be an actor, much as he loved the theater, but since he was the eldest of a large family, he thought it high time that he started earning his own living. Within a few days he made his first appearance on the professional stage, and put a career in painting behind him. He was an extremely beautiful lad and so obviously fitted for a theatrical career that even though *Mary Queen o' Scots* was a failure and quickly closed, he was at once reengaged by Charles Reade to act in the same play for which he had pressured Ellen Terry to return to the theater, *The Wandering Heir.* Johnston met her, and like the rest of the world, fell in love with her. She found him "wonderful" to behold—"a dreamy, poetic-looking creature . . . full of aspirations and ideals." But she thought he was making a mistake in giving up painting, and at the time was not impressed with his histrionic talent.

After Reade's play came an engagement in the important Prince's Theatre at Manchester. The manager Charles Calvert was reviving a number of Shakespeare's plays with, Forbes-Robertson thought, great taste and intelligence. Luckily for the youth, Calvert's company presently was supporting the celebrated Samuel Phelps in *A Midsummer Night's Dream* and *Henry IV, Part II,* in which play Johnston played Prince Hal. Seeing that the youth lacked professional training, Phelps, with his usual kindness, willingly offered to coach the young man, and they grew to be great friends; soon Phelps more often than not enlisted Johnston in the cast of his revivals.

His first great success was at the Haymarket in 1876, which inaugurated a long career as one of the actors most in demand. Two year later he was with the Bancrofts. At the Garrick Club in London there is a portrait of Phelps as Wolsey, the last part he ever played; it was painted by Forbes-Robertson.

Forbes-Robertson's earliest important Shakespearean experience was playing Romeo to Modjeska's Juliet, during her brief sojourn in London (1880); she considered him ideal for the part. In 1882 he went to the Lyceum to act under Irving; he was engaged to be Claudio in *Much Ado about Nothing;* during rehearsals Ellen Terry revised her opinion of his abilities, as she watched him interpret the role with unusual artistry. Shaw had these caustic remarks to make about popular leading men: theatergoers all know "the carefully phrased negation who is careful not to do anything that could help or hinder our imaginations . . . His great secret is to . . . look serious, and, above all, not act." There has been an unwritten law: " 'Be a nonentity, or you will get cast for villains.' . . . Only for certain attractive individual peculiarities which have enabled Mr. Forbes-Robertson to place himself above this law . . . our stage heroes would be as little distinguishable from one another as bricks in a wall."

Forbes-Robertson began to use his spare time for painting again, and, with the encouragement of Millais, he did several commissioned portraits. Henry Irving asked him to paint the scene in the church in *Much Ado,* showing the interruption of the marriage between Claudio and Hero; this painting, which portrays himself, Ellen Terry, and Henry Irving, as well as William Terriss and Evelyn Millard now hangs in the Players Club of New York.

After the Bancrofts retired in 1885 (he had joined them again for the summer seasons), he journeyed to the United States to become Mary Anderson's leading man for an extended tour of the country. She was one of the remarkable beauties of her time, the chief reason for her phenomenal popularity, for she was rather poor as an actress. Forbes-Robertson wasted no time in falling in love with her; he had reason to believe his feelings were reciprocated and they became engaged. But on their return to England she met the very wealthy de Navarro who was, like herself, a Catholic, and she married him—soon to retire from the stage. Forbes-Robertson was stricken for a short time.

He had planned to form his own company while at the Lyceum, but instead he played at various theaters for a number of years, came again to New York, and rejoined Irving twice at the Lyceum, the first time as Buckingham in *Henry VIII*, the second time in a non-Shakespearean part, as Lancelot. About the latter Shaw wrote: "He wears it [his costume] beautifully, like a fifteenth-century St. George, the spiritual, interesting face completing a rarely atttactive living picture. He was more than applauded on his entrance: he was positively adored. His voice is an organ with only one stop on it: to the musician it suggests a clarionet in A . . . [and it] has a richly melancholy and noble effect."

At the age of thirty-eight, in 1895, he thought it time for him to form his own company. He confessed that he would willingly have remained an actor, engaged by whoever wanted him; he had been constantly employed in the theater for twenty-one years, and had acted with all the leading people of his day. The idea of management was distasteful to him, he said, because it was too much of a gamble. Nevertheless, he had before him so many examples of the actor-manager who had taken up that post when much younger than he. Therefore, when Irving quit London that year for an extended tour of the United States, Forbes-Robertson took over the Lyceum to play Romeo to Mrs. Patrick Campbell's Juliet. Shaw did not think him adequate to all the requirements of the hero. "Unfortunately, the 'fire-eyed fury' before which Tybalt falls lies outside the gentlemanly limits of Mr. Forbes-Robertson's stage instinct. . . . [He] fights with unconcealed repugnance: he makes you feel that to do it in that disorderly way . . . without a doctor, shewing temper about it, and actually calling his adversary names, jars unspeakably on him. Far otherwise have we seen him as Orlando wrestling with Charles. But there the contest was in the presence of a court, . . . under Queensbury rules, so to speak. For the rest, Mr. Forbes-Robertson is very handsome, very well dressed, very perfectly behaved. His assortment of tones, of gestures, of facial expressions, of attitudes, are . . . all of the best."

His first season at the Lyceum was unprofitable. When Irving in 1897 was preparing for another American tour, Forbes-Robertson had no money and little incentive to take the theater again. But the combination of his finding a backer and Irving's suggestion that he try *Hamlet* with the offer of lending him the Lyceum sets and props, moved him to play the role that others had been envisioning him as created for. The acclaim was beyond all expectations. Even Shaw let down the barriers, not omitting, however, to take a shot at the same time at his favorite target, Irving.

The Forbes-Robertson Hamlet at the Lyceum is, very unexpectedly at that address, really not at all unlike Shakespear's play of the same name. [Shaw was astounded, for instance, to find] . . . the word "Fortin-bras" in the program, which so amazed me that I hardly know what I saw for the next ten minutes. Ophelia, instead of being a strenuously earnest and self-possessed young lady giving a concert and recitation for all she was worth, was mad—actually mad. The story of the play was perfectly intelligible . . . What is the Lyceum coming to? Is it for this that Sir Henry Irving has invented a whole series of original romantic dramas, and given the credit of them . . . to the immortal bard . . . ? He no sooner turns his back . . . on London than Mr. Forbes-Robertson competes with him on the boards of his own theatre by actually playing off against him the authentic Swan of Avon. [Shaw found it a great success. Forbes-Robertson knew how to] . . . present a dramatic hero as a man whose passions are those which have produced the philoso-phy, the poetry, the art, and the statecraft of the world, and not merely those which have produced its weddings, coroners' inquests, and exe-cutions. And that is just the sort of actor that Hamlet requires . . . Go and watch Mr. Forbes-Robertson's Hamlet seizing delightedly on ev-ery opportunity for a bit of philosophic discussion or artistic recreation to escape from the "cursed spite" of revenge and love and other common troubles . . . how even his fits of excitement find expression in declaiming scraps of poetry; how the shock of Ophelia's death relieves itself in the fiercest intellectual contempt for Laertes' ranting, whilst an hour afterwards, when Laertes stabs him, he bears no malice for all that, but embraces him gallantly and comradely . . . See all that . . . Nothing half so charming has been seen by this generation. It will bear seeing again and again. . . . This is not a cold Hamlet. . . . There is none of that strange Lyceum intensity which comes from the per-petual struggle between Sir Henry Irving and Shakespear. The lines help Mr. Forbes-Robertson instead of getting in his way. . . . We get light, freedom, naturalness, credibility, and Shakespear.

Agate said that of all the Hamlets he had ever seen, Forbes-Robertson had "the winning sweetness of his kindly prince, his grave courtesy in rebuke." When he listened his whole soul seemed to go out to meet the speaker's words. But as for the "wild and whirling words" of which Horatio speaks, this Hamlet was never wild and never whirled. This Hamlet, said Agate, might be compared to "a picture by Watts which can hang in a cathedral and not look silly."

Thereafter Hamlet became Forbes-Robertson's most popular Shake-spearean role.

The restoration of Fortinbras to the play was something of a novelty, and that is why Shaw made a point of mentioning it; the acting editions of the period omitted him, and ended the play with "The rest is silence." (That, of course, gave the actor-manager the privilege of having the final curtain descend on Hamlet's death.) Some critics were foolish enough to insist that everything Shakespeare had written after that line was anticlimactic. Forbes-Robertson's answer to that reveals his own (and, I believe, incorrect) roman-tic interpretation of the prince's character: "It seems to me important that Fortinbras the man of action should be contrasted with the dreamer Hamlet." On another occasion he wrote that while the prince was "not wishy-washy," he "was not a man of action"—a point of view belied by every scene in which Hamlet appears.

Forbes-Robertson had the misfortune to fall in love with Mrs. Patrick Campbell, a beautiful woman and a fine actress, graceful, lovely of voice, and witty. But she was undependable and a demon, raising to the *n*th degree the storms of temperament to which she (and others) felt an actress must be allowed. She seemed to take a particular pleasure in torturing the man who loved her. Why not, when she often tortured her audiences and fellow actors? In this mood, she would turn her back to the spectators, and make faces at her fellow actors. Forbes-Robertson's brother, Ian, disturbed by his brother's sufferings, told her she was destroying him. He was so much affected that after some years of playing opposite her he became ill and had to go abroad. He chose plays with an eye to her wishes, such as Maeterlinck's anemic *Pelléas and Mélisande*, which, without Debussy's exquisite music, is merely silly.

They presently did *Macbeth*. Max Beerbohm found their performances harmonious and beautiful; he made a fairly erroneous deduction: "Indeed, the whole production is a great success. I trust it will be the latest production of *Macbeth* for many years to come."

In 1899 Mrs. Campbell and Forbes-Robertson parted, and his doctor urged him to go away for a long rest. In 1902 he was playing Othello at the Lyric Theatre. The man who had reinstated Fortinbras did far less well with the text of *Othello*. He cut out all speeches and scenes which might offend a Victorian audience (e.g., the word *whore* was changed to *wanton*); Iago's speeches evoking revolting pictures of what he pretended was her sensuality were ruthlessly cut; Othello did not swoon. Max Beerbohm quite justly remarked that Forbes-Robertson did not have the physique for the Moor, who ought to be "a magnificent animal," but rather looked like Hamlet playing an Oriental role. Instead of a calm majestic Othello in the Senate scene, he was a quick-witted, highly refined student. Agate complained that in the part Forbes-Robertson neither harrowed nor froze the blood in the veins of the audience.

In June 1913 he was knighted. Not yet sixty, that year he started on a long farewell tour of Great Britain, the United States, and Canada. He visited great numbers of towns such as Denver, Salt Lake City, Tacoma, Victoria, Calgary, Winnipeg. In 1900 he had married Gertrude Elliott, sister of the fabulously beautiful Maxine Elliott. His wife often acted as his leading lady. Their daughter Jean (1905–1962) became a successful actress.

Forbes-Robertson, after his retirement, admitted that he was glad to be through with his often-performed Hamlet as it had cost him a vast amount of mental and physical strain. He also confessed that he had never once gone on stage without longing for the final curtain. He had never enjoyed his profession, and concluded that he was temperamentally unsuited to it.

22

Jottings on Some Nineteenth-Century Actors

James Fennell (1766–1816), who was six feet tall, with an extremely expressive face, first played Othello in Edinburgh in 1787, and that same year went on to Covent Garden, where he made little impression. In 1792 he came to the United States; he was soon very popular as a member of the American Company, and in Philadelphia with Wignell's troupe. His most applauded role continued to be Othello. Unfortunately he was a man of too great temperament; in Philadelphia, as a result of Fennell's joining the company, Thomas Abthorpe Cooper left in anger for New York. And Fennell caused so much friction within the company that the theater had to be closed for a week. He apologized, but his nature was too fiery for anyone's peace. He went to the Park Theater in New York, was soon dissatisfied, and left to lecture on the Bible and refute Tom Paine's *Age of Reason* and other works to prove the veracity of the "Prophecies and Dissertations on the Miracles." Next, he gave dramatic readings, occasionally returned to the stage, and engaged in various side ventures. On one occasion he speculated too heavily in salt and went heavily into debt. After several "farewell" performances, he retired in 1810.

John Brunton (1741–1822) fathered a family of actors. He was himself first a grocer in Drury Lane, and appeared in 1774 as Hamlet at Covent Garden. He afterwards joined stock companies in Bath and Norwich, and became manager of the latter.

His eldest daughter, Anne Brunton (1769–1808) was first seen in Bath at the age of fifteen, and so well liked that in 1785 she was at Covent Garden. In 1792 she retired to marry Robert Merry, but he was soon bankrupt. So she came to Philadelphia on Wignell's invitation to play at the Chestnut Theater as Mrs. Merry. There she performed Juliet in December of 1796 and became a leading actress of her day, prominent in New York as well as

Philadelphia. Part of her success could be attributed to her great beauty. Merry died in 1798, and in 1803 she married Thomas Wignell, who gave up the ghost shortly after the marriage. For a third time she took a husband, William Warren, part manager of the Chestnut Street Theater. When she died at the age of forty in childbirth, her death was considered something of a disaster to the American stage.

Her brother, John Brunton (1775–1848), made his debut at Covent Garden in 1800, and was the manager of several playhouses. His wife, Anna Ross (1773–?) was also an actress, and their daughter Elizabeth became well known on the English stage as Mrs. Yates.

The youngest of John Brunton's children, Louisa Brunton (1779–1860), was first seen at Covent Garden in 1803. She played Beatrice, Rosalind, and Lady Anne (in *Richard III*). Hazlitt said that she played Rosalind "very agreeably" but *"not exquisitely,"* and that she delivered her lines with intelligence and archness but "was not half giddy, fond, and rapturous enough." He considered her totally unequal to the role of Beatrice, in which part she perpetually introduced "a sort of giggle" which made no sense to the play. Nevertheless, giggle or no giggle, rapturousness or no rapturousness, the Earl of Craven was smitten, and when she married him in 1807 she retired from the stage.

Robert Coates (1772–1848) had a career somewhat similar to that of the "singer," Helen Foster Jenkins, in our own time. He was born on the island of Antigua, the only child (of nine) who survived infancy of a wealthy merchant and sugar planter. When Robert was eight his father brought him to England to begin his first-rate education in the classics. After he had returned to the West Indies, Coates first demonstrated an interest in matters theatrical when he was thirty-three, in 1805, when he took part in some amateur exhibitions. With the death of his father in 1807, Robert Coates became not only extremely wealthy but also the owner of a large collection of magnificent diamonds. He brought them with him when he returned to England to live in Bath and began to indulge a taste for the eccentric which knew no limits. His carriage, for instance, drawn by white horses, was in the shape of a kettledrum, and across the bar of his curricle was to be seen a large bronze rooster, with the motto, "Whilst I live I'll crow."

But it was his passion for the theater that predominated and his great wealth made it easy enough for him to arrange to be "requested" by the ladies to take the role of Romeo at the Bath Theatre on February 9, 1810; he himself, of course, rented the playhouse. The audience roared with laughter at his ineptitude, but, like Helen Foster Jenkins, he took the laughter to be a tribute to his great talents. He was thenceforth known, among other nicknames, as "Romeo" Coates. (He was also called "Diamond" Coates because of the display he made of his precious gems on stage and off; "Cock-a-doodle-doo" Coates because of the motto; "the Amateur of Fashion"; and, as he preferred, "The Celebrated Philanthropic Amateur.") His imagined success impelled him to tour the provinces, and in December

1811 he appeared in London as Lothario. He eventually appeared as Romeo at the Haymarket, wearing a cloak which was a spangled azure, tight red pantaloons, a full wig, and a tall hat. For some time his absurdities drew considerable audiences, so that in February 1813 Charles Mathews produced a satirical sketch of Coates's Romeo in the character of "Romeo Rantall"; it became one of Mathews's most appreciated impersonations, and itself had a long run. Coates, meanwhile, continued to tour Richmond, Birmingham, and other towns. In 1816 he was back at the Bath Theatre.

But it was inevitable that sooner or later audiences would tire of his ridiculous posturing, and begin to hiss rather than laugh at him. Finally, the managers refused to rent him the use of the stage. He was so reckless with his fortune that he went into debt, and was forced to emigrate to Boulogne. Succeeding in making compromises satisfactory to his creditors, he returned to England to live on what was left of his once vast fortune. He met his end when on February 15, 1848, after leaving a performance of a concert at Drury Lane, he was crushed between a handsome cab and a private carriage. He died five days later.

Frances Maria Kelly (1790–1882), English actress and singer, in 1800 played Arthur in *King John* and the Duke of York in *Richard III* at Drury Lane, to great acclaim. Later she revived a number of Mrs. Jordan's famous roles, and for thirty-six years reigned as a great favorite at the same playhouse. She acted with Edmund Kean in 1812, when Drury Lane had been newly rebuilt, playing Ophelia to his Hamlet. She was most often seen in contemporary melodramas. After failing in an attempt to run her own theater, she gave Shakespeare readings and taught would-be actors privately. It was to her that Charles Lamb's "Barbara S——" was written. He was in love with her and proposed marriage in 1819.

When the statesman Fox saw her Prince Arthur, he prophesied to Sheridan, who agreed, that she would become a prominent actress. Mrs. Sheridan, taking part in the same performance, was equally enthusiastic. From 1800 to 1806 Miss Kelly was at Drury Lane and the Italian Opera, where she learned Italian; Mary Lamb later taught her Latin. She also learned to play the guitar and harp. At Drury Lane she was a great favorite until the fire of February 24, 1809. During the summer of that year she was at the Haymarket, and in September went with the rest of the Drury Lane company to the Lyceum. She had a hand, with Edmand Kean, in restoring the health of the new Drury Lane which opened in October 1812. She remained there for thirty-six years without intermission or loss of popularity, though she occasionally gave performances elsewhere.

On February 17, 1816, in the opening scene of a farce being given at Covent Garden, a man named George Barnett fired a gun at her from the pit. Mary and Charles Lamb were present, and some of the shot fell into Mary's lap. When Barnett was tried, and it was shown that he was a total stranger to the actress, he was free on the grounds of insanity. Shortly after, another man fired on her in Dublin, but instead injured a bystander.

She most frequently appeared in melodrama, in which, says Genest, she "was certainly superior to all actresses." She had the doubtful gift of raising minor characters into "unexpected importance." Most of the great actors of her time played with her, including Charles and John Kemble, Mrs. Siddons, Mrs. Jordan, and, particularly, Edmund Kean, opposite whom she often played Ophelia.

Late in life she confessed that she was not indifferent to Charles Lamb's affection for her, but that though she was devoted to him and his sister, she could not entertain the idea of marriage with him because of the strain of insanity in the family.

Henry James Finn (?1790–1840) was an American actor who studied law at Princeton but decided to go on the stage. He appeared at the Charleston Theater and in Boston. After the Park Theater in New York had been destroyed by fire in 1820, he moved over to the Anthony Street Theater, where he was seen as Hamlet, a role he repeated at Chatham Garden Theater in 1824. The Chatham Garden seated thirteen hundred people, and was the first theater in the city to be lighted by gas. The site had been opened by a pastry cook named Barrière in 1819 as a place where open-air music could be heard and punch and ice cream served; in 1823 a theater named the Pavilion opened for the summer season with opera and farces. The Pavilion became the favorite summer resort of New Yorkers, and Barrière therefore decided to erect a permanent theater. His advertisement for the opening on May 17, 1824, assured the public that it was "elegant" and that he had used "his best endeavors to procure such a company of Performers as . . . will meet the wishes, and secure the approbation of the generous and enlightened citizens of New York." A lithograph of the interior shows that it combined the simple with the ornate. Open all year round, it provided a serious challenge to the Park. The company included George Barrett and his future wife, Henry Wallack and his wife, and young Joseph Jefferson. The playhouse flourished until Barrière died in 1826, when Henry Wallack took over the management.

With the success of Finn's Sir Andrew Aguecheek, he decided to concentrate on comic roles; as a comedian he was considered to have no superior. Wemyss, the actor-manager, said that in certain roles Finn's impersonations "have never been equalled on the American stage." Finn died horribly. He was one of the passengers burned to death when the S. S. *Lexington* was destroyed by fire in Long Island Sound.

George Vandenhoff (1813–1885) first acted at Covent Garden (1839) in various roles, including Mercutio in Madame Vestris's production of *Romeo and Juliet.* He came to the United States and was seen as Hamlet at the Park Theater, and then toured the country with considerable success. In fact, he decided to remain in America; he acted in New York, and was for a time leading man at the Chestnut Theater in Philadelphia. When he saw Charlotte Cushman as Lady Macbeth, he accused her of bullying Macbeth: "As one sees her large clenched hand and muscular arm threatening him, in alarming proximity, one feels that if other arguments fail with her husband, she will have recourse to blows." He taught elocution and gave poetry readings between engagements. As Hotspur, Richard III, Macbeth, and Benedick he was praised for dignity, grace, and poetic elegance, but like his father, also an actor, he was deficient in passion and power. Ironically, one of his last appearances was as Macbeth opposite Charlotte Cushman. Among his pupils was Mary Anderson, who took ten lessons from him, the only training she ever received for the stage.

Eliza O'Neill (1791–1872) made her first appearance in Drogheda, where she was born, the daughter of the actor-manager of the town's theater. She went to Belfast and Dublin, quickly made a reputation, and in 1814 was engaged for Covent Garden. As Juliet, to Charles Kemble's Romeo, her debut created a sensation, and for five years she moved from one great success to another.

But we are faced with a difficulty in appraising her abilities. Indisputably Hazlitt (with the exception of very few misreadings, such as that of Portia) was one of the greatest and most sensitive critics Shakespeare has ever had. Nor can we forget his superb appreciation—and objectivity—in considering the acting of Edmund Kean. Yet his judgments of Miss O'Neill, as he always called her, are at such variance with the opinions of others that one almost wonders whether there might have been some personal reason for his comparative harshness with her. Though brilliant as a writer, Hazlitt's private life was more or less a shambles, especially his relationships with women!

The consensus at her debut was that a new Sarah Siddons had come to the London stage. In this view Hazlitt concurred. But he said that though tall and with regular features, she was not particularly graceful. He admitted that she possessed a face which wonderfully projected terror or sorrow; he even granted that she looked like Juliet. However, he found her voice unpleasant. She was at her best, he thought, when listening to the Friar speak of the potion, and also in her change of manner when the Nurse advised her to marry Paris. (He was certainly justified in objecting to the fact that, as usual, the last scene was presented not as Shakespeare had written it.) Her Isabella he found "full of merit," but on the whole disappointing, for she missed the spirit of the character: "She whined and sang out her part in . . . a querulous tone. . . . Her *forte* is in tears, sighs, sobs, shrieks and hysterics." Her Volumnia was too "fleshy" in manner, voice, and person for him—not at all the Roman matron.

Yet other critics say that she had a fine classic face, smooth white skin, dark glossy hair, a beautiful figure, and was beyond praise in tenderness and pathos. She became, they tell us, the Juliet of her day, and the Katherine too. She was described as wonderful as Desdemona. Macready remarked that she "was a remarkable instance of self-abandonment in acting. She forgot everything for the time but her assumed character. She was an entirely modest woman, yet in acting with her I have nearly smothered with her kisses." It is also known that she avoided parts that called for physical force, and on those grounds she refused to do Lady Macbeth. Her reputation was great, and the only flaw her enemies could point to was her meanness with money. She retired very early from the stage, when at the age of twenty-nine she married William Wrixon Becher, M.P., who later became Sir William (and she naturally became Lady) Becher. It was generally felt that her retirement was a great loss to the theater.

Mary Ann Duff (1794–1857) born Mary Ann Dyke, was an American actress born in London. She appeared with her sister Elizabeth (later the wife of Tom Moore) as a dancer in Dublin. She married William Murray of the Theatre Royal, Edinburgh, but he died very soon after the marriage. She married again, this time John Duff (1787–1831), an Irish actor. They went to the United States together, appearing in Boston (1810) as Romeo and Juliet; their performances were well received. In that city, and later in Philadelphia, Mary Ann Duff made her reputation, but in New York she was never quite accepted. Dark, tall, and graceful, she was at her best in tragedy, and is said to have performed the part of every tragic heroine in Shakespeare. The death of her second husband left her with seven young children to support. In dire financial straits she decided in a fit of desperation to marry the eccentric and undependable American actor Charles Young (?–1874), whose performances were occasionally good, but not always so. The marriage was not consummated and was soon annulled. By 1820, after many years of hard work, she was acclaimed the best actress then in the United States. In 1821 when Edmund Kean came to Boston, he asked her to play Ophelia to his Hamlet, and Cordelia to his Lear; acting with him she excelled even her former triumphs—so much so that Kean demanded that she act with less intensity "as he merely desired his efforts to be seconded, not rivalled." Nevertheless, he on many occasions expressed his conviction that she was the superior of every actress on the *British* stage.

Whether or not the *New York Mirror* was simply echoing Kean's opinion we cannot know, but in 1826 that paper stated that the judgment of her as the best living English-speaking actress "has every possibility of being correct"; the more frequently this critic saw her, the more he was convinced that such was the simple truth. Horace Greeley pronounced her Lady Macbeth better than any he had seen.

In 1836 she married an attorney, J. G. Seaver, and went with him to New Orleans, which became their place of residence. Occasionally she would fill engagements in that city.

In the end she became deeply religious, retired from the stage, and lived in deliberate obscurity until her death.

Edward William Elton (1794–1843) was born in London, the son of a schoolmaster whose name was actually Elt. His father used to stage plays in which his students and his son participated. That was, no doubt, the origin of Edward's interest in the theater, and though he was trained for the law at Gray's Inn, he decided to quit that profession. He joined a troupe of strolling players, and appeared in various provincial towns until Charles Mayne Young saw him at Manchester, played with him at Norwich and Cambridge, and brought him to London. Shakespearean parts did not bring him much notice until he came in 1831 to the Garrick Theatre in Whitechapel as Richard III. In the East End he became a favorite. He had experiences of no great length at the Surrey, the Haymarket, and the Adelphi, besides other minor theaters. In January 1837 he won the long-delayed recognition he sought, at Covent Garden. At Drury Lane, 1839/40, he played Romeo, besides non-Shakespearean roles.

He was singularly unfortunate in both of his marriages. He and his first wife separated; his second wife, a Miss Pratt, bore him five of his seven children, and eventually went insane.

Edgar in *King Lear* was perhaps his best Shakespearean part. (He played the original Eugene Aram, which was to be one of Irving's favorite and most popular roles.) He was again at Drury Lane from 1841 to 1842 with Macready, and played Romeo and Edgar with considerable ability. Presently he went to Ireland, and on his return was drowned in the sinking of the *Pegasus*, leaving seven young children behind. He was remembered for his Richard III, Othello, and Brabantio.

Henry Placide (1799–1870), born in the United States at Charleston, South Carolina, of a French gymnast, was considered one of the best comedians of the day. He did the First Gravedigger, Polonius, Peter (in *Romeo and Juliet*), and Feste, among other roles. He was considered "almost a faultless actor," and seems to have been equal to playing anything from farce to high comedy. In three kinds of parts he had no equal: elderly gentlemen, simple countrymen, and drunken servants. He was at the Park Theater in New York for twenty years, acting over five hundred different characters. He did not rely on grimaces, tasteless buffoonery or unjustified exaggeration to achieve his effects. One of those actors who could completely identify himself with the role he was playing, his audiences are said to have recognized him when he appeared on stage only by the lucidity and distinctness of his voice. Even Forrest praised him to the skies, and when asked in Europe who was the finest actor in America, Forrest at once replied: "Henry Placide is unquestionably the best general actor on the American boards, and I doubt whether his equal can be found in England."

Thomas Sowerby Hamblin (1800–1855) was born in London, appeared in leading roles at Drury Lane and came to the United States in 1825. First he appeared as Hamlet at the Park Theater, then toured the country as a tragedian. In 1830 he leased the Bowery Theater, where he was chief actor and manager. But misfortune seems to have pursued him. He rebuilt the Bowery after the fire of 1836. That was but the first of three: in 1838 and 1845 the Bowery was again destroyed. Hamblin understandably gave the Bowery up.

In 1845 he hit upon a scheme to raise $100,000 for a new playhouse by asking 100,000 people to advance $1 in exchange for slips admitting them to one dollar's worth of places in the new theater when it was finished. Because he proposed building further north in the city, he was attacked by the *Broadway Journal.* "We should regret exceedingly," said that paper, "to see a theater erected in Broadway . . . Considering the effect which theaters invariably have in the neighborhood where they have been built, we should expect that the owners of the property would protest the erection of one in that noble thoroughfare." The writer then went on to justify himself. The "little Olympic" was probably of all theaters "the best conducted in the city"; nevertheless it was engulfed by billiard rooms, saloons, "and other equivocal resorts for the profligate and idle." The writer could not understand why a theater should also be "a drinking house, a gambling house and a something else house," as well as a playhouse, but those seemed to be "the real unities of the drama." The theater was now as dissolute as "in the days of Charles the Second . . . We have no reason to believe that Mr. Hamblin would break adrift from the legitimate drama, or that he would do any better in Broadway than he has heretofore in the Bowery." The writer would therefore "rather see him fail" in his present plans, "not that we wish him any ill as an individual, but as a manager he cannot but do harm in the community . . . He would be a fish out of water in Broadway, and his theater would mar the beauty of our magnificent thoroughfare."

Hamblin rented the old Park Theater and opened it on September 4, 1848. Three months later it was ruined by fire. After that he retired.

Harriet Constance Smithson (1800–1854) was born in County Clare, Ireland, the daughter of a man who for years had been manager of theaters in the Waterford and Kilkenny circuit. At the age of two she was adopted by the Rev. Dr. James Barrett of Ennis, with whom she dwelt, far removed from any theatrical concerns. When he died in 1809 she was sent to school at Waterford. Her own father's health was now failing and she unwillingly was induced to enter upon a theatrical career.She made her first appearance at the Crow Street Theatre around 1815 in a part Mrs. Jordan had made popular. In January 1816 she joined Talbot's company at Belfast; her father and mother had been members of that troupe. Though she was given every opportunity to achieve prominence, her lack of training was only too evident. Yet she was liked because she was naive and showed some promise. After other engagements she played at Drury Lane in London in January 1818, making only a slight impression. However, the *Theatrical Inquisitor* praised her looks and figure, which was tall, and her clear voice; she performed "with spirit, over-acting a little in the broadly comic scenes, singing with more humour than sweetness, and dancing gracefully" in the minuet. The *Morning Herald* was more complimentary and was of the opinion that her voice had the "tremulous and thrilling tones giving an irresistible charm to the expressions of grief and tenderness."

After a summer in Dublin, she was again at Drury Lane, where Stephen

Kemble was now manager, and where she was to star in a great many plays. In Shakespeare her best performances were as Desdemona, Cordelia, Juliet, and Imogen. She did Lady Anne to Kean's Richard III and Desdemona to his Othello. In 1823/24 she enacted Anne Bullen in *Henry VIII* and Virgilia in *Coriolanus,* but most of her many roles were not in Shakespeare.

Macready engaged her for a number of provincial performances, and in April 1828 she accompanied him to Paris. As Desdemona she created a great stir, such as she had not evoked in London. In November 1832 she was once more in Paris at the Odéon and the Théâtre Italien on alternate nights. Juliet and Ophelia won her even more admirers.

As far as her acting career went she could not have chosen a more propitious time to be in Paris. The new, young Romantics were in rebellion against their own Corneille and Racine and pedants like Boileau; Anglomania was the style. These young rebels declared that Miss Smithson had revealed Shakespeare to the French; there is no question she established a tradition for presenting the heretofore largely ignored English master in the French theater. Years later the famous Rachel acknowledged her deep indebtedness to Smithson. Her Irish accent, moreover, which had been disadvantageous to her in London, went unnoticed in France. She became the rage; years later Théophile Gautier hymned her outbursts of pathos.

Among those she had enslaved were not only the royal family and its entourage but also the then poor, unknown composer, Hector Berlioz, whose autobiography is full of rapture over *"la belle Smidson,"* the *"artiste inspirée dont tout Paris délirait."* In letters expressing his adoration of her, he flooded her with epistolary extravagances which only alarmed her—to the extent that she told her maid not to accept any more of them.

A German pianist, a friend of Berlioz, suggested that since the composer was being frustrated in his suit, he ought instead to accept a French actress who much resembled Smithson. Berlioz agreed and the Frenchwoman apparently returned his affection. Unfortunately for him and Smithson, the French actress, while he was in Rome, married someone else. In appropriate romantic despair, he threw himself into the sea at Genoa, but was rescued. Two years later he returned to Paris with his *Symphonie Fantastique,* inspired by his love of the Irish actress. He moved to lodgings in Paris right opposite hers.

Her unexpected and exaggerated success led her into extravagant expenditures. Moreover, performances in Amsterdam, Le Havre, Rouen, and Bordeaux were such failures that she had to disband her company. The Parisian public, too (like all publics, by nature fickle), was beginning to weary of her. To cap these new difficulties, she broke her leg above the ankle getting out of her carriage.

Berlioz, nevertheless, in 1833, knowing that she was now heavily in debt, protested his love for her anew. Paradoxically, her success in France had alienated the British public, and rumor had it that her accident was a "theatrical ruse." It is therefore not surprising that she was reluctant to return to Britain. A friend had brought her to a concert to hear Berlioz's new symphony, and she wept to think that she could have inspired that masterpiece. She agreed to meet him the next day. At once he proposed marriage to her.

At the Théâtre Italien a special performance was arranged to help liquidate her debts. The program contained Alexandre Dumas's *Antony*, Act IV of *Hamlet*, and the playing of Berlioz's *Symphonie Fantastique*, *Sardanapole*, and the overture to *Les France-Jugés*. Seven thousand francs were obtained, but the sum was insufficient. Smithson was mortified, and when she rose with difficulty from the stage in the scene from *Hamlet* she received no curtain call, while Madame Dorval, who had performed in the Dumas work, was summoned again and again for applause.

Her marriage to Berlioz turned out catastrophically. He records that she was an exacting and ill-tempered wife. She had no way of making him happy —no one had that secret—and her jealousy was demonic, though the truth is that he gave her frequent occasion to exercise it. In 1851 she became paralyzed. Having long retired from the stage, at the time of her marriage, she died in 1854.

John Baldwin Buckstone (1802–1879), an English actor who left the law for the stage, was for some years in the provinces, where he made himself popular as a low comedian. Kean, after he saw him, encouraged him to develop, and he came to London in 1823, appearing for the next few years at the Surrey, the Coburg, and the Adelphi. During the summer seasons at the Haymarket (1833–1839) he performed and eventually became manager. He was the author of many plays given there, he himself acting in them with characteristic drollery. It is reported that, heard off stage, the sound of his voice, something between a "chuckle and drawl," was sufficient to set the audience into bursts of laughter. For fifty years he was one of London's most liked comedians and fecund playwrights—he composed some two hundred plays, chiefly farces and melodramas. His most popular Shakespearean roles were Launcelot Gobbo and Peter (of *Romeo and Juliet*).

William Evans Burton (1804–1860) was born and educated in England, but after appearing with Kean at the Haymarket had his career in the United States. He first appeared at the Arch Street Theater in Philadelphia, and then in New York. He returned to Philadelphia to convert a circus into what he named the National Theater, and managed it with success. Then he came back to New York to take over Palmo's Opera House on Chambers Street, which by that time was a theater for variety shows; he renovated it and opened it on July 10, 1848, as Burton's Theater, which became one of the most important playhouses in New York. He was a first-rate manager.

Burton was the chief contender for Placide's fame as the best comedian of the day. Many who conceded that Placide was great insisted that Burton was greater. Laurence Hutton said that he was "the funniest man who ever lived." In a then-famous drunk scene in *The Toodles* he could keep the audience in convulsive laughter without uttering a word for fifty minutes. He was a heavy man with a broad face and a very flexible voice; and it appears that he got his funniest effects by use of voice and facial expression. He performed more than two hundred parts, many of them in Shakespeare's plays. Bottom and Caliban were among his most celebrated roles.

In 1856 he gave up his theater and took over the Metropolitan, but this playhouse was too large to sustain the financial crisis of 1857. Despite his featuring Booth, Charlotte Cushman, Mathews, and the Davenports, he had to sell the Metropolitan. He made his last New York appearance in 1859 at Niblo's before setting out for Canada. He died the next year after he returned to New York.

James Edward Murdoch (1811–1893), an American actor, was a famous Benedick, Orlando, and Mercutio. He was particularly praised for the way he delivered his lines. In 1856 he appeared in England in his best-known roles. He retired from acting in 1858.

The reputation of Booth has overshadowed that of Murdoch, yet both men were at the top of their profession during the same period, and cherished similar ideals about acting. Murdoch was more than two decades Booth's senior, but both men attained the height of their careers during the 1850s and 1860s. They acted together in San Francisco in 1853. Three years later Booth was conquering New York, while Murdoch was triumphing in London. An odd coincidence is that their deaths, in 1893, occurred a month apart.

If Booth was more talented, Murdoch had more influence on his profession, for he published three books on his theories of acting. *The Stage* (1880), *A Plea for Spoken Language* (1883), and *Analytic Elocution* (1884). He became a leading teacher of elocution and his ideas more or less directed the course of dramatic training in America. He stipulated that the actor must be faithful to the dramatist's conception and was not free to follow his own fancy. But the actor was "by no means the passive and servile thing" that some think of him as being; he must own a soul which is cooperative with that of the dramatist. Besides that, he must develop the power to express the poet's image and convince the audience of its truth; this faculty is as creative, he said, as the poet's. And truth, he saw, like Booth, was not a matter of everyday reality but an idealization of human experience, for "the natural in expression lies ever nearest to the ideal."

He warned against the actor's employing mannerisms "natural" to himself only, for that would ruin the characterization in a play. An actor who uses his own peculiarities under the illusion that he is being natural is appropriating "the stage and Shakespeare to himself, and swallows them up in the inordinate self-esteem of the individual." (This sounds like a criticism of The Method almost a century before it began to debase the American stage.) What the actor requires is careful study and scholarship and, most of all, a deliberate cultivation of the imagination by studying "the profoundest forms of thought, the noblest moods of sentiment, the most vivid emotions of the soul."

However, he remembered that an actor's identification with his role must stop short of his losing a necessary critical detachment (Hamlet's advice to the players again!). For the purposes of expression he was convinced that the "qualities of voice and speech" were far more important than movements of the body.

When his only son was killed during the Civil War, Murdoch came out of retirement to read and give lectures to the wounded. He died in Cincinnati.

Clara Fisher (1811–1898) was first seen on the stage at the age of six, and won much admiration at that time for her Shylock and Richard III. She played at Drury Lane and Covent Garden, and as a prodigy was considered second only to Master Betty. At the age of sixteen she went to New York to the Park Theater, and thereafter toured the United States in opera and vaudeville, choosing to remain in America for the rest of her long life. Her early successes were due more to her vivacity and lightness of touch than to any great histrionic talent. Her best roles in Shakespeare were as Ophelia and Viola, but it was inevitable that as the years passed and her youthful sprightliness vanished, so should her popularity, since they were her chief props. Nevertheless she continued on the stage for many years, and did not retire until 1880.

Edward Loomis Davenport (1815–1877) was the son of an innkeeper and became in turn the father of a family of American actors. He first was seen at the age of twenty-two in support of Junius Brutus Booth at Providence, Rhode Island. After touring for some years he came to New York in 1843 to support Mrs. John Drew in a number of Shakespearean performances. He went to England in 1848, and remained there for some years, making a reputation for himself as Richard III and Othello. Upon returning to New York he did Hamlet, and then turned to theater management, starring at a number of theaters with his own company. Winter paid him some elaborate tributes: "an actor of extraordinary versatility. I have seen him act, in one evening, Shakespeare's Brutus and Roaring Ralph Stockpole. . . . He was massive and weird in Macbeth. . . . His Othello was, in construction, as nearly perfect as a work of art may be. Mind, grace, force, variety, and occasional flashes of fire were characteristic of Davenport's acting."

He made a fine Iago too. Winter said that Davenport played it with "bluff manliness" and "jovial good nature," and that "virtue, candor, sympathy and sincerity made up the outward show of this personation." (The description indicates that Davenport may indeed have been the perfect Iago.)

His Macbeth was a warrior of "excited imagination," his elocution was excellent, and, Winter was glad to add, he introduced no eccentricities or embellishments into his performance. (What would Winter have said to Roman Polanski's recent movie version of that play?)

Winter admired him no less for his Hamlet as "one of those rare and charming actors who . . . in the whirlwind of passion use all with gentleness." He exhibited in the part delicacy and fine intelligence. But he was insufficiently moving. A great actor, Winter summed him up, who never became a real success.

Davenport was distinguished, had a graceful walk, and a voice which had an unusual combination of harmoniousness, softness, great range, and capacity for great power. Everyone who knew him commented on his inexhaustible kindness. For example, during the long run of *Julius Caesar* at Booth's Theater (1875/76) he suffered so much from an extremely painful case of rheumatism in one hand that he could barely stand to have it touched; yet he continued to hide his agony behind gaiety, kind words, and smiles before the company. He was much loved by fellow actors who considered him a true gentleman.

While he was in England he married Fanny Vining (1829–1891), an actress with much experience who as Mrs. Davenport appeared with him in the United States in leading roles until his death. They had nine children, five of whom went on the stage. Fanny Lily Gypsy (1850–1898) played children's parts with her father, and in 1869 joined Augustin Daly's troupe in New York to become its leading lady. In 1877 she formed her own company and toured the country with it, playing many Shakespearean roles. Blanche Davenport became an opera singer. May (1856–1927) played the Duke of York in *Richard III* at the age of six and in her maturity acted with her father's and Daly's companies. Edgar Longfellow (1862–1918), after some years as a juvenile actor, played with Julia Marlowe and other prominent actresses. Harry George (1866–1949) eventually became a leading man, and then went with his wife into vaudeville. He was one of the earliest actors to appear in films for Vitagraph.

George Washington Lafayette Fox (1825–1877), an American, began acting as a child, and from 1850 to 1858 was an important member of the National Theater Company. In partnership with Lingard he assumed management of the Bowery in 1858 and the New Bowery. In 1867 he gave an excellent performance as Bottom, and a year later a travesty of *Hamlet*, which Edwin Booth saw and is said to have been very much amused by. Fox was called "the peer of pantomimists."

Charles Calvert (1828–1879), although his career and reputation were connected more with his performances in the provinces than in London, deserves attention for his devotion to the cause of Shakespearean production. He was born in London and intended for the law, but after seeing the performances which Phelps was giving at Sadler's Wells was inspired to go on the stage himself. Cheerfully acknowledging his indebtedness, he declared that all he knew about acting and production he had learned from Phelps.

He first acted in 1853 at Weymouth Theatre, then at Southampton and South Wales until (c. 1855) he joined the company in London at the Surrey Theatre. He had been fortunate by this time to have received a fair share of leading roles wherever he had played. A year after his return to London he married Adelaide Biddles, who, as Mrs. Calvert, made out well on the stage. They had many children; five of them, three sons and two daughters, followed their parents' profession. In 1859 Calvert was actor-manager of the

Theatre Royal at Manchester, where he became famous. But his Shakespearean revivals began only in 1864, when he was manager of the new Prince's Theatre. It was a popular belief in that deteriorating era that Shakespeare spelled financial disaster to a playhouse, but Calvert was convinced that Shakespeare, properly presented, could be profitable. The scenery of his productions was, like the costumes, elaborate and historically accurate. The revivals included *The Tempest* (1864), the opener and a great success; *Antony and Cleopatra* (1866); *The Winter's Tale* (1869); *Richard III* (1870); *The Merchant of Venice*, with music by Arthur Sullivan (1871); *Henry V* (1872); *Twelfth Night* (1873); and *Henry IV, Part II* (1874). It is to be noted that he courageously did not begin with the usual *Richard III* (the nearest Shakespeare ever approached to melodrama) but with plays which had been infrequently performed. Even the choice of the second part of *Henry IV*, rather than the far more popular first, is revealing. His stock company was a good one and contained a number of men and women who later became leaders in their field.

But the financial success he had anticipated was irregular. By 1875 he gave up all connection with the Prince's Theatre. He had just produced *Henry V* in New York with great success, and now returned to Manchester, where he presented *Henry VIII* at the Theatre Royal. He spent his last years touring widely.

Not uninteresting were the plans he drew up for founding and subsidizing a Shakespeare Memorial Theatre, but during his lifetime this scheme came to nothing. Eventually, of course, a Shakespeare Memorial Theatre did come into being—but not in London, as he had proposed.

John Edward McCullough (1832–1885), born in Ireland, emigrated to the United States at the age of fifteen. Entirely self-educated, he spared himself nothing in learning the rudiments of the profession to which he aspired. Diligent, hard-working, he joined amateur groups, stock companies, and then touring companies. Forrest saw him and in 1861 took him on for second-lead parts; when he went to San Francisco McCullough went with him. In that city McCullough managed the California Theater, first with Lawrence Barrett as partner, later by himself. Financial troubles caused him to quit the position, after exerting a powerful influence on the city's taste for ten years. He did a great deal of touring from 1875 until 1884, when illness forced him into retirement.

He was a large man of powerful but gentle personality. New York saw him often, and in 1881 he was briefly in London. His speciality was melodrama and certain Shakespearean heroes. McCullough's face was better at expressing perplexity than intellectual conflict or spiritual unhappiness. His Hamlet was bad, lacking subtlety; his talents were rather in the direction of the heroic and noble. Winter said his prince was too "mournful," and that he did not identify with the character, though he gave him credit for sincerity in all his roles. His personal dignity, "commanding stature," bold and regular features, great strength, and "melodious voice" made his Othello, Winter thought, splendid, royal, and simple (as, indeed, Othello should be). Winter's only reservation was that there was a touch of the fantastic in his Moor's makeup and the wild beast's head on the back of one of his robes. Winter considered his a great Lear; he had the requisite imposing figure, natural majesty, and resonant voice; he was marvelous in depicting the gradual disintegration of the old king—and was especially remarkable in his slow passage from agony, to going mad, to the careless volatility of a man already mad. As for Coriolanus, Winter said he "looked Coriolanus to the legs."

His development had been slow but his self-education tireless. While employed as a chairmaker, in one month's time he digested Chambers's *Encyclopedia of English Literature* so well that he could quote from any portion of it. When in Boston doing minor parts for Davenport (1860/61), he was asked late one morning to read the part of the leading man (suddenly ill) on stage that night from manuscript—one of the longest roles in their repertory. He spent the rest of the day in intensive preparation, and appeared that night as though he had had long experience in the part, performing perfectly and without benefit of the script, to the amazement of the rest of the company.

It is understandable that Forrest should have been impressed with him, for they were in many ways much alike—in their power, virility, strength, control of voice, and energy. There is a story concerning them both when they were together in a scene, while playing in Philadelphia. McCullough was determined to impress the older man, and "went after him" with the use of his voice. "He gave me one startled, savage look," McCullough recounted, "and came right back at me with a volley of roars that rattled the big chandelier. We had it out then and all through the evening." Forrest was furious during the encounter, but by next day had forgotten it. The fact is that Forrest retained the younger man for five years, giving him such roles as Edgar, Iago, Laertes, Macduff, and Richmond opposite Forrest's own leads. It was not surprising, either, that McCullough's style became similar to Forrest's. It was a style, said Joseph Clarke of the *New York Tribune*, speaking of McCullough, "virile without virtuosity . . . bold, noisy, direct to the audience . . . [the] carelessness that aimed at 'the gods' with a thunderclap speech, and if a 'hit' was scored, let that suffice."

It was on Forrest's advice that McCullough remained in California, when the older man left, and his parting advice was, "Leave off imitating me," for a lot of "infernal fools" were doing it all over the country. The critics soon noticed a steady improvement in McCullough's style. Years later, when he came back to New York, the same Clarke who had commented on his Forrest-like manner, said that here "was a new McCullough indeed," with "a chaste spirit," a "tempered emotion, utmost grace," and a restraint keeping in check a power "that only flashed out on the mountain tops."

Much loved by his fellow players for his kindness, gentleness, and consideration, as well as by his countless admirers, he was mourned on his death by the entire nation.

Lucy Geneviève Teresa Ward (1838–1922), an American well known, too, in Great Britain, began as an opera singer under the name of Mme. Guerrabella. While performing in Cuba her singing voice was affected by an attack of diphtheria, and she decided to become an actress. She first appeared as Lady Macbeth in Manchester (1873) and the next year was very successful in London as Portia, Emilia, and many other classical non-Shakespearean roles. With a talent for languages, she also played Lady Macbeth in French in Paris where a French critic reported: *"La salle toute entière était suspendue à ses lèvres et frissonait avec elle."* She first came to New York to perform in 1878. Again in London she appeared opposite the young Johnston Forbes-Robertson. On a later visit to London she joined Irving at the Lyceum, playing Queen Katharine in *Henry VIII* and Queen Margaret in *Richard III*. She performed with Benson's company in former roles, and did Volumnia at the Old Vic.

Lawrence Barrett (1838–1891) was an American who began his career on the stage at the age of fourteen, and traveled throughout the United States with many notable companies. He was the son of ignorant Irish immigrants from Paterson, New Jersey, and at the age of ten he left them to begin his endless wanderings. At fourteen he took the job of callboy at a theater in Detroit. Determined to be an actor, he commenced his self-education by concentrating on the only volume he owned, a battered copy of *Webster's Dictionary*, which he very nearly memorized. The plays of Shakespeare he learned by heart as soon as he could procure an edition of them. His persistence resulted in his being given small parts, which he performed with such gauche intensity that the rest of the company laughed at him.

He grew into a tall man with classic features, dark sunken eyes, and a voice of solemn sonority, which nevertheless was capable of much sweetness. He never gave up his thirst for learning and spent the rest of his life in earnest research and scholarship. For years his style was quite eclectic, showing the influences of the actors with whom he worked: Booth, Charlotte Cushman, Hackett, and others, besides Kean, whom he had heard. Although his repertory became vast among plays of his contemporaries, he was at his best in Shakespeare and at one time or another acted all of the important Shakespearean roles. Perhaps his most celebrated role was that of Cassius, whom he played opposite Booth's Brutus. Winter thought his Shylock among his finest achievements; Barrett made him "the implacable avenger of personal wrongs." His Mercutio too was admired, but his Hamlet was felt to be too melodramatic; Winter said that he performed it with "continuous tremor and nervous excitement," and a "strongly accentuated bitterness of feeling."

In 1871 he managed Booth's Theater in New York, and was a good friend of Booth's. In 1884, during Irving's absence from London, he took over the Lyceum, where he was cordially received, but not financially successful.

Despite his interest in the plays of his own time, he would not touch anything realistic, and concentrated on poetic drama. For all his mental vitality and conscientiousness, the public did not find him entirely interesting; they thought him too austere. Doubtless he was overshadowed by the brilliance of Edwin Booth in America and Irving in England. What is hard to explain is the great amount of animosity he evoked, for he was a friendly, in fact too sensitive, man.

Marie Effie (née Wilton [1839–1921]) and Squire Bancroft (1841–1926) were responsible for introducing a number of reforms on the British stage, both in terms of acting style and the kind of play produced.

She was the daughter of provincial actors, and began acting while still a child. She did Fleance in Macready's *Macbeth,* and was highly praised for her Prince Arthur in *King John.* She first was seen in London when she was seventeen, and soon was playing with success in the burlesques, then so popular.

Squire Bancroft was not born into the theater; he began by doing pantomime with the Birmingham stock company in 1861, and for the next four years gained all sorts of experience in various stock and touring companies. In the course of this training he met Marie Wilton, who was still doing burlesque, and who invited him to join her company.

Borrowing £1,000, which was nearly all spent when they opened, they took over the old Queen's Theatre, which had become more or less disreputable, nicknamed the Dust Hole, and situated in a totally unfashionable part of London. They renamed it the Prince of Wales's, decorated it charmingly and managed it well. It opened on April 15, 1865, with Bancroft in a melodrama and Wilton in a burlesque on *La Sonnambula.* Their undertaking was a success.

Two years later they were married, and their theater became one of the most popular in London. Among their innovations was to raise the salary of leading players from the scale of £5 to £10 a week which obtained almost everywhere to £60 to £100 a week; another was their paying for the costumes of the actresses. They were also responsible for working out realistically the possibilities of the box set, using real windows, doors, and ceiling.

They were so eminently successful because, among other reasons, they at first firmly subscribed to the popular prejudice against Shakespeare at a time when public taste was at an all-time low. This view was not likely to be altered by the failure of their elaborate production of *The Merchant of Venice* in April 1875, with Charles Coghlan's inadequate Shylock. And that production is their chief reason for appearing in this book.

Their own autobiography contains too many amusing pages not to include as examples the following letters they received from applicants who wished to join their very competent company.

"HONNERED LADY,—i was borne in allen Street and i am now pottman at the swan with 2 neks i have no art to continue in my persision so I writ to arsk you to putt me on the bords of your theatre i am a borne actor for i citch myself makeing speaches out of plays in the middel of the nite. . . ."

"to Mr. Bangkroft—DEAR SIR—could you be so kind as to teake noites of Ellen _____'s letter which i took the libty of writing asking you if you could for kindly infrom har How she Could become a Balled gril as i have a longing disire to become one—wery tall age 19."

"SIR,—Pleese pardon me for taking the liberty but it is on account of myself wishing to be an Actress I feel I never shall be happy until I am one and I can assure you I will not be long lerning what I have to lern. I can jump about, but I am only just beginning to lern dancing, they tell me I am like a frog jumping about . . ."

The career of the American actor, William Edward Sheridan (1840–1887), though brief, was rewarding. His most notable roles in Shakespeare were as Shylock and Othello, and among his virtues were a melodious, resonant voice and a powerful, virile personality. It was in Philadelphia that he had his first successes. In 1880 he went to San Francisco, where he was extremely popular with audiences. A captain in the Union army during the Civil War, he returned to the stage at its conclusion, at Niblo's Garden, New York, which was at the corner of Broadway and Prince Street. After his first wife died (1872), he married Louise Davenport and went with her to tour extensively in Australia. He died there.

Thomas Wallace Keene (1840–1898), an American actor whose real name was Eagleson—one suspects that the sound of Edmund Kean's name, after his vast reputation, must have been tempting as a pseudonym, for even the celebrated Laura Keene was not born with that name—began at the old Bowery Theater, and earned his first public recognition with Hackett. Supporting many of the leading performers of his day, he toured the United States and England. From 1875 to 1880 he was a member of the California Theater in San Francisco. That playhouse first opened in January 1869, and was built by William Ralston, president of the Bank of California, to provide a place for the performances of two young Irish actors who were in demand in San Francisco, Lawrence Barrett and John McCullough. Intended for only serious drama, the building was magnificent, its exterior supported by Corinthian columns; over the entrance was a bronze figure of Falstaff; the interior was decorated with gold and white scroll work on a blue background; the chairs in the auditorium were gothic and high backed; the seating capacity was 1,478, which could be augmented by additional chairs. These and standing room raised the auditorium's capacity to 2,150 with comfort for all. On opening night, when Barrett played a comedy by Bulwer, there were 2,479 spectators.

Keene proved a valuable addition to the company when Edwin Booth had an engagement there. Later he went on tour. He was a big, ruddy-faced man, quiet and kind, but had no taste for contemporary plays. His best role was Richard III, and he was most in demand in unsophisticated localities.

David Bandmann (1840–1905) was a German-American, who performed in German at the Stadt Theater in New York. He did a Shylock in English in 1867, then toured Australia, New Zealand, and the Orient, as Hamlet, Shylock, Macbeth, Richard III, and Romeo. His Hamlet was (quite correctly) not irresolute. Clara Morris, used to the effeminate prince, by then popular, said of his interpretation: "If Hamlet had had all that tremendous fund of energy, all that love of action, the Ghost need never have returned." The remark is based on the erroneous assumption that the Ghost appears in Gertrude's antechamber in order to spur the prince into action.

While on tour in India Bandmann met a certain Babu Keshub Chunder Sen, a learned man, whom he felt incarnated Othello, and thereafter he applied his makeup so he could resemble Sen as closely as possible. His own description of him reports that his bearing was noble and dignified, that he was six feet tall, broad shouldered and breasted, "a grand, imposing athletic figure," which reminded Bandmann of a "patrician Roman"; his complexion was light olive, his eyes mild and eloquent, his lips firm and set; he wore a black moustache and long black hair which hung carelessly over a fine forehead. Bandmann seems to have been capable of a most unusual perspicacity as to Shakespeare's intentions.

Charles F. Coghlan (1842–1899) was an English actor most of whose career was in the United States. He first appeared at the Haymarket in 1860, where, among other parts, he did Shylock. We have already noted that his inadequate performance of that role caused the Bancrofts to withdraw immediately a lavish and expensive production of the play. It has also been said that he gave the feeblest possible support as Mercutio to Forbes-Robertson's Romeo. Winter, who saw him in New York, said that his Macbeth was "natural," and therefore inept; the interpretation he found sluggish and without definition.

His sister Rose (1851–1932) had, however, a long and distinguished career which began when as a young girl she played one of the three witches in *Macbeth*. She came to New York in 1871, and was for many years leading lady at Wallack's Theater. Her chief Shakespearean role was Rosalind, but she performed many non-Shakespearean roles, including Wilde's *A Woman of No Importance* (1893). She eventually became an American citizen.

Henrietta Hodson (1841–1910) was first seen in Glasgow and Greenock in the same company with young Irving. Together they joined the Manchester stock company at the Theatre Royal, whence she went to Bristol, where she appeared with Kate and Ellen Terry. When she married she gave up the theater but, soon widowed, came back to it. In 1868 she married Henry Labouchère, a proprietor of the Queen's Theatre, where she was acting. At Bath she had enacted Oberon in the same company with Ellen Terry, but thereafter had been seen mostly in modern comedies, extravaganzas, and burlesques. Suddenly in April 1871 she ventured something quite different, the role of Imogen in *Cymbeline*; though she lacked dignity in the earlier scenes, she was very graceful in boy's disguise.

After she took over the management of the Royalty Theatre she produced several plays by William S. Gilbert, the most successful dramatist of his day. For all his infectious good humor and excellent wit as demonstrated in the librettos he wrote for Arthur Sullivan, Gilbert was a very difficult man (as Sullivan, too, discovered), and a martinet in the theater. Henrietta Hodson took serious exception to his behavior at rehearsals, and they had a number of quarrels, even in print.

Her forte was farce; pathos and sentiment were outside her capabilities. It was she, incidentally, who was responsible for introducing Lily Langtry to the theater.

Louis James (1842–1910), an American, first performed in 1863 and was for some years with Mrs. John Drew in Philadelphia. In 1871 he joined Daly at the Fifth Avenue Theater, at Twenty-fourth Street near Broadway, in New York. Daly became a vital force in the American theater, did much to raise the quality of American productions, and for thirty years dominated the legitimate theater. His Fifth Avenue Theater burned to the ground on January 1, 1873. After using temporary quarters, Daly leased a playhouse on Twenty-eighth Street near Broadway and called it the New Fifth Avenue Theater. James was with him as a leading man for some five years.

From 1880 to 1885 he joined forces with Lawrence Barrett, and went with him to London. He set up his own company after that, with Marie Wainwright (1853–1923) as his leading lady, and they toured extensively in a repertory of Shakespearean plays. He continued acting until his death, which occurred while he was putting on his makeup for the part of Wolsey in *Henry VIII*.

An amusing anecdote is connected with a performance he was giving with Clara Morris, "Queen of Spasms," as she was called, in an adaptation of a French play. In one scene her agony was so intense that James was too overcome to speak; the actress, seeing him dissolved in tears, muttered to him, "I say, what ails you? Are you dumb?"

Louis Aldrich (1843–1901), whose name was actually Lyon, was an infant prodigy, "the Ohio Roscius" who toured the country as Richard III, Macbeth, and Shylock, among others. He broke his career to go to school, and as an adult returned to the stage. Having been called various names in the past, including Master Kean, he took the name of Aldrich. He played for five years in St. Louis, was briefly in New York, and joined the Boston stock company. From the 1873/74 season he was Mrs. John Drew's leading man at the Arch Street Theater, Philadelphia. Perhaps because of his childhood performances in Shakespeare, he gave up his plays as an adult. In 1897 he became president of the Actors' Fund, and was the first person to suggest the erection of a home for destitute actors.

Kate Terry (1844–1924) was Ellen's elder sister. At eight she played Prince Arthur in Charles Kean's *King John* and remained with him until his retirement. Among her roles with the company was Cordelia. She was later Ophelia to Fechter's Hamlet. Apparently destined for a brilliant career, she left the stage in 1867 to marry Arthur Lewis. Her daughter was the mother of John Gielgud.

Frank Archer (1845–1917), an Englishman whose real name was Arnold, started acting in 1868, and was in provincial cities as well as in London. He did many Shakespearean roles, including Polixenes, the Ghost in *Hamlet*, Claudius, and Hamlet. He praised Salvini's Othello for not being stilted or unnatural, nor pandering to the audience for applause; but he objected to the Italian's seizing Desdemona by the hair in the last scene and "half dragging her across the stage"; otherwise the interpretation as a whole was "beyond praise."

Wilson Barrett (1846–1904) was remembered by a friend of Agate's as a "very heavy actor—a mass of brawn: he always appeared broader than his height." Other accounts of the English actor-manager, who was a nonpareil in melodrama, speak of him as having been strikingly handsome, with a resonant voice, and a powerful torso, though he lacked something in height. He was less successful in Shakespeare, which he tried often enough. Clement Scott thought well of his Mercutio. He made Hamlet, says Winter, a youthful prince, insisting as he did that in "a little more than kin and less than kind" (Hamlet's first line in the play) *kind* was the German for *child*. Winter also thought he strove too much for novelty, altering lines, presenting the Mouse-trap play before king and queen in a garden, making Gertrude a woman in her mid-thirties, and the chief emotion of the play filial love. Clement Scott criticized his Hamlet for lacking tenderness, inspiration, and imagination. These observations seem a little odd when juxtaposed to Barrett's own thoughts on Hamlet, which I feel to be quite precise: "Hamlet does not hesitate; he does pause and ponder at times, but at others the swiftness of his action is most marvelous." He also quite correctly rejected the idea that Hamlet is mad. He was equally intelligent in specifying that Gertrude ought to be a highly attractive and sensual woman. As for the objection of Agate's friend, Barrett's physique again reminds one that, from all available evidence, the first Hamlet, Richard Burbage, must have had similar dimensions. I concede, of course, that being a highly successful specialist in melodrama, he may very well have been unfit to identify himself in his actual performances with Shakespeare's creations.

Adelaide Neilson (1846–1880), an English actress, was the daughter of a strolling player, and her name was really Elizabeth Ann Brown. Her childhood was a most unhappy one.

Her birth had been illegitimate; her actress mother, giving up strolling, settled in Yorkshire as the mistress of a mechanic. Adelaide was sent to work in a factory, and then worked as a maid. At the age of fifteen she fled from this sort of life to London, where her first employment was as a barmaid. She gave that up to become a member of the ballet. Her extraordinary beauty, slender figure, and dark eyes made her stand out from the rest of the chorus and several kind actors gave her some pointers on their profession. She was advised to read Shakespeare's plays and study them. They fired her ambition and it did not take long for her to decide that nothing would stand in the way of her becoming a leading actress in those plays.

After several years in London and the provinces audiences were full of admiration for her as a Shakespearean actress, but it was not the prominence she thirsted for. That she won in the United States, to which she came in 1872 at the age of twenty-six, more beautiful than ever, and having dyed her brown hair golden. A whole legend was manufactured around her in America: she had been born in Spain of a very wealthy Spanish father and an English mother, had been educated in Europe, had mastered several languages, was a poet, and had settled on the stage partly because her father had suddenly lost all his riches and partly because of her own sparkling imagination.

Her debut was as Juliet, and the critics were wild with enthusiasm. Winter said that she was the most fascinating and irresistible daughter of Capulet he had ever beheld, and that she had a cunning control of subtlety and intensity. She proceeded to add Rosalind, Viola, Beatrice, and Imogen to her repertory, and these were presented with unfailing acclaim on her tours. She engulfed audiences with the surging tide of her emotions and in moments of pathos, when her eyes would fill and real tears stream down her cheeks, the spectators shared her sorrow. Her voice was like silver, and her beauty did not diminish the sympathy of spectators. She eventually rose to the position she had desired and made a large fortune for herself.

She did Imogen first in Philadelphia in the autumn of 1876 and then in New York in May 1877. (By 1892 *Cymbeline* had been revived in New York only five times in one hundred years!) Winter found her innocence, glee, pensive grace, and artless simplicity very moving in the part. Actually, she was no poet at all, but in a theater she knew how to make poetry live and capture the ear of her audience.

In private life she alternated between moods of sweetness and merriment and those of sadness and withdrawal.

London, hearing of her great triumphs in the United States, quickly changed its mind. Edward Sothern, known for his practical jokes (he was an Englishman who had also made a reputation for himself in America in non-Shakespearean plays), came to visit her at the Fifth Avenue Hotel during an engagement at the height of her acclaim. Instead of finding her joyful, as she had every reason to be, he found her sunk in depression. When asking what he could do for her, he was told that she would like a talisman from him to bring her luck on her forthcoming tour—anything would do. Would she care, he jestingly inquired, for a grizzly bear? Why yes, she responded, "Send him up." Sothern obligingly had a young grizzly bear, which had been caged at Wallack's Theater and had just arrived as a gift from California, brought to Miss Neilson's rooms by four porters, the bear "with a chain about as big as the cable of a man of war, and a muzzle like a fire-grate." At the moment, her drawing room was crowded with visitors, who at once went into panic, while Miss Neilson was unruffled. She even attempted to make arrangements to keep the bear, but that proved impossible. The beast eventually was presented to the zoo in Central Park.

Adelaide Neilson made a luckless marriage and divorced her husband in 1877. Her early death at the age of thirty-four was universally held an irreparable loss to the American and British theater.

Clara Morris (née Morrison [1848–1925]), American, began on the stage as a child, and after touring the provinces joined Daly's company at the Fifth Avenue Theater. Though she was not a good actress, and never bothered to learn the technique of her profession, preferring to enact everything with exaggeration, she managed to exert enormous influence over her audiences. She naturally preferred melodrama and seems to have been most successful in such parts as Camille, but she did Lady Macbeth on May 17, 1875, with a blond wig. Her interpretation made Macbeth's wife a fascinating young woman who influenced her husband by her femininity—which is certainly consistent with the play as Shakespeare wrote it—but she was entirely too modern in manner, and did absolutely nothing with the sublime poetry of the tragedy. She had a trick of demonstrating intensity of feeling by distending her nostrils—much as Helen Hayes has done in our own time.

Her mother had deserted her father on learning that the marriage had been bigamous, and Clara's early days were spent in extreme poverty. At thirteen she obtained a job as an extra in a Cleveland stock company. After some years of playing various roles, she was taken on as leading actress by Wood's Museum in Cincinnati. Doing well enough there to fire her ambition, she applied at Daly's in New York wearing shabby clothes and almost penniless. She had a certain wistful prettiness, and during her first interview with Daly exerted herself to be lighthearted and amusing, while stating that she did best in serious roles. Daly assured her that he never had made a mistake in his entire life, and was certain that she couldn't deliver a line of sentiment if her soul depended upon it. She tried to argue the matter, since he had never seen her act, but he repeated that her abilities would definitely lie in comedy. He was underestimating the determination of this twenty-four-year-old woman. At the moment Daly was preparing a production of his own dramatization of a Wilkie Collins novel, *Man and Wife*; the heroine, abandoned by her husband, saves another woman from him by demonstrating that she is still his wife. Clara was given a comic role, and went home with the script utterly depressed. Luckily the actress who was to do the lead rejected the part as "immoral," and Clara was assigned the role instead. Daly became more and more dubious during rehearsals, but on opening night she was given an ovation. She never acted comedy for Daly.

She seemed to be a contradiction. As a private person she was merry, always laughing and in love with fun. On stage she was wildly passionate, incapable of restraint—even crude—but she could rock whole audiences with emotion, and make them weep with her. Tears were always at her command; she had only to think of some misery in her childhood, she said, to start a torrent. Her own explanation of her technique—or lack of it—was that she acted from her heart. Modjeska, who was her exact opposite, said that her performances were her own, her art "apart from any rules." Daly was pleased, increased her salary by $5 a week, and signed her for the following season at $55.

When she acted in Daly's adaptation from the French of *Divorce*, the part she had was that of a woman whom her jealous lover had shot and disfigured, and who eventually went mad. She went to Blackwell's Island to observe the insane. She was also anxious to bear a convincing scar on stage. One day in a horse-car she saw a woman whose throat had been slashed, and she made up her mind to reproduce that gash with makeup near her eye, with gum and plaster. During rehearsals, including the final one, she refused to let the company see what she intended to do during the crucial mad scene. On opening night, when the veil was torn aside to reveal the appalling scar, the audience expressed its shock; encouraged—for Clara never knew what she was going to do next—Clara let out a low "gibbering" laugh, raised it on a long crescendo until it became a shriek, and fell to the floor writhing. As the curtain descended, the house was in an uproar, and the next day the critics declared that she was the greatest emotional actress of the day.

Tears never failed the "Queen of Spasms." When she could not stimulate them by thinking of her childhood, she imagined her own death, or deliberately recalled some tragedy in a book or in the lives of people she had known. She was phenomenally successful despite an ordinary voice, a nasal twang, a not very graceful figure, her monotony and crudity of gestures, and her irritating mannerisms. Her career continued through middle age, though she grew stout and ugly. One periodical in 1880 suggested that if she were thinking of going to London, she had better be advertized "as an Indian star who speaks Choctaw, while the rest of the company speaks English . . . The novelty may be a sensation."

J. H. Barnes (1850–1925), an English actor, made his debut in 1871. In a tour of the United States he became leading man for Adelaide Neilson (1874). He visited America again in 1881. After that he performed frequently in the United States and England as Romeo, Macbeth, Benedick, Leontes, and Polonius. He also acted in various farces and melodramas. He hated the "filthy, sordid, realistic, ugly so-called problems" of the naturalistic dramas as they began to appear with greater frequency in his later years.

Barnes thought Forbes-Robertson's Prince of Denmark—as did many others—the most perfect of the age, "graceful, feeling, pathetic, scholarly, lovable."

He also described Macbeth as possibly the most difficult of all roles to play in Shakespeare because every one of his lines inspires the antagonism of the audience. To enact the part, he said, "is like rolling a barrel up a hill."

Frederick Barkham Warde (1851–1935) acted Shakespeare and lectured upon him. Prepared for the law, he left his studies and in 1867 joined a tiny touring troupe. After that he played in stock companies where he had the opportunity of acting with prominent stars like Adelaide Neilson and Henry Irving. Then he went to Booth's Theater in New York, where he immediately was successful, acting in Shakespeare with McCullough, Booth, and Charlotte Cushman.

In 1881 he had his own company, in which he starred chiefly in Shakespeare. He left the stage in 1919 but made a number of films in Shakespearean plays.

One of the very first five-reel silent movies featured Warde in *Richard III*. The program, dated March 22, 1914, reads: "A Genuine Novelty and Triumphant Success/ The Eminent Tragedian/ Mr/ Frederick Warde/ in Shakespeare's Historical Play/ Richard III/ Five Reels—5000 Feet/A Feature Costing $30,000 to Produce . . . /1500 People, 200 Horses/ 5 Distinct Battle Scenes. A Three-Masted Warship, Crowded with Soldiers, on Real Water . . ." *The New York Times* called the picture "a revelation in many ways. As a picture of conditions as they existed in England . . . it is far and away ahead of any stage presentation." The *Boston Herald* said: "There will hardly ever be a stage presentation . . . comparable with Richard III, as it is shown in picture form . . . This particular attraction is a far greater conception of Shakespeare's play than anything heretofore produced in Boston."

Warde's own account mentions the fact that the play had always been one of the most popular in his repertoire for many years. "An unoccupied estate on City Island, New York, was the location of our labors, and the charming landscape of Westchester County served as the green fields of midland England." There were difficulties, of course. "A picture of Gloucester's ride from Tewkesbury to London was required. Most of the roads in Westchester County are flanked by telegraph and telephone poles. That would not do for England in the fifteenth century." But the director discovered a lane without these utilities. A difficult horse required many retakes. When finally they had a very good shot, examination showed "a modern nursemaid wheeling a baby carriage, with two small children" in the background.

In 1916 the, by now, veteran Warde appeared in the title role of a cinematic version of *King Lear*. When released, it was advertized as "Shakespeare in every detail, except that of course it is produced upon a vastly larger scale than ever was possible on the speaking stage." In all these silent pictures, the substitute for the lines was an occasional subtitle: abbreviated or altered quotations from Shakespeare. The *Moving Pictures World* deplored the inevitable omission of Shakespeare's lines, but thought the five-reel picture well acted and effective. It went on to say, "The plot of *King Lear* when stripped of its wealth of marvelous verse, is a sordid story in which evil passion in many different forms is contrasted with the affection of the old King for his daughter Cordelia, and her love for him." The production was praised for its costuming and settings, which were correct and impressive. Warde and his fellow actors were commended for their ability to express "the soul of the tragedy, as well as its physical action." The greatest value of the picture was that it might lead many "to a study of the poet's works." Warde, no stranger to the role, was praised for the "grand manner necessary to the aged monarch," and for showing his jealousy of his dignity, his rashness, his blindness to everything but his feelings of the moment. A modern critic says that the Cordelia was poor; she merely "looked heavenward in anguish" and rolled her eyes.

George Ormond Tearle (1852–1901), an Englishman, made his first appearance at Liverpool in 1869, and two years later was at Warrington doing Hamlet, a role that he frequently enacted thereafter. Spending six years in the provinces, he came to London and formed his own company, with which he toured Britain. In 1880 he joined Wallack's stock company in New York, making his debut there as Jaques. Soon he was alternating between London and New York. In 1888 he formed a Shakespearean company which had much success at Stratford-on-Avon, and became an extremely valuable training place for young actors. A man of natural elegance and dignity, he was an excellent Shakespearean actor himself, and very popular in the provinces.

His son by his second wife, Godfrey Tearle (1884–1953), acted in his father's company until the elder Tearle's death. He made a good Othello, Hamlet, and Antony. He thereafter had a long and successful career on the London stage and in cinema. He was knighted in 1951.

Edward Smith Willard (1853–1915), an English actor, became celebrated for his villains in melodrama. He once played Hamlet in an attempt to do him realistically and make him modern, emphasizing his cynicism and bitterness and leaving out all the poetry.

His nephew, Edmund Willard (1884–1956) first acted under his uncle's management at Boston (1900) and appeared in London in 1903. After years in the provinces, he played a number of Shakespearean parts at Stratford-on-Avon in 1920/21. He was at his best in strong roles like Othello and Macbeth.

George Weir (1853–1909) was best known as a comedian, a prominent member of Benson's company. As Falstaff in *The Merry Wives* he was much liked. He made a notable Bottom (particularly convincing in his dazed recollection of having been transformed into a donkey); his Fluellen was "natural" as well as admirable; as Launcelot Gobbo he was delightfully comic and contrived business which was entirely in keeping with the play and the role; his Dromio was also admirable. Yet he was also remarkable for his dry humor as the Gravedigger, his grotesquerie as the First Witch and his gravity as the Gardener in *Richard II*.

The Drew family occupies an important place in the history of the American stage. Its importance was further increased by intermarriage with the Barrymores.

Louisa Lane (née Crane [1820–1897]) its first significant member, was herself the daughter of English actors who, in turn, could boast descent from actors in Shakespeare's day. As a child she played with Macready and Cooke. When her father died, her mother in 1827 took her to New York, where she exhibited her virtuosity by taking the part of a number of characters in the same play, and was much applauded for it. She had the opportunity to act with Junius Brutus Booth and Edwin Forrest, both her admirers. At sixteen she was playing Lady Macbeth, and toured the United States in a great many roles. The first of her many marriages was contracted at the age of sixteen.

Her most important work was as manager of the Arch Street Theater in Philadelphia from 1860 to 1892, which was eminently successful under her capable handling. In 1850 she married John Drew and thereafter it was as Mrs. John Drew that she was known.

John Drew (1827–1892) was an Irish actor who had a brief career unconnected with Shakespearean performances. Mrs. Drew had three children; the youngest, Georgiana, became Mrs. Maurice Barrymore, whose children were Ethel, Maurice, and John—of whom more later.

Her son John Drew (1853–1927) became a leading actor of his day. He performed in his mother's company and in 1875 was engaged by Daly to play with Fanny Davenport, and later with Ada Rehan. During the 1880s he was in London for several engagements, including *As You Like It* and *The Taming of the Shrew*; he was especially admired as Petruchio. In 1893 his *Twelfth Night* had an extended run in London. He had been as firmly trained by his mother as any other member of her company. Once when he returned from a tour at 4 A.M. Mrs. Drew, candle in hand, met him at the door and told him not to go to bed, and handed him a script, saying, "You play this tonight." The part was a very long one, and he acted it to perfection—he would not have dared to do otherwise. The success of John Drew and Daly's company in London with *The Taming of the Shrew* is noteworthy as the first triumph of an all-American cast in a Shakespearean comedy in that city.

Lily Langtry (née Le Breton [1853–1929]) was the daughter of the Dean of Jersey, a woman of such phenomenal beauty that she was generally called, after the title John Everett Millais gave to his portrait of her, "the Jersey Lily." At the age of twenty-two she married a rich Irishman, Edward Langtry. She was soon a favorite in the highest circles of London society, and eventually became the mistress (one of many) of the Prince of Wales, the future King Edward VII. She was the darling of society and she smugly observed that wherever she went, "to theatres, picture galleries, shops," she was "actually mobbed," and at social gatherings "many guests stood on chairs to obtain a better view" of her, and she heard herself being discussed wherever she moved. Before the days of press agents, she stood in need of none, and knew how to capitalize on her social success, which only increased when her relationship with the Prince of Wales became common knowledge. Her husband, obligingly, managed to obliterate himself from the scene.

Oscar Wilde, though then only twenty-five, had already realized the value of cultivating what was stylish, and had her to tea.

Edward, Prince of Wales, presently wearied of her, as he did with all his loves, and Lily was faced with financial distress, unable, with her tastes, to accommodate herself to a modest scale of living.

Since she was one of the first of society women prepared to go on the stage, the Bancrofts (also visitors at Wilde's lodgings) employed her at the Haymarket on December 15, 1881, as Kate Hardcastle. The result was a sensation but not because of her acting. Only an enormous salary had persuaded her to enter what she considered a very uninspiring vocation. But no stage fright overcame her; she was used, she said, to looming "largely in the public eye," and among the large audience she knew most of "the occupants of the stalls and boxes, and all in the cheaper parts knew me."

She had had herself coached by Mrs. Labouchère as Goldsmith's heroine, and it was she who first suggested that Lily be allowed to appear under the Bancrofts. Said Mrs. Bancroft: "We took a day to reflect and weigh the many *pros* and *cons* of the startling proposition involved." They agreed because they knew that if they refused, another theater would agree. "We also felt that the extraordinary career of popularity which had been Mrs. Langtry's lot for several London seasons must have destroyed all fear of complete failure," since she had "often and gracefully passed through" facing the public. "Never, perhaps, was a theatre more besieged for seats. All sections of society fought for places, and loud were the lamentations in many a high quarter" when seats were not obtainable. In advance of the opening "public excitement to be present at this exceptional *début* reached fever heat."

At the performance the audience "included the Prince and Princess of Wales, and representatives of great distinction in fashion, art, and literature."

The Bancrofts had further talks with her which made them realize her "desperation for an important stake, and we agreed upon the terms of an engagement until April," when their next production was scheduled. They cast her in parts that required no great talent. Lily felt her new profession doomed her to "a very dull and monotonous existence." Nevertheless, it was her sole way of earning a good living.

In my own college days I was a devotee of Gilbert and Sullivan, and I knew and relished Gilbert's satire of young Wilde walking "down Piccadilly/ With a poppy or a lily," and before that had read that Wilde had in fact publicly paraded his aestheticism by appearing in velvet, bearing a lily in his hand. But many years ago I read a book by Cosmo Hamilton, which I have since been unable to find, in which I remember his saying that what no one seemed to know was that though Wilde did indeed appear quite regularly in London streets with a lily in his hand, he was bearing the lily each time as a tribute to the Jersey Lily after her performance at the theater. I believe charity requires believing that explanation authentic.

Her engagement at the Haymarket was followed by a tour of the provinces, accompanied by many a torchlight parade. She was therefore encouraged to form her own company, and prepared to come with it to the United States.

Her advance publicity was so good that Americans were as eager as the English had been to see her. Among other parts, she appeared as Rosalind in *As You Like It*, in which part, although nowhere was her acting taken very seriously, she was acceptable, and filled Wallack's Theater for two weeks. Interest in her was further augmented by the news that she had a new intimate, the socially prominent millionaire, Frederick Gebhard. He accompanied her, as she went on tour, in her private railroad car. In some cities the financial returns were the highest in their history. She was more than pleased with her wildly enthusiastic reception in the United States, and said that for an actor it was "the promised land." She was probably not the less anxious to remain as a result of Gebhard's providing her with a luxurious house on West Twenty-third Street, where the entertainment was regal. Americans were, characteristically, scandalized by her flagrant immorality and therefore all the more captivated by her. Sarony, the photographer, who, for a very large sum, bought the exclusive rights to her pictures, could hardly supply the demand for them throughout the country.

When she next went on tour, though her acting in no way improved, her railroad cars were decorated on the outside in blue, with wreaths of golden lilies and considerable masses of brass designing the same flower. Within, the bedroom was in green silk brocade, the bath and its fittings were sterling silver, the curtains in both rooms were rosy silk trimmed with lace from Brussels. There was a large drawing room with a piano, two guest rooms, a maid's room, a pantry and kitchen, and sleeping quarters for her staff. There were great ice chests beneath the cars to store provisions. This was her residence, ever in motion, for five years, from which she permitted the United States to view her beauty, her gems, and her elaborate wardrobe. Langtry, in Texas, was named for her, but she did not visit it until the sheriff who had sponsored the idea was dead.

She was apparently not devoid of a sense of humor. She told Daniel Frohman that the funniest slip she ever heard on stage was: "Let us seek some nosey cook."

Fanny Whiteside Brough (1854–1914) came of a family of English actors, and first appeared in Manchester, where she also was the Ophelia to Barry Sullivan's Hamlet (1869). The next year she was in London. She acted under many managers of her day, and was particularly good in comedy, though Max Beerbohm found her a little too farcical.

Her uncle, Lionel Brough (1836–1900), was excellent as a clown in Shakespeare, and played with Tree. He toured extensively, and was very much liked in the United States and South Africa. In 1898 Max Beerbohm said of him that "he plays with such gusto as to make one forget that he was doing this kind of thing when the rest of the cast were in their cradles." He admired his Sir Toby Belch, and described his Host of the Garter in *The Merry Wives* as being "fruity and authoritative as ever."

Robert Bruce Mantell (1854–1928) was born in Scotland, first acted in Belfast, and came to the United States with Modjeska to play Tybalt. After remaining in her company for a while, he went back to England, where he worked hard but achieved little in the way of encouragement from the public. He returned once more to the United States and spent the rest of his life there. Two years with Fanny Davenport (1884 to 1886) brought him some recognition and encouraged him to form his own company. While still young and handsome he played chiefly romantic parts in melodramas, and as he grew older he specialized in Shakespeare; from 1910 he devoted twenty years to a repertory of Shakespearean tragedy and certain classical comedies. His limitations were considerable, but the country owed him one great debt: he brought good theater and plays to innumerable communities in the United States that had no playhouse and so had never seen theater at all.

His technique was a survival of the school of Forrest, of which he was probably the last representative. His powerful voice and physique were at least in accord with his old-fashioned methods. He was married four times to actresses who were for a time his leading ladies.

His Shylock was, like Macready's, a revengeful and formidable Jew, who was "bitterly resentful of the injuries" he had suffered. His Macbeth (1905) was at the beginning undecided and melodramatic, but gradually improved in power and vigor and became a warrior of powerful makeup, calm on the surface but buffeted by conflicting emotional states. He managed to project the correct idea that Macbeth had been brooding on the kingship before the play opens. Throughout he made him a man haunted, with his face growing more and more haggard, scene by scene. Winter thought him the best Macbeth after Edwin Booth, and also thought well of his Hamlet. Other criticisms were less enthusiastic.

Of these matters I cannot speak from personal knowledge, but I did see his Lear when he was about sixty-four and I fourteen. I think it was the first Shakespeare I ever saw on stage. The Bronx Opera House had a new play each week, and I was a regular attendant. I can remember nothing of the others, except the name of Cissy Loftus (I think I saw her as Becky Sharp, but I am not sure)—and years later I was delighted to read that Max Beerbohm had been in love with her. Well, one week it was *King Lear* with Robert Mantell and his company. All I carried away from the theater was that Lear was a very old man with a long streaming white beard (I have always thought of Mantell when I have read to classes Thomas Gray's ridiculous poem, "The Bard,"—whose beard *is* described as streaming in the wind before he takes his suicidal dive) and a great deal more shouting than I was to hear in the theater for a great many years to come. But the thing I remember best —for I had read the play over several times before seeing it—was that Mantell got himself so involved with his emotions during the storm sequence (a thing which Hamlet warns the players they must never do), that it was painfully obvious he had forgotten his lines, and could not go on. But he was a man of resource. He clutched his head, cried: "Oh my God!" and fell to the ground in a swoon—a bit of business which, I suppose, most of the audience took to be part of the play.

Richard Mansfield (1857–1907), son of a prima donna and a London vintner, born in Berlin, and educated in England and on the Continent, is for good reasons accounted an American actor. Going on tour in Gilbert and Sullivan in the English provinces, he eventually took some minor roles in London, then came to New York in 1882 to appear in operetta, but it was the next year that he began his reputation in a *Parisian Romance*, and he enhanced it by playing both roles in *Dr. Jekyll and Mr. Hyde*, in the part of Beau Brummel written especially for him by Clyde Fitch, and other contemporary plays. By temperament he was a romantic actor and had little use for the problem play which was coming into fashion, though he was an admirer of Ibsen's poetic dramas, and introduced Shaw in the United States by appearing as Bluntschli in *Arms and the Man* (1894) and Dick Dudgeon in *The Devil's Disciple* (1897). Beatrice Cameron (1868–1940) became his wife in 1892; she had appeared with him in minor roles, and later took important parts in the Shaw plays.

In 1889 he made his own version of *Richard III* for the Globe Theatre in London. Before his season there opened he went to Bournemouth, taking with him, he wrote, "the half-formulated plans and ideas of a *regenerated* [italics mine] 'Richard III.' " Every day "I was making up my mind more and more . . . as to what sort of man Richard o' Gloster was; and *now* no one can make me think he was otherwise than as I am when I wear his coat and cap. You may not like him, but he is a 'being,' which is more than the ranting, raving, sulking monstrosity you have been accustomed to was." The remark will seem odd when matched with his biographer's assurance that "he had never seen this play performed." But the statement is fully in character, for though to friends he was courteous, witty, and charming, fellow players thought him unbearably conceited and temperamental. Above all, he seems to have been pursued by the demon of originality; he could not tolerate the notion that his interpretations should be other than entirely his own. (In this respect he anticipated twentieth-century directors of Shakespeare.) Few, if any, actors have had more divergent criticisms: he was worshipped and ridiculed; he was loved and detested; he was praised for his versatility, and blamed for lacking variety because he always played himself, Richard Mansfield. Towse said no one could deny his powerful individuality, his unquenchable ambition, his concentrated egotism and his instinct for the best in art. The judgment that he never quit his own personality on stage is clearly an unfair one. In strange, bizarre or unusual characters he could completely transform himself, as in *Dr. Jekyll and Mr. Hyde*, *Monsieur Beaucaire*, or *Cyrano de Bergerac*. What he seemed to require was a role out of the beaten way; in short, an eccentric.

On one point friends and enemies agreed: there was about his playing an "electric" quality which gripped his audiences and held them fast. Even if they thought his gestures awkward or his speech in one key, he was never

boring. This ability to mesmerize his spectators made him the most discussed actor of his age.

His Richard III was a "laughing devil." As his biographer says, "He wiped
out three centuries of tradition with his first entrance. Here was no halting,
grizzled, lowering tyrant. There bounded forth instead, a sleek, sinuous
young Prince of nineteen, beau enough to cover somewhat his deformities,
a creature of blithe villainy." There was assurance of conquest in every curl
of his laughing lip or flash of his eyes. When Mansfield published his version
of the play, he appended a long note giving his reasons for a new interpretation and unusual rearrangements of the text. When Shakespeare wrote the
tragedy, he said he "was either desirous of pleasing the Tudor Court . . .
or drew his history from such corrupt authorities as Hall, Holinshed, and
the work . . . [probably] from the pen of that notable enemy to Richard—
Bishop Morton. Moreover, the great poet, in arranging the principal events
of Gloster's life . . . has so distorted, confused and glomerated deeds and
events" that the results are contrary to history. "Yet we surely may . . .
endeavour in some measure to make him appear as he really was." In
presenting the play, even if it is unhistorical, Mansfield continued, "the
deformity of his *mind*, as drawn by Shakespeare, has to be adhered to,
although history fails to corroborate it. Richard did not slay Edward, the son
of Henry VI, he did not kill King Henry, he did not murder his Queen, the
Lady Anne, and there are grave doubts as to his having been implicated in
the deaths of Edward V and his brother, absolutely no evidence existing that
Henry VII did not find both Princes alive on his accession. Regarding Lady
Anne, his affection for her was sincere. Legge says: 'She had inspired the
dreams of Richard's boyhood.' " (It is interesting to note that a few histori-
ans in our own time have insisted on these very revisions of Richard's story;
but whichever account may be the truth is irrelevant to the play, and if
Mansfield was professing to present Shakespeare's play, it was not for him
to alter it in accordance with what he believed to be historical fact. From all
that we know of what he said and did, Mansfield's passion for presenting
unique interpretations may have been the real motive for his alterations.)

Mansfield went on to say: "When Richard fought at the battle of Tewkesbury and then, according to popular tradition, hastened to London to dispatch Henry [VI], *he was only nineteen years of age.*" Mansfield therefore took
"the liberty of seizing upon the fact to contrast Richard in his earlier and
more careless days . . . with the haggard, conscience-stricken and careworn
tyrant Shakespeare paints him fourteen years later." And in that fashion he
acted him. He was youthful and gay at the opening of the play and more and
more grave, ruthless, and terrifying as the play proceeded. He wished, he
said, to show the progress of Richard's wickedness. Symbolically, in the
throne room he used a ray of red light streaming through a stained glass
window.

In arranging the text "and in curtailing what would be an impossibly long
play," he used some of Cibber's version. He opened the drama with passages from *Henry VI,* and the first act began with a lavish pageant of Queen

Elizabeth and her train entering the Tower of London. Then came Gloster's soliloquy, "Now is the winter of our discontent," which he cut off at "And hate the idle pleasures of these days," and at which point he appended passages from Part III and Part II of *Henry VI.* The last two acts were mostly Colley Cibber's.

Mansfield's statement about his first night of the *Richard III* is very revealing. He was nervous to the point of "actual torture. Yet as I walk down the Strand on my way to the theatre that night, and note the impassive, imperturbable faces of the passers-by, I must confess to myself that I would not change places with them—no, not for worlds. I have something that is filling my life brimful of interest . . ."

His experience in London was a disaster; his debt amounted to $167,000. When he brought *Richard III* to New York, most New York critics, unlike Winter, were unsympathetic, though in 1890 he scored a great hit in *Beau Brummel.*

In 1893 he invited comparisons with Edwin Booth and Henry Irving by performing Shylock on the smallest stage in New York, Hermann's (afterwards the Princess) Theater. The choice of playhouse was a mistake for it gave him no room for his own original ideas. The furniture and hangings were copied from various palaces in Venice; there was a fine string orchestra playing "Venetian" music composed for the occasion by Arthur Mees. The stage was decorated with a frame of flowers and foliage. The only significant Shylock Mansfield had seen had been old Samuel Phelps, who had performed it at Derby School, when Mansfield was a student there.

Mansfield worked on his Shylock for years. At first he played the role as a highly sympathetic one, emphasizing the "poetic tenderness of his domestic passages." (Where are they in the play?) Later he altered, transposed, cut, and condensed scenes—to the destruction of the play. His final analysis was that "Shylock is really the only natural person in most unnatural surroundings. The play itself, if written today, would be either instantly condemned or put down as a farcical comedy." Antonio "cannot find anybody to lend him three thousand ducats, but the man he everlastingly abused, kicked, and spat upon. Bassanio is confessedly a fortune-hunter [!], Gratiano a lick-spittle and time server, Lorenzo is a thief or *particeps criminis,* Jessica is unspeakable, and the Duke condemns Shylock in open court before the trial." This is originality with a vengeance, and a deafness to what the play actually says. Mansfield added that some day he would like to perform the play as it ought to be done "in the realm of poetic farce." He ended by making his Shylock "the embodiment of malignant, implacable hatred based on the endurance of a lifetime of contempt and revilement."

He adopted Irving's introduction of a scene in which Shylock comes home to find Jessica gone; he rushed from his house "in a sigh of heart-bleeding agony . . . and fell overwhelmed with misery, among the fantastics [i.e., the celebrants of the carnival—a scene, of course, not in Shakespeare, but presented again at Lincoln Center, New York, in 1973] as they rollicked away in the pitiless gloom." In the trial scene, when Portia bids him cut "this flesh from off his breast," Mansfield broke "forth in a mad rush to plunge his knife in Antonio's breast"—but was naturally stayed by Portia's "Tarry awhile." He spoke rapidly, assumed a nasal tone for the part, shrugged and bent frequently, and suggested a foreigner among the Venetians by lengthening his vowels, turning his *d*'s into *t*'s (e.g., "My meaning in saying he ees a goot man ees to have you understand me that he ees suffeecient"; "There be land ratz and vatter ratz, vatter tieves and land tieves"), the syllables were cadenced, the vowels were round and melodious, and the consonants crackled.

In New York he lost $8,000 when he presented the play. Sometimes he failed in the metropolis, sometimes he was a success, but he always made money on the road.

In 1900 he gave *Henry V*—his reasons: "its healthy and virile tone [so diametrically in contrast to many of the performances now current]; the nobility of its language . . . the lesson it teaches of godliness, honour, loyalty, courage, cheerfulness and perseverance . . . But perhaps I was influenced beyond any other reason by the desire to drag Henry V out of a slough of false impressions that had materially affected his impersonation on the stage." When presented at Madison Square Garden its curtain rose at 7:45 P.M. and descended after the last act shortly after midnight. There was a great deal of spectacle: the courts of England and France with pages, courtiers, their entourage; waving banners; flashing armor; excited crowds; slum backgrounds for Bardolph, Pistol, and company; the quay at Southampton with the English fleet at anchor; a tumultuous siege of Harfleur, which was stoutly battlemented; a vast hillside of fighters at Agincourt; the marriage of Harry and Kate in the Cathedral at Troyes. In the fourth act he took a hint from Charles Kean's interpolation, with a pantomime of the English returning from Agincourt; the scenery this time showed an open space at the end of London Bridge. The streets, roofs, windows, and bridge were crowded with holiday-makers, flags, banners, and garlands; the cries of vendors, the shouts of boys, the laughter of people, the blare of trumpets, and the bells of Westminster and St. Paul's were heard; the lord mayor and his suite, all in scarlet and ermine, and the civic guard moved on to the Bridge to meet King Harry. The guard came back, pressed the crowd back to make way for the procession, while the mayor and his suite also returned. The trumpets heralded the appearance of the soldiers: company after company of bowmen, archers, men with pikes, and others passed through the cheering mobs, their clothes ragged from war, their faces beaming with rapture. A woman rushed out and kissed her son as he passed by; another pushed her way through the lines to embrace her wounded husband, and marched along with him; a girl searched the faces for her lover, could not find him, asked an officer, who shook his head and whispered to her, and she fainted and was carried along with the crowd; knights and their entourage followed—and everyone in the audience expected at last to see the king; but not yet! First there were dukes, then princes, stopping to line the way for him; another flourish again ushered in not him but a group of white-swathed maidens with palm branches who danced across the stage; next a singing choir of cathedral boys in scarlet were followed by a bishop, the Archbishop of Canterbury and their attendants; and finally, amid trumpet-blasts, bells clanging, drum-rolls, cannon-roars, King Henry rode in amongst them on his white horse.

The role was less taxing than Richard or Shylock (or Cyrano) but he wore seven different costumes during the course of the play. One night as a friend was helping with the wedding raiment, Mansfield said in his dressing room, "If this part kills me, you must inscribe on my tombstone, 'He died of buttoning and unbuttoning.' "

Towse summed up the pros and cons in Mansfield's acting career by saying that when he was performing at his best there were few players who were more interesting than he, and that when he was at his worst there were even fewer who could be more exasperating. As we have seen he was less than amiable; he was, moreover, given to violent outbursts of undirected fury when matters were not going the way he wished. Once, before the curtain went up, a stagehand accidentally dropped a broom against his dressing room door, and Mansfield let out a volley of epithets.

Yet for all that, and although he died while I was still an infant and I therefore never saw him, his name will always be quasi-sacred to me because I believe I can ascribe my passion for the theater to him (and David Warfield) —by surrogate.

My mother's eldest brother, Émile, who functioned as undisputed head of the family circle, was an inveterate theatergoer, and when my mother's large collection of sisters, brothers, nieces, and nephews got together, as they did every Easter Sunday, Thanksgiving Day, Christmas and New Year's Day, Uncle Émile always presided gently but authoritatively. After a sumptuous turkey dinner superintended by my mother—these festivities were always at our house, possibly because my mother was Uncle Émile's favorite, and he himself had been a sorrowing widower since long before I was born —it was an unfailing part of the order of the day that his sisters would clamor, "Do a scene from Richard Mansfield, Émile!" and, presently, "Do that scene from David Warfield, Émile!" As I became more advanced in boyhood I began to understand that, having given an account of that season's Broadway, Émile not only loved the requests—he expected them. He would get up into the center of the room, a tall, handsome, muscular man, and launch into a passage in what I have no doubt was a good imitation of Richard Mansfield's style. How often have I heard "Once more unto the breach, dear friends, once more," and "Now is the winter of our discontent" and (always in demand, though brief) "A horse! a horse! my kingdom for a horse!" and "I have possess'd your Grace of what I purpose." After a few of these, David Warfield would follow, and then a burst of applause from the family, eagerly seconded by me for two reasons: first, because although I had never been taken to a theater, Uncle Émile somehow made me feel that I was in one and that *he* was the legendary Richard Mansfield; and next, because if the applause was loud and prolonged enough, Uncle Émile could be induced to do as an encore my favorite, "The Face on the Barroom Floor," at the final lines of which we would all cry out, "Fall on the floor, Émile, fall on the floor!" Which he sometimes obligingly did.

Mansfield himself had a magnificent and melodious voice, but it was a shock to me many years later to find out that he was, like so many leading actors of the past, below average height, and that he had not much hair, which he therefore combed fairly flat. When he had been my Uncle Émile, he had been very tall, very handsome, with a marvelous mane of black hair.

Philip Ben Greet (1857–1936), born Philip Barling, after experience at Southampton and Margate went to London where he appeared with well-known actors like Lawrence Barrett and Mary Anderson. In 1866 he began to give his many productions of Shakespeare out-of-doors, and formed a company with which he toured Britain and the United States. Many a future star had his early training in Greet's company, and many schoolchildren from 1920 to 1930 owed to his company their introduction to Shakespeare on the stage. Over a million saw his productions in London County Council Schools. Though he spent many years in New York, he returned to England, and was one of the founders of the Old Vic, where between 1915 and 1918 he gave twenty-four of Shakespeare's plays. Though far from a great actor himself, he was an important force in spreading the popularity of Shake-spearean drama both in Great Britain and the United States during a period when their production had fallen off. Shaw thought him quite poor as an actor. As Touchstone, he said, he proved his inadequacy within two minutes of his appearing on the stage, and on another occasion called him "an exasperating placid Polonius." As a producer he was less the scholar than the sympathetic interpreter, but his love and patience for his work were unbounded. In 1929 he was knighted for his services to the theater.

Otis Skinner (1858–1942) first appeared in Philadelphia in 1877 and two years later at Niblo's Garden. He spent some years with Edwin Booth, from whom he learned much, and Lawrence Barrett, and then joined Augustin Daly's company, going with it to London. In 1890 he was seen there as Romeo. With Modjeska he toured in such roles as Benedick and Orlando. As Falstaff (of *Henry IV, Part I*) he was seen in 1926 and two years later as the same person (who is a very different one!) in *The Merry Wives of Windsor.* Late in life he appeared as Shylock to the Portia of Maude Adams, and as Thersites in *Troilus and Cressida.* His training had been in the grand style, which equipped him to develop a wide range of parts. Garff Wilson calls him "the last of the old guard," and Lloyd Morris remarks that Skinner gave great performances in plays like *The Taming of the Shrew* and *The Merchant of Venice,* and could step into such roles right after the slenderest of comedies, but that it was even more impressive that he could make second-rate plays seem important by his superb acting.

His career lasted some sixty years, and in addition to a resonant voice and an agile, athletic body, he was gifted with that mysterious incandescence of which I have spoken in my first chapter. He never failed to hold his audience, no matter how foolish the play. He was long remembered for one such, *Kismet,* an oriental fantasy (1911), which, oddly enough, though one of the silliest of plays, made a first-rate musical comedy in our own time, largely because of a fair amount of faithfulness to the lovely melodies and harmonies of Borodin and the brilliant acting and singing of Alfred Drake.

In 1924 he calculated that he had acted 325 different parts, had taken, at various times, 38 roles in 16 of Shakespeare's plays, and produced under his own direction 33 plays.

Frank Benson (1858–1939) is best known for the English company he formed, and of which he was actor-manager. With them he toured the provinces for many years, constantly keeping Shakespeare in the public eye, and providing invaluable training for many young actors. A graduate of Oxford, he was a man of culture, and made his own earliest appearances on the professional stage under Henry Irving, who had come with Ellen Terry to see the *Agamemnon* of Aeschylus which young Benson had produced himself at Oxford, playing the role of Clytemnestra. Benson had also established himself as an outstanding athlete at the university by winning the three-mile against Cambridge; as a fellow athlete Bram Stoker invited Benson to the Lyceum, and after the show took him to Irving's dressing room.

Irving was very encouraging. "You young men did splendidly," he said to Benson. "If only I had had the opportunity in my young days that you have in yours! Why do you not band together in your troupe, work, study and become a company, the like of which this age has not seen? We have the technical skill upon the stage, we have the traditions; the difficulty nowadays is to get a company that has the literary mind and the trained intellectuality that is associated with university students. Should any of you determine to adopt the stage as your profession I shall be only too glad to render you any assistance I can." (The lack of "literary mind and the trained intellectuality" of which Irving spoke is far more apparent today, even in those who have been to a university. It is these gaps which have made most Shakespearean performances in recent years a painful experience.)

After studying voice production, Benson asked Irving for a role at the Lyceum. When he appeared at the stage door, the keeper showed him a crowd of people waiting in the passage. "They all want to see Mr. Irving." That crowd contained, he went on, peers, M.P.s, painters, poets, "the pick of the land," but they were all told "they can't see the Guv'nor this morning"; Irving was talking over old times with an old crony, would be at it for two hours, and end by thanking his own good fortune and slipping "two tenners" into his old friend's hand. "If you wait for hours you won't see him." Benson protested that he had been told to appear for rehearsal at eleven. (Irving had just lost the actor who was to do Paris in *Romeo and Juliet* and had offered the part to Benson.) The keeper having got matters straight, Benson was introduced to the company, who treated him with kindness. There was a hush as Irving came on stage; seeing Benson, he gave him a friendly nod and said, "Glad to see you—me boy—hope you'll be comfortable."

During the rehearsal Benson lost nearly all his self-confidence. What he was counting upon was his skill as a fencer, in which he was sure he was better than anyone at the Lyceum. In the scene when he had to duel with Romeo, he took the right stance; Irving saw at once that the youth knew nothing about *stage* fencing. Adjusting his spectacles, Irving fell on the astounded youth, seized his foil with one hand, hit him over the knuckles with his sword, prodded him in the belly with his knee, clashed the swords once, and muttered: "Die—me boy—die—down—down," elbowed and kneed him into the opening of the tomb, and stood over him holding his torch. It had all taken a minute. The lessons of the fencing school had been routed by the techniques of stage dueling.

On the first night, he was in too great a state of shock to evaluate his performance, but, with her usual kindness, Ellen Terry had left a note for him: "Well done for first done." Through her backing, he was allowed the privilege of sitting with the prompter to take notes of the performance. Once he had the folly of doing the unheard of—approaching Irving while he was resting on a chair between scenes. "A very beautiful part, that of Romeo," he observed. "Yes," Irving retorted, "and the odd thing about it is that every damn young fool who's been on the stage two minutes thinks he can play it." (This may have been a reference to the one occasion in which Benson had paid three guineas for the opportunity to play Romeo at the Imperial Theatre in 1881.) After that Benson kept his distance until Irving said to him: "You are too modest, Benson—too modest, ye know. Or, at least—you pretend to be."

The following year, 1883, Benson formed his company and took it on tour, in London and the provinces. In the course of his managership he produced every one of Shakespeare's plays except *Titus Andronicus* (no loss) and *Troilus and Cressida*. His brilliance as a manager-producer was superior to his abilities as an actor. Agate said that as Caliban in *The Tempest*, he "used to hang by his toes from the tops of poplars, leaving Prospero to be played by the stick engaged for Duncan." (Agate, who had not much use for the play, congratulated Irving for having had the sense never to attempt Prospero.) Agate further described Benson's figure as "gnarled, . . . sheer botching as an imitation of humanity, yet inspiring as a gargoyle, with some of the demonic fury proper to Hamlet." But he paid him the compliment of being the first to rediscover *Richard II* (a work far superior to the always popular *Richard III*). Despite the defects of his voice and movement the title role of that play and the role of Petruchio were his best performances.

At the height of the success of his companies, there were no fewer than three of them touring the country; he also toured the United States, Canada, and South Africa (1913/14, 1921). Indeed, by 1886 his companies had proved themselves so invaluable that he was invited to take charge of the Shakespearean festival at Stratford-on-Avon at the Memorial Theatre, which by that time was in existence. For the next thirty-three years he produced plays for twenty-eight spring and a half-dozen summer festivals at that playhouse. As acknowledgment of his services, he was given freedom of the borough, an honor granted only once before—to David Garrick. His last assumption of directorship of the Memorial Theatre was in 1919.

At the tercentenary performance of Shakespeare at Drury Lane, on May 2, 1916, he was enacting Caesar in *Julius Caesar,* and at the conclusion George V knighted him in the stage box, the only time an actor was ever knighted in a theater. There was a moment of embarrassment, when it was found that no sword was available; but the ceremony was conducted with a property sword of the company.

Although nearly sixty, Benson served as an ambulance driver in World War I and received the French *croix de guerre.* As John Parker says: "He gave the best years of his life to spreading the love of Shakespeare throughout the world," and, "His genius lay in the opportunities which he afforded to the many capable young artists . . . many of whom achieved greater fame than Benson himself. His company became the nursery for the English stage."

As an actor, despite the numerous parts he attempted, Benson was not very good. Max Beerbohm was astonished at the excellence of his Richard II; Benson "was acting much better than he had acted in other plays— showing . . . just that quality of imagination which one had thought was utterly denied him." However, he appended, "Of his Malvolio, the less said the better." Of Benson's revival of *Antony and Cleopatra* Max wrote: "The gods, I fear, are anxious to destroy Mr. F. R. Benson"; it was the only way to account for Benson's appearing as Antony; "clearly he is on the Olympian black-list." As Hamlet, he was thoughtful rather than imaginative; "his bearing is distinguished rather than beautiful . . . His voice, his face, his limbs, are not safe and ready vehicles for transmission of what is in him . . . He is a made actor, not a born actor"; his gestures rather mar than illuminate the words; "When he says 'The time is out of joint,' he shakes his arms in front of him, as though to imply that he feels it in his own joints. When he says 'There is nothing evil, but *thinking* makes it so,' he taps his forehead with his finger."

Nor as a director was he completely admirable. His interpolations were often as broad as Tree's. In his *Henry V,* the night before Agincourt, French noblemen were frolicking with dancing girls; Henry himself paused in his great speech so the sound of bells ringing in the feast of Crispin could be heard. (Years later, he added a line: "Hark the bells!") The end of the battle terminated in a tableau which reminded one critic of the chorus from *Patience,* "Each is bending on his knee"; soon an archbishop led a contingent of monks chanting a requiem. Max's comment: "A branch of university cricket." When he was middle-aged, Benson, in full armor, in order to suggest Henry's youth, pole-vaulted to the walls of Harfleur.

George Alexander (né George Samson [1858–1918]) started out in 1875 as a businessman, by his father's wish, but four years of business was all he could stomach, and after joining an amateur group, he decided on a theatrical career. He played in the provinces, toured with a company, and in 1881 was with Irving at the Lyceum, though at first he was hesitant about accepting the position; he felt he was still too inexperienced. One of his early roles was that of Paris in *Romeo and Juliet*. On the Canadian tour in 1884 he became the leading "juvenile" of the company; Irving described him as "one of the most gentlemanly and unaffected fellows I've ever met." From Pittsburgh Irving commented on the "petty jealousies" being exhibited by the members of the company; "Alexander is the only actor I ever met who is absolutely free from it. And because he has a finer nature than any of the men with whom he is associated he is made to suffer things which are very hard to bear." In Boston Alexander was given the role of Benedick "at very short notice and, except for a few slips, played it very well." Alexander also played Claudio in the same play, Macduff, and other Shakespearean roles.

There is little reason to believe that he was very good in Shakespeare. In a later production of *Much Ado* (1898), when he had for some years been actor-manager himself, Shaw said of his Benedick: "He smiles, rackets, and bounds up and down stairs like a quiet man who has just been rated by his wife for habitual dullness before company. . . . The charm of Benedick cannot be realized by the spryness of the actor's legs, the flashing of his teeth, or the rattle of his laugh." The judgment was not harsh. The fact is that Alexander's importance as an actor-manager was his eagerness (unlike Irving's aversion) to produce plays by his contemporaries. He gave Pinero, Henry Arthur Jones, Stephen Phillips, and many others (*The Second Mrs. Tanqueray* was first presented by him), and he was responsible for producing one of the most priceless of English comedies, *The Importance of Being Earnest* (1895). In such plays he performed the lead with brilliance. He was knighted in 1911.

Frank Rodney (1859–1902), a member of Benson's company, had the makings of what was later known as the matinée idol, and was a most graceful and attractive Bassanio and Ferdinand. But he was a man of greater scope than that, and Crosse thought him the best Feste he had ever seen; as that delightful clown he gave the audience an understanding of what it meant to be a fool from that professional's own inner feelings. When, for instance, Olivia came on in the first act, he seemed to gather his faculties together as though announcing, "Well, now I must be amusing." He also made a fine, cold and crafty Bolingbroke in *Richard II*. His Macduff arousing the household after Duncan's murder was apparently an experience that spectators never forgot. His untimely death at the age of forty-three was a great loss to the Shakespearean stage.

Louis Calvert (1859–1923) was the son of the English actress Adelaide Calvert, all of whose eight children went on the stage. Louis was the only significant one. He appeared with Irving at the Lyceum in 1887, later seen with a great many of the leading managers in London, and did several of

Shaw's plays. He formed his own company and toured England and the United States, where he acted in a number of Shakespearean plays. He was a first-rate performer, had a fine voice and a robust physique. Equally at home in the classics and modern plays, he was especially noted for his Mercutio, Casca, Falstaff, Hamlet, and Caliban.

His book, *Problems of an Actor,* is very interesting and full of wise suggestions, such as his advice to initiate a passionate role with less violence than a player may be tempted to use, for Shakespeare's passionate characters are difficult and physically enervating to perform; they require complete breath control, and often feats of an athletic nature such as fencing. (The failure to understand the necessity of tempering violence is the chief reason why few actors have been equal to doing Lear, for it is a part that begins *fortissimo* and increases in violence from there.) Calvert was one of the few commentators who had the insight to reject Hamlet as a procrastinator or as a man melancholy by nature; he correctly saw his melancholy as caused by grief and disillusionment; he reminds us, too, that Hamlet was a soldier as well as a scholar; instead of being, as the popular notion had persisted in accepting, a weak man eager to avoid action, he is actually "a strong man pinioned and bound." It is sad that having understood so much of Hamlet better than most interpreters, that (like most critics) not understanding what the Elizabethans thought about ghosts, Calvert should have erroneously concluded that the shock of the Ghost's "revelations" drove Hamlet into insanity. He was very good on Polonius, saw him for what he is, "a kind of clown . . . fond of the sound of his own voice," and "an accomplished liar."

Mary Anderson (1859–1940), an American actress of remarkable beauty, saw Charlotte Cushman, who encouraged her to act. She first appeared in Louisville, Kentucky, as Juliet at the age of sixteen. Later she also did Bianca. She presently was touring the United States and later went to London. In 1885 she performed Rosalind at Stratford-on-Avon, and repeated the performance on her return to New York. She played a wide variety of parts, many of them non-Shakespearean, but she also acted Lady Macbeth and Desdemona. She was gifted with a superb voice, which was marred in performances by faulty elocution. A general criticism was that she was far too self-conscious on stage. One of her celebrated feats, however, was to double as Hermione and Perdita in *The Winter's Tale.* Although immensely popular, the critics found her too cold an interpreter, though some interpreted that as "distinction."

It may be wondered how she managed to be both mother and daughter in *The Winter's Tale,* since the last scene requires both to be on stage at the same time; the solution was to use another girl for that scene and omit Perdita's apostrophe to the statue. She has several times since been been imitated. *The American* waxed lyrical over her Perdita, where she led the dance of the shepherds and shepherdesses; "it was worth traveling miles to see," for her dancing was a "revelation of sylph-like grace and irresistible charm." The play was her favorite, and Winter thought her quite as good as Hermione. At the Lyceum it held the stage for 164 nights, and, as she said, "had not my tenancy of the Lyceum then expired, it would probably have run for another hundred."

One thing she perceived, which most modern directors, more interested in inventing new gimmicks, fail to see, is that the hints for the movements and necessary stage business are more often than not, despite a paucity of "stage directions," indicated by Shakespeare's lines themselves.

One of the oddities of her career is that she began as a star and remained one; another is that while the critics almost always condemned her, the public worshiped her, despite her lack of training and finish. She had the wisdom to retire at the height of her success, and she acted for only a little over thirteen years, refusing all tempting offers to return to the theater.

It is said that she decided to become an actress as a girl after seeing Edwin Booth play in Louisville. It was in the attic of her home that she at once began preparing herself for the stage by reading Shakespeare and books on voice and elocution. The only professional teaching she ever had were ten one-hour lessons in New York from George Vandenhoff; before long she was ready for her debut as Juliet in her native city.

In the South her appearances created a sensation. Seats which usually sold for 75 cents sold for $25, and she drew larger audiences than anyone since Forrest. When she played in Boston and New York the receipts for one day were as high as $9,000. In London she was paid more at the Lyceum than anyone on record, and hundreds were turned away from the doors. On her return to the United States, the newspapers referred to her as "OUR MARY." Her figure and face had some of the perfection of Greek sculpture, and her voice possessed a velvety richness. She satisfied the ideals of her time by presenting a picture of virginal purity and refinement. But her acting range was lamentably limited. Towse, critic of the New York *Evening Post*, said she had "certain formulas" which she applied "to corresponding types of situation with a deadly and unmodified reiteration. In the mechanism of her art she never advanced beyond a moderate proficiency." She was also criticized for the artificiality of her acting, and its utter lack of warmth and artistic sincerity. Above all, she was always the classically beautiful Mary Anderson, never identifying herself with the role she was enacting.

Of course, non-Shakespearean plays engaged her attention too. She seemed made, for instance, for W. S. Gilbert's *Pygmalion and Galatea,* and the pictures of her in that part seem like the *beau idéal* (according to Victorian notions, of course) of what a classical Greek statue (well swathed) must be like. She would have nothing to do with plays that "drag one through the mire of immorality, even when they show a good lesson in the end." Nothing that could not be said in her parlor should be heard in a theater, she observed. Jestingly W. S. Gilbert once said to her: "I hear that you hate gross things so much that you can hardly be induced to take your share of the gross receipts."

When she was engaged by Henry Abbey for the Lyceum in 1883 to appear there for two seasons, he furnished very lavish settings. She longed for "the simple scenery of the old days, when the characters were the chief consideration, and the upholsterer and scenic artist very minor adjuncts!"

It is astonishing that with her fabulous success she should have retired—without any fanfare—before she was twenty-nine! But the truth is that she grew to dislike her profession. She could no longer bear "to live for months at a time in one groove, with uncongenial surroundings, and in an atmosphere seldom penetrated by the sun and air; to be continually repeating the same passions and thoughts in the same words."

A year after leaving the stage she married Antonio de Navarro, a very rich man, and she settled in England, where she lived until she was over eighty.

Ada Rehan (née Crehan [1860–1916]) was born in Limerick, Ireland, but was brought to the United States at the age of five. Her brother-in-law, the dramatist, Oliver Byron, arranged her first appearance at the age of thirteen in a play he had written. After that she joined Mrs. John Drew's company in Philadelphia. There, a printer's error was responsible for the name she retained.

She was with touring groups supporting on various occasions Edwin Booth, Adelaide Neilson, John McCullough, Lawrence Barrett, and other celebrities, and was much beloved by audiences in New York and London (where she first acted in 1884). Under the direction of Augustin Daly she and John Drew became a famous comedy team. A beautiful woman of great charm and lovely voice, she had a large repertory, including the Shakespearean heroines. Critics vied with one another in deciding which was her finest role. One thought her Viola exquisite in its moving tenderness. Another named Katharina in *The Taming of the Shrew*. Winter said that Portia was her favorite role, and that she was "the dazzling white and golden beauty whom the poet had drawn." Shaw, who went to see her Rosalind at Islington, wrote: "I never see Miss Ada Rehan act without burning to present Mr. Augustin Daly with a delightful villa in St. Helena," where he could produce "a complete set of Shakespear's plays. entirely rewritten, reformed, rearranged, and brought up to the most advanced requirements of the year 1856." (Shaw was writing this in 1897.) "And to think that Mr. Daly will die in his bed, whilst innocent presidents of republics, who never harmed an immortal bard, are falling . . . [just because] they assassinate the wrong people! And yet . . . I confess I would not like to see Mr. Daly assassinated," because he trained his company well enough to secure "him a position in London which was never questioned until it became apparent that he was throwing away Miss Rehan's genius." She ought to be tired, Shaw went on, trying "to astonish provincials with versions of Shakespear" which are way below London standards. "I must live in hope that some day she will come to the West End of London." As Rosalind he complimented her on her figure, and the "miracles" of her vocal expression. "But the critic in me is bound to insist that Ada Rehan has as yet created nothing but Ada Rehan. She will probably not excel that masterpiece." Why does she not, Shaw asked, take an example from Duse, who is always Duse but who is a different woman in every part she takes?

Ada Rehan obviously was another one of the fortunates whose inner glow hypnotizes an audience. People who visited her in her dressing room felt it when no one else was present, during careless chit-chat. Her style was classical—that is to say, somewhat artificial for her day—but she was mistress of it and no one thought of criticizing her adversely. Shaw warned that if she persisted in playing those light manufactured (non-Shakespearean) roles which Daly found for her, she was bound to become increasingly oratorical in manner. But she stayed with Daly. And Shaw's advice turned out—unhappily for her—to be have been sound. As the new realistic drama became more and more popular, she discovered that she could not adapt herself to the naturalness required. Moreover, her youthful sprightliness naturally vanished with the years, and in the 1903/04 season Otis Skinner, who was touring with her in three plays which had been great favorites of the public, observed sadly that "the exquisite comedienne" with whom he had had five happy years of association "was no more." In 1905, at the age of forty-five, when a truly great actress ought just be coming into her own, she retired. Eleven years later she died.

John Martin-Harvey (1863–1944) was educated as a Swedenborgian, probably because his grandfather was a minister of that sect; but early in life he joined the Church of England. At school he excelled in drawing, and in later life he drew many fine sketches; he never gave up the idea that he might have done very well if he had chosen the fine arts as his profession. From the one occasion on which I saw him act—or rather *heard* him perform—I suspect that he was right in that belief.

His father was a noted builder of yachts, and while making one for W. S. Gilbert, the latter suggested that young John study with John Ryder, who had been a leading man in Macready's company. John first appeared in 1881 as a boy at the Court Theatre; the next year he joined Irving's company at the Lyceum and remained with it for fourteen years. His earnestness endeared him to the actor-manager, and he made himself useful as a juvenile. In 1889 some of the company, Martin-Harvey being one of the leaders, toured the country with *Othello* and another play. While acting his minor roles at the Lyceum, he was given casual commendation by Shaw in a passing phrase. With Forbes-Robertson he played Osric, the best, said Shaw, he had ever seen.

He left the Lyceum in 1896 for the Court Theatre, where he continued playing chiefly non-Shakespearean parts. In 1899 he made a sensation at the Lyceum, which he was now managing, in a sentimental dramatization of *A Tale of Two Cities*. His sudden success as Sydney Carton has been credited in part to Angelita Helena de Silva (1869–1949), an actress who was of a distinguished Spanish family, and who was his leading lady for years. They married during that eventful year in which he triumphed as Carton (the play was called *The Only Way)* and took over the management of the Lyceum. She had been suggesting the play for years and was the one who finally entitled it. Though he gave many other dramas, he was constantly reviving *The Only Way*, and always attracted an enthusiastic audience.

He did produce *Hamlet* (1904), *Richard III* (1910), and *The Taming of the Shrew* (1913).

In 1910 he took his production of *Hamlet* to Stratford, under the influence of Gordon Craig, who had been revolutionizing the use of scenery. Martin-Harvey gave up all pretense of suggesting by costume or achitecture either the eleventh century or Shakespeare's. The set was made up of immense triangular pillars, shaped like prisms, placed at either end of the stage, and turning upon an axis to indicate different sites by the decorations on them.

To aid the Red Cross during World War I, he gave four plays at His Majesty's Theatre within four weeks. The first was *Hamlet,* in which he abandoned his prisms, as a result of a meeting with Max Reinhardt before the war began, and arranged various curtains against an immense concave white canvas (representing the horizon). As Arthur Machen said of the set: "Everything was suggested, nothing was declared"; he found the scenery admirable since there were no details to distract the attention of the audience. *The Taming of the Shrew* followed in a single set, a magnificent fifteenth-century summer house. *Richard III* was next with the actor-manager giving the traditionally monstrous Richard. The last, *Henry V,* was the least successful; for though appropriate to the times, Martin-Harvey was unable to rise to the stature of its hero. But he had performed a real service, as one critic observed; Martin-Harvey had taught the English-speaking world how little scenery mattered.

In 1912 he gave *Oedipus Rex* (as people persist in calling it) at Covent Garden, which was declared "heart-moving in its sorrow and grief," and caused some to declare that here was proof that he might have risen to greater heights in his profession had he not chosen to be identified for most of his career with melodramatic parts like that of Carton. It was this production that I saw, when he brought it over to the United States in 1923, the *annus mirabilis* of Jane Cowl's superb Juliet, John Barrymore's brilliant Hamlet, Eleanora Duse's farewell tour, the visit of the eye-opening Moscow Art Theatre in Chekhov and Gorki (where no one was a star, and every actor was of star quality), the first production of Shaw's *Saint Joan* with Winifred Lenihan, the Player's Club's delicious revival of *The School for Scandal*, Molnar's *The Swan* with Eva Le Gallienne, unforgettable *Sun Up* with Lucille LaVerne, Philip Barry's *You and I,* Elmer Rice's *The Adding Machine,* Katharine Cornell astounding the town in *Will Shakespeare*—none of which, I am glad to say, I missed (there were others I cannot remember). It was that season that I saw Sir Martin-Harvey's *Oedipus* (he had been knighted two years earlier), a play I have always worshiped. And I am sorry to report that it struck me as the only silly thing of the entire theatrical year—because of Sir Martin-Harvey. I had never heard any actor use his voice that way, like an opera singer, swooping up and down the scale in every sentence, as though he were burlesquing a coloratura soprano in a Donizetti opera. Though I was a very young man, I had had no idea that *Oedipus Tyrannos* could be made ridiculous, but he managed that.

I did hear, however, from a friend who was an actor, a story connected with Sir Martin-Harvey's visit to New York. In 1923 there were not yet any cafeterias in London and he was having his first experiences with one in the interval between a matinée and an evening performance. He apparently relished the whole business of carrying a tray along the railing, picking up whatever he wanted, bringing it to the table. "What fun!" he said to my friend. And then, when both had finished their meal, such as it was, Sir Martin-Harvey turned to my friend, and said seriously and happily, "I say, old fellow, where do we *wash* these things?" It is an endearing touch that almost—though not quite—exculpates him from the crime of his Oedipus.

Benjamin Webster (1864–1947), a Londoner, was the son of William Shakespeare Webster, a solicitor, and the grandson of Benjamin N. Webster, manager of the Haymarket and the Adelphi, under whom many of the earlier Victorian stars, such as Macready, had served. Ben was trained for the law, too, and actually admitted to the bar. But he met May Whitty (1865–1948), well known to our contemporaries as Dame Whitty, and in order to be near her he joined her company (managed by John Hare and W. H. Kendal) in 1887. He was a golden-haired young man with classic features, a great deal of charm, and soon was recognized as an accomplished juvenile lead. The next year he was with Irving at the Lyceum, and played Malcolm.

After a courtship of seven years, he and Miss Whitty were married in 1892. He had been in modern plays with George Alexander, now returned with his wife to Irving in 1895, and remained at the Lyceum until Irving's final season there, having accompanied the actor-manager on an American tour. In 1905 and 1907 he was in the United States again, playing leads for Mrs. Patrick Campbell. He appeared mostly in non-Shakespearean parts, such as the great New York success *Night Must Fall* (1936), with his wife, and the next year he went with her to Hollywood when it was made into a movie.

When he appeared in *Cymbeline* with Irving, Shaw said that he and Gordon Craig were "desperate failures as the two noble savages. They are as spirited and picturesque as possible; but every pose, every flirt of their elfin locks, proclaims the wild freedom of Bedford Park." Craig's verse was the "more musical" of the two, and Webster's fight with Cloten was "very lively; but their utter deficiency in the grave, rather sombre, uncivilized strength and Mohican dignity so finely suggested by Shakespear, takes all the ballast out of the fourth act." It was said of him that he was "too well balanced" to succeed in tragedy and too serious to rise to the demands of the comic spirit.

His daughter by Dame Whitty, as the reader may have already guessed, was Margaret Webster (b. 1905).

Ben Webster's last appearance on Broadway was as Montague in the outrageously bad *Romeo and Juliet* which Laurence Olivier and Vivien Leigh gave in 1940.

Janet Achurch (1864–1916), of whom, oddly enough, the *Dictionary of National Biography* takes no note, was pronounced by James Agate to be the finest Cleopatra of her time—and Shakespeare never created a more difficult role for an actress than the Queen of Egypt. Agate says that she had the looks, conveyed the majesty and the passion of the character, and possessed a voice "which might have quelled provinces." Shaw's rapture was more modified about her in that role. He wrote that she "has a magnificent voice, and is full of ideas as to vocal effects as to everything else. The march of the verse and the strenuousness of the rhetoric stimulate her great artistic susceptibility powerfully; she is determined that Cleopatra shall have rings on her fingers and bells on her toes, and that she shall have music wherever she goes." But Shaw felt "too utterly unnerved" to describe her "often audacious conceptions of Shakespearean music." As he was writing he still could hear "the lacerating discord of her wailings . . . It is as if she had been excited by the Hallelujah Chorus to dance on the keyboard of a great organ with all the stops pulled out." He felt like a "broken man" after the performance.

Miss Achurch toured with Benson for some time and played leading Shakespearean parts for him, but she was more noted for being one of the first actresses to play Ibsen in Great Britain. She also did several plays of Shaw. Touring extensively with her husband, Charles Charrington, she was the first English actress to be seen in Cairo at the Khedivisl Theatre.

She was a beautiful woman, whose bearing was magnificent, and who was mistress of a marvelous voice. In a less Shavian mood, Shaw said that she was "the only actress of genius we now possess."

Mrs. Patrick Campbell (née Beatrice Stella Tanner [1865–1940]) was probably the most difficult actress of her time, despite her extraordinary brilliance in performance. Managers learned to dread her. James Agate called on her when she was in the United States, living in a little hotel on West Forty-ninth Street. She "radiated quicksilver." Her talk was mostly about "flight" in acting as being the prime quality of a great actor. Giving her explanation of why there are only *ten* Commandments, she said that Moses probably decided: "Must stop or I shall be getting silly." Concerning an American actress, she observed: "Her voice is so beautiful that you won't understand a word she says." In self-defense she made what she considered was a vital distinction: "Many people say I have an ugly mind. That isn't true. I say ugly things, which is different." John Mason Brown observed to Agate: "She is committing the wittiest form of hari-kari."

Capable of any sort of temperamental fit, she withdrew at the last minute from the leading role in the premiere of Henry Arthur Jones's *Michael and His Lost Angel* at the Lyceum. During the most emotional scene in Pinero's *The Second Mrs. Tanqueray,* she did an unprecedented thing—she blew her nose in a very realistic way, because of which action "she was discussed at every dinner table for months after." But she was essentially not so much a realistic actor as a thrilling theatrical one, with an enchanting personality onstage, and endowed with physical gifts which enabled her to make the most of surface matters.

Shaw, who was very much involved with her (I do not say deeply emotion-ally involved with her, for I do not believe he was ever deeply emotionally involved with any human being), and created some very important roles for her, gives us a rare insight into her acting methods, though the actor he was "showing up" was Tree. "In *Pygmalion* the heroine, in a rage, throws the hero's slippers in his face. When we rehearsed this for the first time, I had taken care to have a very soft pair of velvet slippers provided; for I knew that Mrs. Patrick Campbell was very dexterous, very strong, and a dead shot. And, sure enough, when we reached this passage, Tree got the slippers well and truly delivered with unerring aim bang in his face. The effect was appalling; and it seemed to him that Mrs. Campbell, suddenly giving way to an impulse of diabolical wrath, had committed an unprovoked and brutal assault on him . . . He collapsed on the nearest chair, . . . whilst the entire personnel of the theatre crowded solicitously round him . . . But his *morale* was so shattered that it took quite a long time . . . before he was in a condition to resume the rehearsal."

Mrs. Campbell's mother was Maria Luigia Giovanna, the daughter of a political exile, Count Angelo Romanini, and from her mother and grandpar-ents she inherited her look of dark Italian beauty. Her expressive voice was rich, and none of her contemporaries on the stage could match her for characterizing passionate and complicated women—as Edmund Gosse put it, "the flash and gloom, the swirl and eddy, of a soul torn by supposed intellectual emotion." Despite her temperamental behavior, she was much in demand to assume the leading role for many important new plays.

In 1884, when she was nineteen, she eloped (as one would have expected) to marry Patrick Campbell, who had an unimportant position in the City of London. Four years later she made her first appearance, in Liverpool. After that she toured with the Ben Greet players, enacting such Shakespearean roles as Rosalind and Viola, and arrived in London in 1890. The next year she was at the Adelphi, acting for the Gattis in melodramas for the salary of £8 per week; they said that her gestures and voice were not effective, and that she did not manage to project anything to audiences. But friends of George Alexander saw her and, aware that he was seeking someone to play Paula Tanqueray in Pinero's new drama at the St. James Theatre, told him about her, and, despite the fact she was still unknown, she was given her great chance. She was truly a sensation; William Archer said of her perfor-mance that from first to last it was a perfect piece of acting, that it was "incarnate reality, the haggard truth."

Her name is actually very little associated with Shakespeare; she did many modern plays by Pinero, Maeterlinck, Ibsen, Henry Arthur Jones, Suder-mann, and others. When she did do Ophelia to Forbes-Robertson's Hamlet, the critics declared her clearly miscast. But Shaw defended her stoutly: She, "with that complacent audacity of hers which is so exasperating when she is doing the wrong thing, this time does the right thing by making Ophelia really mad. The resentment of the audience at this outrage is hardly to be described. . . . This wandering, silly, vague Ophelia, who no sooner catches an emotional impulse than it drifts away from her again, emptying her voice of its tone in a way that makes one shiver, makes them horribly uncomfortable. But the effect on the play is conclusive. The shrinking discomfort of the King and the Queen, the rankling grief of Laertes are created by it at once; and the scene . . . touches us with a chill of the blood that gives it its right tragic power."

About her Juliet to Forbes-Robertson's Romeo, Shaw was less enthusiastic, and perhaps unconsciously explains her unfitness to play Shakespeare. "She danced like the daughter of Herodias. . . . I was taken in by Mrs. Tanqueray—also by Mrs. Ebbsmith, as we all were. Woman's great art is to lie low, and let the imagination of the male endow her with depths. How Mrs. Patrick Campbell must have laughed at us whilst we were giving her all the credit . . . for our silly psychologizing over those Pinero parts! As Juliet she still fits herself into the hospitable manly heart without effort, simply because she is a wonderful person . . . in the extraordinary swiftness and certainty of her physical self-command . . . Her Juliet, nevertheless, is an immature performance . . . There is not a touch of tragedy, not a throb of love or fear, temper instead of passion."

During her maturity, her one other leading Shakespearean role was Lady Macbeth, which Walkley said was done with "a mysterious sensuous charm" —leaving one in the dark as to how she managed it. Crosse says her Lady Macbeth was as poor as her Juliet.

In April 1900 she was overwhelmed by deep personal grief when her husband was killed fighting in South Africa. She played in both the United States and Britain and one famous occasion in 1904 played Mélisande in French to the Pelléas of Sarah Bernhardt, at the Vaudeville Theatre.

For the rest, her performances were almost entirely in modern plays, and she did a considerable amount of touring in them. But by the second decade of the twentieth century, her hold on London was already vanishing, and during the last years of her life she was busy in secondary and minor parts in films in the United States. Agate said that she was one of the six truly great actresses he had seen in his life.

I was told that while she was in Hollywood her comment on Norma Shearer's Juliet was: "And those darling *tiny* eyes of hers!" I cannot vouch for the authenticity of the story, but the remark is entirely in character.

I have already said that I consider the most difficult female role Shakespeare created was Cleopatra's. I have seen every Cleopatra of my time on Broadway, and they were without exception all very bad. Indeed, I have only thrice seen a marvelous performance of that part: Edith Evans's, Zoe Caldwell's, and one in 1951 in Florence. I am ungrateful enough not to have recorded the actress's name, but she was perfect. After one got used to hearing *Antonio* for *Antony* and other such mutations, it was a marvelous experience. She *was* Shakespeare's serpent of the Nile—with all the infuriating, irresistible, chameleonlike charm which has always made such "not very nice" women enchanting to men. I have often wondered whether, if she could have been taught the music of poetry, with her temperament Mrs.

Patrick Campbell might not have made a glorious Cleopatra, the role she never attempted.

Eleanor Calhoun (1865–1957), American born, went to England as a girl. She was trained for the stage by Coquelin in Paris, and acted in London and at Stratford-on-Avon. She married a Serbian of the royal family and became Princess Lazarovich-Hrebelianovich, and quit the stage. The roles associated with her are Lady Macbeth, Rosalind, and Cleopatra. She had some strange ideas about *Macbeth*, which to her was a "kind of grim, exalted comedy" constructed on the paradox that "crime slays the assassin." She regarded Lady Macbeth as a woman actually possessed by the demons she had invoked. For that reason she considered Hecate (who all reputable critics agree was not Shakespeare's creation but a later superfluous addition, possibly by Middleton) as a very important character, an incorporation of the evil spirit which has taken hold of Lady Macbeth. (Any production of *Macbeth* would be the better for omitting the Hecate passages altogether.) Nevertheless, in that role Shaw described her as "modern, brilliant, mettlesome," and striking in appearance.

David Warfield (1866–1951), an American actor, began as a program seller and then an usher in San Francisco; in 1888 he joined a traveling troupe, which he left in a week, and then went into vaudeville and musical comedy. His specialty was an impersonation of a Jew from the New York slums. In 1901 David Belasco starred him in *The Auctioneer*. It was this role of Warfield's which was part of my introduction to drama via my Uncle Émile. Uncle Émile, having done his Richard Mansfield, would take several roles in *The Auctioneer*, and at a certain moment would pause to say, "And this is Warfield's great line," and he would rise on his toes and shout hoarsely, with tears in his eyes, "IF YOU DON'T WANT HER, *I* WANT HER!"

Warfield's sole connection with Shakespeare was the lavish production of *The Merchant of Venice* which Belasco staged, with Warfield as Shylock. It was a tremendously expensive failure, outdoing Tree's superabundance of "effects" and scenery, and vying with Granville* in its hideous distortion of the text. Warfield's Shylock was a petty, forlorn little Jew, who got lost in the extravagance of the sets. On Shylock's leaving the courtroom at the end of the trial, a monk lifted a crucifix before Warfield, while everyone else on stage jeered.

Lyn Harding (1867–1952) was a member of Tree's company, and toured for him with Constance Collier and Godfrey Tearle. He played Enobarbus to Tree's Antony. He had been appearing in several modern dramas on Broadway when, in 1916, he played the king in Tree's production of *Henry VIII*. In 1928 Harding made an impressive Macbeth in New York; I thought

* *The Jew of Venice* (1701)

his performance one of the best I have ever witnessed; Florence Reed, though not glamorous, made a stirring Lady Macbeth and brought considerable feminity to the part; the scenery was an adaptation of Gordon Craig's famous designs for the play, which, though mightily impressive in heightening the ominousness of the atmosphere, are strangely at odds with Duncan's description of Macbeth's castle as a most inviting place to visit.

Violet Augusta Mary Vanbrugh (1867–1942), née Barnes, changed her name at the suggestion of Ellen Terry, who was her close friend. She was the eldest daughter of the Rev. Reginald Henry Barnes, prebendary of Exeter Cathedral. She was educated in England, France, and Germany. At the time she decided to go on the stage it was most unusual for a young woman of her education and social standing to think of such a career. After three months in London, she succeeded in interesting Ellen Terry, through whose influence she was given an extra's part in a burlesque, wearing men's clothes. According to Miss Terry's account, Violet's father had given her "£100 and sent her to London with her old nurse . . . Violet had inherited some talent from her mother, . . . a very clever amateur actress . . . I happened to call on her . . . one afternoon, and found her having her head washed, and crying bitterly all the time! She had come to the end of the £100, she had not got an engagement, and thought she would have to go home defeated. There was something funny in the tragic situation. Vi was sitting on the floor, drying her hair, crying, and drinking port wine to cure a cold in the head! . . . We packed the old nurse back to Devonshire," and Violet came to live with Ellen Terry, who soon got her the part in the burlesque. "This was all I did to 'help' Violet Vanbrugh, now . . . one of our best actresses."

Violet soon had a speaking part, then joined a repertory company at Margate, where she had a new role to learn every week. She next was with the Kendals during their two tours of America. After those two years of hard work she returned to London to rest. One day Henry Irving, whom she knew slightly, stopped a hansom cab in which she was sitting to ask her to take the role of Ann Boleyn in his production of *Henry VIII* at the Lyceum. She made that Shakespearean debut in January of 1892, and at once became the understudy for Ellen Terry as Cordelia. The next year Augustin Daly engaged her to join his company, headed by Ada Rehan, and among the roles she played for him was Olivia in *Twelfth Night*. In 1894 she married Arthur Bourchier, a member of Daly's company.

They both went to the United States to perform, and in 1906 she played Lady Macbeth to her husband's Macbeth for Tree; in 1910 she once again played Beatrice at Stratford. Husband and wife were engaged by Tree that year, and she was much admired as Queen Katharine in *Henry VIII*. The next year she was Mistress Ford to Ellen Terry's Mistress Page in *The Merry Wives*. It is interesting to note that although she did very few Shakespearean roles, and came to them late (most of her career being in modern plays), it was Queen Katharine and Mistress Ford that were her most celebrated roles.

As an actress in modern plays, Max Beerbohm described her at various times as having "much grace and power," as "spirited and graceful," and as a "valuable" actress. Her Lady Macbeth must have been incommoded by her having to do her sleepwalking "on a precipitous zizzag of stairs." The London *Times* said that she went "slowly up and up, always beautifully . . . Beauty is the thing this revival aims at first and last. Of course, we were never shaken with terror." In this production, by the way, Tree added again some silly superfluities. When going to bed, Duncan was led by an entourage which included a harpist, there was singing of a hymn, and the whole company knelt for Duncan's blessing; then, when everyone had quit the stage, the Three Witches entered "cackling."

William Faversham (1868–1940), though born in London, made his career in New York, where he arrived in 1887. He became the matinée idol *par excellence*, or, as it has been put, "a matinée girl's ideal" and the "hero of a thousand matinées." Exceedingly handsome, tall, in fine physical condition because of much exercise and diet, he played innumerable parts, including a Romeo to Maude Adams's Juliet and, when he became actor-manager, Mark Antony in his own production of *Julius Caesar.* He was at his best in parts requiring virile energy and vivacity, but there was nothing subtle about his performances. His *Julius Caesar* ran for a long time in New York and then had an extended tour. He also produced *Othello* and revived once more his Romeo. Then he did a number of new plays, toured Australia, on his return produced other Shakespearean plays, and ended his career by playing the lead, Jeeter Lester, in *Tobacco Road*; it is a choice piece of irony that he should have thus concluded a long acting success built almost entirely upon his aggressive good looks by having to appear as the bedraggled, unkempt, and dirty Jeeter in a production that piled up a record by going on and on for years.

Tyrone Edmond Power (1869–1931), born in London, was the grandson of an Irish actor of the same name, and the father of the movie actor who was so much admired in our time. He was leading man to Mrs. Fiske, Julia Marlowe, Mrs. Leslie Carter, Henrietta Crossman, and other famous actresses. From 1890 to 1898 he appeared in London with Irving and with Tree. His later years were devoted almost exclusively to performances of Shakespeare. His career was developed largely in the United States. In 1922 he played Claudius to the Gertrude of Blanche Yurka in an epoch-making *Hamlet* in which John Barrymore made the most convincing (if not very poetic) prince I have ever seen. Power was all that Claudius should be, forceful, diplomatic, threatening—as the play demanded. (That same year I saw him in the usual week's run of The Player's Club production, this time a hilariously wonderful *The Rivals.*)

His son, Tyrone (1914–1958), much beloved by the cinema public, and whose early death was held a national catastrophe, made his first stage appearance in New York as a page in *Hamlet.* In 1935 he was in the cast of

Katherine Cornell's famous *Romeo and Juliet* and her *Saint Joan* of the next year. Though he continued after that in a few Broadway productions, the rest of his theatrical life was devoted to films.

James Keteltas Hackett (1869–1926), son of the American character actor, was a good romantic actor and a chief competitor of William Faversham as a matinée idol. He too was tall, handsome, and athletic. He joined Augustin Daly's company to play Shakespearean roles. To do himself justice Hackett needed fencing scenes (he was an excellent fencer and liked to exhibit his skill), romantic courtship, and lines of fervid passages. He was unfortunately a little too fond of drink, and Daniel Frohman tells a story of his always excusing himself during rehearsal just when he was due on stage by saying that he had to go to his dressing room to fix his collar. Frohman put an end to this by saying, "Jim, bring the entire bottle of collars out here, so we will not waste time."

In 1914 he inherited a fortune of more than one million dollars from a niece (very much his senior) who had never liked him; but since she died without leaving a will and he was her nearest kin, the money came to him. He was almost fifty when this miracle occurred, and he was able to satisfy an old ambition: to play Othello and Macbeth. This he did, received a singular lack of praise but still took the *Macbeth* to London, where he engaged Mrs. Patrick Campbell to play Lady Macbeth; neither of them was equal to the demands of their parts, but the audiences considered (since the lady could do no wrong) the production wonderful. Hackett was praised for restoring the grand style to Shakespeare. The French government asked him to present the play at the Odéon, and it was highly lauded there too. When his friend, the playwright George Middleton, who was in Paris at the same time, read Hackett a translation of the reviews, Hackett observed that it was very strange; in the United States "they always called me a ham actor," and yet London and Paris had decided he was a great actor—odd, because "I don't feel I am any different." It seems safe to assume that he *was* a ham actor.

His sets for the *Othello* in New York have historical importance; they were designed by Joseph Urban (1872–1933), Viennese by birth, who also designed sets for the Metropolitan Opera House, and built the Ziegfeld Theater. He used broad masses of color and new lighting effects on scenery and costume, such as had been recently in vogue in Europe, and which considerably influenced Anerican productions for some time.

Viola Allen (1869–1948), an American, first appeared on stage in 1882, at the age of thirteen at the Madison Square Theater. Soon she was leading lady to John McCullough, her second role being that of Desdemona, and she also played with him in *Richard III*. Thereafter she performed with Lawrence Barrett, and in 1886 with Salvini. From 1891 to 1896 she was a member of Charles Frohman's stock company at the Empire Theater, a perfect playhouse with a long history of producing quality works until it was unfortunately dismantled, as everything traditional in New York eventually is; upon its boards an endless variety of great performers were seen, such as Maude Adams, Katharine Cornell, John Drew, Nazimova, Gielgud.

For five years Viola Allen was leading lady there. She managed to infuse an atmosphere of nobility into her personations by her refinement and charm. She was assiduous in studying for her parts and appealed to the intelligence of the audience. Viola was her most celebrated role, but she was also popular as Rosalind, Imogen, and Perdita in lavish productions given under her own auspices. They won her great prestige. In 1915 she toured with J. K. Hackett as Lady Macbeth, and in 1916 did Mistress Ford. As was becoming increasingly the tendency from the mid-nineteenth century on, actors and actresses alike gave more attention to modern plays, and she was no exception. She was a tall, dark, handsome, rather than beautiful, woman, who was most in demand in romantic parts.

Ruggero Ruggeri (1871–1953) was an Italian actor who began as a singer. His career was long and active, and he had a preference for roles which called for powerful drama or romantic acting. He was a fine Iago, and a very good, if somewhat old-fashioned, Hamlet. For years he was the leading man of Pirandello's company; he was the original Enrico IV. He acted opposite most of the important Italian actresses of his day.

He came to London with his company in 1926, all of them performing in Italian. Agate thought his Hamlet a true prince in mind and body, with elegant gestures, plastic beauty, and a mobility and grace of feature. A fine actor—but, Agate concluded, not really Hamlet at all. He was, if anything, too princely, too fastidious, too much intellectualized, and by half not human enough.

Maude Adams (1872–1953), daughter of a leading lady in a Salt Lake City stock company, became to the American theater very much what Mary Pickford was to become to audiences of the silent film: a national darling, and the personification of sweetness and purity in a profession which of old had had a fairly seamy moral history among its personnel.

Shy and withdrawn all her life, she was a woman of high ideals and an irreproachable life; on stage she radiated sweetness as easily as she did in private life. She never consented to play the part of an immoral member of her sex, disliked plays that called for violence, and ruled out roles exhibiting jealousy, rage, or hate.

As a child of five she was already a triumph at the San Francisco Theater; young David Belasco was also a member of the troupe. Cast in all the familiar children's roles, including little Eva in *Uncle Tom's Cabin,* she left the theater to pursue her education, and returned to the boards only in 1892 to play opposite John Drew in New York, as part of the Frohmans' company. She was a great success from the beginning and remained with that management for a great many years. In 1899 she performed an excellent Juliet with Faversham, but her sensational popularity, which lasted some twenty years during which she was the public's idol, began with *The Little Minister*. Charles Frohman had been urging James M. Barrie to dramatize his best-selling novel, which the author was unwilling to do. One day while calling at Frohman's office, Barrie found the manager out, so Frohman's secretary suggested that Barrie go to the Empire Theater to kill time. Onstage were John Drew and Maude Adams in a sentimental triviality. He was so enchanted with Maude Adams, that he decided to try the dramatization. Thereafter he wrote no more novels, and became a highly successful dramatist; a great many of his plays were written for Maude Adams. *The Little Minister* began the American public's love affair with the actress who was, indeed, something of a Barrie character herself, without parallel in the theatrical history of the United States.

Billie Burke said that Charles Frohman's talk of her was as though she were "a princess in an ivory tower," and that his eyes would light up with something like religiosity. Miss Burke concluded that he loved Maude Adams "as a hungry spirit loves music and poetry, and as a fine boy loves his heroes and their ideals." She was to Frohman "what she was to everyone else: a sprite." David Gray saw that she was not so much an artist, with all her sweetness and light, "as a public influence," and that the chief force of that influence was "ethical rather than aesthetic."

Viola and Rosalind were the chief Shakespearean roles she assumed, but it is clear that she enchanted her audiences less by great acting than by her elfin quality.

The adoring public never knew her, except as a stage personality. She was, like Garbo later, in absolute terror of any kind of publicity, and Charles Frohman's biographer states that he "spent a fortune sheltering Maude Adams from all kinds of intrusion." The result was that, although being mysterious was certainly not part of her wishes, she was a mystery to the world.

In 1918 she retired from the stage, but she came back to it as Portia to Otis Skinner's Shylock—neither a remarkable performance. She returned again in 1934 to play Maria in *Twelfth Night*. She spent her final years teaching dramatics, but it is an open question as to what she could teach any girl, except, perhaps, to try being another Maude Adams.

Some of the reasons for the disproportion between her fame and the modesty of her theatrical talents, besides the winning quality of her personality, are perhaps illuminated by two observations by Max Beerbohm, not about her—it may be that he never saw her in the theater—but about the period of her astounding triumphs: one, that the feeling against theaters as resorts of wickedness had not yet died out and was still strong among noncomformists; secondly, that among the theatergoing public, popular interest concentrated on actors far more than on the plays. (This latter tendency is probably just as true today as it was during the last decades of the nineteenth century and the early years of the twentieth. And though a man like Mr. Redfield would probably think that is as it should be, it is a meretricious point of view toward drama.)

Maude Adams herself avowed: "I know I was very bad as Juliet. I had thought I was going to be." Yet they pronounced her a completely new Juliet, "the most girlish, the most tender, the most lovable." She was even praised for giving Juliet "a sense of humor"! But Winter observed wryly that "Many schoolgirls, with a little practice, would play the part just as well— and be just as little like it . . . Nature never intended her to act the tragic heroines of Shakespeare. Much of the part was whispered and much of it was bleated. . . . A balcony scene without passion, a parting scene without delirium of grief, and a potion scene without power"—such was her performance of the role.

When in 1908 she was doing Viola, though critics saw that she did not grasp the character, they thought that it was possible to overlook the fact because of her sweetness and grace. It had become a duty to love her, no matter what she did. The *Boston Transcript* averred, after two weeks of Barrie's *A Kiss for Cinderella,* "A week more, and all Boston will be grown young again."

In her Portia of 1931, when she returned to the stage, she was congratulated for not trying to look any younger than her fifty-nine years: "She was still Maude Adams, one of the truly great personalities of the American theater."

It was James M. Barrie who first recommended to Charles Frohman that he present Maude Adams as Katharina in *The Taming of the Shrew* as *not* tamed by Petruchio, but rather as a charming woman who plays with *him*. Thus, her pretense at loving the robes he buys her without consulting her is motivated by the knowledge that he will thereupon tear them up—and have to buy her proper ones. (!) Barrie called his version *The Ladies' Shakespeare.* It was conceived to capitalize on Maude Adams's sweetness; she never could have been a shrew. She was, instead, arch and imaginative.

Helen Haye (1874–1957), an English actress of the old school, accomplished, superb in diction and carriage, spent some time touring with Benson's troupe. She was on stage for sixty years; some of her best performances were her latest, at an age when most actresses, if still alive, are in retirement.

She was not seen in London until 1910; that year she appeared as Gertrude and Olivia. In 1921 she toured Canada, and came to New York in 1925. She was superlative in aristocratic roles. In 1935 she was at the Old Vic. For years she taught acting at the Royal Academy of Dramatic Art; among her pupils were Flora Robson, Celia Johnson, Charles Laughton, and John Gielgud.

Lewis Thomas Casson (1875–1969), an English actor, after gaining experience with an amateur group in Shakespeare, made his first professional appearance in 1903. From 1904 to 1907 he was seen in several of Shaw's plays, and the next year went to Manchester, where he became director at the Gaiety (1911 to 1914). There he met and married the celebrated Sybil

Thorndike, and toured with her, and frequently directed. He himself acted Macbeth, Coriolanus, Shylock, Petruchio, Benedick, and other Shakespearean roles. He was knighted in 1945.

He too entertained some novel notions about *Macbeth*. He was sure, as others (unreasonably, I believe) have been, that there are scenes from the play which have been lost. He rejected the accepted—and clearly correct—idea that Macbeth had pondered on the death of Duncan before the play opens; he was sure that Macbeth first conceived the idea of killing Duncan when the king named Malcolm Prince of Cumberland. In order to fortify this perverse notion he changed the word *murder* to *matter* in Macbeth's soliloquy after the greeting of the Three Witches. He further suggested, finding the scene between Malcolm and Macduff dull, that the scene be played as "fairly broad comedy." (How would that sort with the "He has no children" passage?) Casson also insisted that Macbeth must not win our sympathy (if he were right, how would the play qualify as a tragedy?) because Macbeth is too great a fiend. To him the play builds up to a fight between Good and Evil, of which the climax is the "Tomorrow and tomorrow" speech—a credo of the Devil, "of nihilism and atheism," and that he should say that life is a tale told by an idiot is "the supreme blasphemy."

Margaret Anglin (1876–1958), an American actress, was looked up to by many as one of the very finest actresses of her time. She was actually born and educated in Canada, but came to New York, where she was engaged by Charles Frohman in 1894. She toured with various companies and appeared as Roxane in Mansfield's *Cyrano*. She acted in many modern plays, but had done Viola, Rosalind, Cleopatra, and Katherine on tour. Her fame eventually rested upon her being the leading representative of ancient Greek tragedy, and among her many roles in those revivals were Electra, Medea, Antigone, Phaedra, Iphigenia, and others.

Charles Douville Coburn (1877–1961) and his wife Ivah Willis (1882–1937) in 1906 organized the Coburn Shakespeare Players; both acted the leads in it for many years. In 1946 he played Falstaff for the Theater Guild, and was highly praised. He was for many years a familiar figure in the cinema, often seen in comedies as a crochety old man with a heart of gold.

Alexander Matheson Lang (1877–1948), actor-manager and dramatist, was born in Montreal, a cousin of the Archbishop of Canterbury, and son of the minister of a Scottish Presbyterian church. It was seeing Irving which apparently moved him to hope for a theatrical career. His first work was with Louis Calvert in 1897, followed by membership in Benson's company. In 1902 he toured America with Lily Langtry, and the next year played Benedick to Ellen Terry's Beatrice; he went on to tour with her in repertory. In 1908 his Romeo was pronounced by Max Beerbohm to be excellently romantic and to convey better than any contemporary actor a sense of the hero's youthful spirit. In 1909 he played Hamlet at the Lyceum, a performance which Trewin calls "throbbingly theatrical." Next he toured Australia, and in 1911 started his own company; with a large repertory, chiefly Shakespearean, they went to South Africa and the Far East. He leased the New Theatre in 1920 for matinées of *Othello,* in which he enacted a highly praised Moor. In 1916 he made movies of some of his stage successes, which included a number of modern plays, as well as *The Merchant of Venice,* in which he was Shylock. He was of invaluable assistance to Lilian Baylis, prime mover in the founding of the Old Vic. A tall, heavy-set man of strong features, Lang possessed considerable personal dignity.

He was for a time associated with the producer Richard Flanagan, who by 1896 was managing his own productions, which often ran for more than a hundred nights each. A number of young players later to achieve fame were engaged by him, but it is to be feared that his success was more owing to his eagerness to follow Tree's example of bad taste, so dear to the heart of the public, than to the brilliance of the performances. In his eyes Tree was the greatest of actor-managers. He therefore improved on Tree by having not only rabbits on stage in *As You Like It* but deer as well. He was also devoted to elaborate sets and the intrusion of uncalled-for spectacles when doing Shakespeare. As one observer recalled his scenic effects: "When the moon came out, it came out in six moons, all in different places," not as just one miserly beam of light. Lang tells us, amusingly, how after the balcony scene in *Romeo and Juliet* or the new "tableau" of Othello's being welcomed as Governor at Cyprus, Flanagan was always on the *qui vive* to come out from the wings to acknowledge the applause for scenery or spectacle, with his bowler hat in his hands.

Constance Collier (1878–1955), an English actress, began her long career at the age of three, playing Peasblossom in *A Midsummer Night's Dream.* She made her first appearance in London in 1893 in a chorus, and the same year became one of the Gaiety Girls. But her ambition was to play serious roles, and after appearing in a number of plays, was engaged by Tree and appeared in all his chief productions from 1901 to 1908. In 1908 she came to New York, and thereafter divided her time between London and the United States, equally in demand on both sides of the Atlantic. She was Gertrude in the 1925 London production of John Barrymore's *Hamlet* and had been seen as Cleopatra and Juliet.

Robert Atkins (b. 1886), an English actor whose career was mostly connected with performances of Shakespeare, was engaged by Tree to participate in *Henry IV, Part I* in 1906. He toured with Martin-Harvey and acted in the troupes of Forbes-Robertson and Frank Benson. In 1915 he joined the Old Vic, and after World War I returned to that playhouse in 1920 as producer until 1925. During those years he acted in and produced many Shakespearean plays, including the rarely seen *Titus Andronicus* and *Troilus and Cressida.* Later he established his own company, took it on tour, and then founded the Bankside Players which produced *Henry V, Much Ado,* and *The*

Merry Wives, attempting to re-create the conditions of the Elizabethan stage. He was also at the Stratford Memorial Theatre, and at the Open-Air Theatre in Regent's Park. Even during the Nazi bombings of London he was giving Shakespeare at the Vaudeville Theatre. His own best roles were Touchstone, Bottom, Sir Toby Belch, and Caliban. Crosse says he was a wonderful Falstaff, but that his very best performance was as Caliban, for his artistry conveyed perfectly a "malevolent brute" whose vague, incipient "half-formed human intellect" was dawning. After seeing Atkins for the ninth time as Bottom, Crosse said it was equal to his Caliban. In 1949 Atkins gave one of the most unfamiliar of the plays, *All's Well That Ends Well,* taking the part of Lafeu himself and making it "the central character of the play"—a sort of "grave Sir Toby."

Unlike his predecessors he used little scenery, sometimes, as in *Pericles,* having recourse to settings as simple as unadorned black draperies and white columns; he made full use, too, of his apron stage. Trewin says that he served Shakespeare better than any of his contemporaries.

A few words about the box stage set, which in the nineteenth century and well into the twentieth became the norm for scenery and, as almost a law of dramatic composition, inevitably conditioned the kinds of plays which were written for the stage, as well as the productions of Shakespeare and the classics, works originally written for, and conditioned by, a totally different kind of stage.

Before the introduction of the box set, scenery was a matter of painting in perspective on backcloth, wings, and borders. The box set is an arrangement of flats to form continuous walls, with doors and windows, and a ceiling cloth. It was first used by Madame Vestris at the Olympic in her production of W. B. Bernard's *The Conquering Game* on November 26, 1832, and perfected by her in her production at Covent Garden of Boucicault's *London Assurance* in 1841.

During the Victorian era the "carpenter's scene" was a development of the box-set situation. Because the habit of lowering the curtain between changes of scene or at the end of scenes and acts was a later practice, the carpenter's scene, a short, shallow setting up front, almost always employed in passages subordinate to the main plot, made it possible to change and prepare scenery behind the carpenter's scene backcloth without the audience's being aware of it. Its use in drama was largely dispensed with once curtains were dropped. But the device is still current, as patrons of the musical comedy and review have reason to know.

23

Shakespeare and the Silent Cinema

What a mélange must be the memories of early movies to people of my generation, particularly if, like me, they were addicts from childhood of the nickelodeon! I'm sure mine are: Union soldiers, the Stars-and-Stripes proudly carried in the vanguard, riding gallantly to the rescue of a jerry-built fortress surrounded by Indians; villains chasing around tables distracted heroines (they, poor creatures, clutching in vain at locked doors) with intentions strictly dishonorable until William S. Hart breaks through and saves the girls' honor; the antics of John Bunny and Flora Finch, Chaplin, Turpin, Keaton, Arbuckle, Langdon, Keystone Kops, and other comedians, the pathetic experiences of well-curled Mary Pickford; and then, as the reels became longer, flashes of enchantment such as the adorable Billie Burke, the fascinating wickedness of Theda Bara—and later the sudden, unannounced radiance of Greta Garbo (I can never forget the overwhelming experience of her suddenly appearing at the head of an improvised rude staircase, her Queen Anne's collar framing the most beautiful head the world has seen, in something, I think, called *The Torrent*—at any rate I stayed to see the picture three times, left in a daze of love for her, and was soundly thrashed when I got home for having worried my mother by my unexplained absence.)—and, of course, many other flashes of recollection too numerous to list. But in all this the works of Shakespeare played but a trifling part.

I am sure my coevals would be astonished to know the extent to which the early movies concerned themselves with Shakespeare, in one way or another, and the history, oddly enough, is a much longer one than that of the talking cinema. I have no intention of tracing that entire history for Robert Hamilton Ball has done it full justice in a splendidly documented book, *Shakespeare on Silent Film* (New York: 1968), to which I am indebted for much of what I find worth telling here. I imagine that there are few Shakespearean movies that he has overlooked, but I am grieved not to find in his study any reference to one of the great revelations of beauty with which my early teens were studded because of the nickelodeon. How much of the story of *Antony and Cleopatra* it told I do not know; it must have been a two-reeler, for I must have seen it between 1912 and 1914, the years we were in Denver, and all I remember of it is a resplendent moment when Mary Garden, swathed in (what in black-and-white cinema looked like) shimmering white veils, stepped off a decorated barge on the arm of some courteous man dressed as a Roman (Antony, presumably), lifted one veil and uncovered her lovely face. It was the first Shakespeare I ever saw and I was just crossing into my teens. My mother, when I got home, explained to me who Mary Garden was and who Cleopatra was, and who the man probably was—but I was in no way interested in *him*. I had hoped to find in Mr. Ball's authoritative work material to round out that fragmentary vision of the past, but the film obviously has escaped his notice.

Edison's peep show Kinetoscope was first presented commercially on both sides of the Atlantic in 1894; but there could be no "motion picture" until it could be projected on a screen, as it was the next year. In 1896 Robert W. Paul demonstrated his projector, and the British public was made aware of the cinema. It is astonishing that only three years after that the first attempt with Shakespeare should have been made. And who else would be the pioneer but that enthusiast, Sir Herbert Beerbohm Tree? He was not deterred by the experimental state of films to lend his distinguished reputation by enacting a scene from *King John* in costume and with all the gestures appropriate to the theater, along—of all places—the Embankment. Probably the scene filmed was one that Shakespeare never wrote, but which was introduced as a "tableau" in the play when given indoors, the granting of the Magna Carta, a scene which required no speech, and which, moreover, might suggest Runnymede by the foliage of the trees and the water of the Thames. It is not known that this brief scene was ever shown, but it was a brave effort.

His next brief effort in that new medium was the opening scene from *The Tempest*, which he had presented at His Majesty's Theatre in 1904; of that production the *Era* said: "modern science has enabled Mr. Tree to fairly stagger us by some wonderful storm effects and to produce a magnificent realization of the shipwreck that opens the play. The vessel takes up the whole of the stage." It was that scene which Tree had photographed in the theater; the shipwreck was most realistic, lightning flashed, billows assailed the sinking ship, and the passengers could be seen rushing about in a panic. The film was tinted to give the effect of eerie moonlight. Tree himself was not in this little film for his role in the production was Caliban. This work, which lasted two minutes, was shown publicly in 1905.

In 1910 Tree had given his lavish production of *Henry VIII*, with himself as Wolsey and Violet Vanbrugh as Queen Katharine. This time the filming of the play was made at studios in Ealing. Each scene was rehearsed only once at the studios before being taken. A cast of some two hundred was employed for the undertaking, the sets copied from those at His Majesty's, and the props brought over from that theater. The entire filming, rehearsals included, took two hours. Five scenes were chosen: the cloisters, the banqueting hall, the trial, the antechamber to the king's room, and the coronation. The film was developed at once, and the cast was able to see the result at midnight. It was immediately declared the "Film of the Year"—not that it had many competitors. The proprietor of the film was William George Barker, who had saved enough money from his business operations to go into the film industry and in 1910 opened his own studios at Ealing. He advertised *Henry VIII*, and managed his press-agentry with skill. He warned that showings would be limited—so that naturally orders came streaming in; he printed an illustrated booklet which he sold to the exhibitors at 1,000 for £1, to be sold in turn to audiences; he suggested the employment of orchestras and choruses for the important event. In 1911 the picture at last was shown to the public at various houses, with great emphasis on their exclusiveness (much like today's filmed plays). The theaters were packed. A. E. Taylor, writing from London to the United States, said, "The picture is without doubt the greatest that has ever been attempted." Audience reaction was, however, mixed. It was too much to expect everyone to enjoy seeing excerpts from a play he had never read; those who did know the play were annoyed at all that had been omitted; but there were often cheers at the end.

In 1916 Tree was induced to try again. Reels were longer and after some discussion of the possibilities with David Wark Griffith and John Emerson (who was to write the scenario), *Macbeth* was hit upon as the most cinematic. As Emerson said, the supernatural elements, so difficult to make convincing on the stage, could be done justice by the camera. "The witches are easily given supernatural quality. The same applies to Banquo's ghost." The dagger which Macbeth sees in hallucination, can be shown on the screen "in a very effective and mystical sort of way." Nor are we to forget, said Emerson, that *Macbeth* is "a rattling good melodrama[!]." He found little difficulty in managing the nine-reel scenarios, since "Shakespeare's dramatic structure is more near in form to that of the film than the modern play. . . . We can not only do all the scenes Shakespeare provided for . . . but are able to fill in the lapses of time by adding scenes merely described . . . As, for instance, the fight between Macbeth and Cawdor . . . The coronation of Macbeth . . . jumped over in the play, will be one of the biggest scenes in the picture."

Tree asked Constance Collier to be Lady Macbeth. He was given an ovation on his arrival in California. He was welcomed by cowboys shooting their guns into the air; the official greeting was delivered by a "fair-haired boy of five years, . . . one of the most popular film actors. The infant phenomenon wore a long garment, one which had sewn in large letters the word 'Welcome,' and coming towards me with extended hand, at once put me at my ease by saying, 'Pleased to meet you, Sir Tree.'"

After his first day at the studio Tree observed that it was amazing how much could be done in film "for the tales of Shakespeare that cannot be done on stage." It was possible not only to "illuminate and accentuate many details" but also to heighten the dramatic values." Tree had agreed to do a series of Shakespearean works for Griffith at over $100,000. "I should like," remarked Tree with incredible naïveté, "to call this series of productions *Tales from Shakespeare*. If we can bring to the dramas some such reverent and illuminating interpretation as did Charles Lamb [Charles and Mary Lamb's highly simplified *Tales from Shakespeare* interpret nothing, and are admirably what they set out to be, addressed to children!], I shall be happy indeed."

Some years later, it was admitted that despite Tree's unfailing courtesy, he was very difficult to direct. On stage he always covered the entire area of the boards, and Emerson had his hands full trying to keep him within range of the camera. Besides that, he insisted on reciting all his lines—otherwise he could not *act* Macbeth. It did not matter to him that not a syllable would be or could be recorded; and he put into his words all the passion he used in the theater. The cameraman at last hit on a solution by a dummy machine unloaded with film; Tree's whole text went unphotographed. When the speeches were concluded, the loaded camera took the pictures. Also, since the script required some athletic horsemanship, Tree was sent off somewhere else while a substitute rode for him. When Tree later saw the rushes, he was bewildered at not being able to remember that ride! Constance Collier also tells that when everyone involved in the production saw the completed picture, and eagerly awaited Tree's reaction—for he had said not a syllable during the projection—when the lights went up he was found in his chair sound asleep.

The movie was first shown in New York at the Rialto Theater. *The New York Times* said it was a "fine achievement," that everyone interested in the development of the cinema ought to see it. But its virtues were not the virtues of Shakespeare's play. "What is especially noteworthy is the suggestion of brooding night . . . which pervades all the picture." The critic thought the innovations excellent, such as Macbeth's wincing during the feast given to Duncan at the sight of little Fleance playing with the crown and trying it on his "own boy's head." Quotations from Shakespeare were flashed on the screen (even when unnecessary) to advance the action. A movie magazine thought Tree virile and full of variety in projecting his emotional states. Nevertheless, the movie was a financial failure in the United States and England.

Tree was under contract for ten months. What was the studio to do? A cancellation of the contract was suggested; Tree refused. The only expedient, then, was to ask him to do a role he would, out of sheer self-respect, be obliged to reject. The lawyers thought it would be going too far to ask him to play a Negro in a low-comedy part, so it was decided to cast Sir Herbert Beerbohm Tree as an American farmer in *Old Folks at Home*. To their astonishment Tree accepted, and, worse yet, did a fine job with the part.

New York never saw Bernhardt as Hamlet until she had appeared in a three-minute version of the play, not long after Tree's venture with *King John*. Clément Maurice, who presented the piece, was in 1900 congratulated by *Le Figaro* for his complete and perfect synchronization of film and phono-graph. The scene filmed was the duel with Laertes, and the journal said that the creation of that scene was a marvel of art as well as a masterpiece of precision. Laertes and Hamlet were seen duelling; behind them stood two *"valets d'armes"* to substitute for the court, and a page. Bernhardt herself had padded her slender figure to look more virile and wore a wig of fair, wavy hair in a kind of boyish-bob style.

Paul Panzer, well known as the villain in the episodes of *The Perils of Pauline*, spoke of William V. Ranous, the first salaried director in the old Vitagraph days, when they filmed in Flatbush, Brooklyn. Ranous had toured a great deal with minor troupes; he had also played villains and character roles in road companies which he managed, and unimportant parts with better-known actors and actresses. He had performed some Shakespeare, and, according to Panzer, was of the Salvini school. "Under his direction, Vitagraph produced *Macbeth, Richard III, Othello, Romeo and Juliet, King Lear,* and other Shakespearean plays. They were all in one reel each [!] . . . We built our own scenery and props" and did "carpenter work" and painted canvas "while we were dressed in the costumes of Shakespeare's time . . . For these services we received the magnificent salary of $14 a week; but we got $3 a day extra when we played in pictures."

An article published in 1908 on the Vitagraph *Macbeth, Romeo and Juliet,* and *Othello* observes that considering their brevity and condensation they "are probably as good as any that could have been made." These movies, the critic said, were still in demand in neighborhoods where the patrons would be above average intelligence. The films were exported and praised in London. In Chicago the *Macbeth* was censored. Said the police lieutenant: "I am not taking issue with Shakespeare. As a writer he is far from reproach. But he never . . . saw that his plots were going to be interpreted for the five-cent theater . . . The stabbing scene in the play is not predominant. But in the picture show it is the feature." On the screen "you see the dagger enter and come out and see the blood flow." (What would the good lieuten-ant have said to Polanski's recent all-ensanguined *Macbeth?*)

The *Romeo and Juliet,* which like the others consumed about fifteen min-utes, did not make the police lieutenant unhappy. He was aware that it contained suicide, duelling, and violence, but what counted was the "love element . . . When anyone pays 5 cents to see *Romeo and Juliet* films, he pays to see love. When he pays 5 cents to see *Macbeth* he pays to see a fight."

In the *Othello* Julia Swayne Gordon, a popular star of early movie days, was Desdemona; in 1908 she appeared in *Richard III* and also as Portia; the next year she was Cordelia, Helena (of *A Midsummer Night's Dream*), and Olivia. As an infant, I saw none of these, and when my movie-going days began in seven or eight years, Julia Swayne Gordon seemed to me a woman getting on in years—naturally, to a boy anyone over thirty is ancient—and I cannot picture her as a Shakespearean girl.

Maurice Costello was the greatest matinée idol of the early short pictures, and I saw him many times. I recognized that he was handsome, but could not share my female cousin's particular ecstasy; he rather bored me and I was exclusively interested in the women who played opposite him. His films almost always dealt with contemporary situations, but he did do Lysander with Julia Swayne Gordon; his two daughters, Dolores and Helene, both future stars, were Titania's fairies. In 1912 he was Orlando. The woods of Flatbush became the Forest of Arden; there was an excess of subtitles and far too much mouthing and gestures which meant nothing on a silent screen. The seven ages speech was depicted by views of each of the stages—a pretty schoolboy, a soldier with cannon, a justice taking a nap, etc. The worst error was having Rose Coghlan as Rosalind for she was in fact aging. On stage it is often possible for mature women to appear young, but the camera is merciless about age. This three-reeler, the longest footage Vitagraph had allotted Shakespeare to date, failed to please because, as one critic put it, despite "fine acting, fine directing, fine photography," Rosalind is not herself when enacted by a woman "who was at the zenith of her powers a score of years ago."

In England, Violet Vanbrugh, who had already been filmed in *Henry VIII*, acted with her husband, Bourchier, in *Macbeth*, but the 1913 movie was not a great success, and was fairly damned when brought to the United States. It was ridiculed for the inadequacy of the principals and the photography, as well as a total want of the tragic spirit. Perhaps it is fair to remark that this criticism was made in 1916, when the movie was imported.

In 1911 the Bensons acted in *Julius Caesar*, he playing Mark Antony and she Portia; the work was filmed on the stage of the Memorial Theatre at Stratford-on-Avon; and it was successful enough to be followed by a *Macbeth*, *The Taming of the Shrew*, and *Richard III*. The last named was the poorest; half the footage was taken up by subtitles, leaving some ten minutes for the picture itself. The story was, therefore, far from lucid.

In France, Paul Mounet, younger brother of the famous Mounet-Sully, was filmed as Macbeth in 1910. He was a member of the Comédie Française company. Among the novelties introduced was a scene which opened with the subtitle, "The Coronation. Banquo refuses to acknowledge Macbeth as King." Macbeth enthroned, his subjects bow before him; Banquo will not. Only when the infuriated Macbeth stands up and threatens him does he give in, but he turns his back on Macbeth before quitting the room; the king hands a murderer a dagger with orders to kill Banquo. Another: "The sons of Duncan beg Malcolm, King of England [!] to punish the guilty one. He promises them to do so." When Macbeth comes again to consult the witches, he actually kicks one who is nursing a skull and bones out of the way. Out of a fire with smoke emerges a scroll; the subtitle explains it: "Macbeth, thou shalt have nothing to fear from the King of England until Birnam forest starts to move." These innocent distortions are, comparatively speaking, faithful to Shakespeare when matched with stage and screen productions of our own time. Ball says that the chief trouble with this *Macbeth* was that the persons of the drama were interminably entering and exiting, as if on stage, and with the compression imposed by the brevity of the film and the frequent change of scene, it made identification of who was who nearly impossible.

In Italy, where *Othello* was very popular, a number of film versions were made. Particularly noteworthy was a 1909 opus with Ferruccio Garavaglia as the Moor, Cesare Dondini as Iago, and Vittoria Lepanto as Desdemona —because most of the film was made in Venice, it was the first attempt to use an authentic setting for a Shakespearean movie. Native Venetians were said to have been astounded to see some fifty men and women in brilliant costumes, false wigs and beards pacing Piazza San Marco and the narrow streets. Youngsters followed them, and people came out of their houses to watch. Garavaglia, equipped with armor, sword, and helmet, calmly walked into a tobacco shop to buy cigars and overwhelmed the proprietor. Crowds who had never seen films being made created all kinds of difficulty in their curiosity. Some went pretty far. In one scene Vittoria Lepanto (Desdemona), a beauty, had to lean over a bridge as Iago passed beneath in a gondola. An elegantly dressed young man found her irresistible, followed her up the stairs of the bridge, and as she bent over gave her a pat on her *derrière.* She turned and slapped his face; his reaction was to remind her that she was merely an actress. Her fellow performers were enraged at the insult. Garavaglia and the actor who was playing the duke, both stalwart men, seized the young offender under the arms and threw him in the canal. The onlookers applauded.

In England the movie was commended for its vigor. But it was the opinion of one reviewer that it is hopeless to attempt a Shakespearean performance without words.

We have already discussed Frederick Warde's highly successful *Richard III* and *King Lear.* This American tragedian made a real contribution to the cinema by performing in two of the earliest five-reel pictures to be made.

Helene Gardner, teacher of pantomime, founded her own film company, her studio at Tappan, on the Hudson in New York. In 1912 she announced a *Cleopatra,* adapted from Shakespeare and Sardou's adaptation of Shakespeare. The picture was mostly Sardou. Despite her matronly figure and very limited abilities as an actress, she herself played Cleopatra, and rather monotonously—a disaster for a role that requires more variety than any of Shakespeare's creations. But the film was incredibly successful in the United States and Europe, her acting was declared among the greatest ever seen on the screen, and the film itself "probably the most stupendous and beautiful picture ever produced." David Warfield thought so too. Among the non-Shakespearean elements in the story is a fisherman-slave, who enjoys her favors on the stipulation that he commit suicide at the end of ten days. None of the subtitles was from Shakespeare.

Those moviegoers who were audiences for the wonderful pictures produced in France before World War II will not have forgotten Harry Baur, perhaps the leading actor in French cinema of those days. (After the Nazi occupation of the country, he was killed by the Germans because he was a Jew.) In 1913 he was Shylock in a two-reel version of the play. It would have been impossible for Baur to give a poor performance and his interpretation was highly praised when the film came to the United States. In England, one report said the picture would "make film history"—and remembering Baur very well, I am willing to believe it, even though his Shylock was not precisely Shakespeare's. He made Shylock at times a comic figure, and, said a reviewer, in the trial scene this was especially true in his handling of the knife, "when he takes off his shoe and uses it as a strop, squatting on the floor" like "a wayside cobbler."

This *Merchant of Venice,* again, was treated as though it were a stage play being photographed, with painted backdrops and stage entrances and exits. The signing of the bond took place on screen, in the house of Shylock, who is first seen beside a chest counting his gold; he hears the approach of Antonio and Bassanio, closes the chest, and as they enter sits on the chest. After the bond has been signed and the two leave, Shylock shakes his fist at them. On the whole, for a two-reeler, the film was fairly faithful to the story. Jessica's elopement, Launcelot and Old Gobbo, Shylock's scene with Tubal and other details inevitably were omitted.

The most important Shakespearean film up to that time was the *Hamlet* in which Sir Johnston Forbes-Robertson starred, with Gertrude Elliott as Ophelia and J. H. Barnes as Polonius. In 1913 Forbes-Robertson was making his farewell appearances, and, shy though he was, he may have acceded to the request for the film so that there might be left a permanent record of his performance. The film was made that same year. It was said to cost £10,000, a vast expenditure for 1913, and he was supported by a Drury Lane cast of seventy. But Forbes-Robertson had never overcome his reticence, and hated the idea of being observed by bystanders. His dressing room was across the road from the studio at Walton, and he would wrap his cloak about his Hamlet costume, avoiding looking at anyone until he was escorted to the constructed castle of Elsinore, where he at last was at some ease. He habitually, in the midst of serious moments would emit shouts of laughter, during the showing of the rushes, at his own appearance on screen. "I've got a mouth like a cavern," was one of his comments at his makeup. He also was averse to close-ups until convinced that the medium required them.

An English review said that it was impossible to praise the picture enough. "It is a most perfect production." It lasted for an hour and forty minutes. (*Hamlet* is Shakespeare's longest play by far, and could not be done uncut in twice that time on stage.)

Considering the star's reputation, it is not surprising that the film ran to full houses. The *Daily Chronicle* said it was the most "completely artistic" movie yet made. It attracted large numbers of playgoers who normally avoided the cinema as too coarse a medium, and their applause was noticed to be longer than that of the most ardent movie habitués. But the Pall Mall *Gazette* reminded the public that to present *Hamlet* without its lines was to undertake the "impossible." Nevertheless, it admitted that the medium could do wonders with the Ghost, and conceded that some gratitude was owing when the "ephemeral" art of the actor can thus be rendered permanent.

The picture was acclaimed in Germany the same year and in India in 1915, in which year it also came to the United States. For American showing it was apparently drastically cut. Reviews repeated the objections of the Pall Mall *Gazette* but paid great tribute to Forbes-Robertson and Gertrude Elliott. The photography was still limited to what could safely be done on the combined area of a stage. One of the remarkable aspects of the film is that Forbes-Robertson was then sixty, though he looked younger—but, more importantly, that one forgot his age as the movie progressed. As Ball says, "The truth is that [he] . . . triumphed over his medium." He was perhaps the earliest movie actor to avoid all exaggeration on the screen.

J. H. Barnes played Polonius, incorrectly, I believe, not as a comic personality but a sensible old philosopher. (Of course, without his lines, Polonius's pedantry and clumsy scheming are less evident.)

It is an article of faith with me that burlesque, travesty, or parody can be amusing only when the object of the ridicule is itself inferior. Stephen Leacock was something of a master of this sort of thing when he did his "Winsome Winnie" on the sentimental rubbish of the Laura Jean Libby school, or his "One of Two Things" on the innumerable silly pieces the French have written on Napoleon's heroics. When Fanny Brice did a deliberately clumsy fan dance à la Sally Rand to end all fan dances, and when she advanced to the footlights as a Martha Graham dancer, swathed to her neck in black, with long drooping black sleeves and clenched fists, and uttered one word: "Rewolt!"—I blessed her; but when she did a Juliet in Yiddish dialect I could have guillotined her. It is, naturally, a matter of taste. Some folk think anything can be made funny. I happen to feel that to try to make the sublime ridiculous only proves the vulgarity of the perpetrator. And the movies have had their share of abominable taste in their "take-offs" on Shakespeare.

Romeo and Juliet was the most frequent victim. In England Anson Dyer produced four one-reel animated cartoons: *The Merchant of Venice* (1919), *Romeo and Juliet, Hamlet,* and *Othello* (1920). In the first, Antonio is a man who sells ice cream in Venice; Shylock is a ferocious and greedy miser; Portia causes the plants in her window boxes to grow with amazing speed by weeping upon them, and in court defends her lover from the murderous intent of Shylock by demanding his ration book, and publicly exposes him for having already exhausted his meat stamps.

The *Romeo and Juliet* had the two lovers made in the images of Charlie Chaplin and Mary Pickford, not excluding the Chaplin walk and the Pickford smile. "Chaplin" appeared as Hamlet in Dyer's next—or rather as 'Amlet, who, learning from a ghost that his uncle is a murderer, shoots the culprit with a movie camera; by a projection of film Claudius is confronted with his deed, while 'Amlet watches him with a flashlight. In *Othello* the Moor is a minstrel who in the end smothers Mona with burnt cork and kisses.

Others, enacted by a human cast, during the same years, include an Italian *Othello* with country bumpkin humor; an American Western, *A Sage Brush Hamlet* and a *Romeo and Juliet* with fat Walter Hiers as Romeo. There was also another cartoon by Budd Fisher, with Mutt and Jeff in *Cleopatra*. In 1923 there was a *Juliet and Her Romeo* made in England, and in the United States a *Romeo and Juliet* with Ben Turpin as the cross-eyed hero; in one scene he wiggled his ears. I am sorry to say that Mr. Ball regrets not having seen the last-named. Ernst Lubitsch's last short film was *Romeo and Juliet in the Snow* (1920) in German, a comedy dealing with winter sports. Pathé films showed *The Tempest* in which the hero is shanghaied aboard a ship, cast into the sea by a storm, lands on an island, and falls in love the daughter of the light-house keeper. In 1922 a Danish comedy, *He and She and Hamlet*, with the two popular low-comics, Schenstrom (who was tall and skinny) and Harold Madsen (who was short and fat), much loved in Germany and France, must have been successful enough to warrant its being made again in 1932 with sound.

In 1921 Will Rogers appeared in *Doubling for Romeo*. Rogers said that the reason that film was made (for Samuel Goldwyn) was so they might use the same costumes Geraldine Farrar and a friend had worn in some "costume pictures." Rogers added that he wore Miss Farrar's. In it he was a cowboy who, in order to learn how to make love in a style pleasing to his girl, goes to a studio. A courteous director shows him a variety of love-making techniques and Rogers tries them all, ending with a choice of the "strong-arm method." While reading *Romeo and Juliet* he falls asleep, dreams he is Romeo with the girl he does not know how to sue for Juliet. In a burlesqued balcony scene in the dream, he plays the ukulele in the garden for Juliet; the fight with Tybalt ends with a fist to the jaw; his exit from the Capulet ball is à la Douglas Fairbanks, by means of a rope; and when he lands on the balcony he drinks wine with his Juliet. This was a film in six reels.

In 1922 Buster Keaton, in *Day Dreams*, as a country boy imagines himself to be Hamlet, the skull being supplied too by his fancy. In *Triumph* (1924) Rod La Rocque and Victor Varconi each imagines himself as a Romeo on a balcony with Juliet (Leatrice Joy); the background is a tin can factory. It was even suggested in 1928 that Chaplin himself do Hamlet in two reels, with a supporting cast of Mary Pickford, Douglas Fairbanks, and John Barrymore; luckily it was left to the imagination.

The chief successor to Maurice Costello as a matinée idol in the movies was Francis X. Bushman. Since all the ladies in our home circle when I was a boy thought him wonderful, especially my numerous aunts, it did not occur to me to be openly critical. I did not especially care to see him (I much preferred William S. Hart), but it seemed to me that Maurice Costello was appearing less and less frequently and I was forever seeing Bushman on the screen. I thought him rather pretty, but was disturbed by the curve of his nose. The chief source of speculation about him for me was that X in his name; I was too young to have heard much about saints, and I could not for the life of me decide what name could possibly begin with an X. I ended by concluding that he had put it there just because it did *not* stand for anything, and thus singled him out as not like anybody else. His name was most often associated with that of Beverly Bayne. I had the impression that I was always being pelted by the screen with those two names. He never excited me, and she never brought me to the verge of tears as did that precious Alice Joyce —especially that deeply moving two-reeler in which, having got herself entrapped by huge gambling debts, the sweet-faced Alice, with her long, lovely, waving hair streaming about her, had robbed her own husband's safe, and then, to make it seem like the work of burglars, almost helplessly strew various papers on the floor, looking all the while like an angel straight from heaven. (How I wished then I could have helped her scatter the evidence in the room, since the task seemed so much beyond her strength!)

Well, at any rate, in 1916 Metro announced early in the year that it was going to make what it called "one of the most pretentious features ever offered," a *Romeo and Juliet* with Francis X. Bushman and Beverly Bayne, and by very late summer declared that it had spent $250,000 on the production, with a cast of six hundred "chosen" people. Hearing that a rival production was in the making, Metro in October took a two-page advertisement extolling the wonders of its creation. Seven days later the competitor, Fox, also had a two-page announcement. It was the tercentenary of Shakespeare's death, and William Fox wished the world to know that his contribution to that important year was a new production, a "Tragedy of Love . . . The sweetest story ever told," *Romeo and Juliet,* "with that Renowned Screen Artist, Theda Bara," with an "incomparable cast" in excess of twenty-five hundred.

Both films were released on the same day, October 22, 1916. In rage, Metro advertised again: "Don't be misled. There is one and only one SPECIAL PRODUCTION DE LUXE OF SHAKESPEARE'S LOVE STORY OF THE AGES," and warned against "inferior imitations" of Metro's masterpiece. Fox replied: "What is YOUR VERDICT?"—and reminded the public that comparison was "*now* possible." Metro's next move was to have its stars make a personal appearance on the second night at the Broadway Theater. The press of the eager audiences was all that could have been desired.

Metro's picture was made partly in the New York studio, partly outdoors in Greenwich, Connecticut, and in Brighton Beach, where the streets of Verona were set up. An unusual aspect of the shooting was that the cast learned the lines of the original play and spoke them, even though they were to remain unheard by the audience. For orchestras in theaters, a musical score was provided combining Gounod's saccharine opera and Tchaikovsky's beautiful overture. The *Moving Picture World* said that here at last was a Shakespearean production which disproved that the screen robs the plays of their power because no words are heard. Both Bushman and Bayne were extolled for their excellence. Of the twelve thousand inches of film not a single one was superfluous, and a whole reel was devoted to the balcony scene. I never saw the Bushman-Bayne film myself, for I was not a disloyal youth and therefore naturally went to see Theda Bara's.

I say "naturally" because I was madly in love with Theda Bara all through boyhood and younger adolescence—a matter totally beyond the understanding of my family, for I was a quiet boy and not given to mischief. Vivid as though it were yesterday is the memory of the day her name first flashed across my horizon while I was still in knickerbockers. I was passing our neighborhood movie house to see whether they were still showing the "gigantic spectacle" by someone with the name of D'Annunzio, which I had decided to avoid, and I read that tomorrow would be playing *A Fool There Was* with that great "French actress," direct from a theater called "Antoine in Paris," Theda Bara. I was a credulous youth, never questioning the truth of anything I was told, and for the duration of my one-sided love affair, I never doubted that poster.

I suppose it was the exoticism of her name, the Théâtre Antoine "in Paris," and the sensationalism of the title that attracted me, so I was among the early attendants at the first showing next day. I have seen *A Fool There Was* several times since then in recent years and know how absurd it was. I was properly horrified at the wickedness of the vampire and her cruel laughter, and felt terribly sorry for the poor man as he crawled down the stairs on his hands and knees while she jeered at him; I knew she was evil, and all I wanted was to be one of her victims too, though I had not the faintest idea what her lovers wanted except to "be in love" with her. I never missed a single Theda Bara picture after that. I not only saw every one, and witnessed all the destruction she visited upon various men and women, but I also had an unending series of quarrels with my schoolmates and with my female cousin in particular who, being female, was extremely vicious about Theda Bara; the common verdict was that she must be an awfully evil woman to enact consistently so many wicked roles—and I alone was her champion, often rising to a fever of indignation in maintaining that her acting had nothing to do with her personal character. And then two things happened which gave me the intense pleasure of knowing I had stood alone fighting a worthy cause. One day I was passing the Hotel Plaza's main entrance when out there came a tall woman dressed all in white (broadcloth, I imagine) with a large white picture hat on which fluttered two long white ostrich plumes; over her she carried a white lace parasol and in the other hand she held a leash at the end of which were two elegant white Borzoi dogs—and it was Theda Bara. I stood rooted to the ground, open-mouthed, I guess—and she *smiled* at me! Nobody else, to my astonishment—though indeed, the street was fairly deserted—had recognized her. But I, a knickerbockered school-boy, *had,* and she saw it, and she *smiled* at me! I have spent the rest of my life deploring the paralysis of my tongue at that moment, for she paused a moment as if expecting me to say something. I merely stared, she continued smiling, and, pulled ahead by her Borzois, passed on, giving me a charming glance over her shoulder.

The other thing that happened was an article written by her in a popular movie magazine, which I used to devour every month only for news of her —an article in which she defended herself against just such charges as I had been combatting. She really did not *wish* to play the part of the vampire, she said, but alas! the movie company insisted; however, she had at last pre-vailed and it had been agreed that she was to enact the roles of *good* girls for a change. I proudly showed the article to everyone who had been assailing her character, and read the passages in which it was so clear that privately she was a simple, good woman—all to no avail. No one was convinced, not even my mother, whose face always registered a look of distaste every time I mentioned my adored one's name.

I then saw Theda Bara in several pictures in which she was *very good*. In one she was even a pathetic orphan. In another, at some kind of great personal sacrifice, which I no longer remember, she mounted a small platform in a square to encourage the soldiers to fight the good fight (which, I now suppose, they were reluctant to do until she addressed them). I was happy at this reversal of a career of evil to one of good, though a small voice within me whispered that she was not doing very well in those parts.

When the movies began to talk her career was over, and the reason became only too clear. My last recollection of her was of her coming out of some years of retirement to appear in a Broadway play. I never got the chance to see it, for it closed rapidly. The critics were unanimous in declaring that the most famous vampire of them all had a voice absurdly high-pitched and thin. What a disillusionment! I had always conceived it to have the richness of a clarinet. She died in 1955, and I remember reading years before that she was almost blind from decades of submission to the glare of klieg lights. I could almost envy Mr. Ball even today, for he had a personal interview with her in 1949, but I forgive him for having had the privilege denied me in my adolescence because he says that he found her "a remarkably intelligent woman." That erases the thought of the voice too high-pitched and thin.

Well, I saw her Juliet and, though praised, it did not do as well in the United States as the rival production. She had said (or else her press agent said it for her) that she had studied Juliet a great deal and had concluded that the Capulet heiress had lived in an era of "passionate abandon." The *Moving Picture World* said that to be Juliet one had better be young rather than Bernhardt attempting to look young, since the "screen refuses to be deceived. Theda Bara is young and her long dark curls make many a beautiful picture." The picture was declared "valuable." In Great Britain the movie did much better, and the star was advertized as "Mlle. Theda Bara, the famous Parisian actress." Criticism said it "scored heavily," "its success was immediate," and was "a bounty of beauty." It was shown at Stratford-on-Avon for the Shakespeare festival, and did very well in Australia. I, of course, thought it marvelous on one level, but within me I knew she was not convincing—that her innocence was only skin-deep.

About her name there was a great deal of nonsense. She was born Theodosia Goodman (I think in Cincinnati), and had never been near the Théâtre Antoine. It was explained that Theda Bara, an invention of somebody or other, was an anagram for "Death (ly) Arab." The truth is, she explained to Mr. Ball, that her maternal ancestors had been Italian, named Di Bara, and that she had used the name Bara as a pseudonym for a play she had worked on before going into the movies.

The year after her Juliet, 1917, she did a Cleopatra, which was much more suited to her talents. I remember it very well, because Miss Bara not only wore some very elaborate Egyptian clothes, but also—to my delighted shock and surprise—sometimes wore very little. She was indeed *very* serpentine in her movements, and her old cruelty and power of enslavement were (I was grateful) once more in evidence after all those unconvincing forays into innocence. I remember reading in a movie magazine at the time that the weight of her headdress was such that her head actually bled. I hope I need not say how indignant I was that she should have had to go through all that. I did not know my Shakespeare at the time except for *Julius Caesar*, which I was constantly being taught in each new school I entered—and always incorrectly, with Julius Caesar as the hero, and Brutus and Cassius as the villains—and Lamb's *Tales from Shakespeare*, so I did not see that this *Cleopatra*, as it was named, was somewhat Shakespeare's and somewhat Sardou's adaptation of Shakespeare—and a great deal of the scriptwriter's, Adrian Johnson. In it Caesar figured as prominently as Antony. There was great emphasis laid on Egyptian splendor and luxury, there were three thousand extras, there were elaborate sets of Alexandria and Rome, and eighty boats were burned in battle. It was a long picture, of ten reels. It made a great deal of money and Theda Bara's reputation was further enhanced.

France made its contribution to the tercentenary in 1916 with a brief *Macbeth* film starring Maeterlinck's well-known mistress, Georgette Leblanc. I remember that their long marriage without the ceremony was the subject of several articles of yellow journalism, participated in by public declarations of the principals themselves. In those days it was considered "simply scandalous." The picture, which made little attempt to tell the whole story of *Macbeth* and could have meant little to anyone who did not know it, may very well have been made to let the rest of the world have a look at this notorious woman, who sang at the Opéra Comique and also appeared as an actress in the theater. According to the story, she decided after reading one of his pieces that they were meant for each other, arranged to meet him, and was his mistress and Muse (and, she added, sometimes his collaborator) for many years. Some time before this short picture she had done Lady Macbeth in a private performance of his translation of the play. The criticism of the movie said that one of the most important aspects of the picture was her acting, that "her carriage and every gesture" bespoke "majesty and force."

During the tercentenary the British filmed *The Merchant of Venice*, starring Matheson Lang as Shylock, a role he had been doing at the St. James's Theatre. While the production was having its run, the Broadwest Film Company offered to shoot it just as it was with his entire company and all the stage scenery. They moved everything to their glass-roofed studio and filmed most of it by daylight. Lang was pleased with the results, and so, apparently, was the public. One critic thought that many who went to see the cinema version "for mere amusement" will be moved to read the play now "from start to finish," and then go to hear "the magnificent words" when Lang presents it again on the stage. The same critic made the intelligent stricture that the work was not so much a "photo-play" as a "photograph of Shakespeare's stage play." It was "not a *translation* to the screen." But even though the great lines were not to be heard, the screen performance had the advantage of allowing a much greater number of spectators to see it, people who live in villages and never get to a theater; moreover, the "facial expressions" of the actors can be studied more minutely than in the theater. Lang's performance was especially fine, for he made Shylock seem more sinned against than sinning, and represented his hatred for the "rather priggish" Antonio (!) as almost justified. The actor who performed Antonio, George Skillan, was got up to look like Shakespeare himself. One touch that the film did add to the stage version was a scene in which Shylock gives Jessica her mother's ring. (That was indeed an *addition!*) The picture played in over eight hundred movie palaces.

During the decades preceding World War II the German film company, Ufa, was considered by those limited audiences in the United States interested in foreign films as consistently producing the best movies which were being imported. The chief star of that company was Emil Jannings; he was seen in a great many of their more important productions; those audiences have considerably widened since World War II and Jannings will be familiar to the many who have seen one of the frequent revivals of *The Blue Angel*, in which Marlene Dietrich costarred. (That movie was remade in Hollywood, and if I were Marlene Dietrich I should do what I could to place an embargo on the German version, for it was Hollywood that made her into one of the most beautiful women in the world—and it is only a shock to see how bulbous she was before Hollywood remade her as well as the picture. Jannings was in the American version too, and it was altogether a superior production, though it is never revived.) Jannings was a most excellent actor in his heavy-handed way, paying scrupulous care not only to makeup, but to his gait and gestures, suiting them to the role he was playing. He specialized in provoking pathos—though I saw a magnificent performance by him in *Tartuffe* with some of the simplest and most authentic settings I ever beheld. (I believe it was shown very little in the United States, and I have never met anyone else who saw it.)

In 1922 Jannings played Othello to the Iago of Werner Krauss, with the Emilia of Lya de Putti (who was so excellent in the German *Variety*—with Jannings—and was reduced to committing suicide when brought to California, by the studio's miserable treatment of her). This *Othello* managed to botch the story, rob the Moor of all dignity and poetry, and the Iago of any touch of subtlety in his villainy. This six-reel picture ended with Cassio's coming out on a balcony to address the populace of Cyprus; the subtitle informed one that he was saying to them, "God have mercy on his poor soul." Cassio prayed, eyes lifted to Heaven. Finis.

It was a bad picture, and, perhaps because of Janning's well-earned reputation, a great success in New York. The *Times* said it was "true" and had vitality; the *World* declared it acted "with surpassing strength"; and the *Film Daily* averred that Janning's Moor was "as though Shakespeare's character came to life." Ball, who has, of course, seen it fairly recently, reports that Janning's characterization "is almost animal, gorilla-like in face and passion."

There was some talk of bringing John Barrymore's brilliant *Hamlet* of 1922/23 from the stage to the screen. Griffith objected to making a film of the play on the grounds that there are five murders in it, and "what would the censors say?" Moreover, Hamlet himself is too morbid a character, "who commits suicide" (!!), and Griffith was afraid that the public would have none of such a story. In any event, though Barrymore made a number of films, he never appeared as Hamlet—which is a great pity.

In 1920 a group of Danes in Germany made a *Hamlet* in which the prince was enacted by the actress Asta Nielsen. Basically this version plays ducks and drakes with Shakespeare. How? It will be enough to describe the final scene, from which I have never recovered after seeing the picture decades ago. The whole affair had, indeed, something Wagnerian about it; as Hamlet fell dying all *her* lovely hair tumbled about her head loosely and revealed that Hamlet was actually a woman! At last Horatio understood the nature of his attraction to the prince, and at last the audience could understand why Hamlet would never have married Ophelia. (This was, of course, long before the days either of gay liberation or women's lib.) One was reminded of that incomparable moment in the music-drama when Siegfried, having pierced the Magic Fire, undoes the corselet from the sleeping form of the well-padded Valkyrie, beholds her capacious bosom, and staggers back, crying quite superfluously: "This is no man!" Of course, if the lovely hair tumbled loose on the screen *today*, it would prove nothing about Hamlet's sex.

🌿 24 🌿

The Twentieth Century (I)

Two names inevitably come to mind when one thinks of Shakespearean production in the twentieth century: the Old Vic in London and the Shakespeare Memorial Theatre at Stratford-on-Avon. Both places required traveling by Londoners and visitors to their city. The Old Vic, now the National Theatre, is situated on the south side of the Thames on the Waterloo Road, a most incovenient part of the metropolis to reach. Add to this that tickets for it, unlike the concentration of centrally located theaters on the other side of the river in the West End, cannot be purchased through ticket agents, and you are presented with difficulties enough before you are even seated. Suppose you are in London for three weeks; if you wish you can immediately get tickets for every night of those three weeks, and every matinée too—good seats and at reasonable prices—for every theater in London but one. The tickets can be bought from an agency or if you prefer you can purchase the tickets at the box offices within the course of a couple of hours leisurely stroll because of the close proximity of most West End playhouses. Tickets for all these theaters, I repeat, can be had at an agent's. Not so for the former Old Vic. Indeed, you cannot even reserve seats over the phone, but must risk, after an arduous trip to a most unattractive part of the city, finding tickets unavailable when you get there—if you were counting on attending a performance that day. The once-called Memorial Theatre in Stratford, now the Royal Shakespeare, also requires a trip—a much longer one—plus a consideration of train schedules and, as often as not, arrangements for lodgings for the night. Of course, everyone interested in Shakespeare wishes to see the birthplace and the church and the notorious inscription on the tomb, but when all these have become familiar after many visits, the fatigue of the train ride remains.

Notwithstanding the inconvenience, these two theaters have for a long time been the temples of Shakespearean performance. To them now must be added, happily, the name of the Aldwych in the West End, where the

Royal Shakespeare Company often alternates presenting plays at Stratford and bringing the production to London. (It is interesting, *en passant*, to note that the Aldwych was first opened by an American, the producer Charles Frohman, in 1905, not with Shakespeare but with *Bluebell in Fairyland;* it was not until 1960 that it became the London playhouse for the Royal Shakespeare Company.)

The Old Vic, when it opened in May 1811, was called the Royal Coburg, after Prince Leopold and Princess Charlotte; but it was not a theater devoted to Shakespeare. Its first presentation was *Trial by Battle, or Heaven Defend the Right,* a melodrama based upon a recent murder; the play was sandwiched between a harlequinade and a ballet, and was written by one William Barrymore—with whom the Barrymore family in America had no connections. But crossing over the river to that neighborhood was a risky business which patrons of the West End proved unwilling to undertake; consequently the Coburg soon settled down to catering to people from nearby, and became a playhouse for the most melodramatic of melodramas. Even though the interior was quite handsome—for instance in 1820 it boasted an extraordinary curtain made up of sixty-three mirrors which reflected the entire auditorium—it did not prosper. In 1833 the Coburg was redecorated and reopened as the Royal Victoria, with *Black-Eyed Susan.* Before long it was being nicknamed "the Old Vic." Progressively its audiences became rougher and rougher, and the plays more and more wretched in quality. Later it became a music hall, was sold at auction, reopened as the New Victoria Palace, and closed in 1880.

That year Emma Cons, a woman preoccupied with social reform, bought it and opened the theater again as a "temperance music hall," under the name of the Royal Victoria Hall and Coffee Tavern, with the object of presenting decent family entertainment at very low prices. Despite auguries of dismal failure, the Old Vic now did well.

From 1881 to 1883 it was under the management of William Poel (1852–1934), who was to influence the future of Shakespearean and modern stage productions, and who was eventually to consecrate himself to the Shakespearean and Elizabethan drama. His name was originally spelled Pole; his father was an engineer, musician, friend and sponsor of the Pre-Raphaelite painters and poets. Young Pole was the model for William Holman Hunt's famous painting, *The Finding of the Saviour in the Temple,* and when he grew up his ideas were to a degree formed by these friends of his father. When still very young, he decided to become an actor. There are two stories to account for the change in the spelling of his name: that his father objected to his becoming an actor, and that he therefore changed the spelling; that an early program misprinted his name as Poel, and that he decided to retain the name as his professional one; perhaps both stories are true.

With Salvini he went to Italy for a while; in 1881 he had already begun the work which was to bring fresh air into stage production: he presented the first quarto of *Hamlet*—that in itself was not important, for that edition of the play is assuredly the most corrupt and untrustworthy text of a Shakespearean play ever printed—at St. George's Hall and, what was highly important, presented it without scenery. In short, he was already approximating the conditions under which Shakespeare's plays were first presented. He not only directed the work but acted as Hamlet; his Ophelia was Helen Maude, the future Lady Tree.

After his two-year stint at the Old Vic, he joined Benson's company as Benson's first stage manager. He had for some time been an instructor at the Shakespeare Reading Society, and from the latter grew the Elizabethan Stage Society, which Poel founded in 1895. Under his direction the Elizabethan Stage Society presented seventeen of Shakespeare's plays *in toto;* as well as Marlowe's *Doctor Faustus;* Ford's *The Broken Heart; Arden of Feversham;* Jonson's *Sejanus; Everyman;* Milton's *Samson Agonistes.* Sometimes they were given in halls or inns of court but, wherever, always without scenery. He was, in short, undoing, as far as he was able (for it was to take a long time for other producers and the public to catch up with him), the pernicious popular fashion of drowning the classics in scenery and spectacle. He allowed no tampering with the texts, and no transposing of scenes; his ambition was to give the plays as their dramatists had originally conceived them. He stipulated that his actors speak clearly and rapidly, without oratorical effects. Shaw said ironically and with much point, "What a gigantic reform Mr. Poel will make if his Elizabethan stage should lead to such a novelty as a theatre to which people go to see the play instead of to see the cast!"

In 1888 De Witt's drawing of the Elizabethan playhouse, the Swan, was published, and no one took this revelation more seriously than Poel. The acting of his companies often left much to be desired, but he was determined that the plays should be seen as originally intended, and wherever he was showing his productions of the Elizabethans, he attempted to re-create the Elizabethan theater. Shaw wrote a long and brilliant defense of the method. "The poetry of *The Tempest* is so magical that it would make the scenery of the modern theatre ridiculous. The methods of the Elizabethan Stage Society . . . leave to the poet the work of conjuring up the isle 'full of noises, sounds, and sweet airs.' And I do not see how this plan can be beaten." If Irving were doing the play "he would give us . . . an expensive and absurd stage ship; and some windless, airless, changeless, soundless, electric-lit, wooden-floored mockeries of the haunts of Ariel. They would cost more; but would they be an improvement on . . . [Poel's] arrangement? Mr. Poel says frankly, 'See that singer's gallery up there! Lets pretend that it's the ship.' We agree, and the thing is done. But how could we agree to such a pretence with a stage ship? Before it we should say, 'Take that thing away; . . . or imagination . . . must not be contradicted by something that apes a ship so vilely as to fill us with . . . repudiation of its imposture. The singing gallery makes no attempt to impose upon us; it . . . throws itself honestly on our fancy, with instant success. In the same way a rag doll is fondly nursed by a child who can only stare at a waxen simulacrum of infancy." It is not that one can always imagine things more vividly than art can present them, but that no art can compete with the stimulation of the imagination by Shakespeare's poetry. The dialogue in the first scene of *The Tempest* "would turn the House of Lords into a ship." Of course "modern melodrama is so dependent on the most realistic scenery" that a representation could more easily be spared the dialogue than the sets.

The effect of Poel on later production can be gauged by another observation: "The more I see of these performances of the Elizabethan Stage Society, the more I am convinced that their method of presenting an Elizabethan play is not only the right method for that particular sort of play, but that any play performed on a platform amidst the audience gets closer home to its hearers than when it is presented as a picture framed by a proscenium." A corollary of Poel's theories has been the evolution in our time of the theater in the round.

Obviously, the Old Vic during Poel's two years as manager was not to his purpose, much less would he have been interested in its function as a music hall. *The Bohemian Girl,* its first opera, was produced at the Old Vic in 1900; and when song recitals and orchestra concerts were given, scenes from Shakespeare were appended.

Lilian Baylis (1874–1937), the niece of Emma Cons, had been assistant to her since 1898; in 1912 she assumed management of the Old Vic. She had been trained for the concert stage as a violinist, and had appeared in that capacity at the age of seven in her aunt's theater. Eventually she settled in Johannesburg teaching music and leading a women's orchestra, until in 1898 her aunt persuaded her to join her at the Old Vic.

Emma Cons died in 1912. Lilian Baylis, although sympathetic to her aunt's social and religious objectives as manager of the Old Vic, was determined to elevate the standards of the old theater, now renamed The People's Opera House. In 1906 William Poel had made an offer that Miss Baylis as assistant manager would doubltess have seized upon with delight—that he bring his Shakespearean players to the Old Vic—but the lord chamberlain's restrictions made it impossible to accept the opportunity.

Within less than a decade the governmental limitations were lifted, and World War I made it suddenly possible for the Old Vic to become the home of Shakespearean production; all the playhouses in London were severely hit because of the drop in audience attendance, and leading actors were now only too eager to join a Shakespeare company at the Old Vic at salaries they would have laughed at before the war, if only because it insured their employment. While Miss Baylis took no part in producing them, confining herself to her very able management, from 1914 to 1923 all of Shakespeare's plays were given by various directors at her theater. When the war ended, the Old Vic found itself, despite its location, one of London's most important playhouses, and drew enthusiastic spectators.

Miss Baylis now realized that the work she was carrying on ought to be national in character, so, with help, she acquired the Sadler's Wells Theatre, sacred to the name of Phelps, and in 1931 reopened it as a companion to the Old Vic on the north side of the city. Soon it seemed sensible to devote Sadler's Wells to opera and ballet, and to keep drama for the Old Vic.

Though she had the assistance of others, Lilian Baylis retained firm control of both playhouses until her death in 1937, and was throughout the guiding spirit of both enterprises.

Her transformation of her aunt's temperance institution into a leading theater and an opera-ballet house was a remarkable accomplishment. It is all the more amazing to contemplate when one reads of the unending struggles she faced against insufficient finances, and the fact that she, herself, was—as she freely admitted—untutored; but her instinct for finding cooperative associates was akin to genius. Her intense religious convictions were both deeply humanitarian and open-minded. Her ability to keep her projects afloat is ascribable to an unquenchable idealism as well as to the warm affection she evoked from all who knew her well.

The roster of actors and directors who worked at the Old Vic is an illustrious one—among others, Robert Atkins, Tyrone Guthrie, John Gielgud, Laurence Olivier, Ralph Richardson, Alec Guinness, Robert Helpmann, Michael Redgrave. When Atkins was directing, doubtless taking the hint from Poel's theories, he wasted no time in changing scenery; he would have one or two set scenes, and have the rest of the play given before simple curtains. He stipulated that his actors speak rapidly, intelligibly, with a minimum of by-play. The result was that he was able to give most of the repertory with few cuts. The advantage of his method was to be seen particularly in *Antony and Cleopatra* with its great number of short scenes. (By contrast, Tree in *Julius Caesar* had the opposing generals placed on high rocks with a ravine between them. At the Old Vic they merely marched in from opposite sides before an unadorned curtain.) But Atkins's successors were not of a mind to follow his excellent lead. For example, Harcourt Williams's *Henry IV, Part I* had Falstaff coming in to wake up Hal asleep in bed, along with Poins, equipped with a razor to shave the prince. Productions continued to be more elaborate, and are so still, as I can testify from a recent Olivier *Merchant of Venice.*

The Nazis badly damaged the Old Vic in May 1941, and it was forced to close, though the company was busy enough on tour and in London, temporarily at the New Theatre. While the Old Vic was being repaired, it continued as a school for actors (1947 to 1952); Michael Saint-Denis, its director, later went over to the Royal Shakespeare company at Stratford-on-Avon. By 1950 the Old Vic was able to reopen. From 1953 to 1958 Michael Benthall presented all of the thirty-six plays of the First Folio edition, beginning with Richard Burton in *Hamlet* and ending with John Gielgud and Edith Evans in *Henry VIII.* In 1963 the company broke up and the theater closed.

After considerable interior alterations, the Old Vic a few months later became the National Theatre with Laurence Olivier as director; its first attraction was Peter O'Toole as Hamlet. It went on with some classics non-Shakespearean (*The Recruiting Officer*), non-English (*Uncle Vanya*), more recent (*Saint Joan*), and modern (*The Royal Hunt of the Sun*).

In 1861 there was talk of celebrating the tercentenary of Shakespeare's birth, which would occur in 1864, with the production of a play at Stratford. For many years after Shakespeare's death Stratford-on-Avon seems to have been either indifferent or unaware of the rare swan it had incubated. The man who came to occupy Shakespeare's last residence in the town of his birth, his son-in-law Dr. John Hall, for example, left a book recording the existence and illnesses of many of his patients in Stratford, but has not a word to say about his wife's father. Two generations later, John Ward, vicar of Stratford, made a memorandum for himself that some day he must get around to reading Shakespeare's works. For the remainder of the seventeenth century now and then a lone admirer made his way to Stratford to pay homage to its all-but-forgotten genius. One of these, the great actor Betterton, at the turn of the century, visited the town and came back to London with a small stock of biographical snatches, most of them mere fiction—such as the deer-stealing story. It was in Garrick's time that people began to pay some attention to Shakespeare, and nobody was more responsible for this than Garrick himself, whose Shakespeare jubilee fiasco, postponed from 1764 to 1769, was drowned out by floods of rain and a rising Avon, but nevertheless put Stratford on the map as a center of interest.

The 1861 proposal was to an extent opposed in London and failed to generate much excitement in the public. However, it was a Stratford family, the Flowers, who made of the suggestion a reality. On the tercentenary, in 1864, a temporary wooden theater was erected and six plays were given. E. F. Flower and his son, Charles Edward Flower, despite the ridicule of London, consecrated themselves to the foundation of a permanent Shakespeare Memorial Theatre. When they formed a committee to shape clearly the theater's future, the hostility of London became more vocal; why, London wished to know, should Stratford lay any claim to a special proprietorship of its great son? Charles Flower, deaf to opposition, made a national appeal for £20,000, but only a small part of that sum was forthcoming, so that the major part of the costs came from his own pocket. He also presented Stratford with a site on the Avon. On Shakespeare's birthday, April 23, 1879, the first Shakespeare Memorial Theatre opened with performances by Barry Sullivan and his company of *Much Ado about Nothing*, with Helen Faucit, who came out of retirement, playing Beatrice to Sullivan's Benedick. That first Shakespeare Festival was so successful that Sullivan returned for another the next year. At his insistence, Edward Compton took over in 1881 and Sullivan himself came back the following year. The Shakespeare Festival was now a fact. In 1886, Frank Benson, young and devoted to Shakespeare, began spring and summer festivals which continued for the next thirty years. He produced every play published in the First Folio except *Titus Andronicus* (which can well be spared) and *Troilus and Cressida*. One of Benson's sensational feats was to present what may have been the first uncut *Hamlet* (1899) since Shakespeare's day. That same year Sarah Bernhardt gave the play in French at Stratford at a Saturday matinée. The undying popularity of the Shakespeare Festival may be attributed to Benson, whose appearances in

Stratford were so welcome by the citizens that all were present at the station to greet him, and some would not allow horses to convey him to his hotel, but drew his carriage there themselves.

In 1925 a royal charter was given the Memorial Theatre, and for the first time in its forty-six years the festival made a profit. The theater itself was a typical Victorian horror; the next year, in March, it was destroyed by fire, and from 1926 to 1931 the Festivals were given at the Stratford movie house, through local contributions of £1,600. W. Bridges-Adams had succeeded the Bensons in 1919, and in the cinema theater he was able during six seasons to maintain the audience for a festival.

Charles Flower's nephew, Archibald, took upon himself the raising of funds to build a new theater. The sum needed was vast, and only half of it came from the British public. The other half was raised in the United States, and of that John D. Rockefeller contributed £100,000. The new edifice was designed by Elizabeth Scott, and it was opened by the Prince of Wales (the later Duke of Windsor) on April 23, 1932, with performances of *Henry IV, Parts I and II*. Bridges-Adams extended the season into September, and, satisfied that the theater had achieved permanence, resigned. He was succeeded by Ben Iden Payne, who served from 1935 to 1942. Payne improved the quality of delivering the poetry, and also introduced the practice of making room for other English classics, such as plays by Ben Jonson, Goldsmith, and Sheridan. But it is the plays of Shakespeare which have always been featured at Stratford. After Payne came Milton Rosmer, 1943; Robert Atkins, 1944/45; Sir Barry Jackson, 1946/47; Anthony Quayle, 1948, who in 1953 was joined by Glen Byam Shaw as co-director; Peter Hall, 1960, who was presently sharing responsibility with Peter Brook and Michael Saint-Denis.

For all the difficulties involved, the Stratford theater maintained performances during World War II; despite the shortage of staff, audiences were as large as ever. Sir Barry Jackson, during his directorship, having proved the wisdom of the procedure at Birmingham, chose his actors not on the basis of established reputations, but for the promise they showed. Thus, in his first season he introduced Paul Scofield with Peter Brook as director. In 1948 Helpmann played King John, Shylock, and Hamlet; in the latter role he alternated with Scofield as lead. When Anthony Quayle came to preside, he found a theater in fine repair, with new scenery and costumes, and many stars who were more than willing to leave London to appear there: among them, Peggy Ashcroft, Diana Wynyard, Godfrey Tearle, and John Gielgud. Further renovations were made in 1950, the front curtain removed, and a quasi-permanent set installed for the opening of the 1951 season, on which occasion Michael Redgrave enacted Richard II. That same season he played Hotspur and Prospero; and Richard Burton played Hal and Henry V.

A second company was formed to tour Australia, Canada, and the United States (1952 to 1954). In London the Stratford company took over the Aldwych Theatre in the West End in the winter of 1960, beginning a policy of presenting old and new plays. Some of these were first performed in

Stratford, others only in London. The company has for some time now been known as the Royal Shakespeare Company, and their theater in Stratford, the Royal Shakespeare.

Of recent productions of the Old Vic and the Royal Shakespeare (and Aldwych) we shall have something to say in our last chapter.

The productions of Edward Hugh Sothern (1859–1933) and Julia Marlowe (1866–1950) were characteristic of Shakespearean performances during the early decades of this century. As Lloyd Morris says, without intending irony, they became "a national institution." Indeed they were! Whenever they were in New York my teachers were forever cudgelling us to attend their presentations. I cannot number the times I was dragooned into seeing them. So far as high school teachers were concerned Sothern and Marlowe were apparently the official custodians of Shakespeare. Garff Wilson, again with no intended malice, remarks that they "did their best to create and maintain an interest in Shakespeare." Well, with this auditor they completely failed. I still went to see them in my college days, and after that too, and I cannot remember a single detail of the characterizations of either of them, though of some of their contemporaries on Broadway—Rollo Peters and Jane Cowl in *Romeo and Juliet* or John Barrymore in *Hamlet,* for instance—I have the liveliest recollection of hundreds of unforgettable moments. There was a depressing air of well-meant conscientiousness about their work. I am sure they did do their best to promote interest in Shakespeare; but if I had to choose between their honorable intents and the utter lack of conscientiousness in the majority of Shakespearean productions on Broadway (and some in London, too) with their cursed search for novelty at the expense of the play, I should be hard put to it. It would be a question as to whether it is better to be bored than enraged. Sothern and Marlowe bored me; most contemporary productions of Shakespeare enrage me. I suppose, for health's sake, it is better to be bored. Perhaps a chief reason for the boredom was that Sothern and Marlowe performances were endless. Shakespeare's audiences had no intermissions between acts; Sothern and Marlowe not only had them between acts, but interminable waits between scenes. A scene might take ten minutes to act, and then you would wait twenty minutes while you heard stagehands behind the curtain hammering away on scenery for the next. No play can survive that sort of treatment (I have seen several good modern plays fail for the same reason), and it was against such clumsiness that William Poel conducted his much-needed revolution.

My youthful impressions have, I find, been fortified by the comments of Winter; Sothern's Shylock (of 1907) was "ineffective," for it attempted "to blend greed with benevolence, the crafty usurer with the majestic Hebrew patriarch." Sothern first played Hamlet in 1899, and was seen in it frequently thereafter; Winter agreed that it was intelligent, "conscientious," sincere, but lifted by no tragic prowess; Sothern was unable to project Hamlet's misery and anguish. Nevertheless, he had a large following—probably owing, I fancy, to the schoolteachers.

The son of an English actor and born in England himself, Sothern first toured with McCullough and in 1883 became leading man for Charles Frohman at the Lyceum, where he continued until 1898. He was very popular as a light-comedian and in cloak-and-dagger romances (e.g., *The Prisoner of Zenda*) both in London and New York. Not impressive in stature, he had a handsome face and a certain aristocratic air. His talent was patently for comedy, but he persisted, once he became consecrated to Shakespeare, in converting himself into a tragic actor; his repertory included Romeo, Hamlet, Macbeth, Antony, and Shylock. It is sad that a man who gave so much time to study and desired to be thorough should have been merely adequate. Winter probably hit the mark when he said that Sothern's dominance in the American theater was partly due to the "dearth" of great actors at the time.

Julia Marlowe was also born in England, but became an American while still a child. Her father, a bootmaker and sportsman, mistakenly believed that he had put out the eyes of a neighbor by the flick of his whip, and fled to the United States when she was four. He changed his name to Brough, when he settled in the Middle West, and it was as Fanny Brough that Julia first appeared on stage. Her initiation was in a juvenile production of *Pinafore* (1876) at Vincennes, Indiana. Her mind was already made up: she was going to enact the roles of the great Shakespearean heroines, pictures of whom she had devoured as a child in an illustrated edition of the plays. She came to New York, where she studied for several years. Then in 1887, after a two-week tour of New England in three non-Shakespearean plays, she rented the Bijou Theater in New York for a special matinée of one of them, *Ingomar*. A well-known story is that after the second act many of the audience hurried to nearby florists and emptied their shops in order to present the flowers to her. (I have personal reasons, which will presently appear, for wondering whether that legend was not the invention of Miss Marlowe's fancy.) At any rate, by December of the same year, she had managed to get sufficient backing to appear in a repertory that included Juliet, Viola, Beatrice, and Imogen. Already a star who was accorded a *succès d'estime*, she as yet earned little money.

Her leading man was Robert Taber, and in 1894 they were married, only to separate three years later. He proved a most unsatisfactory husband.

A very few years ago a charming old lady in Massachusetts got in touch with me through one of my publishers; she wrote that she had been an intimate friend of Julia Marlowe and had material the world had never seen or heard, and asked me to come up and speak to her. I did so. It developed that her idea was to give me the material, I was to write the book, and we were to share the royalties. I saw that she had a collection of newspaper clippings and articles such as are available to any researcher at the public library, some photos, some typewritten notes, and a number of personal letters from Julia Marlowe addressed to her. I was not eager, but because of the possibility that the notes and the letters might reveal unknown information, in the interest of theatrical history, I took the notes and the letters home with me to read, with a promise to return them within a matter of days —a promise I was not loathe to fulfill when I had read them. The notes indicated that the dear old lady had made several attempts to write the book herself, but had discovered (as many have still to discover) that writing involves more than a desire to write and a putting down of words on paper; these notes contained no new information outside of the fact that the dear old lady in her younger days had been a close friend of Miss Marlowe's, had worshipped her, had traveled with her, and had somehow managed to make herself the central character of her narrative. The letters revealed nothing new but the fact that the dear old lady and her family had indeed been close to Julia Marlowe but, with the exception of one letter, which I wish I had been allowed to copy, they contained material of no value to anyone else. It was clear enough that what the dear old lady really wished was to let the world know that she had been Miss Marlowe's good friend. But I have no regrets about having gone to Massachusetts, for in addition to repeating a few facts which were already on record, she told me three stories illustrative of the splendor of Miss Marlowe's sensibilities—and then, too, I *had* the opportunity to read that letter. Two of the stories, and that letter I shall deal with presently. I believe the stories for they are consonant with the letter. The other story it is time to relate now.

I was told that the true reason for the failure of Miss Marlowe's first marriage was the extreme jealousy of her husband over his wife's success. The crisis came when (I think it was in Boston) there was a rave review of her performance and no mention of his. He went into a frenzy and started tearing the newspaper into shreds. At this point the dear old lady, reenacting the scene as it had been reenacted for her by Miss Marlowe, rose with difficulty to her feet, extended her right arm fully and pointed to an imaginary door. " 'Go!' she said to him, 'Go at once! And never darken this house again!' And that was how they parted." She sank back into her chair, exhausted with the sheer drama of it.

Julia Marlowe joined forces with E. H. Sothern in 1904 in Chicago, where they first appeared together in *Romeo and Juliet*. They continued the partnership with *Hamlet, The Merchant of Venice, The Taming of the Shrew, Antony and Cleopatra*, and *Macbeth*. They were scheduled to bring some of these plays and *Twelfth Night* to London in 1907.

She was one of those actresses who capitalize on personal beauty, grace, womanliness, and above all in her case, like that of Maude Adams, for being widely known as a woman of virtue.

It must have been at this point in her career that the two other stories related by the dear old lady had their setting. "She was a woman of the strictest morality," said my hostess, "and she made it clear to him [E. H. Sothern] that they could not possibly travel to England on the same boat, lest people talk. Mr. Sothern understood, but insisted that he would come to the dock to see her off. I was going with her, and he did come to the boat —with a gift for her. It was a little dog. 'Take him along in place of me,' he said. 'I shall take the boat next week.' " The old lady's eyes filled with the beauty of the emotion. "And so the three of us traveled to London together. And I will never forget how the poor thing would sit in the hotel with the tears streaming down her face, while she patted the little dog's head and sobbed, 'O why doesn't Pardner come?'—she always called him Pardner—'Why doesn't he come?' She did that every day for a week until he arrived." Her voice was choked with feeling, and she looked at me to see how I was taking it. I repressed the impulse to remark that the question had been superfluous since Miss Marlowe had insisted on Sothern's coming later, but I was already beginning to perceive that, in common with a number of her colleagues, Miss Marlowe was an actress off as well as on stage.

"And then," continued the dear old lady, launching into her third reminiscence, "every night we would have dinner in her room, and she would always have the waiter set an extra chair and all the china, glasses, knives, forks, and spoons for a third person. When she and I sat down, she would say, 'That place is for Pardner.' That's the kind of noble woman she was!"

Sothern and Marlowe were successful on both sides of the Atlantic, and she was highly praised, except for her Cleopatra and Lady Macbeth (a role she disliked), and for the Prince Hal which she was foolish enough to attempt. One thing may be granted her ungrudgingly: her speech was very clear and distinct, and her rich voice could vary from tenderness to harshness and cruelty. Arthur Symons paid her a tribute which, in those days, was most extraordinary from a Britisher to an American—for the British have traditionally been either patronizing or contemptuous of Americans until fairly recently—when he said that no one on the British stage could speak English or deliver English verse as beautifully as Julia Marlowe and E. H. Sothern.

However, on the whole, criticism of her was depressingly similar to that given Sothern: she was very good, she was excellent, she was admirable—but the overtones make it clear that all this proceeded from *her* conscientiousness, and that both of them failed to achieve acting of the first magnitude. In 1911 they were married, and (this was a second marriage for him too) this time the union seems to have been an ideal one.

It must also be admitted that both of them could have made a great deal more if they had not chosen to concentrate on Shakespeare, for both had proved their abilities in other plays that demanded less talent. Sothern's gifts were in light comedy, and it was thought that his best Shakespearean role was Malvolio—though I have my doubts. It is a matter of record that he succeeded in making him a pathetic figure, which, however original, is enough to ruin the play.

Sothern died in 1933, and that is the year of the letter written to the dear old lady—the one letter I wish I had with the freedom to quote it. But though I have neither, I have an exceedingly sharp recollection of its contents, for I read it over several times, scarcely believing my eyes. It was the sort of thing which I believe Thackeray would have prized. The occasion was a sad one: Miss Marlowe was conveying her husband's remains to England, according to his wishes, and she indited the letter from aboard ship as she was in passage. The first three pages did full justice to her sorrow, how wretched she was without Pardner, how inconsolable, etc. But as I turned over the page, a new current was blowing across it. She had had a good night's sleep, she said, and had just eaten a hearty breakfast, and the lines were as cheerful as though penned by Rosalind herself.

Since I read this letter written in her own hand, I have difficulty in discrediting the three stories told me in Massachusetts, for they are all of a piece, though I fear the dear old lady and I give them quite opposite interpretations.

When the distinguished English critic, James Agate, was visiting the United States in 1937 he naturally went to see everything possible on Broadway. His comment on American actors was: "The quickfire comedians beat ours, but otherwise, and apart from Alfred Lunt, there are no actors. There is nobody over here with the quality of Laughton, Gielgud, Olivier, Richardson." If he were alive today to see what the United States stage has to offer in the way of Shakespearean performance, he might have to search for even stronger language, for the numbers of actors turned out by The Method and taught to be *themselves* on the boards has made matters far worse. Agate was also asked by leading critics in America who were then the best actors in Britain; he replied: Gielgud, Edith Evans, and Olivier as the most promising young actor.

As I have hinted before, the blight on twentieth-century Shakespearean production has been, in my judgment, the insistence, not on understanding the play which Shakespeare wrote, but on finding a new gimmick that no one has ever thought of before. When Longinus said many hundreds of years ago that the search for novelty as an end in itself is the greatest of all vulgarities, he was stating an eternal truth, which the contemporary Shakespearean stage continues to prove. When Charles Kean gave *Hamlet* he spent a fortune in reproducing the actual dress of the eleventh century in Denmark—an admissable point of view, which is neither commendable nor damnable. In the twentieth century there have been a number of performances in modern dress. Sir Barry Jackson at the Kingsway Theatre may be taken as an example of how far it can be taken. In 1925 he produced a *Hamlet* in which cigarettes, cigarette lighters, wrist watches, characters playing bridge or mixing a whiskey and soda were seen; outside an auto was heard. The result was total distraction from the business of the tragedy to the silly invented "business." It was naturally necessary to cut such lines as "Hyperion's curls, the front of Jove himself." His *Macbeth* had as hero a general in khaki, with medals and ribbons on his chest; there was also a tentative toying with Scottish dialect—e.g., "Macbaith, weel he desairves that name." His *The Taming of the Shrew* had motor cars, an electric stove, photos taken by flashlight of the wedding group. In 1929 Oscar Asche produced *The Merry Wives of Windsor* in a similar vein; the language of the play was modernized as well, and Falstaff, whenever he left the stage, called for a taxi. In 1938 *Troilus and Cressida* was presented with the Trojans in khaki and the Greeks in German uniform. In 1939 in *Julius Caesar* the rival commanders ex-

changed mutual defiances via the telephone. At Stratford-on-Avon in 1933
Theodore Komisarjevsky (1882–1954) directed; he was born in Venice,
reared in Russia, and learned the theater there before the Bolshevik Revolution; from 1907 to 1919 he was very busy producing plays and operas, and
in 1919 went to England. Before long he was recognized as a leading force
in the European theater; as might be expected, he was at his best in Russian
drama, particularly Chekhov. At Stratford in his *Merchant of Venice*, Launcelot Gobbo was dressed as for a pantomime, Morocco was a minstrel-show
Negro who burlesqued his speeches, Shylock was a fantastic, Portia was
merely flippant. In his *Macbeth*, Shakespeare's greatest poem, all poetry and
color were banished; everything was stark and drab; the scenery was made
of massed aluminum with funnels sticking up everywhere; most of the costumes were a dark green; the supernatural element was entirely eliminated;
when Macbeth thought he saw Banquo's ghost what he actually saw was his
own shadow on the wall (subtle!); the witches told Macbeth's future by
palmistry (comedy!); after the banquet Macbeth went to bed on stage and
had a nightmare in which he heard voices softly spoken from off stage. In
his *Lear*, he was lucky to have one of the finest Lears of his day, Donald
Wolfit, but the director cheerfully transferred speeches from one character
to another. His methods achieved their apogee in *Antony and Cleopatra*,
where he again reassigned speeches and rearranged scenes; there were all
kinds of original touches—for example, when Octavius addresses Antony
in absentia, Antony came on stage to hear it all; perhaps most unfortunate
was his selection of Eugenie Leontovich (b. 1900)—an actress who has
rendered many a brilliant performance in contemporary plays, when her
accent was entirely appropriate or did not matter—as Cleopatra. Agate
called his review, "Anton and Cleopatrova" and transcribed her rendition
of "When you sued staying,/Then was the time for words" as "Wen you suet
staying,/Den was de time for wurst." Agate asked: "What had English tallow
and German sausage to do with this Egyptian passion?"; had it been a great
performance, it would have been as easy to forgive her accent as it had been
Modjeska's; Leontovich was too much by temperament a comedienne; she
was at the sea fight in a Roman helmet, golden breastplate—and a slashed
skirt of blue satin.

Now, there is a perfectly good argument for giving Shakespeare in modern dress, and I have given a highly successful *Merchant of Venice* that way.
On Shakespeare's stage, plays were costumed in "modern dress"; the noblest Roman of them all was accoutred as an Elizabethan gentleman, and the
siren of the Nile as a highly ornamented Elizabethan gentlewoman; in the
first half of the eighteenth century the characters, whatever the period of the
play, appeared usually in eighteenth-century garb. The "historical" approach to costume and scenery came later. Shakespeare may therefore be
costumed in one of three ways: in Elizabethan dress, in historical dress, or
in modern dress. (There obviously is no excuse and, more importantly, no
gain in doing what has so often been done in recent decades, transposing
the period to the Victorian, the Edwardian, the Hispanic-Californian, or the
hippie.) Any of these three will do, so long as no violence is done to the

original meaning of the play and no meaningless, invented "business" (cigarette lighters, cocktail shakers, and the like) detracts from what is supposed to be happening on stage.

I am delighted to find Agate saying that Shakespeare would have trampled upon the best designs of Gordon Craig, Komisarjevsky, Bakst, and Picasso. He refused to believe that Shakespeare would have condoned "a crazy night on a geometrical heath with Lear on a spiral staircase defying an algebraic sky." On the subject no remark has ever hit the nail more precisely on the head than his declaration that the best scenery in Shakespeare is that which gets itself "immediately forgotten." No one was a greater sinner in this regard than Craig, whose designs so powerfully affected stage design in Europe and America—none more than his ideas for *Macbeth*. It is easy enough to see what he had in mind: to reproduce by the setting the play's tone of menace and murder. I had the opportunity of seeing those sets faithfully remade in a performance on Broadway. They were very impressive in themselves, and would have served admirably for *Dracula*. It became highly ridiculous for Duncan to exclaim upon arriving at Macbeth's castle:

> This castle hath a pleasant seat; the air
> Nimbly and sweetly recommends itself
> Unto our gentle senses

when the king is looking up at a towering edifice so terrifying that anyone in his right mind would have preferred to face the dangers of a savage wilderness to spending a night in so threatening a dungeon. Was not the effect Shakespeare planned far subtler than Craig's obvious gothic horror? Later, in the (unintentionally) funniest movie ever made, Orson Welles presented Macbeth's dwelling as a subterranean cave, chill and damp from the constant trickling of water down the overhanging rocks; but the bearskins and Valkyrie helmets of the cast should have been sufficient protection against influenza. In 1936 Mr. Welles gave a much talked about "Harlem *Macbeth*" in which he transposed the setting from Scotland to the Haitian jungle; what was supposed to be so special about it was that all the cast was black. That insured its being highly praised by all those people who rush to demonstrate their political liberalism at the drop of a hat, even when it is, as in the case of this play, totally unconnected with any contemporary political issue. What ought to have counted was whether or not this was a good production of the play Shakespeare wrote; the color of the skin of the performers was irrelevant. If their skin was white, black, yellow, red, or any shade in between, and the production was good, it should have been praised; if bad, it should have been damned. I saw that production and it was abominable. Of it, more later.

And now, to review significant actors of the early twentieth century:

Evelyn Millard (1869–1941), under the actor-manager, Lewis Waller, gave the best Juliet Max Beerbohm had ever seen; she had grace, tenderness, gaiety, and pathos, but no passion; Beerbohm doubted that English girls are capable of any. Waller's Romeo was "from first to last . . . the soldier in love"; there was nothing boyish about him; he made one feel that he was scarred all over, "an heroic document of all the principal Veronese fights in the past fifteen or twenty years."

Sir George Robey (1869–1954) was most successful as a comedian in English music halls, but did an interesting Falstaff in *Henry IV, Part I* in 1932. It was a subject of much discussion in advance as to whether a mistake had not been made in requiring him to give up his tiny flat bowler hat, long and collarless coat, cane, red nose, and raised eyebrows of the music halls. He kept the nose and eyebrows. The public did not know how much he loved Shakespeare, though he had never been on the legitimate stage before, and was astonished at the style and excellence of his interpretation. He did confuse some of the lines and on a few occasions lapsed into his music-hall routines, but one of them, his "basalisk stare" as he delivered the famous speech on Honor, was unforgettable by all who saw it. In 1954 he was knighted for services to the stage and charity, though he did not long survive the honor. He was a remarkable man—an excellent painter who exhibited at the Academy and the Royal Institute for Painters in Water Colours, an Egyptologist, a cricketer, and a violin-maker.

Oscar Asche (1871–1936), whose real name was Thomas Stange Heiss, was born in Australia, the son of a Norwegian and a woman of English stock. His father was a hotel proprietor and a man of extraordinary strength who was able to squeeze a pewter pot in one hand. Educated at Melbourne until he was sixteen, he left with a school friend for a six-month trip to China on a sailboat. Back in Australia, he tried his luck at various occupations without satisfaction; he therefore left again with another friend for a voyage to Fiji. Still a youth, he planned going to Norway to prepare himself for the stage. In Christiania, his father's birthplace, he studied under the son of the famous writer, Bjørnson, met Ibsen, who introduced him to William Archer, the famous translator and populizer in England of Ibsen. Archer advised him, as a man who spoke English, to go to Britain. His first year in London, 1893, was difficult: he slept on the Embankment, and called for cabs outside theaters. But before the year was over he had joined the Benson troupe, his main asset being his cricketing; he was with them for eight years, acting all sorts of minor (Shakespearean) parts. In 1898 he married, and in 1901 his wife joined the company too. In 1904 the Asches became co-managers with a friend of the Adelphi Theatre, where Asche played Bottom, Petruchio, and Angelo (of *Measure for Measure*) in productions that were declared memorable. In 1907 Asche took over His Majesty's Theatre where his most notable performance was Othello, considered one of the best of his time. But it was his own work that brought him his greatest fame: the libretto he composed to while away a rainy week at Manchester, for the musical fantasy, *Chu-Chin-Chow*, which ran for five years (1916 to 1921) for an unheard-of run of 2,238 performances. In 1929 he gave *The Merry Wives of Windsor* in modern dress, with, as we have mentioned, the lines modernized, and Falstaff forever calling for a taxi.

He was a man of "huge stature," and therefore had difficulty with roles more appropriate for a short man. Yet he also did Shylock, and one of his best roles was Claudius, whom he made sensual, savage, and cunning. Beerbohm commended him for remembering that Shakespeare wrote the king's part in verse and for delivering it rhythmically "with reverence for sound," and for comporting himself "with large tragic dignity." Of his Angelo, A. B. Walkley said it was a "fine, not to say fuliginous performance" —which, by the way, on the afternoon of April 28, 1906, had the added attraction of Ellen Terry, who celebrated her jubilee in the theater by appearing to speak the nine lines allotted to Francisca, the nun. When Asche, whom Trewin calls an "agreeably childish giant," presented *As You Like It* at His Majesty's Theatre during Tree's absence in 1907, he vied with Sir Herbert in the creation of his Forest of Arden: two thousand pots of fern, moss-covered logs, bamboo bushes, and wagonsful of leaves from the recent autumn; in one scene the players had to plow through two feet of fern, which naturally had to be replaced each week. Rosalind carried a shepherd's crook and wore a smock as Ganymede. Beerbohm did not care for Asche's Jaques because he was masticating an apple during the seven ages speech and speaking between swallows. That season Asche also played Othello, and flung his Iago around so ruthlessly that the villain must have prayed for the tragedy's early close—though that, at any rate, was far better than José Ferrer's Iago, in our own time, flinging around Paul Robeson's Othello!

Leon Quartermaine (1876–1967) was first seen in London in 1901 with Forbes-Robertson, and in 1913 was a member of Granville-Barker's troupe at the St. James's in Shaw, Galsworthy, and Ibsen. The year before he had appeared for the same producer as the clown in *The Winter's Tale*. After World War I, in 1919, he played Mercutio to Ellen Terry's last great impersonation as the Nurse. When the curtain came down, the house echoed with cries for both actors. In 1922 he was doing Lysander in a production which included the choreography of Michel Fokine. Komisarjevsky's ill-fated *Antony and Cleopoatra* (1936) included as part of its freakishness an Enobarbus, played by Quartermaine, who appeared, one critic said, as "a velvety gallant" with "brocaded tones," though Crosse thought he spoke beautifully "as he always does."

He was with Gielgud at the Queen's in 1937 in *Richard II*. For Ben Greet, in an open-air performance in the Park, he made a splendid Feste (1937). Again he played Antonio to Gielgud's Shylock and Peggy Ashcroft's Portia; in the role he made a pleasant, graceful and dignified merchant.

Walter Hampden (1879–1956), whose name was actually Walter Hampden Dougherty, was born in Brooklyn, New York, and had his theatrical training in England as a member of Benson's company. He returned to New

York in 1907 to appear there for the first time in a season that included
Ibsen, with the brilliant actress Nazimova. Together with other people of the
theater and the world of letters, such as Maude Adams and Mark Twain, the
Doughertys summered in what must have been an interesting community in
the Catskills at Tannersville, New York, the Onteora Club, where there still
will be found the Dougherty house. The center of their community life was
a small theater, well equipped for those days, though now fairly inadequate.
As most of the older generation died, the houses passed gradually into the
hands of a totally different class of people from the creative original posses-
sors. I was invited to direct a play there in 1972, and gave them a professional *The Importance of Being Earnest*, but found, alas, that though there were
still some charming people left, the newcomers, their community more
"restricted" than ever, had little concern for their old theater, and were
interested almost entirely in: (1) drinking scotch, (2) playing golf, (3) drinking scotch, (4) playing tennis, (5) drinking scotch, (6) swimming in the pool,
and (7) drinking scotch.

Hampden's services to the American theater were great, for he staunchly
devoted himself to poetic drama in a period when it was almost banished
from Broadway; he, for instance, had a long run in Brian Hooker's translation of *Cyrano de Bergerac* and in Arthur Goodrich's fine dramatization
of Browning's *Ring and the Book*, *Caponsacchi*. Among the many Shakespearean roles he performed were Romeo, Hamlet, Othello, Macbeth, Shylock, Caliban, and Oberon. I believe that I saw every one of his personations
at the old Colonial Theater, renamed the Hampden Theater, where from
1925 to 1930 he revived all the plays in his repertory with the addition of
others (*Henry V* and the poetic favorite *Richelieu*). In 1925 Broadway was
showing Shaw, *Craig's Wife* and other "problem plays," *The Green Hat*, and
The Wild Duck; in 1926 *The Shanghai Gesture*, *Chicago*, more Shaw and Ibsen;
in 1927 *Burlesque*, *The Trial of Mary Dugan*, *Dracula*; in 1928 *Strange Interlude*,
Diamond Lil, *Marco Millions*; in 1929 *Street Scene*. *Strictly Dishonorable*, *Journey's
End*; and in 1930 *The Green Pastures*, *Grand Hotel*, *Elizabeth the Queen*—to
mention only some great hits and omit the always-thriving musical-comedy
stage—and through all this gallimaufry of the realistic, the prosy serious, the
light comic, the melodramatic and the pseudopoetic, Hampden valiantly
and staunchly held up the banner of poetic drama to large audiences that
were grateful for what he was doing. *Cyrano*, admittedly, is not comparable
to Shakespeare's romantic plays, neither was *Caponsacchi* or *Richelieu*, but all
three are first-rate theater, exciting, gripping, and full of brilliant poetic
moments, in comparison with which, with the exception of the Ibsen plays,
the "hits" of five seasons were tepid theater. Howard Taubman called
Hampden's undertaking "a gallant reversion to the glamor and magnetism
of the great star who served as his own manager." And Hampden was indeed
one of those who luckily radiated magnetism. Mr. Taubman and I had a
similar experience: "As a young New Yorker I was swept up by the panache,
swordplay and romance . . . even as I suspected that his supporting troupe
could not match the sonorous grandiloquence of his style. Do you think I

cared? The play was very much the thing." There were, of course, now and then a few Shakespearean revivals during those five years, but nothing equal to Hampden's sustained loyalty to Shakespeare, and I will go so far as to say that, with very few exceptions, his extensive Shakespearean repertory was the last I have seen which, without any of the oppressive air of conscientiousness of the Sothern-Marlowe productions, captured the spirit, the tone and the magnificence of what Shakespeare wrote, and never stooped to the vulgarity of novelty for its own sake. I, on my part, suspect that Hampden was probably a great actor who was carrying on his battle single-handedly, though his following was large enough to ensure enthusiastic audiences throughout his career; but he had no competitor in America against whom his accomplishment could be measured, and so he has remained—comparatively—unsung. (I say "comparatively" if only because the fine theatrical library at The Players Club in New York has been named after him). Unlike Sothern and Marlowe his sets were not cumbersome; simple and efficient, they made for speed and cumulating drama. The set which Claude Bragdon designed for his *Hamlet* (1925) was not only impressive, but served, with the simplest alterations, for the entire play.

Henry Hinchcliffe Ainley (1879–1945) was born in Leeds and became a clerk at Sheffield, where he took part in amateur theatricals. When George Alexander, actor-manager, was on tour in 1899, the twenty-year-old Ainley was granted the part of an extra. Thereafter he joined Benson's company, and first played in London in 1900 at the Lyceum in *Henry V* in the role of Gloucester. He was doing Lorenzo in *The Merchant of Venice* for the Bensons when Alexander saw him and selected him for the male lead in *Paolo and Francesca*, the most important play of the poetically anemic Stephen Phillips, then considered a first-rate poetic dramatist. The youthful Ainley was so perfect for the romantic part that he became a celebrity with the first performance. In 1903 he came to the United States to be Maude Adams's leading man in several plays (including Maude Adams's greatest success, *The Little Minister*). In 1905 he was in Paris at the Opéra Comique doing the balcony scene from *Romeo and Juliet*. The next year he was in London again in the role of Orlando in Asche's overlavish production; the same year he was an excellent Cassio in Waller's *Othello*. In 1910 he was with Tree in six plays of Shakespeare. But his greatest success began with his Malvolio in a Granville Barker production. After serving in World War I, he appeared in several non-Shakespearean plays, and in 1920 was Antony in *Julius Caesar;* in 1926 he played opposite Sybil Thorndike in *Macbeth;* and in 1930 he did Hamlet. The youthful charm of his early years gave way to a more masterful style, and he was accounted one of the finest actors of his day, the sole objection to his interpretations being, generally, that they did not always harmonize with that of other members of his casts. His Macbeth wore an auburn wig which Agate, always an independent critic of the theater, declared made him look like a Wagnerian tenor. Agate's final judgment on him was that Nature had endowed "this near-great actor" with an excess and an insufficiency: an excess of physical attractiveness and a voice like a "cathedral organ"; an insufficiency in that, having equipped him with the physique and voice for great tragedy, she had given him the instincts of a comedian. Agate thought him "almost the worst" Hamlet he had ever seen, and "quite the worst" Macbeth. Only in the lower reaches of his art, he concluded, was Ainley a great actor—that is, in comic or melodramatic roles in non-Shakespearean plays—and at such times he could be droll, majestic, warmly human, and he always looked magnificent "whether in rags, golden mail, or ultimate white."

John Barrymore (1882–1942) and his elder brother Lionel (1878–1954) and sister Ethel (1879–1959) could trace their antecedents in the theater as far back as the Elizabethans through their maternal grandmother, Mrs. John Drew. Their father, Maurice (1847–1905), an Englishman, was an actor too; he had been born Herbert Blythe but had taken the name of Maurice Barrymore for his profession from an old playbill which he had read at the Haymarket Theatre; he married Georgiana Drew (1856–1893), an actress, Mrs. Drew's daughter; his death was brought about by mental illness, due somewhat to a devotion to the bottle—an obsession passed on to two of his children. Mrs. Drew had had four or five husbands, and multiple marriages became something of a family tendency; John, who maintained the record both for alcoholism and marriages in his generation of Barrymores, was married and divorced four times. He and Lionel both had talent as painters, and hoped to make that their careers; it was only reluctantly that both turned to the theater. Once Lionel and Ethel had decided upon acting, they never gave it up, though Lionel after a while lost interest in the theater, became an early star for Griffith and remained in the movies—and later television —for the rest of his life. He was on Broadway from 1900 to 1902; in 1917 with John in *Peter Ibbetson;* in 1919 with John again, in *The Jest,* a play laid in the Renaissance, in which they both made such a stir that it was suggested that they ought to do Othello and Iago together—they never did; in 1918, 1921 to 1924, after which he preferred the screen. Ethel began on the stage in 1896, became a star at twenty-one in 1901, and in 1903 to 1905 (the last year with John), 1907, 1910 to 1919 (in 1912 with John again), 1921 (with John) to 1924, 1926, 1928, 1930/31, 1934, 1937/38, 1940, and 1944, was every one of those years on Broadway, sometimes in two different plays, even while she was touring in between and making movies—an astonishing record. She was very beautiful with an exciting, husky voice which, in a highly personal monotone, she used with rich dramatic effect. Shakespeare was not her forte for she was not at home in poetic drama, and her Ophelia, Juliet, and Portia were undistinguished. She was at her best in contemporary plays.

The genius of the three was unquestionably John. The producer, Arthur Hopkins, under whom he did his most important work on Broadway, summed him up as that rarest of creatures, the actor who hated to act. He loved to create, but once that had been accomplished, "he was like . . . a writer who was nauseated by a glimpse of some past creation." His brother, on another occasion said similarly, "Once having accomplished something, from a play to a woman, he found it tedious and wanted to start a new quest." All three were well known to nurse crotchets and bad tempers, apparently inherited from their grandmother, Mrs. Drew, and these were satirized in a play by George S. Kaufman and Edna Ferber, *The Royal Family* (1927), at which the audiences were delighted by the extravagant fits of temperament exhibited by the character representing John; but his excesses in that play were nothing to what the real John indulged in with increasing self-destruction as the years went on. He too was frequently seen on Broadway: from 1903 to 1905, 1907, 1909, 1912 to 1922, when, at the height of power and fame, he gave up the stage only to return to it in 1944 to make a public spectacle of himself by the most degrading behavior. He too made a number of films, though not as many as Lionel or Ethel. All three were in their time leading actors in the United States, and their very name—until John made his a mockery—lent an aura of magic to their appearances. John was extraordinarily handsome—and he knew it, for that beautiful Barrymore profile was in evidence on every possible occasion—and had an equally beautiful voice, resonant and melodious, but with a certain furry quality. He wisely trained under Mrs. Margaret Carrington, an ex-singer and authority on voice production, whose theory was, said Barrymore, that the voice could be so freed that one could hear the speaker's "inner essence, the self, the soul, speaking through him." In any case, his voice became through her instruction the most beautiful, lucid, and melodious of any male on the American stage—when he was sober. His earlier roles in light comedy, which charmed the public, gave no indication of his reserve of dramatic power until in 1916, at the age of thirty-four, he appeared in Galsworthy's *Justice.* He was already disgusted with the theater, for he had declared that the audience in a playhouse was a "great hulking monster with four thousand eyes and forty thousand teeth," which "with one great mind makes or breaks men like me." His incapacity for self-discipline was indicated ten years before *Justice* by his uncle, John Drew. When fire and earthquake ruined San Francisco in 1906, John was there in a Frohman company; John Drew heard that his nephew was safe and was helping an army squad clear the ruins, and he said: "It took an act of God to get Jack out of bed, and the United States Army to put him to work."

Two years before *Justice,* his first marriage to a girl from New York society went on the rocks, and he was playing in the popular melodrama *The Yellow Ticket* with the brilliant actress Florence Reed (the best Lady Macbeth I ever saw). He had been difficult from its opening, and when one night he entered upon the stage completely intoxicated, she had had enough and ordered the curtain to be lowered. His understudy took his part, and the play began again.

The great success of *Justice* resulted in a long tour. *Peter Ibbetson* was next, with the main part especially rewritten for him; he did not wish to play so romantic a role, was tired of the public's thinking of him as a "pretty boy," and objected to his costume as making him look like "a marshmallow in a blond wig." The play was a great success, and the critics raved about both brothers, John as the hero and Lionel as the villain. During the entire run of the play and its subsequent tour John avoided drink, but he did nothing to suppress his violent rages when someone coughed in the audience or unforeseen accidents occurred backstage. He could not wait to have done with this role.

He now made an agreement, unwritten, with Arthur Hopkins to perform a series of plays. Hopkins took the Plymouth Theater for three years, and employed Robert Edmond Jones for the scenery, which in every case was superb. Hopkins later revealed that Barrymore had never mentioned financial profits. Although the first of these plays, Tolstoi's *Redemption,* was a great success, at the very height of its run, it was closed because he and Barrymore had the formation of a great repertory in mind. The next play, *The Jest,* laid in Florence at the time of Lorenzo the Magnificent, was an immense hit for both John and Lionel.

John twice performed the lead in Shakespeare, and his next venture in forming the Barrymore-Hopkins-Jones repertory was to do *Richard III.* Realizing that he lacked experience in delivering the broad sweep of Shakespeare's verse, he began to study with Mrs. Carrington. He gave the play as a melodrama, which, of course, is what it is. His Richard was cruel, sardonic, demonic, very winning and very repellent—a truly great performance. His splendid resonant voice steadily improved in quality and command. Barrymore broke with tradition by not emphasizing the physical malformation of the hero. He did this chiefly by use of rapid "spidery" movements. He explained: "I merely turned my right foot inward, pointing it toward the instep of my left foot . . . I did not try to walk badly. I walked as *well* as I could," on the reasonable grounds that a crippled man would do just that. His speech was quiet and mordant, with none of the oratorical effects which have almost always accompanied the rendition of this play. [What he did emphasize was that Richard's spirit was cankered while his mind was quick and intelligent.] Barrymore later confessed that it was the first time he had ever really penetrated the character he was portraying: "In my dreams I *knew* that I was he," and he always thought that this was the peak of his performances. Unfortunately, four weeks after the opening he suffered a nervous breakdown, what Hopkins called "a brief, dazzling sojourn in the high heaven of emotion," and was forced to close. His illness was probably due to a combination of causes: his growing dread of losing his mind as had his father, Maurice; his overidentification of himself with Richard—the sardonic was as much part of his nature as of Richard's; and his mad courtship of Mrs. Blanche Oelrichs Thomas, who wrote under the name of Michael Strange, and who was soon to be his second wife.

His first marriage had been tempestuous; but it was a sea of calm compared to his second, which was responsible for his engaging himself and his sister ill-advisedly to perform in Michael Strange's pseudopoetical, rather silly play, with the pretentious title of *Clair de Lune.* Hopkins had wisely refused to produce it. When staged it was justifiably damned by all critics, and its life was brief.

In 1922 he arranged with Hopkins to do *Hamlet,* the highest point of his career, and as far as the legitimate theater was concerned, about the end of it. I was only a high school student at the time, and did not know a particle of what a lifetime of studying and teaching about the theater has taught me. I therefore was in no position to realize that a number of details in Barrymore's interpretation were, in my later view, dead wrong—but less so than all the other Hamlets I have since seen, and I have seen every one that came to Broadway and a number in London. And the fact remains that Barrymore's Hamlet was so convincing, so clear, so overwhelming in its clarity that I can still pronounce it, granting him his incorrect premises, the greatest Hamlet, along with Gielgud's, which I have seen in my life. I have not forgotten the pictures, the drama, the expressions, the business of any scene as it was enacted by Barrymore, Tyrone Power, Sr. (Claudius), Blanche Yurka (Gertrude), and Rosalind Fuller (Ophelia)—a remarkable cast, which projected a kind of unity rare in Shakespearean productions. Though communicating powerfully with the audience, Power and Miss Yurka made one serious error which led me to misunderstand Shakespeare's intentions for years: by exchanging guilty looks they managed to convey, incorrectly, the idea that Gertrude had been an accomplice in the murder of her first husband. An actress of Miss Yurka's power can do that sort of thing without uttering a word in substantiation. Two decades later, when I got to know her quite well, I chided her gently for having, by the power of her acting, put me on the wrong track; Shakespeare is very clear on the queen's ignorance of the fact that Hamlet's father died by an act of murder. "It took me a long time to correct the impression you stamped on my mind that Gertrude was as guilty of murder as Claudius," I told her. "Oh, did I do that?" she replied innocently. "Actually what I was thinking about was how unfair it was that I had to be a mother when the Ophelia was older than I! I really don't remember *what* I was trying to do. You see, I have always been guided by what David Belasco said to me at the beginning of my career: 'It doesn't matter what you do on stage, my dear, as long as you do it *authoritatively.'* "

Barrymore's Hamlet was wonderful in many places; the interpretation of his sudden outburst of fury against Ophelia was perfectly motivated, as was the exchange of weapons in the duel with Laertes—those were absolutely right.* But he was wrong, as I later realized, in adopting the conventional notion that Hamlet pretends to be insane—as I believe he never does for a moment in the play *Shakespeare* wrote, no matter what other Hamlets or Hamblets do with that issue; and he was most wrong in the scene before swearing Horatio and Marcellus to secrecy and also in putting a division between himself and Rosencrantz and Guildenstern.† When I say that his Hamlet was intelligent and convincing, I do not mean it was right; it was intelligent and convincing from his point of view. And I can say as much for

*I have discussed this in *The Heart of Hamlet,* pp. 220–1, 243–4.
† *The Heart of Hamlet,* p. 73.

only one other Hamlet, John Gielgud's, which was as magnificent in its own way, and as full of error. For the rest, Barrymore *looked* as though he were Hamlet, he looked thirty (which is Hamlet's age), he was sensitive, natural, lucid—you heard every syllable distinctly—he was, of course, a delight to look at, he used that marvelous voice as a dramatic vehicle without any recourse to the oratorical or operatic style. There was none of this Oedipus-complex nonsense invented by Freud; you knew that he loved his father as a son should love a father. The *Tribune* said (with point) that it was a totally "untheatrical" impersonation, and a splendidly "musical rendering" of Shakespeare. With the latter praise I must take mild exception; Barrymore was thrilling every minute, but unlike Gielgud his lines might have been written in a kind of sublime prose.

His Hamlet stopped its run, at his wish, when it had reached 101 performances, one more than Booth's record. In 1923 he went on a brief tour with it, and in 1925 he performed it in London, Constance Collier as Gertrude and Fay Compton as Ophelia. Agate reports that he is said to have knocked down Miss Compton during a performance, for looking "so bloody pure." Agate was delighted with the interpretation and said it was nearer to Shakespeare's creation than any he had seen; quite justly he called the play scene "a miracle of virtuosity," and he had only admiration for Barrymore's handsomeness, intellectual brow, pure diction, perfect enunciation, and touching nobility.

It is to Barrymore's credit that he relished relating the following incident. Most people deny that animals can think, an opinion that experience compels me to disagree with. To confute that unenlightened view I call upon a certain London cat, whose name unfortunately has not come down to us, a cat of literary genius, who was reconnoitering off stage during Barrymore's run of *Hamlet.* It is too bad to have to report that one of Barrymore's lesser errors was to come on stage for the "To be or not to be" soliloquy and take a stance, down-stage center, in the traditional pose, arm supporting fingers at temple, like a professional philosopher abroad without his nurse. Now, as he entered one night this same cat entered too, at a respectful distance, tail upright. Barrymore was unaware; the audience tried not to titter. As Hamlet began to plunge into meditation, the cat scrutinized him with wonder. A very handsome prince—where had the stage beheld a finer profile? A beautiful, expressive voice. But what was the meaning of the figure he was cutting? This was neither the accent of Christians, nor the stand of Christians, pagans, or men, it imitated humanity so abominably. Our intellectual cat had to decipher the puzzle. Quietly it walked to a spot in front of Hamlet, turned its back upon the audience, curled its tail about it, and gazed up in total amazement. It is not recorded whether the cat gave any voice to its critical opinion, but its posture and position were eloquent enough. The audience could no longer restrain its laughter. In the middle of the soliloquy, Barrymore looked down, and then indeed raised his celebrated eyebrow. With great tact, and a great deal more naturalness than he had been employing in the soliloquy, he gently raised the critic, petted it, and quietly conducted it to the wings.

There were two attempts to have him do his *Hamlet* in films, years later, but by then his memory was so undependable that in all his films he had to read the lines from a blackboard, and nothing came of his filming the prince.

And now began that distressing period of his life when his need of self-destruction began to increase in geometric progression. It was as though he took pleasure in being an outstanding example of deliberate devastation of vast abilities through almost endless resources of dissoluteness. The public was forever being treated to the stories of his drunkenness, his involvement with young women, his being in the charge of a nurse to superintend his drinking, his fits of fury. Though he gave some remarkable performances on the screen, that beautiful voice became more and more tainted with whiskey. He aged prematurely, and one would have thought it was time for him to give up when he participated in a movie of *Romeo and Juliet* as Mercutio; all the old charm had become ossified into hideous angular movements and spurts of speech, so that he seemed to me like some resuscitated corpse that had been dug up for the occasion and was being manipulated by strings. But the full measure of the mayhem he had visited upon his genius was reserved for his last Broadway appearance, when he returned to be with his daughter, Diana, in her debut on the stage in 1940, in a stupid play that openly made capital of his vices, *My Dear Children.* He was so drunk during many of the performances that he would abandon his lines and turn to hurl insulting obscenities at the audience. This dreadful exhibition had a *succès de scandale* for four months. The people who came to see it were those who anticipated an exposition of self-degradation, and to laugh at him. It was a terrible conclusion for a brilliant career which should have begun with his Hamlet, instead of ending with it. Yet, as Arthur Hopkins said, when Barrymore gave up the stage "his renunciation was with full knowledge of what he was leaving."

Komisarjevsky's *Merchant of Venice* (1933) opened with some caperings of masquers à la *commedia dell'arte*, and terminated with a yawning Launcelot. The stage itself was forced into every kind of tomfoolery: the Rialto slid one way, the St. Mark's Lion another; Belmont rose unsteadily from the depths. Arragon was burlesqued and Morocco came right out of a minstrel show; in the trial scene Portia wore the spectacles of a bicyclist; the large ruff about Antonio's face made his head look as though it had been brought in on a platter for Salomé's delectation. It was no help that the Shylock was a traditional one; he simply did not belong among these zanies. Komisarjevsky added effects that crippled the verse. Harcourt Williams said that the whole thing was like an infant's experimenting with a new toy "in the shape of a hydraulic lift." Launcelot Gobbo approached being the central character of the play.

Macbeth (1933) exhibited scrolled aluminum screens, curling stairs, howitzers, and rifles, machine guns which went rat-tat-tat-tat, German steel helmets; Macbeth's visit to the Three Witches was converted into an endless nightmare during which he dreamt it, while speaking most of the dialogue himself; the witches themselves, talking with a Scottish burr, were simply fortune-telling ghouls who stole from the dead; Banquo's ghost was merely Macbeth's own shadow. There was some terror but no poetry in this, Shakespeare's greatest poem. Crosse has said that it was the "least enjoyable" performance of Shakespeare he had ever seen.

Though he had gifted people in his cast, such as Donald Wolfit (Antony), Leon Quartermaine, and Ion Swinley, their abilities were simply crippled by Komisarjevsky's direction. Another terrible error was choosing a gifted comedienne (who had recently triumphed in *Tovarich*) to play Cleopatra. Agate's opinion of that performance we have already recorded. But Charles Morgan of *The Times* published a phonetic transcription of a passage which has become part of stage history :

> *"O weederdee degarlano devar*
> *Desolderspo lees falln: yong boisenguls*
> *Alefelnow wimen*

Whoever reading that once in perpetual *tremolo* can interpret it as

> *O wither'd is the garland of the war,*
> *The soldier's pole is fall'n; young boys and girls*
> *Are level now with men*

may attend the performance in peace." But it would be unfair to blame the actress for the tragedy's failure. Komisarjevsky transposed scenes (opened, for instance, ineffectively with Iras, Charmian, and the Soothsayer), had the Soothsayer wandering in and out of the play, uttering lines not allotted to him; Octavius in Shakespeare's version speaking to Antony *in absentia* ("Leave thy lascivious wassails!" etc.) delivered the lines to Antony in person. The cuts in text left it like a bloody battlefield (from which the magnificent poetry had vanished. Said the *Daily Telegraph:* this play would survive any monkeying about with costumes and settings, "but touch the poetry and you are sunk." The production sank.). Crosse makes the point that Komisarjevsky's alteration of the text, rearrangement of the dialogue and transposition of scenes were clearly not made to save scene shifting; one could only conclude that he thought his version better than Shakespeare's.

At Stratford he produced *The Merry Wives* in 1935 and *King Lear* in 1936. His *Lear* was equipped with a staircase "mountaineering on an arrangement of variously-leveled narrow steps"; once more the scenery obscured the actors, despite their excellence. In his *Comedy of Errors* (1938/39) the audience was treated to his notion of the diverting: the men wore plumed pink bowler hats, the women farthingales and modern handbags. In *The Taming of the Shrew* (1939) the prologue was spoken to the accompaniment of Mozart's *Eine Kleine Nachtmusik*—with what appropriateness, let the reader judge; presently on a stage all carnation, blue, lemon, and apple green, the costumes were a combination of *commedia dell'arte* and the Restoration (periwigs included), and a great deal of noise was intended to add to the general merriment.

In 1950 Komisarjevsky directed an open-air *Cymbeline* at Montreal, Canada. Said one critic: in the scene in which outside her bedroom Cloten serenades Imogen, "an element of deliberate clowning was introduced." Nothing in the text justified this tampering, especially "the introduction of the lines, 'We're off to see the wizard, the wonderful Wizard of Oz' as an exit."

Sybil Thorndike (b. 1882), English, early nurtured an ambition to be a pianist, but gave up the idea when she found it impossible to control her nerves. This will seem odd in a woman who as an actress has shown remarkable self-possession, though, like many performers, she admits to stage-fright. She began touring with Ben Greet's company in Great Britain and the United States, and was at first annoyed at being given small parts when she felt she was capable of big ones. As she grew older she became less cocksure. Her training as a pianist proved invaluable, for it taught her the necessity of mastering technique in order to be able to express what one wishes. Younger people in the theater today often vex her because they do not understand how important it is to train their voices and work at the techniques of theater every day of their lives. It is most vital, she feels, to have good health, be impervious to criticism and maintain an impersonal attitude toward one's work—for freedom of expression is a product of discipline.

Her father and mother were devoted to Henry Irving and Ellen Terry, and the first Shakespeare she remembers was her father reading *Hamlet* aloud after having seen them. With Greet she acted in *Macbeth, Twelfth Night, Much Ado,* and about a dozen other plays. While in America she lost her voice, went back to England, saw a specialist who told her that her vocal cords were smothered with growths, said he could not guarantee that she could return to the stage, and ordered her to utter not a word for six weeks. At the end of that time, he examined her, opined she had the constitution of an ox, and announced that her vocal cords were cleared.

She was introduced to the Play Actors, a group that performed on Sunday nights. Bernard Shaw saw the second play she did and sent for her: he asked her to read *Candida.* Into that reading she later said she put everything: Beatrice, Everyman, Lady Macbeth. At the end Shaw rocked with laughter, told her that once she was married and had children she would be a wonderful Candida, but that in the meantime she would do as an understudy for a company that was going to tour with the play. She was next with Miss Horniman's Manchester company. While with them, she met Lewis Casson, and they were married. Casson was a leading actor of the troupe, and did some directing. He helped her with her understudying of Candida. At the outbreak of World War I he enlisted.

It was Ben Greet who engineered her coming to the Old Vic. He wrote to her in November 1914: "There's a strange woman [Lilian Baylis] running a theatre in the Waterloo Road; you'd find her exciting, Syb, because you're as mad as she is. I'm doing some shows for her . . . So come and join us." In those days the Old Vic was still lit by gas on stage; had a vast auditorium; the dressing rooms were hovels; the scenery was ancient and battered; in the grimy horseshoe there were stalls selling jellied eels, and uninviting cafés; at the main entrance there was a café which monopolized most of the area. But everywhere, among staff and cast, there was unquenchable enthusiasm.

Greet wanted Sybil Thorndike to play Lady Macbeth there. Upon reading the tragedy, she remembered Mrs. Siddons's early objection to it as "too awful." Miss Thorndike felt the same way; she knew that she had nothing in her that resembled Macbeth's lady, and she said to Lilian Baylis that she could not play the part because she knew nothing about all "that foulness." I suspect that Lilian Baylis was neither so mad as Benson declared, nor so illiterate as she confessed to being, for her answer to Miss Thorndike proved that she understood Lady Macbeth far better than most of the scholars. She asked Miss Thorndike whether she loved her husband; Miss Thorndike, naturally, said she did. Well, then, Miss Baylis, retorted, what was the problem? "Lady Macbeth loved *her* husband, and what she did was *done for him."* (This is precisely correct.) Miss Thorndike's problems were over.

Agate thought that in the role she showed great intelligence, majesty, and pathos, though her gown was too elaborate, but that she communicated neither awe nor any of the poetry—in which, of course, this play particularly excels. However, two excellent critics were of different mind. Crosse, who thought her the greatest tragic actress since Ellen Terry, pronounced her Lady Macbeth her most superb achievement; among unforgettable moments were her standing in a red dress awaiting Duncan's approach, her form crouched listening against the wall as the murder is being committed, her almost "jaunty" exit with the daggers, and her dull, flat voice in the sleepwalking scene, broken by fitful wails of misery—Crosse said that he had never beheld wretchedness so brilliantly exhibited on the stage as hers during this scene. Trewin, too, affirmed that in the role she gave "true splendour and spaciousness to the night."

Miss Thorndike said that Lilian Baylis had great insight, though she was in many ways "an ignorant woman." Miss Baylis confessed that her perceptions came from prayer, and Miss Thorndike believed it. But Lilian Baylis apparently never stayed to see a play to the end. She used to see pieces of it, then run away to cook a steak at the side of the stage, for a meal between performances. Miss Thorndike said that in the last act of *As You Like It,* you could usually smell steak and chips.

When Miss Thorndike had been at the Old Vic a year she had her second baby. The infant had hardly been born when Miss Baylis asked her to rehearse Ophelia. Miss Thorndike protested that she could not come at once; "I've only just this minute had the baby." But Miss Baylis replied that she could not possibly put off her show; Miss Thorndike went. Her salary was £3 10s. a week! She was there from 1914 to 1918, playing a great many Shakespearean heroines, as well as Hal, Puck, Launcelot Gobbo, the Fool in *King Lear,* and Ferdinand. Her taking on of male roles was not motivated by misguided ambition. Because of the scarcity of men during the war, several actresses did the same thing. Crosse admits that in advance he expected only the worst from the Fool, but he was quickly reassured; she represented the half-cracked youth perfectly, with a stumbling walk, hanging lower lip, and general neuroticism.

As Portia he declared her the finest since Ellen Terry; the quality of her silence during the three casket scenes, her fluctuating emotions made plain but yet under control, was worth a journey to witness; her trial scene was quiet too; there was no traditional scuffle at Shylock's, "A sentence: come prepare." Her authoritative, "Tarry a little," froze all action.

As Hermione in *The Winter's Tale* she radiated, in the statue scene, a spiritual and physical beauty, calm and memorable. As Rosalind her "golden voice and delicious gurgling laugh" were put to marvelous use, though she was guilty of one false touch: she fairly bawled the line, "And I for no woman" into Phebe's face, as though Rosalind had forgotten all about Orlando.

Her Beatrice was disappointing until the climactic church scene; she behaved too much like a monarch dispensing favors instead of being the irrepressibly merry girl Beatrice is; but once Beatrice's passion was given free rein, she was superb.

She made a fine Mistress Quickly, but her Volumnia was too modern, too cheerful, affectionate though proud enough, with nothing of the Roman patrician in the most authentically Roman character Shakespeare ever drew —until the scene with the Tribunes, where she suddenly summoned the requisite grandeur—in Trewin's phrase, "Rome personified." Agate agreed, though he thought she was at her best when Coriolanus comes back from the wars. He also declared that her Queen Katharine in *Henry VIII* proved that that role can be made a great one.

Miss Thorndike has performed in innumerable modern plays, including *Saint Joan,* which Shaw wrote for her, and has often been back in the Waterloo Road theater doing the classics. In 1931 she was made Dame of the British Empire.

Her brother, Arthur Russell Thorndike (b. 1895), was also with the Ben Greet players and at the Old Vic. His best Shakespearean parts were Launcelot Gobbo, Touchstone, Caliban, Pistol, and Pandarus. He too attempted tragic roles. His Richard III was vigorous, though the audience tended to laugh at the wrong places—probably owing to Irving's making Richard something of a comic character. His Hamlet had wonderful energy and romantic passion, but no beauty of voice or personal grace. With all this, Agate pronounced his prince as possessing everything which Ruggeri lacked; he was able to keep the audience excited and amused; there was fire in his heart but no tenderness.

Estelle Winwood (b. 1883), the marvelously goggle-eyed, English-born actress, has been a well-known figure on the American stage ever since her first appearance in the United States in 1916; from then on there have been few seasons on Broadway from which this delightful comedienne with the fetching lisp has been absent. The records do not show her as having ever participated in a Shakespearean play, and the records are the more to blame, for I should consider myself a traitor if I said nothing about her Katharina in *The Taming of the Shrew*, for it was easily the most delicious impersonation of the role I have ever seen. I am not able to pinpoint the date, but I can certify that it was either 1924 or 1925, for a very good reason. I was a very young married man, and my wife, née Francesca Vinciguerra (which translated means "win war"), who was about to have her first book published, was seeking a nom de plume which would be acceptable to the public. I could feel her mounting excitement, which I attributed to the brilliance of Miss Winwood's performance—partially the case, but not entirely. As soon as the curtain fell for the first intermission, she turned to me and whispered, "I've got it! Winwood, Winwar! After all Winwar is what Vinciguerra means!" And that's how her pen name was settled as Frances Winwar. And I *know* that the book was published in 1925.

Estelle Winwood was all that Katharina should be, full of spirit, dashing, challenging, proud, unbending. But what I remember most clearly was the amazing thing she did with her last scene. She delivered her final speech, "Fie, fie! unknit that threatening unkind brow" in a way I have not seen since. She powerfully conveyed the idea, through the coy submission of her words, that she was far from subdued yet, and that Petruchio was going to be managed without his even knowing it. I am not sure that this is what Shakespeare meant, but it is by no means inconsistent with the woman he drew; indeed, it makes rather more sense than her sudden conversion to abject submission to her husband.

Balliol Holloway (b. 1883) as a young man was a member of the company of Millicent Bandmann-Palmer; it was she who gave many a distant town a Hamlet who was apparently a short, stout woman approaching sixty. Before World War I he performed Theseus in Granville Barker's *A Midsummer Night's Dream*, a production which some thought a revelation, while others felt that "pitiless iron" had penetrated Barker's soul. At Stratford in 1923 he made an impressive Macduff; Ruth Ellis said of him that, after Duncan's murder, when the great doors opened, Holloway's voice "brought daylight, fresh air, and the challenge of the good earth." He made one of the best Pistols of his time. At the Old Vic (1925/26) with Edith Evans in the company, Trewin says he knew, already being one of the most experienced of Shakespearean actors, "perhaps better than anyone how to grasp an audience," and was to be accounted as a Shakespearean aristocrat who identified himself completely with the part he was playing, and could go from the Falstaff of *The Merry Wives* (declared "stupendous" by Bridges-Adams) to a terrifying Richard III to a fine Shylock.

He was at the Vic in 1926/27 in *Macbeth*. There is a strong feeling among actors about the dangers attendant on giving this play. I first learned of it in 1947 while I was driving with the English actor, John Abbott, in Hollywood, and chanced to quote something or other from *Macbeth* which seemed appropriate to the confusion of the traffic around us. Abbott slammed his foot on the brake of his car and turned to me in a rage: "Stop it! Stop it! Don't you know the danger of having anything to do with *Macbeth?*" I thought he was joking, but he presently began a long history of the catastrophes connected with productions of that tragedy. According to him, you were risking your neck if you were idiot enough to accept a part in it or quote a phrase from it.

Much as I liked John and enjoyed playing Mozart piano concertos with him, he or I playing the orchestral arrangement on his second piano (my only relief from the insanities of Hollywood), I thought his attitude toward *Macbeth* an unfortunate obsession—until I soon found out in New York that what he felt was pretty general among actors who had done Shakespeare. My researches have, incidentally, lent weight to the superstitions, and no one can blame actors who have come to dread the play. Just to cite the experience at the Old Vic: Lilian Baylis told Sybil Thorndike that she had never presented it without the occurrence of some disaster; Miss Baylis died in 1937 while a rehearsal of *Macbeth* was in progress; Miss Thorndike recalled that at the Prince's Theatre in 1926 there was a series of "dreadful things" which continually occurred and grew in such terrifying crescendo that the manager called her into his room to say, "Sybil, the Devil does work in this play—there is horror behind it—we must do something positive against it"; so they read aloud together, to draw strength, Psalm 91! Holloway, during the 1926/27 season, was rather seriously injured during the final fight in *Macbeth.*

In 1930 he was briefly actor-manager in the West End as he performed Richard III; his casting and staging showed an instinctive feeling for what Shakespeare intended; Farjeon said that Holloway seemed to act even with his fingernails. But the R 101 disaster rocked the nation, and people for a time stopped going to the theaters; Holloway played to a full house on Saturday and to an empty one on Monday.

In 1931 he was the Ghost in *Hamlet* at the Haymarket, Angelo in *Measure for Measure* at the Fortune, and Falstaff of *The Merry Wives* at the Duchess. The next year he was Cassius. In 1933 in an open-air performance in the Park, he was an "overwhelming" Wolsey, his scarlet train snaking "in and out of the bushes"; he presented the cardinal as, on one side haughty, malicious and clever, and on the other stoic and pious—for so Shakespeare has depicted him. In 1934 he returned to Stratford to do Armado, Caliban, Cassius, and other roles. In 1937 he gave a remarkable rendition of Leontes's anguish both as a jealous and a remorseful man. During World War II he acted Kent, a noble Othello, and his usual remarkable Falstaff of *The Merry Wives.*

Agate was a great admirer of this Falstaff; he said he had Falstaff's fatness in "his very bones," acting him "in full sail, trimming with condescension his course to the mean necessities of his purse." Agate thought he spoke

Antony (of *Antony and Cleopatra*) as a poet very well, looked noble, was often moving, but was insufficiently dissolute. His Richard III was alive, very real, and of superior mind; he managed to render the extremely difficult business of the wooing entirely credible. Agate thought his Othello a civilized savage who gradually dropped the mask of civilization and lapsed into the chaotic primitive; he was always the Moor, never an educated Englishman.

Dorothy Green (1886–1961), an English actress, was with the Benson company, the Old Vic, and the Memorial Theatre at Stratford. Her "proud voice and bearing" are spoken of; she made a fine Cleopatra and Lady Macbeth, an exciting Mistress Ford, and a "corrosive" Goneril, which role Agate especially admired; he said she was always magnificent in it. Her Cleopatra was not youthful, but rather a siren approaching middle age; her power of enchantment was not mere superficial beauty, but proceeded from her inner being. But her Goneril won the highest praise. Crosse saw her in the part four times and thought her wickedness superb and very feminine; the intensity of passion in her scene with Edmund, her fury when revealed for what she is in the last act, her ghoulish delight at Regan's illness, and her last exit with drawn dagger were ineradicable memories.

Edith Evans (b. 1888) has been, in all probability, the greatest English actress of her time. She had not only that rare luminosity of which we have several times spoken but the equally rare faculty of completely transforming herself into the character she was enacting, tragic or comic, royalty or nobility or peasant, from Rosalind to Mistress Page, from Queen Margaret to Cleopatra to Juliet's Nurse. As Lady Bracknell in *The Importance of Being Earnest* she was so perfect that you would have sworn that she was born to do *that* role, and you would never thereafter be satisfied with anyone else in the part; yet she was equally marvelous as a simple countrywoman. I would almost entreat the reader not to seek photographs of her in any role but that of Lady Bracknell. She was never a beautiful woman, and to see photographs of her as Rosalind or Cleopatra, because of the bald falsifications of the usual camera portraits, can give only a wrong idea of the magic this remarkable woman could create whenever she was on stage. Beginning with a career as a milliner, she always looks like one in the photos, even as Cleopatra; yet she could always weave a spell that created beauty around her person, when necessary, like a chrysalis. Zoe Caldwell, who in my opinion could be the greatest English-speaking actress of *her* generation, if she wished to, told me recently that it was absolutely astonishing to watch Edith Evans at close quarters, and her ability to subtly suggest sensuality by the very way she touched objects—a table, a dress, a glass, a box. Dame Edith Evans is the cardinal example in our century of how unimportant personal beauty is for great acting.

She was the daughter of a worker in the post office who, to keep his wife happy, which meant keeping her busy, took a house in Ebury Street, London —as it happened, next to a house where Noel Coward's parents lived. As

seas" of wit gracefully launched; she was buoyant, carefree and understanding; once she became transformed into Ganymede she was not a girl in breeches, but a mooncalf of a youth; yet when alone with Celia she was enchanting, coaxing Rosalind again. As Juliet's Nurse she was "slow as a cart-horse, cunning as a badger, earthy as a potato." Her Queen Margaret in *Richard III* was done with a great gust of passion and her diction was magnificent; Agate said of this performance that she could walk and rant as only a queen should.

In 1935 she returned to the Old Vic to do a vulgar, informal Emilia, and managed to suggest her entire life with Iago; her final fury was superb. The same year she joined Gielgud, Olivier, and Peggy Ashcroft in a *Romeo and Juliet* in which she so much enlarged upon an already marvelous Nurse to the extent that Agate, for the only time in his criticism, objected to her performance; he said that she made the Nurse the center of the play and thus knocked the tragedy out of balance. It is the sort of thing that a great actor taking a lesser role must be careful not to do. However, there may have been another reason: neither Gielgud nor Olivier had yet come into his own. Miss Evans employed a voice "caked with the earth of all the counties"; her gauche tottering for help upon finding Juliet apparently dead upon the bed was massive and never to be forgotten. Where, in that vulgar outburst of agony, one critic asked, was the elegance of Millamant and the youth of Rosalind?

Her Rosalind of 1937 was again a marvelously new revelation. In her blue coat and breeches she was like "the goddess of a Watteau forest." Alan Dent said that, though like a Meredith heroine in richness of mind, she was still Rosalind herself. Her beautiful panic on the line "Alas the day! What shall I do with my doublet and hose?" was sheer music. As the Shrew the same year to Leslie Banks's Petruchio, she raised a veritable tornado such as audiences had rarely heard before.

Her Cleopatra of 1946 to Godfrey Tearle's Antony, her incomparably great performance, was, says Crosse, the best he had ever seen. I believe him. It was the best I had seen. In 1959 her Volumnia was Rome victorious in mourning weeds. The same year her Countess of Rousillon was the perfect compassionate aristocrat that she must be; here she was lucky to have a fresh and moving Helena in Zoe Caldwell.

This account naturally omits all of Edith Evans's triumphs in non-Shakespearean and modern plays. She was created Dame of the British Empire in 1946.

Esmé Percy (1887–1957) at the age of seventeen did Romeo for William Poel's Elizabethan Stage Society with a Juliet, Dorothy Minto, who was fourteen. On December 10, 1912, he was Troilus on the historic occasion when Edith Evans played Cressida. Then he joined the Benson company and had the opportunity to play in many Shakespearean roles.

In 1930 there was no dearth of Hamlets. Percy enacted him at the Court Theatre in February, Henry Ainley at the Haymarket in April, Gielgud at the

Old Vic the same month and in May at the Queen's, and Alexander Moissi at the Globe in June. Percy was forty-two and an actor of considerable nervous energy. The production moved rapidly, and though Desmond Mac-Carthy thought that his was not a prince to whom military honors at his funeral seemed called for, he was both tender where tenderness was called for and ferocious in his movements at other times; he was always "fascinating to watch." During the bombing of London in 1940 he performed a "blazing" Hotspur.

Highly regarded in London, he toured South Africa, and joined the army in World War I, was placed in control of entertainment for the troups and produced over one hundred forty plays for them. When he returned to the stage he was notably successful in a great many Shavian roles, including Tanner, Androcles, Higgins, Dubedat, and Magnus, and was eventually made president of the Shaw Society. All his colleagues spoke of his rare intelligence and versatility. A great lover of dogs, he lost the sight of one eye through an accidental bite, which in no way abated his affection for them. After he died, some of his friends erected a drinking fountain for dogs in Kensington Gardens as a tribute to him.

Ernest Milton (b. 1890) did Hamlet at Plymouth in 1924, and proved that he possessed that rare magic which no training can provide; he was passionate, with a great surge of emotional conviction; he was above all, a Hamlet who had indeed seen the Ghost. He also made a subtle comic part of Ford in *The Merry Wives of Windsor*. The same year he did King John, Angelo, and Romeo. The next year he repeated what Trewin has called "the most romantically moving Hamlet of his generation." During the 1927/28 season he revived a role long neglected, that of King Lear, and brilliantly portrayed Lear's being "cut to the brains."

In 1932 he became actor-manager and began with an unsuccessful Othello, whom he made too intellectual. But his Shylock, which followed immediately, was proud (as he should be) and inflammable. After two months he gave up management. In 1941 he performed a finer King John at the Old Vic, pale and subtle. In 1944 his Macbeth, though not the warrior Shakespeare created, was the man of imagination incarnate, an easy prey to hallucinations; the audience, carried away, saw that dagger in the air.

Agate thought his Othello of 1932 too much like a cat and too little like a lion; and he, too, complained that Milton had made the Moor too much the thinker, nor did he develop the hero's suspicions slowly enough (a common fault with Othellos). He praised Milton's delivery of Macbeth's lines as beautiful throughout, without wailing or moaning, and for his remarkable delivery of the banquet scene.

At the Old Vic he had been delightfully youthful and charming as Hamlet, very impressive as Banquo, and a fine comedian as Autolycus and Parolles. Crosse says that he owes some of his most vivid memories to Milton.

Florence Saunders (1890–1926), a beautiful woman whose life was a losing battle against crippling arthritis, appeared at the Old Vic during

World War I—because of the lack of men she even appeared as a "distinguished" Lucio in *Measure for Measure*—and did Emilia for the Ben Greet company. During the early 1920s she was in repertory at Stratford-on-Avon. At the Old Vic she was to be seen in almost any role from Ophelia to Goneril, made a notable Katherine in *The Taming of the Shrew,* and an excellent Rosalind. In 1920 she had taken on the role of the Countess of Rousillon. At Stratford again she revived her well-loved Rosalind in 1925, less than a year before her death.

Crosse considered her swagger as Lucio a real triumph. He also praised her gifts as an authentic repertory actress. Her Ophelia was "really and miserably" mad without the jerkings and screaming of many an Ophelia; her splendid-looking Goneril dominated the scene whenever she appeared, and she projected with subtlety a savageness and libidinousness perfectly suiting the part; Paulina was one of her finest portrayals: by her torturing of Leontes she dominated the first three acts of the play; her Portia of *The Merchant of Venice* was the equal of the best of Crosse's time, and he especially admired the differences she introduced in her reactions as each of the three suitors was considering the caskets. He had seen her Rosalind several times, and, as was everything she did, it was "beautiful and distinguished." Her concluding words in the epilogue, "Bid me farewell" had a tragic quality he never forgot, for in a few months she was dead and the Memorial Theatre at Stratford had been burned to the ground.

Nothing in my researches has astonished me more or made me more indignant than that no one seems to have written a book about one of the most gifted, versatile and popular actresses of our century, Jane Cowl (1890–1950), and that the voluminous *Oxford Companion to the Theatre* (1,088 pages of double columns in small type), while taking note of countless actors of far less importance, has remained ignorant of her existence. Not only was her career of interest for the enormous variety of roles she assumed on Broadway, the frequency with which she appeared there and for her succession of triumphs, but her life—at least in the snatches which it is my unhappy privilege to know—was itself dramatic in its admixture of acclaim and tragedy.

Born in Boston, she made her first appearance on Broadway at the age of thirteen. The next year, 1904, she had a role in that melodrama which so much impressed my Uncle Émile, David Warfield's *The Music Master.* Her first important role was offered her in 1909; the next year she was in another play; and in 1912 she became a star in a melodrama which was a smash hit, *Within the Law,* which ran for 541 performances. Thereafter she took the lead in romantic plays, melodramas, tragedy and comedy. In 1915 she starred in the popular *Common Clay;* in 1917 she coauthored and starred in the highly successful *Lilac Time;* in 1918 I saw her in the first play I ever saw her or anyone else in on Broadway, *The Crowded Hour;* in 1919 she starred again in one of her own works, *Smilin' Through,* which had a long run.

At last in 1923, happily teamed with a gifted actor, Rollo Peters, she attempted Shakespeare—and enacted the greatest Juliet I have ever seen in my life; it was one of the major triumphs of her career. Perhaps because of it, that same season, with Peters again, she was Mélisande in Maeterlinck's pseudopoetic drama *Pelléas and Mélisande* (which, without Debussy's inspired music, is fairly silly stuff), and did the role so exquisitely that one forgot the hollowness of the play. The next year she and Peters gave *Antony and Cleopatra*. In 1925 she was the lead in a Noel Coward comedy; in 1927 *The Road to Rome* was one of her great successes; in 1929 she returned to the poetic drama with Stephen Phillips's anemic tragedy, *Paolo and Francesca* (which in 1902 in London had been credited with inaugurating a new epoch of poetry in the theater), but whose shortcomings were concealed by the delicacy and pathos of her rendition. In 1930 she was doing Shakespeare again, this time with Leon Quartermaine in a *Twelfth Night* that was loved for its sparkle; later that year she appeared in Benn Levi's delightful *Art and Mrs. Bottle*, with Katharine Hepburn in the supporting cast. Ninteen thirty-two found her in a new play; 1934 in S. N. Behrman's delicious and thoughtful *Rain from Heaven;* 1935 in the very popular *The First Lady;* 1938 in Thornton Wilder's *The Merchant of Yonkers* (which he later revised as *The Matchmaker,* which, in turn, was converted into the long-running musical *Hello, Dolly!*). No one who saw her brilliant comic-pathetic performance in *Old Acquaintance* of 1940 will ever forget it. In 1947 she revived *The First Mrs. Fraser.* She made comparatively few films, but when she appeared in one, somehow without her attempting to capture it, and ill as she already was with the cancer from which she soon died, she held the center of interest.

In Shakespeare only her Cleopatra was a disappointment. She looked the part, she brought much variety to the role, but that determination to keep her hands busy, of which she spoke to me, was in this one instance overdone; indeed, she made the fatal mistake of using those hands to simulate the clichés of Egyptian movements—somewhat in the style of the ballet from *Aïda;* the result was unintentionally ludicrous. But her Viola more than atoned for the error, and was a joy to behold. Besides being blessed with the most beautiful of faces, she had a voice unsurpassed in richness and color, and she never used it for coloratura effects. She had the rare secret of speaking Shakespeare's poetry, while doing it full justice, for the *meaning* of every word. She never accented the wrong one, as most Shakespearean actors do, and never elided an important one.

It was the Juliet of 1923, however, which is so memorable that I can recollect today every scene of it; and one very important scene most vividly of all for it contained something approaching a miracle of acting—a scene, moreover, which is usually botched in all productions of *Romeo and Juliet.* Shakespeare was more or less committed to the idea that his lovers fall in love at first sight. Though psychologists, marriage counselors, et al. may protest to the contrary, it is a simple fact that some people *do* fall in love in just that way, and I know of at least a dozen cases, including my own, in which a more or less permanent attachment had just such a beginning.

Now, in this tragedy Shakespeare has written no lines and left no stage directions for that all-important moment of first sight and immediate love.

Indeed, the first lines either of them speaks after that meeting at the Capulet ball, where they first see each other, are Romeo's question to the serving man:

> What lady is that which doth enrich the hand
> Of yonder knight?

In the preceding scene Romeo has told his friends that he will not dance at the festivities which they are about to crash, and prefers to enact the part of a servant: *"A torch for me . . . I'll be a candle-holder, and look on."* What almost inevitably happens, therefore, in productions of the play is that the stage is crowded with dancers and the loud strains of the musicians playing for them rise above the hubbub; Romeo observes Juliet among the dancers, plunges in among them, and returns with her to the front of the stage to begin their dialogue: *"If I profane with my unworthiest hand,"* which they must shout at the top of their lungs in order to make themselves heard. So it was, for instance, in the famous Katherine Cornell production (by the way, one of Miss Cornell's very top performances was as Juliet). This sort of thing avoids the great challenge of allowing us to witness the lovers' first meeting and falling in love.

Though the box stage of the Cowl-Peters production had fundamentally nothing in common with the Elizabethan theater, I am convinced that that scene was staged exactly as Shakespeare would have wished it. We know that at the back of the Elizabethan stage there was a recessed space, "the inner stage," and what would have been more natural and appropriate than that the guests at the ball, after having been greeted by Capulet, should drift off into that inner stage for their dancing and that the music should be so subdued as to be barely audible, not to interfere with any dialogue on the stage proper? In the Cowl-Peters production the stage proper was a kind of antechamber to a larger room (the equivalent of the Elizabethan inner stage) where, though we see no one, we are to assume the dancing and the serving of refreshments are taking place. After the masked Montague intruders were welcomed, all of them except Romeo drifted into the other room to participate in the dancing. He alone remained behind, standing on the threshold to watch them. Presently Juliet entered on Paris's arm; he whispered something to her (probably having to do with refreshments) and left her for a few moments on the stage proper. For those moments Romeo and Juliet were the only persons on the stage, while we heard the music faintly in the background. It was natural and inevitable that they should look at each other. He slowly removed his mask so that his face might be seen. At the movement, she quickly turned her head away, but not before she had caught a glimpse of him. Now she just as quickly turned back to look at him. And although they were separated by half a stage, she managed the miracle: to project with her eyes and her entire countenance, and her hands suddenly dropped to her sides, that she had fallen completely in love. It is a look I have never forgotten, and how she managed it I cannot begin to guess, but it was certainly one of the greatest moments in my entire and crowded experience in the theater.

Another miracle occurred when the photographer perfectly caught that moment for the cover of the *Theatre Arts*. He was obviously as haunted by it as I.

Blanche Yurka, one of the great performers of Ibsen and an actress with an extensive repertoire, was a great friend of hers, and in her usual generous fashion freely admitted to me that Miss Cowl had taught her most of what she knew about acting. It was in Blanche's dressing room at a theater that, as I have already recounted, I first met Miss Cowl sometime in the early 1940s. I have good cause to remember that first meeting. Some of the conversation I have already reported in my opening pages; what I did not indicate was the elaborately unfriendly way she conducted herself during our introduction and with which she colored her first few remarks. Here was a woman I had worshipped for years, and I was so shocked at her rudeness that, before I knew what I was saying, I asked her, "Miss Cowl, is your dislike directed at me personally, or at me only because I happen to be a man?" At that, she threw her head back, laughed a thrillingly rich laugh, and when she had recovered her breath, she said, "I'm sorry. No, I have nothing in the world against *you*. I guess I have it in for all men generally." When, later that evening, Blanche outlined her story, I could scarcely blame her for being on the defensive.

She had married Adolph Klauber (b. 1879), a producer-manager, who was drama critic for *The New York Times* from 1906 to 1918. During her career Miss Cowl had made a fortune, particularly from the two works of her own composition, but being either inexpert or bored with matters financial, she had gladly allowed her husband to manage them for her. She was unaware for years that he was not only squandering her earnings on his own plea- sures, which included a string of mistresses, but that he had never once bothered to pay a single one of her income taxes. I imagine it was when the authorities caught up with this failure, which had continued for an extended period of time, that she at last learned the bitter truth: her indebtedness to the government, Blanche told me, exceeded a million dollars, and he had left her not a cent to pay the debt. All Miss Cowl ever said to me about him, when I knew her better, was, "When my husband had worked himself deeply enough into a hole, he retired into insanity."

Through Blanche she gradually warmed toward me. I think the first time I succeeded in her accepting an invitation to a small party I was giving was when she understood that it was for Blanche's birthday. After that, though she would come to visit us, it was some time before she agreed to stay for dinner, even though Blanche had praised my cooking. Eventually that bit of ice was broken too.

It was customary for my friends to ask me to play the piano after dinner, and one night I shall never forget, Jane Cowl asked me to play one of my especial favorites, Schumann's *Fantasy*, opus 17. I was only too happy to oblige. When I looked up at the conclusion, I saw that she was weeping profusely, inconsolably. When she was quiet again, she thanked me with deep sincerity, apologized for her tears, and said that she had needed that good cry for a long, long time.

The last time I saw her was at the Wellington Hotel, where she was staying with her little Pomeranian. While we were there a bellboy brought in a good-sized dish of fresh-looking meat and vegetables for the dog. Blushing, she said, "He always brings much too much," and gave her pet a third of it, which was indeed quite enough for a dog of that size. After we left, Blanche explained to me: "She told me on the phone yesterday that she has at last paid up that million or more she owed the government. In order to do it, she has been depriving herself of everything, including food. Do you know why she divided the dog's food that way? Every night her dinner is her share of what the boy brings for the dog." I expressed my horror at the situation, but Blanche assured me that she thought the boy guessed the fact, and always brought the best from the kitchen. At last I understood why it had taken so long to get Jane Cowl to agree to being on my list of dinner guests. Pride, tragic pride.

And what a conclusion to the life of the greatest of Juliets!

Leslie Banks (1890–1952) first appeared in Benson's company in the provinces, toured the United States and Canada, and came to London in 1921. He was a man of distinguished appearance, with a fine voice, imagination, and quiet humor in his performances. In 1937 he was Petruchio opposite Edith Evans, and at the Haymarket (1944/45) played Claudius and Bottom, an indication of the range of his talents. *The Taming of the Shrew* was a Claude Gurney production and in contemporary fashion characteristically mangled: Petruchio and his servants dressed themselves as ghosts to frighten Edith Evans, and a "pantomime horse galumphed" across the stage. The piece, said Trewin, "romped itself to bits."

Ion Swinley (1891–1937) was Lysander in Granville Barker's *A Midsummer Night's Dream,* a production which John Palmer denied was Shakespeare's, but rather the product of Barker's excessive sanity with, in it, "pitiless iron." Young Swinley in 1913 played Troilus to Edith Evans's Cressida; in 1916 he was at Stratford for Ben Greet as Polixenes. In 1923 when he played Henry V, Agate found him very "decorative" in figure, giving a good performance up to a point but lacking in lightness of voice. That same year he made a good Troilus, emphasizing his giddiness. The next season he did Orlando for the Old Vic, and an eloquent Hamlet—though Agate protested that he did not melt one—as audiences had become accustomed by Forbes-Robertson, though he (very properly) introduced more awe and presented the prince as basically sane; moreover, his movements were dignified and graceful. In 1935 he gave a very good Mark Antony in *Julius Caesar,* but his Macbeth that year was recited rather than acted, with too many errors in the lines, and his mood alternating between the glum and the animated. Crosse, on the other hand, considered his tragic heroes and Mark Antony as better than average.

Phyllis Neilson-Terry (b. 1892) in 1912 enacted a Desdemona in Tree's company and was highly commended for avoiding a too-drooping interpretation; Laurence Irving made a cold, intellectual villain of Iago, though he did little justice to the poetry. In 1933 she was Rosalind to Jack Hawkins's Orlando; their mock-marriage was found very moving. In the same park Agate declared her Olivia to possess the colors and perfumes of a botanical garden, with something "of Queen Elizabeth thrown in." Her Katharine in *Henry VIII* was in its beauty, dignity, and strength the best performance of the play. A niece of Ellen Terry's, when she later played Lady Macbeth opposite Donald Wolfit, she adopted her aunt's emphasis on her love for Macbeth and, without relinquishing her purposefulness, she influenced him by her sensual, clinging devotion to him—which is, of course, entirely in keeping with the play Shakespeare wrote.

Sir Cedric Hardwicke (1893–1964), though associated in the public mind with modern plays, and perhaps particularly with Shaw's *Caesar and Cleopatra*, began with Benson's company and toured with it (1912/1913). A year later he was at the Old Vic, but was in World War I, and did not return to the stage until 1922 when he joined the Birmingham repertory company. At the Old Vic he was one of the best Sir Tobys Crosse had ever seen. He also played, in a modern-dress *Hamlet,* the Gravedigger in a bowler hat. When Olivier did *Richard III* for the films, Hardwicke was Edward IV. And that about sums up his career as a Shakespearean actor.

Leslie Howard (1893–1943), best remembered for his elegant, refined style in modern plays, was Romeo to Norma Shearer's Juliet in a film made during the 1930s. It was a production done in the very worst Hollywood tradition of excess. When Romeo first saw Juliet at the Capulet ball, the dance turned out to be a ballet in which Juliet was *première danseuse,* and the hall in which this unexpected exhibition took place was something of a replica of the Roman baths at Bath (without the water, of course). Romeo kept dashing around the place from column to column to catch a closer look at her, according to the positioning of the dancers and to flirt with her—in a refined way, naturally, before they had a chance to speak. The garden in the balcony scene would have made the one at the Villa d'Este puny in comparison, and the stars as though directed by Stokowski in the heavens obligingly twinkled in perfect time to the love passage in Tchaikovsky's lovely overture. Howard was fairly good in the role. As for Miss Shearer, she was advertised as having asked for time to study it, and then began what Agate described as one of the most "rigorous novitiates" since the time of Loyola; she withdrew herself into fifteenth-century Italy, but ended by playing it to the best of her ability as Ellen Terry had performed it. Of course, Howard made Romeo, as was his wont in all parts, very much the Englishman, but, on the other hand, what would be more astonishing than to have a very Italian Romeo? Certainly Shakespeare did not make him so.

Agate has left a perfect summation of Howard's manner. It seems that

Howard was considering doing a movie of *Hamlet* and thought of beginning with the second scene so as to commence with brilliant and noisy notes, instead of the quiet of the sentries' dialogue. He was going to alternate making this film with another by James Hilton about a shy little Presbyterian minister. But then, said Agate, all the men Howard played were shy little Presbyterian ministers, and he performed them perfectly, "always the English gentleman, the slow-of-answer sort"; one felt that his favorite readings were the whimsies of A. A. Milne. He was not only English in manner, but in appearance as well as speech, "pipe, slacks, and golf-jacket." (The fact is that he was of Hungarian extraction!) Everyone remembers his Professor Higgins (as well as Wendy Hiller's Eliza) as absolutely the ideal. (But Shaw insisted that he was entirely wrong and would have preferred Charles Laughton; according to the dramatist, it was Howard's fault for making a love story out of *Pygmalion*, and Shaw insisted that Higgins was not supposed to marry Eliza.)

It was Howard's misfortune to try an extremely short-lived Hamlet on Broadway during the same season as Gielgud. Hamlet, alas, is not a very English prince, nor as shy and sensitive as Howard was bound to make him. A friend of mine who saw him during the few days the production ran said, rather cruelly, that Howard throughout behaved like a man looking down through gratings in the streets to see if he could find the end of a cigarette.

Wilfred Lawson (1894–1961), remembered by all who saw him in the film version of *Pygmalion* as a superb Doolittle, had his fling with Shakespeare in 1934 at the Old Vic as Antony to Mary Newcombe's Cleopatra. Agate was almost kind when he said of him that he neither looked nor spoke the part, but seemed more like "a leading member of Peter Quince's troupe." He was already established as an idiosyncratic character actor, and it was a strange role for him to undertake. He wore a gold band to keep his hair in place, but it kept slipping over one eye, and his speech was so muffled and came out in such spurts that he was not understood even in the fifth row.

Fay Compton (b. 1894) acted in plays by Barrie (*Mary Rose* was especially written for her) and was a success in many contemporary plays. For the British Council she toured Europe in Shaw and Shakespeare. She played a heart-breaking Ophelia to John Barrymore's Hamlet, when he brought the play to London (1929) and again with Gielgud (1939). In Regent's Park she was seen in a number of Shakespearean roles in the open-air theater. Later she appeared in Gielgud's *King Lear* as Regan.

David Hay Petrie (1895–1948) was, in Agate's opinion, the finest Shakespearean low-comedian he had ever seen; he compared him to Bernhardt and Irving for possessing a flame within himself such as had illuminated those two famous tragic actors. This praise was forthcoming for his Thersites, a role which is rarely performed well; Agate said that "lurking in the shade," he dominated the whole of *Troilus and Cressida* (1923). Trewin, on the other hand, describes him as "a young Scot who had the easy directness of the Elizabethan clown."

In 1924 in a great cast which included Martita Hunt and Gielgud, he gave an outstanding performance as Puck, his first triumph in the West End after his triumphs at the Old Vic, where his Costard in *Love's Labour's Lost* was the great performance of the evening; as Costard he breathed the very spirit of the Elizabethan fools and yet contrived to make it all seem modern. Crosse declared that Petrie was one of the two best Shakespearean clowns of his theatrical experience. Just remembering his Costard could cause Crosse to laugh. In roles such as that of Launcelot Gobbo it was necessary to keep your eye on him all the time he was on stage, for unexpectedly he would come out with some piece of drollery, and even when he stood still his silly facial expression was enough to tickle one.

With unexpected courage Atkins cast Petrie as Shylock (1924). He did not, said Agate, try to make another Lear out of the character; he did not uproot stout trees, "leaving them lying around." His grief for Jessica was subordinated to the affront to his house—and even that came second. He restored, Agate declared, the balance of the play. He did not, Crosse added, revert to the comic pre-Macklin Jew, nor was he grotesque, nor did he attempt the "Major Prophet style." He made Shylock just a shabby little Hebrew, and by word, gesture, and look made that insignificant figure tragic. Best of all, he made no attempt to make Shylock the central figure of the play—which few actors avoid.

In 1929 in Asche's modern-dress version of *The Merry Wives*, Petrie scored a triumph as Evans, whom he portrayed as a little, shabby, and shaggy Welsh parson, "endearing" in his "speckled straw hat," and arriving on a bicycle with a wireless set. In 1934 he made a marvelous Fluellen, never too jerky, as most actors are in the part, but full of "choleric joviality" which was both hilarious and natural. Even the way he sprang to attention when Henry addressed him was touched with comic genius.

Gwen Ffrangcon-Davies (b.1896), who had been in Birmingham doing Shaw, in 1924 played Juliet to an inexperienced boy of twenty, John Gielgud; in six weeks she had three Romeos: Gielgud (who became ill), and Ernest Milton, Ion Swinley, and then Gielgud again. She did well, and looked most fetching with a wreath on her reddish-golden hair and in her high-waisted dresses à la Botticelli. In 1938, whereas Donald Wolfit had spoken the choruses to *Henry V* with great elegance and power, though with his arms kept too tightly against his sides, she delivered them with great energy at Drury Lane, though it was felt her expressive gestures went too far when to illustrate the word *hourglass* she outlined one in the air. After a South African tour she returned to England in 1942 to play Lady Macbeth opposite Gielgud; she was very effective in dominating her husband in the first half of the play, and in being dominated by him for the rest of the tragedy. She managed also to convey an interesting idea; that of narrowly keeping watch over Banquo after Duncan's murder. She played in a number of important non-Shakespearean plays with Gielgud, and during his 1950 season at Stratford she was engaged to play Regan to his Lear, by common consent, one of his greatest roles.

John Laurie (b.1897) was graduated from minor to major roles when he performed Hamlet at the Old Vic in the 1920s, envisioning the prince as sharp, not sweet; his nunnery scene was particularly convincing. He made an even better Macbeth, barbaric and weak, conceived with intelligence and a fine balance between the two extremes of his nature. In 1930 he played Claudius to Esmé Percy's Hamlet at the Court Theatre. At Stratford he was Orlando opposite his wife, Florence Saunders, and in 1935 an inflammable Douglas in *Henry IV, Part II.* Just before World War II began in earnest, he played a demonic Richard III at Stratford; he was very loud and fierce, as Benson had been in the part, and, like Benson, he threw away his prayer book with a shout at the end of III, vii; but his scenes of wooing Elizabeth and Anne were well done; his chief fault was in being too quick to feel the strings of conscience, and in actually shrinking from his mother's curse. (Irving and other actors had done much better with that scene by accepting the curse with ironic humor.)

Cecil Trouncer (1898–1953), celebrated as a "character actor," first appeared in London in 1921. He was at the Old Vic for several years, where he was often praised for creating an interesting persona of minor characters. For instance, in *Much Ado,* Leonato is almost always a nonentity; Trouncer made him into a real human being. In a 1937 *Hamlet* at the West End, a production based upon Professor J. Dover Wilson's odd theories, his Polonius was a figure of "spreading pomp"; Trouncer had a rich and warm voice, and Trewin said that as Polonius he "chiselled the phrases, shaping them into carved leaf and flower." This must have been charming to the ear, but it is scarcely in keeping with the old muddlehead whom Shakespeare drew. In Gielgud's 1945 revival of the play, Trouncer was the First Player, doing a first-rate job of swelling the inflated lines it is his duty to speak about the Hecuba business.

Morris Carnovsky (b.1898) was born in St. Louis, Missouri, and first appeared in New York at the Provincetown Theater in 1922. Soon he had joined the Theatre Guild, for whom he appeared in plays by Shaw, O'Neill, Anderson, Chekhov and an adaptation of *The Brothers Karamazov.* In 1931 he joined the Group Theatre, doing plays by Odets and other contemporaries; the Group Theatre was, of course, the fountainhead of The Method in this country. It was not until 1957 that Mr. Carnovsky began performing for the American Shakespeare Festival at Stratford, Connecticut. Since then he has appeared in *Measure for Measure, The Tempest, The Taming of the Shrew, Hamlet, A Midsummer Night's Dream, The Merchant of Venice,* and *King Lear.* Mr. Carnovsky is an extremely handsome man with an imposing figure and a beautiful resonant voice. His only shortcoming is that while he enunciates every word with clarity and intelligence, there is a Yiddish lilt when he speaks, even as an ancient Trojan, a lilt which is quite appropriate to his Shylock, but is otherwise disturbing. I hasten to add that I do not doubt that he picked up that lilt as a result of his association with the Group Theatre, for I note that many a product of The Method, whether the actor be Irish, Italian, Southern, or New England American, has a far more omnipresent Yiddish inflection than Mr. Carnovsky.

Mr. Carnovsky has always proudly espoused The Method, and he is a good example of how unimportant *theory* is in the arts when compared with practice. He is so excellent an actor, his performances are so thoughtful and fundamentally in the *right* tradition, that even though he tells himself that in his acting he is expressing himself, what he actually does is identify himself with the character he is portraying—and that is as it should be. It disturbs me not at all that Mr. Carnovsky *thinks* he is doing something far different and inferior to the excellence he always exhibits on the stage. He looks upon the Group Theatre as the one permanent company of his career. He quite accurately states that the American Shakespeare Festival in Connecticut "is not yet a company . . . It changes too much; it has no fundamental artistic policy." Every syllable of that accurate judgment continues to be borne out as the years roll by. Indeed, rarely has the Connecticut company been blessed with a cast that included even one actor of Mr. Carnovsky's stature.

One of his most astonishing admissions is that though the Group Theatre's choice of plays was conditioned by the bread lines and the poverty of the depression years (they never, he asserts, would have accepted a play like *Dinner at Eight*—one assumes that for them laughter was a kind of indecency), what he himself particularly learned from that association was *consciously* to examine "the materials" of his craft, to develop consciously a technique. He has in truth done so, and he seems to have been the only one who did.

Among his particular triumphs in Shakespeare have been his Shylock, first given in 1957 and then again in the mid-1960s, and his Lear (1963). The Lear was noble and the tragic tone sustained with perfect control. As for the Shylock—granted Carnovsky's mistaken premises that Shylock is surrounded by "a group of men-about-town, wastrels, fortune hunters, gamblers, heiresses (by law and theft), businessmen," and Shylock "in the midst of it all, a desperately serious man galvanized by revenge, committing his life and fortune to the wild pursuit of retributive justice,"—granted, I say, his totally incorrect assumption, Carnovsky's second Shylock of the 1960s, was superb because of its dignity and concentration. All the more so because he was surrounded by a totally inadequate cast, and further hampered by the hideous interpretation of the director that Antonio, Bassanio, and all their friends were either totally or somewhat homosexual! Antonio was made so outright, and the play ended with his standing in misery because his friend Bassanio was now happily married. There is some danger that this may become a new tradition. In the 1972 production of the play at the

Beaumont Theater in Lincoln Center, New York, the idea was carried even further. Antonio and Bassanio were obviously lovers—not in the Elizabethan sense of "great friends"—but in the meaning attached to the phrase by Gay Liberation. In the trial scene Bassanio made such obvious love to Antonio, carressing his body to express his love, that all that seemed to be lacking—even if Antonio's life at the moment was at stake—was a bed for them to continue.

As for Carnovsky's Portia, Barbara Baxley, whose own interpretation of the role was that Portia is a brazen bitch, nothing could have been worse. It was therefore inevitable that with such a cast Shylock should have dominated the entire play—not Portia, as Shakespeare intended.

Carnovsky's Lear has been singled out by Howard Taubman as a great classic performance. "Building on years of wide experience and approaching the role from a backlog of other Shakespearean parts, he tackled Lear with the boldness of a veteran willing to risk everything on a big conception." He worked at it at Stratford, Connecticut, then further in Chicago, Los Angeles, and again at Stratford, "seeking answers to questions that had eluded him and finding new heartrending depths."

Judith Anderson (b.1898) was born and educated in Australia, and first appeared there in Sydney in 1915. In 1918 she came to the United States, where she has since pursued her distinguished career. After playing small roles in stock, she had her first New York success in 1924. Soon after that she took the city by storm with her marvelous performance in Pirandello's beautiful play, *As You Desire Me*. I shall never forget the illusion she created of great beauty and voluptuousness. It was only years later, when I came to know her a little, that I understood that they were indeed illusion, created (and created again and again by her on the stage) by that priceless incandescence of which I have said enough. She is also gifted with an extraordinarily beautiful voice of great range and variety. Everyone who saw her in Robinson Jeffers's version of Euripides' *Medea* or Jeffers's *Tower Beyond Tragedy* in which she was Clytemnestra, must count both as among the most overwhelming experiences he has had in the American theater. Howard Taubman did not exaggerate when he spoke of her Medea as burning up the stage "in the raging inferno of her performance." Rosamund Gilder said further that her Medea was "pure evil, dark, dangerous, cruel, raging, ruthless," and that from her opening passage she sustained "an almost incredible intensity," which, nevertheless, was varied in mood so consistently and her movements were so skilled, that she seemed to have penetrated "the unexplored regions of pain and despair." She had the audience in her grasp every moment that she was on stage.

Of course, Miss Anderson has been the lead in a great many plays, but her two outstanding Shakespearean performances have been as Gertrude in Gielgud's *Hamlet* in New York (1936) and as Lady Macbeth with Olivier at the Old Vic (1937), and thereafter in the United States with Maurice Evans. John Mason Brown considered her Gertrude a failure for so great an actress, but that may have been because he did not know that the whole conception of the Gielgud *Hamlet* was based upon J. Dover Wilson's *What Happens in Hamlet,* and that the (apparently now accepted as silly) notion, originating with Freud, that what was bothering the prince was an Oedipal love for his mother, was at the heart of the production. Given this interpretation, which is idiotically at variance with the lines Shakespeare wrote, Miss Anderson can only be praised for the subtlety and conviction with which she conveyed such a smothering love. The scene in Gertrude's chamber was so compellingly a scene between two lovers that it was downright embarrassing. On the other hand, her behavior at the performance of the Mouse-trap was perfect in showing her unawareness of its applicability to her own situation. And again, of course, she radiated, somehow, great beauty and voluptuousness.

For her Lady Macbeth I have no end of admiration. John Mason Brown said that with a little more consistency, it "could be the perfect Lady Macbeth of this generation." What I admired about it above all else was the complete femininity of it, the total absence of the tigress (a creature Shakespeare never intended for the role), and perhaps, especially, the sense of her great love for her husband and the transmission of the feeling that all she did and all that she urged were done for his sake because she knew that what she did and urged was what he himself wished to have done. It was indeed one of the great Lady Macbeths of our time. What a catastrophe that an actress of such scope and power should have suddenly in 1970, at an advanced age, decided to enact Hamlet!

It should be mentioned that in 1960 during the Birthday Honours Miss Anderson was created Dame Judith Anderson.

Katherine Cornell (1898–1974) was the daughter of a theatrical manager in Buffalo, New York, and first acted with the Washington Square Players in 1916, remaining with them for two years. In 1919 she was a great success in London as Jo in *Little Women.* Returning to New York, she took a variety of parts until in 1923 she won acclaim in a rather poor play, *Will Shakespeare,* in which she played Mary Fitton. The next year she made theatrical history in New York as Candida, a part that seemed to have been created for her, thought it was an old one by that time. Unkind critics have said, with a certain amount of justice, that no matter what the play, she more or less enacted Candida ever since. From that judgment I should certainly exempt her charming Juliet and deeply touching Elizabeth Barrett.

In 1921 she married Guthrie McClintic, who usually directed the works in which she starred. She never had a more sensational success than in *The Barretts of Wimpole Street,* a play on the love affair of Elizabeth Barrett and Robert Browning (superbly personated by Brian Aherne). It was an effective play, but among other things it gave the public an utterly false and libelous portrait of Elizabeth's father as having been motivated by an incestuous love for her—for which there is not an iota of evidence—a portrait which, it is to be feared, will not be eradicated until someone comes along with a corrective drama equally impressive. In the meantime, I recommend, for a juster view, Frances Winwar's brilliant biography, *The Romantic Lovers*. The play ran for a year in New York, and was taken on tour throughout the country. Two years later on a tour of thirty-one states Miss Cornell and her company gave that play, *Candida*, and *Romeo and Juliet* in repertory. In Seattle, Washington, they had a thrilling experience. They were to give *The Barretts* there on Christmas night, but were prevented from getting to the city because of a washout on the railroad which lasted until midnight; greeted by the manager, they were informed that the audience was still waiting at the theater. They swiftly went there, rang up the curtain while they were getting into costumes and making-up, and began the performance at 1 A.M., ending three hours later. The spectators cheered endlessly and demanded dozens of curtain calls. It was probably the most memorable night of Miss Cornell's life.

Brooks Atkinson felt that she had that special incandescence of which I have several times spoken; "something psychological happened," he said, "when she made an entrance." I myself felt this only once, when she was doing Juliet in 1934, with Basil Rathbone as Romeo and Brian Aherne as Mercutio. She seemed, although thirty-six, a very young girl in voice and movement, and was quite wonderful throughout: in the balcony scene, where the very enchantment of the night breathed through her lines; with the Nurse, where a childlike impatience with the teasing was most fetching; in parting from Romeo, where her despair was keyed perfectly, not unmixed with hope; in the soliloquies, where imagination or terror were marvelously expressed.

But her Cleopatra of 1947 was very bad—bad in a way quite different from Jane Cowl's. Taubman said that she "manhandled" the role, and had very unwisely undertaken it. I myself found her on some occasions giving us Candida again, and on others, instead of being the irresistible serpent of the Nile, to one's great discomfort she was heavy almost to the point of the bovine. But then, as I have said, of the many, many Cleopatras I have heard on the English-speaking stage, only two were superb: Edith Evans and Zoe Caldwell.

Paul Robeson (b.1898), the most celebrated black actor of his age, abandoned a legal career for the stage. He first acted in 1921, and the next year was in England playing with Mrs. Patrick Campbell. When he came back to New York, he achieved notice with the Provincetown Players in works by Eugene O'Neill, and scored a great triumph in that dramatist's *The Emperor Jones*. He had a magnificent bass voice and a fine stage presence which he used to good effect in *Show Boat*. In 1930 he was in London again, this time as Othello, an undertaking which could not then have been made in the United States because of his race and Desdemona's; as it was, a great deal of indignant comment was heard from across the Atlantic.

However, by 1943 the average "intellectual" in New York was parading his "social conscience"—even if he did not really own one—and for some reason the idea that a black man was going to bed with a white girl became a symbol of freedom, especially among those who would have committed suicide if their own daughter had but dreamt of following suit. There was no impediment to Robeson's reviving *Othello* in the United States and his performance was greeted with great acclaim—not, of course, on its actual merits. The play had a long run.

A social conscience is a very good thing; one might venture to state that a social conscience is imposed upon one as a practicing Christian or Jew or humanist, but there is nothing in the Bible or humanism which prescribes that a method for compensating the injustices so long visited upon the blacks—and more recently visited upon the blacks by other blacks in Africa, Detroit, and Harlem—is to consider that all you have to do is place a black man on the stage and what he does is automatically divine. When Paul Robeson appeared on the boards as Othello, and opened his mouth to speak, he looked and sounded as though he were indeed Othello. His bearing was noble and his deep voice was sheer music. But alas! As the play progressed his nobility quickly vanished, his beautiful voice spoke lines that were clearly meaningless to him, and by Act III he had lost all identity with Shakespeare's hero. In the third scene of that act, on seeing Cassio about to leave, he began, with no provocation, to manifest terrible jealousy even before Iago began to poison his mind. By the time Iago began his dirty work, Othello was already so choked with jealousy, he could hardly speak. (This error was not peculiar to Robeson; many an Othello I have seen becomes unaccountably jealous at the mere sight of Cassio [III, iii], and does not allow the jealousy, as Shakespeare intended, to grow.) But, worst of all, Robeson let Othello's jealously paralyze, even incapacitate, him. The Moor whom Shakespeare drew would have decapitated a man who laid a hand on him; José Ferrer as Iago was soon throwing Robeson about the stage as though he were a bag of rags. This Othello was pitiful and without dignity. He evoked sympathy but no awe. I asked myself what character he thought he was playing, and I decided that it must be Uncle Tom in Harriet Beecher Stowe's classic. I was not far from the truth as I discovered when I read that Robeson considered the play dealt with discrimination against the blacks!

Now, it is true that an element in the play is the difference in race between Desdemona and her husband, but it is *not* what the tragedy is *about*. The difference in race only accentuates the love she felt for him, emphasizes the fact that her love was so great that it could ignore that difference.

A very dangerous tradition was begun with Robeson's Othello; not only were J. Dover Wilson and Howard Barnes convinced that a black man was indispensable in the role if the play was to be understood, but that conviction was considered axiomatic for a long time thereafter. When I directed the tragedy myself in 1951 and publicized the day for auditions, some forty black men appeared among the others for the lead. Naturally, if any one of them had seemed equal to the demands of the part, I would have chosen him gladly; the sad fact was that not one of those forty had the faintest notion of how to read verse, and most of them were unequal to pronouncing the simplest words. The actor I eventually chose was brilliant, easy to direct, but white. Before we opened I was asked a hundred times whom I had chosen, and when I replied I was almost always greeted with: "Don't you think it dangerous not to choose a Negro for the role?"

At cocktail parties and other gatherings, when my opinion of Robeson's performance was solicited, I gave it, and was treated like a pariah—a bigot —a man perversely insistent upon being original—usually by people who may never have seen another *Othello* or who had skimmed through a reading of it.

However, I was not alone in my judgment. Of the London performance Trewin has since said that Robeson spoke his speeches with "sonorous monotony" and "wanted any real command," and of his London revival of 1956 that Robeson's voice "fixed itself in a monotonous and strangely distant bass rumble." Of the American production Farjeon justly said that Robeson was too much the underdog; "the cares of *Old Man River* were still upon him. He was not noble enough"; and Stark Young, with his usual perspicacity, observed that Robeson's being a Negro was irrelevant and that he lacked "the fine tragic style"; and Rosamund Gilder remarked that there was no core to his violence.

Unhappily these and similar criticisms seem to have escaped the notice of everyone I encountered who had seen the play (I myself did not read them until I was researching this book). But *The Daily Worker* (read in those days by people whose incomes came from clipping coupons—was not the Soviet Union our ally? And did we not, in fact, hand over to her all those countries now behind the Iron Curtain, and make possible the Berlin Wall?) was thrust again and again upon me with *its* evaluation of Robeson's performance. (I believe Mike Gold was the critic.) What, the critic asked, had the part of Othello been before Robeson bestowed upon it its true significance? (Apparently Kean had never existed.) And what Robeson had finally revealed was the true theme of the play: the oppression of a Negro by (and this phrase I have never forgotten) the "Trotskyite-Fascist" Iago!

It was no secret, of course, that Robeson was, to say the least, sympathetic to the Communist cause. He preferred to educate his children in the Soviet Union, a very odd decision, since if there was one black man in this country who had no reason to complain of his treatment it was Paul Robeson; of him it may be said that he was a success—and a financial one too—*because* he was a black man. No white actor with so average a talent as Robeson's could have ended up owning a mansion in Riverdale on the Hudson.

Charles Laughton (1899–1962), also inexplicably omitted from the *Oxford Companion to the Theatre*, was, as everyone knows, one of the most popular actors of the century. It was never observed of him, so far as I know, that whatever his role—whether a king, a beachcomber, a detective, a murderer, a great scientist, a butler, a great painter, a Roman Emperor—it was always Charles Laughton we were seeing and hearing. It was truly remarkable that that pudgy-faced, fat little man with a countenance that might have been considered the *beau idéal* of the lower class, uneducated Britisher, and who never failed to speak in that measured careful way of his as though every sentence contained dangerous ice on which he might slip, but who was lifted above all possibility of mediocrity by the masterly twinkle in his eye and an inner radiance that never failed him, should have convinced us all that he was in succession an endless variety of diverse persons, when he never ceased being himself.

He was born into a family of hotel keepers at Scarborough. After doing service in World War I, despite his family's objections he decided to pursue his ambition to become an actor by enlisting as a student at the Royal Academy of Dramatic Art, where he studied under Komisarjevsky.

No doubt the most universally known of his performances was his Henry VIII in the 1933 film, and the most celebrated of his gestures, the king's throwing of chicken legs over his shoulder. Indeed, for movie audiences that gesture seemed to constitute the clue to Henry's character. Later that same year he played Henry VIII under Tyrone Guthrie's direction at the Old Vic; of his stage performance Agate said that he brought to the theater all the vulgarities of the film, though he no longer threw the legs of chicken onto the rugs. A few months later, under the same direction, he played Prospero in *The Tempest* rather like "Father Christmas," said Agate, with a "naughty twinkle in his eye"; his face was "cherubically set against spirits," and he seemed "only too anxious to pass the port." Guthrie had cast Laughton's wife, Elsa Lanchester, as Ariel, who played that difficult role to perfection; as Agate observed, Ariel must never appear to be a girl got up to be a boy, or even a boy appearing to be a boy; you ought to be able to cry, said Agate, "Hail to thee, blithe spirit! Boy thou never wert!" Lanchester was more than airy, said Agate; she actually "took away weight." He thought Roger Livesey made of Caliban a "delicious monster," part Frankenstein and part Petrouchka.

That same season at the Old Vic Laughton was in *Measure for Measure* and *Macbeth*. Agate thought his Angelo excellent, though Laughton lacked the resonance required for blank verse; he was dressed in black watered-silk, and looked like a "distressful eagle," though never like a vulture. Livesey was excellent as the duke—the most difficult role in the play to make convincing. But it is strange that so excellent and sensitive a critic as Agate should have declared that he had no use for *Measure for Measure,* for he thought it expressed contempt for every man in the audience who, if honest with himself, would ask his sister to give up "what in comparison with his death is a trifling service." Agate obviously missed the whole point: Isabella was willing to be whipped to death to save her brother's life, but she could not buy his freedom by agreeing to an act for which he himself was to be executed; her battle was against corruption in high places—and in the year 1974 the play seems more relevant than ever. Agate compounded his felony by declaring the duke's "Be absolute for death" speech to be "the most absolute bosh that ever fell from human lips." If I had to limit myself to ten of the hundreds of great speeches in Shakespeare to show the poet at his best, that speech would certainly be one of them. (T.S. Eliot thought so too,

57. Samuel Phelps as Macbeth. Phelps, more than any other actor of his century, was influential in restoring Shakespeare's texts after centuries of their mutilations. *(Courtesy of the Victoria & Albert Museum, London)*

56. Judith Anderson, who has proved herself often to be a magnificent actress, indulged the folly of playing Hamlet in 1971 at the age of seventy-three. *(Courtesy of the Museum of the City of New York, Theatre and Music Collection)*

58. Phelps as Henry IV. His transformation of Sadler's Wells, despite its unsavory history and its distance from the West End, into an important theater, was a noble and courageous undertaking. *(Courtesy of the Harvard Theatre Collection)*

59. Henry Irving as Hamlet. At the summit of his career he reflected how strange it was that he should have achieved so great a reputation "with nothing to help me—with no equipment. My legs, my voice, everything has been against me. For an actor who can't walk, can't talk, and has no face to speak of, I've done pretty well." *(Courtesy of the Walter Hampden Memorial Library, The Players)*

60. Irving as Shylock. He was responsible at his theater, the Lyceum, for introducing elaborate scenery and interpolating scenes Shakespeare never wrote—such as the one in which Shylock returns in misery to his house to find it empty after Jessica's elopement— which unfortunately established a tradition now usually followed. *(Courtesy of the Museum of the City of New York, Theatre and Music Collection)*

61. Ellen Terry as Beatrice, a role which, like that of Portia, was one of her most adored by the public. For years she played opposite Irving in many Shakespearean plays. *(Courtesy of the Museum of the City of New York, Theatre and Music Collection)*

62. Adelaide Ristori as Queen Katharine in *Henry VIII*. After performing in Italian, this forceful actress began to study English so that she could enact the roles in English. *(Courtesy of the Walter Hampden Memorial Library, The Players)*

63. The French actor Albert Fechter, as Hamlet. He was complimented for moving acting closer to everyday realism, but his broken accent caused much adverse comment. *(Courtesy of the New York Public Library)*

64. Scenes from Fechter's production of *Hamlet*, which was the rage of London at the time. Winter considered his English and his blank verse "execrable." What he actually did was to convert the play into the "gentlemanly melodrama" then very much in favor. *(Courtesy of the Victoria & Albert Museum, London)*

65. Tommaso Salvini as Othello, his most celebrated role. Henry James considered him the perfect Moor. He was acclaimed throughout Europe in the part. Winter complained that he began to be jealous too early in the play, in Act I. *(Courtesy of the Walter Hampden Memorial Library, The Players)*

66. Salvini as King Lear. He was also seen an heard (always in Italian) as Hamlet, Macbet and Coriolanus. He performed frequently England and had four seasons in the Unit States. Of all foreign actors he made the gre est impact upon the English-speaking stag *(Courtesy of the Museum of the City of N York, Theatre and Music Collection)*

67. Helena Modjeska as Viola in *Twelfth Night*. Though born in Poland, we think of her correctly as an American actress. She was thirty-two when she came to this country, after acting Shakespeare in Polish for more than ten years. Despite her accent, which she never lost, she was looked upon as one of the finest actresses of her day, both in comedy and tragedy. *(Courtesy of the Museum of the City of New York, Theatre and Music Collection)*

68. Modjeska as Rosalind in *As You Like It*, o of her most popular roles. *(Courtesy of the M seum of the City of New York, Theatre a Music Collection)*

69. Herbert Beerbohm Tree as Hamlet. W. S. Gilbert said his acting in the role was funny without being vulgar. Nevertheless, Tree had a great following in his time. *(Courtesy of the Walter Hampden Memorial Library, The Players)*

71. Johnston Forbes-Robertson as Hamlet, his most celebrated role. Shaw, for a change, was full of enthusiasm for *his* acting of Shakespeare, and Agate said that of all the Hamlets he had ever seen, Forbes-Robertson had "the winning sweetness of his kindly prince, his grave courtesy in rebuke." *(Courtesy of the Walter Hampden Memorial Library, The Players)*

70. Tree and Violet Vanbrugh as Macbeth and Lady Macbeth. He loved display for its own sake, and in *Macbeth* there was an elaborate scene of Duncan being escorted to bed; to make time for it great chunks of one of Shakespeare's shortest plays had to be omitted. *(Courtesy of the Victoria & Albert Museum, London)*

72. Forbes-Robertson as Claudio in *Much Ado*, acted under Irving. *(Courtesy of the Museum of the City of New York, Theatre and Music Collection)*

73. Forbes-Robertson started out as a painter, and here, in 1882, after he had joined Irving at the Lyceum, he painted the church scene in *Much Ado*. The painting now hangs at The Players, New York. Ellen Terry, at the left, is Beatrice; Forbes-Robertson, right of center, is Claudio; Henry Irving, two men to the right of him, is Benedick. *(Courtesy of the Walter Hampden Memorial Library, The Players)*

74. Lawrence Barrett as Cassius, self-educated, became one of America's leading Shakespearean actors. His Cassius, performed opposite Booth's Brutus, was his most celebrated role. *(Courtesy of the Museum of the City of New York, Theatre and Music Collection)*

75. Clara Morris, who exerted enormous influence over her audiences without ever mastering the technique of her profession. She demonstrated intensity of feeling by distending her nostrils. She was known as the "Queen of Spasms." *(Courtesy of the Walter Hampden Memorial Library, The Players)*

77. Lily Langtry, reclining; the photograph is inscribed with her married name, Lille de Bathe, 1900. With little or no acting genius, she became the rage because of her beauty, and became one of the numerous mistresses of the Prince of Wales (the future Edward VII). Her most popular role was Rosalind. *(Courtesy of the Museum of the City of New York, Theatre and Music Collection)*

78. Robert Bruce Mantell as Macbeth. He was the last representative of the school of Edwin Forrest. Despite his limitations, the United States is in his debt because he brought some of the best plays to innumerable communities that had no theater and to thousands who had never seen a play. *(Courtesy of the Museum of the City of New York, Theatre and Music Collection)*

5. John Drew, a leading actor of his day. Ie became the uncle of Ethel, Maurice, nd John Barrymore. Drew, who acted in is mother's company, was especially ad-ired as Petruchio. *(Courtesy of the Wal-r Hampden Memorial Library, The Iayers)*

79. Robert Mantell as Hamlet. (*Courtesy of the Walter Hampden Memorial Library, The Players*)

81. Ada Rehan as Katharina in *The Taming of the Shrew*. A beautiful woman of lovely voice and charm, she had a large Shakespearean repertory. Portia was her favorite role, and she was a notable Viola. (*Courtesy of the Walter Hampden Memorial Library, The Players*)

80. Richard Mansfield as Richard III, whom he made a "laughing devil." My Uncle Emil was fond of giving impersonations of Mansfield's various roles when I was a child, and from those sessions I date my passion for the theater. (*Courtesy of the Walter Hampden Memorial Library, The Players*)

82. Mary Anderson as Hermione in *A Winter's Tale*, in which she also took the part of Perdita. An extraordinarily beautiful woman, gifted with a superb voice and great charm, she nevertheless marred her performances with faulty diction. (*Courtesy of the Museum of the City of New York, Theatre and Music Collection*)

83. Mrs. Patrick Cambell as Ophelia. "Despite her extraordinary brilliance as an actress, she was one of the most difficult. Managers dreaded having to deal with her. Agate said she "radiated quicksilver." (*Courtesy of the Walter Hampden Memorial Library, The Players*)

85. E. H. Sothern and Julia Marlowe in *Hamlet,* 1921. "Our high school teachers were forever cudgeling us to go to see them do Shakespeare, most conscientiously and boringly. They became, says Lloyd Morris, "a national institution." (*Courtesy of the Museum of the City of New York, Theatre and Music Collection*)

84. Theda Bara, the great "vamp" of the silent cinema. "I was a schoolboy in knickerbockers when I saw her first film, *A Fool There Was,* and from that time on I never missed a Theda Bara picture and yearned to be one of her victims. She made a wicked Cleopatra and a saccharine Juliet—for once in a while she played the part of a good woman. (*Courtesy of the Walter Hampden Memorial Library, The Players*)

86. Walter Hampden as Othello. "Hampden's services to the American theater were invaluable. He devoted himself to poetic drama in a period when it was almost banished from the stage. (*Courtesy of the Walter Hampden Memorial Library, The Players*)

F: Dear Margaret Carrington —
with the Greatest love and gratitude
from her offspring —
old Pop Hamlet. 1923

87. John Barrymore as Hamlet in a photograph by the great Edward Steichen. His Prince of Denmark, if somewhat lacking in poetry, was one of the great performances of the century for power, clarity, and brilliance. *(Courtesy of the Walter Hampden Memorial Library, The Players)*

88. John Barrymore as Hamlet and Blanche Yurka as Gertrude. After a career of wonderful performances in the United States and London, and an equally successful one in the movies, John Barrymore embarked on a course of self-destruction, which augmented in geometric progression until the public could no longer bear his drunkennesss and obscenities. *(Courtesy of the Museum of the City of New York, Theatre and Music Collection)*

89. Estelle Winwood, she of the bulging eyes, who gave the most enchanting and clever performance of Katharina in *The Taming of the Shrew* I have ever seen. *(Courtesy of the New York Public Library)*

90. Edith Evans as Rosalind and Michael Redgrave as Orlando at the Old Vic in November 1936. The costumes were inspired by Watteau. Miss Evans has been almost beyond dispute the greatest English actress of her time. There seems to have been no role that she could not act to perfection. *(Courtesy of Frank Lockwood)*

91. Jane Cowl as Juliet. The photograph catches the moment when she first sees Romeo in the greatest performance of *Romeo and Juliet* I have ever seen (1923). The photographer has caught wonderfully well the manner in which Miss Cowl was able to project love at first sight. *(Courtesy of the Harvard Theatre Collection)*

93. Katherine Cornell as Juliet, one of he finest performances, and Edith Evans as th Nurse (1934). I should place that produ tion second only to Miss Cowl's *(Courtesy the Walter Hampden Memorial Library, Th Players)*

92. Judith Anderson as Gertrude with John Gielgud as Hamlet (1936). Miss Anderson has been the lead in a great many plays, always (except when she was Hamlet) with distinction. She is one of the few fortunates who are incandescent when on stage. Gielgud's Hamlet was the greatest of our century. *(Courtesy of the Walter Hampden Memorial Library, The Players)*

94. Set design for *Hamlet* by the great scenic designer Jo Mielziner. *(Courtesy of the Walter Hampden Memorial Library, The Players)*

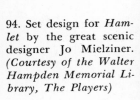

5. Maurice Evans as Hamlet in an uncut ver-
ion of the play, 1933. He performed it again
1 New York in 1938. Audiences, unused to
eeing the whole play as Shakespeare had writ-
en it, were ecstatic; they thought they were
eeing a new interpretation only because they
ere seeing Shakespeare's play for the first time.
Courtesy of the Museum of the City of New
ork, Theatre and Music Collection)

7. John Gielgud as he appeared in his bril-
ant *The Ages of Man*. (Courtesy of the Walter
Iampden Memorial Library, The Players)

96. Flora Robson and Charles Laughton at
the Old Vic in Guthrie's production of *Macbeth*, 1934. Suprisingly, Miss Robson, who
is well known for her ability to project
brooding power, did not give the traditional
and incorrect tigress, but, as Shakespeare intended, a loving wife ambitious for her husband. (*Courtesy of the Victoria & Albert Museum, London*)

98. Laurence Olivier as Hamlet. The London
Times said of the performance that Olivier
"has looked for himself in the part and the
part in himself." (*Courtesy of the Walter
Hampden Memorial Library, The Players*)

99. Ralph Richardson in one of
his most celebrated roles, Falstaff
(Courtesy of Frank Lockwood)

101. Orson Welles in his one brilliant
Shakespearean performance, as Brutus, which
he also directed, at the age of twenty-two
(Courtesy of the Walter Hampden Memorial Library, The Players)

100. Alfred Drake. In 1964 he performed the
finest Claudius in *Hamlet* I have ever seen.
Despite the general messiness of a production costumed in "rehearsal clothes" with
nothing but the brick wall at the back of
the stage as scenery, his portrait of the king
was incisive; he made of him an intelligent
and dangerous adversary, worthy of the
prince, and a man who loved his wife and
who had committed murder for her sake as
well as the crown's. *(Courtesy Friedman-Abeles)*

102. Paul Scofield as King Lear (left) with Tom Fleming and Alec McCowen. *(Courtesy of the Walter Hampden Memorial Library, The Players)*

103. Richard Burton as Hamlet and Hume Cronyn as Polonius, 1964, in the "rehearsal clothes" version of the play, directed by Gielgud. Burton carried the assumed madness of the prince to the point of the ridiculous (jumping up and down on the king's throne, for instance, like a three-year-old). The only distinguished acting in this production was Cronyn's Polonius and Drake's Claudius—both of which were superb. *(Courtesy Fried-man-Abeles)*

104. Zoe Caldwell as Cleopatra at Stratford, Ontario, in one of the two greatest performances of that difficult role in our century (the other being Edith Evans's). She could be *the* actress of our time, if she wished to. *(Courtesy of Miss Caldwell)*

105. Judi Dench as Ophelia. Miss Dench, whose services are in constant demand in the London and Stratford-on-Avon theaters, has shown herself to be a leading actress in every sort of play from tragedy to comedy to satire to musical comedy. *(Courtesy of Christina Call)*

apparently, for he inserted—without quotation marks—some of its greatest lines in one of his own poems!)

As Macbeth, Agate thought Laughton's round face unsuitable and the actor guilty of too much "elvish expostulation"; the role was beyond Laughton's physical means; he had, however, a complete intellectual comprehension of the character. He was very good in the banquet scene, when he bounded away from Banquo's ghost up the staircase "like an india-rubber cat." There were many subtleties in the performance, too, such as his first meeting with his wife; but all the poetry was gone from the play.

In 1959 he participated with Olivier and Edith Evans in a cycle of the historical plays. That same year he played Lear at Stratford; it was a meticulous performance but it lacked the essential emotional power.

Obviously, it is not as a Shakespearean actor that Laughton will be remembered. The truth is that I find it hard to think of him without seeing him wearing (as in *Ruggles of Red Gap* and other works) a bowler hat.

Martita Hunt (1900–1969), who gave a stunning performance as the Madwoman of Chaillot in later years, was a gracious Helena in *A Midsummer Night's Dream* in 1929, a fine Regan in 1930 and a too likeable Lady Macbeth the same year. As the queen in *Hamlet*, also during 1930, she brilliantly conveyed the woman's stupidity, and Crosse thought her conception of the Nurse in *Romeo and Juliet* was fascinating in its total dissimilarity to Edith Evans's conception. Miss Hunt, he thought, had never been better than as a brown Italian peasant, grim, sinister.

Tyrone Guthrie (1900–1971) gave up acting for directing; he was twice appointed producer at the Old Vic (1933 and 1936) and from 1939 to 1945 was administrator of the Old Vic and Sadler's Wells. He also produced plays at the Shakespearean Festival Theatre at Stratford, Ontario, from 1953 to 1957. In 1963 he was in charge of a theater fashioned after the Ontario model in Minneapolis; its purpose, he declared, was to establish outside of New York a permanent repertory company to give Shakespeare, the classics, and American plays. He was knighted in 1961.

He must be considered in our study because after Komisarjevsky, no director showed more persistence in his search for novelty in Shakespeare, and the temper of the times being what they were, he was considered a genius for his efforts. Posterity may decide otherwise, when this devotion to eccentricity in giving Shakespeare will have exhausted itself.

When Guthrie took over the Old Vic and Sadler's Wells in 1933, he seemed not only to have no relish for Shakespeare's verse but to distrust it, for he began to create all kinds of business which he imposed upon the plays he directed, as though he hoped to distract the ear by engaging the eye. He decided to diminish the cuts made because of changes in scenery by using a permanent set which was, as Trewin puts it, "both contemporary and obtrusive"; it also involved a great deal of climbing for the actors. (The designer was the architect, Wells Coates.) It is to Guthrie's credit that he had faith in the possibilities of Flora Robson—not an actress to decorate the stage, but a woman of intelligence and emotional energy; he cast her, surprisingly, as Isabella (to Laughton's Angelo). Her Lady Macbeth was affectionate and without imagination. Guthrie refused to open *Macbeth* with the witches on the grounds that to do so was falsely to attribute to them the "governing influence" of the tragedy. (The intention was, of course, in the right direction.)

When he returned to the Old Vic in the autumn of 1936, the great sensation of his season was *Hamlet*. Guthrie had been impressed by the ridiculous elaborations of Dr. Ernest Jones on the Freudian concept that what was at work in the prince was an Oedipus complex. Olivier did his best to illustrate what he thought a "profoundly interesting" notion, but the innovation seemed to escape the notice of the audience (as it could never have done in the Gielgud projection of the same idea). Guthrie's novelties further intruded themselves by having the queen in her death fall backwards from a height. His *Twelfth Night*, again with Olivier as an overacting Sir Toby, "like a veteran Skye-terrier, ears pricked for mischief," and Jessica Tandy doubling as Viola and Sebastian (which made obvious difficulties for the scene when the brother and sister recognize each other—a mute actor had to be brought on as Sebastian); Alec Guinness's Sir Andrew was a "walking wraith." When he gave *Henry V* that year, Katherine and Alice, for no good reason, were elevated on a palanquin for the lesson in English. The season ended when he took his *Hamlet* to the little town of Helsingör in Denmark (the Elsinore of Shakespeare's play). Olivier was again the prince, Vivien Leigh, Ophelia, Anthony Quayle, Laertes, Leo Genn, Horatio, and John Abbott, Claudius. During rehearsals there was a steady downpour of rain in the courtyard where the performance was to be held, and John Abbott appeared with an umbrella and spoke with understandably intense feeling Cladius's line, "Is there not rain enough in the sweet heavens?" The rain continued next day, and it was obvious that the performance could not open at the old castle. Then Guthrie was inspired: he quickly set everything up in a neighboring hotel. The audience's chairs were arranged in the ballroom; the place was jammed that night and the Prince and Princess of Denmark were present, with the storm still raging appropriately outside. Though the castle courtyard was available the next night, Guthrie never forgot the improvised theater in the ballroom; it fortified his objection to the proscenium stage for Shakespeare.

Crosse objected to Guthrie's omitting, in *Macbeth*, not only the first scene, but the opening thirty-five lines of the witches' second scene as well. Guthrie in a program note had said that there was "overwhelming evidence" that these passages were not authentic—a statement which Crosse quite justly challenged as sheer fabrication. The apparitions of the fourth act were also omitted, and the cauldron was a "small kettle" which could not possibly have held all that the witches were throwing into it.

By 1938 Guthrie was even more eccentric. His *Midsummer Night's Dream* of that year was costumed in a mixture of the early Victorian and the "pseudo-classical." What, Crosse asked, could that sort of thing add to anyone's enjoyment? The fairies were in white ballet skirts; Vivien Leigh's Titania was got up to look like an old engraving of Taglioni, the celebrated ballerina; Robert Helpmann's Oberon was a shining beetle.

That same year he cast Alec Guinness at the Old Vic in a modern-dress *Hamlet;* at Ophelia's funeral there were dripping umbrellas and mackintoshes, though he had said three years earlier that he disliked modern-dress performances of Shakespeare. After *Hamlet* he directed *The Taming of the Shrew* "in a world pulped with custard-pies"; Petruchio wore red, white, and blue corsets at his wedding; Grumio was a clown with a string of sausage.

In 1941 Guthrie gave a *King John* in lavish style with heraldic curtains and waving banners, a great deal of armor, but a much too arch use of hobby horses before the walls of Angiers; the First Citizen wore spectacles and a woolen beard. In 1952 he ventured with a play rarely performed, and only partially the work of Shakespeare, *Timon of Athens*; Guthrie called it a satire on the delusions produced by riches as well as on a philosophy of materialism. Again the extraneous was ample: the senators, for instance, were a bevy of persecuted grotesques.

By this time it was plain that when Guthrie directed you came to see the production not the play. When he directed *Troilus and Cressida* in 1956, the setting was placed circa 1930, as a contention between "Ruritania," the Central European powers, and the locale, Potsdam. The Trojans, looking, according to Trewin, like musical-comedy dragoons, were in yellow, with brass helmets and "heliograph-winking" breastplates; the Greeks wore spiked helmets and Teutonic mustaches; Cressida first appeared in a riding habit with a hobble skirt—when the Old Vic came to New York that year with this play in its repertory, I left the theater after that intolerable first act— Helen of Troy was an Edwardian commanding the world with waltzes at her grand piano, bewigged Pandarus was an effete who could not speak without drawling, Ajax a general in scarlet and Ulysses an admiral; Thersites was "a civilian attached to the Expeditionary Force," who sported a sketchbook and a camera.

In 1959 he gave *All's Well That Ends Well* at Stratford-on-Avon in which he was coauthor with Shakespeare. There were drastic cuts and in III, iii he expanded a passage by ten lines with new comic business; at court the costuming was Edwardian, in camp contemporary.

In 1961 he was knighted for his services to the theater; it would have been more accurate to have said for "disservices to the future of the theater," for Guthrie did more than anyone else to encourage the vulgar innovations which are practiced in our time.

He opened his Minneapolis Theater in 1963 with a new modern-dress *Hamlet.* Howard Taubman reported that it was "ludicrous and infuriating," though not unprovocative. The tragedy was set in a twentieth-century principality; Laertes wore a trench coat with a holster and pistol over it "like a comic secret agent of films on TV." Ophelia was in "outdoor whites with a brace of tennis racquets under her arm" while she saw Laertes off. During the Mouse-trap spotlights were used to "rake the audience," and for the sword play between Hamlet and Laertes there was a courtier to cry, "Most irregulah!"

Maurice Evans (b. 1901) first became noted as an actor in 1928 when he appeared in his native England in *Journey's End*. In 1934, he joined the Old Vic, and enacted a great many roles. As Richard II, slight yet sturdy-looking, he demonstrated very well how the king's arrogance and self-indulgence disintegrated into uncertainty and thence into an agony born of his inability to understand what had happened to him. His ringing voice delivered Richard's lines with the requisite rhetorical splendor. Agate thought he did very well considering that in figure he was the last person one would imagine in that role; Agate thought he was more suited for Hotspur, quick in body and mind, the very opposite of Richard's indolence. Nevertheless, he did full justice to the early scenes of the play, though this critic thought the serious half of the play was beyond his physical scope. After all, Agate reflected, one must remember that this Richard is one of the most difficult of all of Shakespeare's parts.

Later that season Evans performed an Iago which was eager and (quite properly) youthful, full of variety, but perhaps too light. The last production of that season found Evans as the prince in an uncut version of *Hamlet*.

The following year, 1934, he came to the United States to play Romeo to Katherine Cornell's Juliet, which she revived in 1935. Evans so much impressed a member of the American audience that the man wrote to him to ask whether he should like to have money for another play. It was arranged that they meet at a bar, where the man apologized: in the meantime he had engaged his capital in another enterprise. But would $25,000 be of any use, and what would Evans' next venture be? *"Richard II,"* Evans replied, and the man at once wrote out a check for the amount he had mentioned. Later when asked what share of *Richard II's* profits he thought he ought to have, the philanthropist said he had not donated the sum for profits, and would be satisfied with the payment of 6 percent interest. As a result Evans found himself suddenly very well-to-do, or, as Agate put it, Evans was now a rich man.

Actually, in 1936, Evans was in two plays before appearing in *Richard II* in 1937: in *Saint Joan* with Katherine Cornell and as Napoleon in *St. Helena*. But his *Richard II* was assuredly the surprise hit of 1937: it had not been seen in New York since 1878 when Booth presented it, and it now ran for an astonishing 133 performances, closed for the summer, reopened in September for 38 performances, and was then taken on tour across the country. It was his Richard that established Evans for a while as the leading Shakespearean actor in the country; after all, no American actor of his generation had had the advantage of learning his vocation in Shakespearean repertory as do most English actors; in Evans's case, he had had training before coming to the Old Vic with the Cambridge Festival Theatre.

As a consquence of Evans's success with it, *Richard II* suddenly began to be included in college Shakespeare courses, and after its long neglect as a play marred by dramatic weakness, which it certainly possesses, scholars began to write papers about it. What emerged from this new interest, however, was the discovery that the tragedy is brimming over with marvelous poetry.

Although there had been several uncut productions of *Hamlet* in England during that decade, New York had never seen one, and Evans took advantage of his new prestige to present his uncut *Hamlet* in 1938. It is the longest play Shakespeare ever wrote, doubtless the longest masterpiece ever written for the theater; Evans's production began at 6:30 P.M. (unheard of in a city in which 8:30 or 8:40 was the rule) and continued for four and one-half hours, with one long intermission for the audience to snatch a bite to eat. The critical acclaim was enormous; what everyone said was that this was a new, revealing Hamlet, which effectively routed all the complicated discussions about the "difficulties" of the play. If I may quote what I have said elsewhere on this subject:

On the occasion of Mr. Evans's production, even though the direction [by Margaret Webster] attempted little more than to exploit the surface meaning of individual scenes without relevance to the whole design, the drama-critics all acclaimed Mr. Evans's "new" interpretation of the hero—although they were rather vague about identifying what that interpretation was! . . . All that was actually new . . . was that for the first time . . . the lines that Shakespeare had written were at last to be heard in their fullness. Naturally the resulting play was "new!" Every *Hamlet* the critics had seen before Mr. Evans's had necessarily been a distorted one because of the annihilation of whole portions of the tragedy. Not because of any profound understanding of the play, but because the lines at least were there, was Mr. Evans's the first . . . attempt in our time to give the play as Shakespeare conceived it.

"Despite the notable success of Maurice Evans's uncut revival, nearly all of Shakespeare's plays have proved too long for the endurance of most audiences," says Mr. Hazelton Spencer. [Yet because it has been the *in* thing to do, our audiences have sat through the intellectual vacuities, embarrasing sophomorism, and the endless repetitions of some of Eugene O'Neill's equally long plays, such as *Mourning Becomes Electra* and *The Iceman Cometh.*] "Why Shakespeare," he continues, "who almost lived in the theatre, habitually wrote in excess of its requirements is a pretty question." An equally pretty question is how, knowing those "requirements" well enough to become the most successful dramatist of his time, Shakespeare contrived to write so much "in excess" of the artistic "requirements" of his theatre that he created not for his age but for all time. . . . Is it not just possible that Shakespeare gauged correctly the length of each of his masterpieces? that he made the length of each conform to the "requirements" of his art rather than to a modern director's guess of the possible "endurance of most audiences?" Besides, how long should a tragedy be? . . .

Obviously every work of art must be as long as it needs to be.

. . . In the arts no attribute partakes less of the absolute than that of length. *Vanity Fair* and *The Egoist,* for all their pages, are immeasurably briefer in their effect than many a novelette that could be mentioned; *Paradise Lost* seems much shorter than *Peter Bell.* The relativity of length was forcibly illustrated years ago during several seasons' attendance at the Wagner-cycle at the Metropolitan Opera House [before Rudolf Bing]. During the regular subscription nights *Götterdämerung, Parsifal, Die Meistersinger,* and *Tristan* had quite tedious and long-winded spots, though the performances were each cut down by an hour or more. But at the special Wagner-cycle performances, where they were presented uncut, often with the same casts, they never seemed a note too long. A performance lasting more than an hour longer than the cut version inevitably became a swifter one. In short, one decided, Wagner knew more about the ideal length of his masterpieces than his editors!

For like reasons Mr. Evans's uncut performances were the most rapid of contemporary *Hamlets.*

And that was no mean virtue. In the work from which I have quoted, I have tried to show that all the many "problems" which critics have discovered in that play are nonexistent, and have emanated largely from the cut versions to which audiences have traditionally been subjected.

In 1939 Margaret Webster staged *Henry IV, Part I,* with Evans as Falstaff; in 1940 he did Malvolio to Helen Hayes's Viola for her; in 1941 Macbeth opposite Judith Anderson. None of these was very good, with the exception of Miss Anderson's wonderful Lady Macbeth, to which Evans was unequal. In 1945 he gave his so-called G. I. version of *Hamlet;* a highly amputated *Hamlet,* which he had already played in the South Pacific war zones for the soldiers; the excuse for the cuts—such as the omission of the graveyard scene—was that they had been made out of delicate consideration for the soldiers; but there was no such excuse for presenting it on Broadway. (In the meantime Mr. Evans had become a citizen of the United States—in 1941.)

When Agate paid a visit to America he was shocked to find Evans rated as a better actor than Gielgud, and was puzzled, especially considering Evans's "baby face" when compared with the "august masks" of Irving and Forbes-Robertson, which Americans had seen.

It is a judgment of which audiences in the United States would no longer be guilty. Evans came to America at a propitious moment, and his early successes there sustained for a while his reputation in the face of later performances, which were by no means so impressive. Evans has since proved himself a very good actor, who is much better when *not* playing Shakespeare.

Donald Wolfit (1902–1969) was an English actor-manager, who devoted himself chiefly to Shakespeare. His first appearance on stage was as a walk-on at York in *The Merchant of Venice* (1920). In 1922 he was doing the First Witch for Charles Doran's touring company. In 1929 he was invited to join the Old Vic company, which that season boasted the youthful John Gielgud as the leading actor. Wolfit was soon cast as Claudius to Gielgud's Hamlet and Martita Hunt's Gertrude; he was praised by the director, Harcourt Williams, as the best Claudius in his memory. (Wolfit's makeup resembled a Velásquez portrait of Philip IV of Spain).

In 1936 he had the misfortune to be cast as Antony in the Komisarjevsky production which featured Eugenie Leontovich as Cleopatra. Wolfit managed superbly under conditions which might have destroyed an inferior actor, but it was to little avail when his crisp diction had to deal with a very Russian enchantress of the Nile. Under the same direction he executed a first-rate Kent to Randle Ayrton's Lear, but an elaborate stage construction, with its multilevel narrow steps, fairly defeated the most valiant efforts of a fine cast. The same year, 1936, he gave, also at Stratford, with Iden Payne as director, a Hamlet which delighted John Masefield; this prince was aware at every turn of the dangers among which he moved. Unfortunately Payne, as was common in that decade, followed the theories of J. Dover Wilson, and Wolfit was passionate (rather than passion's slave) and romantic.

In September of 1939 the festival at Stratford-on-Avon was shut down because of the war, and Wolfit had already been chosen to be actor-manager, with a company that toured Britain. After nine weeks, during which he was seen as Petruchio, Malvolio, Shylock, Macbeth, and Hamlet, he had almost made expenses. Later he added Othello, Benedick, and Touchstone to his personal repertory, toured for another ten weeks, and early in 1939 he added Romeo. When the war began he started on his "black-out" tour of the provinces. He had taken upon his shoulders the invaluable work that the Bensons had formerly done. Early in the war he also gave lunch-hour excerpts from the plays. He offered these, with the inclusion of the sonnets, at the Strand Theatre in London, during 1940, the year of the heavy bombing. During the Battle of Britain he continued even after the back of the theater and the dressing rooms had been shattered. In recollection, Wolfit described their offerings: "Anything that came into our heads as a suitable short scene: the three casket scenes from *The Merchant of Venice,* the Orsino and Viola scenes and the box-trees scene from *Twelfth Night;* potted versions of *Othello, Richard III, Hamlet, The Merry Wives of Windsor,* and *As You Like It,* and always a group of sonnets." Sometimes they contrived to present an entire play—e.g., *Hamlet* and *Othello.* In 1942 at the Strand he was able to give a fuller Shakespeare season, with the enthusiastic backing of the critic, James Agate. Whatever the weaknesses of his casts, Wolfit's own great talents were enough to carry the weight of every performance. Agate especially praised Wolfit's Richard III as being as terrifying as it should be, and for making Richard a "constructive villain," though avoiding the macabre.

In the early part of 1943 Wolfit produced his *King Lear* against a massive Stonehenge setting. At first Agate, though granting the actor immense talent, declared that Nature had deprived him of the requirements of a great tragic actor: his face was too broad and his baritone voice had no resonance;

as Lear he was, thought Agate in 1943, admirable but not overwhelming. Lear remained in Wolfit's repertory just the same. If Cleopatra is the most difficult female role in Shakespeare, Lear is assuredly the most difficult male part, if for no other reason than that it begins *fortissimo* and then continues to increase in volume from that point on. Few actors since Garrick have known how to husband their resources so that they may be equal to the second part of the tragedy. In 1946, after not having seen Wolfit in the role for fifteen months, Agate declared that this Lear "was the greatest piece of Shakespearean acting I have seen since I have been privileged to write for the *Sunday Times.*" He did, as a great actor should, make the audience feel in the heath and hovel scenes that it was in the presence "of a flaming torch beside which Michael Angelo and Bach are but tapers." He swept the spectators off their feet, and projected everything required of that marvelous role —majesty, grandeur, mind, kingliness—and, above all, he was a *man.* To this rhapsody Crosse added his opinion that Wolfit's Lear was the best since Irving's. I did not ever see Irving, but I did see Mr. Wolfit's Lear, and I can heartily endorse everything Agate and Crosse felt about his performance. Years later, it was my task to edit the Living Shakespeare recordings, and I can truthfully say, hearing Mr. Wolfit in Lear for the second time, that his disc is perhaps the most dramatic in the whole series of Shakespearean plays.

Unfortunately Mr. Wolfit did not please Agate as Macbeth (1945), for he lacked the necessary introspection, vacillation, and remorse; Macbeth was bloody, bold, and resolute in this production *before* the witches enjoined him to be so. Crosse's opinion was that Wolfit's Othello equaled his Lear.

In 1957 Wolfit was knighted for his services to the stage and to Shakespeare in particular. Indeed, although Sir Donald appeared in other plays —though even here his preference was for dramas either not modern or modern plays whose setting was not contemporary—his career stands out among his contemporaries for his consecration to the greatest of all poets and dramatists.

Brian Aherne (b. 1902), who made an indelible impression as Robert Browning in *The Barretts of Wimpole Street* opposite Katherine Cornell's Elizabeth, also appeared as Mercutio when she was doing her celebrated Juliet. Orson Welles had originally been designated for that role on Broadway since he had been playing it on a pre-Broadway tour. Aherne asked Guthrie McClintic, the director, for the part, and McClintic agreed. Aherne believes that Welles never forgave him, though he was allotted the role of Tybalt in exchange. During the well-known duel scene, Aherne says, "I often had the impression that he slashed at me with unnecessary venom, and twice he broke my property sword off at the hilt, leaving me defenceless."

Some years later, J. R. Rubin and Irving Thalberg tried to get Mr. Aherne to take the part of Romeo in a film opposite Norma Shearer. He thought himself too tall and too mature for the young lover, and advised them to get someone younger: the result was that they engaged Leslie Howard, who was years older than Mr. Aherne.

While he was staying at a remote country inn in North Wales, Mr. Aherne received a telephone call from the producer, Max Gordon, who said that his *Othello,* with Walter Huston in the title role, was "dying on the road." It was due to open in New York in three weeks; would Mr. Aherne come at once to take over the part of Iago? Mr. Aherne replied that he did not think he could manage to come to the United States just then. His reasons were romantic.

But when the *Othello* opened in New York in January 1937, Aherne was playing the villain. He was the *only* Iago I had seen, or have ever seen, who convinced me that he was the Iago Shakespeare had in mind when he wrote the play. For me, every other Iago had been made to look much too old. The text tells us quite specifically that he has "looked upon the world for four times seven years" (I, iii, 312), and it does not require a course in higher mathematics to conclude that he is twenty-eight. The usual Iago is made to look at least as old as Othello, if not older. Alfred Drake complained to me that though he knew that Iago should be a young man, his director at Stratford, Connecticut, insisted that since Earle Hyman made a youthful-looking Othello, Alfred would simply have to be his senior; it was also thought logical that the manipulating villain be older than the Moor. But, more importantly, every Iago I have seen, with the exception of first Brian Aherne, and, years later, Alfred Drake, was made up to look so villainous that anyone in his right mind would have kept such a man at the greatest possible distance instead of, as Othello does, having him acting as his ensign ("ancient") constantly by his side. Now, the only way to explain Iago's long success before his unmasking at the end is to make him the kind of man who invites companionship. It is true that he is often caustic, bawdy, rude in his speech—but that is part of the game he is playing as the blunt, frank, *honest* soldier; let others be courteous and gallant but as for himself, he implies, he prefers to say just what he thinks, which, of course, is what (save in his soliloquies—and not always in them) he never does. Brian Aherne was never handsomer, never more dashing than as Iago. And that was obviously perfect for the part. Such a man is a thousand times more dangerous than one whose villainy breathes through every pore of his body.

A few years ago at Founder's Night at The Players Club I told Mr. Aherne that he was the first and thus far only completely satisfying Iago I had ever seen, the only one who had made the part truly credible. He was, I am glad to say, pleased, for I was not trying to flatter him, and he told me something astonishing. A few days after the phone call from Max Gordon, Aherne was being asked about his acting plans by Douglas Fairbanks. He mentioned the Iago he had rejected. Fairbanks looked at him in amazement, gave him a considerable blow on the chest, called him a damned fool, and commanded him to call up Gordon at once and accept. Didn't Aherne realize it was one of the greatest parts Shakespeare had ever created? Fairbanks admitted that he would have given his eyeteeth for such an opportunity. Fairbanks then went on to discuss his understanding of the part. Iago must not be made "senselessly malevolent"; he is a highly intelligent fellow, gifted with biting wit; his bitterness about having been superseded by the much less able

Cassio was perfectly valid. (The latter observation is, of course, a serious oversimplification, though it is true that Iago is a better soldier than Cassio. I did not bother to speak of my objections to Mr. Aherne. After all, the lines in the play do not justify such a simple-minded explanation, no matter what Iago says in the opening scene, and there was therefore no way for Mr. Aherne to show that *that* was the root of his wickedness. I am happy to say that no one would have guessed from his dashing performance that such was his interpretation.)

Pursued by "feminine recriminations," he called Gordon back and accepted the part. Now, Walter Huston, though damned by the critics as too much like Dodsworth, too American an Othello, certainly made of the hero a highly intelligible creation, but a man without poetry in his soul. And, of course, an Othello without poetry is not Othello. Aherne said that noting Huston's shortcomings he decided that he would give Iago "a bravura performance, with all the flash, fire, and humor that I could." He certainly lived up to his intentions. Walter Huston generously insisted that Aherne be listed as costar with him. It is amusing to know that Robert Edmond Jones, who directed, was in despair over Aherne's interpretation, and left little notes for him saying things like, "Brian, Iago is *evil, slimy,* and *dark.* He must *horrify* the audience, not fascinate them!" But Aherne would not abandon what he was sure was right, the Muses be praised. Huston himself never objected. One critic had the wisdom to declare that this was "the greatest Iago of our generation." But the production ran for only three weeks. Huston's comment was only, "Well, I'm afraid they didn't like me." He had invested heavily in the production, and lost a great deal of money. The production did not deserve to fail. With all his weaknesses, Huston was a far better Othello than many I have seen.

A few years later Aherne married a very young girl who unexpectedly became a movie star. One day she discovered the notices for his Iago on his desk, and, overcome with jealousy, destroyed them.

Flora Robson (b. 1902) had a season with the Ben Greet Players, then joined Fagan's company in Oxford at the Playhouse, and in 1924 quit the stage for four years. After returning to the theater, she by degrees continued to rise in importance as a West End actress, as well as in the cinema, chiefly in modern plays. She is particularly remarkable in roles calling for a suppressed inner intensity.

A tall woman, and rather plain, she contrived something of a miracle, Agate thought, in her performance of Bianca in *Othello* (1932). Tyrone Guthrie became interested in her potential; to his credit he understood the great reservoir of power which she possessed. In 1933, he took a great chance in casting her in the most unlikely of all roles for such a woman, Isabella, of whom one thinks as all purity and marblelike whiteness; Agate complained that she was all "warring bronze." But for the second half of the play that must have been quite perfect. Shakespeare's characterization of Isabella is that of a young woman who does not understand herself very well at first; we find her, at the beginning, about to enter a convent, the last place on earth, as it turns out, for her; as the revolting hypocrisy of Angelo is at last revealed to her, her personality begins to unfold as her heretofore untapped capacity for anger develops; her anger is magnificent and makes of her a kind of Joan of Arc brandishing a sword against corruption in high places. Flora Robson was well equipped to do magnificently by such requirements.

Again she was surprising in the *Macbeth* which followed (1934). With her figure and ability to project brooding power, one would have expected her to make Lady Macbeth the traditional—and incorrect—tigress. Instead, she wonderfully made of her a loving wife, ambitious for her husband, who could reveal the extremes of agonized remorse in her sleepwalking scene.

Seventeen years later she was performing a fine Paulina to Gielgud's Leontes and Diana Wynyard's Hermione.

She was created Dame of the British Empire in 1960. Despite her successes in the few Shakespearean roles she performed after her apprenticeship, Agate thought that although she is a superb actress, and manages all the mechanics of a role, she is not essentially a Shakespearean tragedienne. Rightly or wrongly, she seems to have been of his opinion; appearing constantly in the West End and sometimes in New York, she has done little Shakespeare during her career.

25

Gielgud and Olivier

Sir John Gielgud and Lord Laurence Olivier for nearly half a century have, beyond possible cavil, been the two leading male Shakespearean actors of our times. No others have achieved more fame in the English-speaking world or have devoted so much of their energies and talents to the plays of Shakespeare. Both men, of course, have appeared in countless non-Shakespearean dramas, serious and comic. Among the very greatest performances I have seen I count Olivier's Oedipus in *Oedipus the King*, Astrov in Chekhov's *Uncle Vanya*, and the title role in Osborne's *The Entertainer*; and Gielgud's Jack (as well as his direction) in *The Importance of Being Earnest*, his Raskolnikov in *Crime and Punishment*, and his (and Richardson's) acting (1970) in Storey's *Home*—acting so magnificent on the part of Gielgud and Richardson that they caused the work to seem very much of a play, while, in fact, like Storey's other pieces for the theater, it is not a play at all. (English actors, as we have noted, because of apprenticeship in classical repertory—Edith Evans is the grand exception—frequently manage to convince you that you are witnessing a fine dramatic work, even though, once the final curtain falls, you realize that what you have been attending is second rate; contemporary American actors can almost never do that.)

Gielgud and Olivier have both been aware for a long time that they are rivals. Alan Dent, who has been involved in some of Olivier's presentations (disastrously in the film of *Hamlet*) and is a good friend, asks why it is necessary to compare the two. Does anyone bother, he demands, to ask the traveler who knows Italy whether he prefers Florence to Venice? Well, I know that if Dent asked me I could answer that question without hesitation and institute all sorts of comparisons between the two cities, in both of which I have lived for long periods of time. Florence is masculine, Venice feminine; Florence's splendor is powerful and stern in all its exteriors; Venice's is that of an enchantress and is chiefly a matter of *externals*; the almost forbidding elegance of Florence's old buildings is to be seen on all sides of the edifice; the exquisite facades of Venice's old buildings front the canals, but the approach along the sides to the entrance is usually through mean and cramped streets; Florence, like New York, is too hot in the summer and uncomfortably cold in the winter; Venice has only two weeks of fiercely hot weather, and its winters are much milder; Florence is a city to live in: it has opera, concerts, theater, recitals, ballet—all of high quality, all year long—yes, it is still the "Athens" of Italy; Venice has all these things for the very few months of the tourist season, and most of it is supplied by visiting companies and orchestras and performers: for the rest of the year its one open theater, a jewel indeed, the Fenice, is closed most of the time, and owns a third-rate opera company and orchestra. After the tourist season Venice is a highly unintellectual and inartistic city, where an individual who is alone might die of aesthetic starvation. Finally, inside the uncompromising severities of Florence's old palaces everything is luxuriant beauty; behind the lovely facades of Venice's *palazzi* are rooms crowded with spurious Tintorettos and Titians, except for the museums and churches, and endless paintings of Venetian scenes.

I could go on, of course. Why should not Gielgud and Olivier be compared, since they know themselves to be rivals?

Audiences more addicted to the cinema than theater doubtless think of Olivier as the superior, because of the five films in which he starred as Orlando, Henry V, Hamlet, Richard III, and Othello. (As I write this it is announced that he will soon be seen as Shylock on TV in the United States.) Gielgud has never starred in a Shakespearean movie, and it is significant that Roger Manvell's huge triple-columned 574 pages of small type, the *International Encyclopedia of Film*, while having a sizeable article on Olivier, does not even mention Gielgud's name. Yet, for all Olivier's brilliance as an actor, of the two Gielgud is by far the greater Shakespearean. The proof of the matter can be witnessed in two Shakespearean movies in which Gielgud did take part. When Joseph Mankiewicz assigned him the role of Cassius in his *Julius Caesar* (1952), with James Mason making a very weak and unconvincing Brutus, Marlon Brando a beautiful-looking Mark Antony who spoke as though his mouth were filled with mashed potatoes, Louis Calhern a well-thought-out but very American Caesar, and the settings in their obvious rectangular concrete looking more like Nazi Berlin than ancient Rome, Gielgud, despite all the shortcomings surrounding him, by simply doing his best by the role, walked away with the picture without trying to do so. He also made Cassius as Shakespeare had depicted him, not villainous or insidious, but intelligent, as patriotic as Brutus but more human, and sympathetic. It was a beautiful performance, and the only question plaguing one was why *he* had not been cast as Brutus.

One had a more precise basis for comparison of Olivier and Gielgud in *Richard III*. Olivier's Richard was wonderful in its serpentine viciousness, and one was filled with admiration for him—until Gielgud was on screen in the very minor role of Clarence. (The part is so subsidiary that Ronald Hayman's biography of Gielgud makes no reference to it.) Yet, after his brief appearance, when Gielgud made his final exit, one suddenly became aware of the fact that Olivier has no end of cleverness in his technique, but that one never forgot that he as Richard was *acting,* and that his skills added up to a bag of marvelous tricks, in contrast to Gielgud's simple eloquence and identification with the role. Once more, in a part far less important than that of Cassius, he dwarfed everyone else in the film.

If I speak in terms of an implied competitiveness between the two men, it is no more than Olivier himself has expressed. He has said, for instance, that his reason for accepting Tyrone Guthrie's invitation to go to the Old Vic to do Hamlet was that Gielgud had already shown himself to be the Hamlet of his generation, and that he knew he was putting himself up "in a kind of stupid rivalry." He has also stated a lifelong admiration for Gielgud "with complete devotion," but he also knows that each of them is a different kind of actor; Gielgud has been "all spirituality, all beauty," while Olivier thought of himself as "all earth, blood, humanity,"—even the more ignoble parts of humanity without the beauty; he felt that Gielgud missed the human realism, and that was why Olivier concentrated upon it; he was conscious that this difference implied a rivalry between them both "that might last all our lives."

On the other hand, when Gielgud and Olivier alternated the roles of Romeo and Mercutio, Gielgud said that Olivier started out, as Romeo, with the advantage of "looking like a handsome young Italian" (Does anyone think of Romeo as other than English? Shakespeare certainly did not.) and fulfilled and went beyond all expectations in the role, but that his flaw was a noticeable "deficiency in poetic feeling." (Romeo *is* the most lyrical of Shakespeare's tragic heroes.) Gielgud further conceded that Olivier had "a great advantage over me" in vitality, handsomeness, "brilliant humour, and passionate directness"; he was, moreover an excellent fencer, and as Mercutio his fight with Tybalt was "breath-taking" as a prologue to Mercutio's death.

I do not admit Olivier's contention that Gielgud is more "abstract" because he does more for the beauties of Shakespeare, and that he himself is more convincing because he is more earthy. Quite the contrary. Olivier is a man who spares no pains in making himself *look* the role he is playing— he constantly changes the shape of his nose and the effect of his own face —and has a most fertile invention for details that enlarge his interpretation of the part, and when he is at his best he is always impressive and exciting. But he has never, when doing Shakespeare, allowed me to forget that I am to admire his skill, which I gladly do, or that he is *playing* a part. Even so, if Gielgud were not there to invite comparisons, I should probably think Olivier our best Shakespearean actor, when *he* is at his best. But Gielgud *is* there, and when he is doing Shakespeare I am not aware of his skill or his technique, but only of the character he is portraying and the beauty of the lines he delivers.

I have seen both men quite frequently in Shakespearean and non-Shakespearean roles, and I feel strongly that Gielgud is always at his best in

Shakespeare, often good in plays by others, and sometimes very poor—as when he did Jason to Judith Anderson's Medea, and in a hopelessly muddled play by the usually gifted Edward Albee, *Tiny Alice.* Yet his performances as Hamlet, Benedick, Prospero, Richard II, and Lear were perfection. Olivier, on the contrary, though a first-rate Coriolanus, Mercutio, Henry V, and Hotspur, was one of the worst Hamlets and Romeos (though in the latter case the production I saw in New York was so idiotically staged that no one could have survived it) I have ever seen, and his Othello was beneath contempt. Yet, when he is not doing Shakespeare, no one is better, as witness his Stanhope in *Journey's End,* Julian in *The Green Bay Tree,* Bothwell in *Queen of Scots,* Oedipus, Astrov, Macheath, Berenger (in *Rhinoceros*), Archie Rice (in *The Entertainer*), and in many movies like *Wuthering Heights, Pride and Prejudice,* and *Spartacus.* Perhaps he is the greatest non-Shakespearean actor of our time, despite his devotion to Shakespeare's plays. An important segment of the disparities between these two great actors is the early hint of Gielgud's; it is to the poetry of Shakespeare that Olivier pays the least attention, while no one in our time has revealed a more sensitive ear to it than Gielgud. While Shakespeare is the world's greatest dramatist, he is also incontestably the world's greatest poet—and the great Shakespearean actor must do justice to both.

There is another matter which had also better be gone into briefly, and that is Olivier's notion that he is doing better by Shakespeare by being "more realistic." Gielgud has made the wise point that modern actors think that all parts of a Shakespearean play should be made naturalistic; instead, they ought to select those moments which should be made naturalistic, for the simple reason that when Shakespeare wishes to be naturalistic he is quite plainly so; e.g., Lear's "Pray you, undo this button" or Cleopatra's "Do you not see the baby at my breast that sucks the nurse asleep?" or Lady Macbeth's "All the perfumes of Arabia will not sweeten this little hand." Such moments could not be simpler or more moving, but they are moments which are more beautiful when combined, as Gielgud says, "with the rich scaffolding" already erected around them. As for realism, Edith Evans once told Gielgud that she would never enact the role of a mother losing her child unless she could make the women in the audience say that that actress on stage "knows more about a mother losing a child than I do,"—and that requires acting the part not in terms of everyday realism, but larger than life. That is a principle, of course, governing everything that is done on stage.

John Gielgud (b. 1904) is a grand-nephew of Ellen Terry, and doubtless it is from her that he inherits his histrionic gifts. When he was seven he received as a Christmas present from his mother a toy theater, all gold and cream, three feet wide, with a red velvet curtain. Little Jack at once transformed his toy soldiers into actors, costumed them and painted them; he supplemented these figures with others from his sister's dollhouse, including furniture and a tiny grand piano. That sister, Eleanor, was often the sole audience; when other children were present, she functioned in the "box office." The youthful Gielguds were still enjoying their miniature theater when Jack was fifteen. Their grandmother, the former Kate Terry, Ellen's sister, had given up the stage early, but she often took the children to West End matinées, where they usually sat in a box; frequently she would take them behind the scenes to meet the actors whom they had been enjoying. Among the plays which the youngsters invented and exhibited were such as had the thrilling titles of *Kill That Spy!*, *Plots in the Harem*, and *Lady Fawcett's Ruby*. By the time Jack was ten he was considering becoming an actor himself.

At school he took part in dramatics and at the age of eleven was stage manager for *The Merchant of Venice*, in which he also was the Shylock.

Next he fell in love with stage designing, and went as often as he could to see plays and the ballet. While still in school at Westminster, although his parents wished him to specialize in history at Oxford, he definitely made up his mind at the age of sixteen to be an actor. They agreed to allow him to try the profession on the promise that if he had not become a success by the age of twenty-five, he was to turn architect. At this period he was rather taken with the possibilities of his looks; he was forever washing his hair to make it look fluffy—he has for years now been completely bald—and even sported a monocle on a string.

During the holidays he was participating in amateur theatricals. In an open-air production he was Orlando—catastrophically so at the first performance. Brandishing his sword as he crossed the grass to intrude on the duke's repast, with the line, "Forbear and eat no more!" he tripped over a log and fell headlong on his face; in the last act, as he pointed in the direction whence Rosalind was to appear, on the line, "Ah, here comes my Ganymede," he was dismayed to see no Ganymede appearing. He repeated the line much more loudly, without result. From the other side the prompter was trying desperately to make him understand that Ganymede had changed clothes into those of Rosalind one scene prematurely.

In the spring of 1921 he was at the drama school conducted by Rosina Filippi (a former creditable member of Tree's company), who was so much pleased with Jack's Mercutio that she wrote to his parents predicting a fine future for him. In July he applied for a scholarship at Lady Benson's drama school, and he won a year's tuition free.

Learning that students of the drama could, without salary, take walk-on parts at the Old Vic, he went there. It was very exciting to be in a real theater at last, even though it was a dirty one, and the supernumeraries had to change clothes in an upper box with only a curtain to shield them from the audience.

His first professional appearance occurred in November of 1921, as the Herald in *Henry V*. He had one line only: "Here is the number of the slaughtered French," but he did that so badly that he was demoted to a walk-on part in the plays that followed.

In 1922 he was invited by his second cousin, Phyllis Neilson-Terry, to go on tour with her in a small part and understudy the lead in a modern play.

Once he was called upon to play one of the major roles, though not the lead which he had understudied, and he did very well in it. A month later, when the company was at Oxford, his second cousin allowed him to play the part again for his parents' sake. This time he did very badly.

He next won a scholarship at the Academy of Dramatic Art (now the Royal Academy), and among his teachers he was most impressed by Claude Rains. He deliberately imitated him as well as other actors whom he admired.

Nigel Playfair, a friend of Jack's mother, offered him the role of the Poet Butterfly in the Capek Brothers' *Insect Play,* which though a great success in New York (as *The World We Live In*), an unforgettable experience, ran for only six weeks during its London première. Claude Rains was in the cast. During all this time Gielgud was still studying at the Academy.

Gielgud has said that the first time he was convinced he could act was when he took the part of Trofimov in *The Cherry Orchard* (1924) at the Oxford Playhouse. But ever since he had been a walk-on at the Old Vic it was Shakespeare that he yearned to do. He read everything he could get his hands on about the classic actors, and he was burning to do Hamlet and Richard II.

In 1924 he was playing Romeo opposite Gwen Ffrangcon-Davies at the Regent Theatre, and by his own confession he made "a frightful mess of it." His costume was wrong, his wig was frightful; he was only nineteen but he did not know how to move; in short, he was not yet ready for the great plays.

After playing a considerable number of parts at various theaters, Gielgud went to the Old Vic in 1929, and in September appeared as Romeo, with Martita Hunt as the Nurse and Donald Wolfit as Tybalt. Harcourt Williams, the director, declared that Gielgud's performance was the least interesting he had seen during his own two years at the Old Vic. So much for our greatest Shakespearean actor when he was twenty-five.

But in November he began to come into his own with Richard II. By this time Williams listened eagerly to Gielgud's many suggestions for the various productions, and often sought his help with various scenes. Williams later testified that Gielgud's ideas were never advanced for the sake of glorifying his own part, and that his effect upon the whole company was now "electric."

Richard II is an ideal role for him. He is gifted with an extraordinarily beautiful voice, capable of exquisite lyricism, yet having nothing in common with the old oratorical, coloratura style once so popular. The play itself, as Gielgud understood, has innumerable "graphic descriptions of things and places," and he taught himself to summon up the same color images for such passages in every performance. For that play and for many others, Gielgud has one extraordinary advantage. He has admitted that his tear ducts are ready to flow as his voice gives off certain cadences. A friend of mine who was in the cast of the recent Richard Burton *Hamlet,* which Gielgud directed, told me that when Gielgud would stop an actor and demonstrate the way he should like to hear a passage sound, his eyes would overflow at his own eloquence. (This facility with tears was of invaluable help in his performance of *Home*; indeed, it was probably the chief ingredient in so profoundly moving the audience.) His last scenes as Richard were so touching that at the final curtain the audience went wild. Ivor Brown, who had described Gielgud's Romeo as meaningless "from the waist down . . . He has the most meaningless legs imaginable," called his Richard "exquisite." Williams said that his performance of the abdication scene was one of the great things of the modern theater.

His next part under Williams was as Oberon, and he has said that the beautiful language moved him so much at rehearsals that "tears would spring to my eyes." What really astonished everyone was when, in March 1930, he made so great a success with Macbeth. Like Irving, he entered for his first appearance with his sheathed sword over his shoulder, but he could not figure how to get rid of it until it occurred to him to let it drop in his surprise as being hailed king; he managed to increase his age and weight by rehearsing in heavy robes, and like Ellen Terry he knew how to make a cloak act. (Gielgud now objects that the photographs of that production make him look too much like a Wagnerian hero.) James Agate hurried into his dressing room to tell him that he had never seen the murder passage better performed; and when he wrote about it in the *Sunday Times* he said it was the first time he had witnessed a Macbeth who maintained "his hold upon the play" until the finish. Ivor Brown praised the actor for having "ripened into a rich masculinity."

On April 28, 1929, at half-past six he opened an uncut *Hamlet*. Gielgud was twenty-six, and the records are scant of young Hamlets; Forbes-Robertson had been forty-four, Irving thirty-seven, John Barrymore forty. His youth only aided him in providing great variety of tone and pitch, and a physical energy to equal his mental celerity. In *Richard II* he had allowed the verse to captivate him; in *Hamlet* he penetrated to the perplexities of the prince's mind, situation, disgust with his surroundings, and love for his murdered father. It was perhaps his first complete triumph in losing John Gielgud to become the hero he was portraying.

Richard II is a play which had been, and is now, rarely performed. Garrick, Kemble, Cooke, and Irving never gave it, and others who did attempt it had mercilessly cut or altered it. Harcourt Williams never forgot Gielgud's tall, slender figure garbed in black in the Westminster Hall scene, his blond head and his pallid "agonized" countenance beneath the radiant crown. When Gielgud did Richard again in 1929, Agate wisely observed that the success of the play depends upon Richard's wedding disaster with the "passion of a bridegroom"; he thought Gielgud missed the artist side of Richard, but did full justice to the "elegiac." He spoke the lines exquisitely but failed to show Richard "revelling in the woes anticipated."

The same season he made a memorable Oberon in a performance which Ivor Brown declared was a production that put the fantasy into the heart of a moonstruck Warwickshire, although one critic found the Oberon sinister; Agate declared it "terrifying" because the makeup reminded him too much of the Ghost in *Hamlet*; later Agate praised Gielgud's Oberon for the exquisite diction which belonged to an age "when it was manly to recite poetry."

Soon Gielgud was making a "radiant" Antony in *Antony and Cleopatra* and a fine Antony in *Julius Caesar*; his sardonic laughter in the latter play at Cassius's offer of a share of the spoils was a master stroke; in the former tragedy Ivor Brown spoke of him admiringly as a "grizzled, bearded Elizabethan who might have sailed with Drake or sonneteered with the Mermaid boys, valiant, melting, melancholy, and yet marching as a Roman to his fall."

The next year, 1931, he was, although only twenty-seven, doing Lear (with Richardson as Kent), and gave notice of the great future awaiting him. One of Harcourt Williams's treasured memories was of Gielgud treading down a steep slope between spears to climb up to his elevated throne, giving an unusual twist of Lear's neck "as if the head were too heavy for it, which gave at once a sense of mental danger." In recollection the actor himself said that he had been "wholly inadequate" in the great storm scenes, lacking, as he did, both the physique and the voice for them: "Lear has to *be* the storm, but I could do no more than shout against the thunder-sheet"; the only scene which satisfied him was the one with the Fool when he takes leave of Goneril. The critics, however, imply that Gielgud was far too severe with himself for his bold undertaking. (*King Lear* was still held, as Charles Lamb had implied, to be unactable, and in his curtain speech the young actor declared that the tragedy "shrieks aloud to be acted.")

He had performed *Hamlet* in 1930, and in November of 1934 he produced it himself in the West End. Trewin has called that performance, which ran for 155 consecutive times—a record shorter only than Irving's original production at the Lyceum—the "key Shakespearean revival of its period. It was a West End victory" for the production of Shakespeare. (Incidentally, Gielgud gave Alec Guinness, who at the time was almost penniless, his first opportunity by engaging him as Osric.) It is odd that at first the critics, though favorable, were not as enthusiastic as they should have been; perhaps, as Hayman suggests, it is unfair to judge an actor on opening night, when he is likely to be exhausted by rehearsals and particularly so when, as in this case, he has also been harassed by the thousand concerns of a director. Agate had declared the 1930 Old Vic venture as fine a performance as could within reason be demanded, but perhaps a little deficient in pathos and a little too musical in the closet scene with Gertrude; however, he conceded, it was "noble in conception." Nevertheless, for the new Hamlet he decided that it was a trifle disappointing in everything that followed the interview with the Ghost (I,v), though never failing to rise to the "highest of its poetry" or sensitivity to its philosophy; the whole interpretation abounded "in loveliness" but Agate felt that Gielgud's "treasury could yield more." Less than five years later the same commentator found "an immense advance" and "an increasing vigor" in Gielgud's prince. But Charles Morgan wrote of Gielgud's Hamlet that "it is of such a rank as will entitle it to be remembered and debated for years to come," and W. A. Darlington called it "The first Hamlet of our time," adding, "There can have been few to equal him in the long history of our English stage."

In 1936 he brought the production to New York. Rosamund Gilder, who wrote a book on the subject, praised it for never being blurred in conception. As she saw it, we first found the prince "frozen in grief, rage and futility." The violent nausea he has experienced over his mother's second marriage was clearly evident in his first soliloquy; what followed was a series of climaxes which were the mirror of his imagination, sufferings, actions—all of which violated his own basic nature, which was contemplative, reasoning, and analytical. That is, indeed, an excellent summation of Gielgud's interpretation.

I saw that production in 1936, and I count it and Barrymore's the two greatest Hamlets I have seen in my lifetime; Barrymore's was perhaps a more unified interpretation but not at all a poetic one; Gielgud's was equally powerful and, of course, marvelously true to the poetry. It matters not that, after more than thirty years' study of the play, I find myself in total disagreement with the interpretations of both actors. This is not the place to argue my objections, for I have already published a book expounding what I believe Shakespeare meant by the play—among other things, that Hamlet is never mad, never pretends to be mad, and never procrastinates. But granting Gielgud his premises, his was a piece of virtuosity, not one detail of which I can ever forget.

One overpowering section at the end of Act I, which was absolutely right and performed with a brilliance that staggers description, was after the Ghost has made his revelations and departed. If I may quote myself:

It was acting of sheer genius. Here only, if anywhere in the tragedy, is Hamlet near nervous collapse:

> Hold, my heart,
> And you, my sinews, grow not instant old,
> But bear me stiffly up!

He staggers about, clasping his head between his hands as though the beating inside it would deprive him of his reason ("in this distracted globe"). To most men the narrative of the Ghost might have indeed proved too much: to hear that solemn voice . . . of a deeply loved father —to learn of that spirit's endurance of the flames of Purgatory . . . —to hear of his mother's adultery, of his father's murder, of his hated uncle's criminality—to have the burden of vengeance thrust upon him —all this, without preparation, laid upon him suddenly—and to have the horrible tale cap the bitterness in which his father's death and mother's hasty marriage have already plunged him—even the mightiest of men might have been undone by such a stroke. But not Hamlet. Small wonder, however, that he reels; the world . . . has just tumbled about his ears.

But he is given no time for ordered reflection; before his whirling thoughts have spent themselves—in a mere twenty lines—Horatio and Marcellus are upon him. He has not even had time to recover some degree of self-control.

Only Gielgud has understood how ill-prepared Hamlet is at this moment to speak to anyone. He is bursting with what he has been told, and the lines prove that he is *on the verge of disclosing everything*:

MARCELLUS: How is 't, my noble lord?
HORATIO: What news, my lord?
HAMLET: O, wonderful!
HORATIO: Good my lord, tell it.
HAMLET: No, you'll reveal it.
HORATIO: Not I, my lord, by Heaven.
MARCELLUS: Nor I, my lord.
HAMLET: How say you, then, would heart of man once think it?
    But you'll be secret?
HORATIO & MARCELLUS: Ay, by Heaven, my lord.
HAMLET: There's ne'er a villain dwelling in all Denmark . . .

He is about to add "like my uncle." Characteristically, Hamlet . . . is on the point of ruining everything. Human, all too human, he rushes to the comfort of sharing the weight of what he has heard. But, characteristically too, just in time he stops the torrent of his words. Gielgud conveyed all this marvelously; at the end of the last line quoted, he suddenly ceased, looked in dazed bewilderment at both men, clapped a hand over his mouth to dam the current, and staggered away almost drunkenly, while muttering

> But he's an arrant knave.

Words—anything to finish the sentence which he has nearly terminated by a revelation that could have proved fatal to his cause. . . . Surely this is precisely what Shakespeare intended. . . .

—even though Kittredge described the passage as Hamlet's speaking "flippantly of the Ghost," and J. Q. Adams found the words to be "so much nonsense."

John Barrymore's interpretation, wonderful in many places, was annoyingly consistent with such views; he took each of the men around the shoulder, led them up to the footlights, assumed at first a conspiratorial air, played up the suspense of what he was about to reveal, and delivered "But he's an arrant knave," as though it were all a great joke, and moved off in handsome profile with an airy wave of his hand. It was a rather flip and revolting moment.

What weaknesses the Gielgud *Hamlet* demonstrated were a result of his accepting as Gospel some of the wild theories of J. Dover Wilson, who had recently published *What Happens in Hamlet*. J. Dover Wilson, editor of the Cambridge edition of Shakespeare, was for several decades held to be the high priest of Shakespearean scholarship, and in that lofty position enunciated some fairly incredible assertions and inventions concerning the plays. He did some astonishing glossing of words, which tended to be immediately accepted, coming from so eminent a source: e.g., when Hamlet sees Ophelia reading in her little holy book, after his "To be or not to be" soliloquy, his:

> Soft you now!
> The fair Ophelia! Nymph in thy orisons
> Be all my sins remembered!

was interpreted by Wilson thusly—*fair Ophelia* lacks warmth (though *Fair Portia* [*Merchant of Venice*, I, i, 162] does not!), there is a "touch of affectation" in *nymph* and *orisons* (though apparently not in *Romeo and Juliet* [IV, iii, 2–4] or in *Paradise Lost,* when at a very solemn moment Milton uses the latter word!) and of "sarcasm" in *Be all my sins remembered.* (Sam Johnson's sensibilities were more alert when he said of the same passage that it was a "touch of nature. Hamlet . . . makes her an address grave and solemn, such as the foregoing meditation excited in his thoughts.") Wilson was also fond of announcing that scenes and stage directions were missing in various plays, and the nonsense we have cited about the brief words of Hamlet to Ophelia was obviously invented to bolster one of Wilson's "discoveries" earlier in the play, a "discovery" which Gielgud unhappily at once adopted. In the second scene of Act II, Polonius informs the king and queen that he has uncovered the fact that Hamlet is mad and that the cause of the madness is Hamlet's love for Ophelia; he promises to "loose" her to the prince at a time and place where the king and himself can overhear the results of his little plot. Wilson insisted that the prince must overhear this plan to trick him, and that a stage direction has been lost. He obligingly supplies it: "Hamlet, disorderly attired and reading a book, enters the lobby by the door at the back; he hears voices from the chamber and pauses beside one of the curtains, unobserved." Gielgud later admitted that his employing this "restored" stage direction did not clarify "the meaning sufficiently to warrant the trouble we took with it"; he was increasingly sure, when playing this bit, that "if Shakespeare had meant Hamlet to overhear something, he would surely have made it clear in the text. The play has much spying in it . . . but in each case it is Hamlet who is spied upon." This judgment is sound, and Gielgud might have added that: 1. when both sides spy on each other, we are in the realm of comedy, not tragedy, and 2. this gratuitously "restored" stage direction makes the later scene with Ophelia, instead of being better explained, almost unplayable. The reason I have gone so much into the matter is that because of the great prestige of Gielgud's wonderful production, *it has more or less become a tradition to play the scene in the second act the same way.* There have been few *Hamlets* since the mid-1930s which do not introduce what is essentially a ridiculous and crippling, not to say spurious, action.

In 1935 Gielgud and Olivier presented *Romeo and Juliet* at the New Theatre, exchanging the parts of Romeo and Mercutio, with Gielgud as director. Agate commended Olivier as looking the part of a lover and a moving one as such, but complained that he missed all the poetry of the lines, ran the words all together in a line, and cut off each verse from the following one in a staccato style; Gielgud's Mercutio he found beautiful, but not Shakespeare's, for it was an interpretation built around the Queen Mab speech; Peggy Ashcroft "implied" Juliet, without playing her. When Gielgud did Romeo, Agate thought him marvelous in the poetry, though he seemed in love only with himself. One night, as Mercutio, Gielgud made so large a gesture with torch in hand that the soaked wadding fell out and ignited the stage cloth; valiantly Gielgud stamped on it, but his shoe caught fire; he trod one foot on the other until the flame was extinguished. The audience applauded him loudly. But thereafter the lighted torches were banned as a hazard. In a broadcast, Agate eventually gave his preference to Gielgud: if the lover "were just a lovesick gumph," who occasionally, falling into a trance, speaks "unaccountable poetry," then Olivier is Romeo; but if what you wish is Shakespeare's "analytical and critical lover, then Gielgud is your man." Of the production itself Gielgud later declared he had been rather "showy" as Romeo, and remembered Ralph Richardson saying to him that when Olivier leaned against the balcony and looked up, the audience immediately had the whole scene; Gielgud admitted being jealous of Olivier for being like "a young panther," while he himself had been "draping myself about the stage . . . thinking myself very romantic." It is possibly this capacity for self-criticism, not common among actors, which has enabled Gielgud to be the greatest Shakespearean of his age.

It is a further tribute to his integrity that when he was Shylock in 1938 at the Queen's Theatre, he miraculously followed Shakespeare's intentions by making the Jew subordinate in the play to Portia. (I have never seen that done except when I directed the play.) His Shylock looked drab, was not sentimentalized, bore a scraggy beard, and seemed to have bleary eyes; he was very much the outsider in Venice.

Agate was dissatisfied with his Lear of 1940; the actor lacked the physique on which to build the "patriarchal" become prematurely old; this shortcoming Agate felt most in the storm scenes, where Lear "must be as old as the elements." Nevertheless, there was, as always with Gielgud, great beauty in the verse.

The same year he was Prospero in a set that aimed to "make the pageant insubstantial"; he was compared to an El Greco in appearance. The date coincided with the fall of Dunkirk and the collapse of France. It was a decade before this theater opened again. The Old Vic retained its organization in the provinces during the autumn of 1940. In 1942 Gielgud produced *Macbeth* again in London; Agate declared it a performance of great variety. In the succeeding years he repeated some of his former successes: Hamlet (1944) and Oberon (same year) among them. He did Benedick in 1950 as well as Lear and Leontes in 1951, Prospero, Benedick and Lear again, and Othello (1961). In 1959 he was Benedick to Margaret Leighton's Beatrice; I have never seen a more perfect *Much Ado about Nothing*. She was an irresistible woman, matching wit for wit with him, yet both managed to convey, beneath their barrage of insults, that they were powerfully drawn to each other, and the Church scene was enchanting in its romantic smashing of the walls which had never really divided them. Brooks Atkinson of *The New York Times* believed that Gielgud's Benedick was exactly what Shakespeare had had in mind.

Gielgud has appeared in some one hundred fifty plays, many of them in several productions. His highly successful one-man show *The Ages of Man* was created as a result of an invitation to give a "recital" at the house of Lady Astor in St. James's Square, with interspersed pieces played on the lute by Julian Bream. The title was taken from George Ryland's anthology of the same name, and Gielgud used a similar division: youth, maturity, and old age. He had no idea that what he was putting together would ever be seen by the general public. He made a wonderful collection of speeches and poems, ordered with perfect taste and style, and delivered with all the resources of his eloquent voice: some characters he merely indicated, concentrating on the poetry; others, like Richard II, Hamlet, Leontes, Macbeth, and Lear he acted out fully. In August 1957 he was asked to give the program at the Edinburgh Festival, where he presented passages from seventeen Shakespearean plays; a member of the audience was heard to remark on leaving that it had been like listening to a program of great music by an orchestra. In October he took the program to Berlin and Paris, then to Milan and the Holland Festival. In September of the next year he embarked on a tour of Canada and the United States, and was heard in Toronto, Kingston, Ottawa, Montreal, Corning, among other places. In thirteen weeks he had traveled eighteen thousand miles and his audiences varied in number from a few hundred to five thousand at a time. After a brief rest, including Christmas in Cuba, he opened in New York at the 46th Street Theater: his first-night audience included such stars as Lillian Gish, Katherine Hepburn, Marlene Dietrich, and Mary Martin. Brooks Atkinson in the *Times* declared it an event of the first importance, and the program a masterpiece. Walter Kerr observed that whatever Gielgud was seeing during his renditions, the audience saw too, "the fusion of mind and matter is perfect." Basil Rathbone said it was "the ultimate," something he could never have anticipated hearing; John Steinbeck felt uplifted as if by great music, "which, of course, this is." The season had to be extended for two weeks, and there was a lively traffic in black-market tickets.

Trewin has proved unhappily clairvoyant in his thoughts on the effect of this great presentation. Because of the actor's "triumphant command of the vocal line," it was speech just as Shakespeare's should be spoken; but for the newer generation of actors and spectators it was wasted genius, for they have come to expect speech which is "rough and lumpish," filled with belligerent "swagger"; a new snobbery, Trewin foresaw, would disdain fine speech, would deliver verse without shape or form, like the acting it would approve, would prefer lumping vowels and consonants together like the contents of a "junk shop."

It was a matter of astonishment to me that a man who could be so cool and critical in appraisal of his own work should have been capable of expressing to me one of the most exaggerated pieces of misjudgment I have ever heard. When *Home* and two other British companies were in New York a few years ago, The Players invited members of all three casts to a Christmas celebration; on that occasion Sir John, after an affable chat, urged me not to miss the Peter Brook *Midsummer Night's Dream* which was due in New

York very soon; he said, "It is a very great production." I took his advice and saw it: I have rarely seen anything worse, more vulgar, and even obscene. But of that, more later.

Laurence (first Sir, now Lord) Olivier (b. 1907) was born in Dorking, the son of an Anglican clergyman, and was sent to All Saints Choir School when about nine years of age. In contrast to the drabness of low-church ceremony, that of the high Anglican was, Olivier has said, deliberately flamboyant and even theatrical. The priests were pleased to think they were on good terms with actors like Sybil Thorndike and Forbes-Robertson; the theater was eminently respectable—Irving had made it so. The youngsters, therefore, were very much involved in their own dramatic enterprises and celebrated stars would come to see them.

When Forbes-Robertson saw the young Laurence in *Julius Caesar,* he remarked to the lad's father, "He *is* Brutus." He was ten at the time. Eventually Ellen Terry came to see the play, and she said: "The boy who plays the part of Brutus is already a great actor." When Laurence asked his father how soon he could follow his brother to India and become a rubber planter, since he did not care to go to the university, the Rev. Mr. Olivier said, "Nonsense, you're going to be an actor."

But his father also made it clear to him that he would not go on stage unless he finished the Central School, where he came under the influence of Elsie Fogarty. At the age of seventeen he had to take his examination for a scholarship, and was placed upon a platform some ten yards away from Miss Fogarty. He recited the "Seven Ages of Man" speech, after which she called him to sit beside her; she told him that he gave too much importance to action, and pointed out to him that it had been unnecessary to indulge in the motions of fencing at "Sudden and quick to quarrel." Then she added something peculiar: she ran her little finger down the middle of his forehead, and said: "You have a weakness here and remember that." Olivier thinks it was that remark which for years made him "slap on all that putty" on his face.

In his early career he was given parts at the Court Theatre with Barry Jackson, and after various roles was playing Uncle Vanya when only nineteen. After that he was starred in very "showy" parts in the West End, such as Stanhope in *Journey's End* and *Beau Geste;* there were no indications that he would ever be interested in the classics. He knew he wished to be seen in the West End, that he wanted money, "violently" wished to get married, and to be a great success. He was fairly confident that he would reach the heights. He thoroughly enjoyed playing with Noel Coward in *Private Lives,* and was more than grateful to him for his brilliant criticism, and for being the first person to cut him off when he was talking nonsense. Coward also encouraged him to read *Wuthering Heights, Of Human Bondage, The Old Wives' Tale,* and *The Forsyte Saga.* From those he went on to Dickens, which his master at the choir school had said would be invaluable to an actor. Coward also did something else important for him. Olivier had been fired twice, and

Coward noticed that he was a giggler; during the run of *Private Lives* in London and New York, he helped Olivier cure himself of the habit, taught him to giggle when the play called for it, and only then.

All his early ambitions have been fulfilled: the West End, money, success, getting to the top, and his "violent" desire to be married, for he has been married three times, first to the actress Jill Esmond, next to Vivien Leigh, with whom for years he acted—both these marriages ending in divorce—and in 1961 he married his present wife, Joan Plowright, with whom he has also frequently appeared.

His penchant for strenuous physical action in the parts he performs he has explained as originating in his being "absolutely swept overboard" as a youth by the films of Douglas Fairbanks, John Barrymore, Rudolph Valentino, Ramon Navarro (in *Ben Hur*), and Milton Sills; he thought of himself as "a sort of Tarzan," and he worked hard to develop the virile biceps, chest, and torso of his cinema heroes.

As we have noted, he joined Gielgud at the New Theatre in 1935, where they alternated in the roles of Romeo and Mercutio. He was already determined to challenge Gielgud's preeminence. Although, as we have seen, Gielgud admired and even envied his success as Romeo for his tremendous energy, Agate, as we have also noted, was displeased with the way he murdered the verse. The contrast between Gielgud's classic elegance and Olivier's realism, although there was but three years' difference between the two young men, seemed very broad indeed. Against Gielgud's wishes as director, Olivier played Romeo as a "tousled" rash Italian adolescent, almost suffocating with emotion. St. John Ervine and Herbert Farjeon thought him the best actor they had seen in the role; Ivor Brown praised his sincerity, but declared him a prosaic Romeo; most of the press was unsympathetic. As Mercutio he was more generally praised. "I was trying to sell realism in Shakespeare," he later reminisced.

During the long run of *Romeo and Juliet* Olivier made a film in which he played Orlando to the Rosalind of Elizabeth Bergner (b. 1900). This Viennese actress, for a while greatly overrated because of her exaggerated coyness which expressed itself in the most eccentric mannerisms (someone once said that he was always prepared to see her wrap a leg around her neck and suck on a toe to express an emotional state), certainly put Olivier at a great disadvantage, though his efforts were noble. There is surely no accent in English more disagreeable than the Germanic, and in Shakespeare's poetry—! Even Olivier's insufficient command of verse seemed satisfactory in comparison. Agate protested that her performance was too *gamine* and too wilting under stress; Rosalind, he reminded us, was a patrician. Bergner's Rosalind at sixty, he averred, would be a "sousy" *Hausfrau*, whereas Shakespeare's Rosalind at that age would be another Lady Bracknell.

Olivier joined the Old Vic in 1937, and it was there that he made his reputation as a Shakespearean actor. That year, under the direction of Tyrone Guthrie, he enacted Hamlet. Guthrie had been impressed by the nonsense Dr. Ernest Jones had written about Hamlet's problem—an ad-

vanced case of the Oedipus complex. This psychoanalyst had said that the
prince was a victim of psychoneurosis—which is to say that the "buried" part
of Hamlet's mind, which was once his as an infant, was still living with "the
adult mentality" which should have replaced it; Hamlet hates Claudius for
successfully doing what he himself unconsciously wished to do—go to bed
with Gertrude; but Hamlet never denounces the king with the same passion
with which he upbraids his mother, for that would merely "stimulate to
activity his unconscious and 'repressed' complexes"; Claudius incorporates
"the deepest and most buried part of his own personality, so that he cannot
kill him without killing himself." Thus wrote the eminent Freudian doctor.
Luckily, the audience was totally unaware of all this during the *Hamlet*
performance—it *is* rather difficult to drag into the lights of the proscenium
anyone's unconscious mind!—and the energetic enactment of the prince,
though puzzling to some, brought Shakespeare's intentions closer to realization than perhaps anyone suspected. His was, as it should be, not some
young member of a philosophy department wandering around without his
nurse, but a strong, virile Hamlet. Agate, limited by the old sentimental view
of the prince's character, found it too jaunty, too much like Beau Geste,
though he liked the vitality and excitement; again, however, he found
Olivier totally deficient in variety of expression, sympathy and poetry, with
the exception of the soliloquies. The London *Times* called it a highly original
performance; Olivier neither aped other Hamlets, nor departed wildly from
convention "but has looked for himself in the part and the part in himself."
In making him quite properly a man of action, Olivier was clearly influenced
by the Hamlet of Barrymore, which he had justly admired. Raymond Mortimer found this prince completely credible and living: "quizzical, protean,
mercurial . . . playing a new part every minute with himself for audience.
[Mortimer here hits upon what I have already hinted is Olivier's chief weakness as a Shakespearean actor. He seems almost always, in Shakespeare, to
be playing as if he himself were the audience.] Mr. Olivier has as many voices
as a ventriloquist, one for each facet of Hamlet's nature." This was an uncut
Hamlet, and Olivier himself may have given the answer to the endless variety
Mortimer had seen and heard. There had been very few rehearsals, and
before the first night Olivier hadn't had the opportunity to go through the
entire uncut version, and therefore, he later said, never knew "what it was
like to go from one scene to another." He had never had the chance to
decide where to take a rest, where breath would be needed, where he dared
let himself go.

He has described himself as a collector of details. A studious observer of
people's behavior, he sometimes has kept what he has seen in his memory
for as many as eighteen years; sooner or later he finds that one or another
of these details serves his needs in a play. He declares that he works "mostly
from the outside in. I usually collect a lot of details . . . and find a creature
swimming about somewhere in the middle of them."

In this connection he considers himself a heretic against what the world
of actors has been talking about for years, the Actors Studio and The

Method. His valid objection to their procedure is that an actor who begins "from the inside" is more apt to "find himself in the parts he plays, than to find the parts in himself." This, inexplicably enough, is, as we have seen, exactly why Morris Carnovsky approves of The Method.

His next undertaking was Sir Toby Belch. With that role began Olivier's elaborate use of makeup to transform his normal appearance probably more than has any other British actor. He gave Toby a beaked nose, a longish mustache, pouches under the eyes, and full scarlet cheeks. It was impossible to discern the Olivier countenance beneath the disguise. He was criticized for overdoing the staggering and stumbling of the old souse, of being *too* comical for the health of *Twelfth Night.* Trewin says his overplaying was like a "veteran Skye terrier, ears pricked for mischief." Jessica Tandy played both Viola and Sebastian, causing the inevitable embarrassment in the recognition scene.

After that came Henry V, a role for which his talents seemed perfect, as the general public was to witness years later in the best Shakespearean movie Olivier ever made. The choice of play was all the more suitable, for this was the coronation season of 1936. But he disliked the play and its glorification of war, and this time underplayed Harry's role; his resemblance to the king's portrait was remarkable—even though his friend, Alan Dent, thought he looked too Chinese, the Oriental impression further accentuated by the actor's "keeping his eyes half-closed throughout the play." The wonderful "tirades" abounding in this history were spoken, Dent said, "as if the verse were an unending series of iambics mounting semitone by semitone," and the variations in volume were entirely arbitrary. Dent was reminded of "the monotonous rise and fall of telegraph wires along a railway track, seen from the rushing train."

But after some weeks, he was suddenly helped into identifying himself with Henry by a few words of Charles Laughton, who told him that the king was "England" and that was all there was to it. His greatest interpretation of the part came later, in 1944, in the best of all his Shakespearean films.

Late in 1937 he appeared as Macbeth at the Old Vic and the New Theatre; the night before the tragedy opened Lilian Baylis died. In an atmosphere that was inevitably unhappy, Olivier, as Agate thought, did not look as though he could cope with Hyrcan tigers, and spoke the lines in too high a voice; the actor was not naturally a bass, and it was difficult for him even to be a baritone; but the last act was fine in the white heat of its energy; Agate thought that Olivier would play the role twice better when he should be twice as old. The effect of the whole production was hindered by the "barbaric décor," the grotesquely scaly witches and a Banquo's ghost which was masked. The incidental music by Milhaud was hopelessly inadequate and upset the whole cast.

Guthrie again had recourse to the theories of Dr. Ernest Jones in presenting *Othello*—this most preposterous of premises, that Iago's conduct is to be explained by a subconscious homosexual desire for the Moor. Richardson, who played Othello, was unaware of the theory—would probably have refused to endure it—was a rather heavy-handed Othello, and Olivier, carrying out Guthrie's (that is to say, Jones's) idea, was a highly "demonstrative" Iago. The result was, inevitably, a confused performance.

But Olivier once more shone when he undertook a role that Garrick had avoided, Coriolanus, in 1938. Agate was profoundly impressed with this characterization both in action and voice, though he did wish that Olivier would stop altering his face with every role. Dent was rhapsodic at the brilliance and fire of the acting, his "Horatian" disgust with the mob, and the delicate tenderness to wife and mother which, by contrast, was all the more eloquent; his very walk spoke pride and eminence, and he proved at last that Shakespearean verse was not beyond his mastery. Ivor Brown observed that the actor's voice had developed wonderfully since he had joined the Old Vic, both in dynamics and passion. Agate elsewhere declared that Olivier, despite his "clowning" and superfluous makeup was the closest of any actor in England to the "heroic tradition"; the only thing that remained to render certain the honor was whether or not he was going to develop a genuine sensitivity for poetry. Olivier himself was not convinced by this laudation, but felt he had been better in his earlier Shakespearean performances; what had impressed the critics, he thought, was the business of his death scene, when he fell down a stairway in a somersault and, rolling over thrice, stopped just behind the footlights.

The London theater was not to see him for six years, during which time he was in films, in New York, and in the Fleet Air Arm. In 1940 I saw him with his wife, Vivien Leigh, on Broadway in *Romeo and Juliet*—or to be honest, I saw the first part of the performance, for our party found the production unendurable. I cannot say whether Olivier was good or bad; it was the production which was insufferable. As I remember it, for the last scene of the first act, there was a large platform on the stage on which all the Capulet guests were huddled, and in the very front, Romeo and Juliet sat, legs dangling, and exchanging their love talk in a spotlight, while all the guests remained silent and immobile; it was an artifice irritating beyond words and had the undesirable effect of a movie. What made us resolve to give up was the opening of the second scene of the next act. Mercutio had exited on the line,

> 'tis vain
> To seek him here that means not to be found.

Whereupon, Olivier popped up like a jack-in-the box on the other side of the wall to declare,

> He jests at scars that never felt a wound.

Another annoyance was the thin shop-girl quality of Miss Leigh's voice. To our amazement, having left the theater and gone to a near-by movie house just in time to see and hear Vivien Leigh receive her award for her Scarlett

O'Hara, we could hardly believe that that rich voice belonged to the same woman whose presence we had fled; electrical amplification, of course, was the reason for the difference.

In 1944 Olivier was with the Old Vic company at the New Theatre in *Richard III*. He fused intellect and dramatic power in a role that is extremely difficult to make convincing; he was, as Trewin has said, "thinker and doer, mind and mask." He limped but there was no limping of mind; his speech raced; his deviltry, his sardonic thoughts, his kingliness were delivered in bravura style. Agate said that he had converted the traditional cyclonic storm to a "polar blast"; his high-pitched voice was a wind that penetrated the ribs; but Agate felt that this was not really Shakespeare's Richard, that at the end it would have been less appropriate to say over the dead villain, "The bloody dog is dead," than "We have scotched the snake *and* killed it." Olivier admitted that Hitler was not far from his mind as he performed the part. The audience, who had been through sufficient nightmares because of the Nazis, even if unconscious of Olivier's analogy, were well prepared to understand the manipulative treachery he projected.

The next year he did Hotspur for the Old Vic company, using the device of making that valiant warrior and tender husband stammer on the consonant *w*. The idea may have originated with Hotspur's last words, that he was now "food for—" as Hal finishes "For worms"; in any case, Olivier's Hotspur died struggling to pronounce the word which Hal supplied. His end, characteristically acrobatic, saw him staggering from Hal's blow on his neck, and suddenly plunging in his suit of armor down a few steps onto his face —an end which Agate thought touching; Olivier, that critic said, had humanized all the heroics of the role.

Olivier told Sam Behrman an amusing incident connected with his make-up for Hotspur. He had determined to play Hotspur in a red wig, and once he had decided that, it was necessary for him "to make up for it all over." "To live up to that red wig" took the actor at least three hours in his dressing room. At one performance he was annoyed from the very first appearance he made on stage by a "flamboyant commercial type" who was sitting up front with a young woman. Throughout, this pest kept whispering to her, every time Hotspur made an entrance. He became so much of an obsession that Olivier tried not to see him; in vain, he saw nobody else. On Olivier's next entrance, this creature gave him a special welcome. In a clear loud voice he said to the young woman: "Well, here comes Old Ginger again!"

(Incidentally, Sam, while trying to cheer up Robert Sherwood after Olivier had refused to act in one of his plays, assured the playwright that the best actors in the world cannot "read plays; they just read parts." To substantiate the assertion, Sam confided to Sherwood that Olivier was of the opinion that "Christopher Fry was as good as Shakespeare.")

That same season he was also playing Shallow to Richardson's Falstaff, and one critic said that he seemed to have lost ten inches and gained thirty years overnight, with his shrill ancient scarecrow figure, crackling voice, goatee, and sharply pointed nose.

Next came what I consider to be the highest point of his career, his *Oedipus the King*. It was one of the few great performances I have seen in my life. John Mason Brown has said that it mixed blood and electricity, that it pulled lightning from the sky, that it was thrilling without ever losing majesty. I shall never forget the two amazing, harrowing groans Olivier emitted at the moment when Oedipus at last confronts the truth about himself; those sounds bespoke, as could no words, the horror he was experiencing; they seemed to rise unbidden from the very depths of his being. No doubt William Butler Yeats's direct (and amputated) version was perfect for a masterful actor who was always better in prose than in verse.

In the autumn of 1946, he gave an unconventional Lear for the Old Vic, injecting into the role unanticipated humor, new ideas, and his bent for realism; many thought these compensated for his lack of stature, kingliness, and weight of voice. In the earlier scenes he was less the impetuous, still physically powerful old monarch than, as Findlater puts it, "a fey, whimsical, almost comic grandfather, with touches of Shallow." Agate again complained about the high-pitched voice, and thought Olivier brilliant but not moving. This critic touched upon what has possibly been the core of Olivier's problem with Shakespeare: by instinct he is a comedian and a tragedian by art—that he calls too much attention to how well he is doing this or that bit of pathos. Irving, said Agate, never did that and had acted as though he himself was engulfed in Lear's tragedy.

In 1948 Olivier's film of *Hamlet* appeared. I can only say that for a hundred reasons I hated it, all of them, no doubt, due to the actor's increasing conviction that one had to do Shakespeare in new ways. The film was very popular, was (and still is) frequently revived, and during the many years I was teaching the play to college students, I had to battle incessantly against the misconceptions they had imbibed from it. All the errors introduced are far too many to list, but here are the important ones:

1. Alan Dent, who arranged the script, left out more than a third of the play. The characters of Guildenstern and Rosencrantz, so important to the plot and the conclusion, were entirely cut out. Hamlet was therefore never shipped off to England.

2. The movie opened with Olivier saying in a ghostly voice that *Hamlet* was a play about a man "who could not make up his mind." (Talk about oversimplification!)

3. The camera played lovingly, and with nauseating obviousness, upon Gertrude's bed, to underline Hamlet's incestuous love for his mother, which was acted (figuratively, of course!) up to the hilt in the scene in her closet.

4. (One of the most serious.) In the last scene, Gertrude apparently knew that the chalice was poisoned and very well projected the idea that in drinking of it she was committing suicide to warn her son not to partake of it. This was outrageously out of character for the superficial sentimentalist who was Shakespeare's Gertrude, and proved one of the most persistent convictions which students carried away from the movie.

5. When Hamlet greeted the players in the second act, his, "welcome all. I am glad to see thee well" was addressed to a poodle. (Most original!)

6. The whole recitation of the First Player was cut out, beginning with "I heard thee speak me a speech once"; we therefore never understood how Hamlet got the idea of presenting the play before Claudius.

7. At the performance of that play the whole court was busy watching the king's terrified reactions rather than the play itself; they seemed to know that he had been guilty of murdering Hamlet's father!

8. In the last scene at Hamlet's line, "Treachery! Seek it out"—delivered by Olivier as "Seek it ou—ou—out!"—the hero rushed up a staircase to a balcony overlooking the scene, and jumped therefrom in fine Fairbanks style to stab the king. (It is recorded that in the filming of this scene, Claudius insisted upon having a stand-in; a professional strong-man was fitted into the king's robes. But even strong-men have their limits; this one was knocked unconscious and lost two teeth.)

9. Horatio made no attempt to die too.

10. There was no Fortinbras. His concluding speech was allotted to Horatio.

11. At the very end there was a long procession down steps, then up again, up, interminably up, as Hamlet's corpse was very slowly carried past Gertrude's bedroom (subtle!), then further up to the top of the battlements. Why? Would Hamlet's body presently be hurled fathoms below onto the rocks bordering the sea?

Yet years before the picture was made, Olivier agreed with Tyrone Guthrie that it was revolting that *Hamlet* should be cut to suit the "convention of a two and a half hours' entertainment"; a cut *Hamlet*, Olivier at that time declared, could never be the play Shakespeare wrote; "the thought of this awful sacrilege brought a brooding silence." But the film was described by Mr. Olivier and his colleagues as "a simplified essay in *Hamlet*; . . . if it was to be a *good* film, it was necessary to be quite ruthless." Such a decision might well have called anew for a brooding silence!

In 1947 he was knighted. Four years later he and his wife, Vivien Leigh, presented alternately *Caesar and Cleopatra* and *Antony and Cleopatra*. In the Shaw play her thin voice and coy manner worked admirably for the kittenish queen; but for Shakespeare's complicated serpent of the Nile they were a disaster. As Caesar, Olivier was efficient, but too elderly; as Antony he was good, but too much a victim of the *Weltschmerz*. It is thought he deliberately played down both roles to enable his wife to shine the more; in Shakespeare the sacrifice was in vain.

In 1961 he was appointed director of the National Theatre, which opened and continued across the Waterloo Bridge at the Old Vic's premises. Five years after that he made a movie of *Othello*, which made no pretense of being more than a faithful filming of the tragedy as it had been given on stage. To my mind this was the worst performance of his career. Excessively blackened, the Moor became a member of a minstrel show; the shadow of Ernest

Jones's homosexual theory hung over the production; perhaps it was for that reason that Othello appeared with a rose in his hand? But the most inexplicable aspect of his behavior was the odd way he used his hands and legs—gesticulations and shuffle which brought to mind the wraith of Old Black Joe. The reason for this strangeness was later revealed by Sammy Davis, Jr., on the David Frost TV show (rebroadcast on May 11, 1970). Frost and Davis were talking about Olivier when Davis said to the world: "Laurence Olivier! . . . That was it! Because the greatest compliment ever—and I don't know if this story is known—but I'm sure Larry, which I am now close enough to he and his wife Joan to say it: when I was in England at the Prince of Wales's Theatre he used to come at least four to five times a week and sit in the wings and watch my performance. Now, need I tell you what a compliment that is? You know, all right. I said, 'Why?' He says, 'Because I'm going to do Othello.' Now funny as that sounds, and I did the same thing, ah ha ha ha . . . What he wanted was a rhythmic movement which he achieved in the piece. His opening move is a move that I use on stage with a microphone. For instance, if this is a mike, I do this. [Here Davis made a kind of half-S movement of hand and torso forward, and then leaned back and made another half-S movement to the rear, a kind of arabesque in the air.] His opening move you will see in the film; he walks out and he goes . . . [Davis repeated the half-S movements] and then stands, but all of his movements are here [indicating the upper portion of his body]. I'm *so complimented!* So now you can imagine—what can you do? Are you gonna run to somebody and say, 'See what he's doin, he saw me do dat'? They gotta go like this: 'Get outta here!' " In this instance Olivier was working from "without" with a vengeance; he might also have remembered that Othello was a Moor, not a Negro.

In 1970 Sir Laurence Olivier became Lord Olivier, the first actor ever to be raised to the peerage. Not even the Beatles were so honored.

After a considerable amount of advance publicity, including protests of the Jewish Anti-Defamation League, *The Merchant of Venice* was presented in the United States on TV, March 16, 1974. Though this was not a photographed stage performance, it was, with a few exceptions, the same production which I had suffered through in London at the National Theatre in October 1970. (The major difference was that I did not see Olivier but Robert Lang as Shylock in London, for illness had caused Olivier to withdraw from the cast.) The Anti-Defamation League is quite wrong in thinking that Shakespeare in this play was attacking the Jews; nor was he defending them—truths which I have attempted to demonstrate at length elsewhere. What we do need is a Society Against the Defamation of Shakespeare by directors and actors. To list the sins of this production would take a volume. Let me mention a few. Lord Olivier has expressed the view on the air that to make people come to see Shakespeare he must be presented always in a new way. This time the setting was placed in the 1880s, even though the Victorian Age is further removed from us than the Elizabethan or the Italian Renaissance. Antonio was elderly, Bassanio young—the disparity in their ages making it difficult to imagine the intensity of their friendship. Joan Plowright, in all the Shakespearean roles in which I have seen her, projects, I feel, an unpleasantness quite foreign to a Shakespearean heroine (I felt it in London and I felt it here anew, and others agree with me)—and as Portia she spoke her lines as though she did not mean a word she said; there was the usual excess of invented business with Portia in the second scene, for example, reviewing the characters of her suitors with Nerissa while looking at a series of stereopticon slides (were these their portraits?); Shylock was forever tapping others, notably Antonio on his breast where he was planning to take the pound of flesh (very subtle!), with his elegant cane, just as Portia tapped Bassanio with her riding crop; perhaps the most serious defect was the omission of Shylock's first soliloquy, beginning with "How like a fawning publican he looks" and going on to the all-important revelation, that his reason for hating Antonio is that

> in low simplicity
> He lends out money gratis, and brings down
> The rate of usance here with us in Venice . . .
> and he rails
> Even there where merchants most do congregate
> On me, my bargains, and my well-won thrift,
> Which he calls interest;

Old Gobbo was omitted and Launcelot became a cockney; when Launcelot, coming to invite Shylock to Bassanio's dinner, trips over English, as is his wont, and grandly says, "My young master doth expect your reproach" (for "approach") and Shylock answers with the wonderful thrust, "So do I his," Olivier said this with a laugh while exchanging smiles with Jessica, as though she knew and approved his designs on Antonio's life. Another major outrage was casting as the bold, arrogant Arragon a decrepit nonagenarian who seemed to have both feet already in the grave (though in the movie he did not invent to the same degree the quite unwarranted comedy of his wheezing repetition of "Who chooseth me"); Jessica's elopement was not shown, though Shylock wept copiously over it; during the great speech, "Hath not a Jew eyes," which Shylock proudly uses as a lash, Olivier instead achieved the limit of pathos, weeping until his voice was so choked he could hardly speak; all the comic overtones, while Tubal alternately rejoices and tortures Shylock, were disregarded to allow Olivier to weep first over Jessica's photo, then his dead wife's; there was no warmth on Portia's side toward Bassanio; in the all-significant song, "Tell me where is fancy bred," which gives more than a hint to Bassanio about the caskets, not a word could be made out as *two* Victorian songbirds warbled away in coloratura style; when Shylock loses the trial we heard him weeping aloud once more off stage; twice Portia simply couldn't remember Jessica's name (to emphasize anti-Semitism, of course), a thing gracious Portia would never be guilty of; in their beautiful last act Lorenzo and Jessica kept as far apart as possible in their love scene;

at the close of the play, when all others had gone off, Jessica was left reading the document of her inheritance all alone while in the distance was heard the voice of a cantor singing what I am told is the Hebrew prayer for the dead; all through the play the word *Jew* was spoken with disparagement (as it is only by Gratiano in Shakespeare), whereas it is only a designation, no more significant than Othello's being called "the Moor" or Cassio a "Florentine" to show they are not native Venetians. In addition to these distortions a great deal could be mentioned. It is a wonder that Shakespeare survives at all when his purposes are so constantly twisted.

26

The Twentieth Century (II)

Sir Ralph Richardson (b. 1902) has unquestionably been one of the leading actors of our time. He is one of the lucky ones who possesses that inner radiance which comes across the footlights with unmistakable force. I have, however, one reservation concerning him. I have seen him often on both sides of the Atlantic, and have never left the theater other than delighted with him, and I have seen him in all sorts of plays and roles; but almost more than any other important actor he has never permitted me to forget for a moment that I was seeing and hearing Ralph Richardson rather than the character he was portraying, probably because his facial expressions, voice, and enunciation are, however agreeable, always the same. He never loses his identity in the role.

He first appeared as Lorenzo in *The Merchant of Venice* at Brighton in 1921, was with the Birmingham Repertory in 1926, came to the Old Vic in 1930, and the next year when Sadler's Wells was reopened played Sir Toby Belch. At the Old Vic he was seen in a wide variety of roles from Petruchio to Bottom to Falstaff; in 1952 he was Prospero at the Royal Shakespeare Theatre; later he returned to the Old Vic, where he was much praised for his Timon.

In 1931 Agate found his Henry V too modern, too little the warrior; but his Kent perfect, and his Faulconbridge quite as good; in these parts the critic declared him master of a "direct and manly pathos." But as Othello, the same year, Agate thought him a complete failure; that was inevitable with Olivier attempting to indicate Ernest Jones's notion of Iago's homosexual cravings for the Moor, and poor Richardson, unaware of this, making a ponderous Othello.

Of all his Shakespearean parts, that of Falstaff in the two *Henry IV* histories (1946) has been the most admired. A correspondent wrote Agate that Richardson had created a spoiled-baby Falstaff, "bigger, brighter, funnier than ever before." Agate himself declared that the actor had injected into the characterization everything needed: exuberance, mischief, and gusto; it was, the critic said, great acting; he called it a beautiful moment when Falstaff, having bilked Shallow of so much money, was content to sit and reflect upon the folly of his benefactors. I saw these performances and must agree with all the enthusiasm, except for one thing which much disconcerted me—an irritation I have felt with most Falstaffs. They are always too obviously stuffed with false padding; in Richardson's case, the padding was so excessive that one was able to pay little attention to anything else, except by special effort. The college professor who, when I was a student, first read the great Falstaff passages (which he obviously loved) was a man of elegant build; when he read Falstaff's speeches, he merely protruded his tummy a little bit and the illusion of the fat knight was perfect. I see no reason why actors feel that they have so much to overdo Falstaff's circumference.

Sir Ralph himself considers the costume Alex Stone designed for him in the role to have been "wonderful," and loved its "two or three stomachs, two or three chests, and two huge arms."

He admits that he has been at his best in comic roles, and that despite the fact that he earnestly wished to play Othello and Macbeth, they were "disasters. . . . I just damn well didn't see the dagger [before me] and neither did anybody else." He concedes that for tragic parts he does not possess the requisite "emotional imagination."

Dame Peggy Ashcroft (b. 1907), who has appeared in so many plays, has never said to herself before going on stage, "I'm going to give a great performance"; that, she says, would be enough to sink any actress. Like Tallulah Bankhead, she confesses to getting bored with long runs or having to do any role over and over again. She feels that because a dramatist's creations can give one much insight into human motivations and behavior, acting is a good preparation for life. (Since the record proves that many actors have made at least as much of a mess of their lives as the rest of us, this conclusion seems open to question.)

She first fell in love with Shakespeare at school, and this decided her to act. First she was excited by his language, later by his depiction of character and his power as a dramatist. It was stimulating, she found, to become involved in a character apart from one's self. After studying with Elsie Fogarty, she started working in the theater at eighteen. She was an exquisite Desdemona to Robeson's Othello in 1930.

When she was twenty-five she was Rosalind with the Old Vic company at Sadler's Wells in 1932. The artist Walter Sickert sketched her in the act of putting the chain around Orlando's neck. Agate said that she projected great depth of feeling, but none of the poetry. The same year she was Portia to Gielgud's Shylock; *Punch* reported that she delivered the "quality of mercy speech" in the trial scene not as a "purple patch, but almost in confidential tones, hands behind back . . . a quite indefensible reading but surprisingly interesting." When she was in the role again twenty-one years later, she made a confident Portia to Redgrave's Shylock, and Eric Keown said that she might have been "a Newhamite with a first in law, but I felt that she would also have been among the toasts of May Week so charming were her scenes with Bassanio and so civilised her sense of a social occasion."

With Gielgud at the New Theatre, she for the first time understood the value of a permanent company; she played Juliet with him in 1935. Her Juliet was greatly admired; the childlike quality of her early scenes was especially touching, and Agate said they could not have been better; but he found her unequal to the great moments, and thought that she implied the role without playing it. However, a month later he declared she had made great gains in depth and power.

In 1938 she was enacting Viola, and stood out from the rest of the company for her excellence, except for Michael Redgrave's Sir Andrew Aguecheek; when she appeared in the part again in 1950 she was highly praised for projecting her loyalty to the duke, her quietness in the face of despairs and frustrations—all somehow eloquent in answer to her brother's final questionings, as she paused before saying, "Of Messaline."

She played Ophelia to Gielgud's "most fluent, . . . eloquent and his bitterest" Hamlet in 1944. In 1946 as Titania she seemed an immortal to Agate, who nevertheless complained that her running her words together made it difficult to understand what she was saying.

In 1950 at Stratford-on-Avon she was Beatrice to Gielgud's Benedick, and was admired for never tossing "herself about the stage like one of those Gilbertian contadine dancing a cachucha" or bolero. (The reference is to Gilbert and Sullivam's delicious *The Gondoliers.*) The same season her Cordelia was "goodness incarnate."

In 1953 she played opposite Redgrave as Cleopatra, a role for which one would have thought her temperamentally unfitted, but she was, as usual, excellent. She tried to make the queen a Greek, not an Egyptian, as indeed she was historically, and has stated that she evolved her interpretation from the text (something actors in Shakespeare rarely do). Interestingly enough, she found Cleopatra the most rewarding and exciting of all the many parts she had played.

Her Imogen of 1957 was thoroughly credible, and her Margaret of Anjou in 1963 was a full-length portrait. At Stratford-on-Avon John Barton had arranged the three parts of *Henry VI,* the first two retaining their title, the third confusingly renamed *Edward IV,* and he had added *Richard III.* Appearing from the moment she was seen as the Princess of France through her misfortunes to the half-insane queen of *Richard III,* Peggy Ashford achieved one of the major triumphs of her career.

Sir Michael Redgrave (b. 1908), a son and grandson of actors, and the sire of another generation of thespians, has had what might have been the disadvantage of being three inches over six feet in height. He was born at Bristol, and with his mother followed his father to Australia, where he first appeared on stage in his father's arms at the age of two. A year later his parents separated and he never saw his father again. He was back again in

England, living the uncertain life connected with a touring company to which his mother belonged. When he was nine, she married again, and his stepfather planned for him a different social milieu, intending him for a public school and a university; of course, he was not to think of acting as a profession, a decision with which his mother heartily concurred.

Nevertheless, he acted constantly while he was at school at Clifton and made an impression as Lady Macbeth. He first set foot on a professional stage when he was thirteen in a walk-on part at Stratford in *Henry IV, Part II* as a result of his mother's being in the company. His own ambition was to be a writer. At Cambridge he continued to appear in plays. It was his height which made him endorse his mother and stepfather's prohibition of the stage. He therefore was for three years a teacher of modern languages at a public school in Cranleigh. While there he staged a series of plays, performing the duties of leading actor, director, and manager in *As You Like It, Hamlet, The Tempest,* and *King Lear.* These amateur productions attracted considerable attention among critics and scholars. Wilson Knight was enthusiastic about *King Lear* and said the young man's production had afforded him some of the most poignant moments of his experience in the theater, and J. Dover Wilson lauded Redgrave's Lear as "unimaginably beautiful." Redgrave admits to having been "highly conceited" while performing the leads in these great plays.

He then auditioned for Lilian Baylis at the Old Vic. It appeared that she was not interested, but while he was in Liverpool, he received from her an offer of a contract at £3 a week. Because of it William Armstrong agreed to give him £4 as a member of the Liverpool Repertory. Among the many plays it presented, that company gave Shakespeare once a year, a program which matched Redgrave's ambitions at the time. Having appeared as Hamlet, Prospero, and Lear at Cranleigh, he was anxious to concentrate on modern plays. At Liverpool in two seasons he was seen in twenty-seven parts. He also married there; Rachel Kempson, who had been Juliet at Stratford two years earlier, became his wife.

At the end of the second season Guthrie, who had seen performances by Mr. and Mrs. Redgrave, asked them to come to London to join the Old Vic company as juvenile leads in plays with Olivier and Edith Evans. Redgrave acknowledges a great indebtedness to Miss Evans, to whose Rosalind he played Orlando, in which role, a critic said, he proved his control of verse and the knowledge of "how to wear a costume and still look a man." Once Edith Evans asked him a question which he says altered his whole career: did he wish to be like Olivier and Gielgud or like Peggy Ashcroft and herself? She was cryptically asking what sort of standards was he aiming at. The idea that he had to set himself certain goals was a new one to him. She also gave him many helpful hints: on another occasion, when he was appearing with her in *The Country Wife,* she asked him during a rehearsal to place his hand on her diaphragm as she spoke the words, "Perfectly, perfectly, Mr. Horner," and pointed out that she was using more strength of voice for that whisper, which carried through the house, than she required for speaking loud. It was her gentle way of letting him know that he had the shortcoming of sometimes dropping his voice until it was inaudible—a shortcoming which, despite his excellence, I have found he never completely overcame.

His readiness to undertake in his youth parts of huge emotional range he explains as owing to his ability to "switch on" an emotion—a capacity he ascribes to the glands. Of course, some emotions come to him more readily than others; the volcanic anger of Lear, for example, he found difficult.

In 1937, the season of his Orlando, he made a stir with his Laertes. Agate thought him excellent, and Raymond Mortimer called his interpretation ideal and had particular praise for his superb voice and wide emotional range. The next year he made of Sir Andrew Aguecheek, Peggy Ashcroft being the Viola, "an immensely likeable, companionable fop," with no justification whatsoever. Agate thought it a diverting piece of clowning, while disapproving of the interpretation.

He had already made a number of films, and was making them anew. During the 1939/40 season he was asked to rejoin the Old Vic to play Richard II and either Romeo or Macbeth; but World War II broke out and it was ten years before he was playing again in Shakespearean drama. At the Aldwych Theatre his Macbeth was severely criticized; he has said that he was unfortunately judged by the first night, which he admits may not have been very good; but he feels that his later performances needed no apology. His guess is that the critics thought it presumptuous of him to be playing Shakespeare after so many years devoted to the cinema; besides, he had never, in his maturity, attempted a Shakespearean role of the dimensions of Bellona's bridegroom. Just the same, the production ran for three months and made money. He concedes that he would approach the part again only with dread, for there are portions of the tragedy which appall him. Part of his failure he later ascribed to the great influence his reading of Stanislavski had had upon his acting of modern plays: he had tried, he said, "to rationalize and understand Macbeth, instead of just presenting him."

In 1949 he was again asked to join the Old Vic, and he began with Berowne in Love's Labour's Lost; instead of doing him in the familiar interpretation, as an artificial creature, he understood, as Ivor Brown observed, that there was a man beneath the exterior "and Redgrave gave us that man." The next year he attempted Hamlet, which had been a stipulation for his rejoining the company. His was a clear and precise prince but lacked fire; Ivor Brown said that his performance was intelligent, exciting, true to the plot but "less lyrical, less ethereal" than the greatest Hamlets, though more real and "agonized." Harold Hobson wrote that at Hamlet's first entrance Redgrave established the tone of bitter sorrow over his father's death, reinforced by the first sound of his pained voice suggesting a man so much paralyzed by unhappiness that it abolished the question of why the prince did not kill Claudius. (In my opinion, as I have fully explained elsewhere, that, like the flowers which bloom in the spring, tra-la, has nothing to do with the case.) When he did the role eight years later at Stratford, his Hamlet was far richer and nobler in personality, while retaining the intellect with lucidity and no overcomplicated subtleties.

His Richard II, Hotspur, and Prospero came to Stratford in 1951. As the young king who was more poet than monarch, Redgrave well balanced the oppositions in Richard's makeup: the inability to act and the irresistibility of dramatizing his situation. This role he recreated in the selections of the play recorded in The Living Shakespeare series, which I edited, and it was my favorite among all the discs because of Redgrave's beautiful voice and command of the verse. His Hotspur was wild and uncompromisingly unromantic, a soldier who, because he was supposed to speak "thick," talked in the flat Northumbrian burr. As Prospero he united profound humanity to the dignity of a seer. In that role Redgrave found Stanislavski of no help at all; there was no point in trying to re-create Prospero's past as Duke of Milan; instead Redgrave made him an old man whose powers had been acquired with much labor, and who felt that his own life was approaching its terminus. Interestingly, in this part Redgrave for the first time wore a false nose.

At Stratford in 1953 he was Lear, Shylock, and Antony. Although the production of *King Lear* left a great deal to be desired, Redgrave correctly presented a king old and tired, but unwilling to face the fact that he was no longer a heroic figure full of vitality; his lost strength would come back in fits and starts. Robert Speaight said that the performance frequently overwhelmed him by its sweep and wonderful acting; Philip Hope-Wallace pronounced it the best interpretation since the war—that no other actor had so well succeeded in making one consistent Lear. His Shylock was fierce, gray-bearded, and "sibilant"; Peggy Ashcroft was Portia. Both of them rose to heights in *Antony and Cleopatra*; Trewin says the production surged ahead like "the flood waters of the Nile," and that both of them "took it at the flood." Redgrave indicated by his first entrance his carelessness, love of laughter, and "abandoned magnificence." He was in truth one of the triple pillars of the earth, large of heart and heroic. (His great height did him in good stead in this role.) When the play was brought to London he was astonished at its great success, and he reflected that in the past he had always "*tried* too hard," and did not as Antony.

Though he had played eleven classic roles in four years, he had made very little money; so between 1954 and 1958 he did a dozen films to improve his income, as well as three modern plays. In 1958 he was seen on the stage as Benedick in a production of *Much Ado about Nothing* set in the mid-nineteenth century; he was bearded, wore a straw hat, and smoked cigars, but never abandoned elegance.

Among creators there is often enough disparity between theory and practice (e.g., Wordsworth's often writing at his best when *not* using the language of the average man; the Pre-Raphaelite poets and painters working under the delusion that they were imitating nature; Hardy's strange impression that his tragic novels showed the force of Circumstance), but, after all, in the arts it is the result that counts. In view of Sir Michael's triumphs, some of his ideas sound strange indeed—but then, actors have never been remarkable for articulating what they do on stage. He is thoroughly right in rejecting the Oedipus-complex explanation of Hamlet's conduct and Olivier's theory that the play was the tragedy of "a man who could not make up his mind." He is equally perceptive in saying that the major fault of Shakespearean criticism is that the scholars have developed their ideas by taking lines out of context.

But he makes the odd admonition that we ought to remember that the female parts in Shakespeare's day were taken by boys and that the dramatist could not have foreseen that someday women would enact those roles; therefore, says Redgrave, the love scenes in Shakespeare's plays are severely limited by the fact that the company's *boys* were going to appear as women! Are there any women more feminine in all literature than Portia, Beatrice, Viola, Olivia, Rosalind, Isabella, Imogen, or Cleopatra, and are there any greater love scenes in drama than those between Romeo and Juliet, Portia and Bassanio, Rosalind and Orlando, Othello and Desdemona, Antony and Cleopatra—to mention only a few? Antony is described as noble, says Redgrave, eight times, but except for his treatment of Enobarbus we never see him doing a noble thing; yet, as we noted, Redgrave was remarkable for the nobility *he* established in the character. He finds Macbeth an even more unsatisfactorily written part, calls him a murderer, and fails to find him much of a poet; this is the more astonishing in that the world has long recognized that *Macbeth* is perhaps Shakespeare's greatest poem, and that it is because Macbeth *is* so great a poet that he retains the audience's sympathy.

Robert Helpmann (b. 1909), born in Australia, has been an actor, dancer, choreographer, and director. Whenever I have seen him in a play he has seemed to me more dancer than actor. His first appearance in a leading role occurred in 1937 when he was Oberon at the Old Vic; at the same theater he was Shylock, Petruchio, Angelo, Richard III, and Launcelot Gobbo. In 1946 he was seen as Hamlet, Shylock, and King John at Stratford. For the Old Vic he directed *The Tempest, Antony and Cleopatra,* and *Romeo and Juliet.*

From the beginning, Agate was comparing him to Sarah Bernhardt; his Oberon in "glittering black" was "first cousin" to her Hamlet. When Helpmann acted Hamlet Agate thought that at the beginning he made a "heart-taking little figure . . . And how like Sarah!" Helpmann had the same tousled hair, the same profile, the same collarette, and his acting was on "the androgynous plane of pure poetry." But, Agate continued, he merely recited Hamlet's lines; they did not seem to come from within him; he reduced the prince to a charming little person. Crosse found him too passive and undistinguished. Trewin thought him fretful rather than passionate, and remembered his beating a nervous tattoo on a drum at the line, "The play's the thing . . ." Trewin declared his Richard III too melodramatic.

Jessica Tandy (b. 1909), whose silvery voice has graced many a modern play on Broadway, in 1934 was sadly miscast as Ophelia; though Gielgud, the Hamlet, was pleased with her, she was found insignificant just when she should have been most touching. To Olivier's Sir Toby she took on both the role of Viola and that of her brother. In 1940 she played Cordelia to

Gielgud's Lear—all these roles at the Old Vic. Since then she has wisely demonstrated her very great dramatic ability in contemporary plays, very often with her husband, the brilliant Hume Cronyn.

José Ferrer (b. 1912), an actor of considerable gifts, whose performances vary from the inspired to the quasi-ham, or, as in *Cyrano,* an admixture of both, was Paul Robeson's Iago in the United States. Surely a more villainous Iago was never seen, nor a more deliberately malign-looking one. Stark Young objected to its lack of dignity and elegance. My own objections, which I have already indicated, are summed up in the fact that he distorted the play by making the villain the chief character in the tragedy.

Sir Alec Guinness (b. 1914), familiar to cinema audiences for his many witty performances, was seen in 1934 as Osric in Gielgud's *Hamlet.* During 1936/37 he repeated the role at the Old Vic, and was also praised for his Andrew Aguecheek, in which latter part Trewin says he was a "walking wraith." He then joined Gielgud's company at the Queen's as a sympathetic and pathetic Aumerle in *Richard II* and Lorenzo in *The Merchant of Venice,* in the last act of which Ivor Brown was delighted with his "unspectacular, meditative, star-struck beauty" of expression. When he was only twenty-four Guthrie cast him as Hamlet in a modern-dress uncut version of the play, a performance sincere and straightforward. His next Shakespearean triumph was as the Fool in *King Lear,* where he was quiet, wry, and utterly devoted to the king. At the New Theatre as Richard II (1947) he portrayed the weak king as ironic but did little justice to the poetry; he was Menenius the next season in *Coriolanus.* Though it was hard to imagine him in the part, he performed with delicate balance, never ranting or harsh. In 1953 he helped inaugurate the first season at Ontario, Canada, as Richard III under Guthrie's direction. My own feeling about Guinness is that I would much rather see him in modern satirical comedy, where his tendency to be always himself masquerading as someone else is never objectionable, as it is in Shakespeare's serious plays.

Alfred Drake (né Capurro [b. 1914]) is a native of New York and has been the finest singer-actor of his generation on Broadway as well as in London. The extraordinary beauty of his baritone singing voice—I can testify to his having been one of the finest lieder singers I have ever heard—has in a way kept him from doing what he most wished to do, and proved himself entirely able to do on the few occasions when he had the opportunity to demonstrate those abilities—acting leading roles in the great classics. It was because of this ambition that he refused to accept an offer to sing with the Metropolitan Opera Company of New York.

At Brooklyn College of the City University of New York, he was seen in lead roles in plays such as those by Pinero. He was hardly out of college when he began to appear regularly on Broadway in musicals. His thought was that when he reached the top he would be able to choose roles in serious and important plays. He had every reason to indulge this hope when in 1941 he played Orlando to Helen Craig's Rosalind at the Mansfield Theater; Eugene Bryden's direction was poor and the production was not long-lived but Drake's performance was singled out for high praise.

But the beauty of his voice and his magnetism on the stage, which had made him highly desirable for revues and musicals ever since *Babes in Arms* (1937) and continued with *One for the Money* (1938), *Two for the Show* (1940), and which brought him to stardom as singer and actor in *Oklahoma!* (1943), *Sing Out Sweet Land* (1944), *Kiss Me Kate* (1948), and *Kismet* (1953)—all of which had long runs—made it difficult for producers and directors to think of him in any work in which he did not have to sing. It is true that during these years he had appeared in some nonmusical comedies and serious plays, but the public thought of him primarily as a singer.

In 1957, however, he had the opportunity to play Iago opposite Earl Hyman, John Houseman directing, at the Stratford (Connecticut) Playhouse. Since Hyman was young, Drake was forced to play, against his judgment, an older man, though no one was better equipped than he to play a dashing villain of twenty-eight. As it was, his Iago was otherwise perfect. The same season he played Benedick to Katharine Hepburn's Beatrice. Again he was ideally suited to the role, but John Houseman and Jack Landau had bowed to Hepburn's perverse insistence that the comedy be set in a Latin American background (sombreros and all), and Katharine Hepburn was far too brittle to make an adequate Beatrice. His one chance to show how brilliant he can be in Shakespeare came in 1964 in New York when he enacted Claudius to Richard Burton's hopelessly inadequate Hamlet. He was the best and most intelligible Claudius I have ever seen, and he was aided only by the perfection of Hume Cronyn as Polonius. The rest of the cast was poor. I feel I owe it to Drake to add that when in 1961 he took the lead in *Kean* (a musical based on Sartre's play), he proved again how much the American Shakespearean stage has lost because Drake is so magnificent a singer. He is president of The Players, the club Booth founded.

Carmen Matthews (b. 1914), who was born in Philadelphia, has had a very busy life as an actress, though not often in Shakespeare. Her first appearance was at Stratford-on-Avon in 1936. Two years later she accepted a minor role in a New York *Hamlet.* In 1939/40 she exhibited considerable gifts as Lady Mortimer, Ophelia, and the queen of *Richard II.* In 1964 her Gertrude at Stratford, Connecticut, was the outstanding performance of the season's *Hamlet.* But on the whole she is more associated with contemporary drama.

Orson Welles (b. 1915) is the conspicuous case in his generation of an actor who never fulfilled the promise of his early career. He was born in Wisconsin to parents who had made an unsuccessful marriage. At their separation, when he was six, he lived with his mother for two years. When she died, he went to his father, where he moved in the society of actors, sportsmen, and people of social station. Before he was eleven he had twice traveled around the world, and already evinced his precocity. After his father died, he set out for Ireland, where he was accepted as an actor at the Gate Theatre at the age of sixteen; it is said the Dublin management took him on chiefly in admiration of his cheek, for he valiantly claimed to be a famous star in his own country. Returning to America, he played Mercutio and other non-Shakespearean roles on tour with Katherine Cornell (1933/34). He was not yet twenty.

At the age of twenty-one he was fairly established in radio, and became the director of the Negro People's Theater, where he presented an unforgettably ridiculous *Macbeth* (1936)—popularly known as the "Harlem *Macbeth.*" Here he was precocious with a vengeance. He transported the scene to Haiti, transformed Hecate to a man, and made him the leading character, a sort of witch doctor who continued to reappear on the stage, lashing a whip and repeating ad nauseam, "He shall peak and he shall pine." (Shakespeare never wrote the part of Hecate, and her brief appearances in the play—later insertions—are merely a nuisance in *Macbeth.*) The black cast seemed thoroughly to enjoy parading about in their lavish court costumes, strangely out of place in the jungle, but did not indicate that they understood a word they were uttering.

The next year, with John Houseman, Welles was appointed director of the Federal Theater Project, and presently they founded the Mercury Theater. There he directed a remarkable *Julius Caesar,* himself playing Brutus, a production in modern dress which drew a thoroughly intelligent and undistorted parallel between Caesar and Mussolini. It was, in my opinion, very important as a corrective to the almost universally perverse interpretation of the tragedy as taught in our schools; for generations teachers of the young have been standing the play on its head by making Caesar (who is almost a caricature) the hero, Brutus and Cassius (the most admirable figures in the play) the villains, and the truly villainous Mark Antony the noblest Roman of them all. Welles's production is perhaps the best I have ever seen of the play.

But the danger sign was already to be found in the program notes; there one read that Orson Welles, who had reached the advanced age of twenty-two, was one of the world's leading authorities on Shakespeare! This was something like his pretentions at the Gate Theater six years earlier, only more serious. Welles never again as a stage or screen actor achieved the heights of that year. I ascribe the decline to his exaggerated opinion of himself at twenty-two.

In 1938 he gave his now notorious radio broadcast announcing that inhabitants of Mars had just invaded the earth; he succeeded in creating hysteria and panic among thousands of idiots who heard his announcement. The wide credulity accorded his trick can have done little to direct his temperament toward modesty.

The first film he made in Hollywood, written with Herman Mankiewicz, in which he starred and which he directed, *Citizen Kane* (1940), made cinema history; the invaluable aid of his cameraman, Gregg Toland, and his editor, Robert Wise, resulted in an innovative movie which has since been imitated; technically it was a fascinating work, though few people have noticed that it has very little to say for all its elaborate skillfulness. His next picture, *The Magnificent Ambersons* (1942) was quite as remarkable for its directing and was actually far superior. After that Welles appeared in America and Europe in numerous inferior films in which his style became more and more hammy in voice and facial expression.

There is an old story which I first heard thirty years ago. Some wit was in a Hollywood studio commissary with friends when Welles passed by on his way to another table. "There," said the anonymous clever man, "but for the grace of God, goes God!"

He first appeared in London in 1951 as Othello, in a stage production he directed. Crosse says that the text was hideously mangled; scenes and bits of scenes were for no reason transposed, and there were numerous and important omissions; Welles had a terrible weakness for long and meaningless pauses; Othello killed his wife by wrapping her up in the bedclothes; when he asked Cassio's pardon after that, he kissed him; and before stabbing himself he waved his dagger about in the air. The next year he made a film of the play, with Ralph Richardson as a repellent Iago; it included a great deal of walking by Othello while he delivered his lines. It was as poor as the stage version.

The film he made of *Macbeth* was the (unintentionally) funniest movie I have ever seen. Welles spoke throughout with a pronounced Scottish burr and was forever rolling his eyes; the rest of the company were dressed in what looked like costumes borrowed from the opera's garb for Wagner's "Ring" cycle; in the midst of these Valkyries and their mates appeared a figure who may have been, for all I know, Friar Laurence wandered into the wrong play, for a monk with a cross several stories high was usually present in the throng; Macbeth's lines were allotted to his lady and vice versa; the Macbeths, despite Shakespeare's description of the charm and fairness of their castle, seemed to be living in some subterranean cave with water trickling down the rocks. It was all very "atmospheric."

In 1966 he was Falstaff on the screen, with all his worst habits to the fore, and of all the overstuffed Falstaffs Welles succeeded in excelling them by the quantity of his padding.

Pamela Brown (b.1917), who was as superb a Gwendolyn in *The Importance of Being Earnest* as Edith Evans was a Lady Bracknell, has done nobly in many a film. At the age of seventeen she appeared as Cressida for the first time at Stratford since Edith Evans had been seen in the role; Miss Brown employed a lisp to indicate the girl's instability. Later (1946) she was Ophelia to Helpmann's Hamlet; Agate thought she gave a marvelously realistic study of a traumatized personality, praised her for not attempting prettiness, and declared her a fine actress. She was Goneril in Olivier's *King Lear*, Margaret Leighton being Regan; the critics particularly noted an effective piece of business when Lear curses her: She had been busy with her needlework, insolently indifferent to him, but she was troubled by his words, dropped her sewing, took it up again, and with a great effort tried to resume her former indifference.

Margaret Leighton (b.1922), who has also appeared in many films as well as in many modern plays, was first seen at the Birmingham Repertory in 1938. After her experience there and on tour, she joined the Old Vic company in 1944, playing a considerably wide range of parts, chiefly in modern and non-Shakespearean roles. In 1952 at Stratford she capitalized on her ethereal quality to make a good Ariel, used her great resources as a comedienne to make a very gay Rosalind, and then played a moving Lady Macbeth. At the Old Vic to Olivier's Lear and Pamela Brown's Goneril she gave an ideal portrait of Regan as icy, spiteful, and chillingly wicked.

In 1959 on Broadway she and Gielgud made the most satisfying and quite perfect Beatrice and Benedick possible.

Paul Scofield (b. 1922), who is perhaps best known to the larger public for his brilliant portrayal of Sir Thomas More in *A Man for All Seasons* (1960), has had a long and varied career in Shakespeare and modern drama. After taking many parts in a students' repertory company and touring during World War II, he joined the Birmingham Repertory company in 1945. That year he attracted considerable attention for his acting as the Bastard in *King John* under the direction of Peter Brook, twenty-one and two years younger than Scofield. In their hands the Bastard became the focus of interest in the play. Trewin says that he looked miraculously Elizabethan, with high cheekbones, deeply furrowed brow surmounted by thick curly hair, dark eyes under heavy brows, and a "tense nobility" of face; at that age his voice could swell or fall as the lines required.

In 1946 he was at Stratford-on-Avon and remained there until 1948, playing Henry V, Don Armado in *Love's Labour's Lost*, Cloten in *Cymbeline*, Lucio in *Measure for Measure*, Pericles, Mercutio, Sir Andrew Aguecheek, Hamlet, Troilus, Bassanio, Roderigo, and the Clown in *The Winter's Tale*. His Mercutio was pronounced the outstanding performance of the play; memorable was Mercutio's Queen Mab speech as he lay flat on his back in torchlight, eyes in a trance, his hand raised while the lines sang out to the attentive grotesquely masked friends.

At the Lyric Theatre in 1952 Scofield, under Gielgud's direction, performed Richard II "with heavy-lidded eyes," in which every word was distinct and separated. In 1955 he did Hamlet again in London and then took it to the Moscow Art Theatre, the first English company to be represented there since the revolution. This expedition led to his being appointed Commander of the British Empire on New Year's 1956. Scofield's prince was a man suffering without histrionics, a Renaissance man with "rifted" voice which suggested light playing on a broken column; some thought him too restrained, others deplored the change from his earlier youthful Hamlet.

At Stratford in a 1962 Peter Brook production he enacted a much-disputed Lear. Brook's setting was a series of coarse off-white screens against which were placed various rusted metal forms; the costumes were made of leather. On the king's first appearance, he was a very arrogant man, and we were made to feel (injuriously for the play) that Goneril and Regan had had to endure too much from him; later in his leather coat and boots reaching to the thighs he seemed like an obstinate, weather-beaten skipper astride the bridge of his vessel as he defied the elements. Toward the close he became a gray ghost, his tough voice frayed to a thin wisp. The end found the stage empty to intensify the tragedy. Harold Hobson in *The Sunday Times* declared that the deliberate limitation of the scale of Brook's production conveyed the "dark and terrible import" that "man is being watched, . . . his presumption will not be forgiven," and that the meek shall inherit the earth "only if an earth is left them to inherit."

I have seen and heard Paul Scofield several times since *A Man for All Seasons,* and it seems to me that he has settled for always being Sir Thomas More no matter what role he is playing, with the same low-keyed, wearied voice.

In 1971 Peter Brook issued his film version of *King Lear* with Scofield in the title role. *The New Yorker* opened its review of the work with the remark that it is "gray and cold, and the actors have dead eyes." The critic went on to say that "I didn't just dislike this production—I hated it." Brook's deliberate intentions were to make the world of the tragedy gray, bleak, and dead —even Cordelia was sullen, a "walking corpse" like all the other actors. Lear became less the center of the work than did the icy barren landscapes of northern Denmark, where the picture was made; the idea seemed to be to enforce the notion that the world is chaos, and there is no hope for mankind. Everyone in the cast appeared sightless—even before Gloucester had his eyes put out (in a giant close-up). Brook, the critic went on to say, undoubtedly had a conception, but it was not a good one; instead of giving dimension to the play, it canceled it out. The acting was "dry" throughout and stiffly mannered, and the main plot was cut so much that all the subplots seemed of equal importance—or nonimportance. The result was not a tragedy, for the plot evaporated, dealing as it did with soulless people. There were unsettling changes from close-ups to distance shots, and the camera kept shifting its angle. Everything seemed devoid of meaning, and the critic sums up by saying, "You may feel dead while you watch." Famous as Scofield's stage Lear had been, on screen he froze you, kept aloof from you, so that you could not once identify with him. For Brook to have confined himself to a single second-rate idea was "an excruciating folly."

Newsweek described Scofield's Lear as a "great gray condor whose tired wings will no longer bear him."

Perhaps Brook's incomprehensible success earlier that same year with a revoltingly vulgar *A Midsummer Night's Dream,* staged with a not dissimilar aridity, may have encouraged him to push barrenness even further in this film.

Richard Burton (b. 1925) was born Richard Jenkins, the son of a miner, in Wales. The man who later adopted him, to whom he owes so much, and whose name he took, Philip Burton, has told me that Richard was one of his students at a secondary school in Port Talbot, Wales, when Philip was himself a young schoolmaster. Richard's mother had died when he was a year old, and he was living with a married sister, much older than himself, with children of her own. He was a boy who had a talent for getting into trouble, Philip says, and Richard's sister came to Philip to plead for his special interest in the lad. The language spoken at home was Welsh, and Philip had to work hard to get the boy over his Welsh accent which, as is characteristic of the industrial towns (though not of the rural areas), was quite ugly. But Richard learned easily: he had an instinctive love of language and poetry.

Philip Burton's adoption of Richard was a gradual process; it never became completely legal because of a stupid complication: the older man lacked the twenty days necessary to give him the required twenty-one years the boy's senior. Instead Richard became Philip's legal ward.

The boy wished to sing too, and he brought home a song by Sullivan; when they were practicing with Philip at the piano, the older man had difficulty suppressing his laughter: the song was keyed for a soprano and Richard's voice was changing. At last Philip could no longer control himself, and the enraged Richard cried out, "I'll show you. Someday I'll show you." Fifteen years later, after the opening performance of *Camelot*, Richard said to his foster father, "Well, I showed you, didn't I?"

Richard Burton made his debut as an actor in 1943. In 1953 he joined the Old Vic company, and during that season performed Hamlet, Coriolanus, the Bastard, Sir Toby Belch, and Caliban. In 1955 he alternated the roles of Othello and Iago with John Neville, and later that season was Henry V. Although I had seen him in a number of modern plays and many films, I had never seen him in Shakespeare until his 1964 Hamlet, which was directed by Gielgud. Up to that performance I had thought him the lucky possessor of that inner glow which I have spoken of as so invaluable to an actor, and additionally endowed with a beautiful voice. But it would seem that if one must be born with that special illumination, one can lose it too. Burton has more or less lost his. My own explanation is that with the years, ever since his romance with Elizabeth Taylor (I mean before they were married, and of course even more so after they were both divorced from their spouses and married to each other), he has chosen to live his private life screamingly and vulgarly in public, and that this wallowing in public vulgarity has debased his acting. (Another factor might be mentioned—his willingness to take part in so many worthless films; as for his films I make two great exceptions in which his old magic resulted in great performances: in *Becket* and *Who's Afraid of Virginia Woolf?* he was superior to the actors who had performed the roles on the stage.)

Trewin thought his first Hamlet merely "solid and painstaking." In an interview with *Playboy* Magazine Burton dismissed *Hamlet* as a play utterly elementary and primitive in idea, and accused Shakespeare of elaborately "dressing up the obvious"; if the play has seemed obscure that is simply a result of the dramatist's being a genius with words. He considers it a work entirely "boring to perform."

As the Bastard Trewin found him strangely cold, though he made a straightforward English patriot obviously brought up in Wales. As Henry V the same critic thought him too stiff and too unvaried in tone.

In the 1964 *Hamlet,* I have been told, Burton was very popular with the cast, with a fund of stories and by his good fellowship, but Gielgud had much difficulty and little success in getting him to adopt his suggestions. It would probably be impossible to assess the value of his performances, for it seemed that he changed the details frequently, according to his mood. When I saw him I thought his prince without charm or magnetism; he was very elaborately pretending to be mad, and the way he jumped up and down on the king's throne like a three-year-old was fairly nauseating. Of course the production was very popular because of the Taylor-Burton scandal, and I do not remember whether it was staged before or after Burton wrote an article for a slick magazine extolling the beauty of Elizabeth Taylor's breasts. In the March 1974 issue of *The Ladies' Home Journal* he wrote another article extolling Sophia Loren, and concluded: "Have spent all night in bed with Elizabeth for real and all day in bed with Sophia for unreal. Not bad when you've come from the bowels of the earth." Earlier in the piece he had said that Miss Loren has treated him as though he were a "clown prince. So she should; I am both."

I look upon him as having deliberately debased himself, as did John Barrymore, though in a somewhat different way. There is something unforgivable in the waste of such a remarkable talent.

It is life's coincidences which make it so unpredictably fascinating. I had just finished the preceding paragraph when my doorbell rang; it was a neighbor with some pages from today's Sunday *News,* the issue of April 14, 1974, which he thought might interest me. Joe Pilcher has written a piece called "The Slings and Arrows of Outrageous Burton," and with the subtitle, "With Liz away, the finest Hamlet of his day plays the clown prince for kicks in the California sticks." The occasion was a press conference called for Burton at Oroville, California. Facing innumerable photographers and questioners, Burton sat with a large ice-filled glass of vodka in his hand. He was asked why his wife was not there, whether there was anything between him and an eighteen-year-old waitress, and what he thought of life. Then Mr. Pilcher quoted a sage observation that someone had once made: "Had he hewed to the hard road of self-denial, he might have been greater than Olivier, but instead he chose $30,000,000 and Elizabeth Taylor." In answer to the persistent questions about his wife he said various things: that she had sprained her ankles by "falling off her sandals," that she was in Los Angeles for an examination after an operation five months ago when her "exquisite stomach" had been "ripped open." About the girl who was recently chosen Miss Pepsi, why had he given her a $450 ring? Well, he replied, "that was a drunken night"; he was looking for a present for Elizabeth but the other girl was so sweet that he bought her the jewelry. What interests me most is the greatest coincidence of all; the journalist finds a "startling parallel" to John Barrymore forty years ago, "his greatness lost in the swamp of alcoholism."

Zoe Caldwell (b. 1933), it would probably be agreed by those who went to see her in a most inconvenient part of New York and in the dingiest of theaters enacting the title role of *Colette* (1970), has the potential to be the greatest English-speaking actress of her generation. The work was hardly a play at all, being a collage of various of Colette's autobiographical writings, but Miss Caldwell's performance was so great a *tour de force* that I went to see her three times during its run. In my opinion it might still be running had she not left for England to take the lead as Emma Hamilton in a Rattigan play. The producer did not seem to realize that it was Miss Caldwell who was bringing the crowds; after her departure the play opened with a new Colette and closed after seven performances. As the fascinating French novelist, Miss Caldwell traced her entire life from girlhood to adulthood, through maturity to old age, all the while projecting the gamut of emotions from delicate poetry to outright farce, from pathos to tragedy, to philosophic acceptance. Having already seen her Cleopatra, I was not as astounded as the New York critics, who unanimously raved about her performances. I honestly can declare that the greatest actresses I have seen during my life have been Eleanora Duse, Edith Evans, and Zoe Caldwell.

I have been lucky enough to have had several interviews with Miss Caldwell in London and New York, and her delicious sense of fun made each visit a joy. She was born at Melbourne, Australia, and began acting under the tutelage of Winifred Moverley Browne at the age of seven. With her she studied voice, dancing, eurhythmics, "everything." By eighteen all preparation for a career was behind her, and she was ready to work. I thought it very touching that she should give full credit to a woman surely no one in the western world had heard of; for it is just the sort of thing most people, unfortunately, would omit.

In Australia she was Desdemona, and never wishes to play her again; Rosalind, and thinks she would not be too good at it if she tried it anew (that I doubt); Viola, in which role she cut her hair to Sebastian's length, but he was so effeminate that the audience was truly confused as to who was the girl and who the man; Maria; and Ophelia. She now feels she understands Ophelia, but the first time she took her on, she made her so introverted that she wore a cap covering both sides of her face (something like a horse's blinders) and dared not look out from beneath those sides! She would love to play Beatrice, but has never had the chance to do so.

Having worked her way up to being the leading actress in Australia by the time she was twenty-four, she came to England in 1957 to do a walk-on at Stratford-on-Avon, and understudied Ophelia for Redgrave's Hamlet, profiting from the opportunity to learn more about the role. She was given the part of Margaret in *Much Ado about Nothing* and of the daughter of Antiochus in *Pericles.* Guthrie saw her and that season chose her to play Helena to Edith Evans's countess in *All's Well That Ends Well;* Trewin was delighted with her freshness in her scenes with the countess and her poetic control in those with the king.

She played Bianca in Paul Robeson's *Othello* (1959), years after his New York performance, and was Cordelia to Laughton's Lear. In our conversation on this play, I was delighted that she understood the strength in Cordelia's character.

At Stratford, Ontario, she performed Lady Macbeth, and then went to Minneapolis to Guthrie's theater, where in her performance of Ophelia she felt that she at last understood her. She told me she was content with her performance and quickly added that *she* has nursed no desire to perform the part of Hamlet!

Back in Ontario, she was seen as Mistress Page, Lady Anne of *Richard III,* and, her greatest Shakespearean performance, Cleopatra. I was much interested in her ideas concerning this complicated part, and her description of the character was a perfect summary of the way she performed it: she understood the Queen of Egypt to be very voluptuous, witty, "bitchy," a girl with "a thousand facets." She made the observation that an actress who sees the character that way does not have to worry about putting the pieces together, because (which is the simple truth) every time you see Cleopatra, she shows herself in a new light. Miss Caldwell mixed perfumed oils into her makeup so that her body was fragrant from head to foot. Her Antony, Christopher Plummer, she praised to the skies. I have never seen a Cleopatra superior to hers for faithfulness to Shakespeare's intentions. It was in 1967 that she played the role with Plummer. Elliot Norton, drama critic for the *Boston Record,* saw that performance too and made some keen observations about it. When Miss Caldwell first appeared on stage, she was not striking, for Cleopatra theoretically should have been taller than Miss Caldwell's small, compact figure; she should be tall because she should be regal. But within a minute she had proved that Cleopatra must be small, compact "and wildly, exhilaratingly vital" and not at all tall. "God created Zoe Caldwell to play Cleopatra." (That seemed an act of faith beyond dispute.) Norton lauded her voice, which encompasses the purr of a lioness, the hiss of an adder, the bellowing of a boat whistle. When she and Antony came on in the first scene, she was purring like a panther "whose claws were showing." She was sure of herself as she played her "own game, nagging and needling Antony until he blushed at her effrontery—her mockery that he had better hear the messenger, who might be from his master, the boy Caesar. The scene, for all its brevity, formed a firm basis for the rest of the play. Can any actress, Mr. Norton asks, in so brief a span project persuasively Antony's rapt address to her:

> Whom every thing becomes—to chide, to laugh,
> To weep; whose every passion fully strives
> To make itself, in thee, fair and admired!

and suggest all these qualities? "Miss Caldwell did."

In what followed, sometimes moving rapidly, sometimes sitting languidly, sighing, taunting, smiling, shouting in a burst of anger, "raging like a savage," quizzing a messenger like an adolescent about Octavia's face, she finally achieved a Roman grandeur in her last scene. At every moment she "was the woman Shakespeare drew in opulent understanding of all women." Yet, no matter what the mood, even when talking most rapidly, she was always "easily and clearly audible," always true to the beautiful music of the verse.

There is only one reason which could prevent Miss Caldwell from becoming the leading actress of her generation, and why she is not seen often enough on the stage. She is married to the producer Robert Whitehead, by whom she has two children, and she feels her life complete as wife and mother, and is therefore reluctant to accept roles which separate her from her family. It is only when the itch to act becomes irresistible that she will yield to it.

Judi Dench (b. 1934) was born at York and had intended to become a scenic designer. I was also fortunate in having an interview with her in London, during which she was most generous in giving me the facts of her career. In 1954 she entered the Central School of Speech Training and Dramatic Art, then located at Albert Hall, and won a great many medals; during her last year, 1957, Michael Benthall, then running the Old Vic, was looking for an Ophelia to play opposite John Neville for the August season, and asked her to take what she thought was to be a walk-on part; when told she was to be Ophelia, she burst into tears.

That same season she found herself engaged for Julietta in *Measure for Measure*, Maria in *Twelfth Night*, and the Princess of France in *Henry V*.

In 1958 she went to Paris, Edinburgh, the United States, and Canada with *Hamlet* (as Ophelia) and the Princess of France with Laurence Harvey. In 1959/60 she was in many non-Shakespearean roles as well as the queen in *Richard II*. In 1960/61 she played Juliet at the Old Vic in Franco Zeffirelli's production; Trewin thought she might be the Juliet of her age, impulsively young as she was, but the work as a whole was impaired by Zeffirelli's deafness to English verse. That season she was also Hermia.

In 1962 she was at Stratford-on-Avon for the Royal Shakespeare Company as Titania and Isabella. Trewin found in her role in *Measure for Measure* "a gleam of truth in every phrase," and in her Titania a spirit who seemed to be made of "spun crystal"; it had been years since Oberon (Ian Richardson) and Titania had been presented in Shakespeare's native town "more fittingly and mellifluously."

The next year she was in West Africa as Lady Macbeth and Viola; she also reenacted her Titania for a film of the play. At Nottingham she was Isabella again in a modern-dress production. In 1969 she doubled as Perdita and Hermione at Stratford (I later saw her magical interpretations of both roles in London at the Aldwych Theatre), and she also took the role of Viola. The next year she was in both plays in Japan, and then in London.

Miss Dench is very droll about her occasional mishaps. In the Zeffirelli *Romeo and Juliet*, friends of hers who were members of the ballet were in the audience and she was so busy showing them that *she* could dance too that she fell flat on her face. (She adds that she is subject to falling easily.) In *Twelfth Night* she had on a black wig as Maria in Edinburgh, but lost it; with complete calm she returned it to her head in full sight of the audience, who greeted the gesture with applause.

I found her very sound on Shakespeare and what he meant to convey during our discussion; she was particularly splendid on Isabella. I have seen her in many parts, including non-Shakespearean, and have never seen her turn in a performance of less than the highest quality.

27

Some Recent Productions

We have noted performances in our own time which have been brilliant, excellent, good, acceptable, poor, and deplorable. But I cannot conclude this book without paying specific attention to some productions of the immediate past and present which have flagrantly violated Shakespeare out of ignorance, bad taste, or inferior judgment. The reader and I are both living in the present, and without this representative survey I should be avoiding the goal toward which everything in this work points.

I have already mentioned plenty of examples of the particular curse under which the Shakespearean theater operates: that worst of all vulgarities, the search of novelty as an end in itself. Lord Olivier has said that people will not come to see Shakespeare unless he is done each time in a new way. I suggest that nowadays the newest way of all would be to give the plays in the *spirit* in which they were written—that is to say, without transporting them to some meaningless milieu (e.g., the Victorian, the Edwardian, the Haitian jungle), without transposing scenes and speeches, and, most of all, without burying the play under all kinds of superimposed "business." To introduce the last named with the excuse that they make the play more "meaningful today" is to say that it is the exterior of the play which counts, not what the poet-dramatist truly intended; to argue that any such alterations are justifiable in order to make the greatest works ever written for the theater more "relevant" to the contemporary world is tantamount to arguing that it is perfectly right to substitute saxophones for clarinets and horns, electric guitars for violins and cellos and a hard-rock chorus for the sublime Hymn to Joy in Beethoven's Ninth Symphony, inserting or substituting such gracious "relevant" modern phrases as, "Baby, baby!" or "I've been invited to an orgy!" No vulgarian would object to *that!* Indeed, in terms of drama that is pretty much what Peter Brook did to *A Midsummer Night's Dream,* as we shall see.

The first line of the trial scene in *The Merchant of Venice* is the duke's

"What! Is Antonio here?" Now, every college sophomore has already learned that *What*, one of the oldest words in our language and the very first in *Beowulf* (where more logically it is spelled *Hwaet*) is no more than an exclamation, roughly equivalent to "Hey there!" or "Ho there!" It appears frequently in Shakespeare—"What Juliet!" "What Jessica!"—where it is no more than a summoning call. Yet in the 1970 London production of the play at the National Theatre upon which the recent TV movie was based, there was the duke sitting at the head of a board-room table, with Antonio and Bassanio plainly in view to his right; but the director could not be bothered finding out the simple meaning (or lack of it) in *What!*, and with extravagant ingenuity arranged to have a subordinate first whisper something in the duke's ear, and then had the duke blast out in astonishment: "WHAT?? Is ANTONIO here?" (i.e., if he is here, how dare he be?). After all, they were convened for Antonio's trial, and where else should he have been? This is but one instance of the willful ignorance of directors these days. (The movie omitted this original touch.)

When Zeffirelli directed the *Romeo and Juliet* movie, he was proud of the fact that neither Leonard Whiting nor Olivia Hussey, hero and heroine, had ever read the play. Thus blissfully ignorant, they were in a perfectly impartial position to agree with Zeffirelli that "it is a contemporary drama." Whiting went on to say, "I find Shakespeare very boring," but in Zeffirelli's movie there was so much action that "I don't think of it as poetry at all." (This in the play containing the greatest lyrical poetry in our drama!) Zeffirelli's own account was that Juliet must be strong, Romeo gentle, and the story one of young people "finding identity in a troubled era, just like today." He added that like kids today these two *"were* quite revolutionary." He did not explain how.

This new cult of ignorance, it must in all fairness be conceded, comes in part from a not altogether unwarranted distrust of a large portion of Shakespearean "scholarship." For a long time Shakespearean "scholars" have been writing to illuminate not the plays nor the actors nor the public. They write for one another in "learned" periodicals or merely to be promoted in their teaching jobs. Moreover, they rarely remember that they are writing about *plays*, and that in plays you must not approach the work *a priori* with a thesis based first on some passage in Act IV, then bolstered by some passage in Act II, then supported by some passage in some other act. In a play, you must take Lewis Carroll's advice: begin at the beginning, go on until you come to the end, and then stop. Your passage in Act IV dare not be interpreted until you reach it, for its meaning depends upon all that precedes it. It is this habit of squeezing a play into a theory founded upon some speech midway in the play which has resulted in all the confusion concerning Hamlet, Shylock, and Othello, among others. All this is sorry fact. Still, it is not an excuse for a director's failure to insist that his and his actors' performances be built on a complete understanding of the meaning of every word in the play.

I do not mean to imply that director and actor are not free to *expand* upon the fundamentals of a Shakespearean character, so long as they do no violence to the dramatist's conception. At a Pipe Night at The Players Club a few years ago, Frank McHugh was vastly entertaining in a story he related about Frank Bacon, who established a record run in the stellar role of *Lightning* on Broadway. Years before that triumph Bacon was playing the First Gravedigger in a California stock presentation of *Hamlet.* Walter Catlett, the Second Gravedigger, prepared to do his job conscientiously, was astonished to see Bacon putting on what seemed an endless series of vests, one over the other, while they were putting on their costumes. When they were on stage Catlett, digging away for all he was worth, could not understand why the audience began to howl with laughter, which rose every few moments in volume and delight. Then he looked up and saw that Bacon, after every line or two, would take off one vest and lay it aside before peeling off the next one, until he was literally divested of them. Now, *that* I wish I could have seen. The First Gravedigger is a clown, and Bacon's little trick made him only more of one, without offense to Shakespeare's purposes.

In 1969 Nicol Williamson came to New York as Hamlet, after having performed it in London under the direction of Tony Richardson at the Round House. There, Williamson's prince was described by Thomas Quinn Curtiss as "nasal and non-U," and more anxious to "shake things up generally" than to avenge his father's murder, and more a commoner than a potential king. The performance Quinn described as "harsh, insistent and shrill," doing no justice to the lyric possibilities, and becoming inaudible when the actor turned his back on the audience. Richardson's alterations of the text did "not improve the unfolding of the play," and the cast's styles of acting varied from one another and frequently "clashed."

When the production was brought to New York, on the second night an angry member of the audience, leaving the theater during the intermission, shouted aloud, "It's a phony, I can only take one half, and that cost me ten bucks!" I sympathize with that spectator, though, as I rarely do any longer, I sat through the entire performance. It is recorded that during that second night, "many in the audience yawned, others fell asleep," and numbers departed before the play was over. Clive Barnes of *The New York Times* did think the production shabby and the supporting cast inadequate but he hailed Williamson for putting an end to the Gielgud or Olivier Hamlets.

For reasons of his own Williamson assumed the rising inflection of the English Midlands, or, as Allan Lewis put it, "more like the Barbados blacks" (Williamson has red hair). Throughout the evening he kept his hands stiffly at his sides, which I assumed was intended to show Hamlet's inability "to communicate"—a favorite bromide of our day. Allan Lewis said Williamson was able to find "ugliness everywhere and is equally ugly, more like a Black Panther or an SDS rebel, which I suppose provides the relevance in these days." Allan Lewis correctly reflected that Hamlet cannot "live in a vacuum" and relate to nothing else. Thus our "greatest tragedy" became a play without tragedy. Nothing seemed at stake, no one fell from a height. It may indeed make a new Hamlet, says Lewis, by having him speak in strange rhythms and behave like a "petulant dropout," but it is hardly a valuable one. Lewis accounts cogently for the critical acclaim heaped upon William-son by saying that whatever "defies tradition" and can sound contemporary enough is manna for the press agents. That summation accounts for most of the Shakespeare seen since then in New York and much that is seen in London and Stratford-on-Avon.

No production of recent years lingers in my memory as more revolting than the 1970 Peter Brook *A Midsummer Night's Dream*, even though all the critics I read (except Brendan Gill of *The New Yorker* and John Simon of *New York* Magazine, who thought of it as "Bardocide") went wild with enthusi-asm. Peter Brook has said that whereas the theater began as magic, "magic at the sacred festival or magic as the footlights came up," nowadays the director must open up his "empty hands" and show that he has "nothing up his sleeves." Well, he certainly was successful. *Time* praised him for presenting an "explosive, gaudy circus" (*gaudy* seems peculiarly inappropri-ate for the glaring white box in which the entire play took place) which was "howlingly funny" and "genuinely sexy." Now this, certainly not one of the dramatist's greatest plays, is not howlingly funny (except, perhaps in the Pyramus and Thisbe section) nor sexy. The Lord knows that Brook made it sexy enough. As for the howlingly funny comedy, bored with the perfor-mance, I began to watch the audience attentively. They did laugh uproari-ously, but *never once* at anything Shakespeare had written—only at the gim-mickry Brook had added to the play. No one was, for instance, the least bit amused at the Pyramus and Thisbe episode, which was merely thrown away; as I have said, I have often seen students do it better. The production was indeed like a three-ring circus. The white box was topped by a gallery fenced off with lead pipes; from there the members of the cast, when not on stage, looked down upon the action, and regained it by ladders when they were through with a scene. Oberon was lowered from this gallery and lifted to it on a trapeze; Puck climbed up and slid down on a rope. Pease-blossom, Cobweb, Moth and Mustardseed, the Fairies, were husky mustached men dressed hippy style. (The reason for this was presently seen.) The "little western flower," the juice of which Oberon bids Puck drop upon the eyelids of Titania and the lovers, became a juggler's stick on the end of which Puck caught a spinning plate which Oberon threw him; when Puck (dressed throughout as Harlequin) stood astride Lysander, I thought he was going to put his eye out with the stick; then, as the love effects of the "nectar" began, Lysander, half-asleep, began to caress the legs of Puck until he came to his genitals. *Then* we saw it was working! Later Helena felt Lysander's body until she reached his penis; *then* she knew it was a man! When the Fairies sang it was quasi-rock, quasi-Oriental, with quasi-Oriental gestures. When Bottom had the ass's head on him, he was lifted up by these stevedore Fairies, and one of them bared his arm to the shoulder, thrust it through Bottom's legs, and made a fist, so that naked arm and fist together made an enormous throbbing phallus. It was at these obscenities the audience howled with delight—not at the play which Shakespeare had written. Was it possible that Alan Howard, who was Theseus and Oberon in the play and who spoke both roles in the same bored manner, as though he had a pain in his tummy, was the same man I had seen shortly before this at the Aldwych in London making an admirable Benedick and a first-rate comic in Ben Jonson? Passages which were not written as songs were sung to a strumming rock-band accompaniment. At the end of the play, when all was cleared up for the lovers, there was a scene of mutual groping of private parts by all hands. The whole thing was shocking, not morally, but for the outrageous vulgarity visited upon a work which has the refinement of the music Mendelssohn later wrote for it. It exposed public and critic alike for paying tribute to such desecration. Anything but anything for a laugh was the order of the evening. The *Time* critic praised it as a dream which was "not an escapist fantasy but a vision of order and regeneration."

In November of the same year it was my privilege to sit through the first half of a special presentation of *King Lear*, renamed, because it was "a contemporary impression" of that play, *K. L. Lear*, at The Actors Studio, "conceived and directed by Maya Kenin." We were told that only six months had been spent thus far on the masterpiece. K. L. Lear was an American tycoon, the Fool was a woman who was Lear's mistress. Regan and Goneril both had daughters who called Lear in the appropriate voice, "Grand-daddy." These two monsters, by the way, seemed anything but vicious—but why go on?

In 1971 the National Theatre in London presented a new *Coriolanus* staged by Manfred Wekwerth and Joachim Tenschert from East Berlin, both associated with Brecht. They gave London a very Brechtian *Coriolanus*, from which, during rehearsals, Christopher Plummer very understandably withdrew. He was replaced by a young actor, Anthony Hopkins. The stress, naturally, was upon "class struggle and the glorification of war." Coriolanus himself emerges as a fascist beast, rather than an uncompromising aristo-crat. Though Shakespeare, as he wrote the play, took no sides, this produc-tion was entirely proletarian in its viewpoint. Despite Mr. Hopkins's real ability, Coriolanus, as the directors intended, evoked no sympathy and was downright obnoxious.

The change that has come over Mr. Joseph Papp, director of the New York Shakespeare Festival, during the years is disappointing, though easily ex-plained. In the early days at Central Park he was a vigorous champion of Shakespeare, doing his best by him. In 1961 he was saying: "The challenge for the director . . . is to achieve this modernity [i.e., presenting characters that are believable and with whom the audience can identify] *without sacrific-ing the form and poetry of Shakespeare and without vulgarizing the period*" (italics mine). Yet within that same decade he was presenting a *Hamlet* in which the prince came on stage in a coffin with wheels, and from which, continuing the transposition of scenes and speeches, Hamlet rose to recite the "O that this too too solid flesh" speech as referring to Gertrude and Claudius, as the hero ripped off the coverlet from the bed on which they reposed. Since then, and since his appointment at Lincoln Center (when he has not directed them himself), he has preferred to select Shakespearean directors who have had no experience with the plays, but who have "interesting new" ideas. Obviously Papp now wishes to be à la mode.

In August 1971 he allowed A. J. Antoon to direct *Cymbeline* in the Delacorte Theater in Central Park. The comedy in this tragicomedy was more often than not burlesqued; King Cymbeline was turned into a clown "at least 160" years of age, and in his "dotage, limping around like a lost Lear," lapsing into an "L. B. Johnson drawl." However, when he wins over the Romans, he hot-stepped "into a cakewalk." The Roman legions were got up like wild animals, and the British like "an army of Big Birds." The absurdities of the production were overwhelming. The year before, in Ontario, Canada, the same play was made, as it should, to revolve around Imogen, in an uncut, no-absurdity emphasis upon the dramatic values of the play. In Antoon's production she became more or less lost in the midst of spurious invention.

Another critic said of this performance: "Sometimes Mr. Antoon tries to make jokes at the expense of the script; sometimes a lot of business obscures the script; there are transpositions and interpolations. But nothing holds together. Iachimo, as written, is a strange, slick, clever villain, with much delicate poetry to speak; William Devane's Iachimo is intolerably cloddish."

In New York at Lincoln Center's Vivian Beaumont Theater and in Stratford, Connecticut's Shakespeare Playhouse, both of which approximate the Elizabethan stage in shape, the record of production, with very few exceptions, is appalling.

In the spring of 1972 Ellis Rabb directed *Twelfth Night* at the Vivian Beaumont. It was done with most elaborate *chinoiserie* effects in the scenery (why?) and even the priest who marries Olivia and Sebastian was clothed in Chinese garb. It made, said Brendan Gill, a most "tiresome evening." Moses Gunn, who is black, was, said Gill, "an ideally unsuitable Orsino, and Cynthia Belgrave, also black, as Maria, squeaks and gibbers in a fashion conspicuously inappropriate to the bawdry of Old England." I should add that to me she seemed to be not at all the little devil Shakespeare invented. There was again, a great deal of needless running about, and for no explicable reason Olivia preferred to speak with her body and face prone, close to the ground (to show mourning for her brother?). Feste, most delightful of clowns, was here merely a bore.

John Simon admired the set and was apparently prepared to have, for a change, a delightful evening at the Vivian Beaumont. But as soon as Gunn appeared to speak his opening line, everything was ruined. Gunn's "mixture of croak and quaver" constitutes the "most unstrung" delivery now on the American stage. Moreover, he had not the slightest notion of the meaning of what he was saying. His stare was meaningless, his eyes rolled about wildly. Simon thought the other blacks in the cast even worse. The Maria was "a black stereotype well worth avoiding"; Simon thought her a "crudely unappealing actress." Her unintelligibility was exceeded only by Harold Miller's black Fabian. Mr. Simon raises some cogent considerations. He says, "Casting a Negro in a white Shakespearean role is a hopeless proposition." He bids liberals keep up their ranting, but a black simply will not work as Orsino. He adds that neither appearance nor voice of a black actor can be made to suit the plot's logic or the tone of the language. He asks us to consider what would happen if an all-black play were cast with some white actors. As for Rabb's direction, it becomes absurd that "sooner or later everybody flops down or sprawls out, as if Illyria were hit by an epidemic of sleeping sickness."

Papp had already done *Two Gentlemen of Verona* as a rock musical; I did not much care because that play, for all its occasional charm, is not a particularly good play. But *Much Ado About Nothing!* The most brilliant comedy in English, with incomparable Beatrice, Benedick and Dogberry in the cast—to be set in a scaffolding filled with the faces of Theodore Roosevelt, Keystone Kop Ford Sterling, "with a Model T Ford and an iron-maiden corset ad thrown in"—and having "midway up the rigging a brass band blaring," with a "Scott Joplin rag can" rattling through the amplifiers, a Benedick just returned from the Spanish-American War and a Claudio in khaki? All this achieved again by Antoon's direction! Walter Kerr, like many of the critics, liked it, but he added: "The Keystone Kops do not help, though Barnard Hughes—with helmet and billy and a nose like a cigar-glow—is an exceptionally able Dogberry." He and "his colleagues have been hurtled on stage in a shivering yellow car to pile up in twos and threes and then leap" for the theater's aisles. To my surprise, even Gill liked it. But though it had a long run, I would not go to see it for I knew I should be restless to make my exit. John Simon found it out of character for Beatrice to mount a chair for a clearer sight of the returning Benedick, and equally wrong for Dogberry, who ought to take himself most seriously, to "dance around waggishly holding up his coattails"; nor would Don John, when defeated, wilt on the floor in a burlesque of Chaplin's travesty of Hitler; moreover it was a "soggy joke" to have "a wistful number with umbrellas under the rain" in the penultimate scene. Simon found Glenn Walken's Claudio very bad, a kind of Andy Hardy. I have seen Mr. Walken far too often; he seems to be greatly admired in some quarters; his technique is unquestionably modern, possibly suitable for the "relevant" plays of today, but unbearable in Shakespeare.

At about the same time they were doing *Macbeth* at Stratford, Ontario. Julius Novick described it as "erratic, fierce and odd," and added that almost everyone disliked it. There was an unexplained crowd of "Poor People" who kept appearing and reappearing, particularly in the witches' scenes, along with other original touches: Lady Macbeth appeared in her bare feet; Macduff wore a ridiculous hat, Italian comic-opera style—such details were somehow connected with the thoughtful "directorial 'concept' " of Peter Gill.

In 1972 appeared the nauseating film version of *Macbeth* produced by Roman Polanski. A more deliberately blood-soaked production of the play can never have been given, and it is all the more remarkable that it should have followed the massacre of Polanski's pregnant wife and his wife's guests by the Manson gang. One would have thought that he could face anything but needless, meaningless spilling of blood and sickening violence, but his *Macbeth* was saturated with both. When asked why, his unacceptable reply was that the superfluous bloodletting and violence were intended to discourage both in life! As Pauline Kael pointed out, "the movie is full of correlations with what happened in Hollywood; . . . one sees the Manson murders in this *Macbeth* because the director has put them there." This critic went on to remark that it is customary to go to see this tragedy in order to watch some famous actor; on this occasion the actor, Jon Finch, "is barely featured. Slaughter is the star of this *Macbeth.*" The corpses and murders which Shakespeare arranged off stage were here brought on the screen. There was, indeed, such a heaping up of violence and blood pouring that the poetry was almost inaudible. Miss Kael sagely observed that the movie "says that nothing is possible but horror and more horror." At the very end, a Polanski addition, "the new king's crippled, envious brother" has gone to find the witches, "and the cycle of bloodletting is about to begin again."

Unhappily, for the sake of this book, I felt obliged to view this monstrosity, where there was no one to sympathize with, no one to admire, no poetry to stir the imagination. Macbeth, instead of a stout warrior-chief, was a youth, very lithe in movement and totally unheroic; Lady Macbeth was a slip of a girl, who could not possibly have known what it is to give suck to babes—much more like Ophelia throughout than Macbeth's wife. Roman Polanski interviewed nearly one hundred actors before choosing the little-known Jon Finch to play Macbeth, and had decided that *all* the actors should be in their twenties. Kenneth Tynan, creator of *O Calcutta!,* the all-nude show, wrote the screenplay for this production—it was therefore not unexpected that there would be scenes in which characters would wear no clothes —and the picture was financed by Hugh Hefner, of *Playboy* fame. To increase the horror, all kinds of changes and additions were made: the hallucinated dagger of Macbeth's imagination was very much in the air for all of us to see, and it quite literally marshalled him (I could honestly say, *marched* before him) into Duncan's chamber to do the murder; the scene of that murder was in no way less than what the members of Manson's "family" could have been equal to—Macbeth first pricked the sleeping Duncan awake with his dagger, then savagely stabbed him, almost joyously, many times, until the king's eyes popped out of his head before us; surely Macbeth's hands were bloodier than those of any Macbeth on record. Presently we beheld the drunken Porter urinating; one wondered why Lady Macbeth would have dragged her train through a muddy courtyard. Such soliloquies as were allowed to remain soliloquies were partly spoken, partly "thought" while the character moved no lips. Everybody looked as though he knew that Macbeth was going to murder Duncan; the killing of Duncan's servants was shown, accompanied by grins of the murderer. There was a bear-baiting scene. Macbeth confided to his wife that he intended to kill Banquo ("To be thus is nothing," etc., originally a soliloquy). The bear seemed the chief guest at the banquet scene; this bear, as well as Banquo's murderers, came to an untimely end; Banquo's ghost entered lavishly besmeared with blood; Macbeth's soliloquy on the occasion was delivered to the guests. Macbeth's second visit to the witches (in a cave) introduced us to a large covey of them, all naked, many with enormous pendulous breasts. It was Malcolm who delivered the Burnam Woods prophecy. The man who warned Lady Macduff was one of her murderers, and the Macduff household was again a scene of general slaughter. Lady Macbeth was also naked in her sleepwalking scene, and while washing her hands moved them as if she were playing the piano. Macbeth heard of his wife's death without emotion. When Burnam Wood began to march it looked like a collection of Christmas trees that had been discarded in January. The last scenes were naturally a splendid opportunity for a great deal more bloodshedding; we saw Macbeth literally decapitated, as his head fell from the throne on which he was seated, and the exposed interior network of the neck clearly shown. Nothing more dreadful or un-Shakespearean can ever be contrived with his play.

In 1972 the Royal Shakespeare Company was of course showing Shakespeare at Stratford-on-Avon and at the Aldwych in London. John Barton's production of *Othello* was laid in the mid-nineteenth century, with the Venetian soldiers as "colonial militia men" and Othello himself a bore, and far too "unctuous." There were the now-expected innovations, and as Clive Barnes said, "There is a kind of decadence in such gimmickry, as every director tries desperately hard to put his fingerprints all over the play, encouraging audiences all too often to say, 'How clever!' rather than 'How true!' "

In the late summer of 1972 the Royal Shakespeare Company at Stratford-on-Avon was busy with the Roman plays, *Julius Caesar, Antony and Cleopatra, Coriolanus,* and *Titus Andronicus;* the director, Trevor Nunn, claimed that the four plays "show the birth, achievement and collapse of a civilization." Mr. Nunn had better read his Aristotle, who emphasizes the fact that drama is *not* history—a doctrine to which Shakespeare, without reading the *Poetics,* instinctively subscribed. He is forever compressing what in history took years into a few weeks or months; indeed, the Antony of one play is a totally different person from the Antony of the other. Why not? Each appears in a different play, under different circumstances, and at a different time of his life. Mr. Nunn (unlike his East German predecessor) gave a Coriolanus destroyed by his own pride. In both of the plays in which Antony appears Mr. Nunn apparently had the courage to direct the plays as Shakespeare had conceived them.

In the spring of 1973 Ellis Rabb directed at the Vivian Beaumont Theater in New York one of the most outrageous of all possible performances of *The Merchant of Venice.* The direction and the cast were almost equally offensive. Salario became Salaria; Belmont became not Portia's estate, but a yacht (called The Belmont) anchored somewhere or other on which all the guests went about in the scantiest bikinis and lolled on beach chairs—just as though they were at the Lido; indeed, most of the characters were practically naked except at the crotch, and it may have afforded pleasure to some members of the three sexes—such as had paid phenomenal prices for front-row seats at the all-nude *O Calcutta!*; people like that are almost to be envied for this low emotional threshold! Bassanio, one of the most aristocratic and elegant of Shakespeare's men, was an insufferable prosaic hippy in the person of Christopher Walken, who would do better to use no gestures at all than the mean, half-hearted little jerks he indulged in. There were, of course, long meaningless silences (to which Pinter has accustomed us) as well as much mangling of the text; Morocco's scimitar, by which he takes an oath, was a little pin; at parting with Shylock in the third scene, Antonio, under the delusion that he was speaking Yiddish, said, *"Auf wiedersehn!"*; Launcelot Gobbo had no soliloquies, but spoke to the cigarette-smoking hippies; his father was cut out of the text; hippy women were all over the place; Shylock was endearingly sweet to Jessica (Shakespeare wrote him not one such line), and was generally a very gentle person, who as a rule ad-dressed himself exclusively to the audience, and never once looked at the duke during the trial scene; Portia saved Antonio not by any prepared plan but by a sudden flash of inspiration—thus robbing the entire play of its meaning, and during that same scene Bassanio's love for Antonio was made blatantly homosexual by the nature of the caresses he bestowed upon him (the way for such an interpretation having already been prepared some years earlier at Stratford, Connecticut). There was a great deal of manufactured business throughout, in the way of cigarette smoking and highball drinking; Lorenzo seemed far more in love with himself than with Jessica and in their beautiful scene at Belmont in the last act, they never so much as touched each other; their dialogue was an argument rather than a series of love speeches; there was no fun about the rings on Portia and Nerissa's return —indeed, Portia gave Bassanio a resounding slap. Generally, all through the play, everyone looked miserable, especially Antonio; Jessica came to regret her marriage to Lorenzo, and it seemed a question as to whether poor Bassanio ought to have married Portia or Antonio.

Concerning this production, John Simon, one of the few critics who hates to see Shakespeare mangled, said it "would be unfair to many other direc-tors to call Ellis Rabb the worst in America, but he is certainly the most perverse"; he found the performances "viscous, pulpy and nerveless" and done in a pseudorock style. He objected that Venetian society should consist of "campy homosexuals and idle tourists"; the direction reduced the play to a "shambles." Christopher Walken, as a "seemingly un-Platonic" friend of Antonio's "struts about like a male model showing off the latest Bill Blass collection while mumbling his lines in a barely audible, breakneck mono-tone, like some lobotomized valedictorian at an idiot school." What was called for, said Simon, was "not a critic but a neurosurgeon."

In the summer of that year *As You Like It* was given in Central Park with the costuming for the exiled noblemen in white satin right out of Watteau. The performance was boring, the impression of one auditor being that they must have added lines to the play to make it endless. Actually it was only a nearly uncut version. Simon objected to the Papp production because the acting was "almost garish," without any effect of ensemble playing. The Corin was like a "scat singer" and the Adam like a "Borscht-belt" comedian; Le Beau and Charles seemed to come "out of the seedier gay bars"; you could almost smell Johnson's Baby Powder on Celia; Orlando came right out of a *West Side Story* Puerto Rican street gang, and Amiens (played by Meat Loaf [sic]) looked, but did not sound like, "a castrato"; Jaques (played by an actor named Coffin) was a "leering, scowling, growling and guffawing churl"; the Rosalind looked believable "only as a boy"—Kathleen Widdoes, who did the role, understood acting to be a profession in which you make love to yourself "in public."

As to the Stratford (Connecticut) Playhouse, so admirably fitted to do justice to Shakespeare, its sins extend farther than those of the Vivian Beaumont Theater—but only because it was built earlier. John Simon, after a season which included *Antony and Cleopatra,* concluded his review with the remark that he would not soon return to that Stratford, for the way the great play was performed was enough to make the angels weep. He did not bother to tell us, but undoubtedly he must ask himself: What is the use of having a playhouse on the Elizabethan model when every effort has for years been made to depart from the meaning of Shakespeare's plays? Poor Mr. Simon, despite his declaration, will as a critic have to go there again in the future. Luckily, I do not have to. One gets an idea of what went on in that tragedy by his description of its Caesar as a small fellow whose voice and behavior lacked any dignity, but who did "strut" rather more than did his colleagues, and wore his nightshirt like a Klansman's, and by telling us that the Cleopatra was more like a "lounge lizard" than Shakespeare's bewitching queen.

I have walked out of too many Stratford performances to bother taking the trip up to Connecticut again merely to be irritated. Even when I have seen fine individual performances (e.g., Alfred Drake as Benedick and Iago; Morris Carnovsky as Lear and Shylock), the rest of the production was either poor or intolerable. After I had waited for years to see *Measure for Measure,* it was merely disgusting to see that most vitriolic of plays filled with some of Shakespeare's finest poetry turned into slapstick farce, despite the valiant efforts of Arnold Moss* as the duke. It was, as I have already remarked, nauseating to see Carnovsky's Shylock surrounded by a bevy of homosexuals, the Antonio-Bassanio crowd, and to see Antonio at the end desolated by his friend's happiness with Portia—nauseating not because I have any objection to homosexuals leading their own lives, but because Shakespeare

*Arnold Moss is a good actor and I have seen him three times in Shakespeare, each time with admiration for his talents. But he has each time been unlucky in the production. He made an admirable Prospero in 1945 under Margaret Webster's direction; but his Ariel, Vera Zorina, was forever assuming ballet stances and making one shudder each time she said: "Pchospe-chro" (the *ch* as in German); his Trinculo and Stefano had their own Slavonic pronunciations; and his Caliban, Canada Lee, was ungainly enough without any of the earthy poetry written for the role. When I saw him as Malvolio he was easily the finest actor in the cast, though the conception was all wrong. In his dressing room I congratulated him on his acting but asked why he had made Malvolio a tragic figure. His remarkable answer was: "I'm glad you said that and that I made him come across as tragic. I felt that Shakespeare had been unfair to him."

never invented a single homosexual in any of his plays (with the possible exception that homosexuality in Patroclus is *spoken* of), and my allegiance is to Shakespeare.

In the summer of 1973 they gave *Macbeth* at Stratford, Connecticut. John Simon's opening comment was that the stainless steel set for the play was the "only stainless thing" in the performance; the set itself, looking like a "giant sawtoothed bank vault" did not increase the horror of the tragedy, was repetitious, and ended by being merely "cute." He thought that the "clever" ideas of the director, Michael Kahn, were hit-or-miss and caused the production to "die on its feet of neglect," and that these clever ideas themselves, when put together, added up to nonsense. For example, the witches were ladies of Duncan's court leading a double life; he was thus able to place the opening scene not on the stormy heath but at a holy communion service. Mr. Simon observed that not since Paul Robeson's Othello had he heard a Shakespearean hero sing his part in such a tuneless, deadening "recitative." This Macbeth was Fritz Weaver. On the other hand, Rosemary Murphy played Lady Macbeth, said Mr. Simon, as drawing-room comedy; besides looking like Columbine, in the sleepwalking scene she wore ballet slippers; in that scene she was a puzzled housewife who could not understand "why that damned spot" could not be washed off "with the usual detergents." The review was headed, "Signifying Nothing," and concluded with the tart remark that the whole was "invincibly ignorant."

Julius Novick in the *Times* was also of the opinion that not all of the director's original ideas "seem to have a great deal to do with one another." The great metal wall designed as the set by Douglas Schmidt created a "barren world, haunted by its own emptiness, profoundly inimical to human life." Mr. Novick wondered what "kind of acting would be right for this anti-human scenic world." As Falstaff might say, "A question to be asked!" And I ask what has an antihuman world got to do with tragedy?

In the late summer of 1973 the New York Shakespeare Festival presented *King Lear* "as a lackluster farce," said John Simon. The staging, he continued, was "one part Peter Brook (whose *Lear* . . . was also offensive), . . . one part weird excogitations, and one part letting the actors do whatever they can come up with." James Earl Jones's Lear was largely "slow-witted and subdued, somewhat in imitation of Paul Scofield's" but not as consistent. What ruined Jones's performance was his "arbitrary fragmentation" of passages and pauses without significance; some of the most tragic lines were given, intentionally or not, as if intended for laughs: at any rate, the audience guffawed at words that should provoke tears, like, "Let me wipe it first" or "Kill, kill, kill." And his dying lines, written to be said as he gazed down at Cordelia's dead body, "Look on her, look, her lips," were "barked straight at the moon or one of the planes flying overhead." Even so excellent a performer as Paul Sorvino proved "what a lack of training" can do to American actors: his Gloucester was a bad "joke" throughout, mumbled or raced at "breakneck speed," and with a tendency to overemphasize words of no importance. Lee Chamberlain's Cordelia was "either unduly aggressive or exceedingly dull." Again, there was no sense of ensemble playing, for the "looks, voices, acting styles" were as lacking in uniformity as a collection of immigrants on "Ellis Island." Mr. Simon concluded with a message I have insisted upon from the very beginning of this book: "Our actors and directors, lacking any real training in classical and verse drama, remain hopelessly imprisoned in contemporary offerings." Thank you for the endorsement, Mr. Simon.

Michael Feingold reviewing the same production for the *Times* found this *King Lear* to be not the tragedy he knew but a play "written by Peter Brook and Jan Kott—inspired by Beckett's *Endgame*—a play full of senility and meaningless violence and barrenness, dead pauses, dead feelings, living-dead characters." Edwin Sherin calmed Shakespeare down and made Lear "the most changeable" of human beings.

I did not have to go to the festival (I was, in any case, not in town during the summer) to see this performance produced by Joseph Papp; by turning on my TV set on a Wednesday night in early 1974 I was able to see it, with the original cast. I was pleased to hear how James Earl Jones has vastly improved in diction since I first heard him years ago in Shakespeare; he now speaks clearly and even with elegance; by contrast Paul Sorvino talked without any dramatic meaning. But there my pleasure ended. Jones's Lear was disabled by age from the very beginning, barely able to move without a cane; Shakespeare's Lear—that is part of his tragedy—when we first meet him is still physically powerful but unaware of his mental deterioration—we even see him at Goneril's come in from hunting and call out, like the robust man he is, for his dinner, as soon as he enters. Ellen Holly's Regan had a voice too high pitched and near hysteria; Regan is a cold snake, and Miss Holly was therefore better equipped to do Goneril. Cordelia used far too many gestures in the first scene, where she has so little to say. Lear started shouting from the first scene; how was he going to manage his mounting wrath to a *fff* as the play requires?—I already knew I should not be able to watch much of this. Raoul Julia's Edmund was good, but showed his villainy too plainly. Gloucester was intolerable; he read his lines like a schoolboy, produced laughs as though he were in a comedy, and always managed to accent the wrong word. The Fool was far too old, did not wear a clown's costume, and in one scene made two obscene gestures. Lear fell down and wept before Goneril's cruelty. Meanwhile, the audience laughed at all the most inappropriate places. I turned off the set, and picked up a book.

But there was, up to a point, a certain unfamiliar consistency in this *King Lear*. Lear was black and so were all his three daughters—though the consistency went no further, with the rest of the kingdom white. May we *dare* go into a matter which no one seems to have had the courage to broach? Of course, I wish to see *every* black man given equal opportunity with white, yellow, and red men. In rock music they seem to have almost a monopoly —and *that* I wish they would keep along with their white counterparts. In TV commercials they certainly give the impression of having already won places possibly even in excess of their proportion to the population. In plays, on and off Broadway, they are no longer ignored; here again the number of all-black plays and musicals is probably proportionate to the black population; more power to them, since they are able to draw the audiences. In music we have some great interpreters who are black: Henry Lewis, of the New Jersey Symphony, is a first-rate conductor; Martina Arroyo, Leantyne Price, Shirley Verrett, George Shirley, and Sidney Johnson are among the great singers of our time. When I see Mr. Johnson's name on a program at the Clarion Concerts, where I often hear him, I am always delighted; it does not disturb me that he will be singing a role written for a white man, for it was the singing that I came to hear. The same is true even of performed opera of the Italian school, where one wishes more to hear the music than mind the drama. (I am not so sure that I would be comfortable with a black Wotan, Parsifal, Sieglinde, Baron Ochs, or Octavion.) But when Morris Carnovsky played Lear against Ruby Dee; when the Vivian Beaumont Theater gives me a black Orsino and Maria, I *am* upset —not out of racial prejudice, but out of respect for Shakespeare's plays. After all, a white man doing Othello blackens face, arms, legs, and hands. Is there any reason why a black actor should not whiten his when doing a white role? My argument is reinforced, however unpopularly it may be received, by the simple fact that Leontyne Price as Donna Anna and George Shirley as Don Ottavio in *Don Giovanni* both are artists enough to have worn without shame light makeup, even though it was not necessary. This is a question that must be resolved sooner or later unless, what would be manifestly wrong, black actors will hereafter be barred from doing Shakespeare.

In January 1974 John Houseman, who had collaborated with Jack Landau years ago in Connecticut in a production of the same play, staged for the City Center Acting Company, made up of recent Julliard School graduates, a *Measure for Measure,* which by all accounts was a staging similar to the one on which I walked out. For this production too is made into a "cute farce," for, as John Simon observed, Mr. Houseman had not yet learned that "the arbitrary transfer of Shakespeare to another period almost never works (here to a Vienna that extends from Mozart to Mack the Knife.)" The earlier production had been changed to a Venice running over with Venetian blinds. After all, Venice and Vienna both begin with a V.

Grants from the City of New York, the New York State Council on the Arts, the National Endowment for the Arts, the Samuel I. Newhouse Foundation, the Ford Foundation, the Rockefeller Foundation, the Andrew W. Mellon Foundation, the J. M. Kaplan Fund, the Shubert Foundation, and IBM Corporation—this list is incomplete, the program informs us—makes possible the further desecration of Shakespeare at Lincoln Center in New York. During the 1973/74 season at the Mitzi E. Newhouse Theater (formerly called The Forum) in the basement below the Vivian Beaumont, where Joseph Papp's *Boom Boom Room* was being performed by the "New York Shakespeare Festival," *Troilus and Cressida* and *The Tempest* were given.

Walter Kerr's review of the direction of David Schweizer perfectly coincides with my reactions to the first half. (I naturally left at the intermission.) The program informed us that Mr. Schweizer "is the kind of bright, new talent that Joseph Papp likes to put to work. It was Mr. Schweizer's innovative production ideas got him this particular assignment." The note on him, listing his former work, implies that he never before had had the opportunity to destroy Shakespeare. Mr. Kerr, to quote him, says that the actors chosen by the director "seem not only indifferent to verse but altogether unacquainted with the English language." There was no deciphering Madeleine le Roux's Cressida-Cassandra-Helen at all. (She took all three roles.) She "possessed . . . no consonants—or none she was willing to part with," and finished serious speeches "with burlesque stripper's moues"; she trotted down the ramp "like a trained pony," and embraced her succession of wooers "so woodenly that" one felt they were going "to hang up their shields on her." Her "pahn me, pahn me," apparently meant "Pardon me." Christopher Walken's Achilles spoke in monotone, indulged in "furtive giggles, coy simperings," and "every ten minutes" behaved as though he had "just come out of *The Godfather*"; once he even fell into "those Puerto Rican inflections that seem mandatory in all recent Shakespeare Festival productions." It was not surprising that this Achilles should lose his climactic battle, "considering that he has come on for it in a green-spotted feather boa, looking rather like Tarzan with seaweed."

To Mr. Kerr's I add my own observations: all the Greek and Trojan heroes were clothed thus: the young, in brief bikinis; the older, in shorts (what a treat again for some!); there was actually a steam room on the plains before Troy; Thersites was a poor spastic creature; Troilus's shield was heavily stitched to look like a huge baseball; all through the play a dead horse lay at one corner of the stage—some characters sat on it, some kicked it; Pandarus seemed an habitué of the Bowery. Agamemnon emphasized every other word, Ulysses only every third word; nobody seemed to understand what he was saying; Helen-Cressida-Cassandra sounded and looked like Mamie Van Doren.

Later in the season in the same theater, Sam Waterston as Prospero was got up to look like a young hippy, and Ariel was a huge lout, who leaped over him.

In January 1974 at the Brooklyn Academy of Music, New York, the Royal Shakespeare Company presented *Richard II*, with Ian Richardson and Richard Pasco alternating the roles of the king and Bolingbroke. Richardson played Richard disastrously "as a kind of drag queen"; the "epicene" robbed the audience of any pity for him; in a play "laced with some of Shakespeare's most musical poetry," he delivered his lines "with inflexible metronomic monotony." Walter Kerr found some interesting details in his performance but no "cumulative shape." John Simon thought Richardson's king "a distasteful, flaming queen" and Pasco's Bolingbroke "adequate," but as Richard, Pasco spoke too much in falsetto and was like a "yokel" at times, while Richardson's Bolingbroke was a "slimy, effete villain."

As we are about to go to press, in July 1974, Stratford, Connecticut, continues its mockery of Shakespeare with a *Twelfth Night* and a *Romeo and*

Juliet. For the latter play the setting naturally was changed—this time to 1866 and the times of Garibaldi. The director, Michael Kahn, took his cue from the movies, beginning the play with the ending and then proceeding with flashbacks; he added Sonnet 116 to the middle of the play and Sonnet 55 to the end, in order, as John Simon said, to "explain the obvious." But he also did not hesitate to embellish the play by affixing a subplot in which old Capulet and a young Lady Capulet wage a continual sexual feud. When he wishes to take her to bed, she does not want him, and when she wants him, he does not want her. Very original and very "in." Walter Kerr said of this Verona that it was more like a sleepy Sicilian town, where people sip vermouth at sidewalk cafés and Mercutio sports a black patch over one eye, suggesting trouble with the Mafia (or a certain well-known brand of men's shirts?); in his costume of "floppy panama," frock coat, and bow tie he seemed to Kerr "directly off a Mississippi riverboat."

Puppets, said Mr. Kalem of *Time*, would have sounded more emotionally convincing. In a "stridently monotonous" tone, Miss Roberta Maxwell's Juliet was a "fishwife haggling unsuccessfully over a flounder." Mr. Simon was irritated by her "tomboyish" manner and the "comic rasp" of her voice. David Birney's Romeo was "limp and bland"; David Round's Mercutio was like some "nightclub comic."

In Director David Williams's *Twelfth Night* "the prankishness and the poetry" were divorced. John Simon observed that when Moses Gunn "mouthed" the opening line, it was as if he were singing Calypso; in this production Larry Carpenter spoke the line in "tones made of fruit mush interlarded with arthritic pauses" so that the critic considered running away. The comics were disastrous; Fred Gwynne's Toby was a "leaden oaf" who neighed his speeches "without inflection," every syllable devoid of "wit and significance." Summing up this year's Stratford, Mr. Simon says, "The pain it paineth every day."

Aside from these comments, two critics reflected on matters that ought to cause those schoolteachers who drag thousands of students to Stratford to do some reflecting too. "There is no law that requires," one of them says, the Connecticut playhouse "to vary its productions between the barely adequate and the eminently atrocious. It is just the sloppy custom of the place. . . . This tampering with Shakespeare, trampling on Shakespeare" can hardly harm adults who know the plays. But what of the youngsters forced every summer to go to Stratford? "They are being aesthetically defrauded and deluded. Here is a cultural center that confirms the worst popular myth —that culture is a humorless, tiresome, deadly bore." Mr. Simon is even more indignant. "Will no one save us from these foolish directors who must remake the masterpieces in their own image? [Mr. Simon might have used a stronger word than "foolish."] Will no one tell them that love of drama is not love which alters a text when it finds alteration amusing? Can they not learn that the true director triumphs through subservience to his author, not through arrogance that enthrones him as a supposedly greater artist than the playwright?" These words should be engraved upon the façade of every playhouse which presents Shakespeare. The sentiments were never more needed.

I had originally wished to call this book, from a line wherein Hamlet teases Polonius, *Then Came Each Actor on His Ass* (meaning *donkey*), but the title was rejected on account of the *double entendre*, that being the very reason I liked it. For that is how many actors have been doing Shakespeare for centuries, and now more than ever.

Oscar Wilde, in a serious moment, said (what I have believed all my adult life to be true): "If one cannot enjoy reading a book over and over again, there is no use in reading it at all." There are many books that I have reread often, and as for my favorites—*Vanity Fair, Bleak House, Great Expectations, Martin Chuzzlewit* (because of Sarah Gamp), *The Egoist, Madame Bovary, Zuleika Dobson, The Importance of Being Earnest*—I have read each at least a dozen times. Most of Shakespeare's plays I have read not less than a hundred times (never without discovering some new wonder), and I expect to be found reading him on my deathbed. For like reasons I have gone to every performance I could find of Sophocles, Molière, Racine, Ibsen, Chekhov, the Wilde play and—until recently—Shakespeare. But this criminal distortion and "modernization" through gimmickry of Shakespeare's plays have forced me to walk out of most performances during the last fifteen years. In the same essay Wilde said: "Pure modernity of form is always somewhat vulgarizing. It cannot help being so. The public imagine that, because they are interested in their immediate surroundings, Art should be interested in them also." (He might have added that nothing becomes old-fashioned more rapidly than "pure modernity of form,"—because those interested in it are concerned only with exteriors.) Who would willingly go to see even twice a performance of a Shakespearean play loaded with "modernizations" through gimmickry? That is the test.

Until the public wearies of this sort of thing, though no plays were written more entirely to be *seen* in a theater, eventually all but the feather-brained and the vulgar will be driven to the library, where they at least can conceive the plays being performed as their author intended. To say that every time a Shakespearean play is given it must be done in a "new" way is to say that nobody will come to hear Claudio Arrau do a Beethoven sonata more than once—whereas I have recognized many of the same faces returning to hear this great master perform the same works innumerable times; the same was true of Toscanini's performances of Mozart, Beethoven, and Wagner; the same is true of most of the world's great musicians, who, because they are great, do not vary much their interpretations; they are great not because they are "original" but because they endeavor to deliver what the composer intended. The audiences at the Comédie Française are delighted to know that their Molière and Racine are being acted just as Molière and Racine wanted them to be, and might start a riot if any serious departure were made from the seventeenth-century conception of how the play should be done. Shakespeare is more spacious, to be sure, and he may be acted in Elizabethan, modern, or historical settings but not with gimmickry, not with the cheap resort to "originality" that today exists as an end in itself.

Bibliography of Works
and Periodicals Consulted

Academy, The.

Agate, James, *Anthology, An* (ed. by Herbert Van Thal), New York, 1961.

————, *Brief Chronicles*, New York, n.d.

————, *Contemporary Theatre, 1923*, London, 1924.

————, *Contemporary Theatre, 1924*, London, 1925.

————, *Contemporary Theatre, 1925*, London, 1926.

————, *Contemporary Theatre, 1926*, London, 1927.

————, *Contemporary Theatre, 1944*, London, 1945.

————, *Contemporary Theatre, 1945*, London, 1946.

————, *Ego 1*, London, 1935.

————, *Ego 3*, London, 1938.

————, *Ego 6*, London, 1944.

————, *Ego 8*, London, 1946.

————, *Ego 9*, London, 1946.

————, (ed.) *English Dramatic Critics, The (1660–1932)*, New York, n.d.

————, *First Nights*, London, 1934.

————, *My Theatre Talks*, London, 1933.

————, *More First Nights*, London, 1937.

————, *Red Letter Nights*, London, 1944.

————, *Their Hour Upon the Stage*, London, 1930.

————, *Those Were the Nights*, London, 1946.

Aherne, Brian, *A Proper Job*, Boston, 1969.

Alger, William R., *Life of Edwin Forrest, The*, Philadelphia, 1877.

Allen, Shirley S., *Samuel Phelps and Sadler's Wells Theatre*, Middletown, Conn., 1971.

American, The.

Anderson, James R., *An Actor's Life*, London, 1902.

Anderson, Mary, *A Few Memories*, New York, 1896.

Angelo, Henry, *Pic Nic*, London, 1800.

Anon., *Account of the Life of the Celebrated Mrs. Cibber, An*, London, 1857.

————, *Account of the Life of the Celebrated Tragedian, Mr. Thomas Betterton, An*, London, 1749.

————, *Apology for the Conduct of Charles Macklin, Comedian, An*, London, 1773.

————, *Case of Mr. Macklin, The*, Edinburgh, 1775.

————, *Case of the Present Theatrical Disputes, The*, London, 1743.

————, *Case of the Stage in Ireland, The*, Dublin, 1758.

————, *Epistle from Tully, An*, London, 1755.

———, *Green Room Gossip*, London, 1809.

———, *Life of Mrs. Abington, The*, New York, 1969.

———, *Life of James Quin, Comedian, The*, London, 1766.

———, *M-ckl-n's Answer to Tully*, London, 1775.

———, *Memoirs of the Life and Writings of Samuel Foote*, London, n.d.

———, *Mr. Garrick's Conduct and Management of the Theatre Royal in Drury Lane*, London, n.d.

———, *These Were the Actors*, London, n.d.

Appleton, William W., *Charles Macklin, an Actor's Life*, Cambridge, Mass., 1960.

Archer, Frank, *An Actor's Notebook*, London, n.d.

Archer, William, *Henry Irving, Actor and Manager*, London, 1883.

———, *Masks on Faces*, New York, 1957.

———, *Theatrical World of 1895, The*, London, 1896.

Archer, William, and Lowe, Robert (eds.) *Dramatic Essays by John Forster and George Henry Lewes*, London, 1896.

——— (ed.), *Hazlitt on Theatre*, New York, n.d.

Armin, Robert, *Fools and Jesters*, London, 1842.

Armstrong, Cecil F., *Century of Great Actors, A, 1750–1850*, London, 1912.

Arthur, George, *From Phelps to Gielgud*, London, 1936.

Arundel, Dennis, *Story of Sadler's Wells, The*, London, 1965.

Asche, Oscar, *Oscar Asche; His Life*, London, 1929.

Ashley, Leonard, *Colley Cibber*, New York, 1965.

Aston, Anthony, *Supplement to Cibber's "Apology"* (q.v.), *A.*

Atkinson, Brooks, *Broadway*, New York, 1970.

Aubert, Charles, *Art of Pantomime, The*, New York, 1969.

Ayres, Alfred, *Acting and Actors, Elocution and Elocutionists*, New York, 1894.

Baker, David E., Reed, F. A. S., and Jones, Stephen, *Biographica Dramatica, or a Companion to the Playhouse*, London, 1812.

Baker, Henry Barton, *History of the London Stage and Its Famous Players, A, 1576–1903*, New York, 1904.

———, *London Stage: Its History and Tradition, The*, London, 1889.

Baker, Herschel, *John Philip Kemble*, Cambridge, Mass., 1942.

Baker, Richard, *Theatrum Triumphans*, London, 1670.

Baldwin, Thomas W., *Organization and Personnel of the Shakespearean Company*, Princeton, 1927.

Ball, Robert H., *Shakespeare on Silent Film*, New York, 1968.

Bancroft, George P., *Stage and Bar*, London, 1929.

Bancroft, Squire and Marie, *Bancrofts On and Off the Stage, Written by Themselves, The*, London, 1888.

———, *The Bancrofts* (8th Edition), London, 1891.

Barker, Felix, *The Oliviers*, New York, 1953.

Barker, Richard H., *Mr. Cibber of Drury Lane*, New York, 1939.

Barnes, J.H., *Forty Years on the Stage*, New York, 1915.

Barrett, Wilson, *On Stage for Notes*, London, 1954.

Barry, John D., *Julia Marlowe*, Boston, 1907.

Barton, Margaret, *Garrick*, London, 1948.

Bax, Clifford, *All the World's a Stage*, London, 1946.

Baxter, Beverley, *Five Nights and Noises Off*, London, 1949.

———, *First Nights and Footlights*, London, 1955.

Beerbohm, Max, *Around Theatres*, New York, 1954.

————, *Last Theatres*, London, 1970.

————, *Mainly on the Air*, London, 1957.

————, *More Theatres*, London, 1957.

————, (ed.) *Herbert Beerbohm Tree*, New York, n.d.

Behrman, S. N., *People in a Diary*, Boston, 1972.

————, *Portrait of Max*, New York, 1960.

Belfrage, Bruce, *One Man in His Time*, London, 1951.

Bellamy, George Anne, *Apology for the Life of George Anne Bellamy, An*, 6 vols., London, 1785.

Bellchambers, Edmund, *Memoirs of the Actors and Actresses Mentioned by Cibber* (an appendix to Cibber's *Apology*, q.v.)

Bennett, Arnold (ed. by Newman Flower), *Journals 1911–1921*, London, 1932.

————, *Journals 1921–1928*, London, 1933.

Benson, Dorothy C., *Arnold Bennett*, London, 1935.

Benson, Constance, *Mainly Players*, London, 1926.

Benson, Frank, *My Memoirs*, London, 1930.

Bernard, John, *Retrospectives of the Stage*, London, 1830.

Bentley, Gerald E., *Jacobean and Caroline Stage*, 2 vols., Oxford, 1941.

————, *Shakespeare and His Theatre*, Lincoln, Nebraska, 1964.

Betterton, Thomas, *History of the English Stage, The*, London, 1741.

Birmingham Post, The.

Bishop, George W., *Barry Jackson and the London Theatre*, London, 1933.

————, *My Betters*, London, 1957.

Blum, Daniel, *A Pictorial History of the American Theatre 1860–1970* (3d Edition, enlarged and revised by John Willis), New York, 1969.

Boaden, James, *Life of Mrs. Jordan, The*, London, 1831.

————, *Memoirs of Mrs. Inchbald*, London, 1833.

————, *Memoirs of Mrs. Siddons*, London, 1834.

————, *Memoirs of the Life of John Philip Kemble*, London, 1825.

Boas, Guy, *Shakespeare and the Young Actor*, London, 1962.

Booth, Edwina, *Edwin Booth*, New York, 1894.

Booth, John, *The Old Vic*, London, 1917.

Boston World, The.

Boswell, James, *Private Papers* (ed. by G. Scott and F. A. Pottle), Mount Vernon, N.Y., 1928–1934.

Bradbrook, Muriel C., *Elizabethan Stage Conditions*, Cambridge, England, 1932.

————, *Rise of the Common Player: A Study of Actors and Society in Shakespeare's England, The*, Cambridge, Mass., 1962.

Brereton, Austin, *"H.B." and Laurence Irving*, London, 1922.

————, *Henry Irving: A Biographical Sketch*, London, 1883.

————, *Lyceum and Henry Irving, The*, London, 1903.

————, *Some Famous Hamlets from Burbage to Fechter*, London, 1884.

Bridges-Adams, W., *British Theatre, The*, London, 1944.

————, *Irresistible Theatre, The*, Cleveland and New York, 1957.

Brook, Donald, *Pageant of English Actors, A*, London, 1950.

Brook, Peter, *Empty Space, The*, New York, 1969.

Brown, Ivor, *How Shakespeare Spent the Day*, New York, 1964.

————, *Shakespeare*, London, 1947.

————, *Shakespeare and the Actors*, London, 1970.

————, *Shakespeare Memorial Theatre, The, 1954–1956*, London, 1956.

———, *Shakespeare Memorial Theatre, The, 1957–1959*, London, 1959.

———, *Shakespeare in His Time*, Edinburgh, 1960.

Brown, John Mason, *Dramatis Personae*, New York, 1963.

Bull, Peter, *I Know the Face, But*, London, 1959.

Burnim, Kalman A., *David Garrick, Director*, Pittsburgh, 1961.

Burton, E. J., *British Theatre, 1100–1900, The*, London, 1961.

Burton, Hal, *Great Acting*, New York, 1967.

Burton, Philip, *Early Doors*, New York, 1969.

Byrne, M. St. Clare, "The Stage Costuming of Macbeth in the 18th Century," in *Studies in English Theatre History*, London, 1952, pp. 52–64.

———, "Fifty Years of Shakesperian Production" in *Shakespeare Survey 2*, Cambridge, England, 1949.

Calvert, Louis, *Problems of an Actor*, New York, 1918.

Campbell, Mrs. Patrick, *My Life and Some Letters*, London, 1822.

Campbell, Thomas, *Life of Mrs. Siddons, The*, London, 1834.

Cardus, Neville, *Autobiography*, London, 1947.

Carlisle, Carol J., *Shakespeare from the Greenroom*, Chapel Hill, 1969.

Carritt, E.F., *Calendar of British Taste, A*, London, 1948.

Carter, Huntley, *New Spirit in the European Theatre 1900–1924, The*, London, 1925.

Carter, Lionel (ed.), *Masque Library, The*, London, 1950.

Cavanagh, Peter, *Irish Theatre, The*, Tralee, 1946.

Century Magazine, The.

Chambers, Edmund, *Elizabethan Stage, The*, Oxford, 1930.

Charke, Charlotte, *Art of Management, The*, London, 1735.

Chekhov, Anton, *Letters on the Short Story, the Drama and Other Literary Topics* (ed. by Louis S. Friedland), New York, 1924.

Chetwood, William R., *General History of the Stage, A*, London, 1749.

Cibber, Colley, *Apology* (ed. by Robert W. Lowe), London, 1880.

Cibber, Theophilus, *Life and Character of the Excellent Actor, Barton Booth, The*, London, 1753.

———, *To David Garrick, Esq.*, London, 1759.

Clarke, Asia Booth, *Elder and the Younger Booth, The*, Boston, 1882.

———, *Passages, Incidents and Anecdotes in the Life of Junius Brutus Booth by His Daughter*, New York, 1870.

Clarke, I.C., *My Life and Memories*, New York, 1925.

Clarke, Mary, *Shakespeare at the Old Vic, 1955–1959*, 5 vols., London, 1959.

Clement, Clara E., *Charlotte Cushman*, Boston, 1882.

Cochran, Charles B., *I Had Almost Forgotten*, London, 1832.

Cole, Toby, and Chinoy, Helen K., *Actors on Acting*, New York, 1970.

Coleman, John, *Fifty Years of an Actor's Life*, 2 vols., New York, 1904.

———, *Players and Playwrights I Have Known*, London, 1885.

Coleman, John and Edward, *Memoirs of Samuel Phelps*, New York, 1969.

Collier, Constance, *Harlequinade: the Story of My Life*, London, 1929.

Collier, John Payne, *History of English Dramatic Poetry to the Time of Shakespeare, and Annals of the Stage to the Restoration*, London, 1831.

———, *Memoirs of the Principal Actors in the Plays of Shakespeare*, London, 1846.

Collins, Charles E., *Great Love Stories of the Theatre*, New York, 1911.

Colman, George, *Posthumous Letters*, London, 1820.

Congreve, Francis, *Authentic Memoirs of the Late Charles Macklin, Comedian*, London, 1798.

Connoisseur, The.

Cook, Dutton, *Hours with the Players*, London, 1881.

———, *Nights at the Play*, London, 1881.

———, *On the Stage*, London, 1883.

Cook, James, *Actor's Notebook, The*, London, 1841.

Cooke, William, *Elements of Dramatic Criticism*, London, 1775.

———, *Memoirs of Samuel Foote*, London, 1805.

———, *Memorials of the Life of Charles Macklin*, London, 1804.

Cornhill Magazine, The.

Cornwall, Barry, *Life of Edmund Kean, The*, London, 1835.

Cotton, William, *Story of the Drama in Exeter, 1787–1823, with Reminiscences of Edmund Kean, The*, London, 1887.

Crawford, Lane, *Acting, Its Theory and Practice*, New York, 1969.

Craig, Edward Gordon, *Ellen Terry and Her Secret Self*, London, 1931.

———, *Henry Irving*, London, 1930.

———, *Index to the Story of My Days*, London, 1931.

———, *On the Art of the Theatre*, London, 1951.

———, *Theatre Advancing, The*, London, 1921.

Crofte-Cooke, Rupert, *Feasting with Panthers*, New York, 1967.

Crosse, Gordon, *Shakespearean Playgoing 1890–1952*, London, 1953.

Darbyshire, Alfred, *Art of the Victorian Stage, The*, Manchester, 1907.

Darlington, W.A., *Actor and His Audience, The*, London, 1949.

———, *I Do What I Like*, London, 1947.

———, *Literature in the Theatre*, London, 1925.

———, *Six Thousand and One Nights: Forty Years a Dramatic Critic*, London, 1960.

———, *Through the Fourth Wall*, London, 1922.

Davies, Thomas, *Memoir of the Life of Garrick*, London, 1780.

———, *Life of Garrick, The*, Boston, 1818.

Davies, W. Robertson, *Shakespeare's Boy Actors*, London, 1939.

Day, M.C., and Trewin, J.C., *Shakespearean Memorial Theatre, The*, London, 1932.

Denham, Reginald, *Stars in My Hair*, London, 1958.

Dent, Alan, *Mrs. Patrick Campbell*, London, 1961.

———, *Nocturnes and Rhapsodies*, London, 1950.

———, *Preludes and Studies*, London, 1942.

Dent, B.J., *Theatre for Everybody, A*, London, 1945.

Derwent, Clarence, *Derwent Story, The*, New York, 1953.

Dibdin, James C., *Annals of the Edinburgh Stage, The*, Edinburgh, 1888.

Dickins, Richard, *Forty Years of Shakespeare on the London Stage*, London, 1907.

Dictionary of National Biography.

Disher, Maurice W., *The Last Romantic, Martin Harvey*, London, 1948.

Donaldson, Francis, *Actor Managers, The*, London, 1970.

Doran, Dr. John, *Annals of the English Stage from Betterton to Edmund Kean*, 2 vols., New York, 1880.

Downes, John, *Roscius Anglicanus* (ed. by Montague Summers), London, n.d.

Drama.

Drinkwater, John, *Discovery*, London, 1932.

Dublin University Magazine, The.

Duerr, Edwin, *The Length and Depth of Acting*, New York, 1963.

Du Maurier, Daphne, *Gerald: A Portrait*, London, 1934.

Dunbar, Janet, *Flora Robson*, London, 1960.

———, *Peg Woffington and Her World*, London, 1908.

Dunlap, William, *Memoirs of George Frederick Cooke*, New York, 1813.

Dunn, E. C., *Shakespeare in America*, New York, 1939.

Eaton, Walter P., *Actor's Heritage, The*, Boston, 1924.

Ellis, Ruth, *Shakespeare Memorial Theatre, The*, Winchester, 1948.

Eustis, Morton, *Players at Work; Acting According to the Actors*, New York, 1937 and 1969.

Examiner, The

Fagg, Edwin, *The Old Vic*, London, 1936.

Farington, Joseph, *Farington Diary, The* (ed. by James Grieg), London, 1923.

Farjeon, Herbert, *Shakespearean Scene: Dramatic Criticisms, The*, London, 1949.

Faucit, Helena, *On Some of Shakespeare's Female Characters*, London, 1887.

ffrench, Yvonne, *Mrs. Siddons, Tragic Actress*, Verschoyle, 1954.

Field, Kate, *Charles Albert Fichter*, Boston, 1882.

Findlater, Richard, *Michael Redgrave, Actor*, London, 1956.

———, *Player Kings, The*, London, 1971.

———, *Unholy Trade, The*, London, 1952.

Fitzgerald, Percy, *Art of Acting, The*, New York, 1892.

———, *Kembles, The*, New York, 1969.

———, *New History of the English Stage, A*, London, 1882.

———, *Romance of the English Stage, The*, Philadelphia, 1875.

———, *Samuel Foote*, London, 1910.

Foote, Samuel, *Table Talk and Bon Mots* (ed. by William Cooke), New Southgate, 1889.

Forbes-Robertson, Johnston, "Ellen Terry," in *The London Mercury*, 1928, pp. 492–96.

———, *Player Under Three Reigns, A*, London, 1925.

Fordham, Hallam, *John Gielgud*, London, 1952.

Foss, George R., *What the Author Meant*, Oxford, 1932.

Fowler, Gene, *Good Night, Sweet Prince*, London, 1940.

Frohman, Daniel, *Encore*, New York, 1937.

Funke, Lewis, and Booth, John E., *Actors Talk about Acting*, New York, 1961.

Furness, Horace H. (ed.), *Variorum Edition of Shakespeare's Plays*, Philadelphia, n.d.

Gaisford, John, *Drama in New Orleans, The*, New Orleans, 1849.

Garrett, John (ed.), *More Talking of Shakespeare*, London, 1959.

Garrick, David, *Letters of David Garrick, The* (ed. by David M. Little and George M. Kahrl), Oxford, 1963.

———, *Private Correspondence* (ed. by James Boaden), London, 1831–32.

Geisinger, Marion, *Plays, Players and Playwrights*, New York, 1971.

Genest, John, *Some Account of the English Stage from the Restoration in 1660 to 1830*, 10 vols., Bath, 1832.

Gentleman, Francis, *Dramatic Censor, The*, London, 1770.

Gentleman's Magazine, The.

Gibbs, Lewis, *Sheridan*, London, 1947.

Gielgud, John, *Early Stages*, London, 1953.

———, *Stage Directions*, London, 1963.

Gilder, Rosamund, *Enter the Actor*, Boston, 1931.

———, *John Gielgud's Hamlet*, New York, 1937.

Gildon, Charles, *Life of Mr. Thomas Betterton, The*, London, 1710.

Glasgow Citizen, The.

Glasgow Herald, The.

Goldie, Grace W., *Liverpool Repertory Theatre, 1911–34, The*, Liverpool, 1935.

Goodwin, John (ed.), *Royal Shakespeare Theatre Company, 1960–63, The*, New York, 1964.

Gould, Thomas R., *Tragedian, The*, New York, 1868.

Granville-Barker, Harley, *On Dramatic Method*, London, 1931.

———, *On Poetry in Drama*, London, 1937.

———, *Prefaces to Shakespeare*, 4 vols., London, 1963.

Grebanier, Bernard, *Great Shakespeare Forgery, The*, New York, 1965.

———, *Heart of Hamlet, The*, New York, 1960.

———, "Lady Macbeth of London," in *Shenandoah*, Summer, 1962, pp. 28–36.

———, *Truth about Shylock, The*, New York, 1962.

———, *Uninhibited Byron, The*, New York, 1970.

Greene-Armytage, R. N. (ed.), *Book of Martin Harvey, The*, London, 1930.

Greville, Charles C. Fulke, *Greville Diary, The* (ed. by Philip W. Wilson), London, 1927.

Guthrie, Tyrone, *Life in the Theatre, A*, London, 1960.

———, *Theatre Prospect*, London, 1932.

Hackett, James H., *Shakespeare's Plays and Actors*, New York, 1863.

Haddon, Archibald, *Green Room Gossip*, London, 1922.

Hale, Lionel, *Old Vic, 1949–50, The*, London, 1950.

Halliday, F. E., *Cult of Shakespeare, The*, London, 1957.

———, *Shakespeare Companion, A*, London, 1955.

———, *Shakespeare in His Age*, London, 1956.

Halliwell-Phillips, J. O., *Memoranda*, Brighton, 1879.

Hamilton, Cicely, and Baylis, Lilian, *Old Vic, The*, London, 1926.

Hammerton, J.A. (ed.), *Actor's Art, The*, New York, 1967.

Harbage, Alfred, *Shakespeare's Audience*, New York, 1961.

Hardwick, J.M.D., *Emigrant in Motley, the Unpublished Letters of Charles and Ellen Kean*, London, 1954.

Hardwicke, Cedric, *Let's Pretend*, London, 1932.

———, *Victorian Orbit, A*, London, 1961.

Harker, Joseph, *Studio and Stage*, London, 1924.

Harper's Monthly Magazine.

Harrison, G. B., *Elizabethan Plays and Players*, London, 1940.

Harrison, Gabriel, *Edwin Forrest, the Actor and the Man*, New York, 1889.

Hartnoll, Phyllis (ed.), *Oxford Companion to the Theatre, The* (3d Edition), Oxford, 1967.

Harvey, John Martin, *Autobiography of Sir John Martin Harvey, The*, London, 1933.

Haslewood, John, *Secret History of the Green Room, The*, London, 1793.

Hatton, Joseph, *Henry Irving's Impressions of America*, London, 1884.

Hawkins, F. W., *Life of Edmund Kean, The*, London, 1869.

Hayman, Ronald, *John Gielgud*, New York, 1971.

Hazlitt, William, *Characters of Shakespeare's Plays, The*, London, 1906.

———, *Complete Works* (ed. by P.P. Howe), London, 1933.

Hedgecock, Frank, *Cosmopolitan Actor: David Garrick and His French Friends, A*, London, 1912.

Henderson-Bland, R., *Actor-Soldier-Poet*, London, 1939.

Hiatt, Charles, *Ellen Terry and Her Impersonations*, London, 1898.

Hill, John, *Actor, The*, London, 1750, 1755.

Hitchcock, Robert, *Historical View of the Irish Stage, An*, Dublin, 1788.

Hobson, Harold, *Ralph Richardson*, London, 1958.

———, *Theatre*, London, 1948.

————, *Theatre 2*, London, 1950.

Hogan, C.B., *Shakespeare in the Theatre 1701–1800*, Oxford.

Holmes, Martin, *Shakespeare's Public*, London, 1964.

House, Edward H., "Edwin Booth in London," in *The Century Magazine*, December 1897, pp. 269–279.

Hudson, Lynton, *English Stage, 1850–1950, The*, London, 1951.

Hunt, Leigh, *Dramatic Essays*, London, 1894.

————, *Town, The*, Oxford, 1907.

Hutton, Lawrence, *Curiosities of the American Stage*, New York, 1891.

Ireland, John, *Anecdotes of Mr. Henderson*, London, 1778.

————, *Letters of the Late Mr. John Henderson*, London, 1786.

Irving, Laurence, *Henry Irving*, London, 1951.

————, *Successors, The*, London, 1967.

Jaggard, Gerald, *Stratford Mosaic*, London, 1960.

James, Henry, *Scenic Art, The*, New York, 1957.

Jameson, Anna, *Shakespeare's Heroines*, London, 1898.

Jerdan, William, *Personal Reminiscences* (ed. by Richard H. Stoddard), New York, 1875.

Jones, Henry Arthur, *Shadow of Henry Irving, The*, New York, 1969.

Joseph, Bertram, *Tragic Actor, The*, London, 1959.

Kane, Whitford, *Are We All Met?*, London, 1931.

Kelly, Hugh, *Thespis*, London, 1767.

Kelly, Michael, *Memoirs* (ed. by Richard H. Stoddard), New York, 1875.

Kemble, Frances A., *Records of Later Life*, London, 1882.

Kemp, T.C., *Birmingham Repertory Theatre, The*, Birmingham, 1948.

Kemp, T.C., and Trewin, J.C., *Stratford Festival, The*, Birmingham, 1953.

Kennard, A., *Mrs. Siddons*, London, 1887.

Kenny, Charles L., *Mr. Phelps and the Critics of His Correspondence with the Stratford Committee*, London, 1864.

Keown, Eric, *Peggy Ashcroft*, London, 1955.

Kirk, John F., "Shakespeare's Tragedies on the Stage," in *Lippincott's*, June 1884, pp. 604 seq.

Kirkman, James T., *Memoirs of the Life of Charles Macklin*, London, 1799.

Knepler, Henry, *Gilded Age, The*, New York, 1968.

Knight, Esmond, *Seeking the Bubble*, London, 1943.

Knight, G. Wilson, *Golden Labyrinth: A Study of British Drama, The*, London, 1962.

Knight, Joseph, *Theatrical Notes*, London, 1893.

Komisarjevsky, Theodore, *Myself and the Theatre*, London, 1929.

Ladies' Home Journal, The.

Landstone, Charles, *Off-Stage*, London, 1953.

Landstone, Charles, and Williamson, Audrey, *Bristol Old Vic, The*, London, 1957.

Lang, Matheson, *Mr. Wu Looks Back*, London, 1940.

Lanier, Henry W., *First English Actresses, from the Initial Appearance of Women on the Stage in 1660 till 1700, The*, New York, 1930.

Leach, Joseph, *Bright Particular Star*, New Haven and London, 1970.

Lee, Sidney, *Shakespeare and the Modern Stage*, New York, 1906.

Leeper, Janet, *Edward Gordon Craig*, London, 1948.

Lehmann, John (ed.), *Orpheus*, London, 1948.

Lelyveld, Toby B., *Shylock on the Stage*, Cleveland, 1960.

Lewes, Charles L., *Memoirs*, London, 1805.

Lewes, George Henry, *On Actors and the Art of Acting*, London, 1875.

Lichtenberg, G.C., *Letters from England* (ed. by Margaret L. Mare and W.H. Quarrell), Oxford, 1938.

Locke, Robinson, *Collection of Dramatic Scrapbooks*, Toledo, Ohio, 1920.

London Evening Standard, The.

London Times, The.

Lounsbury, Thomas R., *Shakespeare as a Dramatic Artist*, New York, 1965.

Lowe, Robert, *Thomas Betterton*, New York, 1969.

MacCarthy, Desmond, *Drama*, New York, 1940.

_____, *Theatre*, London, 1954.

Mackenzie, Henry, *Anecdotes and Egotisms* (ed. by Margaret L. Mare and Harold W. Thompson), London, 1927.

Macklin, Charles, *Case of Charles Macklin, Comedian, The*, London, December 5, 1743.

_____, *Mr. Macklin's Reply to Mr. Garrick's Answer*, London, 1743.

Macliammoir, Michael, *All for Hecuba*, London, 1946.

Macqueen-Pope, W.J., *Carriages at Eleven*, London, 1947.

_____, *Footlight Flickered, The*, London, 1959.

_____, *Haymarket*, London, 1948.

_____, *Ivor*, London, 1951.

_____, *Theatre Royal, Drury Lane, The*, London, 1945.

Macready, William C.M., *Diaries, The* (ed. by William Toynbee), New York, 1912.

_____, *Reminiscences and Selections from His Diaries and Letters* (ed. by Frederick Pollock), London, 1875.

Magarshack, David, *Chekhov: A Life*, New York, 1953.

Maltby, H.F., *Ring up the Curtain*, London, 1950.

Manchester Courier, The.

Manchester Examiner and Times, The.

Manchester Guardian, The.

Mander, Raymond, and Mitcheson, Joe, *Artist and the Theatre, The*, London, 1955.

_____, *Hamlet Through the Ages*, London, 1952.

_____, *Picture History of the British Theatre, A*, London, 1951.

_____, *Theatres of London, The*, London, 1963.

Manvell, Roger, *Ellen Terry*, London, 1968.

_____, *International Encyclopedia of Film, The*, New York, 1972.

_____, *Sarah Siddons: Portrait of an Actress*, New York, 1970.

Marshall, Herbert, and Stock, Mildred, *Ira Aldridge, and the Negro Tragedian*, New York, 1958.

Marshall, Norman, *Other Theatre, The*, London, 1947.

_____, *Producer and the Play, The*, London, 1962.

Marston, Westland, *Our Recent Actors*, Boston, 1888.

Masefield, John, *"Macbeth" Production, A*, London, 1945.

Mason, A.E.W., *Sir George Alexander and the St. James's Theatre*, London, 1935.

Mason, E.T., *Othello of Tommaso Salvini, The*, New York, 1890.

Mathews, Charles, *Memories* (ed. by Mrs. Mathews), London, 1838–39.

Matthew, Anne, *Memoirs of Charles Mathews*, London, 1838–39.

Matthews, Bache, *History of the Birmingham Repertory Theatre, A*, London, 1924.

Matthews, Brander, and Hutton, Lawrence, *David Garrick and His Contemporaries*, Boston, 1900.

_____, *Edwin Booth and His Contemporaries*, Boston, 1900.

_____, *Kean and Booth and Their Contemporaries*, Boston, 1900.

———, *Kembles and Their Contemporaries, The*, Boston, 1900.

Matthews, Brander, and Thorndike, Ashley H., *Shakespearian Studies*, New York, 1962.

McDowell, John D. et al., *Selected Bibliography and Critical Comment on the Art, Theory and Technique of Acting*, Ann Arbor, 1948.

Melville, Lewis, *More Stage Favorites of the 18th Century*, London, 1929.

Menpes, Mortimer, *Henry Irving*, London, 1906.

Miles, Bernard, *British Theatre, The*, London, 1948.

Minney, R.J., *Bogus Image of Bernard Shaw, The*, London, 1969.

Mitchell, R.J., and Leys, M.D.R., *History of London Life, A*, London, 1958.

Molloy, J. Fitzgerald, *Life and Adventures of Edmund Kean, The*, London, 1888.

Montague, C.E., *Dramatic Values*, London, 1911.

Monthly Mirror, The.

Moody, Richard, *Astor Place Riot, The*, Bloomington, 1958.

———, *Edwin Forest*, New York, 1960.

Moore, Thomas, *Memoirs of the Life of the Right Honourable Richard Brinsley Sheridan*, London, 1827.

———, *Personal Reminiscences* (ed. by Richard H. Stoddard), New York, 1875.

Morris, Clara, *Life on the Stage: My Personal Experiences and Recollections*, New York, 1901.

Morris, Lloyd, *Curtain Time: The Story of the American Theatre*, New York, 1953.

Moses, Montrose, *Fabulous Forrest, The*, Boston, 1929.

———, *Famous Acting Families in America*, New York, 1906.

Murdoch, James E., *Analytic Elocution*, New York, 1884.

———, *Plea for Spoken Language, A*, New York, 1883.

———, *Stage, The*, Philadelphia, 1880.

Nagler, A.M., *Shakespeare's Stage* (translated by Ralph Manheim), New Haven, 1958.

Nashe, Thomas, *Pierce Penilesse* (ed. by G.B.Harrison), London, 1924.

New Haven Register, The.

New Republic, The.

Newsweek.

New York Dramatic Mirror, The.

New Yorker, The.

New York Herald-Tribune, The.

New York Magazine.

New York Times, The.

Nicholson, Watson, *Antony Aston, Stroller and Adventurer*, South Haven, Michigan, 1920.

———, *Struggle for a Free Stage in London*, Boston, 1906.

Nicoll, Allardyce, *Development of the Theatre, The*, New York, 1927.

———, *English Theatre, The*, London, 1936.

———, (ed.), *Shakespeare Survey*, Cambridge, England, 1948– .

Norman, Charles, *Rake Rochester*, New York, 1954.

Observer, The.

Odell, George C. D., *Shakespeare from Betterton to Irving*, 2 vols., New York, 1963.

O'Keeffe, John, *Recollections* (ed. by Richard H. Stoddard), New York, 1875.

Oldys, William, *Choice Notes*, London, 1862.

Oman, Carola, *David Garrick*, London, 1958.

Ormbee, Helen, *Backstage with Actors*, New York, 1969.

Parry, Edward, *Charles Macklin*, London, 1891.

Parsons, Mrs. Clement, *Garrick and His Circle*, New York, 1906.

———, *Incomparable Siddons, The*, London, 1909.

Peake, R.B., *Memoirs of the Colman Family*, London, 1841.

Pearson, Hesketh, *Beerbohm Tree, His Life and Laughter*, New York, 1916.

———, *Last Actor-Managers, The*, London, 1950.

———, *Life of Oscar Wilde, The*, London, 1946.

Penley, Belville S., *Mrs. Siddons and Bath*, London, n.d.

Pepys, Samuel, *Diary and Correspondence*, 4 vols., New York, n.d.

Phelps, W. May, and Forbes-Robertson, Johnston, *Life and Life-Work of Samuel Phelps*, London, 1886.

Philadelphia Inquirer, The.

Philadelphia Public Ledger, The.

Playfair, Giles, *Kean*, New York, 1939.

———, *Prodigy: A Study of the Strange Life of Master Betty, The*, London, 1967.

Playfair, Nigel, *Kean*, London, 1950.

Poel, William, *Shakespeare in the Theatre*, London, 1913.

Pollock, W.G., *Impressions of Henry Irving*, London, 1908.

Porter, William S. ("O Henry"), *Complete Works, The*, 2 vols., New York, 1953.

Proctor, Bryan W., *Life of Edmund Kean, The*, London, 1835.

Prynne, William, *Histrio-Mastix*, London, 1632.

Purdon, C.B., *Producing Shakespeare*, London, 1850.

Raby, Peter (ed.), *Stratford Scene, 1965–68, The*, Toronto, 1968.

Ralph, James, *Taste of the Town, The*, London, 1731.

Rankin, Hugh F., *Theatre in Colonial America, The*, Chapel Hill, 1965.

Redfield, William, *Letters from an Actor*, New York, 1966.

Redgrave, Michael, *Actor's Ways and Means, The*, London, 1953.

———, *Mask or Face*, London, 1958.

Reed, Rex, *Conversations in the Raw*, New York and Cleveland, 1969.

Rees, James, *Life of Edwin Forrest, The*, Philadelphia, 1874.

Rhodes, B. Crompton, *Stagery of Shakespeare, The*, Birmingham, 1922.

Rice, Charles, *London Theatre in the 1830's, The* (ed. by A.C. Sprague and Bertram Shuttleworth), London, 1950.

Ristori, Adelaide, *Memoirs and Artistic Studies* (ed. by G. Mantellini), New York, 1907.

Robbins, Phyllis, *Maude Adams*, New York, 1956.

Robinson, Crabbe, *London Theatre, The* (ed. by Edmund Brown), London, 1966.

Robinson, Mrs. Mary, *Mrs. Mary Robinson, Written by Herself*, London, n.d.

Rogers, Samuel, *Recollections*, London, 1859.

Rosenberg, Marvin, *Masks of Othello, The*, Berkeley, 1961.

Ross, Lillian and Helen, *Player, The*, New York, 1961.

Rowe, Nicholas (ed.), *Shakespeare*, London, 1709.

Rowell, George, *Victorian Dramatic Criticism*, London, 1971.

———, *Victorian Theatre, The*, Oxford, 1956.

Royde-Smith, Naomi, *Outside Information*, London, 1941.

———, *Pilgrim from Paddington*, London, 1953.

———, *Private Life of Mrs. Siddons, The*, London, 1933.

Ruggles, Eleanor, *Prince of Players*, New York, 1953.

Russell, Charles E., *Julia Marlowe, Her Life and Art*, New York, 1926.

Russell, W. Clark, *Representative Actors*, London, 1888.

St. John, Christopher (ed.), *Ellen Terry and Bernard Shaw: A Correspondence*, London, 1931.

Sands, Dorothy, *Life and Times of Colley Cibber, The*, New York, 1927.

Sartre, Jean-Paul, *Kean* (translated by Kitty Black), London, 1969.

Saturday Review, The.

Scotchman, The.

Scott, Clement, *Ellen Terry*, London, 1900.

_____, *Drama of Yesterday and Today, The*, London, 1899.

_____, *From "The Bells" to "King Arthur,"* London, 1897.

Seilhamer, George D., *History of the American Theatre, The*, Philadelphia, 1888.

Shattuck, Charles H., *Hamlet of Edwin Booth, The*, Urbana, 1969.

Shaw, George Bernard, *Dramatic Criticisms from the "Saturday Review"* (ed. by John F. Matthews), New York, 1959.

_____, *Our Theatre in the Nineties*, 3 vols., London, 1932.

_____, "Point of View of a Playwright, The," in Max Beerbohm's *Herbert Beerbohm Tree*, New York, n.d., pp. 240–52.

Shaw, Martin, *Up to Now*, Oxford, 1929.

Sheldon, Esther K., *Thomas Sheridan of Smock Alley*, Princeton, 1969.

Sheridan, Richard B., *Letters, The* (ed. by Cecil Price), Oxford, 1966.

Short, Ernest, *Sixty Years of the Theatre*, London, 1951.

Siddons, Sarah K., *Reminiscences, The* (ed. by William Van Lennup), Cambridge, Mass., 1942.

Sillard, Robert M., *Barry Sullivan and His Contemporaries*, London, 1901.

Simpson, Harold, and Braun, Mrs. Charles, *Century of Famous Actresses 1750–1850, A*, New York, 1969.

Skinner, Cornelia O., *Madame Sarah*, New York, 1966.

Skinner, Otis, *Last Tragedian, The*, New York, 1939.

_____, *Mad Folk of the Theatre, The*, Indianapolis, 1928.

Sothern, E.H., *Julia Marlowe's Story* (ed. by Fairfax Downey), New York, 1954.

_____, *Melancholy Tale of "Me," My Remembrances, The*, New York, 1916.

Southern, Richard, *Changeable Scenery: Its Origin and Development in the British Theatre*, London, 1952.

_____, *Georgian Playhouses, The*, London, 1948.

Speaight, Robert, *Acting*, London, 1939.

_____, *Drama Since 1939*, London, 1947.

_____, *William Poel and the Elizabethan Revival*, London, 1954.

Spectator, The.

Spencer, Hazelton, *Shakespeare Improved*, Cambridge, Mass., 1927.

Sprague, Arthur C., *Shakespeare and the Actors*, New York, 1963.

_____, *Shakespearean Plays and Performers*, Cambridge, Mass., 1953.

Stanislavski, Constantin, *My Life in Art*, New York, 1956.

Steen, Marguerite, *Pride of Terrys, A*, London, 1962.

Stirling, Edward, *Old Drury Lane*, London, 1881.

Stockwell, La Tourette, *Dublin Theatres and Theatre Customs, 1637–1870*, Kingsport, Tenn., 1938.

Stoker, Bram, *Personal Reminiscences of Henry Irving*, London, 1960.

Stopes, Charlotte C., *Burbage and Shakespeare's Stage*, London, 1913.

Stubbs, Jean, *Eleanora Duse*, New York, 1970.

Sunday News, The (New York).

Tatler, The.

Taubman, Howard, *Making of the American Theatre, The*, New York, 1965.

Taylor, John, *Memoirs* (ed. by Richard H. Stoddard), New York, 1875.

Terry, Ellen, *Ellen Terry's Memoirs* (ed. by Edith Craig and Christopher St. John), London, 1933.

————, *Story of My Life, The,* London, 1908.

Theatre, The.

Theatre Arts.

Theatre Magazine.

Theatre Workshop, The.

Thompson, Laurence, *Behind the Curtain,* London, 1951.

Thorndike, Russell, *Sybil Thorndike,* London, 1939.

Thorndike, Sybil and Russell, *Lilian Baylis,* London, 1938.

Timbs, John, *Anecdote Biography,* London, 1860.

Time.

Times, The (London).

Towes, John P., *Sixty Years of the Theatre,* New York, 1916.

Tree, Herbert B., *Henry VIII and His Court,* London, 1911.

Tree, Viola, "My Father," in Max Beerbohm's *Herbert Beerbohm Tree,* New York, n.d., pp. 171–80.

Trewin, J.C., *Benson and the Bensonians,* London, 1960.

————, *Drama 1945–50,* London, 1951.

————, *Shakespeare on the English Stage 1900–64: A Survey of Productions,* London, 1964.

————, *Theatre Since 1900, The,* London, 1951.

Tuckerman, Henry T., *Edmund Kean, the Actor,* Boston, 1857.

Tynan, Kenneth, *Alec Guinness,* London, 1953.

————, *Curtains,* London, 1961.

————, *He Who Plays the King,* London, 1950.

Vandenhoff, George, *Dramatic Reminiscences,* London, 1860.

Victor, Benjamin, *History of the Theatres of London and Dublin,* London, 1961.

Village Voice, The.

Wagenknecht, Edward, *Merely Players,* Norman, Okla., 1966.

————, *Seven Daughters of the Theatre,* Norman, Okla., 1964.

Walbrook, H.M., *Nights at the Play,* London, 1911.

Walker, Alice, and Wilson, J. Dover, *Othello,* Cambridge, England, 1957.

Walker, Katherine S., *Robert Helpmann,* London, 1947.

Ward, Genevieve, and Whiteing, Richard, *Both Sides of the Curtain,* London, 1918.

Watkins, Ronald, *Moonlight at the Globe,* London, 1946.

————, *On Producing Shakespeare,* London, 1950.

Webster, Margaret, *Same Only Different, The,* New York, 1969.

————, *Shakespeare Today,* London, 1957.

Weglin, Oscar, *Beginnings of the Drama in America, The,* Greenwich, Conn., 1905.

Westwood, Doris, *These Players: A Diary of the Old Vic,* London, 1926.

White, T.H., *Age of Scandal, The,* London, 1950.

Whitman, Walt, *November Boughs,* Philadelphia, 1888.

Whyte, Frederic, *Actors of the Century,* London, 1898.

Wilde, Oscar, *Intentions,* New York, 1909.

————, *Poems,* New York, 1909.

————, *Reviews,* New York, 1909.

Wilkes, Thomas, *General View of the Stage, A,* London, 1733.

Wilkinson, Tate, *Memoirs of His Own Life,* Dublin, 1791.

————, *Wandering Patentee, The,* York, 1795.

Williams, E. Harcourt, *Four Years at the Old Vic,* London, 1935.

————, *Old Vic Saga,* London, 1949.

———— (ed.), *Vic-Wells: The Work of Lilian Baylis,* London, 1938.

Williams, John, *Children of Thespis,* Dublin, 1787.

———, *Pin Basket to the Children of Thespis, A*, London, 1797.

Williamson, Audrey, *Contemporary Theatre 1935–56*, London, 1956.

———, *Old Vic Drama*, London, 1948.

———, *Old Vic Drama 2*, London, 1951.

———, *Theatre of Two Decades*, London, 1951.

Wilson, A.E., *Edwardian Theatre, The*, London, 1951.

———, *Lyceum, The*, London, 1952.

———, *Prime Minister of Mirth*, London, 1956.

Wilson, Garff B., *History of American Acting, A*, Bloomington, 1966.

Wilson, J. Dover, *Hamlet*, Cambridge, England, 1936.

———, *Othello*, Cambridge, England, 1957.

———, *What Happens in Hamlet*, Cambridge, England, 1936.

Wilson, J. Dover, and Worsley, T.C., *Shakespeare's Histories at Stratford 1951*, London, 1952.

Wilson, John Harold, *All the King's Ladies*, Chicago, 1958.

Wilstach, Paul, *Richard Mansfield, the Man and the Actor*, New York, 1908.

Winter, William, *Other Days*, New York, 1908.

———, *Shadows of the Stage*, Edinburgh, 1892.

———, *Shadows of the Stage, 2d Series*, New York, 1894.

———, *Shakespeare on the Stage*, New York, 1911–1916.

———, *Vagrant Memories*, New York, 1915.

———, *Wallet of Time, The*, New York, 1913.

Winwar, Frances, *Oscar Wilde and the Yellow Nineties*, New York, 1940.

———, *Wingless Victory*, New York, 1956.

Wolfit, Donald, *First Interval*, London, 1954.

Worsley, T.C., *Fugitive Art, The*, London, 1949.

Wyndham, Henry S., *Annals of the Covent Garden Theatre*, London, 1906.

Young, Julian C., *Personal Reminiscences* (ed. by Richard H. Stoddard), New York, 1876.

Young, William C., *Documents of American Theater History*, 2 vols., Chicago, 1973.

Abbreviations Used in the References to the Text

The following abbreviations have been used in the reference notes; see the Bibliography for full title and date:

AA Agate, *Anthology.*
AB Agate, *Brief Chronicles.*
AE3 Agate, *Ego 3.*
AE6 Agate, *Ego 6.*
AE8 Agate, *Ego 8.*
AE9 Agate, *Ego 9.*
AM Appleton, *Macklin.*
AS Aston, *Supplement to Cibber.*
BA Burton, *Great Acting.*
BB Bancroft, *The Bancrofts.*
BE Bellchambers, *Memoirs.*
BHB Beerbohm, *Some Memories.*
BI Brereton, *Henry Irving.*
BL Brereton, *Lyceum and Henry Irving.*
BR Brown, *Shakespeare and the Actors.*
BS Ball, *Shakespeare on Silent Film.*
CA Cibber, *Apology.*
CC Carritt, *Calendar of British Taste.*
CG Carlisle, *Shakespeare from the Green-room*
CS Crosse, *Shakespearean Playgoing.*
CT Cole & Chinoy, *Actors on Acting.*
DD Doran, *Annals.*
DNB *Dictionary of National Biography.*
DR Dent, *Nocturnes and Rhapsodies.*
FE Frohman, *Encore.*
FP Findlater, *Player Kings.*
FV Furness, *Variorum Edition.*
GBS Shaw in the *Saturday Review.*
GG Grebanier, *Great Shakespeare Forgery.*
GJ Gilder, *John Gielgud's Hamlet.*
GH Grebanier, *Heart of Hamlet.*
GR Goodwin, *Royal Shakespeare Co.*
GT Grebanier *Truth about Shylock.*
GU Grebanier, *Uninhibited Byron.*
HG Hayman, *John Gielgud.*
HL Hutton, *Curiosities.*
HO Hartnoll, *Oxford Companion.*
HS Halliday, *Companion.*

HW Hazlitt, *Complete Works.*
IH Irving, L., *Henry Irving.*
JT Joseph, *Tragic Actors.*
KM Kirkman, *Macklin.*
LO Lewes, *On Acting.*
MA Moody, *Astor Place Riot.*
MB in SR, Max Beerbohm in *Saturday Review.*
MC Morris, *Curtain Time.*
MD Matthews & Hutton, *Garrick,* etc.
ME Matthews & Hutton, *Edwin Booth,* etc.
MH Mander & Mitcheson, *Hamlet.*
MI Manvell, *International Encyclopedia of Film.*
MK Matthews & Hutton, *Kean, Booth,* etc.
MKB Matthews & Hutton, *Kembles.*
MS Manvell, *Sarah Siddons.*
NY *The New Yorker.*
NYD *New York Dramatic Mirror.*
NYM *New York Magazine.*
NYT *New York Times.*
OS Odell, *Shakespeare.*
PD Pepys, *Diary.*
RM Rosenberg, *Masks of Othello.*
RP Ruggles, *Prince of Players.*
RS Raby, *Stratford Scene.*
RT Rankin, *Theatre in Colonial America.*
RV Rowell, *Victorian Dramatic Criticism.*
SI Spencer, *Shakespeare Improved.*
SM Skinner, *Mad Folk.*
SR *Saturday Review.*
TO Trewin, *Shakespeare on English Stage.*
TS Terry, *Story of My Life.*
WH Wilson, *History of American Acting.*
WM Wagenknecht, *Merely Players*
WS Wagenknecht, *Seven Daughters.*
WW Winter, *Shakespeare on the Stage*

References to the Text

PAGE	LINE		PAGE	LINE	
21	32	BR, pp. 21–22.	32	15	PD, I, p. 102.
22	19, 22, 25	HO, pp. 9, 288, 186.	32	23, 26	CA, I, pp. 178–79, 180.
22	28	Winter, William, *Shadows of the Stage, First Series*, p. 13.	32	30	AS in CA, II, p. 358.
			33	10	*Ibid.*, 307.
			33	21	OS, I, pp. 12–13.
22	35	HO, p. 63.	34	6	*Ibid.*, pp. 15–16.
23	21	DD, I, pp. 31–34.	34	21	CA, I, pp. 157–62.
24	20, 28	DD, I, pp. 39, 42.			
			34	44	PD, I, p. 131.
24	37	HO, p. 219.	35	1, 3	*Ibid.*, p. 211, 426.
			35	5	Victor, Benjamin, *History of the Theatres of London and Dublin*, III, p. 13.
	Chapter Three				
26	16	CC, p. 114.			
26	18, 23, 27	PD, I, pp. 261, 329.			
26	30, 31, 33, 36	PD, II, pp. 72, 142, 372, 431.			
			35	9	SI, quoted p. 26.
26	42	PD, III, p. 36.	35	24	AS in CA, II, p. 309.
27	15, 19	CC, quoted pp. 84, 93.			
27	26	HS, p. 563.	35	30	WW, I, quoted p. 237.
27	29	CC, quoted p. 129.	35	36	Rowe, Nicholas (ed.), *Shakespeare*, I, p. xxxiii.
29	1	OS, I, pp. 4–6.			
29	8	HO, p. 153.			
29	10	HS, p. 153.			
29	14, 25	OS, I, pp. 7, 9.	35	46	GG, pp. 4–5.
30	2	Miles, Bernard, *British Theatre, The*, p. 17.	36	7	SI, p. 63.
			36	9	CA, I, p. 221.
			36	25	AS in CA, II, pp. 336–37.
30	12, 20	HO, pp. 255, 629.	36	35	CA, I, pp. 190–91.
30	24, 30, 37, 43	PD, III, pp. 224, 229, 296–99, 440.	37	3	*Tatler, The*, No. 134.
31	19	Prynne, William, *Histriomastix*, p. 208.	37	9, 24	CA, I, pp. 191–92, 196–97.
			37	27, 29	SI, pp. 79, 73.
31	41	Davies, Thomas, *Memoir of the Life of Garrick*, p. 19.	37	32	DNB, I, p. 1237.
			38	2	DD, I, p. 105.
			38	8	CA, I, p. 219.

Chapter Four

Page	Line	
		rence, *Curiosities of the American Stage,* p. 261.
51	25, 34	RT, pp. 155, 157.
51	42	HO, p. 1008.
52	4	*Ibid.*, pp. 520–21.
52	30	MKB, pp. 237–40.
52	38, 45	Dunn, E. C., *op. cit.*, pp. 94, 39.
53	6, 11, 14	*Ibid.*, pp. 221, 245, 246.

Chapter Five

Page	Line	
54	8	Miles, Bernard, *British Theatre, The*, p. 17.
54	9	DD, I, quoted p. 154.
55	18, 20	RM, pp. 99, 267.
56	17	DD, I, pp. 265–78.
56	20	HO, pp. 117–18.
56	39	DD, I, pp. 279–81.
57	1, 5	*Ibid.*, pp. 272, 226–28.
57	13	DNB, II, p. 837.
57	16	DD, I, p. 275.
57	20	GG, p. 88.
57	32	DD, I, quoted pp. 282–83.
58	1, 20	Miles, Bernard, *loc. cit.*
58	37	DD, I, p. 371.
59	11, 20	*Ibid.*, pp. 377, 383.
60	1, 12	*Ibid.*, pp. 387–89, 384.
60	16	DNB, XVI, p. 550.
60	24	DD, I, p. 320.

Page	Line	
60	25	HO, p. 784.
60	29	DD, I, p. 321.
60	35	HO, *loc. cit.*
60	37	DD, I, p. 322.
61	9, 23	*Ibid.*, pp. 321–22, 394–95.
61	28	CG, quoted p. 460.
62	17	DNB, IV, pp. 359–62.
62	22	AM, p. 28.
62	31	DD, I, p. 395.
62	33	DNB, *loc. cit.*
62	36	WW, I, p. 459.
62	43	MD, quoted p. 36.
63	1	Agate, James, *English Dramatic Critics, The,* p. 57.
63	3	MD, p. 29.
63	6	Fitzgerald, Percy, *New History of the English Stage,* II, p. 49.
63	9, 14	MD, p. 32, quoted p. 41.
63	17	RM, pp. 38–39.
63	18	*Gentleman's Magazine,* November 1734.
63	21	HO, p. 784.
63	24	MD, p. 30.
63	30	DD, I, p. 396.
63	32	MD, p. 32.
64	7, 17, 31	DD, I, pp. 402, 403–4, 400–1.
65	9, 16	*Ibid.*, pp. 397–99, 404.
65	21	Cooke, William, *Memorials of the Life of Charles Macklin,* p. 19

PAGE	LINE		PAGE	LINE	
		Other First Nights, quoted p. 213.			*Romance of the English Stage,* p. 229.
72	6	Barton, Margaret, *Garrick,* p. 73.	78	39	HO, pp. 546–47.
			79	1	MD, pp. 5–6.
72	23	Davies, Thomas, *Memoir of the Life of Garrick,* I, p. 75.	79	7	*Apology for the Conduct of Charles Macklin, An,* p. 30.
72	45	AM, pp. 68–70.	79	29, 31	KM, II, 112–13
73	6	HO, pp. 329–30.			and 138–216,
73	11	OS, I, p. 339.			217–56.
73	31	DD, II, pp. 119–32.	80	5	HO, p. 830.
			80	11	*Ibid.,* p. 715.
74	4	O'Keeffe, John, *Recollections,* pp. 42–45.	80	19	DD, II, pp. 59–60.
74	11	MS, p. 44.	80	33	Taylor, John, *op. cit.,* p. 276, and CG, p. 461.
74	13	Wilkinson, Tate, *Memoirs,* III, p. 147.			
74	20	MS, p. 70.	80	38	HO, p. 1015.
74	21	AM, p. 70.	81	5	DD, II, pp. 113–16.
74	33	HO, pp. 1013–14.	81	7	HO, p. 241.
75	7, 23	DD, II, pp. 6–7, 12–13.	81	10, 14, 21	DD, II, pp. 132, 201, 208.
75	29	AM, pp. 80–82.	81	31	Taylor, John, *op. cit.,* pp. 279–80.
75	39	Cooke, William, *op. cit.,* p. 157.			
75	45	WW, I, p. 243.	81	45	DD, II, p. 209.
76	3, 10, 15, 23	MD, pp. 125, 127, 132, 136–37.	82	21	Taylor, John, *op. cit.,* pp. 280–84.
76	32, 40	DD, II, pp. 96–99, 103–4.	82	31	HO, p. 439.
77	19	DNB, I, p. 1229.	82	41	WW, I, pp. 144–45.
77	28	DD, I, pp. 104–6.	82	42	RM, p. 50.
77	31	MD, pp. 128–29.	82	44	HO, *loc. cit.*
77	36	DNB, *loc. cit.*	83	12	DD, II, pp. 237–38.
77	42	AM, p. 83.			
78	9	*Ibid.,* pp. 89–92.	83	42	O'Keeffe, John, *op. cit.,* pp. 50–51.
78	26, 32	MD, pp. 173–76, 178.			
78	38	Fitzgerald, Percy,	84	3, 5	HO, pp. 783–84, 715.

PAGE	LINE		PAGE	LINE	
115	22	WW, I, pp. 92–96.	119	27	MKB, pp. 123–24.
115	24	MKB, pp. 3–19.	119	31	HO, pp. 309–10.
115	39	DD, II, p. 286.	119	42	*Ibid.*, p. 271.
116	1	*Ibid.*, p. 293.	120	8	*Ibid.*, pp. 273–74.
116	7	MKB, pp. 3–17.	120	26, 33	MKB, pp. 163, 183.
116	12, 22	DD, II, pp. 289, 290.	120	37	Sprague, Arthur C., *op. cit.*, p. 143.
116	37	Kelly, Michael, *Memoirs*, p. 169.	121	5	DD, II, pp. 348–49.
116	39	WM, p. 40.			
116	46	Dunlap, William, *Memoirs of G. F. Cooke*, I, pp. 123–25.	121	15	Hunt, Leigh, in *Tatler, The*, July 10, 1831.
117	2	*Ibid.*, II, p. 351.	121	29	Lamb, Charles, in *Englishman's Magazine, The*, August 1831.
117	4	AM, p. 55.			
117	17	Dunlap, William, *op. cit.*, II, pp. 350–52.	121	31	HO, p. 274.
			121	40, 46	Sprague, Arthur C., *op. cit.*, quoted pp. 42 and 65.
117	26	Sprague, Arthur C., *op. cit.*; p. 194.			
117	29	AM, p. 247.	122	9, 17	HO, pp. 656, 631.
117	31	Dunlap, William, *op. cit.*, I, p. 187.	122	22	HL, pp. 262–63.
			122	26, 30	Sprague, Arthur C., *op. cit.*, quoted pp. 135 and 212.
117	38	Sprague, Arthur C., *op. cit.*, quoted pp. 23–24.			
118	17	Lamb, Charles, in *The Morning Post*, June 4, 1801.	122	31, 38	HL, pp. 265, 270.

Chapter Nine

PAGE	LINE		PAGE	LINE	
118	24	DNB, IV, p. 1009.	123	3	HW, V, p. 345.
118	28	MKB, pp. 3–17.	123	10	HO, pp. 437–38.
118	43	DD, II, pp. 291–92.	123	14	DD, II, p. 265.
			123	26	HO, *loc. cit.*
119	9	*Ibid.*, p. 295.	124	12	Hunt, Leigh, *Dramatic Essays*, pp. 3–8.
119	15	DNB, p. 1009.			
119	19	HW, V, p. 207.	124	16	HW, XVIII, p. 199.

PAGE	LINE		PAGE	LINE	
124	17, 20, 24	WW, I, pp. 329, 331, 416.			in the *London Times*, June 15, 1817.
125	3	OS, II, quoted pp. 57–58.	133	2, 17, 42	GG, pp. 92–95, 127, 300.
125	16, 20	Sprague, Arthur C., *op. cit.* quoted from *London Magazine, The*, pp. 326–28.	134	16, 22, 27, 35,37	*Ibid.*, pp. 157, 159, 171, 175, 201.
			135	7	*Ibid.*, pp. 202–6.
125	27	*London Times, The*, Dec. 16, 1811.	136	4, 29	*Ibid.*, pp. 209–15, 216–19.
			137	21	*Ibid.*, pp. 221–24.
125	35	Sprague, Arthur C., *op. cit.,* quoted from *Quarterly Review, The, loc. cit.*	137	38	Jerden, William, *Personal Reminiscences*, pp. 186–91.
			138	11	Young, Julian C., *Personal Reminiscences*, p. 169.
125	39	RV, quoted from Hunt's *Critical Essays*, p. 9.	138	20	RV, quoted pp. 8–12.
127	25	Taylor, John, *op. cit.,* pp. 218–27.	138	28	FP, quoted p. 58.
			139	22	*Ibid.*, pp. 63–66.
127	35, 39	OS, II, pp. 4, 45.	139	31	Jerden, William, *op. cit.*, p. 190.
128	3	*Ibid.*, pp. 49–50.			
128	17	HO, pp. 155–56.	139	36	HO, *loc. cit.*
128	32, 35	WW, I, pp. 239–40, 249.			

Chapter Ten

PAGE	LINE			
128	39	HO, p. 871.	140	5	HO, p. 886.
129	3	MKB, p. 275.	140	13	AE9, quoted p. 119.
129	6	HO, p. 533.			
129	19	*Monthly Mirror, The*, January 1808.	140	17, 22	HW, XVIII, pp. 278, 274.
			140	27	Funke, Lewis, and Booth, John E., *Actors Talk about Acting*, pp. 141–42.
129	25	AE3, quoted p. 74.			
129	37, 39	JT, pp. 189, 191.			
129	41	OS, II, p. 54.			
130	8, 23, 31	Kelly, Michael, *op. cit.,* pp. 120, 135–37, 170.	141	7	Agate, James, *English Dramatic Critics, The*, p. 63.
132	9	Hazlitt, William,			

PAGE	LINE		PAGE	LINE	
141	18	DD, II, pp. 262–63.			ollections," in *Harper's Monthly Magazine*, December 1862.
141	22	HO, *loc. cit.*			
141	26	FE, p. 227.			
142	9, 33	DD, II, pp. 240–41, 243–44.	147	32	MS, quoted p. 130.
142	36	MS, pp. 21, 23, 39, 59.	147	35, 37	Sprague, Arthur C., *op. cit.*, pp. 241, 243.
142	41	DD, II, pp. 243–44.	147	42	Genest, John, *op. cit.*, VI, p. 338.
142	43	MS, p. 69.			
143	2	DD, II, p. 245.	148	2	Boaden, James, *op. cit.*, p. 260.
143	9	MS, p. 71.			
143	19	GU, p. 19.	148	15	Grebanier, Bernard, "Lady Macbeth of London," in *Shenandoah*, Summer 1962.
144	22	FE, quoted pp. 169–70.			
144	24	Boaden, James, *Memoirs of Mrs. Siddons*, p. 217.			
144	38	Siddons, Sarah K., *Reminiscences*, pp. 12–22.	148	32	Sprague, Arthur C., *op. cit.*, quoted pp. 269 and 270.
145	8	Sprague, Arthur C., *op. cit.*, quoted p. 110.	148	38	Boaden, James, *op. cit.*, p. 262.
145	22	DD, II, pp. 249–50.	148	42	Hunt, Leigh, *op. cit.*, p. 235.
145	47	Boaden, James, *op. cit.*, pp. 170–72.	148	44	Sprague, Arthur C., *op. cit.*, quoted p. 271.
146	32	Siddons, Sarah K., *op. cit.*, pp. 17–20.	149	18	Mathews, Charles, *Memoirs*, II, p. 107.
146	46	DD, II, p. 304.	149	28	MS, quoted from Campbell, pp. 120–21.
147	5	Siddons, Sarah K., *loc. cit.*			
147	7	MS, p. 25.	149	30	MS, p. 93.
147	21	Hunt, Leigh, *Dramatic Essays*, p. 212.	150	3, 7, 8	*Ibid.*, pp. 138, 284, 388.
			150	18	AE3, quoted pp. 314–15.
147	26	Siddons, J. H., "Random Rec-	150	23	Campbell, Thomas, *Life of*

PAGE	LINE	
		Mrs. Siddons, The, II, p. 61.
150	29	*Variorum Edition* of *The Winter's Tale,* pp. 389–90.
150	39	AE3, *loc. cit.*
150	43	Macready, William C., *Reminiscences,* p. 43.
150	45	JT, p. 218.
151	5	Campbell, Thomas, *op. cit.,* pp. 30–35.
151	21, 24	Boaden, James, *op. cit.,* II, pp. 158–59, 282.
151	31	Campbell, Thomas, *op. cit,* 59, 380–83.
152	6, 7, 15	MS, pp. 290–95, 296–97, 380.
152	37	Hazlitt, William, in *Examiner, The,* June 16, 1816.
153	8	Moore, Thomas, *Personal Reminiscences,* p. 138.

Chapter Eleven

154	3	HO, p. 533.
154	5	DD, II, p. 265.
154	12	HW, V, p. 340.
154	17, 20	Sprague, Arthur C., *op. cit,* pp. 83–84, 374 n. 93.
155	40	Taylor, John, *op. cit.,* pp. 250–53.
155	42	MKB, p. 219.

PAGE	LINE	
156	7	HO, p. 533.
156	16, 34	OS, II, pp. 85–109, 169–72.
157	7	DD, II, pp. 279–82.
157	14	CG, quoted p. 106.
157	23	Sprague, Arthur C., *op. cit.,* quoted p. 13.
157	30	DD, II, p. 283.
158	6	HO, pp. 533–34.
158	16	Hunt, Leigh, *op. cit.,* pp. 148–49, 155, 205.
158	29, 37	HW, XVIII, p. 252, 277.
158	41	MKB, pp. 142–44.
158	46	HO, p. 525.
159	11, 44	SM, pp. 180–81, 182–85.
160	7	GG, p. 176.
160	15, 17, 20, 23	SM, pp. 190, 195, 197, 199.
160	27	*Manchester Courier, The,* May 9, 1846.
160	32	Hazlitt, William, *Dramatic Essays,* pp. 70–72.
160	40	Taylor, John, *op. cit.,* p. 244.
161	7, 18, 27	GG, pp. 176–77, 180–81, 212.
161	20	HW, V, p. 252.

Chapter Twelve

| 162 | 11 | MKB, pp. 300–1. |
| 164 | 16 | DD, II, pp. 296–301. |

PAGE	LINE		PAGE	LINE	
164	29	MKB, pp. 305–8.			*op. cit.,* pp.
165	17	HL, pp. 238–43.			52–53.
			172	43	GU, pp. 198–99.
		Chapter Thirteen	173	10	Hunt, Leigh, in
167	8	GT, pp. 328–29.			*Examiner, The,* February 26, 1815.
167	15	HW, V, p. 175.			
167	21	Hazlitt, William, *Characters of Shakespeare's Plays, The,* p. 212.	173	23	Hazlitt, William, in *Times, The,* October 27, 1817.
168	4	Hazlitt, William, *Morning Chronicle, The,* January 27, 1814.	173	28	HW, V, pp. 242, 294.
			173	36	DD, II, p. 309.
			173	45	WM, pp. 36–37.
			174	12	HW, XVIII, pp. 277–78.
168	7	WM, p. 31.	174	14	Molloy, J. F., *op. cit.,* I, p. 213.
168	10	DD, II, p. 377.			
168	25	Molloy, J. F., *Life and Adventures of Edmund Kean, The,* I, pp. 3–5.	175	33, 42	*Ibid.,* I, pp. 233–43, II, p. 43.
			177	15	*Ibid.,* II, pp. 72–80.
168	29	WM, *loc. cit.*	178	26	*Ibid.,* II, pp. 77–90.
168	33	DD, II, p. 378.			
168	38	WM, p. 32.	179	33	*Ibid.,* II, pp. 90–103.
169	31	DD, II, pp. 379–81.	179	45	CG, quoted p. 273.
170	11	AE6, quoted pp. 150–51.	180	28	Molloy, J. F., II, *op. cit.,* pp. 106–8
170	35	DD, II, pp. 381–84.	183	3	*Ibid.,* II, pp. 110–28.
170	38	WM, p. 32.			
171	14	DD, II, pp. 384–86.	183	6	WM, p. 38.
171	25	WM, p. 35.	183	43	Molloy, J. F., *op. cit.,* II, pp. 129–33.
171	31, 44	HW, pp. 180–81, 187–88.			
171	45	WM, p. 36.	185	42	*Ibid.,* II, pp. 133–77.
172	23	Molloy, J. F., *op. cit.,* I, pp. 202–3.	186	32	*Ibid.,* II, pp. 178–83.
172	36	Moore, Thomas,	187	25	*Ibid.,* II, pp. 189–205.

188   23   *Ibid.*, pp. 223–28.   pp. 225–38,
189   3   *Ibid.*, II, pp.   291–93.
                   228–33.   194   19   RM, p. 18.
189   13   DD, II, p. 407.   194   25   HW, V, p. 41.
189   18   WM, p. 39.   194   26, 30   DD, II, pp. 308,
189   27   DD, II, pp.   351.
                   413–14.   194   34   RM, quoted p.
189   35, 40, 41 HW, V, pp.   120.
                   189–90, 207,   194   38   MKB, p. 271.
                   187.   195   23   Young, Julian C.,
189   42   *Ibid.*, XVIII, p.   *Personal Remi-*
                   290.   *niscences*, pp.
190   2   *Ibid.*, V, p. 338.   153–55.
190   26   Lewes, G. H.,   195   28   MKB, p. 272.
                   quoted in RV,   196   26   Young, Julian C.,
                   pp. 56–60.   *op. cit.*, pp.
190   31, 33, 36 MK, pp. 2, 7, 29.   157–59.
                                                197   35   *Ibid.*, pp. 164–69.
         Chapter Fourteen   198   7   MKB, pp.
191   6   DNB, IV, p. 984.   273–76.
191   19   Fitzgerald, Percy,   198   13   HW, V, p. 234.
                   op. cit., pp.   198   25, 33   HO, pp. 996–97,
                   241–42.   887.
191   25   DNB, IV, p. 985.   198   38   NYD, January
192   4   Fitzgerald, Percy,   1885.
                   op. cit., p. 252.   198   46   HO, p. 432.
192   8   HO, p. 67.   199   4   MK, p. 163.
192   23   Marshall,   199   10   Dunn, E. C., *op.*
                   Herbert, and   *cit.*, p. 149.
                   Stock, Mildred,   199   13   HO, p. 424.
                   Ira Aldridge, pp.   199   31, 36   Moses, Montrose,
                   25–30.   *Famous Acting*
193   9, 14, 20, *Ibid.*, pp. 39–66,   *Families in*
       22, 25, 36 79, 92–116,   *America*, pp.
       40, 42, 46 121, 130,   145–46, 20.
                   175–81, 204–6,   200   12   SM, pp. 263–64.
                   203–11, 219,   200   42   Moses, Montrose,
                   225.   *op. cit.*, pp.
194   5   Sprague, Arthur   20–24.
                   C., *op. cit.*, p.   201   38   Molloy, J. F., *op.*
                   214.   *cit.*, II, pp.
194   13, 17   Marshall, Herbert   7–12.
                   and Stock, Mil-   202   33   SM, pp. 266–68.
                   dred, *op. cit.*,   Also Moses,

PAGE	LINE		PAGE	LINE	
		Glasgow Herald, The, March 14, 1848; *Glasgow Citizen, The,* April 1848.			Tragedies on the Stage," in *Lippincott's,* June 1884, pp. 604 seq.
218	17, 24	Moses, Montrose, *Fabulous Forrest, The,* pp. 124, 136.	224	17	Moody, Richard, *op. cit.,* pp. 385–86.
218	31	Whitman, Walt, *November Boughs,* p. 90.			**Chapter Sixteen**
			225	3	HO, p. 117.
			225	12	Moses, Montrose, *Famous Acting Families in America,* quoted pp. 35–36.
218	33	WM, p. 74.			
220	6	FE, pp. 20–26.			
220	20	WW, I, pp. 333–35.			
220	22	HO, pp. 272, 331–32.	225	19	WM, p. 126.
			225	23	HO, *loc. cit.*
220	44	WW, I, *loc. cit.*	226	3	Moses, Montrose, *op. cit.,* p. 36.
220	46	Ayres, Alfred, *Acting, Actors, Elocution and Elocutionists,* p. 101.	226	5	HO, *loc. cit.*
			226	12	WM, p. 126.
			226	20	HO, p. 531.
			226	46	Moses, Montrose, *op. cit.,* pp. 41–42.
221	24	Young, William C., *Documents of American Theater History,* I, pp. 76–77.	227	38	RP, pp. 90–94.
			228	7, 39	FE, pp. 89–90, 112.
222	5	FE, pp. 29–30.	229	29	RP, pp. 94–96.
222	10	WM, pp. 94–96.	229	33	See GH.
222	17	WW, I, pp. 474–76.	230	12, 19, 28	RP, pp. 94–96, 96–98, 100, 107–09.
222	23	Harrison, Gabriel, *Edwin Forrest,* p. 64.	230	31	Moses, Montrose, *op. cit.,* p. 42.
222	37	Moody, Richard, *Edwin Forrest,* pp. 245–48.	231	27	RP, pp. 111–20
			232	19, 39	*Ibid.,* pp. 120–24, 125–31.
223	25	*Ibid.,* pp. 258–62.	233	19	*Ibid.,* pp. 133–37.
223	35	WM, p. 109.	234	36	*Ibid.,* pp. 138–51.
223	37	RM, p. 92.	235	20	*Ibid.,* pp. 155–60.
223	41	Kirk, John F., "Shakespeare's	236	5	*Ibid.,* pp. 161–66.
			236	9	WM, p. 127.

PAGE	LINE		PAGE	LINE	
236	36	RP, pp. 173–80.	249	45	WW, I, pp.
237	10	*Ibid.*, pp. 181–83.			108–9.
237	17	FE, pp. 94–95.	250	4, 5, 9, 14,	*Ibid.*, pp. 155,
237	22	RP, pp. 184–85.		17, 22, 33	268, 271, 340,
237	29	FE, p. 95.			342, 347,
238	24	RP, pp. 185–94.			477–80.
238	38	*Ibid.*, pp. 195–97.	251	1	*Variorum Edition*
238	41	WM, p. 127.			of *Othello*, p.
239	5	RP, pp. 205–6.			214.
240	1, 8	WM, quoted pp.	251	6	RM, p. 129.
		123–24,	251	15, 29, 40	Shattuck,
		129–30.			Charles, *Hamlet*
240	11	Moses, Montrose,			*of Edwin Booth,*
		op. cit., p. 48.			*The*, pp. 123,
240	22, 30	RP, pp. 234,			152–54, 190
		224–27.	252	4	*Ibid.*, p. 308.
240	38	Moses, Montrose,			
		op. cit., pp.			
		49–50.		***Chapter Seventeen***	
241	6, 34	RP, pp. 245–51,			
		255–58.	254	20	*New York Dramatic*
242	20, 45	*Ibid.*, pp. 260–65,			*Mirror*, Febru-
		267–70.			ary 16, 1901.
243	9	House, Edward	254	25	MH, p. 21.
		E., "Edwin	254	28	*New York Dramatic*
		Booth in			*Mirror, loc. cit.*
		London," in	254	30	MH, p. 24.
		Century Mag-	254	39	*Theatre Magazine,*
		azine, The,			July 1916, p.
		December			21.
		1897, pp.	255	1	MH, *loc. cit.*
		269–70.	255	4	WW, I, p. 429.
244	10	*Ibid.*, pp. 270–76.	255	13	GG, pp. 211–
244	43	RP, pp. 277–87.			25.
245	30	House, Edward	255	14	DNB, XVI, pp.
		E., *op. cit.*, pp.			236–37.
		277–79.	255	20	*New York Dramatic*
246	41	RP, pp. 288–303.			*Mirror, loc. cit.*
248	24	FE, pp. 138–40.	255	22	MH, *loc. cit.*
248	39	RP, pp. 324–41.	255	24	*New York Dramatic*
249	9, 22	*Ibid.*, pp. 343–48,			*Mirror, loc. cit.*
		350.	255	28	DNB, VIII, pp.
249	27, 31	WM, pp. 148,			4–5.
		139.	255	41	MH, *loc. cit.*
			256	4	*New York Dramatic*
					Mirror, loc. cit.

PAGE   LINE

256   22   WW, I, p. 430.
256   35   *New York Dramatic Mirror, loc. cit.*
256   39   MH, *loc. cit.*
256   46   WH, p. 48.
257   12   WW, I, p. 209.
257   19   Leach, Joseph, *Bright Particular Star*, p. 116.
257   29   WH, p. 48.
257   35   Leach, Joseph, *op. cit.*, p. 118.
257   38   WW, I, 500.
257   44   RP, p. 115.
258   3   WW, I, pp. 500–6.
258   13, 19 RP, pp. 94, 115–16.
258   31   Leach, Joseph, *op. cit.*, p. 129.
258   36   WH, p. 40.
258   43, 44 Leach, Joseph, *op. cit.*, pp. 151, 230.
259   1, 5   *Ibid.*, pp. 113–14, 157.
259   7   Booth, Edwina, *Edwin Booth*, p. 263.
259   16   WH, p. 53.
259   19   HO, pp. 224–25.
259   26   *New York Dramatic Mirror, loc. cit.*
259   31   Leach, Joseph, *op. cit.*, pp. 175–77.
259   39   Clement, Clara, *Charlotte Cushman*, pp. 66–67.
260   2   WH, p. 55.
260   7   Taubman, Howard, *Making of the American Theatre, The*, p. 87.
260   11, 17, 19 Leach, Joseph, *op. cit.*, pp. 207–10, 222–23, 229–30.
260   26   HO, pp. 224–25.
260   37   WS, p. 71.
260   41   AA, pp. 244 and 276.
261   3   HO, p. 105.
261   8   Skinner, Cornelia O., *Madame Sarah*, pp. 260–61.
261   9   *New York Dramatic Mirror, loc. cit.*
261   11   Skinner, Cornelia O., *loc. cit.*
261   14   AA, quoted p. 244.
261   42   Beerbohm, Max, from *Saturday Review, The,* quoted in *Around Theatres,* pp. 34–37.
262   10   WW, I, pp. 431–42.
262   17   *New York Dramatic Mirror, loc. cit.*
262   18   Atkinson, Brooks, *Broadway*, p. 6.
262   22   AA, p. 35.
262   25, 27 Shaw, George Bernard, in *Saturday Review,* June 18 and June 15, 1895.
263   4   *New York Times, The,* January 3, 1971, Section 2.

PAGE LINE

263 35 MH, p. 24, and
GH, p. 101.

Chapter Eighteen

264 11 DNB, XV, p.
1032.
265 8, 19 Allen, Shirley S.,
*Samuel Phelps
and Sadler's
Wells Theatre*,
pp. 13–15, 26.
265 23 Macready, William C., *Reminiscences*, p.
414.
265 24 DNB, XV, p.
1033.
266 3 Allen, Shirley S.,
op. cit., pp.
30–34.
266 14 Phelps, W. May,
and Forbes-
Robertson,
Johnston, *Life
and Lifework of
Samuel Phelps*,
p. 50.
267 17 Allen, Shirley S.,
op. cit. pp.
36–44.
268 34 *Ibid.*, pp. 45–59.
269 11 *Ibid.*, pp. 63–65.
270 2, 9 *Ibid.*, pp. 60–70,
75.
271 6, 36 *Ibid.*, pp. 75–81,
85–90.
272 17, 43 *Ibid.*, pp. 164–73,
174–78.
273 22, 33 *Ibid.*, pp. 179–88,
201.
274 6, 10, 23 *Ibid.*, pp. 293–99,
301, 310–11.
274 27 WW, I, p. 114.
274 41 HO, p. 778.

PAGE LINE

275 3 WW, I, p. 339.
275 21, 22 IH, pp. 279–80,
289.
275 37, 45 Shaw, George
Bernard, in
*Saturday Review,
The*, July 13
and December
14, 1895.
276 6 *Ibid.*, December
26, 1896.

Chapter Nineteen

277 2 HO, pp. 478–80.
277 5, 10, 15, IH, pp. 39, 47,
24 55, 62–84.
278 10, 21 *Ibid.*, pp. 79–82,
94–97.
279 13 TS, pp. 72–74.
279 15 HO, *loc. cit.*
279 16 RM, p. 77.
279 19 AE9, April 25,
1882.
279 20 RM, *loc. cit.*
279 27 TS, p. 74.
279 38 HO, *loc. cit.*
279 40 AE3, pp. 279–80.
280 1 AE6, p. 182.
280 12 AE3, *loc. cit.*
281 14 *Ibid.*, p. 283.
281 15 Minney, R.J.,
*Bogus Image of
Bernard Shaw,
The*, pp. 42–
43.
281 19 AE3, p. 285.
281 25 IH, pp. 132–33.
281 40 TS, pp. 72–73.
283 17 BI, pp. 81–85.
283 24 DNB, Supplement
1901–11, p.
252.
283 37 IH, pp. 155–58.
283 39 DNB, *loc. cit.*

PAGE	LINE		PAGE	LINE	
329	2, 12	Winwar, Frances, *Wingless Victory*, pp. 116, 138.			*of Beerbohm Tree*, pp. 87–88.
329	14	Shaw, George Bernard, in *Saturday Review, The*, June 8, 1895.	333	26, 33	Pearson, Hesketh, *op. cit.*, pp. 85–103, 107.
329	25	Agate, James, *More First Nights*, pp. 249–50.	334	4, 28, 43	Beerbohm, Max, *op. cit.* pp. 189, 199, 197–98, 198–99.
			334	46	Donaldson, Francis, *Actor-Managers, The*, p. 161.
		Chapter Twenty-one			
330	7	HO, pp. 955–56.			
330	11	HS, p. 659.	335	1, 10	*Ibid.*, pp. 153, 162.
330	19	OS, II, p. 315.	335	15	Blum, Daniel, *Pictorial History of the American Theater*, pp. 157, 159.
330	21	CS, p. 36.			
331	1	WW, I, 386–88.			
331	8	Behrman, S. N., *Portrait of Max*, p. 46.			
331	21	GT, p. 335.	335	24	"My Father," in Beerbohm, Max, *op. cit.*, p. 171.
331	33	CS, pp. 36–37.			
331	38	HO, *loc. cit.*			
332	4	CS, p. 39.	335	28, 36, 41	Pearson, Hesketh, *op. cit.*, pp. 172, 68–72, 137–78.
332	7	AE6, p. 126.			
332	10	Behrman, S. N., *op. cit.*, p. 59.			
332	14	AB, p. 86.	335	44	Shaw, George Bernard, in Beerbohm, Max, *op. cit.*, pp. 240–41.
332	21, 24, 30	Shaw, George Bernard, in *Saturday Review, The*, May 16, 1896, May 30, 1896, January 29, 1898.	337	15	Donaldson, Francis, *op. cit.*, pp. 123–27.
332	32	Pearson, Hesketh, *Beerbohm Tree*, pp. 22–41.	337	23	*Ibid.*, p. 128.
			337	26	IH, p. 402
332	37	HO, p. 956.	337	34	Shaw, George Bernard, in *Saturday Review, The*, March 23, 1895.
333	7	Beerbohm, Max, *Some Memories*			

PAGE	LINE	
338	5	Donaldson, Francis, *op. cit.,* pp. 128–29.
338	9, 10	IH, pp. 542, 567.
338	15, 36	Shaw, George Bernard, in *Saturday Review, The,* January 19 and September 28, 1895.
338	42	Donaldson, Francis, *op. cit.,* p. 131.
339	30	Shaw, George Bernard, in *Saturday Review, The,* October 2, 1897.
339	37	AA, p. 242.
340	3	CG, p. 93.
340	15	Donaldson, Francis, *op. cit.,* pp. 133–34.
340	19	Beerbohm, Max, in *Saturday Review, The,* October 1, 1898.
340	21	Donaldson, Francis, *op. cit.,* p. 134.
340	27	TO, pp. 22–23.
340	28	Beerbohm, Max, in *Saturday Review, The,* December 20, 1902.
340	32	AB, p. 303.
340	45	Donaldson, Francis, *op. cit.,* pp. 139–40.

Chapter Twenty-two

PAGE	LINE	
341	6	HO, p. 314.
341	15	Taubman, Howard, *op. cit.,* pp. 62–63.
341	17	HO, *loc. cit.*
342	12	HO, pp. 136–37.
342	15, 17	HW, XVIII, pp. 249, 264.
342	20	HO, *loc. cit.*
342	38	DNB, IV, p. 595.
342	45	HO, pp. 185, 180.
343	17	DNB, *loc. cit.*
343	27	HO, p. 532.
344	10	DNB, X, pp. 1237–38.
344	15, 20	HO, pp. 318, 166.
344	31	Young, William D., *op. cit.,* I, pp. 72–73.
344	35	WH, quoted p. 163.
344	37, 43	HO, pp. 318, 982.
345	9	WH, p. 95.
345	15	HO, p. 697.
345	33, 36, 38	HW, V, pp. 199, 284, 350.
346	6	MKB, pp. 289–92.
346	7, 16	HO, *loc. cit.,* pp. 261–62.
346	17	MK, p. 8.
346	20, 22	HO, *loc. cit.,* p. 1021.
346	24	MK, *loc. cit.*
346	42	WH, p. 45.
347	4	HO, p. 274.
347	14	DNB, VI, pp. 755–56.
347	20	CG, p. 462.
347	25	MK, pp. 145–53.

PAGE	LINE		PAGE	LINE	
347	36	WH, pp. 157–58.	355	1, 3, 8, 9	*Ibid.*, pp. 282,
347	44	HO, p. 426.			353, 191, 194,
348	22	Taubman,			204.
		Howard, *op.*	355	6	WH, pp. 30–37.
		cit., pp. 78–79.	355	18, 30	WH, pp. 30–37,
348	24	HO, *loc. cit.*			quoted from
349	10	DNB, pp.			*Vanity Fair*, p.
		576–79.			31.
349	18	HO, p. 890.	355	37	Clarke, I. C., *My*
349	20	DNB, *loc. cit.*			*Life and Mem-*
349	24	HO, *loc. cit.*			*ories*, p. 266.
349	26	DNB, *loc. cit.*	355	40	Winter, William,
349	32	HO, *loc. cit.*			*Other Days*, p.
349	45	DNB, *loc. cit.*			214.
350	2	HO, *loc. cit.*	355	44	Clarke, I. C., *op.*
350	16	Fitzgerald, Percy,			*cit.*, p. 267.
		op. cit., pp.	356	7	HO, p. 998.
		253–55 seq.	356	9	IH, p. 330.
350	26	HO, p. 137.	356	14, 17	HO, *loc. cit.* p.
350	29	MK, pp. 183–			83.
		84.	356	25	WH, p. 91.
350	38	HO, pp. 142–43.	356	26	Winter, William,
351	13	*Ibid.*, 663.			*Shadows of the*
351	20	WH, pp. 80–85.			*Stage, 1st Series*,
351	39, 44	Murdoch, James			p. 216.
		E., *The Stage*,	356	27	HO, *loc. cit.*
		pp. 27–37,	356	29	WH, p. 92.
		252.	356	31	Winter, William,
352	6, 8	HO, *loc. cit.*, p.			*op. cit.*, p. 224.
		319.	356	34	WH, p. 93.
352	10	HL, p. 234.	356	35	HO, *loc. cit.*
352	18	WH, pp. 142–	356	37	WW, I, p. 169.
		43.	356	40	CG, p. 457.
352	32	HO, p. 233.	356	42	HO, *loc. cit.*
352	35, 39, 43,	WW, I, pp. 281,	356	43	IH, p. 380.
	45	469–72, 281,	356	45	HO, *loc. cit.*
		337.	357	2, 4	Winter, William,
353	4	WH, pp. 87–88.			*Shadows of the*
353	23, 30	HO, *loc. cit.*, p.			*Stage, 1st Series*,
		333.			pp. 216, 219.
354	25	DNB, III, pp.	357	30	HO, pp. 77–78.
		718–19.	357	36	DNB, Supplement
354	37	HO, p. 599.			1920–1930, p.
354	43	WW, I, p. 353			50.

PAGE	LINE		PAGE	LINE	
358	9	Bancroft, Squire and Marie, *The Bancrofts*, p. 255.	364	23	MC, pp. 218–21.
			364	33	WH, pp. 124–32.
			364	38, 40, 43, 46	CG, pp. 457, 14, 93, 363.
358	16, 17, 27	HO, pp. 681, 687, pp. 531–32.	365	10	HO, p. 998.
			365	22, 33	BS, pp. 155, 151–62
358	38	Young, William C., *op. cit.*, I, pp. 248–56.	366	6	*Ibid.*, pp. 241–44.
			366	21, 30	HO, pp. 935, 1009–10.
358	42	HO, *loc. cit.*	366	33	TO, pp. 6, 18.
359	4	CG, p. 456.	366	39	CS, pp. 23–24.
359	7	Morris, Clara, *Life on the Stage*, pp. 158–59.	367	14	HO, pp. 353–54.
			367	18	Taubman, Howard, *op. cit.*, p. 122.
359	18	CG, quoted p. 193.	367	24	HO, *loc. cit.*
359	21	HO, p. 187.	367	27, 31	MC, p. 227.
359	26	CS, p. 19.	368	13	*Ibid.*, pp. 250–52.
359	28	WW, I, p. 472.	368	34	Bancroft, Squire and Marie, *op. cit.*, pp. 330–32.
359	34, 39	HO, pp. 187, 445–46.			
360	2, 12	DNB, Supplement 1901–1911, pp. 275–76, 111.	369	33	FE, p. 123.
			369	37	HO, p. 134.
360	27	HO, pp. 501–2.	369	38	Beerbohm, Max, in *Saturday Review, The*, May 4, 1901.
360	32	WH, p. 130.			
360	43	HO, p. 18.			
361	6	*Ibid.*, p. 927.			
361	10, 11, 13	CG, pp. 456, 187, 203–5.	369	41	HO, *loc. cit.*
			369	43, 44, 45	Beerbohm, Max, in *Saturday Review, The*, September 24, 1898, February 9, 1901, June 14, 1902.
361	17	AE6, p. 16.			
361	20	HO, p. 83.			
361	27	WW, I, pp. 363, 375.			
361	33	Barrett, Wilson, in *Lippincott's Magazine*, April 1890, pp. 2–3.			
			370	6	HO, p. 618.
			370	9	MC, p. 287.
361	41	HO, p. 681.	370	15, 22	WW, I, pp. 210, 493–98.
362	45	MC, pp. 242–44.			
363	15	HO, p. 656.	371	17	HO, p. 617.
363	23	WW, I, pp. 505–9.	371	21, 25, 27	Wilstach, Paul, *Richard*

PAGE	LINE		PAGE	LINE	
		Mansfield, pp. 169, 171, 166.			March 24 and April 7, 1900,
371	35	WH, pp. 206–11.			March 30, 1911.
372	3	WW, I, p. 119.	379	45	TO, p. 7.
372	39	Wilstach, Paul, *op. cit.*, pp. 178–82.	380	2	DNB, Supplement 1911–1920, pp. 3–4.
372	43	WW, I, p. 119.	380	5, 7, 12, 13	IH, pp. 383, 444, 448, 450.
373	5, 11	Wilstach, Paul, *op. cit.*, pp. 177, 175.	380	14	DNB, *loc. cit.*
			380	21	Shaw, George
373	15	MC, p. 267.			Bernard, in
374	3, 9, 28	Wilstach, Paul, *op. cit.*, pp. 250–54, 423, 341–52.			*Saturday Review, The,* February 26, 1898.
375	10	*Ibid.*, pp. 352–58	380	37	CS, p. 24.
375	14	WH, p. 211.	380	40	TO, p. 61.
376	14	HO, p. 411.	381	10, 19	Calvert, Louis,
376	16	DNB, Supplement 1931–1940, p. 361.			*Problems of an Actor,* pp. 145–49, 15–21.
376	22	HO, *loc. cit.*	381	22, 24	CG, pp. 110–11, 133–34.
376	25	Shaw, George	381	34	ME, p. 11.
		Bernard, in *Saturday Review, The,* May 15, 1897.	381	37, 42	Winter, William, *Shadows of the Stage, 1st Series,* pp. 98, 105.
376	36	HO, p. 887.	381	45	*American, The,*
377	16	*Ibid.*, p. 102.			January 19,
377	20	IH, pp. 396–97.			1889.
378	26	*Ibid.*, pp. 397–400.	382	1	WW, I, p. 105.
			382	3	*Variorum Edition*
378	29	HO, *loc. cit.*			of *The Winter's Tale,* p. 398.
378	34	AB, p. 17.			
378	36	AA, p. 242.	382	7	CG, pp. 12–13.
378	37	AB, p. 97.	382	33	WM, pp. 63–70.
379	14	DNB, Supplement 1931–1940, pp. 71–72.	383	9	MC, pp. 252–54.
			383	18	Winter, William, *Shadows of the Stage, 1st Series,* p. 260.
379	22, 26, 35	Beerbohm, Max, in *Saturday Review, The,*	383	19	HO, p. 792.

PAGE	LINE		PAGE	LINE	
394	3	Young, William C., *op. cit.*, I, p. 232.	398	1	TO, pp. 61–62.
			398	9	DNB, *loc. cit.*
			398	25	TO, pp. 11–12.
394	7	WH, pp. 145–50.	398	33	HO, p. 189.
394	9	MC, p. 285.	399	3	*Ibid.*, p. 49
394	10, 20	HO, *loc. cit.*, p. 816.	399	6, 7, 9, 12	CS, pp. 148, 58, 121, 149.
394	26	Agate, James, *Contemporary Theatre, 1926,* pp. 12–13.	399	16	TO, p. 91.
			399	29, 38	HO, p. 123, 156.
394	28	HO, p. 12.			**Chapter Twenty-three**
394	33	WH, pp. 159–60.	401	29, 40	BS, pp. 22–23, 30–32.
395	1	HO, *loc. cit.*	402	6, 8	*Ibid.*, pp. 78–82, 77.
395	18	MC, pp. 280–84.	403	41	*Ibid.*, pp. 229–35.
395	20	WH, p. 150.	404	32, 37, 40	*Ibid.*, pp. 41–44, 45, 48.
395	21	HO, *loc. cit.*	405	5, 16, 18, 22, 28, 42	*Ibid.*, pp. 55, 143–45, 78, 186, 82–84, 90–94.
395	29	MC, *loc. cit.*			
395	31	HO, *loc. cit.*			
395	42	Beerbohm, Max, *Mainly on the Air,* pp. 52–53.	406	2, 25, 40	*Ibid.*, pp. 95, 102–3, 147–48.
396	2, 9, 13, 16, 18, 26, 28	Robbins, Phyllis, *Maude Adams,* pp. 55, quoted p. 56, 122–23, 178, 242, 147, 163–64.	407	16	*Ibid.*, pp. 177–80.
			408	12	*Ibid.*, pp. 198–99.
			409	33	*Ibid.*, pp. 264–71.
			410	42	*Ibid.*, pp. 236–39.
			412	24, 37, 46	*Ibid.*, pp. 365, 239–41, 365.
396	33, 44	HO, pp. 439, 158.	413	20	*Ibid.*, p. 253
397	3	CG, p. 459.	414	12	*Ibid.*, pp. 245–52.
397	25	HO, p. 27.	415	3, 9	*Ibid.*, pp. 279–84, 271.
397	28	WH, p. 279, and MC, p. 286.	415	26	GH, pp. 100–1.
397	32	HO, p. 186.			**Chapter Twenty-four**
397	40	DNB, Supplement 1941–1950, p. 473.	418	13	DNB, Supplement 1931–1940, p. 708.
397	43	Beerbohm, Max, *Last Theatres,* p. 357.	418	22	Shaw, George Bernard, in

PAGE	LINE		PAGE	LINE	
		Saturday Review, The, July 11, 1896.	429	31	Atkinson, Brooks, *Broadway*, pp. 305–6.
418	24	HO, p. 872.			
419	4	Shaw, George Bernard, in *Saturday Review, The,* November 13, 1897.	430	5	Beerbohm, Max, in *Saturday Review, The,* February 11, 1908.
419	11	HO, quoted p. 747	430	16	TO, pp. 150–51.
420	12	DNB, Supplement 1931–1940, pp. 53–54.	430	20	HO, p. 803.
			431	1	DNB, Supplement 1931–1940, pp. 18–19.
420	25, 28	CS, pp. 56–57, 59.	431	5	CG, p. 25.
420	46	HO, pp. 695–96.	431	6	CS, p. 25.
421	19	GG, pp. 4–5 and 11–24.	431	9	Beerbohm, Max, in *Saturday Review, The,* April 8, 1905.
421	22	HS, p. 389.			
421	30	HO, p. 921.			
423	3	*Ibid.,* pp. 921–22, and HS, pp. 589–90.	431	24	TO, pp. 46–49.
			431	28	HO, p. 782.
423	9	MC, p. 287.	431	29, 31, 33, 36	TO, pp. 84–85, 105, 154–55.
423	15	WH, p. 189.			
423	42, 43	WW, I, pp. 208, 388–92.	431	37, 38, 39, 40, 41	CS, pp. 98, 157n., 110, 142.
424	5	HO, p. 892.	432	23	HO, p. 427.
424	9	WH, p. 214.	432	31	Blum, Daniel, *op. cit.,* pp. 222–49.
424	35	WS, pp. 119–20.			
425	38	WH, p. 148.	433	1	Taubman, Howard, *op. cit.,* pp. 163–64.
426	37	HO, p. 892.			
426	38	WH, p. 215.			
427	15, 21	AA, pp. 166, 158.	433	18	MH, pp. 2, 7, 64, 100.
428	1	CS, pp. 89–93.			
428	6	HO, p. 540.	433	42	DNB, Supplement 1941–1950, pp. 6–7.
428	23	CS, pp. 94–97.			
428	34	Agate, James, *Those Were the Nights,* pp. 309–10.	434	2	Agate, James, *Their Hour upon the Stage,* pp. 85–86.
429	10	AB, pp. 34–35.			

PAGE	LINE		PAGE	LINE	
476	36	HO, p. 804.	488	8	Wilson, J. Dover,
476	38, 44	AB, pp. 295, 33.			*What Happens*
477	12	TO, pp. 159–60.			*in Hamlet*, p.
477	14	HG, p. 177.			192.
477	15	HO, *loc. cit.*	488	13	See GT, pp.
477	18	AB, pp. 33,			216–17, 259,
		232–33.			263.
			488	24	Wilson, J. Dover,
	Chapter Twenty-five				*op. cit.*, p. 43.
478	23	DR, p. 15.	488	29	GJ, pp. 51–52.
480	12, 19	BA, pp. 18, 17.	489	2	Agate, James,
480	30	DR, p. 22.			*More First*
482	11	HG, pp. 6–10.			*Nights*, pp.
483	6	*Ibid.*, pp. 13–23,			183–86, 205.
		and Funke,	489	11	HG, pp. 94–96.
		Lewis, and	489	16	BA, p. 139.
		Booth, John E.,	489	24	TO, p. 172.
		op. cit., p. 6.	489	29, 35	AB, pp. 195,
483	15	HG, pp. 24–29.			202, 244–45.
483	20	BA, pp. 136–38.	489	45	HG, p. 209.
483	34	HG, pp. 24–29.	490	30	*Ibid.*, pp. 202–5.
483	39	Funke, Lewis,	491	5	CT, p. 408.
		and Booth,	491	19	BA, pp. 11–12.
		John E., *op. cit.*,	492	3, 15	*Ibid.*, pp. 13–15,
		p. 19.			16.
484	7, 31	HG, pp. 28, 57,	492	29	FP, p. 211.
		58–62.	492	42	AE3, p. 19.
484	33	AB, p. 91.	493	10	GH, pp. 69, 97.
484	36	TO, p. 116.	493	15	TO, p. 164.
484	41	AB, pp. 93–94.	493	21	AB, pp. 270–74.
484	44	TO, p. 117.	493	31	FP, p. 213.
484	45	AA, p. 257.	493	38	BA, p. 18.
485	1	CS, pp. 67, 69.	493	44	CT, pp. 410–11.
485	11	TO, pp. 138–39.	494	8	FP, p. 213.
485	21	HG, p. 70.	494	14	TO, p. 164.
485	26	TO, p. 150.	494	20	FP, *loc. cit.*
485	33	HG, pp. 86–88.	494	27	DR, pp. 22–23.
485	36, 39, 42	AB, pp. 258,	494	31	FP, p. 215.
		264–69,	494	33	TO, p. 192.
		278–79.	494	39	AB, pp. 241–43.
485	46	GJ, p. 6.	494	42	AE3, p. 239.
486	8	*Ibid.*, pp. 16–18.	495	3	TO, pp. 173–74.
486	16	GH,	495	7	AB, p. 168.
487	36	*Ibid.*, pp. 142–44.	495	11	DR, p. 23.

PAGE	LINE	
495	21	FP, pp. 215–16.
496	13	AA, p. 253.
496	15	FP, p. 217.
496	25	TO, p. 195.
496	27	AA, p. 259.
496	38, 41	Behrman, S.N., *People in a Diary*, pp. 231–32, 228.
496	46	FP, p. 219.
497	4	Brown, John Mason, *op. cit.*, pp. 286–88.
497	16	FP, p. 220.
497	22	AE9, pp. 237–39.
498	15, 30	GH, pp. 245, 430–31.
499	39	GT,
500	21, 36, 29	*Ibid.*, pp. 147–213, 207–8, 253–55.
501	17	*Ibid.*, pp. 176–78.

Chapter Twenty-six

502	18	HO, p. 800.
502	21	AB, pp. 112–13, 196, 89, 303.
502	25	TO, p. 173.
502	29	AE9, p. 176.
503	3	AA, pp. 259–61.
503	21, 35	BA, pp. 69, 89–92.
503	36	AB, p. 20.
504	3	TO, pp. 140–41, 233.
504	10	AB, pp. 61, 215.
504	13, 16, 18	TO, pp. 153, 223, 194.
504	20, 25, 28	AA, pp. 258, 215–16, 233–34.
504	32	BA, p. 92.
504	39	TO, p. 250.
504	40	HO, p. 791.

PAGE	LINE	
505	18	FP, pp. 238–40.
505	29	BA, pp. 100–2.
505	31	FP, p. 241.
506	7	BA, pp. 102–6.
506	9	AB, p. 274.
506	11	FP, p. 241.
506	12	TO, p. 178.
506	14	FP, p. 243.
506	23	TO, p. 207.
506	27	BA, p. 106.
506	30	FP, p. 248.
506	39	TO, pp. 213–14.
506	42	FP, p. 249.
506	46	TO, p. 237.
507	11	*Ibid.*, pp. 232–39.
507	23	FP, pp. 256–57.
507	26	TO, pp. 233–34.
507	37	FP, pp. 257–58.
508	2, 4, 9, 21	Redgrave, Michael, *Mask or Face*, pp. 71, 74, 78, 79–82.
508	28	HO, p. 438.
508	30	AE3, p. 269.
508	35	AA, pp. 244–45.
508	37	CS, p. 126.
508	39, 42, 44	TO, pp. 191, 228, 149, 164.
509	1	*Ibid.*, p. 186n.
509	8	*New Republic, The*, November 1, 1944.
509	12	HO, p. 421.
509	15, 18	TO, pp. 164, 176.
509	20	HO, *loc. cit.*
509	27	TO, pp. 207, 240 n.
511	6	MI, pp. 500–1.
512	19	CS, p. 152.
512	44	AA, p. 245.
513	4	CS, pp. 130–31.
513	9	HO, p. 552.
513	13	CS, *loc. cit.*

PAGE	LINE		PAGE	LINE	
		New York, March 19, 1973.	535	32	*The,* December 9, 1973. Simon, John, in *New York,* January 28, 1974.
531	9	*Ibid.,* July 19, 1973.			
532	10, 22	*Ibid.,* July 14, July 21, 1973.	536	14	Kerr, Walter, in *New York Times, The,* July 7, 1974.
532	29	Novick, Julius, in *New York Times, The,* July 15, 1973.	536	20	Kalem in *Time,* January 1, 1974.
533	6	Simon, John, in *New York,* August 20, 1973.	536	29	Simon, John, in *New York,* January 1, 1974.
533	13	Feingold, Michael, in *New York Times, The,* August 12, 1973.	536	39	Kalem, in *Time, loc. cit.*
			536	46	Simon, John, in *New York, loc. cit.*
534	31	Simon, John, in *New York,* January 14, 1974.	537	10, 25	Wilde, Oscar, *Intentions,* pp. 20, 18.
535	19	Kerr, Walter, in *New York Times,*			

Index

In the index which follows, when Shakespeare's name, the titles of his plays, or the names of their characters are mentioned only *in passing*—i. e., if nothing of special interest is involved —these are not recorded below. For example, if the actor is said to have played the roles of Hamlet, Othello, Macbeth (etc.) and there is no occasion to discuss the performance or its importance, the reference is omitted. However, the names of *all actors* dealt with in this book are listed below.